IRISH SOCIETY:
SOCIOLOGICAL PERSPECTIVES

EDITED BY:
Patrick Clancy
Sheelagh Drudy
Kathleen Lynch
Liam O'Dowd

Institute of Public Administration
in association with
The Sociological Association of Ireland

First published 1995
by the Institute of Public Administration,
57-61 Lansdowne Road,
Dublin, Ireland.

Reprinted 1997

British Library Cataloguing in Publication Data

Cover design by Butler Claffey Design

ISBN 1 872002 87 0

Typeset by Phototype-Set Ltd.
Printed by ColourBooks Ltd., Dublin

CONTENTS

CONTRIBUTORS

Patrick Clancy — Department of Sociology, University College Dublin

Patrick Commins — Economic and Rural Welfare Research Centre, Teagasc, Dublin

Robert Cormack — Department of Sociology and Social Policy, Queen's University, Belfast

Damien Courtney — Department of Business and General Studies, Cork Regional Technical College

Chris Curtin — Department of Political Science and Sociology, University College, Galway

Sheelagh Drudy — Department of Education, St. Patrick's College, Maynooth

Tony Fahey — Economic and Social Research Institute, Dublin

Mary Kelly — Department of Sociology, University College Dublin

Madeleine Leonard — Department of Sociology and Social Policy, Queen's University, Belfast

Kathleen Lynch — Equality Studies Centre, University College Dublin

Evelyn Mahon — Department of Sociology, Trinity College, Dublin

Ciaran McCullagh — Department of Sociology, University College Cork

Eithne McLaughlin — Department of Sociology and Social Policy, Queen's University, Belfast

Robbie McVeigh — Centre for Research and Documentation, Belfast

Valerie Morgan — Department of Education, University of Ulster

Máire Nic Ghiolla Phádraig   Department of Sociology,
University College Dublin

Liam O'Dowd   Department of Sociology and
Social Policy, Queen's University,
Belfast

Denis O'Hearn   Department of Sociology and
Social Policy, Queen's University,
Belfast

Robert Osborne   School of Public Policy,
Economics and Law, University
of Ulster at Jordanstown

Michel Peillon   Department of Sociology,
St. Patrick's College, Maynooth

Bill Rolston   Department of Sociology,
University of Ulster

Mike Tomlinson   Department of Sociology and
Social Policy, Queen's University,
Belfast

Tony Varley   Department of Political Science
and Sociology, University College
Galway

Christopher Whelan   Economic and Social Research
Institute, Dublin

Steven Yearley   Department of Sociology,
York University, England

1
Sociology and Irish society

PATRICK CLANCY, SHEELAGH DRUDY,
KATHLEEN LYNCH and LIAM O'DOWD

The end of the twentieth century seems an appropriate time to reflect on Irish society. *Fin de siècle* life has become extremely complex, even complicated. Ireland is small in terms both of geographical area and of population. The population of the entire island is less than that of a large city in many other parts of the world. Nevertheless, Ireland contains within it a similar level of complexity and a comparable diversity of social forces to many much larger societies.

Despite its size Ireland has made, and continues to make, a very distinctive contribution to European, and even to global culture. The Irish experience, historically and contemporaneously, mirrors that of many other societies. In ways, the Irish experience may be viewed as a microcosm of that found within a number of other post-colonial states and peripheral economies in the capitalist world order. Ireland is subject to global, social, economic and political processes, as well as to national and local ones. Irish people must struggle to make sense of their everyday lives and to understand these forces and processes as they affect their families, their social networks, their access to resources, their culture and their general quality of life.

The objectives of this book are fourfold. Firstly, it seeks to present up-to-date information on key areas and issues in Irish society. It presents research from both north and south of the border. Some chapters deal with the whole of Ireland, others with north and south separately. There are twin chapters on some issues, such as development and education. In presenting sociological accounts of both parts of Ireland, we reflect the current research interests of sociologists in Ireland rather than a mechanical presentation of matching chapters on each jurisdiction. Our second objective is to illustrate the perspectives that sociologists bring to the analysis of society. Thirdly, the book aims to stimulate systematic and critical reflection on the nature of our society. Finally, through the process of critical analysis and reflection, it is hoped that the book will stimulate the reader to identify alternative, and perhaps better, routes and futures for Irish society as it moves into the beginning of the third millennium.

In this chapter we attempt to provide an introduction to the discipline and its differing perspectives. We begin by looking at the scope of sociology in comparison to other social science disciplines. We discuss the origin and evolution of the different approaches in sociology and highlight the most important theoretical and methodological areas in current debates. We trace the origins and development of sociological inquiry in Ireland. We then outline the issues covered in the remainder of the book.

The scope of sociology

Sociology is the systematic study of social relations, institutions and societies. Such a simple definition does not, of course, delimit the precise scope of the discipline since social relationships, institutions and societies are complex phenomena which can be studied in a variety of ways. The fundamental assumption behind the sociological approach is that men and women are relational beings, that is, that human beings are formed by their relationships with others.

Our individual behaviour reflects the context of our social experience.

While sociologists share with psychologists an interest in individual behaviour the levels of analysis used are different. For the most part, psychologists take the elements of the person (e.g. motives, emotions, traits and skills) as their units of analysis while sociologists are primarily interested in the relations between persons and the more or less enduring patterns of relations between individuals and groups. The focus of sociological inquiry is on people as social beings, the way in which they structure their relationships – the manner in which their social ties with others are formed, sustained and changed. In seeking to study the impact of the social, sociologists concern themselves with both the collective and cultural aspect of human behaviour. Thus, sociology involves the study of groups, organisations and social institutions, as well as norms, values and ideologies which give meaning to social behaviour.

It is frequently remarked that, because of its broad scope and its interest in all social behaviour, sociology is the most diffuse of the social sciences. For example, while economics can be said to deal with the production, distribution, exchange and consumption of goods and services, sociology includes within its remit a concern for the institutional and cultural context within which such processes transpire (Smelser, 1994). This very diffuseness is, however, part of the appeal of sociology. Short (1992, p. 2176) claims that no other discipline addresses such a broad range of phenomena; no other discipline is so responsive to human concerns, to the ever-changing nature of social life, and to humankind's relationship with its environment; and no other discipline is so successful in generating data and theory that are relevant to such matters.

Origins of the sociological tradition

While it is necessary to go back to the work of the Greek philosophers Plato and Aristotle to find the first systematic reflections on the nature of society, modern sociology has its origins in nineteenth century western Europe. Its origins stem largely from the work of social theorists who were endeavouring to understand the sweeping social changes occurring at the end of the eighteenth and early nineteenth century. The rupture to traditional society was caused by the twin revolutions – the industrial revolution which occurred between 1780 and 1840 and the democratic revolutions of the United States of America in 1776 and France in 1789. These revolutions were viewed as having precipitated unprecedented social changes in the organisation of society. The social, economic, political and ideological ferment which prevailed induced a number of thinkers to seek to explain the social changes which they were witnessing. In so doing they explored the nature of the bond between the individual and society.

Prominent social theorists at this time included Max Weber, Ferdinand Tonnies and Georg Simmel in Germany; Claude Henri Saint-Simon, Auguste Comte and Emile Durkheim in France; Herbert Spencer in England; and Karl Marx, who although born and educated in Germany, spent most of his life in England. Although Comte was the first to use the term 'sociology', having earlier used the term 'social physics', the writings of Marx, Weber and Durkheim have had the most enduring influence in the shaping of the discipline. Moreover, their works, which contain widely divergent views on the nature of society, continue to provide a focus for much contemporary debate within sociology.

In seeking to understand social change Marx advanced a materialist conception of history, arguing that economic influences are the main determinants of change. Marx described the transition from the medieval 'feudal' mode of production to the 'capitalist' mode of production, which he predicted would ultimately give way to socialism or communism (he used these terms interchangeably). He saw class struggle as the engine of social change. Each mode of production, prior to socialism, was defined by two antagonistic classes locked together in struggle over the means of production. While actual capitalist societies contained several classes, the capitalist mode of production was defined by the struggle between the capitalist class and the proletariat or working-class. The former owned and controlled the means of production – land, capital, including banks, factories and machinery. The latter had nothing to sell but its labour-power, having been forced off the land into cities and factories. Yet, it was the proletariat which Marx saw as the key to the ultimate overthrow of capitalism and the setting up of the future classless socialist society.

While Weber was strongly influenced by Marx he was also highly critical of some of Marx's views. He rejected the materialist conception of history and did not see the class conflict as having the significance which Marx attributed to it. Instead, he argued that ideas and values have as much impact on social change as economic conditions have. In this context he pointed to the crucial role played by the Reformation and Protestant ideas in the rise of capitalism in western Europe. Weber suggested that *rationalisation* constitutes one of the master trends of western capitalist society. Rationalisation is the process whereby every area of human relationships is subject to calculation and administration. The growth of bureaucracy, which represents a persistent concern in Weber's work, represents one expression of this movement away from traditional authority towards a rational form of authority.

While the interests of both Marx and Weber extended into a range of disciplines, including philosophy, economics, comparative history and (in the case of Weber) law, Durkheim's concerns were focused more explicitly on the establishment of sociology as a separate discipline. However, like the other major founders of sociology he was also preoccupied with the changes transforming society. He argued that European society was moving from a society based on mechanical solidarity to one based on organic solidarity. The former was characterised by shared moral values, especially religion, and by a simple division of labour. Organic solidarity was based on the growing inter-dependency engendered by an ever more complex division of labour. Like Marx and Weber, he argued that religion was losing its force in urban industrial society.

In addition to the theoretical work of leading figures such as Marx, Weber and Durkheim, another important influence on the development of sociology was the growing tradition of statistical surveys including government sponsored enquiries. This tradition, much of which was initially associated with political economy, was committed to fact-gathering on a wide range of issues, such as demographic processes, industrial conditions, crime, suicide, health and poverty. It was generally part of the social reform movement developed by government and voluntary agencies alike. In Britain, Charles Booth's pioneering work on the extent of poverty was especially influential.

While sociology originated in western Europe, it was in the United States that most development took place during the first half of the twentieth century. This coincided with the establishment of many new universities and the development of research oriented graduate schools. The first department of sociology was established at the new University of Chicago in 1892 (twenty-one years before Durkheim was appointed to the first ever European chair of sociology). In contrast to the European emphasis on developing general theories of social change, American sociology was characterised by a social problem focus, by a tendency towards specialisation in a variety of subfields (such as rural sociology, sociology of religion, deviance) and by a strong emphasis on empirical research. For a long time the most influential American social theory was the social-psychology oriented theory developed by C. H. Cooley, G. H. Mead and W. I. Thomas. Collins (1994, pp. 42-3) suggests that this theoretical orientation matched the political orientation of most American sociologists, whom he characterises as liberal reformers, not radicals nor conservative cynics. Given their desire to see America as a land of equality and opportunity, social psychology was conveniently focused on the individual and the small group, and thus away from embarrassing questions about the larger structure of stratification, wealth and power.

Contemporary sociology has moved far beyond that envisaged by its nineteenth century originators, and beyond the somewhat homogenising influence of American sociology which prevailed through much of this century. The internationalisation of the discipline is reflected in the membership of the International Sociological Association which is drawn from more than ninety countries. The accelerated pace of scientific and technological change, the spread of multinational corporations, the rise of a global economy, the development of new patterns of work, all call for a re-evaluation of general theories of social change. The widely divergent experiences of change in Latin America, Africa and Asia, the great transformation of eastern Europe, and the emergence of newly independent states have had a major influence on sociology. One result has been to increase greatly the richness and diversity of the discipline. It now draws on an ever-increasing range of societies and social experience, and on a large number of theoretical perspectives, methodologies and techniques of investigation.

The discipline of sociology

Sociology as a science
Nineteenth century social theorists were deeply impressed by the development of the natural sciences and by technological advances in the Europe of their time. The promise of science emanating from the Enlightenment was great; scientific rationalism appeared to offer solutions for understanding and controlling the natural order. Marx and Durkheim accepted such premises, and argued that social science could develop general theories and laws in the manner of the natural sciences. It was believed that scientific rationalism could inform the development of the social as well as the natural order.

Weber, on the other hand, did not regard the methods of the natural sciences as being adequate for understanding social reality (although he undoubtedly shared the belief in the value of scientific rationalism). He sought to develop a more interpretive model for social science which would allow for the distinctiveness of its subject matter. He observed how the subjects of social research actively interpret and redefine their own reality, and claimed that these active and interactive interpretations need to be part of any objective account of social life. These different approaches to sociology as a science inform two major theoretical perspectives, the structuralist and the interpretive.

Structuralism: consensus, conflict and the influence of Marx

In terms of its epistemology and methodology, the structuralist tradition is closer to the natural science model, while the interpretive paradigm, with its focus on patterned subjective interpretations emanated from the work of Weber and his followers. Marxist theorists generally worked within a structuralist framework, albeit a conflict-based one. They did not share the consensus assumptions of the Durkheimian functionalists. In addition, many Marxists viewed knowledge as *praxis*; knowledge was not a set of pre-defined facts and theories without history or future; it was a dynamic in its own right and its very existence created new realities which shaped and formed existing realities.

Durkheim made the most explicit attempt to model sociology on the natural sciences. He sought to establish social facts as the specific subject matter of sociology. Such facts included, for example, language and religion. He saw them as the product of social groups, not of individuals; as external to individuals and shaping their behaviour. Sociology is then, for Durkheim, a study of objective social facts:

> A social fact (being) every way of acting, fixed or not, capable of exercising on the individual an external constraint; or again, every way of acting which is general

throughout a given society, while at the same time existing in its own right independent of its individual manifestations (Durkheim, 1938, p. 13).

Durkheim sought to model sociology on the natural sciences of the time by emphasising its objective nature, its reliance on quantitative data, and its capacity to formulate general laws of behaviour. Broadly speaking, therefore, we can see that Durkheim sought to apply the scientific method to what he saw as the central problem of sociology – social order or how societal cohesion was maintained.

The structuralist perspective has two dimensions: one seeks to address the question of social order, that is, how societies persist, cohere and remain stable and generally integrated units. The assumption here is that societies strive always to maintain cohesion around shared values. This is the consensus approach advanced by major theorists such as Durkheim and Parsons (1951). The conflict approach traces its origins to Karl Marx. It assumes that societies are built not around consensus or shared values but around the conflicting interests of capital and labour and that order is maintained through considerable coercion. The main focus here is on change as generated by class conflict and struggle (Wright, 1979). A classical empirical work in this field is Bowles and Gintis' (1976) *Schooling in Capitalist America.* It analyses the relations between education and the economy in terms of the structural constraints of capitalism: it claims that schools reproduce the existing hierarchical social relations of economic life and that they also reproduce a consciousness which accepts the unequal ordering of relationships under capitalism.

Both the conflict and consensus approaches share the view that the organisation and structure of society strongly influences the attitudes, values, institutions and relationships we develop. Similarly, both approaches tend to give quantitative, statistically aggregated data a priority over non-quantitative evidence. The most commonly used quantitative evidence is information collected by means of social surveys and official statistics. The procedures used in social surveys follow a natural science, or 'positivist', model of sociology. Use is made of scientific sampling, structured interviews and or questionnaires, and statistical analysis. Data are frequently presented in the form of correlations and tabulations. Generalisations or 'law-like' statements may be made, although these will be couched in terms of probability or tendencies.

The Interpretive Perspective

While Weber held that, like all scientific observation sociology 'strives for clarity and verifiable accuracy of insight and comprehension' (1947, p. 90), he argued that social science could not be modelled on the natural sciences. Social science was set apart by its subject matter – human beings or social actors. It must therefore allow for the meanings that people attach to their actions, and take full advantage of social scientists' capacity to understand and interpret human intentions and meanings. Sociology was therefore not inferior to natural science; rather it was a different type of science:

> ... a science which attempts the interpretive under-standing of social action in order thereby to arrive at a causal explanation of its course and effects. In 'action' is included all human behaviour when and in so far as the acting individual attaches a subjective meaning to it (Weber, 1947, p. 88).

The epistemological assumptions which underpinned Weberian methodology were of paramount importance to interpretive sociology. This approach is concerned with subjective meanings and human intentions. It argues that there could be no unity of method because the social world is a meaningful place, a world full of active subjects not passive objects; it emphasises the importance of agency as opposed to structure. Within this tradition, data are more likely to be

drawn from informal, unstructured and open-ended inter-
viewing. When the whole way of life of a social group is the
object of inquiry, ethnography is a method which is
frequently used. Originating in anthropology, it involves
participant observation on the part of the researcher, who for
a time becomes a member of the group. The keeping of
detailed notebooks, tape-recordings, and more formal
interviews are also part of the method. Data are often
presented in narrative style rather than in the form of
statistics and tables.

The interpretive tradition has been developed
considerably in the USA in the work of Mead (1964),
Goffman (1962) and others, and a number of variants of the
approach have been developed. For example, one of the
most important of these, often termed symbolic
interactionism, seeks to illuminate how individuals interpret
and define their own situations and roles. Studies are
generally small in scale, focusing on particular places such as
hospitals and prisons and on small group interaction.
Ethnomethodologists such as Cicourel (1964) and Garfinkel
(1967) are also within the interpretive tradition. Like
symbolic interactionists, they study inter-personal interaction
using qualitative research methods. They are primarily
concerned, however, with studying the methods whereby
social actors produce meaning. For ethnomethodologists the
common social world is constructed from the sense-making
work of individuals. They differ from symbolic interactionists
insofar as they focus on the methods of constructing
meaning, rather than on the subjective meaning itself.

*Postmodernism and feminism and the impact of new social
movements*
In the last twenty years there have been a number of
challenges to the dominance of structuralist and interpretive
paradigms in sociology. Most importantly, sociology has been
confronted by the failure of the project of the Enlightenment.
Scientific rationalism has not led to the development of a new

world order which is stable, predictable and manageable (not to mention egalitarian, just or environmentally safe). The failure of modernism has presented sociology with an enormous challenge. It has meant that the methodologies and theoretical assumptions which were the bed-rock of social scientific analysis have now been subjected to more critical analysis than hitherto. The challenge from post-modernists such as Foucault (1972, 1980) has been especially strong for structuralists working out of the natural scientific model within the social sciences. He and others have challenged the modernist belief in development and progress, including the belief that science itself is part of the developmental project heralding progress and emancipation. They have rejected grand narratives, such as Marxism and structuralism, which attempted to explain social phenomena according to the canons of positivist logic of cause and effect. Foucault, by linking his analysis of knowledge to the analysis of power, has shown how the theoretically objective methodologies of the natural and social sciences are, in many respects subjective, and dictated by particular interests which construct and control the relevant discourses. The post-modernist critique is most applicable to research and theory within the strong positivist (natural science) tradition. In so far as Weberian sociology recognises the importance of subjective realities, it is less vulnerable to the postmodernist critique, albeit not totally so, given its own grand narratives. Although post-modernism represents a clear rupture with structuralism, its critique of objectivity in particular is not a new one within the social sciences. It has generated an ongoing debate between positivists and phenomenologists, and more recently between feminists and other social scientists.

Dorothy Smith (1987), Duelli Klein (1983) and Sandra Harding (1987) are among the many feminist critics of traditional positivist research methodologies within the social sciences. And the claims which they, and other feminist sociologists, make about the failures of social science research are similar in some respects to post-modernists, although they arrive at these from different premises. Feminists claim that sociology is a patriarchal discipline and that the claim to objective and value-free research is untenable, due to male biases in both the subjects of research investigation and in the methodologies employed. They claim that prior to feminism all schools of sociology systematically privileged male knowledge, experience and interests, but without acknowledging that this was the practice. Feminists show how many sociological issues of major interest to women, such as hierarchical power relations within the family have been either ignored or interpreted as 'natural' by leading sociologists (Delphy and Leonard, 1992). In addition, they demonstrate how women have often not been counted in sociological studies, especially in major studies of social mobility which claimed to speak for the whole of society (such as Goldthorpe *et al*, 1980 and Whelan and Whelan, 1984).

Feminists point to the need for alternative methodologies which will not only account for the reality of women's lives but will provide some perspective on how women can be emancipated from oppression. Marxist theory of knowledge as praxis has therefore had a direct impact on feminist thinking about research, although the influence of Marxism is not always recognised in the literature. And the pressure to make sociological research open and accountable to women is part of a more general trend to make social researchers more accountable to the subjects of their research (especially those who are vulnerable or oppressed) (Lather, 1986). Those who purport to examine oppressed or marginalised groups are increasingly being asked to explain the ways in which their research is of value to those whom they investigate (Oliver, 1992; O'Neill, 1992). The feminist movement, the disability movement, the black movement, the Traveller movement – all have begun to question the 'hit and run methods' of social research whereby the researchers came, collected data and left. They have queried the practice whereby dialogue about the research was confined to other academics or policy makers, and generally excluded the research subjects. Low income and marginalised peoples have been frequent subjects of social investigation; questions are being asked about the way research itself is conducted. There is a growing demand for a change in the ordering of the social relations of research production.

Sociology is constantly evolving and changing as a discipline. While the nineteenth century founding *fathers* (sic) of sociology (Durkheim, Marx and Weber) have exercised an overriding influence on its development, the last twenty years have produced major new developments in sociological theory which have their roots in late twentieth century intellectual and social movements, notably post-modernism and feminism. Differences in theoretical orientation within sociology are parallelled by differences in research methodology. Challenges to the dominance of positivist research methodologies have grown consistently in recent years; the demand for more qualitative and interpretive research has, in certain quarters, notably in feminist sociology, been superseded by a demand for more emancipatory research approaches.

Sociology in Ireland: origins and development

Professional sociology in its modern sense is relatively new in Ireland, reaching an important milestone in 1973 with the founding of the Sociological Association of Ireland which has sponsored this book. Various forms of proto-sociology were in evidence in Ireland long before that date, shaped by two broad intellectual traditions. One was associated with the British administration in Ireland under the Union, the other with the Catholic Church. The former, of course, was part of a broader British tradition and was developed in Ireland by colonial administrators, lawyers and political economists. It was largely empirical, even empiricist, although sometimes informed by theories of political economy or social evolution.

Underlying much of the British tradition was an attempt to understand why nineteenth century Ireland appeared to be a land of 'strange anomalies'; anomalous, that is, with respect to England, in terms of economic conditions, religion, politics, demography and land tenure. Political independence and partition greatly weakened this tradition. Social reform based on detailed and systematic empirical analysis had little place within official nationalist and unionist thinking. The empirical tradition that survived was represented by a small number of statisticians employed by government; by some medico-social research, especially in Belfast; and by occasional small-scale poverty and housing studies carried out by academics and others.

The second major tradition influencing Irish sociology derived from 'Catholic sociology'. This had its origins in continental western Europe, in the social encyclicals of successive popes, and in the Catholic social movement of the late nineteenth and early twentieth century. It was meant to counteract the rise of socialism and secularism in Europe, and the social theories advanced by Marx, Durkheim and other contemporary non-christian social theorists. It had an explicit social ideal – a society which would be a *via media* between capitalism and socialism, founded on Catholic social principles. This was advocated strongly in the Republic of Ireland, after partition, by a large number of Catholic, especially clerical, writers. It advanced a series of prescriptions for a vocationalist or corporate order. It advocated a rural way of life, strong family units, and the widest possible diffusion of private property. It was also suspicious of growing state involvement in welfare services.

By the 1920s Cronin's *Primer of the Principles of Social Science* (1927) was available in Catholic schools. While it never matched the circulation levels of Archbishop Whately's famous *Easy Lessons in Money Matters* (see Boylan and Foley, 1995) among nineteenth century schoolchildren, it did reflect the way in which the dominant social ideology had changed – the principles of political economy had given way to the principles of Catholic social thought. By the 1930s, there were professors of Social Science and Catholic Action in Dublin's Jesuit seminary and Maynooth College respectively. In 1937, a lectureship in sociology was established in University College Cork and sociology was first offered as a degree course at University College Dublin in 1953.

By the 1950s, however, the limitations of this type of sociology were becoming very apparent. The social ideal which it contained seemed farther than ever from realisation, in the wake of economic stagnation, large scale emigration and the continued disintegration of Irish rural society. Even sympathetic commentators began to be critical of the lack of empirical analysis in this tradition. Newman (1955, p. 9) wrote that 'in Ireland there had been practically no attention at all given to factual studies; what are called sociological studies are usually expositions of social principles'. In Northern Ireland, prior to the 1960s, there was even less interest in empirical social research: the practice of government was informed by data from sources other than social science.

By the early 1970s, chairs were held by academic sociologists in the colleges of the National University of Ireland, and Maynooth College (initially Catholic priests) and in Trinity College. Sociological research began to be undertaken in a number of research institutes such as the Economic and Social Research Institute and the Agricultural Institute (Foras Taluntais). In general, sociology became more responsive to the modernisation agenda of the state rather than to the Catholic church and began to undertake policy-related research. In Northern Ireland, the setting up of modern sociology departments coincided with the outbreak of the 'troubles', the expansion of sociology in British universities and the arrival of many visiting social scientists to study the conflict. Sociology in Ireland now became more integrated into the international mainstream of the discipline. Initially, however, the discipline conjoined a number of diverse and loosely connected strands. It juxta-posed the remnants of Catholic sociology with the strong influence of American and British sociology in the courses taught in, and personnel appointed to, Irish universities. Whereas disciplines such as history and literary studies were able to develop on an all-Ireland basis, initially this proved more difficult in sociology with the latter's tendency to equate state and society. Moreover, the conflict between theoretical paradigms in international sociology in the 1960s and 1970s found echoes in Ireland, however faint.

From the early 1980s, however, a number of factors helped to generate a somewhat more coherent sociological research agenda. The conflict in Northern Ireland focused attention on the state and the various dimensions of communal division – economic, ethnic and national. Northern Ireland was a reminder of the problems of equating economy, state and society and this equation was rendered even more problematical by Ireland's membership of the European Union. Sociological research began to locate Ireland within a broader comparative context which transcended the Irish-British, Irish-English comparisons which had dominated social thought since the nineteenth century. Some of the dominant research themes which have emerged are reflected in the contributions to this book – the development or underdevelopment of Ireland as a European periphery, its particular patterns of demography, social stratification and mobility, Ireland in the context of the European Union, and the impact of feminist thinking on Irish social research.

New approaches and research themes are beginning to lay the basis for sociology in Ireland. These transcend the border, encourage north-south comparisons and locate the whole of Ireland within a wider international context. Even where research is more policy-directed, and hence more tied to the administrative and political agenda of each state, as in the sociology of education and the sociology of poverty and inequality, a firm basis for comparison is being created. Research on the state, community action, rural development, religion, the environment and the mass media provide subjects for research by postgraduates and others in both parts of the country.

Gaps remain of course. Ethnographic work generally has been left to anthropologists, most of them from abroad. There is relatively little research in urban sociology or in the sociology of organisations and few detailed workplace studies. Given the power and influence of the major professions in Irish life, sociologists have paid scant attention to medicine, law or other leading professions. Irish sociological research has been biassed more to structural rather than cultural analysis although there is a growing interest in the forms of popular culture. The controversial turn towards post-modernism in sociology has generally had relatively little influence in Ireland to date. Literary critics, journalists and other social commentators have been quicker to embrace post-modernist analysis than sociologists.

Clearly the intellectual environment within which sociology is located has changed in the last two decades. New fields such as mass communications, women's studies, cultural studies, equality studies, policy studies, even Irish studies have laid claim to much of the subject matter of sociology. Other disciplines such as history, political science and economics have developed, to varying degrees, a sociological dimension of their own. Sociology itself remains in danger of fragmentation into various sub-specialisms which have little contact with each other. There are countervailing trends, however, linked to the small size of the country, the gradual emergence of a series of major sociological studies of Irish society, and the focal point provided by the Sociological Association of Ireland and the Irish Journal of Sociology. The response to globalisation, European integration and to a revived economic neo-liberalism would appear to encourage Irish sociologists to think more wholistically as they struggle to interpret the lack of fit between economy, state and society on the island.

This volume draws together research into a range of key

areas of Irish life. The sociological research community is inevitably a small one. Nevertheless, although we have indicated some of the gaps in sociological inquiry, the breadth of issues covered in this volume indicates the richness and diversity of sociological research in Ireland. This book does not purport to be comprehensive in the number of areas of research included, nor does it represent all Irish sociological research. It would take many volumes to draw together the fine research on Ireland being done by sociologists in higher education institutions and research institutes within Ireland and abroad. However, the book does focus on certain important themes. These are assembled under three broad headings: (i) Population, Work and Social Change; (ii) Class, Politics and the State; and (iii) Education, Culture and Social Movements.

While many of the themes are closely interrelated, the reader will note that the authors approach them from a variety of analytical perspectives. The editors feel that this is one of the distinct strengths of the book. As we have already pointed out, there is no one single approach in sociology. Rather there are different, and sometimes competing, ways of interpreting social reality.

Outline of the book

Population, work and social change
Seven chapters dealing with population, work and social change form the first section of the book. Since an analysis of population processes is essential for an understanding of any society this section commences with Damien Courtney's comprehensive overview of demographic structure and change in the Republic of Ireland and Northern Ireland. The author includes a short discussion of the approach, methods and sources used in demography. The main focus of the paper is on the changing demographic profile of Ireland, paying particular attention to the similarities and differences in the experience of both parts of the country. Courtney

contrasts the long period of population decline in the
Republic, which was reversed only in recent decades, with the
slight but steady growth achieved in Northern Ireland
throughout the twentieth century, with the exception of the
1970s. He documents the decline in marital fertility, which
has been especially dramatic in the Republic since 1980, and
notes how this has been partially offset by a rise in extra-
marital births. The chapter contains an extended discussion
of migration, especially emigration, which continues to be
the main determinant of population structure and change.
Some of the implications of this migration are examined;
these include effects on the age structure, dependency levels,
economic development and, in the case of Northern Ireland,
its impact on the denominational composition of the
population.

The chapters by O'Hearn and O'Dowd build on the
demographic framework outlined by Courtney, by examining
the processes of socio-economic development which have
shaped patterns of work and unemployment in both parts of
Ireland. Both chapters engage in the intensifying debate over
the nature and implications of socio-economic change on the
island of Ireland. They reflect the ambivalent and uneven
effects of the process of modernisation on the two peripheral
economies on the island, and outline the limitations of the
neo-liberal development strategies which have held sway in
the European Union and other advanced industrial
economies since the early 1980s.

In Chapter 3, on the Republic, O'Hearn discusses the
consequences of export-led industrialisation, the gap
between the performance of multinational and indigenous
industry, the phenomenon of jobless growth and the
problem of mass unemployment. He highlights the growing
critique of the accuracy of Irish economic statistics which
currently suggest high levels of growth, a widening gap
between gross domestic product (GDP) and gross national
product (GDP) and the possibility that the country's trade
surplus is largely illusory. He suggests that Irish policy-makers

have been forced to register some of the criticisms of modernisation approaches put forward by dependency theorists, even if this has not fundamentally altered national economic policy. O'Hearn critically reviews the dominant explanations of socio-economic development, pointing in particular to the potential of new studies of global restructuring which link institutional economics, business history, labour studies and the sociology of institutions and world systems. He concludes by outlining some of the options for Irish development policy: continued liberalisation, niche development and dependency reversal.

Whereas the Republic's economy is critically dependent on investment by multi-national corporations, Northern Ireland depends heavily on public expenditure and a massive subvention from Britain. O'Dowd begins Chapter 4, on Northern Ireland, by outlining three broad historical phases in its socio-economic development: its period of initial industrialisation, the post-war period of modernisation, and the final period since the early 1970s in which a state dependent economy emerged. He then considers three themes which are interwoven in the literature on socio-economic development in the North. The first concerns general perceptions of progress and decline. Common-sensical views that living standards have improved over time co-exist with strong perceptions in the social science literature of relative decline. The second theme focuses on a series of critical development issues: the radical restructuring of Northern Ireland's productive base since the 1960s, equality issues concerning class, gender, locality, and the persistent gap between Catholic and Protestant unemployment rates. The third orientation in the literature emphasises the largely negative impact of state dependency and governance structure on socio-economic development. O'Dowd concludes by arguing that any application of general theories of development to Northern Ireland must take into account the way in which the regional economy is embedded in non-economic institutions and in social relationships. In this respect, existing inequalities in Northern Ireland, ethno-national divisions and the nature of the British governance structure combine to inhibit socio-economic development.

In Chapter 5, Commins explores the impact of European integration on rural economy and society in the Irish Republic. In particular, he focuses on the changing impact of the Common Agricultural Policy (CAP). He examines in turn the impact of the CAP's price and market support policy and its structural policy, the reform of these policies in the 1980s, the linking of CAP structural policies to the re-organisation of the Regional and Social Funds, and the development of broader policies for promoting rural development. Commins suggests that, in a general sense, both agricultural producers and consumers have been beneficiaries of the CAP. However, he also identifies a number of its negative consequences. Firstly, the social goal of a more equitable distribution of farm income has been negated by a price policy which is biassed in favour of large producers. Secondly, the CAP has failed to resolve the structural problems of Irish agriculture. Thirdly, the high expectations surrounding EU regional policy in the early 1970s have not been realised. The concluding section of the chapter explores what the operation of the CAP reveals about the process of policy formation and change. Commins argues that policies are the result of bargaining processes among diverse interests with unequal influence. In the context of the CAP, producers have proved to be better organised and more politically effective than consumers or taxpayers. He identifies a move from a sectoral to a more diversified territorial strategy aimed at regenerating rural society generally, but notes that the special provisions for regional and rural development conflict with the overarching principles of competition policy in the Single European Market.

In Chapter 6, Fahey moves from the transnational and national levels to consider the impact of social change on family and household in the Republic of Ireland. He begins by reviewing the treatment of the family within the sociological tradition in the work of Le Play, Engels, Parsons, and Arensberg and Kimball in Ireland. He then points to two approaches which have undermined the factual adequacy of the distinction between the traditional and modern family: empirical social history and feminist approaches. The former has, inter alia, demonstrated that nuclear families were prominent in some traditional societies, whereas the latter demonstrate that the subordination of women in family and household survived the so-called transition from traditional to modern societies. Fahey then explores some of the complex influences on family life in Ireland: emigration, the land system, industrialisation, the changing role of education, and moves to greater gender equality within the family. He goes on to identify three stages in the evolution of the household economy: the pre-industrial Irish farm household, the 'breadwinner' husband/stay-at-home housewife economy of the industrial era; and the smaller households unable to sustain a full-time unpaid houseworker where both the man and the woman can be in paid work. Fahey suggests that Irish households are still largely in the second stage but points to the growing preoccupation with the 'the crisis of the family' in popular debate, fuelled by stories of criminal violence, rape and sexual abuse. Finally, he discusses factors which are influencing and changing family life in Ireland: the legislative prohibitions on divorce and abortion, more frequent marital breakdown and the rise in non-marital births.

In Chapter 7, Leonard explores a neglected area of the household economy – informal activity – which comprises paid and unpaid economic transactions that occur outside the mainstream market economy and which are not registered by government agencies. Drawing on detailed research in a disadvantaged area of Belfast she concentrates on women's involvement in various forms of informal economic activity. These include: self-provisioning within the household; reciprocal transactions among friends, neighbours and relatives outside the household; the informal provision of goods and services for money within the community; and, finally, the informal selling of labour power to formal employers operating outside the community. The chapter suggests that narrow definitions which equate active labour with the formal production and exchange of goods and services fail to grasp the full economic significance of the varied forms of labour undertaken by women. Leonard's analysis illustrates how informal economic activity may be 'an economy of last resort' for women, how it reproduces the gender roles in the formal economy and how it challenges artificial distinctions between active and inactive labour and between use value and exchange value production.

The final chapter in Section 1, by Lynch and McLaughlin, further challenges conventional concepts of work in the social sciences by focusing on caring and love labour – the largest area of work in which people are engaged and in which women are disproportionately involved either in a paid or unpaid capacity. The authors seek to clarify the distinctions and the relationships between three forms of work: love labour (labour involved in developing solidary bonds), caring and paid employment; they explore the tensions which exist between these, tensions which impinge most heavily on women. Recognising the distinction between 'caring for' and 'caring about', Lynch and McLaughlin point out that not all work can be commodified, especially work that has to do with maintaining the quality of relationships. They highlight the extent to which care work and love labour are central to social relationships yet are devalued as contributions to economy and society. The authors locate caring and love labour within the wider sexual division of labour in Ireland, where childcare, domestic tasks and informal care are carried out largely, if not exclusively, by women. Such work often limits the access of carers to paid employment, limits their earning capacities or forces them to remain outside the paid workforce altogether. Lynch and McLaughlin conclude by a detailed analysis of how social policy in both parts of Ireland shapes, and is shaped by, the nature and scope of care work and love labour. They conclude that equality debates and employment and social welfare policies have failed to date to provide non-exploitative care arrangements which would be in the interests of those providing and those needing care.

Class, politics and the state
This section of the book deals with a number of interrelated themes and fundamental questions for Irish society, relating to class, social mobility, political interest groupings and the state. It begins by focussing on the concept of class itself and on its applications. In Chapter 9, *Class Society, Inequality and the Declassed,* Drudy argues that a very central tool of social scientific analysis – that of class theory – has led to an incomplete understanding of the conditions of a number of important segments of contemporary societies. The chapter traces the development of the main concepts used in class theory, with particular emphasis on the period from the 1970s onwards. It presents the contrasting perspectives offered in functionalism and in Weberian and Marxist class theory. In empirical studies, all of the perspectives make use of classifications of occupations to assess class position. This gives rise to one major difficulty: that of classifying the very large number of people in society who do not have a paid job. The chapter then focuses on a number of current debates, including those ranging round the impact of mass unemployment on the class structure, the question of the existence or otherwise of an underclass, and the relationship of women to the class structure. Examination of official figures on the Irish labour force illustrates that reliance on occupation to indicate class position frequently results in the elimination from class analysis of over two-thirds of the adult female population and more than a third of the adult male population.

Chapter 10, *Class Transformation and Social Mobility in the Republic of Ireland,* focuses on closely related issues. Arguing that the study of prevailing patterns of social mobility is of critical importance to an understanding of modern Irish society, Whelan suggests that inequalities of mobility opportunities are not simply one additional inequality but are, in fact, the crucial mechanism by which resource differences become perpetuated across generations. It is through the operation of restrictions on social mobility that closed social groupings emerge which are characterised by disparities in material and cultural resources, contrasting employment experiences and residential segregation. He argues that changes in the class composition of the Irish workforce emerged from industrial development that was more rapid, occurred later, and was more state-inspired than in most western societies. However, international comparisons suggest that Ireland is characterised by less open mobility patterns than many other countries. Although the primary focus of Whelan's analysis is on male mobility rates, nevertheless he does examine female social mobility and concludes that differences in female mobility patterns are almost entirely a consequence of gender segregation in the labour market. His analysis suggests that the logic of Irish industrial development, involving the dispersal of industrial location to rural areas in the 1960s and 1970s, involved particular costs for the urban working class.

Peillon's analysis of the relationship between state and society raises the question of the kind of rapport which has developed between them. In Chapter 11, *Interest Groups and the State*, he points to the complexity of this relationship. On the one hand the state may be viewed as the upholder of the collective interest, the common good. On the other hand, when society is divided into classes with competing interests, the activities of the state tend to benefit some classes and to disadvantage others. For example, in the Irish situation, because the capitalist class possesses a strategic and scarce resource (capital), and because the state wishes to foster capital investment and to promote a particular type of economic development, state policies tend to favour capital investment and to satisfy the needs of the capitalist class. Nevertheless, one of the central characteristics of the state's orientations and actions is their complexity. The state seeks to encompass a diversity of orientations of action which may appear contradictory. Indeed, the state itself constitutes a social force and manifests autonomy. Peillon examines in this context not only the impact of various social groups on the state, but the impact of the state on society. He argues that a pluralist play of interest groups can be observed in the Republic of Ireland. Ireland, he suggests, has also had frequent recourse to corporatist practices. In the corporatist system, some organised groups are granted a special and even official status, and they are treated as privileged partners by the central powers. They participate directly in the process of public decision-making, not from outside through external influences, but from inside. However, Peillon concludes that in Ireland such incorporation remains voluntary, and has not become part of the formal institutions of the state. It thus does not threaten or deny the autonomy of interest groups. Corporatism, as experienced in Ireland, is primarily concerned with the conflict between the two major social categories of advanced capitalism: employees and employers. It reaches right to the core of the play of class interests.

The relationship between a particular type of interest group (i.e. community groups) and the state is explored in Chapter 12, *Community Action and the State*, by Curtin and Varley. They identify two types of community group in Ireland. One type displays 'integrationist' tendencies, an 'all-together' ideology concerned with the common good and is epitomised by the representative community councils of Muintir na Tíre. The other type is characterised by an 'oppositional' tendency and is classically found in the social action elements of the first EC anti-poverty programme. These focused not on whole localities but on certain disadvantaged categories such as low-income farmers or unwaged women. The form of analysis used by oppositional community groups suggests that the state plays an important role in underpinning patterns of disadvantage. Curtin and Varley argue, however, that the dominant integrationist tendency has received a powerful boost over the past decade or so as the state in Ireland, faced with a complexity of crisis conditions, has sought to mobilise communities and community groups for certain purposes such as job creation, social service delivery or the legitimation of new area-based special interventions. The authors point out that there are instances where integrationist and oppositional tendencies may be linked together even within the same community groups. For example, while many women's groups have chosen to present themselves as community based, an underlying oppositional tendency can be detected when community action is built upon feminist principles and the critical perspective these imply. Even among 'integrationist' groups there is growing dissatisfaction with short-term schemes. The temporary nature of area-based 'partnership' schemes is such that, far from being empowered in the longer term, community partners can be left dangerously exposed once projects are wound up. Thus, Curtin and Varley draw our attention to the complexity of community action in Ireland today.

Chapter 13, *Getting the criminals we want: The social production of the criminal population,* turns to an examination of the role played by the legal institutions of the state regarding the way in which different forms of crime (particularly middle class and working class crime) are defined, and the manner in which the law in relation to different types of crime is enforced. McCullagh argues that the criminal population that we have is a product of the means through which society responds to the socially harmful behaviour of different sections of the community. Some of these means enable the powerful and socially respectable in Irish society to escape criminal sanction when they engage in socially harmful behaviour. He suggests that three of these means are of central significance. The most important is the process of law-making. This is the means through which the criminal label is distributed in society. As it operates in Ireland the process of law-making distributes this label in an uneven manner. It sanctions some kinds of socially harmful behaviour and ignores others. It is, he argues, aided and abetted by an enforcement system that devotes more resources to the pursuit of some kinds of law-breaking than to others. The final element is a court system in which some people and some offences are treated more harshly than others. The result is a criminal population in which the poor, uneducated and unskilled are disproportionately represented. McCullagh argues that the existence of corporate and middle class crime challenges the way we view the causes of crime in Irish society, in particular our perceptions of the links between poverty and deprivation as causative factors in criminal or socially harmful behaviour.

In Chapter 14, *Fortress Northern Ireland: a Model for the New Europe?*, Tomlinson focuses on some of the key features of the Northern Ireland conflict and its management, in the context of the emergence of pan-European structures of inter-state co-operation and regulation, and debates over the nature of the European Union. The chapter seeks to show that while Northern Ireland might be peripheral and insignificant in terms of the European economy, it assumes a much greater importance in shaping Europe's emerging security policies. Until the IRA ceasefire in September 1994, Northern Ireland was the foremost source of armed conflict within the EU, often with consequences for mainland European countries. In particular, Tomlinson indicates how the conflict has produced the most developed counter-terrorist policies in Europe. The chapter is concerned with the implications of the institutionalisation of the conflict for questions of state power and accountability, human rights and for the emerging shape of EU integration. Northern Ireland, he argues, provides a model of forms of conflict and policing which have both tested the boundaries of the permissible within Europe and which have contributed to the construction of fortress Europe.

Education, culture and social movements
In this third section of the book there are eight chapters dealing with education, culture and social movements. The

centrality of education in contemporary Ireland is reflected by the inclusion of three papers dealing with this topic. There are separate papers which deal with education in the Republic and in Northern Ireland, together with a paper on gender and education which deals with both north and south.

In his analysis of education in the Republic in Chapter 15, Clancy starts with an overview of the main theoretical perspectives in the sociology of education. The paper draws heavily on two of the dominant structuralist perspectives, functionalism and neo-marxism, to examine the working of the education system. It is suggested that education involves two key processes. The first involves socialisation and the moulding of consciousness as evidenced by the role of the school in fostering religious, nationalist and economic interests and values in society. In Ireland the concern for the moral curriculum is linked to conflicts about the control and governance of the education system. The second key social process with which education is involved concerns status attainment and role allocation. The paper examines the operation of the school's selection function and its role in the perpetuation of the prevailing system of class relations.

In Chapter 16, on education in Northern Ireland, Cormack and Osborne centre their analysis on the struggle for equality, taking into account class, gender and religious differentials in participation and attainment. However, the chapter also provides an over-view of the historical development of the system and a detailed outline of the structure of current provision in education. In relation to equality the authors argue that, taking a century-long perspective, great gains have been made. By the early 1990s Catholics constituted half of all entrants into higher education although they remained significantly over-represented among those who leave school without any qualification. Likewise for females the story is one of continuing improvement. Females now out-perform males in secondary education and constitute half of higher education entrants. However, they remain somewhat disadvantaged on entry to the labour market, a disadvantage which the authors attribute to the bias towards arts and humanities in their choice of subjects studied. The working class has made least gains. It is suggested that the problem of underachievement of students from working class backgrounds remains as pertinent now as it was at the turn of the century.

One of the conclusions reached by Morgan and Lynch from their analysis of gender and education in Chapter 17 is that, while gender differentiation in education is often subtle and complex, paradoxically it may require more direct policy initiatives and interventions if it is to be tackled effectively. An interesting feature of their review of the situation, north and south, is their concern with the hidden curriculum which determines the ethos of schools. They point to a major lacuna in the education literature which has not systematically examined the type of male (often macho) culture which develops in all-male schools and which, at times, is the dominant culture in co-educational schools. They argue that while some attention has been given to the analysis of how women learn to be subordinate, insufficient attention has been given to the analysis of how boys learn to dominate and the ways in which schools perpetuate the culture of male domination.

The broadcasting institutions in both Northern Ireland and the Republic are the subject of Kelly and Rolston's analysis in Chapter 18. The first part of the chapter presents a critical comparative analysis of the role played by both radio and television in the formation of national cultural identities north and south. Although the values of the upper middle classes were strongly reflected in radio programming in the south, this did not lead to conflict, not least because of the high level of consensus which existed on the nationalist cultural project of the station. Furthermore, there was no strong intellectual basis either within or without the media from which such a critique would emerge. The Chapter argues that there was no cultural consensus on which BBC

Northern Ireland could draw, so its response was to align itself with the unionist government, at least until the 1950s. The advent of Ulster Television did not alter the nature of broadcasting in the north as it was owned and controlled by unionist interests.

The impact of censorship on broadcasting is the subject of the second part of the chapter. It shows how, for the duration of the war in Northern Ireland, censorship of the media operated directly, but mostly indirectly through self-censorship, on both sides of the border. The system of censorship through self-policing mainly affected the reporting on the conflict and did not extend systematically to other areas. Its implications, for the operation of the war itself, and for creating a culture which tolerates censorship are not yet known.

Turning to another type of cultural institution, Nic Ghiolla Phadraig in Chapter 19 shows that the Catholic Church still exercises considerable influence through its controlling interest in first and second level education especially, and, but to a lesser degree, through its ownership of several health and welfare institutions. However, this power is increasingly contested as the struggles between secular and religious interests are becoming more public in educational fields (such as the disagreement over the boards of managements in schools following the publication of the Green Paper on education in 1992) and in the health sector (the issue of denominational control and influence in the Tallaght hospital). Nic Ghiolla Phadraig's paper also suggests that the Catholic Church is not characterised by unanimity of purpose in its approach to public policy; while certain groups within the church are fighting for equality and justice, others are more comfortable with a church which subvents elite institutions perpetuating inequality in the health and educational spheres. Overall, however, she suggests that the social project of the church has been the maintenance of political stability. To this end it has provided the state with independent legitimation; the state, in turn, instituted laws and policies in line with church teaching. She claims, however, that the net outcome of the 'social stability project' has been the perpetuation of major structural inequalities which have not been challenged by either the church or the state.

Chapter 20 on sectarianism, by McVeigh, addresses another aspect of religion which is of central importance in Irish political culture, yet it is one which has been under-theorised and generally unanalysed both internationally and within Ireland. McVeigh suggests that the issue of sectarianism cannot be understood apart from the issue of colonialism. He claims that sectarianism was at the heart of the colonial legacy, as early colonisers believed that there was something uniquely problematic about Irishness whatever its religious formation. In the post-reformation era, Roman Catholicism became a signifier of Irishness or non-Irishness as the case may be, and superordinate and subordinate relations were defined accordingly. He suggests that the northern state was founded on sectarian principles which had their origins in a colonial past; the result was a state that operated in the interests of unionism; the response from the south was to establish what he calls a 'pluralist theocracy which established the Catholic Church but also incorporated other religious blocs'.

McVeigh claims that sectarianism also constitutes a structure, and that its formation and development is closely linked to the operation of the state, and to that of other structures such as race, class and gender. Sectarianism is, he suggests, also about difference and otherness, and involves asymmetrical power relationships. Whatever the inter-relationship between Catholic and Protestant sectarianism in terms of cause and effect, McVeigh claims that Protestant sectarianism is a product of powerlessness vis-a-vis the British State, a by-product of the fear of being subordinate within a majority Catholic state. Finally, the paper argues that the religious labels associated with sectarianism in Ireland, namely Catholic and Protestant, are primarily signifiers of ethnic rather than religious identity.

In Chapter 21 Yearley examines the social shaping of the
environmental movement in Ireland, a topic which has only
recently attracted sociological investigation. In reviewing the
factors which account for the growing support for New Social
Movements, including the environmental movement, the
author attributes particular significance to the growth in the
'knowledge class' within a changed class structure. Turning
to the specifics of the development of the environmental
movement in the Republic and Northern Ireland, he points
to a number of factors which account for the way in which
ecological politics in Ireland deviate from the typical pattern
found in other advanced western countries. These include
the nature of the class structure with a somewhat smaller
middle class, the strong involvement of the state in
promoting industrialisation, the heavy reliance on foreign
owned industry, the action of the environmental social
movement organisations and, in Northern Ireland, the way in
which politics have been monopolised by the sectarian divide.

Finally, in Chapter 22 Mahon provides an overview of the
development of the women's movement in the Republic of
Ireland over the last twenty five years. Somewhat in contrast
to Nic Ghiolla Phadraig's analysis, she suggests that the power
of the Catholic Church is waning in terms of its impact on
sexual politics in Ireland. She highlights the fact that in the
1970s a liberal agenda of institutional reform dominated
public discourse. Demands for equal pay, access to
contraception and equality in educational and welfare
provisions were dominant. The fact that there was a strong
focus on liberal legislative change was not surprising given
the impact of the European Community directives at that
time, the fact that there were few basic equality provisions for
women in either labour law or family law, and the fact that
politics in the south was not organised around radical
socialist or feminist agendas. The chapter also shows how the
agenda for political action changed in the 1980s with a rise in
the influence or radical feminism and the emergence of the
Women's Right to Choose Group campaigning around the

issue of abortion. The failure of this group to have its demands addressed satisfactorily was matched by the meteoric rise of the anti-abortion lobby led by the Society for the Protection of the Unborn Child (SPUC). The pro-life amendment campaign of the early 1980s culminated in an anti-abortion clause being inserted into the constitution in 1983. The paper argues that, in many respects, the lessons of the 1980s have created a women's movement which operates with new vigour and determination in the 1990s. The election of Mary Robinson as President in 1990, the Supreme Court decision in the X case which permitted abortion under particular circumstances, and the affirmation of women's right to travel and to receive information on abortion were important milestones challenging the seeming immutable cultural attitudes to women in the mid-1980s. Mahon attributes these changing attitudes to a variety of factors including better education, the pluralist influence of the media and the waning power of the clerical wing of the Catholic Church in Irish political life.

References

BOWLES S., and H. GINTIS, 1976. *Schooling in Capitalist America*, London, Routledge and Kegan Paul.

BOYLAN, T. and T. FOLEY, 1995. 'From Hedge School to Hegemony: Intellectuals, Ideology and Ireland in the Nineteenth Century', in L. O'Dowd (ed.), *On Intellectuals and Intellectual Life in Ireland*, Belfast/Dublin, Institute of Irish Studies/Royal Irish Academy, forthcoming.

CICOUREL, A., 1964. *Method and Measurement in Sociology*, New York, Free Press.

COLLINS, R., 1994. *Four Sociological Traditions*, Oxford, Oxford University Press.

CRONIN, M., 1927. *Primer of the Principles of Social Science*, Dublin, M. H. Gill and Son Ltd.

DELPHY, C., and D. LEONARD, 1992. *Familiar Exploitation: A New Analysis of Marriage and Family Life*, Polity Press, Cambridge.

DURKHEIM, E., 1938. *The Rules of Sociological Method*, Chicago, University of Chicago.

DUELLI KLEIN, R., 1983. 'How to Do What We Want to Do:

Thoughts About Feminist Methodology', in G. Bowles and R. Duelli Klein, *Theories of Women's Studies,* London, Routledge and Kegan Paul.

GARFINKEL, H., 1967. *Studies in Ethnomethodology,* New York, Prentice Hall.

GOFFMAN, E., 1962. *Asylums: Essays on the Social Situations of Mental Patients and Other Inmates,* Chicago, Aldine.

FOUCAULT, M., 1972. *The Archaeology of Knowledge,* trans. by A.M. Sheridan Smith, London, Routledge.

FOUCAULT, M., 1980. 'Truth and Power', *Power/Knowledge: Selected Interviews and Other Writings, 1972-1977* (ed. Colin Gordon), Brighton, Harvester Press.

GOLDTHORPE, J.H. *ET AL,* 1980. *Social Mobility and Class Structure in Modern Britain,* Oxford, Clarendon Press.

HARDING, S. (ed.), 1987. *Feminism and Methodology,* Bloomington, Indiana University Press.

LATHER, P., 1986. 'Research as Praxis', *Harvard Educational Review,* Vol. 56, No. 3, pp. 257-277.

MEAD, G., 1964. *On Social Psychology: Selected Papers,* A. Strauss (ed.), Chicago, University of Chicago Press.

NEWMAN, J., 1955. 'Towards a Catholic Sociology', *University Review,* Vol. 1, No. 4, pp. 3-12.

O'NEILL, C., 1992. *Telling It Like It Is,* Dublin, Combat Poverty Agency.

OLIVER, M., 1992. 'Changing The Social Relations of Research Production', *Disability, Handicap and Society,* Vol. 7, No. 2, pp. 101-114.

PARSONS, T., 1951. *The Social System,* London, Routledge and Kegan Paul.

SHORT, J. F., 1992. 'Sociology', in B. R. Clark & G. R. Neave, (eds.), *The Encyclopedia of Higher Education,* Oxford, Pergamon Press.

SMELSER, N. J., 1994. *Sociology,* Oxford, Blackwell.

SMITH, D.E., 1987. *The Everyday World as Problematic: a feminist sociology,* Milton Keynes, Open University Press.

WEBER, M., 1947. *The Theory of Social and Economic Organisation,* T. Parsons (ed.), Glencoe, Ill., The Free Press.

WHELAN, C.T., and B.J. WHELAN, 1984. *Social Mobility in the Republic of Ireland: A Comparative Perspective,* Dublin, Economic and Social Research Institute Paper No. 116.

WRIGHT, E.O., 1979. *Class Structure and Income Distribution,* New York, Academic Press.

PART ONE
Population, Work and Social Change

2
Demographic Structure and Change in the Republic of Ireland and Northern Ireland[1]

DAMIEN COURTNEY

Introduction

Demography provides a statistical description of human populations. The nature of human society cannot be fully understood without a clear comprehension of the integral role played by population processes in the dynamics of social life. The components of population consist of the ultimate vital events of birth and death. Natural movement of population is complemented by migration within and between countries (Courtney, 1991a). The basic actions in every population system, of entering and leaving, determine changes in population size. The pre-occupation of sociologists with social change which has led them to the study of demography as social change involves population change. Demographic structures and events are, therefore, of particular interest to sociologists. They may utilise them in various analytical frameworks which enhance their understanding and explanations. Demography was included by Durkheim in one of seven sections in *L'Année Sociologique*, the first sociological journal. Today demography is used by, among others, sociologists, social scientists, public servants and entrepreneurs as a basis for strategic planning and development in social and economic affairs throughout the public, voluntary and private sectors.

In spite of some explanatory limitations, modernisation theory, which is functionalist inspired, is of considerable descriptive value and has been the key theoretical perspective used in explaining social demography and population change. The central analytical issue concerns the interaction between demographic processes of population change, i.e. fertility, mortality and migration on the one hand, and socio-economic characteristics of modernisation on the other. In addition, an examination of the social differentials of fertility, mortality and migration is complementary and crucial in understanding social groups and communities within societies (Goldscheider, 1971). In sociology, comprehensive data are essential for the construction of theories and whilst demographic material has been of considerable adminis-trative and biographical value, both to civil and religious authorities, over-emphasis on empirical analysis of it has generally been to the detriment of its theoretical develop-ment. In fact, interactionist, phenomenological and other micro approaches consider demography more an adminis-trative method than a sociological one. Nevertheless, we will consider at the outset the essential features of two separate frameworks which attempt to make sense of demographic change.

Malthus (1958) was the first to provide, in 1798, a consistent theory of population in his *Essay on the Principle of Population.* Most attention centres around his global argument that population, when unchecked, doubles every generation i.e. increases in a geometrical progression (1, 2, 4, 8 ...) whereas, in the most favourable circumstances, the food supply, or subsistence, increases in an arithmetical progression (1, 2, 3, 4 ...). A positive check, however, is achieved through 'misery' due to increasing mortality as a result of disease, famine, wars and excesses. Preventive checks bring about decreasing fertility and are achieved by 'moral restraint' through late marriages without any extra-marital sex or, alternatively, by 'vice' resulting from birth control. He was correct in anticipating population growth but he greatly under-estimated the subsequent advances in industry, technology and communications. Malthus's more specific argument concerning families and social groups in particular cultures states that the balance between population and subsistence depends on a range of economic, social and political factors.

The second analytical framework grew out of the demo-graphic and socio-economic development of advanced societies during the nineteenth and early twentieth centuries. These changes gave rise to the theory of demographic transition which distinguished five phases:

- a stationary phase in which mortality and fertility are high
- an early expanding one when mortality begins to decline and fertility remains unchanged at a high level
- a late expanding one, when the decline in fertility follows the decline of mortality
- a low stationary one, when mortality and fertility are both at a similar level
- a diminishing one, when fertility declines below the level of mortality, which ceases to decline, and so the population begins to diminish (Blacker, 1947).

What happens between the 'transitional' and 'modern' societies is only vaguely explained by the theory. Like modernisation theory it is uni-directional and under-estimates the importance of regional and local variations in the developmental process. (See Andorka, 1978, for a more com-prehensive account of this theory of demographic transition).

In western Europe the Malthusian transition or what Hajnal described as the (western) European pattern of late marriages and high rates of celibacy occurred after the sixteenth century whilst the neo-Malthusian transition of the nineteenth century was characterised by a decline in marital fertility (Coale, 1969). The role of migration in demographic transition theory may be conceptualised in two ways. The first position argues that migration provides a short-term safety valve relieving population pressure and delaying fertility decline. The second is a modified Malthusian argument of multiphasic response: migration, along with mortality and fertility, is one of various responses to the pressures of population growth and relative socio-economic deprivation (Goldscheider, 1981).

ᵉ Van da Kaa (1987) describes what the population of Europe has experienced since the mid-1960s as its 'second demographic transition'. Whilst considerable heterogeneity remains between different European countries and regions, clearly emerging population trends and changing lifestyles are in evidence. They include later motherhood, more voluntary childlessness, declining fertility, lower replacement levels, greater longevity, an ageing population and labour force, greater female education and labour force participation, more persons living alone especially the elderly, fewer legal marriages, more consensual unions, extra-marital births and one-parent families, increasing levels of marital instability, separation and divorce, more couples gainfully employed outside the home and a greater sharing of household activities (Courtney, 1992). 'Population implosion' is characterised by stabilisation of the above demographic indicators resulting in increasing ageing of the population and, in the absence of immigration, in long-term population decline at a time when the world population continues to experience extraordinary growth (Hoffmann-Nowotny and Fux, 1991).

The world population increased from 2.5 billion persons in 1950 to 3.7 billion in 1970 and 5.2 billion in 1990. Meanwhile, the European population fell from 15.6 per cent of the world's total in 1950 to 12.4 per cent in 1970 and to 9.5 per cent in 1990. Paradoxically, it was only in the late 1960s that Europe and in particular western Europe became a continent of net immigration *vis-à-vis* the rest of the world. (See Courtney, 1991a and 1992, and Cruijsen *et al*, 1991, for a

review of European demographic trends during the 1980s
and projections for the future).

Demographic sources

Generally, the sociologist personally observes the phenomenon to be studied. However, population statistics are
collected, compiled, analysed and published by government
agencies which have statutory powers and the resources
necessary to undertake such diverse and complex operations.
The Central Statistics Office (CSO) carries out this function
in the Republic of Ireland (RI) on its own behalf and that of
the Department of Health (Punch, 1992) whereas in
Northern Ireland (NI) this is undertaken primarily for the
Department of Health and Social Services by the Registrar
General and the Census Office and also for the Department
of Finance and Personnel through its Policy Planning and
Research Unit (PPRU) (McQueen and Johnston, 1992).

The *Census of Population* gathers demographic, social,
economic and administrative data at a given time relating to
all persons and households in a country. It provides
information about a population's structure such as sex, age,
conjugal condition, place of birth, principal economic status,
occupation, industry, housing and household composition,
language, religion, fertility, migration and education. All the
Irish census years with their populations are indicated in
Tables 1 and 2. Throughout the twentieth century and
especially in recent decades the census of population has
been taken more frequently in the RI. In 1991 it was held on
the same date in the RI and throughout the United Kingdom
(UK) including NI. The greater availability of small area
population statistics and unpublished cross-tabulated census
data provide an invaluable base for a wide range of
sociological research.

The compulsory registration of births, deaths and marriages
in Ireland since 1864 provides continuous and complementary data which are available in quarterly reports for each

Table 1: **Population and average annual rates of change (per 1,000) in the Republic of Ireland, 1871–1991**

Intercensal period	Population (000s)[1]	Marriage rate[2]	Birth rate	Death rate	Rate of natural increase	Migration rate	Rate of increase
1871–81	3,870	4.5	26.2	18.1	8.0	–12.7	–4.6
1881–91	3,469	4.0	22.8	17.4	5.3	–16.3	–10.9
1891–01	3,222	4.5	22.1	17.6	4.5	–11.9	–7.4
1901–11	3,140	4.8	22.4	16.8	5.6	–8.2	–2.6
1911–26	2,972	5.0	21.1	16.0	5.2	–8.8	–3.7
1926–36	2,968	4.6	19.6	14.2	5.5	–5.6	–0.1
1936–46	2,955	5.4	20.3	14.5	5.9	–6.3	–0.4
1946–51	2,961	5.5	22.2	13.6	8.6	–8.2	+0.4
1951–56	2,898	5.4	21.3	12.2	9.2	–13.4	–4.3
1956–61	2,818	5.4	21.2	11.9	9.2	–14.8	–5.6
1961–66	2,884	5.7	21.9	11.7	10.3	–5.7	+4.6
1966–71	2,978	6.5	21.3	11.2	10.1	–3.7	+6.4
1971–79	3,368	6.8	21.6	10.5	11.1	+4.3	+15.4
1979–81	3,443	6.3	21.5	9.7	11.8	–0.7	+11.0
1981–86	3,541	5.5	19.1	9.4	9.7	–4.1	+5.6
1986–91	3,526	5.1	15.7	9.0	6.8	–7.6	–0.8

[1]Population at end of intercensal period. The following populations (000s) were enumerated at previous censuses in 1821: 5,421; 1831: 6,193; 1841: 6,529; 1851: 5,115; 1861: 4,402; 1871: 4,053.

[2]The marriage rates, 1871–1926, are averaged around end of year rather than April, e.g. 1871–80.

Source: *Census of Population and Reports on Vital Statistics.*

Table 2: **Population and average annual rates of change (per 1,000) in Northern Ireland, 1871–1991**

Intercensal period	Population (000s)[1]	Marriage rate[2]	Birth rate	Death rate	Rate of natural increase	Migration rate	Rate of increase
1871–81	1,305	NA	26.7	18.8	7.8	–11.9	–4.1
1881–91	1,236	NA	24.6	18.9	5.7	–11.1	–5.4
1891–01	1,237	NA	25.5	19.9	5.6	–5.5	+0.1
1901–11	1,251	NA	24.9	18.5	6.4	–5.3	+1.1
1911–26	1,257	5.8	22.9	16.9	6.0	–5.7	+0.3
1926–37	1,280	6.7	20.1	14.3	5.8	–4.1	+1.7
1937–51	1,371	6.9	21.9	13.3	8.6	–3.7	+5.0
1951–61	1,425	6.9	21.4	10.9	10.5	–6.6	+3.9
1961–66	1,485	7.3	25.1	11.7	13.4	–5.2	+8.2
1966–71	1,536	7.9	19.7	9.6	10.1	–3.3	+6.8
1971–81*	1,533	6.3	17.9	10.9	7.0	–7.2	–0.2
1981–91	1,573	5.8	17.7	10.2	7.5	–4.8	+2.6

[1]Population at end of inter-censal period. At previous Censuses the following populations (000s) were enumerated in 1821: 1,380; 1831: 1,574; 1841: 1,649; 1851: 1,443; 1861: 1,396; 1871: 1,359.
[2]Marriage rates are for the particular year at the end of the inter-censal period but are not available (NA) before 1926 in official publications.
*1981 figures, as revised by NI Census Office, take account of non-response.
Source: Censuses of Population and Registrar General Annual Reports.

jurisdiction and are later published annually in the *Report on Vital Statistics* (RI) and *the Registrar General's Report* (NI). Births are tabulated by sex, age of mother at maternity and number of previous children. Deaths are classified by sex, age and detailed information on the cause of death. Marriages are given by religious denominations. The reports provide data for births, deaths and marriages and equivalent rates per 1,000 population for the RI, NI, Scotland, England and Wales. In NI, information on live births and infant mortality by social class is of great value, especially to sociologists. A summary of net migration has been greatly enhanced by the publication since 1985 of an estimation of the number of persons who have immigrated and emigrated. In the RI the *Registrar General's Report* (which became the *Report on Vital Statistics* in 1953) provided a summary of the number of immigrants and emigrants by destination prior to 1940. The second world war effectively ended this practice although a migration balance was published subsequently.

Sample surveys which are also widely used by sociologists are becoming increasingly important as a source of demographic statistics although it is unlikely that they will ever fully replace the above methods of data collection. The Labour Force Survey (LFS) which was undertaken throughout the European Union, biannually between 1975 and 1983 and annually since then, provides comprehensive information on employment, unemployment and related topics. The RI data on households and family units is particularly useful to sociologists especially as Household Budget Surveys are held irregularly. In NI, on the other hand, a Continuous Household Survey (comparable to the General Household Survey in Britain) has been held annually since 1983 and provides a valuable data base for demographic and social research.

Population registers which exist in some of the Scandinavian and Benelux countries facilitate the continuous observation of biographical details of individuals from the cradle to the grave. They enable such demographic and social data to be centralised from a variety of sources and used in aggregate form, confidentially, for analytical purposes. They have the advantage of providing at any given time the exact size and structure of a population. Population registers provide better migration statistics than is otherwise possible, e.g. in Ireland and in Britain they do not exist. (See Courtney, 1994a, for a comprehensive review of official demographic sources in the RI).

In addition, international bodies such as the European Union (EU), the Council of Europe, the Organisation for Economic Cooperation and Development (OECD) and the United Nations Organisation (UN) publish different demographic reports as part of a series, or occasionally as commissioned research on public policies. They provide an appropriate comparative framework for socio-demographic studies, e.g. of the young or the elderly, the employed or the unemployed.

Information is collected in response primarily to the needs of governments, their ministries or departments and agencies. Thus, sociologists undertaking research may have to rely on demographic data collected for other purposes. This highlights the need for a preliminary critique of the questions used and the manner in which the information is collected. Improvements are desirable in reducing publication time-lags and providing more accurate details of migration. The importance of appropriate data collection cannot be over-emphasised. Though it is often difficult to accomplish, the collection of pertinent population data must precede demographic analysis and explanation. Analysis of population movement is essentially concerned with its primary components, i.e. fertility, mortality and migration (See Pressat, 1978, for a short and eminently clear introduction to basic statistical techniques in demographic analysis).

In what follows, directly comparable data between the RI and NI are not always provided. This is due in some respects to the desire to furnish a greater variety of information types and examples in what is, of necessity, a brief chapter on Irish demography. It also reflects different sources and ways of presenting some data in both parts of Ireland.

Population change

Demographic change may be explained by means of the following population components equation:

$$P_1 = P_0 + (B - D) + (I - E)$$

where P_0 and P_1 represent a population at the beginning and end, respectively, of a specified interval, usually a year, where persons enter the population through births (B) and immigration (I) and leave it through deaths (D) and emigration (E). The combination of births and deaths constitutes a natural increase while the addition of net migrants indicates total change. The corresponding rates used in Tables 1, 2 and 3 are ratios (per 1,000) of the different components of population change to the mean population, e.g.

$$\text{Rate of natural increase} = \frac{\text{Natural increase}}{\text{Mean population}} \ (\times 1{,}000)$$

This crude rate of natural increase is of course the difference between the (crude) birth and death rates.

In Ireland, the late eighteenth and early nineteenth centuries were times of rampant population growth for which the economic system proved inadequate. In 1841 the Irish population was a little more than half that in England and Wales (15.9 million). After the famines of the 1840s Malthus's 'ideal' was achieved when the Irish population overall declined dramatically and continuously until 1926, from 8,177,744 to 4,228,553, i.e. by 48 per cent. Thereafter, with the exception of the 1950s, it grew to 4,514,313 in 1971 and to 5,096,683 in 1991, an increase of 20.5 per cent. The Censuses of Population taken in 1991 reveal that there are more than 5 million persons living on the island of Ireland for the first time since 1881.

In 1922 Ireland was partitioned. The Irish Free State (which became the Republic of Ireland in 1949) achieved independence from the United Kingdom while Northern

Table 3: **Population and change, distribution by broad age groups, dependency ratios and density in some western European states, 1991–1993**

State	Population (000s) (1.1.1993)	Population change per 1000 in 1992			Age group (years) %				Dependency ratio (%)	Population density (km²)
		Growth rate	Rate of natural increase	Net migration rate	0–14	15–44	45–64	65+		
Austria	7,909,6	6.2	1.5	4.6	17.6	44.5	22.6	15.3	49.0	94
Belgium	10,068,3	4.6	2.0	2.6	18.2	43.7	22.7	15.4	50.6	330
Denmark	5,180,6	3.6	1.3	2.2	17.0	43.9	23.6	15.5	48.1	120
Finland **	5,055,1	5.2	3.4	1.7	19.2	44.5	22.7	13.6	48.8	15
France	57,526,6	5.4	3.8	1.6	19.9	44.4	21.1	14.5	52.5	104
Germany **	80,274,6	6.5	–1.0	7.5	16.3	43.5	25.2	15.0	45.6	225
Greece **	10,280,0	15.7	0.7	15.0	18.1	42.8	24.7	14.3	48.0	78
Italy ***	57,746,0	2.9	0.6	2.3	16.3	45.0	24.0	14.8	45.1	192
Luxembourg	395,2	13.7	3.2	10.8	17.9	45.2	23.3	13.6	46.0	153
Netherlands	15,238,6	7.3	4.6	2.8	18.3	46.8	21.9	13.0	45.6	373
Norway	4,299,2	6.0	3.7	2.4	19.2	44.1	20.5	16.2	54.8	13
Portugal	9,859,6	0.4	1.3	–1.0	18.9	44.5	22.5	14.1	49.3	107
Spain	39,114,3	1.5	1.0	0.5	18.1	45.8	21.9	14.1	47.6	77
Sweden	8,692,0	5.5	3.3	2.4	18.5	40.8	23.0	17.7	56.7	19
Switzerland	6,904,6	9.5	3.5	6.7	17.5	44.5	23.5	14.6	47.2	167
United Kingdom *	57,960,0	3.6	2.5	1.0	19.4	42.7	22.1	15.8	54.3	237
England	48,378,0	3.5	2.8	0.8	19.2	43.1	21.9	15.8	53.8	371
Wales	2,899,0	2.4	1.4	0.7	19.5	40.7	22.6	17.2	58.0	140
Scotland	5,111,0	0.8	1.2	–0.4	18.9	43.8	22.3	15.1	51.4	66
Northern Ireland	1,610,0	10.0	6.9	3.1	24.2	43.7	19.5	12.6	58.2	119
Ireland *	3,556,5	4.2	6.0	–1.7	26.3	44.4	17.9	11.4	60.5	50

* Ireland refers to the Republic of Ireland. The population estimates for England, Wales, Scotland and Northern Ireland are mid-1992 unlike the UK as a whole where the population is provided for the beginning of 1993 like most of the other countries.

** 1992 population with population change in 1991.

*** 1991 population with population change in 1990.

Source: *Council of Europe, 1993, Tables 1.1 to 1.5.* OPCS, 1994, *Population Trends No. 75,* Tables 5 and 6.

Ireland remained part of it. In the RI the population continued to decline until the 1960s apart from a small increase during the inter-censal period, 1946-51. Table 1 shows that the high rates of natural increase were surpassed by even higher levels of net emigration which had the most profound and devastating effect on values, attitudes and behaviour patterns. *The Commission on Emigration and Other Population Problems* (1954) stated that, on balance, the RI population was likely to be 2.5 million in 1986. The presence of over 3.5 million in spite of a resurgence in emigration and population decline in the late 1980s demonstrates the transformation that has occurred since 1961.

The decline in population was arrested in NI by the turn of the century when a slight increase of 0.1 per cent was recorded during the inter-censal period, 1891-1901. Table 2 indicates that the population continued to grow over each inter-censal period with the exception of 1971-81 when it declined a little. This growth was achieved as a result of relatively high rates of natural increase and in spite of high levels of emigration. The small decline in population during the 1970s was the result of a falling birth rate and a decline in the rate of natural increase combined with an increase in the (net) emigration rate.

In most countries population change is largely determined by natural increase yet in spite of its generally high level in both parts of Ireland, as Tables 1 and 2 indicate, it has consistently been less important than migration. Table 3 provides data on the population size, rates of growth, natural increase and net migration in a number of western European countries in the early 1990s. There were 80.3 million persons in Germany (of whom about 21 per cent reside in former East Germany), 58.0 million in the UK, 57.7 million in Italy and 57.5 million in France. The high growth rate in Greece, Luxembourg, Switzerland and the Netherlands in 1992 was due especially to immigration to those countries which was significantly higher than during the 1980s. Germany too had a high level of immigration in recent years together with a negative rate of natural increase which Denmark too experienced in 1984.

Since 1981 there has been population growth in each of the countries listed, though in some instances this has been small. Furthermore, the following experienced short-term population decline in the years specified: Austria (1982-83), Belgium (1981 and 1983), Denmark (1981-84), West Germany (1982-85), Luxembourg (1982), the UK (1981-82), the RI (1987-90), Italy (1990-91) and Portugal (1987-91). Within the UK the smallest population is in NI, yet it had the highest growth rate from mid-1991 to mid-1992 due to its high rates of natural increase and net immigration. Scotland which experienced a small amount of net emigration has a population comparable in size to the total number of persons on the island of Ireland.

Fertility and nuptiality

Natality is used to describe the number of births which has occurred *in toto* in a population and is expressed by the birth rate whereas fertility is not used as an absolute value in itself but as a phenomenon relating to individuals directly concerned with it, namely women in their childbearing years. In spite of an increase in cohabitation, consensual unions and extra-marital births in Ireland, most births still occur to married couples. As the propensity to marry, therefore, is important it is necessary to consider nuptiality along with fertility. The two are interwoven, one having a behavioural influence on the other.

The number who marry and the age at marriage are matters of great social significance especially in Ireland where relatively high permanent celibacy and late age at marriage provided the classic example of the Malthusian preventive check. Such marriage characteristics have been attributed in the RI to the large proportion of the population engaged in agriculture, the family system of inheritance, lack of urbanisation, poor economic conditions, low incomes and the indirect effects of emigration (Coward, 1978). It was not until the late 1950s that marriage patterns underwent change in the RI. Whilst nuptiality in NI was traditionally closer to that in the RI than elsewhere its characteristics were not as accentuated.

In the RI there was almost a 50 per cent increase in the age-specific first marriage rate for women between 1961 and 1971 although it declined again by nearly 46 per cent from 1971 to 1989. A significant decline over twenty years in the median age of brides and grooms ended in 1977. This too has risen since then along with a fall in the number of marriages. In fact, western European countries have generally experienced a decline in marriages with an increasing incidence of cohabitation. During the 1980s the average age at marriage has increased almost universally. In 1990 the average age of persons marrying for the first time was 28.3 years for men and 26.3 for women in the RI compared with 26.2 years and 24.3 years for men and women, respectively, in NI. In the RI the predominant influences on the fall in the number of marriages may be the protracted economic recession, the effects of a high level of unemployment, growing materialism, increasing marital breakdown and the absence of divorce. The earlier and greater decline in the age of grooms reflects a greater degree of similarity in the spouses' ages than in the past whilst the proportion who are single has fallen to a level more in line with other western European countries. In NI the proportion of ever-married females increased until 1971 from when it has fallen a little overall. The decline is particularly significant among younger age groups reflecting a greater delay in persons marrying for many of the same reasons outlined above for the RI.

Divorce, which exists in NI since the last century, albeit initially on a very restricted basis, increased from 1,653 (on all grounds), i.e. 2.5 per 1,000 in 1983 to 2,310 or 3.4 per 1,000 of the married population in 1991 when 36.5 per cent of divorces took place within ten years of marriage. In the RI divorce is not legally available although judicial separation is.

In 1986 a proposal to remove the constitutional ban on divorce was defeated by 63.5 per cent to 36.5 per cent. The 1991 census reveals that there were 55,143 separated persons in the RI (including some divorced elsewhere) compared with 37,245 in 1986. The 21,350 males and 33,793 females separated in 1991 represent 3.1 per cent and 4.8 per cent of the ever-married (excluding widowed) male and female populations, respectively. The government which came into office in 1994 has promised a further referendum on the matter.

The traditional marriage pattern in the RI was counter-balanced by high levels of fertility. By 1946 families were on average twice as large as those in Europe's low fertility countries in spite of the prevalence of late marriage (Walsh, 1980). A decline in completed family size has occurred in the RI since 1911 due particularly to a fall in the number of very large families. The modal completed family size for women aged 25-29 years at marriage and married for 25-29 years was seven to nine children then whereas in 1981 it was four to six children (Clancy, 1991). Cohort analysis underlines the prevalence of the four child family in the RI and illustrates a broad similarity in the distribution of families by number of children between 1961 and 1981. The largest families are found among those of long marriage duration and young age of the wife at marriage. The recent data provide evidence of younger brides having achieved a reduction in fertility for all marriage durations in contrast with the situation for over a century up to 1961.

Neither the stem family system nor the standard of living thesis[2] explain fully the traditionally high level of marital fertility. This is paradoxical as they were frequently advanced, until the 1950s, as explanations of other Irish demographic peculiarities: postponed marriage, permanent celibacy and high emigration (Kennedy, 1973). An extensive analysis of economic records, ethnographic studies and census data from 1926 to 1971, along with an intensive sample survey of farm families during 1970 and 1971, illuminate the relationship between fertility patterns and value systems in both 'peasant' and modern type societies (Hannan, 1979). The value system in the peasant economy provided an incentive to family formation which was relatively independent of economic factors whereas in a modern market economic system such is not the case.

Cohort analysis which provides essentially a longitudinal perspective is limited by data availability. In contrast, period analysis for a calendar year is the summation of different cohorts each with their own fertility histories. The difficulty in correctly interpreting the relative effects of variations either in total fertility or in the length of interval between births is a serious drawback. For that reason it was difficult initially to establish with certainty whether recent fertility decline was merely a temporary phenomenon or of fundamental long-term significance. Table 4 suggests such a fall in marital fertility, especially among older women. The total (period) marital fertility rate which comprises age-specific marital fertility rates declined by 46.0 per cent between 1961 and 1991. Preliminary evidence from the CSO suggests a post-ponement effect or lag between the time of marriage and the birth of the first child due probably to the use of contraception as an instrument of birth control. If the 1961 total marital fertility rates endured there would have been about 95,600 births to married couples in 1991 instead of 43,155 in the RI, a decline of almost 55 per cent in thirty years.

We lack a clear understanding of the processes involved in establishing new family size goals but it has been suggested that the breakdown of kinship dominance, improvements in living standards and mobility aspirations are of crucial impor-tance (Goldscheider, 1971). Specifically, fertility changes in the RI are attributed to varying patterns of nuptiality and migration, occupational changes from agriculture into production and service industries, increasing regional development and urbanisation, EU membership with greater general receptivity to new ideas and increasing numbers of married women in the labour force (Coward, 1982). Adult

Table 4: **Total marital fertility rates (per 1,000) and annual percentage change in the Republic of Ireland, 1961–1991**

Age Group (years)	1961	1971	1981	1986	1991	Annual Percentage Change			
						1961-71	1971-81	1981-86	1986-91
15–19	612.6	681.6	549.5	523.1	417.8	+1.1	–1.9	–1.0	–4.0
20–24	478.0	459.3	326.5	291.9	257.7	–0.4	–2.9	–2.1	–2.3
25–29	392.4	350.5	262.5	225.6	209.4	–1.1	–2.5	–2.8	–1.4
30–34	298.6	249.1	188.2	162.1	146.2	–1.7	–2.4	–2.8	–2.0
35–39	202.4	160.7	105.7	80.4	68.9	–2.1	–3.4	–4.8	–2.9
40–44	77.1	58.7	30.7	23.4	16.0	–2.4	–4.8	–4.8	–6.3
45–49	5.8	4.3	2.9	1.8	1.1	–2.6	–3.3	–7.6	–7.8
15–49	206.7	196.4	146.6	118.5	111.7				

Source: *Censuses of Population* and *Reports on Vital Statistics*.

male and female relationships have evolved in response to changing expectations, especially among women. A growing proportion of the younger generation are planning their families, with profound effects on the life-cycle of the average married woman. The labour force participation rate for (ever)-married women has increased from 8 per cent in 1971 to about 28 per cent in 1992. This trend is likely to intensify in coming decades when a substantial number of Irish women will have reared their families at a much younger age than hitherto. The reduction in fertility has been facilitated by the liberalisation of family planning legislation which was introduced initially in the RI as recently as 1979 unlike NI where it has existed since the 1930s.

In NI the number of economically active married women is relatively higher than in the RI and lower than in England and Wales. Like other western European countries it has continually increased since the early 1950s. In NI it more than trebled between 1961 and 1991 from 55,000 to 168,573 at a time when the total number of economically active persons remained largely static. While the proportion of married women who were economically active increased from 33 per cent in 1971 to 47 per cent in 1981, such participation rates remained lower than in England and Wales for women over thirty years of age. Compton and Coward (1989) suggest that this may be due to women in NI having larger families and longer periods of childbearing in a depressed economy where employment is difficult to find. Between the censuses of 1971 and 1991 there was a small decrease in the proportion of men, and a big increase in the proportion of women, defined as economically active (Cormack *et al*, 1993). The high number of married women in part-time employment, 38 per cent in 1991, may reflect attempts to reconcile the conflicting roles of childcaring and working for remuneration. In contrast with the situation in NI, it is estimated in the 1992 LFS that only 27.6 per cent of married women in the RI are in the paid labour force and fewer of these (27.1 per cent) are in part-time employment.

In general, fertility in NI has been consistently lower than in the RI albeit higher than that found in most western European countries including Britain. This may be due to a relatively young age structure, a high proportion of its population engaged in agriculture, low levels of economic development, personal incomes, industrialisation and modernisation. Official statistics are supplemented by the results of the 1983 NI Fertility Survey (NIFS). This comprehensive survey about fertility, family planning and related socio-economic and cultural variables is the first such study undertaken in either part of Ireland. High fertility levels are found, particularly among Catholics, compared with those in England and Wales. Compton and Coward (1989) suggest that 'fertility in NI may be characterised as the overlapping of the high fertility regime associated with the RI, typical of Catholics, and a low fertility regime more reminiscent of Britain, typical of Protestants'. The consistency of this differential across the socio-economic structure suggests that the cause is due to some form of cultural rather than denominational distinctiveness (Compton, 1991). In general, an inverse relationship between social class (as defined by the male's occupation) and family size exists. However, it is the skilled non-manual who have the lowest completed family size in England and Wales and among the 'Other Denominations' in NI. In contrast, along with the skilled manual they have the highest completed family size among NI Catholics (Table 5).

Following the baby boom of the late 1940s the birth rate in NI fell to a low in the mid 1950s before rising to a new peak in 1964. The total period marital fertility index also peaked in 1964 thus minimising the impact of the age structure of the population. The close correspondence of the two measures from the 1950s through to the 1980s may be attributed to changes in marital fertility. Compton and Coward (1989) affirm that the increase in marital fertility prior to 1964 encompassed an advancement in the timing of births whereas the subsequent decline was associated with birth deferrals.

They conclude that between 1964 and 1969 the greater decline in marital fertility (TMFR) occurred at a time when nuptiality was increasing whereas between 1970 and 1977 the greater decline in the birth rate happened because of the decline in nuptiality. They attribute the renewed increase in the live birth rate in the late 1970s almost entirely to a revival in marital fertility. Such changes in nuptiality and the timing of births help to explain the short-term fluctuations of period measures compared with the gradual decline in cohort fertility. The rapid decline in the total period fertility rate (TPFR) in the RI, especially during the 1980s, caused it to fall below that in NI between 1986 and 1990. However, following further declines the TPFR in 1992 was 2.09 in NI compared with 2.11 in the RI.

Table 5:   **Completed family size by social class in Northern Ireland and England and Wales, 1971–1983**

Social class		N. Ireland 1983 RCs	ODs	England and Wales 1971
I	Professional	3.82	2.42	2.11
II	Intermediate	4.19	2.62	2.02
IIIN	Skilled non-manual	4.54	2.41	1.90
IIIM	Skilled manual	4.62	2.70	2.24
IV	Semi-skilled	4.46	3.10	2.29
V	Unskilled	4.21	3.68	2.57

Data for England and Wales refer to couples married 20-24 years in an uninterrupted first marriage (1971 data are the most recent available; family sizes have probably declined somewhat since then). Note: RCs are Roman Catholics, ODs are Other Denominations.
Source: *Compton and Coward (1989, p. 201).*

 Overall, completed fertility in NI has fallen from 4.0 children for couples marrying in the aftermath of the second world war to 3.3 children for those marrying in the early 1960s. Like the RI there have been significant and sustained changes in the distribution of family sizes. Between 1961 and 1983 the two- and three-child family became more dominant especially since 1971. The increase in four-child families may reflect the decline in larger families whilst childlessness and one-child families have also become less prevalent. Average family size by marriage duration is a useful measure where childbearing is planned. After increasing during the 1960s family sizes were between 7 and 12 per cent lower in 1983 compared with 1971, apart from those of less than five years' marriage duration. Fertility decline in NI is related to a number of demographic, socio-economic and cultural changes as in other countries, including the RI and the remainder of the UK. In particular, the importance of changing contraceptive technology and use, increasing individualism, consumerism and secularisation, notwithstanding the geographical isolation of NI, have been advanced as explanations.

(In the RI, the Protestant population has been in decline for many years due initially to a high number emigrating in the aftermath of independence and in modern times as a result of inter-marriage with Catholics who were required by the *ne temere* decree to bring up their children as Catholics.)The number of Protestants (persons belonging to the Church of Ireland, Presbyterian and Methodist Churches) declined from 4.6 per cent of the population in 1961 to 3.0 per cent in 1991 at a time when the overall population increased by 18.4 per cent. In NI the lower incidence of inter-marriage reflects the low level of social integration between Catholics and Protestants as well as the large absolute and relative size of the minority Catholic population (Walsh, 1970). The 1983 NIFS suggests that the number of mixed marriages is rising. Whilst it does not differ a lot by social class, education or even region, there are noticeable geographical differences at local level. Mixed marriages are more common in peaceful areas where high levels of segregation and sectarian conflict are absent.

The emphasis up to now on marital fertility reflects the importance of the relationship between nuptiality and fertility and the fact that in both parts of Ireland as in many other European countries most births occur within marriages. Nevertheless, a steady rise in the proportion of marriages in which a first birth is recorded in the year of marriage suggests a significant increase in the number involving pre-nuptial conceptions. This is most common among teenage brides and younger women generally. A significant increase has taken place in the number of extra-marital births. In the RI there were 9,303 births outside marriages in 1992, equivalent to 18.0 per cent of all births registered, compared with just 975, i.e. 1.63 per cent in 1961. The proportion of first order extra-marital births has fallen too. This reflects a more liberal and permissive society today than in the past. In addition, some are probably the product of post-marital relationships which, in the absence to date of divorce in the RI, cannot be legalised. The number of single parents has also increased significantly as more unmarried mothers prefer to keep and rear their own children instead of handing them over for adoption or fostering (Courtney, 1991b). In 1991 there were 75,337 lone mothers living with children and 15,569 fathers in similar circumstances including widowed persons, i.e. 7.9 per cent and 1.6 per cent, respectively, of all family units living in private households. In 1992 over 66 per cent of extra-marital births in RI were to women under the age of twenty-five years. In NI too the number of extra-marital births has risen from 815, i.e. 2.5 per cent of all births registered in 1960 to 5,603, or 21.9 per cent of all births in 1992. A little over 64 per cent of them were to mothers under the age of twenty-five years. In spite of the sharp increase in extra-marital births in recent years in both parts of Ireland there are fewer proportionately than, for example, in England and Wales where they account for 31.2 per cent of all births in 1992. The incidence of extra-marital births varies from being almost non-existent in some Mediterranean countries, e.g. 2 per cent in Greece, to being extremely prevalent in the Nordic countries, e.g. 55 per cent in Iceland.

Abortion is, in principle, illegal in both parts of Ireland

and although a small number are carried out in NI on medical grounds, in practice some women from NI go to England for abortions, as do some from the RI. The situation in the RI is somewhat confused. A referendum held in 1983 on the right to life of the unborn was carried, with 66.9 per cent voting in favour and 33.1 per cent against. The inclusion by the Irish government of a protocol in the Maastricht Treaty to uphold the 1983 amendment to the constitution and subsequent related court cases led to further referenda. In 1992 the people voted in favour of the Maastricht Treaty, the right to information about abortion and the right to travel for one, but against the availability of it in the RI. The UK Office of Population Censuses and Surveys (OPCS) has documented a steady increase in the number of abortions carried out in England and Wales since abortion was legalised in 1967. The official number of women from the RI who had abortions there increased from 3,320 in 1980 to 4,254 in 1992, i.e. an average increase of 2.6 per cent per annum whilst those from NI rose from 1,565 to 1,794, an increase of 1.3 per cent per annum in the same period. They represent 2.5 per cent and 1.0 per cent, respectively, of all legal abortions undertaken in England and Wales in 1992. Many of the women are unmarried. The proportion under twenty years of age is 16.8 per cent from the RI and 21.0 per cent from NI.

Throughout western Europe fertility has been in decline for many years with the total period fertility rate below the replacement level of 2.1 in many countries. The fact that some of them have experienced a small increase in their total period fertility rates during the 1980s requires careful interpretation. There appears to be a pattern whereby women in countries with low levels of fertility are relatively older at childbirth. This is especially true for first order births where the average age of mothers has increased in almost all countries.

In conclusion, the overall transformation that has occurred in recent nuptiality and fertility trends in both parts of Ireland is neo-Malthusian in essence and reflects a significant shift in culture, behaviour and value systems.

Mortality

Mortality decreased very significantly during the last half of the nineteenth century. This decrease has continued throughout the twentieth century albeit on a less dramatic scale. The level of mortality in both parts of Ireland compares reasonably well with other countries although it is marginally higher than most other western European ones and it is now the least volatile of demographic components. While variations according to sex and age may be indicated by age(sex)-specific mortality rates, in the same way as for marriage and fertility, the most complete statistical profile is provided by life tables.

Mortality statistics reveal that life expectancy at birth is highest in Sweden where in 1988-89 it was 74 years for men and 81 years for women. The comparable data for Turkey, however, is 63.5 and 68.5 years, respectively. Table 6 provides details of life expectancy at different ages for males and females in the RI and NI. Increased longevity has been accompanied by a widening gap between that for males and females with the disappearance of the traditionally and relatively high female mortality in the RI. Females can now expect to live, on average, five to six years longer than males in Ireland. Life expectancy at birth is marginally higher for males in the RI than in NI while it is identical for females. Life expectancy at birth for males in the RI has increased from 57.4 years to 71.0 years and in NI from 55.4 years to 70.6 years between 1925-27 and 1985-87. Life expectancy at birth for females in the RI has increased from 57.9 years to 76.7 years and in NI from 56.1 years to 76.7 years in the same period.

Since the mid-1920s the increase in life expectancy at birth has been greater in NI than in the RI. This decline in mortality has been most significant among infants. There has been some improvement in the life expectancy of women aged 65 years (life expectancy for females at 65 years of age in NI is 16.6 years compared with 16.2 years for those in the RI) and whilst NI men of that age have experienced a small

Table 6: **Expectation of life at ages 0, 1 and 65 years for males and females in Ireland 1841, the Republic of Ireland and Northern Ireland, 1925–1927 to 1985–1987**

PERIOD		Males			Females		
			Age (years)			Age (years)	
		0	1	65	0	1	65
1841	CD	24.0	30.7	9.6	24.2	30.3	10.5
	RD	29.6	37.8	10.9	28.9	36.1	10.8
1925-27	RI	57.4	61.2	12.8	57.9	60.8	13.4
	NI	55.4	59.9	11.9	56.1	59.5	12.7
1960-62	RI	68.1	69.3	12.6	71.9	72.7	14.4
	NI	67.6	68.7	12.2	72.4	73.2	14.4
1970-72	RI	68.8	69.2	12.4	73.5	73.8	15.0
	NI	67.6	68.3	12.0	73.7	74.1	15.2
1980-82	RI	70.1	69.9	12.6	75.6	75.4	15.7
	NI	69.3	69.3	12.4	75.7	75.4	16.1
1985-87	RI	71.0	70.7	12.6	76.7	76.3	16.2
	NI	70.6	70.3	12.8	76.7	76.4	16.6

RI: Life Tables for the Republic of Ireland; NI: Life Tables for Northern Ireland;
CD: Civic District, population of towns containing 2,000 inhabitants and upwards;
RD: Rural District, population of all towns containing less than 2,000.
Source: *Report of Census Commissioners 1841 (Appendix, pp. lxxx-i), Commission of Emigration and other Population Problems (Table 79), Irish Life Tables (various),* and *Registrar General NI Annual Report 1991 (Table VI).*

increase, the life expectancy in the RI of men aged 65 years has surprisingly only declined from 12.8 years in 1925-27 to 12.6 years in 1985-87.

Thus life tables also reveal the significance of the decline in infant deaths and the impact which this has had on overall mortality. Even since 1971 the infant mortality rate (deaths of children under one year of age per 1,000 live births) has fallen. Significantly, in NI it declined from 22.7 to 6.0 in 1992 and in the RI from 18.0 to 6.6 in the same period. It compares favourably with other western European countries. After surviving the first year of life the probability of death decreases considerably and is not as high again until about the age of sixty years. However, some male age groups have in recent years experienced a small increase in mortality against the overall pattern, e.g. the rise in mortality during the early 1970s among males aged twenty to thirty-four years in NI has been attributed to the higher incidence of traffic accidents and an increase in violent deaths arising from 'the troubles' (Coward, 1986). International data suggest that lower socio-economic groups are prone to higher mortality risks and this is especially true in cases of perinatal (stillbirths plus deaths during the first week of life), neonatal (deaths of infants aged under four weeks) and infant mortality. NI statistics reveal that in 1992 perinatal, neonatal and infant mortality rates ranged from 5.3, 2.7 and 4.0 among professionals to 13.4, 5.2 and 6.2 respectively, for the unskilled. Perinatal mortality rates are expressed per 1,000 births (live and still) while neonatal, like infant mortality rates, are given per 1,000 live births. Similarly, Nolan (1990) found significant differentials in standardised mortality rates in the RI between professional/managerial occupational working groups and semi-skilled or unskilled manual categories based on 1981 data for men aged fifteen to sixty-four years. Infant mortality is also influenced by high parity births, birthweight and the mother's biological attributes.

Coward (1986) attempts to explain the higher mortality rates in NI compared with England and Wales by a variety of economic and social lifestyle factors which are influenced by lower living standards, more widespread poverty, differences in diet, smoking habits and the possibility of proportionately higher emigration among healthier individuals. Marginally higher mortality levels in urban areas throughout Ireland also reflect differing lifestyles and environmental conditions. Finally, changing patterns of mortality are influenced by changes in the cause of death. Heart disease continues to be the single biggest cause of death though its rate has declined recently compared with an increase in the prevalence of cancer. The death rate from all forms of heart disease has fallen from 4.14 per 1,000 population in 1961 to 3.18 in 1990 in NI and from 3.93 to 2.84 in the RI. In the same period the death rate from cancer has risen from 1.53 to 2.17 in NI and from 1.61 to 2.04 in the RI. Meanwhile, deaths from tuberculosis, especially among younger age groups, have fallen significantly since the 1940s. In recent years cases of, and deaths from, AIDS have risen though they remain relatively small in number. There were forty-two deaths from AIDS in the RI during 1992 and five in NI between April 1992 and 1993.

Migration

Migration is the most difficult component of population change to define, record and analyse. It is generally defined in terms of the area to be studied. It can be either internal or international and inward or outward. Immigration to western Europe which began in the early 1960s, reached its peak between about the middle of that decade and 1974 at the time of the first oil crisis; since then it has declined and in recessionary times return migration has been stimulated in some host countries. The predominant receiving countries of such Mediterranean and third world migration are now found in southern Europe (Hoffmann-Nowotny and Fux, 1990). Meanwhile, intra-European migration is declining in almost all western European countries. During the 1980s, such traditional emigrant countries as Portugal, Greece and Italy all experienced a surplus of immigrants over emigrants who came mainly from North African and third world countries. Higher fertility among immigrant couples has a rejuvenating impact on age structures and dependency ratios and directly affects overall population change. In addition, the contribution of immigration is relatively important where there are low or falling rates of natural increase amongst the indigenous population. Such differentials, whilst having a positive impact on population size and growth, are sometimes perceived by reactionary groups as increasing ethnic minorities and heightening disharmony and tensions in society. This is especially so when unemployment is high although the presence of immigrants is frequently due to (wo)manpower needs in receiving countries. Return migration is often related to falling employment in times of economic recession (Uner, 1990). Immigration to former West Germany grew significantly throughout the 1980s prior to the removal of the Berlin Wall and its reunification with East Germany. The predominantly younger age profile and higher family size of many recent German ethnic immigrants has rejuvenated its population which had fallen by almost 200,000 persons between 1980 and 1988.

The absence of compulsory registration in Ireland, such as exists in some other western European countries as outlined above and, more particularly, the absence of border controls makes the estimation of Irish migration for intercensal periods a hazardous business. Difficulties brought about by the under-estimation of the RI population in 1979, when compared subsequently with the census results, has compelled the CSO to consider and develop other method-ological means of measuring migration (Courtney, 1994a). They include net passenger movements, child benefit for children under sixteen years of age, children enrolled at first and second level schools, the aggregate register of electors of all persons aged eighteen years and over, Labour Force Survey estimates of gross migration flows, the number of immigrant visas issued to Irish persons by the United States of America (USA), Canada and Australia and new registrants with the National Health Services and the National Insurance Scheme in the UK. Data are available since 1992 from the administrative records of the Department of Social Welfare in the RI to identify returned migrants amongst newcomers on the unemployment 'Live Register' (Punch, 1994). In NI estimates of migration have been based similarly on the transfer of National Insurance and National Health Service records along with the International Passenger Survey. The Census of Population in Britain provides useful information on migration within one year preceding the census and by country of birth for those from both parts of Ireland. Reciprocal data for Britain are available in both the RI and NI Censuses of Population. Some information on cross-border movement between the RI and NI is provided below.

The human tragedy of emigration from Ireland reached catastrophic proportions during and after the famines of the 1840s. Between then and 1925 almost 4.75 million Irish persons went to the USA, 670,000 to Canada and over 370,000 to Australia and New Zealand. Total overseas emigration in that period was 5.8 million. From 1876 to 1921 only 8 per cent of emigration from the RI went to Britain compared with 28 per cent from NI (Commission on Emigration and Other Population Problems, 1954). Tables 1 and 2 indicate that from the 1880s onwards emigration from the RI has been of greater significance than from NI and, with broadly similar levels of natural increase in both parts of Ireland, resulted in continuing population decline in the RI whilst NI experienced a steady growth in population. The situation changed fundamentally in the early 1930s when Britain replaced the USA as the major destination of Irish emigrants. This situation continued during the second world war and afterwards. In the 1950s the pattern was one of heavy emigration from the RI of single persons who married and had their children abroad. During the 1960s net emigration declined and the population growth was significant. A proportion of those took advantage of new opportunities to return with their families during the 1970s. Industrial developments assisted by capital grants and tax incentives and accessibility to EU markets provided highly skilled jobs in the RI for many of those migrants of whom 19,000 were born in NI, 69,000 in Britain and 21,000 elsewhere (Garvey, 1985). In 1980-81 the largest occupational group of immigrants consisted of professional and technical workers. In contrast, many others in the labour force, especially farmers on marginal holdings and unskilled labourers, remained in residual classes and were particularly vulnerable to emigration (Rottman *et al*, 1982).

The first evidence of a return to net emigration after nearly ten years came during the short intercensal period, 1979-81, when population increase was lower than the natural increase by 5,045, i.e. by about 0.7 per 1,000 population per annum. The situation deteriorated during the 1980s when the average annual level was 14,377, i.e. 4.1 per 1,000 population and 27,297, i.e. 7.7 per 1,000 population for 1981-86 and 1986-91, respectively. Annual estimates of gross migration for April 1982-88 using Labour Force Survey data on 'one-year immigrants' indicate a steady increase in emigration (Courtney, 1989). Detailed annual estimates of gross inward and outward migration flows classified by sex, age group and country of origin/destination from 1987-93 published for the first time by the CSO in 1994 confirm that this trend peaked in 1988-89 when there was emigration of approximately 70,600 (39,200 males and 31,300 females) at a time when such economic indicators as manufacturing output, the trade surplus and gross national product were increasing. Between April 1982 and 1993, it is estimated that there were approximately 472,300 emigrations from the RI. Thus, there is an inability to translate economic growth into sufficient employment to sustain the large numbers entering the labour force each year. The decline in emigration since 1988-89 due to the world-wide recession has resulted in increasing unemployment with the seasonally adjusted standard unemployment rate reaching an average of 15.8 per cent of the labour force in 1993. It is likely, however, that emigration will increase again with improvements in the world economy and continue into the twenty-first century. In the same period, 1982-93, there were approximately 263,500 immigrations, thus an annual volume of migration (emigration plus immigration) of approximately 66,900, i.e. 19.0 per 1,000 population.

Between 1987 and 1993 marginally more males migrated than females: approximately 182,900 males and 160,500 females emigrated while approximately 106,700 males and 99,300 females immigrated. Most of the emigrants were aged fifteen to twenty-four years (63.2 per cent) with females a little younger than males: 30.4 per cent were aged twenty-five to forty-four years and 9.1 per cent 0-14 years. In the case of immigrants there was also a high number of persons aged 0-14 years (16.0 per cent) and twenty-five to forty-four years (40.6 per cent), reflecting the movement of families into the RI. The relatively high number of immigrants aged forty-five years and over (14.0 per cent) suggest persons moving on retirement. From 1987 to 1993 about 60.3 per cent emigrated to the UK, 10.2 per cent to elsewhere in the EU, 14.2 per cent to the USA and 15.1 per cent to the rest of the world. More males emigrated to the UK and more females elsewhere. There were about 52.8 per cent who immigrated to the RI from the UK, 15.2 per cent from other countries in the EU, 13.3 per cent from the USA and 18.9 per cent from elsewhere in the world. Similarly, the number of males was higher from the UK and there were more females from elsewhere in the EU and from the USA. However, there were marginally more males immigrating from the rest of the world (CSO, 1994).

Sexton, Walsh, Hannan and McMahon (1991) attempt to explain the reasons for emigration from the RI by using a sample of school-leavers in 1981-82. They found that by the end of 1987 about one in three of the cohort had emigrated whilst a further 8 per cent intended to migrate. Expectations and belief in finding employment abroad coupled with failure to do so at home are the principal causes of emigration. Although income dissatisfaction is much less important it does provide some with a reason to emigrate. Emigrants who fail to attain their desired occupational status are most likely to come from middle class backgrounds with better education. 'The upwardly mobile middle classes are about twice as likely to have emigrated as those from stable or downwardly mobile working class or small farm origins.' This represents a fundamental change from earlier emigration. Previous migration experience and involvement in migrant networks are surprisingly important in decision-making. Many seek employment or alternative employment in the RI before going. In general, 'push' and 'pull' factors appear to influence the decisions of the poorly educated and better educated middle-class, respectively. In addition, the life-cycle is important insofar as single persons or those married without dependants are more likely to migrate.

In NI emigration exceeded that of the 1950s during the 1970s, especially in the early years of the decade, due to severe economic problems and the effects of the troubles. The decline in emigration since then reflects the recession in Britain and the difficulties of finding employment there (Coward, 1986). Like the RI the preponderance of migrants are young. Table 7 provides details of migration by sex and age group of persons born in the RI and NI who were resident in England and Wales in 1991. The Irish stock both from the RI and NI was slightly lower than in 1981. The 788,280 persons born in Ireland are uniformly representative of many generations of migrants. There are many in their late twenties whilst the number of teenagers from NI is relatively high by comparison with those from the RI.

In a recent survey of emigrants from NI, Compton and Power (1991) found that over 50 per cent of those who leave are motivated by job-related factors. Many leave to further their education and training in Britain. Others emigrate for marriage, family reasons and a desire for independence. A mere 2.5 per cent of the sample gave 'the troubles' as their main reason for emigration. Using LFS data, Forsythe and Borooah (1992) suggest that migration between NI and

Table 7:   **Migration by sex and by age group of persons born in the Republic of Ireland and Northern Ireland and resident in England and Wales in 1991**

Age Group (years)	Republic of Ireland			Northern Ireland		
	Persons	Males	Females	Persons	Males	Females
0–4	3,272	1,716	1,556	2,167	1,081	1,086
5–9	7,333	3,749	3,584	3,828	1,925	1,903
10–14	6,848	3,408	3,440	4,338	2,220	2,118
15–19	7,889	3,668	4,221	6,609	3,407	3,202
20–24	28,130	11,875	16,255	16,010	7,834	8,176
25–29	35,636	17,646	17,990	20,377	10,417	9,960
30–34	30,525	14,788	15,737	18,163	9,122	9,041
35–39	37,449	17,536	19,913	19,397	9,228	10,169
40–44	50,028	23,631	26,397	21,001	10,359	10,642
45–49	57,978	27,799	30,179	20,808	10,582	10,226
50–54	59,705	29,130	30,575	16,426	8,368	8,058
55–59	59,395	28,864	30,531	15,549	8,115	7,434
60–64	55,421	25,994	29,427	14,602	7,437	7,165
65–84	123,821	53,005	70,816	37,136	16,208	20,928
85+	6,329	1,586	4,743	2,110	555	1,555
Total	569,759	264,395	305,364	218,521	106,858	111,663

Source: OPCS, *1991 Census, Ethnic Group and Country of Birth, Great Britain*, Table 2.

Britain is strongly bi-modal involving on the one hand a 'brain drain' and on the other many with low skills and poor employment prospects. The latter are more likely to return to NI and contribute to the unemployment problem unlike the former who deprive it of potential innovators and entrepreneurs and who may be more favourably disposed towards a political solution (Compton, 1991). Finally, this situation is accentuated by the high mobility of graduates in industries which are considered important for economic development. Most of the outflow from NI is, however, internal within the UK unlike the RI where graduates with expensively acquired skills are lost to competitor countries (Compton and Power, 1991). Educational institutions in NI are, nevertheless, the net losers of many high quality students who pursue their studies abroad, mostly in Britain (Osborne *et al*, 1987). It is estimated (Jardine, 1994) that over 4,000, i.e. 40 per cent of NI higher education entrants have taken up places in Britain in 1992-93.

The contrasting migration experiences of the RI and NI during the 1970s and 1980s have also been reflected in the movement of persons between the two parts of Ireland. The PPRU in NI has estimated that during 1971-81 approximately 22,000 more persons migrated from NI to the RI than in the opposite direction. This number declined gradually from about 6,000 in 1972-73 to about 1,000 per annum at the end of the decade. During the 1980s and early 1990s the balance was reversed with net movement from the RI to NI rising to approximately 1,424 (2,824 RI to NI and 1,400 NI to RI) in 1991-92 and 1,157 (2,757 RI to NI and 1,600 NI to RI) in 1992-93 (PPRU). This is in contrast with the overall situation in NI where net emigration to Britain and elsewhere increased during the 1980s.

Internal migration has traditionally been much less prominent in Ireland than elsewhere. Nevertheless, it is becoming increasingly important and deserves much more consideration than is possible in this short chapter. It is highest among teenagers, especially the unmarried and the economically active, and declines with advancing years. Shorter mobility in urban areas reflects changes in residence and marital status, with movement of longer distances due to labour force considerations. Industrial development provides greater opportunities for skilled manual and white-collar workers.

In the RI, population growth in the 1960s was confined generally to urban areas. During the 1970s a growth rate of 1.55 per cent per annum – over four times the EU average – was widely diffused encompassing most parts of the country. In 1991, 57 per cent of the population live in towns of 1,500 persons or more compared with 32 per cent in 1926. The medium-sized towns have been the major beneficiaries of this growth. Dublin city has, however, experienced decline from a total population of 567,866 in 1971 to 478,389 in 1991 while the contiguous counties of Dublin, Kildare, Meath and Wicklow have increased from 494,354 to 872,206 in the same period. The other cities too have experienced decline at the expense of their suburbs and adjacent satellite towns where substantial growth has occurred.

In NI, a fall in emigration during the 1980s contributed to a return to population growth which was reflected in almost all of the twenty-six local government districts. Nevertheless, the population remains unevenly balanced between the less-developed rural areas of the west and the more industrialised urban ones in the east. The population in the Belfast District Area (DA) has continued to decline from 416,679 in 1971 to 279, 237 in 1991 due to the troubles and redevelopment whilst its suburbs and nearby towns have grown in size. (The real decline in Belfast is unclear as the DA is that portion of the city remaining after Castlereagh DA was formed.) The largest growth during the 1980s was experienced in Lisburn which reflects the development of the Poleglass and Twinbrook housing estates on the western hinterland of Belfast. The populations of Ards, Banbridge and Carrickfergus also increased significantly. Cookstown and Magherafelt were the only local government districts west of the River Bann to grow by more than 10 per cent between 1981 and 1991.

Population composition and dependency

The two most important demographic variables used in
sociological studies and surveys to understand and explain
the structure of society are those of sex and age. Further
characteristics of population composition such as place of
residence, stratification and class, education, occupation and
unemployment, are discussed in other chapters. The
composition of a population by sex and age affects the entire
social, cultural, economic and political fabric of a society. Its
effect on marriage patterns, fertility, mortality and migration
determines population size and specifically influences
dependency levels, (wo)manpower availability and
employment opportunities.

The population pyramid provides the best graphical
representation of such variables. Its socio-economic profile
demonstrates the need for service provision and public
expenditure priorities, e.g. a young population calls for
education and child care facilities whereas an ageing one
requires a contracting labour force to sustain more elderly
persons (Jardine, 1994). Figure 1 indicates changes in
population structure from the traditional triangular pyramid
characteristic of young populations through to the present
time. The first observation to make is that the population of
what is now the RI was almost four times as large as that of NI
in 1841 compared with 1991 when it is a little more than twice
the size. In fact, the differential evident today was achieved by
1881 with particularly significant changes occurring during
the 1860s. By using five-year age groups the irregularity
displayed in the 1841 pyramid may be attributed to the over-
enumeration of persons in the decimal years (Figure 1a). The
age structure was broadly similar in both parts of Ireland
then. The 1841 age pyramid for Ireland just prior to the
famine is that of a population characterised by high fertility
and low life expectancy. The broad based pyramid narrows
quickly and is indicative of a pre-transition demographic
régime. The pyramid for 1926 provides dramatic evidence of

the effects of the famine, eighty years after the event (Figure 1b). The populations have contracted fundamentally due to unprecedented high levels of mortality and emigration. The effect on family formation and the decline in fertility coupled with increasing life expectancy subsequently, have resulted in an ageing process. The year 1961 marks a watershed in the recent demographic history of the RI and the extremely irregular pyramid for that year is due to previously heavy emigration especially during the 1950s (Figure 1c). The less ill-proportioned structure in NI reflects the lesser impact – albeit high – of emigration prior to 1961. Further gains in life expectancy are reflected in more pronounced ageing. One of the disadvantages of using a small number of pyramids at such wide intervals is that they may not adequately illustrate short-term fluctuations which occur in the interim such as the rejuvenation of the RI population during the 1970s due to the high birth rate and the unprecedented net immigration. The decline in fertility, increased longevity, further ageing and a recurrence of net emigration from the RI is evident in the 1991 pyramid (Figure 1d). In spite of a more post-transitional look to the NI pyramid both populations continue to display a younger age structure than that found elsewhere in western Europe.

The sex ratio (of males to females) in the RI has also been exceptional throughout the twentieth century until 1986. Like NI, however, there are now more females than males in the RI. The higher number of male births is usually offset by the greater longevity of females which also contributes to their significantly higher number over the age of sixty-five years. Sex imbalances have social and psychological repercussions with a depressing impact on marriage patterns especially in rural areas. Farming populations have an older age structure and higher levels of celibacy. The urban/rural divergence – though decreasing – remains because of the increasing importance of internal migration. A younger urban population at each census also reflects urban/rural differences in family patterns and occupational structures.

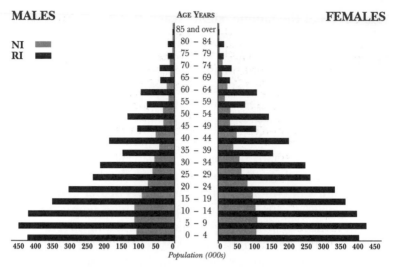

Fig. 1a   **Populations of the Republic of Ireland and Northern Ireland, classified by sex and by age group, in 1841**

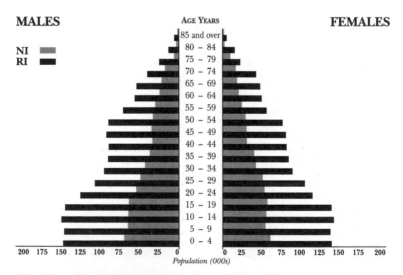

Fig. 1b   **Populations of the Republic of Ireland and Northern Ireland, classified by sex and by age group, in 1926**

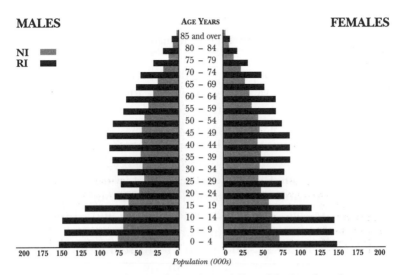

Fig. 1c   **Populations of the Republic of Ireland and Northern Ireland, classified by sex and by age group, in 1961**

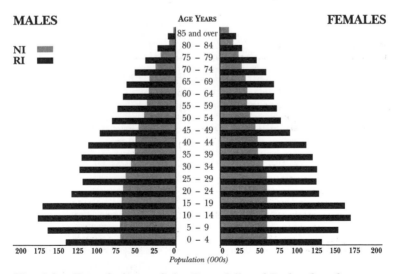

Fig. 1d   **Populations of the Republic of Ireland and Northern Ireland, classified by sex and by age group, in 1991**

Dependency is crucial in understanding the relationship between population, the formulation of public policies and the provision of associated services. The *dependency ratio* is defined as the ratio of persons in dependent ages, i.e. persons aged under fifteen years together with those aged sixty-five years and over to those in the economically productive age groups (fifteen to sixty-four years). Eurostat (of the EU) has used the broad groups of 0-19 years, twenty to fifty-nine years and sixty years and over to reflect the increasing concentration of the labour force aged twenty to fifty-nine years and higher education participation rates among teenagers (Cruijsen *et al*, 1991). Between 1926 and 1961 the dependency level, both young and old, increased at almost every census in the RI. The greater increase in the 1950s was due to the effect of emigration on the young active population. Dependency levels have since decreased and the sustained fall in fertility indicates a continuation of this trend, though increasing unemployment represents additional real dependants. Nevertheless, in 1991 age dependency of sixty-three for every one hundred persons in the active category is higher in the RI than in NI where it is fifty-nine which in turn compares unfavourably with all of the other western European countries given in Table 3. This is an indication of the difficulty the Irish have in maintaining or improving the standard of living. The declining proportion of young persons – which still constitutes the largest component of dependency – does not any longer necessarily imply an easing of the economic burden. An increase in those of working age may require a continued high level of social security transfers unless employment increases. In addition, the resource costs of health and personal social services for the elderly, especially for the very old, are far greater than for the young. This has serious implications for public expenditure and the taxpayer. Notwithstanding heavy expenditure by countries on health and social welfare, old age is often associated with poverty and loneliness. In general, the demographic structure as characterised by sex, age and the extent of

dependency can affect the degree of either vitality or conservatism in a society and ultimately through voting behaviour
influence the choice of policy priorities including the type
and level of social service provision.

The population distribution by broad age groups,
dependency ratios and density in some western European
countries in the early 1990s are, as we have observed,
provided in Table 3. The RI with 26.3 per cent and NI with
24.2 per cent have significantly more of their populations
under fifteen years of age than any of the other countries.
The smallest proportion of children is found in Germany and
Italy with just 16.3 per cent. The oldest populations with the
highest proportion of elderly persons are in the Scandinavian
countries of Sweden with 17.7 per cent, Norway (16.2) and
Denmark (15.5). The UK has 15.8 per cent and Belgium 15.4
per cent. The rejuvenation of Germany's age structure since
re-unification has already been noted. The highest
dependency ratio exists in the RI (60.5 per cent), NI (58.2),
Wales (58.0), Sweden (56.7), and Norway (54.8). Italy's 45.1
per cent represents the lowest among the countries listed
with many others also having a dependency ratio below 50
per cent.

In NI it is important to identify the socio-demographic
relevance of the denominational composition of its
population. Since the question on religion was first asked at
the 1861 census the proportion of Catholics fell from 40.9
per cent to 33.5 per cent in 1926. Since 1937 it rose a little
and reached 34.9 per cent by 1961. It is more difficult to
determine what happened after that as there was a
significantly high level of non-response among Catholics in
1971 and in 1981 due to the adverse political situation and
whilst the results of the 1991 census are considered to be
comprehensive the introduction of the category 'no religion'
has compounded the situation. The PPRU estimates the
Catholic population at 42.1 per cent based on the premise
that in 1991 non-response was more prevalent among non-
Catholics whilst it was predominantly Catholics who failed to

state a religion (Jardine, 1994). Ó Gráda and Walsh (1994), however, believe the Catholic share to be higher than the 43.9 per cent estimated when half of those in the 'non stated' and 'none' categories are presumed to be Catholic. The age profile of Catholics in 1991 is much younger than that of non-Catholics although among those under ten years of age the proportion is lower among the youngest children (Jardine, 1994).

The sectarian demography is compounded by the concentration of populations of one denomination or the other in different geographical locations in NI. Catholics are found predominantly in the west, in the local government districts of Newry and Mourne in the south and Moyle in the northeast. In absolute terms, there are many Catholics in Belfast and its surrounding areas although they are in a minority. Segregation by housing increased during the troubles especially in the larger urban areas and it is probably also evident in rural border areas (Coward, 1986). Nevertheless, the Catholic proportion of the economically active population increased in all district council areas between 1981 and 1991 (Cormack et al, 1993).

The changing religious demography of NI is of considerable political and social significance. The Anglo-Irish Agreement in 1985 and the Downing Street Declaration in 1993 affirm that any change in the constitutional position of NI would only occur with the consent of a majority of the electorate. Concern about the future religious balance in NI is, therefore, of paramount importance. Population projections incorporate assumptions which are uncertain about the main components of demographic change. The value of the New Year survey considered above (Compton and Power, 1991) is also demonstrated in the information furnished by it on migration from NI by religious denomination. It was found that Protestants who were disproportionately represented among the outflow of students were also more likely than Catholics to have already acquired employment before arriving in Britain. Catholics were more likely to return to NI. As the numbers leaving are about the same, they conclude that the Catholic rate of emigration has fallen to about half that of Protestants.

Ó Gráda and Walsh (1994) consider the significance of this differential migration from one which was predominantly Catholic in the past to one where Protestants are now predominant, and explain it in terms of greater opportunities abroad for the better educated and more incentives for Protestants to leave, induced by strong enforcement of equal employment legislation combined with uncertainty about the constitutional status of NI. Thus, migration even more than fertility is set to become the most problematic and difficult component of projecting population change within and between the two communities (Eversley, 1989). Whilst fertility is falling and converging it is likely to remain relatively higher among Catholics. The higher proportion of deaths in the Protestant population, due to its older age structure with its better socio-economic profile, will also result in relatively lower growth *vis-à-vis* the Catholic population. However, Jardine (1994) reasons from the consistent evidence of surveys and opinion polls, undertaken during the 1970s and 1980s, that the stereotyping of Protestants with unionism and particularly Catholics with nationalism is too simplistic and is 'fundamentally flawed' as an expression of constitutional preference. Whilst one would be foolish to under-estimate the strength of aspirations among either nationalists or unionists, Whyte (1990) concludes that Catholics in NI are less resolutely for a united Ireland than Protestants are against it.

In the RI it is interesting that, with the exception of Dún Laoghaire-Rathdown and County Wicklow, it is the border counties of Cavan, Donegal and Monaghan which had in 1991 the highest proportion of Protestants including Church of Ireland, Presbyterian and Methodist in their populations, with 8.9 per cent, 9.8 per cent and 8.8 per cent, respectively of those who stated they had a religion (3.2 per cent for the RI). The total number of Protestants, which fell significantly at the time of partition, steadily declined thereafter. Between 1961 and

1991 the Protestant population fell by 22,222, i.e. by 17.1 per cent from 129,645 to 107,423. This situation is compounded by the older age structure of the Protestant population. In 1981 the proportion aged sixty-five years and over was 18.4 per cent compared with 10.7 per cent for the total population of the RI.

Conclusion

This chapter provides a necessarily limited account of the demographic characteristics of the RI and NI, particularly during the 1980s and early 1990s, with reference also to population developments elsewhere in the UK and in western Europe. The most striking overall feature is the contrasting situation whereby the RI experienced almost consistent decline in population, except for the intercensal period 1946-51 and between 1961 and 1986, whereas NI has grown steadily if unspectacularly throughout the twentieth century except during the intercensal period 1971-81 which, ironically, was the only period of substantial immigration to the RI in modern times.

Fertility and nuptiality have followed a pattern which is prevalent in many other western European countries. The numbers marrying peaked during the 1970s at a time when persons in the RI and NI married at a younger age. Since then the number of marriages has fallen and the age at which persons marry has risen considerably. Marital breakdown has been increasing. Completed fertility has been in decline throughout the twentieth century. The total period fertility rate has been decreasing in the RI and in NI since the early and late 1970s, respectively. It was consistently lower in NI except between 1986 and 1990. The number of extra-marital births and abortions has risen significantly especially since the early 1980s. Mortality levels, while somewhat higher, compare favourably with many other western European countries and are the most predictable component of population change. Migration continues to be a major deter-minant of population change in the RI and NI as recent emigration affects in particular the young and active and leaves its mark throughout the island both in urban and rural areas. Like other parts of the developed world the populations of the RI and NI are ageing, yet they retain particularly young age structures, especially in the RI, which makes the creation and maintenance of sufficient employment critical and difficult. The higher dependency ratios have implications for fiscal policies and the provision of social and other public services. The religious composition of the NI population is of immense socio-political importance and impinges in many ways on population distribution and movement, social integration, differential levels of fertility, emigration, unemployment and ultimately peace and stability. The long-term decline of the Protestant population in the RI has diminished a vital element of its composition.

A typical demographic study would include other important characteristics such as a detailed breakdown of the population by regions and local government areas. The limits set here prevent the consideration of differences not merely between north and south but also in terms of east and west. Differential patterns of nuptiality, fertility, mortality and migration are interwoven with differences in sex ratios and age structures. A related matter is the extent of economic and social development in evidence, e.g. in NI the area west of the River Bann is considered disadvantaged, likewise the area west of the River Shannon in the RI. A recent initiative by the Catholic bishops of Connacht and Donegal received the financial support of the European Union and facilitated a study of the West of Ireland (Euradvice, 1994) which was followed by the Report of a Government Task Force (1994). Similarly, the population is usually analysed along with the labour force, employment and unemployment. Issues of particular interest include labour force participation rates by sex, age, marital status and economic sector. The relationship between occupation, socio-economic status, life cycle and family size are of immense sociological interest. More sociological studies on the various components of population movement and structure like the NI Fertility Survey and the RI NESC Report on Emigration are essential. Demography provides an essential basis for a lot of sociological analysis and is of particular relevance to the study of society. Demography and sociology should, therefore, be further integrated, new research methods developed and more studies undertaken.

In the RI and NI, as in other countries, demography benefits from the state regularly furnishing essential statistics. This has the advantage of using some of the state's substantial resources, human and otherwise. The disadvantage is that providing information primarily for the planning and development of public policies and services leaves little possibilities for 'outsiders' to influence the design of questionnaires and the operation of data collection. In recent years official statistical agencies regularly prepare and publish population and labour force projections. In the RI the CSO has established a working group comprising statisticians, civil servants, academics and researchers with the intention of updating and publishing projections. Similarly, population projections for NI, England, Wales and Scotland are prepared by the Government Actuary Department of the UK and published annually. In addition, Eurostat and the OECD systematically do so for their member states. Although population projections are not predictions they enable us to chart future broad trends such as that of demographic ageing (Courtney, 1994b). A set (two or three) of high, medium and low projections are usually prepared. Their reliability is ultimately dependent on the accuracy of the data used and the related assumptions adopted.

In conclusion, population structure and change provide the basis for identifying social needs and establishing and prioritising policies to develop appropriate services to meet them. Demographic knowledge is a prerequisite for well planned and efficiently administered services. Precisely up-dated information and data constitute the basis for strategic economic and social planning and development throughout the public, voluntary and private sectors.

Notes

1. This chapter is dedicated to the memory of John Coward who wrote, among other things, the demographic chapter on Northern Ireland in *Ireland, A Sociological Profile* (1986) and who lost his life en route from London to Belfast in the MI plane crash at East Midlands in January, 1989.

    I wish to acknowledge the assistance provided by the Central Statistics Office in the Republic of Ireland and the various government departments concerned with population matters in Northern Ireland for their encouragement and assistance in the preparation of this chapter. I am particularly grateful to Aidan Punch and Catherine Finneran in Dublin and to Jacquie Hyvart in Belfast for their time and very special interest in this work. I am also thankful to many others who helped in various ways. The usual disclaimer applies.

2. In Ireland the stem family system meant that only one child in each generation inherited the family holding whereas the standard of living thesis considered one's status and standard of living to be more important than marriage.

References

ANDORKA, RUDOLF, 1978. *Determinants of Fertility in Advanced Societies*, London, Methuen.

BLACKER, C.P., 1947. 'Stages in population growth', *Eugenics Review*, Vol. 39, pp. 81-101.

CENTRAL STATISTICS OFFICE, 1994. 'Annual Population and Migration Estimates 1987-1993', *Statistical Release*, Dublin, Government Information Services (30 May).

CLANCY, PATRICK, 1991. 'Irish Nuptiality and Fertility Patterns in Transition', in Gabriel Kiely and Valerie Richardson (eds.), *Family Policy; European Perspectives*, Dublin, Family Studies Centre (Belfield).

COALE, A.J., 1969. 'The decline of fertility in Europe from the French Revolution to World War II', in S.J. Behrman, L. Corsa Jr. and R. Freedman (eds.), *Fertility and Family Planning: A World View*, Ann Arbor, University of Michegan Press.

86 Irish Society: Sociological Perspectives

COMMISSION ON EMIGRATION AND OTHER POPULATION PROBLEMS, 1948-54. *Reports*, Dublin, Stationery Office.

COMPTON, PAUL A., 1991. 'Demography – The 1980s In Perspective', *Studies*, Summer, pp. 157-168.

COMPTON, PAUL A. and JOHN POWER, 1991. 'Migration from Northern Ireland: A Survey of New Year Travellers as a Means of Identifying Emigrants', *Regional Studies*, Vol. 25, No. 1, pp. 1-11.

COMPTON, PAUL A. and JOHN COWARD, 1989. *Fertility and Family Planning in Northern Ireland*, Aldershot, Avebury.

CORMACK, R.J., A.M. GALLAGHER and R.D. OSBORNE, 1993. *Fair Enough? Religion and the 1991 Population Census*, Belfast, Fair Employment Commission for Northern Ireland.

COUNCIL OF EUROPE, 1993. *Recent Demographic Developments in Europe*, Strasbourg.

COURTNEY, DAMIEN, 1994a. 'A Demographer's Perspective', *Proceedings of Seminars on Labour Market and Demographic Statistics*, Dublin, Central Statistics Office, pp. 51-62.

COURTNEY, DAMIEN, forthcoming (1994b). 'The Demographic Picture', Southern Health Board Conference Proceedings, *The Years Ahead – Five Years On*, Cork, SHB.

COURTNEY, DAMIEN, 1992. 'Future Demographic Trends in the European Community', The Retirement Planning Council of Ireland Annual Conference, *The Future of Retirement*, Dublin, 14 October.

COURTNEY, DAMIEN, 1991a. 'Demographic Trends in Ireland and Western Europe during the 1980s', Dublin, Irish Council of the European Movement *Conference Proceedings on Migration and Mobility of Labour, Future Trends in Europe*.

COURTNEY, DAMIEN, 1991b. 'The Changing Demography of Irish Women in the 1980s', Strasbourg: Council of Europe Seminar Proceedings on *Present Demographic Trends and Lifestyles in Europe*, pp. 347-9.

COURTNEY, DAMIEN, 1989. 'Recent Trends in Emigration from Ireland', *Development Studies Association Annual Conference*, The Queen's University of Belfast.

COURTNEY, DAMIEN, 1986. 'Demographic Structure and Change (in the Republic of Ireland)' in P. Clancy, S. Drudy, K. Lynch and L. O'Dowd (eds.), *Ireland: A Sociological Profile*, Dublin, SAI/IPA, pp. 22-46.

COWARD, JOHN, 1986. 'Demographic Structure and Change (in Northern

Ireland)' in P. Clancy et al
(eds.), op. cit, pp. 176-197.
COWARD, JOHN, 1982.
'Fertility Changes in the
Republic of Ireland during
the 1970s', Area, Vol. 14,
No. 2, pp. 109-117.
COWARD, JOHN, 1978.
'Changes in the Pattern of
Fertility in the Republic of
Ireland', Tijdschrift voor
Economische en Sociale Geografie,
Vol. 69, No. 6, pp. 353-361.
CRUIJSEN, HARRI, MARJA
EXTERKATE, RON
LESTHAEGHE, ALAN
LOPEZ, PHILIP MUUS and
FRANS WILLEKENS, 1991.
Two Long Term Population
Scenarios for the European
Community, Eurostat
Luxembourg Conference on
Human Resources in Europe at the
Dawn of the 21st Century.
EURADVICE LTD., 1994.
Developing the West Together. A
Crusade For Survival, Galway,
Final Report of Study of the
West of Ireland.
EVERSLEY, DAVID, 1989.
Religion and Employment in
Northern Ireland, London,
Sage.
FORSYTHE, FRANK P. and
VANI K. BOROOAH, 1992.
'The Nature of Migration
Between Northern Ireland
and Great Britain: A
Preliminary Analysis Based on
the Labour Force Surveys,
1986-88', The Economic and
Social Review, Vol. 23, No. 2,
pp. 105-127.

GARVEY, DONAL, 1985. 'The
History of Migration Flows in
the Republic of Ireland',
Population Trends, No. 39,
(Spring), pp. 22-30.
GOLDSCHEIDER, CALVIN,
1971. Population,
Modernisation, and Social
Structure, Boston, Little,
Brown and Company.
GOLDSCHEIDER, CALVIN,
1982. 'Societal Change and
Demographic Transitions:
Selected Theoretical Issues
and Research Strategies',
Population et Structures Sociales,
Chaire Quetelet, Louvain-la-
Neuve, Cabay and
Département de
Démographie.
GOVERNMENT TASK FORCE
ON 'A CRUSADE FOR
SURVIVAL', 1994. Report,
Dublin, Stationery Office.
HANNAN, DAMIAN, F., 1979.
Displacement and Development:
Class, Kinship and Social
Change in Irish Rural
Communities, Dublin, The
Economic and Social
Research Institute, Paper
No. 96.
HOFFMANN-NOWOTNY,
HANS-JOACHIM and BEAT
FUX, 1991. 'Present
Demographic Trends in
Europe', Strasbourg: Council
of Europe Seminar Proceedings
on Present Demographic Trends
and Lifestyles in Europe.
JARDINE, EDGAR F., 1994.
'Demographic structure in
Northern Ireland and its

implications for constitutional preference', *Statistical and Social Inquiry Society of Ireland*, Dublin (5 May).

KENNEDY, ROBERT, E. JR., 1973. *The Irish: Emigration, Marriage and Fertility*, Berkeley, University of California Press.

MALTHUS, THOMAS R., 1958. *Essay on the Principle of Population* (2 vols.), London, Everyman's Library. (Introduction by Michael P. Fogarty, the first edition was published in 1798).

McQUEEN, ALISON and JACQUIE JOHNSTON, 1992. 'Northern Ireland Sources of Demographic Information', The Department of Health and Social Services Conference on *Statistical Sources for Local and Regional Development*, Belfast, 3 April.

NOLAN, BRIAN, 1990. 'Socio-economic Mortality Differentials in Ireland', *The Economic and Social Review*, Vol. 21, No. 2, pp. 193-208.

Ó GRÁDA, CORMAC and BRENDAN WALSH, 1994. 'Recent Trends in Fertility and Population North and South', Working Paper, *University College Dublin*.

OSBORNE, R.D., R.J. CORMACK, R.L. MILLAR and A.P. WILLIAMSON, 1987. 'Graduates: Geographical Mobility and Incomes', in R.D. Osborne, R.J. Cormack and R.L. Millar (eds.), *Education and Policy in Northern Ireland*, Belfast, Policy Research Institute, pp. 231-244.

PRESSAT, ROLAND, 1978. *Statistical Demography*, London, Methuen. (Translated and adapted by Damien Courtney from *Démographie Statistique*, 1972, Paris, Presses Universitaires de France).

PUNCH, AIDAN, 1994. 'Demographic Statistics – The CSO Perspective', *Proceedings of Seminars on Labour Market and Demographic Statistics*, *op. cit.*, pp. 31-40.

PUNCH, AIDAN, 1992. 'Measuring Population Structure and Change in the Republic of Ireland', Conference on *Statistical Sources for Local and Regional Development*, *op. cit.*

ROTTMAN, DAVID B., DAMIAN F. HANNAN, NIAMH HARDIMAN and MIRIAM M. WILEY, 1982. *The Distribution of Income in the Republic of Ireland: A Study in Social Class and Family – Cycle Inequalities*, Dublin, The Economic and Social Research Institute, Paper No. 109.

SEXTON, J.J., B.M. WALSH, D.F. HANNAN and D. McMAHON, 1991. *The Economic and Social Implications of Emigration*, Dublin, National Economic and Social Council, Report No. 90.

UNER, SUNDAY, 1990. *The Changing Structure of the*

European Labour Force,
Strasbourg, Council of Europe
Seminar, *op. cit.*
VAN DA KAA, DIRK J., 1987.
'Europe's Second
Demographic Transition',
Population Bulletin, Vol. 42,
No. 1, pp. 3-57.
WALSH, BRENDAN, 1980.
'Recent Demographic
Changes in the Republic of
Ireland', *Population Trends,*
Vol. 21 (Autumn), pp. 3-9.
WALSH, BRENDAN, 1970.
*Religion and Demographic
Behaviour in Ireland,* Dublin,
Economic and Social
Research Institute, Paper
No. 55.
WHYTE, JOHN, 1990.
Interpreting Northern Ireland,
Oxford, Claredon Press.

3
Global Restructuring and the Irish Political Economy

DENIS O'HEARN

During the 1980s, debates about Irish economic change
followed the broader literature on economic change and
'development'. One approach, more often from economics
than sociology, maintained that Ireland since the 1950s went
through a process of 'modernisation', characterised by the
increasing prominence of industry and urbanisation in Irish
economic life. Ireland had become more like developed
Europe and North America in its consumption habits, its
relatively equal income distribution, and (increasingly) the
demographic behaviour of its people. Some even argued that
the main engines of modernisation were the transnational
corporations (TNCs) and other transnational institutions
that had become influential in Irish economic life, while
others emphasised the modernised character of the Irish
state (for a characterisation of this literature, see Wickham,
1986; see also O'Malley, 1980). Historically, proponents of
this approach claimed that Ireland started on the road to
modernity when Finance Secretary T.K. Whitaker
'introduced' modern planning and welcomed foreign
industry in 1957/58.

Another approach (this time including more sociologists)
argued, tentatively at first, that Ireland was going through an

entirely different transition. Rather than becoming more like industrialised Europe, Ireland was becoming dependent on foreign industrial investment like industrialising countries in Latin America and Asia (Jacobsen, 1978; Wickham, 1986; O'Hearn, 1989; Jacobsen, 1994). Not only had foreign industrial domination excluded significant indigenous industry, but the foreign sector brought with it a series of negative features. Some studies concentrated on the failure of foreign sectors to link with other parts of the Irish economy (Stewart, 1976). TNCs imported nearly all of the material inputs they used in production and exported nearly all of their output, so that they did not create demand for Irish products (*backward linkages*), nor did they supply downstream Irish companies which used their semi-fabricated products in the production of something else (*forward linkages*).

An IDA advertisement of the 1970s quoted the US Department of Commerce to the effect that liberal Irish incentives to foreign firms helped them achieve profit rates of twice the European average. Yet the TNCs failed to reinvest these resources in the Irish economy, instead removing the vast majority of their profits from Ireland. By the mid-1980s, observers began to refer to a 'black hole' through which capital was sucked out of the Irish economy. While such observations of Irish 'dependency' were not well-received for some time, the severe recessions of the late 1970s and 1980s eventually led even some orthodox observers to agree with semi-official reports, such as the Telesis Report (1982) and Culliton Report (1991), that were highly critical of Irish export-led and foreign-dominated policies.

The recession of the 1980s also provoked scepticism about prevailing explanations of the failure of the Irish regime of *import-substitution industrialisation* (ISI) and its transformation to *export-led industrialisation* (ELI) under Whitaker and Seán Lemass. O'Malley (1989) compared the Irish transition to strategies in South Korea and Taiwan, and suggested that a more rational response to the recession of the 1950s would have been to increase protection of capital goods, inducing the 'deepening' of indigenous industrialisation from basic consumer goods to higher-tech capital goods. Girvin (1989, pp. 198-9) argued that the recession was concentrated in Irish agriculture, rather than industry, indicating that it was Irish farming that required modernisation and that the transition to TNC-led industrialisation was almost beside-the-point. O'Hearn (1990) questioned the historical significance of the so-called Whitaker/Lemass revolution, and therefore of the connection between recession and economic transformation, by tracing the beginnings of free trade and TNC-domination to Ireland's participation in the new European project after the Second World War. Once Ireland accepted Marshall aid, it was forced by the US and European bodies to dismantle industrial protection and attract export-oriented foreign capital by setting up bodies such as Bord Tráchtála and the Industrial Development Authority (IDA) and by introducing incentives such as capital grants and export profits-tax relief. These institutions and policies were in place before Whitaker published his famous *Economic Development* in the late 1950s.

The first ambitious critique of the modernisationist perspective was Crotty's (1986) analysis of 'capitalist post-colonial undevelopment' in Ireland. In a manner similar to Frank's early dependency analysis, Crotty insisted that Ireland was unique in Europe because it had been *un*developed as a British colony. Its economic structure was oriented toward the profitability and advantage of colonial (British) capital and was seldom to the advantage of Irish development. Crotty paid special attention to conditions on the land and to the creation of the Irish state by local *comprador* elites who had benefited from colonialism (and who continue to benefit from dependent post-colonialism). This class helped reinstate dependence after the Second World War so that '... now too Irish society has been forced into dependence on foreign resources as complete as that of the exotic potato 140 years ago' (Crotty 1986, p. 80). Post-colonial (or neo-colonial) underdevelopment has been a more popular theme in radical analyses of British imperialism in the north since the 1970s, as is reflected in O'Dowd's chapter in this volume.

Changing problems: the 1980s recession and after

The decade of the 1980s was particularly severe on the Irish economy. While global recession elicited efforts to 'restructure' national and transnational economies, the recession was deeper in Ireland than in the rest of Europe. Several Irish crises of the 1980s lent support to critics of Irish economic policy and forced Irish policymakers to respond. Mass unemployment was the most obvious crisis. Yet unemployment was the result of deeper economic trends that were related to Ireland's liberal and foreign-dominated economic policies. These included a growing disparity between official economic growth rates and domestic economic results due to foreign debt and TNC profit repatriations, the return of involuntary emigration, and the failure of the foreign sector to link with indigenous economic sectors.

Employment as a failed policy-goal
The numbers of unemployed and unemployment rates in Ireland began to increase after accession to the EC in 1972 because competition from free trade caused indigenous firms to close. Unemployment rates rose more rapidly after 1980 when indigenous industrial decline was complemented by TNC disinvestments and the failure of new TNCs to invest in adequate numbers. Between 1980 and 1985, unemployment rates in the south of Ireland doubled from about 10 to 20 per cent, making unemployment the major crisis of public policy.

Although timid economic reforms were introduced, the major reductions of recorded unemployment came from changes in the definitions of unemployed and in the structure of work. Government training programmes temporarily remove many people from official unemployment. By 1992 some 40,000 people were on training schemes (including compulsory schemes that were tied to the receipt of social welfare payments) and nearly 20,000 were on pre-retirement schemes. Optimism from an increase of 30,000 jobs in 1993-94 was tempered by the fact that half of the increase consisted of places in temporary government schemes. In addition, a growing but unknown proportion of the employed are in temporary and part-time jobs rather than permanent full-time employment. As a result of these anomalies, estimated unemployment rates diverge quite significantly. The OECD (1993) reported two unemployment rates for 1992, ranging from 16.7 per cent (based on the labour force survey) to 21 per cent (based on registered unemployed). Such discrepancies can have an important impact on public relations, as the Irish government claimed in 1990 to have reduced the unemployment rate to 13.7 per cent, while the OECD reported an unemployment rate of more than 17 per cent. Figure 1 shows three different estimates of Irish unemployment between 1983 and 1993. At the beginning of the 1980s the three estimates are quite close. After 1986, however, as the unemployment crisis deepened, surveyed unemployment levels dipped below the registered unemployed while Irish government claims were below the survey numbers.

Regardless of these discrepancies, unemployment rates clearly rose since the 1970s. Short-term drops occurred during 1987-1991 and 1994, but even the 'jobs boom' of 1990 resulted primarily from a short-term construction boom (followed by an equally impressive bust in 1992) and a rise of professional service employment, with only a moderate rise of manufacturing employment. These increases were short-lived and, by 1993, the numbers on the live register in the 26 counties reached record highs of nearly 300,000 before dipping in 1994.

A particularly worrying aspect of Irish unemployment is its long-term nature. During the 1980s southern unemployment changed from predominantly short-term to predominantly long-term. While 36.9 per cent of unemployed were 'long-term unemployed' (twelve months and over) in 1983 – one of

Figure 1.   **Three estimates of Irish unemployment (26 counties), 1983-1993**

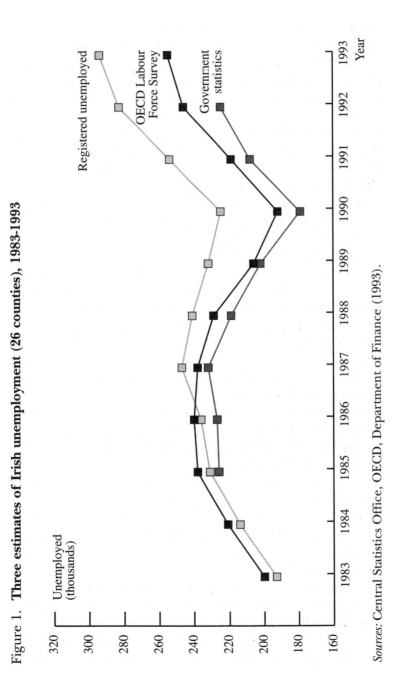

Sources: Central Statistics Office, OECD, Department of Finance (1993).

the lowest proportions in Europe – 67.2 percent were long-term unemployed by 1990 (OECD, 1992). In the north, 50 per cent were long-term unemployed in 1992 (Borooah, 1993, pp. 6, 15), along with a sectarian bias that is discussed by O'Dowd in this volume.

Emigration and unemployment
Some would argue that people have a basic right to remain in their country of origin, if they wish, as productive citizens. Irish unemployment totals would rise considerably if we added those who involuntarily emigrated because they could not find work in Ireland. The emigration crisis of the 1980s hit both working-class youth and professionals (for details see Courtney's chapter in this volume). Annual emigration rose from 8,000 in 1981-85 to 30-45,000 since 1987 (Mac Laughlin, 1994). Yet public reactions to emigration do not universally regard it as a crisis. A well-known economic journalist called emigration 'part of the natural order of things' while the southern Tánaiste spoke approvingly of emigration as a policy alternative in the US magazine *Newsweek* (Waters, 1992). In the north, an emerging unionist analysis proposes higher emigration as a policy alternative to high rates of Catholic unemployment.

As with unemployment, the official statistics may not capture the true dimensions of the emigration crisis. Mac Laughlin (1994) argues that actual emigrants are only a subset of the much wider pool of potential emigrants. They are also members of families that are dislocated by the loss of sons, daughters and even fathers (one quarter of the families surveyed by Mac Laughlin have at least one immediate family member living abroad, while 13 per cent had three or more emigrants). Finally, the net figures do not reflect the uprootedness caused by a rapid increase in the frequency of emigration and return emigration. Transport and communications technologies make it possible for many people to move back and forth between Ireland and other countries several times during an intercensal period. This causes

instability in communities, families and labour markets that
are not reflected in the global net emigration statistics.

Growth and employment
A third crisis of the mid-1980s was one of economic growth.
After rapturous claims about the Irish economic model in the
1960s and early 1970s, growth slowed significantly by 1979.
During 1979-87, real annual economic growth never reached
3 per cent and was negative or practically nil in most years.
Like unemployment, however, there is disagreement about
how poor Ireland's economic growth performance was
during this period (and, conversely, how good it has been
since 1987). Part of the disagreement regards relativity – as a
relatively poor region, Ireland requires very high rates of
economic growth to 'catch up' with the European core. The
East Asian NICs, for example, recorded annual real growth
rates of around 10 per cent during most of the 1970s and
1980s. Ireland's average growth rate of only 3.1 per cent
during 1972-90 was among the lowest in Europe.

Since 1987, however, the south has grown more rapidly
than a sluggish Europe. Some observers optimistically
forecast that this trend will continue into the next
millennium and predict convergence between Irish and
European income levels (ESRI, 1994). Ironically, this is
worrying for the Irish state because it stands to lose EU
transfers (structural fund grants) if its per capita GDP
exceeds 80 per cent of the EU average. Some observers claim
that Ireland is doing 'too well'.

This is a serious misreading of Ireland's recent dependent
economic performance. While the region's level of economic
activity, as measured by GDP, converged moderately toward
the European average (which was itself suppressed by the
inclusion of East Germany) in the 1990s, there are serious
problems with using GDP for this purpose. Figure 2 shows
that 26-county GDP and GNP were practically equivalent
until 1976. Since then, a large gap opened between them
with GNP now almost 15 per cent below GDP. The growing

Figure 2.   The growing gap between Irish output and incomes (26 counties), 1960-1991

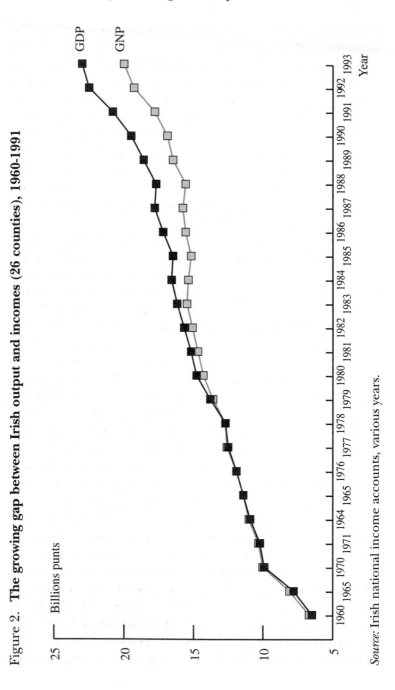

Source: Irish national income accounts, various years.

gap is a direct result of Ireland's dependent economic model since the difference between GNP and GDP is net capital transfers abroad. This huge outward flow of capital – the 'black hole' – consists primarily of repatriated TNC profits (which comprise 11-13 per cent of GDP) and interest paid abroad on Irish government and other foreign debt (recently about 9-11 per cent of GDP). GDP measures economic output, but GNP more accurately measures what the Irish population or economy retains for its efforts. This is not important in economies where the two measures are practically equal, but in Ireland GDP seriously overestimates the level of economic welfare.

Some Irish economists argue that all published output figures – GDP *or* GNP – are unrealistic because official trade statistics are grossly inaccurate. Estimates of southern GNP growth for 1993 ranged from 0.9 to 3.6 per cent (the highest figure being the Central Statistics Office estimate that is quoted by the government). An economist for a leading Irish stockbroker argues that official estimates of output in the 1990s are too high because of inflated export figures and understated profit repatriation figures (Mangan, 1994). Between 1990 and 1993, the export surplus of manufactured goods grew by 3 billion punts while official figures for profit repatriations rose by only 850 million. Mangan estimates that as much as 2 billion punts of the official trade surplus was phantom because it was created by intra-company transfer pricing rather than actual Irish output. In order to avail of low Irish company tax rates, TNCs either deflate their intra-company import prices and inflate export prices or account goods made in other countries as Irish-made to increase the added-value of their Irish operations. He reckons that Irish GNP figures were overstated in 1993 by more than a billion punts (the difference between the phantom trade surplus and the amount that was officially recognised as profit repatriations), or nearly 5 per cent. By the same logic, GDP overstated actual output by more than 2 billion punts, or nearly 10 per cent. In unstockbroker-like language, he suggested that the government's figures should be filed 'under childrens' fairytales, science fiction or horror stories'.

It is worth briefly examining the issues of profit repatriations and debt since they have had such an impact on the Irish economies. Profit repatriations are the direct result of TNC activities and are high precisely because Ireland relies so heavily on foreign investments. As the IDA attracted electronic and pharmaceutical firms in the 1970s, their inflated profit rates and low reinvestment rates led to a rapid rise in capital 'leakages' from Ireland. Figure 3 shows that TNC profit repatriations rose rapidly after 1974 in absolute terms and relative to GDP. O'Hearn (1990) and Munck (1993, p. 155) argue that this *decapitalises* the Irish economy because resources that might have been available for economic expansion are removed from the island. Others (O'Malley, 1992b; Mjoset, 1993) counter that repatriations are largely irrelevant because Ireland does not suffer from a lack of capital relative to investment opportunities. Regardless of the effect of repatriations on economic growth, they represent a phantom element of current economic activity because they accrue to companies and capitalists abroad.

Comparative profit rates between the foreign and indigenous sectors indicate the depth of the problem, since the overwhelming proportion of profits in industry accrue to the foreign sector and are subsequently repatriated. IDA survey data reveal that average profit rates in the foreign sector are consistently much higher than indigenous rates. Throughout the 1980s, foreign profit rates (profits as a percentage of sales) averaged about 20 per cent while indigenous profit rates averaged less than 3 per cent. Profit rates of US firms in leading sectors like pharmaceuticals and electronics were consistently above 30 per cent (O'Hearn, 1993). Some of the difference between foreign and indigenous profit rates may be the result of transfer-pricing activities, for which sectors like pharmaceuticals are notorious. Yet a significant part of the gap can only be explained by differences in structures of production and market positions of the two sectors – a subject that will be taken up below in the discussion of restructuring and innovation.

After profit repatriations, interest payments on debt are the most serious drag on retained incomes from Irish economic effort. The debt crisis occurred in many industrialising countries after western banks, flush with oil revenues in the 1970s, encouraged them to borrow their way out of recession at attractive rates. While Ireland was not plagued to the same degree as many Third World countries with the problems of corruption or debt-financed 'show projects' (from dams to iron mines to hotels), it had its own reasons to incur debt. Entry into the EC eliminated the state's greatest source of revenues (tariffs and other import taxes). Income taxes and VAT could not make up the lost revenues, particularly with recession and falling employment levels. On the other hand, severe social welfare cuts were difficult while the European project was legitimised precisely by its 'modernising' effects on Irish social welfare. Nor could the state cut its welfare programmes for foreign industry, which were the basis of its hopes for future economic expansion. The result was a rapid rise in debt from about 94 per cent of GNP in 1981 to more than 130 per cent in 1987. Debt interest rose from 8 per cent of GNP in 1981 to 12.5 per cent in 1985. A combination of good luck (changing foreign exchange rates) and a government austerity programme after 1987 helped the Irish government reduce its still-high foreign debt below 100 per cent of GNP in the mid-1990s. But public debt continues to be an issue because much of it was simply shifted to local hands so that the state pays domestic interest rather than foreign interest.

Finally, many people have noted a disparity between economic growth and employment growth after 1987. Apart from short-term reductions, the numbers of registered unemployed continued to rise into the 1990s. One of the more optimistic forecasts of rapid economic growth through the end of the century (ESRI 1994) forecasts only a moderate decrease in the numbers unemployed.

The disjunction between economic growth and employment growth, however, is not just a feature of the most recent
economic upturn. It has been true of the whole dependent
period of Irish development. Figure 3 compares growth of
industrial output and industrial employment between 1980
and 1992. Throughout the period, industrial output grew (in
volume terms) while employment either declined or
stagnated. The most rapid periods of growth (1982-4, 1986-8,
1991-2) were periods of *downturn* in employment growth (or
upturn in job losses). While lag effects may distort the
relationship between output and employment, two developments are significant. First, the slower rate of job losses after
1985 is partly because the EC-induced round of failures of
indigenous firms after 1972 was practically finished (there
were few indigenous jobs left to lose). Second, the disparity
between industrial output growth and industrial employment
after 1985 was primarily due to the restructuring of older
TNC operations (with accompanying job losses) and the
entry of restructured TNCs (which created few jobs). Some
economists might point to the disparity as a sign of economic
health because labour productivity must have been rising
throughout the period. Yet this would be positive only if
rising productivity induced enough economic expansion to
create replacement jobs for the old ones that were lost.

Despite continuing economic crises, Irish policymakers have
had neither the desire nor the ability to basically transform
Irish economic policy. Instead, the regime hid unemployment
by massaging its official figures while it publicly de-emphasised
the unemployment problem by emphasising economic growth
as its primary policy goal. The media paid increasing attention
to Irish economic growth rates in the 1990s – a supposedly
'miraculous' success relative to the rest of Europe – and less
attention to continuing unemployment (particularly long-term
unemployment) and its devastating social effects.

The above-mentioned disparities – between growth and
employment, between divergent estimates of unemployment,
emigration and growth – obfuscate public understanding of

Figure 3. **Relationship between growth of industrial output and employment (26 counties), 1980-92**

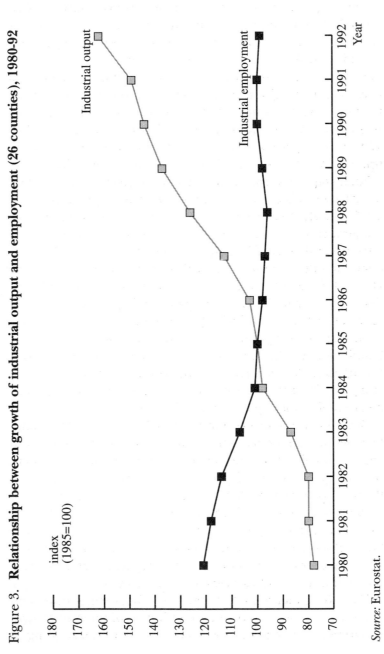

Source: Eurostat.

the precise nature of Irish economic and social crisis. A well-known Dublin journalist (O'Toole, 1994), quoting James Thurber – 'we live, man and worm, in an age where almost everything can mean almost anything' – argues in post-modern fashion that Irish society has 'ceased to exist' in any recognisable form. Because of TNC domination of the economy, the Irish diaspora, informal work and the like, we do not know the true levels of production, exports, profits, emigration or unemployment, or practically anything that the economic and social sciences generally profess to measure or understand. Since we cannot estimate them, we cannot say much about how they interrelate. There is no longer an Irish economy, just a 'black hole' through which TNC profits, jobs and Irish citizens vanish. Even denationalised Irish history has become a reconstructed, sanitised, consumerised commodity. While O'Toole wryly puts his finger on the confusion that surrounds contemporary Irish political economy, there *is* a rate of unemployment and a relationship between economic activity and employment; there *is* a flow and a net amount of emigration and a certain number of people living and working in Ireland at a given time; there *is* an Irish economy which has become increasingly integrated into the global strategies of international firms and capitalists. And there *are* many histories of Ireland – real and imagined – that effect the island's economic change. It is up to the social sciences to clarify these supposed post-modern confusions.

Changing perspectives: restructuring and the sociology of economic change

Many criticisms from the dependency approach were at last recognised by Irish scholars and policymakers in the late 1980s. The IDA introduced 'linkage programmes', however ineffective, to address the disarticulation of foreign firms from the local economy. Economists admitted that repatriated profits were a problem, although they were more enthusiastic about addressing the 'black hole' with austerity programmes to reduce the debt than with reducing repatriations. Overdependence on foreign capital was a major topic of the Culliton Report. Even world-systems concepts such as peripherality were incorporated into the official lexicon, although peripherality was given an exclusively geographical meaning without the world-systems emphases on the logical hierarchy of global production or the historical processes of peripheralisation. The Irish government produced a 'peripherality policy' which concentrated on infrastructure and transport (Government of Ireland, 1987) and the Northern Ireland Economic Council (1994) began to discuss the effects of peripherality during the 1990s.

The 1982 Telesis Report emphasised the inadequacies of an industrial strategy based on foreign investments. It prescribed substantial reductions in grants to foreign firms along with an increase in aid for indigenous firms that currently exported or could be expected to increase exports. Yet little was done to change Irish policy – in these or other directions, by the 1990s. While Telesis proposed a target of 75 per cent of grants to indigenous firms by 1990, the actual shift in grants to indigenous firms was only from 51 to 54 per cent during 1985-9. Grants were no more selective by 1990, and there was little switch by the IDA from grant aid to equity participation.

Thus, the Culliton Report of 1992 contained essentially the same conclusions and prescriptions as the Telesis Report, despite a decade of severe recession and global restructuring. It recommended a reduction in grant aid to foreign firms and a switch to equity participation. Following the popular literature on competitive advantage (Porter, 1990), the report recommended the promotion of industrial clusters (closely related to the Telesis concern with the lack of linkages between foreign firms and local economies). It also recommended the break-up of the IDA into two bodies that would be concerned solely with indigenous and foreign firms, respectively. The state followed the last recommendation and broke up the IDA in 1993. Yet, despite widespread agreement that future development strategies must emphasise indigenous industry, it remains to be seen whether the indigenous industry division will be simply a 'poor relation' to the foreign-oriented IDA. Criticisms of the Culliton Report include its inadequacy, even at the best forecasts, for creating jobs at the required levels; its recommendations to extend tax-breaks to corporations, implying a continuing tax overburden on workers; and its emphasis on cutting industrial-promotion expenditures instead of more efficient use of current expenditures (Sweeney, 1992).

While mainstream policies and reports generally acknowledge that the Irish economy has been in crisis and that change is required, there is little official response to radical critiques of the Irish emphasis on free trade and free enterprise. If anything, the Irish economies became more liberal in the late 1980s and early 1990s. In the north this was due to Thatcherism but was partly attenuated by special exemptions of the north from some privatisation and austerity programmes (again, at least partly explained by legitimacy constraints and the dual policy of reform and repression; O'Dowd *et al*, 1980). In the south, austerity and privatisation policies were a response to the cost of servicing state debt.

Irish trends toward liberalisation in the 1980s were similar to many Latin American industrialising countries where the IMF and World Bank tied loans and debt renegotiations to liberal reforms (or *structural adjustment*) in the receiving countries. But the Irish state response exceeded Latin American responses in its enthusiastic adherence to budgetary cuts and privatisation. Irish liberalisation was also mandated by the European plans for monetary and fiscal union, the creation of the Single European Market (SEM) in 1992, and most recently by strict debt-management requirements under the Maastricht treaty.

Pressures on industrialising countries to liberalise their trade and local economic relations were part of a larger effort by the richer industrialised countries to increase their industrial competitiveness and pull the global economy out of recession. Liberal trade regimes and openness to foreign investments, which were already a feature of the Irish economy, were combined at the firm level with new structures of 'flexible' production that were intended to increase firm profitability. Essentially, this involved the retrenchment of trade union power, instability of employment, more part-time and temporary work, and falling real wages for workers throughout the first world. Such 'restructuring' was also prescribed for 'developing' regions, although trade union power and wages were already less highly developed there than in the core. Significantly, many of the most effective liberalisation and austerity programmes were introduced by socialist and populist governments, from socialist regimes in Chile and Spain to the populist Fianna Fáil coalitions in Ireland.

In Ireland a local ideological justification for austerity was provided by a group of neo-liberal economists popularly called the 'Doheny and Nesbitt school of economics' because of their favourite Dublin drinking establishment. Academics and business columnists such as Paul Tansey of the *Sunday Tribune* popularised the view that the debt was the single overriding cause of the Irish economic crisis and, therefore, the most important policy priority. The reduction of public debt through the hard medicine of state expenditure cuts was necessary, despite high levels of poverty and falling standards of living throughout Ireland.

The southern government under Haughey introduced severe cuts in public spending in areas such as health in 1987 and subsequently legitimised the cuts by claiming that austerity was the cause of several years of rapid (although not employment-inducing) economic growth. Privatisation and cutbacks of state-owned companies, another major plank of the liberal agenda, were also introduced by the southern state and continued into the mid-1990s with moves to restructure Irish Steel, Team Aer Lingus and the Electricity Supply Board.

The introduction of neo-liberal policies in Ireland corresponded with a broader resuscitation of intellectual justifications for such policies throughout the 'developing' world. It is generally accepted in the field of development studies that classical modernisation approaches were severely weakened by dependency and other critiques of the 1960s and 1970s (although academics often underestimate the extent to which modernisationism still prevailed in official circles and the popular media). The decline of modernisation theory among academics hardly affected liberal economic and social policies, however, which maintained legitimacy partly because they were compared to statist policies in the former Soviet bloc and corrupt state regimes in the periphery. Liberal models also continued to dominate neo-classical economics. Outside of economics, however, the absence of a theoretical approach to legitimate current liberal policies created a sort of vacuum. This vacuum was filled by a 'new modernisationism' (the term was used with slightly different emphases in meaning by O'Hearn, 1989 and So, 1990).

According to So, the new modernisationism agrees with classical modernisation analysis on a variety of issues. It analyses development basically at the national level, focusing on internal factors (such as cultural values and social institutions) that must become 'modern' if society and economy are to successfully develop. Both versions rather uncritically accept modernisation and industrialisation as ends to which nations should and will aspire. On the other hand, the new modernisation accepts that there may be variant paths to development and even that some *traditions* can be modernising (for example, Asian forms of social organisation which induce efficient work practices). This means that concrete case studies are necessary to pinpoint factors that promote or obstruct development in specific cases. Finally, the new modernisation approach accepts that some external factors (for example, global markets) may be important, although it continues to focus on internal factors that allow countries to respond to external markets in efficient and modernising ways. In this respect, the new modernisation tends to view global markets and institutions as essentially neutral in their impact on local modernisers, except to the degree that they provide opportunities for market exploitation. This is exemplified by their use of the Korean and Taiwanese 'newly-industrialising countries' (NICs) as examples of how third world countries can combine traditional forms with outward-oriented liberal policies as a route to modernisation. Yet neo-modernisationism's newly-found recognition of variant development paths does not go so far as to admit the possibility of non-liberal (much less socialist) development policies, the centrality of states to some development models (including South Korea and Taiwan) or the possibility that global firms and institutions may block peripheral attempts to develop.

The disastrous slump of the 1980s provoked several sociological 'explanations' of Irish economic failure. Some were modernisationist while others invoked dependency and world-systems explanations. There was also a division between those who explained Irish failures primarily by local factors, and those who explained it by placing Ireland in its global context. Girvin (1989), while ostensibly analysing the specific problems faced by Ireland due to its location 'between the first and third worlds', insists on a localised analysis. Regardless of Ireland's colonial restrictions, he argues, it is now only *constrained* by external forces. Constraints, he insists, do not involve 'direct control over decision making', which is autonomous in an 'independent state' like Ireland. Constraints can be 'removed or reduced by negotiation or adaptation' and, thus, 'the behaviour of individuals, institutions or political parties' within Ireland must be the main obstacle to economic growth and development. 'Individuals, institutions or political parties' still leaves a lot of room for variation in the apportionment of blame, however, and there are varying analyses of the specific locations of Irish failure.

Lee (1989, pp. 390-96, 511-687), for example, blames the lack of local modern thinking and behaviour for Irish social and economic 'backwardness'. He claims Irish people have a 'possession ethic' rather than a 'performance ethic'. Unlike efficient Asian cultural characteristics, Irish farming experience and climate imposed a tradition of short-term economic calculation, preoccupation with security, and a preference for extensive property holdings rather than intensive and efficient use of smaller holdings. These characteristics spread to the professional and middle classes and suppressed entrepreneurship in Irish culture. Repeated attempts by Seán Lemass and others to encourage entre-preneurship met with failure, creating the eventual necessity to import it in the form of the TNCs. The failure of Irish entrepreneurship, in private and public sector alike, continues to this day in the form of an insufficient 'demand for, and supply of, social thought' (Lee, p. 605). The Irish state failed to induce an intellectual infrastructure, leading to insufficient innovative thought in social institutions from the state to the universities and media. The importation of ideas, in the form of foreign consultants and TNCs, substituted for local enterprise and intellect, but failed to take root because of the continuing local resistance to (or even indifference about) innovation. Thus, the specificities of Irish culture, which permeated its national institutions, made the country unable to avail of the considerable advantages of its closeness to Europe just as earlier generations had been unable to exploit the advantages of proximity to Britain.

Breen *et al* (1990) similarly place Irish failure in a local context, although their explanations lie in the neo-Weberian tradition of emphasising the failures of the Irish state. Following Evans *et al* (1985) they emphasise the distinction between state autonomy (its ability to make policies indepen-dently of forces in civil society) and state capacity (its ability to successfully implement those policies). Invoking Evans *et al*'s suggestion that the more a state exercises autonomous economic policymaking powers, the more it loses the capacity to succeed, they examine the effectiveness of state policy since 'the state seized the initiative as the main force in Irish society in 1958' (Breen *et al*, 1990, p. 31). From this point of view, two internal factors were primarily responsible for the Irish crisis of the 1980s. First, the Irish state took a more active role in 1958 in establishing policies and providing resources for social change and development, without establishing effective control over the institutions that would use the resources and implement the policies (e.g. the church). This had a major impact, for instance, on education, with obvious implications for development. The second reason for failure was that the state pursued industrialisation by attracting ready-made capital (TNCs). The problem was not so much with the TNCs or their activities, but with the degree to which resources that went into that sector might have been applied elsewhere. The state overspent on the attraction of the TNCs and had too little left to implement policies that might induce local innovation. It thus incapacitated itself by overspending on foreign firms that were obviously outside the realm of state autonomy.

Neither the modernisationist nor the neo-Weberian models, however, explain precisely where the impulse for development lies. Lee's 'market for ideas' is vague in the extreme and fails to examine how or where an alternative performance-based ethos might be applied to induce successful economic activity. It says little about the structures of capitalism or industrialisation – about what, besides desire, is necessary for success. In a sense, the neo-Weberian model explains even less. It explains to some degree how existing policies have failed in their implementation (although the dependency model says much more about the sources of failure of export- and TNC-led models). Yet it assumes that a 'capacitated' state would be more successful without articulating what kind of policies at the state level could work.

In other words, what are the precise mechanisms that drive industrialisation and economic expansion, where are they located (e.g. at the state level, the world-system level, the firm level, the individual level), and can they be captured by local states or other local actors?

Restructuring, innovation, and the core-periphery structure

It is these questions that another recent literature addresses. Some of this work is economically technical, in the sense that it identifies structural economic conditions for success and attempts to identify where they exist or could exist in Ireland. Another approach, however, is more conceptual, and attempts to identify how 'economic evolution' (in Schumpeter's words) proceeds and, moreover, who participates in certain forms of economic change and who does not. Both of these approaches address the issue of how Ireland's position in the EU, particularly under restructuring and the Single Market, affects its development possibilities.

One of the most exciting recent literatures in the social sciences is on innovation and competitive advantage. It combines institutional economics, business history, the sociology of institutions and world-systems, and labour studies to account for the success or failure of certain regions during periods of economic change. Most of the literature specifically addresses the recent period of global *restructuring*, during which Japan's strategies of production organisation, labour relations, and access strategies for raw materials and markets appear to have created a competitive advantage for its industrial producers. It asks what gives a region such a competitive edge, particularly in the leading high-tech sectors that drive periods of expansion. In so doing, it necessarily takes industrial history into account, comparing the present stage with earlier periods of competition over such sectors as cotton and automobiles. Part of the excitement of this literature is that it combines a broad range of social disciplines – the history of technology and business organisation, the histories of colonialism and imperialism, the institutional economics of scale and scope, the politics of global power and trade policy. When it is economic, it is not in the formal sense but in Polanyi's (1957) substantive world of *social embeddedness*, where markets are not the pure mechanisms of the neo-classicists and post-neo-classical mathematicians but are manipulated and created by individuals and institutions within hierarchies of social power. Regions and firms do not come to the market to sell their goods equally, but have unequal access to technologies, capital, markets and regional and global power institutions. While this literature has seldom been combined explicitly with critical approaches to development like dependency and world-systems, a few Irish case studies have begun to do so.

Among the primarily economistic approaches, O'Malley (1992a) extends his previous analysis of Ireland as 'late industrialiser' to the problems of restructuring in the 1990s. In particular, he analyses which regions will and will not benefit from the Single European Market (SEM) primarily in terms of whether their firms participate in activities that have significant economies of scale. He argues that the most important restrictions on late developers are market imperfections that create barriers to entry through unequal access to economies of scale. The SEM increases these barriers by raising the threshold, or minimum efficient size (MES) beyond which firms must produce in order to compete. Thus, activities that are widely tradable and have significant economies of scale will be most sensitive to the SEM.

O'Malley's conclusions, which he divides between foreign and indigenous sectors, are sometimes equivocal (although he tries hard to be optimistic). TNCs operating in Ireland are concentrated in the sensitive sectors (e.g. computers, pharmaceuticals) where the increased size of the SEM will enable firms to capture scale economies. This means the SEM may encourage them to expand. Yet TNCs can capture scale economies without expanding in Ireland, because their Irish operations are simply the gateway into the European market.

A US electronics firm, for example, can increase its scale of operation in Singapore and still move more of the final product through an unexpanded Irish subsidiary. This is especially relevant where the stages of production that have the largest economies of scale are not located in Ireland.

Few indigenous industries, however, are in sectors that have significant economies of scale (23 per cent by employment, compared to 63 per cent of TNCs). The few that are in such sectors are mainly non-traded because of high transport costs (bricks) or are in subsectors that do not have scale economies (ornamental glass). Thus, the SEM cannot be expected to induce significant expansion of indigenous industry. On the positive side, O'Malley contends, the destruction of uncompetitive Irish firms in the 1970s and 1980s was so thorough that surviving ones are unlikely to suffer from increased liberalisation. Unlike his earlier analyses (1989), O'Malley makes no prescriptions about how the Irish state might enable firms to participate in the sensitive sectors through selective protection and incentives. This may be a tacit recognition of the fact that such policies are impossible to pursue within the liberal structures of the EU, yet his failure to discuss how the rules of the EU restrict Irish policy choices is unfortunate.

While O'Malley and others concentrate on the formal aspects of Irish economic organisations, an emerging literature takes a more 'substantive' view of economic development. Following political economists like Polanyi (1957) and Schumpeter (1939), they treat economic activities and markets as embedded in social institutions that mix economic and non-economic rationalities. Such perspectives emphasise the longer view (history matters) and concentrate on the relationships between innovation and socio-economic change. Although work in this vein is still sparse, it includes Mjoset's (1992) study of Ireland in a north-European comparative context, Munck's (1993) explicitly non-partitionist review of Irish economic history and prospects, and work-in-progress by O'Hearn (1992, 1993, 1994).

Mjoset is solidly within the sociological tradition of
development theory because he explicitly addresses the
socio-economic problems mentioned above (disparities
between economic growth rates and unemployment,
emigration, poverty) by distinguishing between simple
economic growth and socio-economic development
(improvement of conditions for the fulfilment of human
needs; the development of social institutions and practices
that underlay economic change; the participation of
different social groups or classes in economic change). His
'comparative institutional perspective' compares Ireland to a
series of small but richer countries of the European core and
Scandinavia. By comparing Irish 'failure' to European
'successes', he hopes to uncover institutional preconditions
of development that are missing in Ireland but present in the
other cases. Insofar as these institutions and practices can be
identified and replicated, the study is prescriptive. But Mjoset
does not rule out the possibility that Ireland might be unable
to replicate successful elements of other countries. This
makes him more agnostic of Irish development within
Europe than the neo-modernisationists or even O'Malley.

Mjoset derives patterns of success ('virtuous circles of
development') and failure ('vicious circles') by combining
neo-Schumpeterian political economy with the dependency
framework of Samir Amin (1972) and its application to
European economies by Senghaas (1985). Schumpeter
(1939) argued that the most important economic changes
are not continuous processes of equilibrium growth, as
proposed in neo-classical growth theory, but discontinuous
surges of growth caused by clustered innovations. Economic
change moves in 60-70 year *long waves* of expansion and
contraction (usually called Kondratief or k-waves), where
each expansion is caused by linked clusters of innovations
concentrated in leading sectors (historically cotton, railroads,
automobiles; currently microelectronics and biotech-
nologies). A dual process of *innovative expansion* and *creative
destruction* of outmoded activities restructures capitalist

economies. According to Mjoset, such processes are extremely important to small economies because those who can 'hook on' to innovation will develop and prosper, while those who do not will face crises. The ability to 'hook on' depends, says Mjoset, on a series of institutional factors called *national systems of innovation*.

Mjoset identifies innovation, therefore, as a highly localised process. Successful *national* systems of innovation, following Porter (1990), contain factors – human and knowledge resources, capital resources, and infrastructure – that are created and nurtured by institutions of education, research, capital markets, and the state. Successful institutional structures create demanding buyers, linkages between firms and sectors, competitive specialisation and productive interfirm rivalry. Unlike Porter, however, Mjoset concentrates on national institutions and clusters of national industries rather than firms and inter-firm behaviour.

Where such institutions or national systems exist, Mjoset argues, one finds *growth with development*. True development, following Amin, is *auto-centric*: it favours products and productive processes related to mass rather than luxury consumption; the modernisation of leading industrial sectors is linked to modernisation of other sectors including agriculture; wages and demand are relatively high and, as a consequence, there is relatively full employment. *Peripheral* or *non-autocentric growth*, on the other hand, favours exports and luxury products, the production of which is largely unlinked to other indigenous sectors. Thus the growth of leading sectors is not linked to the development of 'traditional' sectors such as agriculture; wages tend to be low, especially in the undeveloped sectors; and generalised lack of development means high unemployment is likely. According to Mjoset, successful small European countries with national systems of innovation have conformed to the autocentric model of virtuous circles of development. Ireland, on the other hand, has no highly-developed national system of innovation because its growth path conforms more closely to the characteristics of peripheral nonautocentric growth.

The central question, however, is 'why'? Why did some small European countries establish autocentric growth while Ireland did not? Amin, like other dependency analysts, places national success or failure in its global context. The closer a dependent country's economic relations with industrialised capitalist countries, the more likely it is to be exploited and underdeveloped by the more developed country. But Senghaas (1985) insists that the thesis of dependent underdevelopment breaks down in Europe. Small countries such as Switzerland and Sweden had close external links with larger more developed neighbours that did not stifle their development. Indeed, they developed because of their proximity to Europe, not in spite of it. They 'hooked on' to expansive innovations that were centred in the core of Europe because they had institutions that made up 'national systems of innovation'.

Mjoset infers from this evidence that the locus of innovation depends on *national* variables. His comparative work aims to locate those national innovation-conducive institutions that are present in continental European states and missing in Ireland. Yet he also explores the comparative historical development of these institutions (or, in Ireland's case, histories of institutional failure). It is this analysis that is potentially most fruitful in Mjoset's work but also potentially most controversial. Its fruitfulness lies in the hope that by identifying the nature and evolution of innovative institutions and development strategies of 'hooking on', it may be possible to construct policies to recreate such institutions and strategies in Ireland. Its controversial aspect lies in the very assumption that Ireland, after centuries of historical development (or underdevelopment) that differed so fundamentally from Mjoset's comparative cases, could even contemplate mimicking their institutions and strategies.

Taken independently, perhaps all countries have the potential to create so-called national systems of innovation. But Ireland's capacity (as Mjoset recognises) was restricted and even reversed by eighteenth- and nineteenth-century British colonial policies which deindustrialised and depopulated the island. Alone among today's small outward-oriented European economies, Ireland was subjugated in the 1700s and 1800s, while small countries like Switzerland and Sweden maintained political autonomy and independence of economic policymaking. Dependency analysis, Senghaas and Mjoset notwithstanding, would never propose that *any* connections between small countries and large developed industrial countries will be destructive to the small countries. Rather, the *dependent* nature of the external relationships of small countries (Ireland) and large countries (Brazil, Mexico) alike – including colonialism, informal colonialism, and post-colonialism – restricted their development or even *under*developed them.

As I have already discussed, this historical identification of external relationships that limit indigenous development (including the creation through colonialism of indigenous classes and institutions that are anti-development) is taken up by Crotty (1986). But his solutions are strictly neo-classical. Colonial and post-colonial institutions and classes, particularly state institutions, cause Irish underdevelopment primarily by manipulating market mechanisms. The state keeps the cost of holding land and obtaining capital artificially low so that the propertied classes can maintain their advantages, while it keeps the cost of labour artificially high, inducing property owners to substitute capital for labour. The solution is to 'get prices right' by taxing land and capital, by subsidising labour, and by remunerating socially useful labour that is not presently paid. Crotty claims to be disinterested in 'development' in the formal sense; he cares little about growth or industrialisation, but much about the fulfilment of basic needs. This places him in sympathy with emerging green and post-modernist *antidevelopment* theorists (Sachs, 1992). Yet his economistic 'solutions' appear naïve insofar as the social institutions and classes who benefit from the status quo will oppose policy changes tooth and nail.

A less economistic analysis of the historical legacy of colonialism and imperialism – world-system analysis – identifies processes of *peripheralisation* which remove national or regional capacities to innovate or even to 'hook on' to innovation. Peripheralisation refers to the subordination of local productive systems to the interests of leading core capitals and economies. This includes the obvious transformation of peripheral agriculture away from subsistence production into export-oriented activities that are labour-intensive, pay low wages and return relatively low profit rates. In the middle-income *semiperiphery*, it also entails the promotion of industrial activities with similar characteristics (labour-intensity, relatively low wages and profits) but which also have few linkages with the innovative clusters that one finds in core industrial sectors. Semiperipheral industry may be profitable to core firms and sectors for various reasons – cheaper or more repressed labour, access to state subsidies, the absence of state regulations – but they do not have the same capacity as core activities to expand, innovate or induce other linked activities.

In my analysis of the subjugation of the Irish cotton industry by Britain, I argue that systems of innovation are not national or regional, but global (O'Hearn, 1994). I argue that British policies before and after the union of 1801 peripheralised Irish industry and agriculture alike, as part of the process by which English industry captured innovations. Global economic and political power (*hegemony*, in world-systems terminology) was necessary for British industry to obtain cheap and stable access to critical raw materials, labour and markets and to restrict similar access for existing or potential competitors. Access to such global assets was necessary if linked innovations in industry, transport and distribution were to be profitably undertaken. Without equal access to the world-system, and therefore facing unequal competition from British cotton manufacturers and linked industries, Irish entrepreneurs rationally switched to the less innovative and semiperipheral linen industry.

Elsewhere (O'Hearn, 1993), I argue that similar world-systemic processes and structures still block innovation in contemporary Ireland. The restructuring of the European region in the 1980s was based on the desire of the strongest core states and firms to successfully compete in leading innovative sectors of today's global economy. In order to compete, however, the European 'state' (or coalitions of European core states) must provide structures that enable their strongest firms to capture innovations. The Single European Market aims to increase market size so that the most advanced European firms can attain the scale they require if they are to bear the vast costs of innovation and research that are necessary to compete profitably with US and Japanese firms. EU and intergovernmental technology programmes are intended to encourage innovation while liberal merger and monopoly regulations enable inter-firm collaboration to increase the larger firms' market power. This, however, may encourage processes of *agglomeration* of firms and sectors in European core regions. Many observers consider agglomeration to be central to restructuring because regional concentration enables flexibility (Piore and Sabel, 1985).

On the other hand, EU policies to counter 'peripherality' may be both ineffective and ill-conceived because they define it as a purely geographical concept rather than a logical one. Efforts to 'bring the periphery closer to the core' by improving transport and other infrastructures may simply make Ireland more vulnerable to penetration by the core (for example, imports of core products that replace indigenous products and producers). Without policies that actually create jobs, programmes to improve 'skill infrastructures' will simply make foreign labour markets more attractive to Irish emigrants. While there are countervailing factors, the agglomeration of key activities in the European core may marginalise Irish labour within Europe and thus increase the pressures of unemployment and emigration that became critical in the 1970s.

Alternatives

Given the nature of the Irish economic crisis, what are the alternatives? Notable suggestions include: (1) continued liberalisation, (2) niche development or 'hooking on', and (3) dependency reversal.

The ascendant mainstream approach (not just in Ireland but throughout Europe and the world) is liberalisation. The basic argument for liberalisation is that state institutions and regulations stifle flexibility and innovation, while distorting prices in ways that send false signals to private economic actors. The strength of the core states and institutions in the global economy, including the world bank and the international monetary fund, is shown by the fact that liberal strategies have been consistently introduced not only by governments of the right but also by governments of former socialist and social democratic parties.

Aside from its academic and professional adherents, recent Irish liberalisation was originally advocated by the more right-wing parties (Fine Gael and the Progressive Democrats), but was introduced and fostered by the more populist Fianna Fáil and the Fianna Fáil/Labour governments. Despite high official growth rates since 1988, however, the social impact of liberalisation is questionable because of the persistence of unemployment, emigration and poverty. Even strictly economic variables such as growth may be drastically overestimated in official statistics, while the performance of indigenous firms and the creation of linkages among economic sectors and firms are disappointing.

Although liberal policies are ascendant, there is little evidence that they have improved the innovative capacities of Irish economic institutions. Instead, Ireland has become increasingly dependent on transfers – EU structural funds for the south and British subventions for the north. As the numbers of manufacturing jobs decline, job creation depends more heavily on transfers to fund state employment schemes and construction. As a result, an increasing proportion of jobs are temporary, part-time and low-paid. Not only is this pattern inadequate for long-term development, but there is increasing evidence that both the EU and Britain are unwilling to maintain subventions at the current levels.

Institutional approaches arose in response to perceived inadequacies of the liberal model in the core economies of Europe, Japan and the US. Many leading social scientists recognise that recent economic successes – Japan and Germany, as well as ascendant economies such as South Korea and Taiwan – were based on managed trade rather than free trade, on strategic state intervention and control of interfirm and intersectoral strategies rather than free enterprise. Thus, although core states and institutions prescribe liberalisation for the third world, they implement interventionist, state-managed policies for themselves.

An Irish proposal for strategic intervention based on East Asian successes was O'Malley's (1989) positive assessment of South Korean policies of protection for export. Rather than following Irish-style free trade and foreign-dominated policies, South Korea nurtured its large indigenous holding companies (*chaebol*) by extending special credit terms, preferential access to imports with cheap foreign exchange rates, and protection against competing imports, in exchange for satisfactory corporate performance toward introducing innovations, deepening production into machinery and consumer durables, and expanding exports in leading sectors.

Unfortunately, such comparisons are largely moot. EU regulations leave Ireland no control over the central instruments used by East Asian states including foreign-exchange rates, import protection and export subsidies (not to mention the less attractive policies of extreme labour repression). Even without these EU restrictions, however, it is doubtful whether Ireland could institute such policies. Cumings (1987) persuasively argues that the US allowed South Korea and Taiwan to introduce protectionist and interventionist policies as a trade-off for their front-line support in the cold war. They also had a special position as subcontractors to Japanese industry that is very different from the situation of most other dependent economies (but which may have important parallels in Senghaas and Mjoset's successful European cases). Other countries that attempted interventionist strategies, e.g. Latin American countries – faced extreme pressures and sanctions from the US and international bodies, culminating in the debt crises of the 1970s and 1980s and the dismantling of intervention in favour of free trade and free enterprise. O'Hearn (1990, 1993) argues in his comparison of Ireland and East Asia that Irish interventionist alternatives have been preempted by threats of expulsion and isolation from Europe, an outcome that is generally regarded to be even more frightening than the present crises.

Failing systemic change that would enable effective intervention, the most popular strategy proposal is *niche development.* This involves identifying and exploiting small opportunities, or niches, that are left open by the expanding and innovating European economies. Opportunities to fill such niches are supposedly left because the large European firms cannot be bothered to perform many small but necessary (and profitable) activities. Mjoset (1992) and O'Malley (1992) clearly favour a strategy of inducing indigenous Irish firms to exploit niches, as a way of 'hooking on' to the innovative expansions in Europe. Niche strategies are compatible with analyses that concentrate on state capacities (e.g., Breen *et al,* 1989 and Lee, 1989) because the ability of firms to enter niches may depend on the state's capacity to identify them, pass on information to indigenous investors and induce investors to enter them. They can also be compatible with neo-liberal approaches, because the market will supposedly induce firms to enter niches that provide attractive profits.

In broader political terms, niche strategies are compatible with programmes of economic harmonisation put forward by the British Labour Party and the northern Social and Democratic Labour Party (SDLP). This perspective regards Irish unification as a long-term process that will follow from the harmonisation of the northern and southern economies. In turn, harmonisation is considered to be the most positive economic strategy in the context of a liberalised Europe under the SEM. This is because national borders are seen to lose their economic relevance as trade barriers come down, leaving regional markets and more 'natural' territorial economic units to take their place. Munck and Hamilton (1993, p. 145) relate the harmonisation perspective to the economic analysis of the 1984 New Ireland Forum, which asserted that Irish economic reunification would increase the 'home market' for the south by half and more than treble the northern 'home market'. Support for harmonisation on these grounds has come from key business figures such as Ulster Bank chair George Quigley. Obviously, a larger harmonised 'domestic' market would increase Irish firms' ability to co-operate and capture economies of scale, and thus compete for important export niches. Presumably, an Irish state (or states) that was less preoccupied with war would have a greater capacity to concentrate resources on the development of selected industries and firms that might successfully compete for identified niches. The removal of economic policymaking from the British state to an Irish state would also enhance such a strategy.

There are several arguments against niche strategies. First, there is no evidence that niches exist in adequate numbers to satisfy the employment needs of all EU states. On the contrary, the persistence of high unemployment rates in Europe suggests that the niche market is a sellers' market with far more prospective entrants than the market will bear. Any advantages gained by a peripheral country like Ireland will simply be to the disadvantage of others like Spain, Portugal or Greece. Second, there is no reason to expect core economies to forego niches simply because they are small. All successful core economies contain a mix of large and small producers. Indeed, the modal innovative firm in the age of microelectronics may be smaller than in previous waves of expansion (for example, the automobile wave). German success comprises both large firms and small firms that populate innovation-intensive corridors such as Baden-Wurttemburg. Third, a central element of restructuring in the 1980s and 1990s was the increased importance of close but flexible relations between large firms and their suppliers. Insofar as this involves agglomeration of smaller activities around large industrial nodes, niches are more likely to be filled by proximate producers in the smaller continental countries that surround the European core, especially since these countries have historically developed systems of innovation, training and infrastructure. Peripheral regions such as Ireland are more likely to participate where their advantages overcome those of the small continental countries – advantages such as lower labour costs or state subsidies and grants, which are associated more with dependent niches than with innovative niches.

Finally, even if a niche strategy contributed to Irish economic growth it would be incomplete without a broader strategy to combine growth with development. Arguably, growth is necessary for development because it provides the resources and employment that are necessary to meet the broader social needs of a population. Yet growth is not sufficient for development because an economic strategy cannot by itself guarantee how resources will be applied. They may be used primarily for the enrichment of a privileged elite class, especially if niche development is combined with neo-liberal policies.

The distinction between simple growth and growth with development is the basis for more radical alternatives which Munck and Hamilton (1993, p. 148) term 'democratic economies'. The elements of such strategies are vague, perhaps necessarily so since we have yet to see a working model. But the strategy is decidedly not a return to De Valera's self-sufficiency because it is disdainful of the radical free enterprise and autarchy that were inherent in that model. Nor is it a reverie for Soviet-style 'socialism-as-it-actually-existed', for the obvious reason that these systems were undemocratic and overcentralised. It does, however, have affinity with concepts of development for basic needs that come from third world sociologies of development, as well as neo-Marxian models that are based on prioritising use values over exchange values as the basis for distributing resources among different economic activities (see, e.g. Harvey, 1982). It is also consistent with models of grassroots development 'from below', which emphasise economic democracy and decentralised planning institutions.

I have been skeptical, however, whether successful democratic development strategies can be implemented by single semiperipheral countries such as Ireland within the capitalist world-system (O'Hearn, 1993). Upward mobility by semiperipheral countries into the core is rare. World-system analysts consider this immobility to be the result of the semiperiphery's subjugation by core powers whose interests require the maintenance of the core-semiperiphery-periphery structure (see, e.g. Arrighi and Drangel, 1986; Chase-Dunn, 1989). I do, however, argue that systemic trans-formation can be encouraged by building regional solidarity in movements that demand the reversal of regional marginalisation and the semiperiphery's (and periphery's) full participation in core economic sectors and activities.

In the shorter term, however, networks of local movements are realistic building blocks for dependency reversal and democratic development. Such networks build confidence within communities about their members' abilities to partici-pate in democratic development projects. In Ireland, local groups have resisted corporate and state activities, from ecologically destructive chemical plants in Cork to cutbacks of health services under austerity programmes in both the north and south. Grassroots development forums have encouraged small but important projects that aspire to implement democratic economic structures and to prioritise development for community needs. A particularly important aspect of this activity is co-operation among grassroots organisations, such as the Social Economy Network, an action-research partnership between groups in West Belfast and Ballymun in Dublin. Other Irish groups participate in international grassroots networks comprising trade unions, community groups, women's groups and other organisations.

Finally, grassroots approaches are common both to radical developmental approaches and to the new anti-developmental approaches. Deep green and post-modernist approaches are skeptical about the very concept of development. To quote a leading proponent, 'the idea of development stands today like a ruin in the intellectual landscape. Its shadow obscures our vision' (Sachs, 1991, p. 1). Although this approach is not widespread in Ireland its growth may be indicated by the initial success of the Green Party in Irish elections of the 1990s. Crotty (1986) is partly anti-developmental, because his proposals for change eschew traditional visions of industrialisation and affluence and, instead, concentrate on redistributing current incomes for a more equitable outcome. He shares with Marxism, third-world approaches and feminism the emphasis on basic needs and the revaluation of devalued labour. Yet he breaks with those traditions by denying that the general development of society's productive capacities is a prerequisite for an equitable and affluent society. A more direct, but less specified, anti-developmentalist (or at least agnostic) approach is Tucker's work on the *myth of development* (1992). He emphasises the disempowering nature of a concept of 'development' that is based on European core cultural values, yet his alternatives centre on the development of locally-appropriate concepts of social development rather than completely denying the validity of any concept of development. The new anti-developmentalism contains elements that many social scientists (including radical ones) would consider to be overly negative in terms of its unwillingness to consider the potentially liberating aspects of technological and productive change, if only they could be removed from the oppressive social context of (Eurocentred) world capitalism. Yet green approaches have vital potential to blend with other radical approaches that aspire to elaborate society-centred development strategies that can distinguish the negative aspects of European development thought from its more progressive history of movement toward empowerment and liberation.

References

AMIN, SAMIR, 1972. 'Accumulation and development: a theoretical model', *Review of African Political Economy* 1.

ARRIGHI, GIOVANNI and JESSICA DRANGEL, 1986. 'Stratification of the world-economy: an explanation of the semiperipheral zone', *Review*, 10:1, pp 9-74.

BOROOAH, VANI, 1993. 'Northern Ireland – Typology of a regional economy', in Paul Teague (ed.), *The Economy of Northern Ireland: Perspectives for Structural Change*, London, Lawrence & Wishart.

BREEN, RICHARD, D. HANNAN, D. ROTTMAN, C. WHELAN, 1989. *Understanding Contemporary Ireland*, New York, St. Martin's.

CANTILLON, SARA, JOHN CURTIS and JOHN FITZGERALD, 1994. *Medium-term Review: 1994-2000*, Dublin, ESRI.

CHASE-DUNN, CHRISTOPHER, 1989. *Global Formation*, London, Basil Blackwell.

CROTTY, RAYMOND, 1986. *Ireland in Crisis: A study of Capitalist Colonial Under-development*, Dingle, Brandon.

CUMINGS, BRUCE, 1987. 'The origin and development of the Northeast Asian political economy: industrial sectors, product cycles and political consequences', in Fred Deyo (ed.), *The Political Economy of New Asian Industrialism*, Ithaca, Cornell University Press, pp. 44-83.

Department of Finance, 1993. *Economic Review and Outlook, 1993*, Dublin, Stationery Office.

EVANS, PETER, D. RUESCHEMEYER, T. SKOCPOL (eds.), 1985. *Bringing the State Back In*, Cambridge, Cambridge University Press.

GALLAGHER, A., R. OSBORNE and R. CORMACK, 1994. *Fair Shares?* Belfast, Fair Employment Commission.

GIRVIN, BRIAN, 1989. *Between Two Worlds: Politics and Economy in Independent Ireland*, Dublin, Gill & Macmillan.

GOVERNMENT OF IRELAND, 1990. *Operational Programme on Peripherality: Roads and Other Transport Infrastructure, 1989-1993*, Dublin, Stationery Office.

HARVEY, DAVID, 1982. *The Limits to Capital*, Chicago, University of Chicago Press.

HITCHENS, D., J. BIRNIE and K. WAGNER, 1993. 'Economic performance in Northern Ireland: a comparative perspective' in Paul Teague (ed.), *The Economy of Northern Ireland*, pp. 24-59.

INDUSTRIAL POLICY REVIEW GROUP, 1992. A *Time for Change: Industrial Policy for the 1990s* [Culliton Report], Dublin, Stationery Office.

JACOBSEN, KURT, 1978. 'Changing utterly? Irish development and the problem of dependence', *Studies*, Winter.

JACOBSEN, KURT, 1994. *Chasing Progress in the Irish Republic*, Cambridge, Cambridge University Press.

LEE, JOSEPH, 1989. *Ireland 1912-1985: Politics and Society*, Cambridge, Cambridge University Press.

MANGAN, OLIVER, 1994. 'No longer a joke', *Davy Stockbrokers Weekly Market Monitor*, 22 July.

MAC LAUGHLIN, JIM, 1994. 'Emigration and the peripheralization of Ireland in the global economy', *Review*, 17:2, Spring, 1994, pp. 243-73.

MAC LAUGHLIN, JIM, DENNIS PRINGLE, COLM REGAN, FRANCIS WALSH (eds.), 1980. *Antipode, Special Issue on Ireland* 12:1, Summer.

MJOSET, LARS, 1993. *The Irish Economy in a Comparative Institutional Perspective*, Report No. 93, Dublin, National Economic and Social Council.

MUNCK, RONNIE, 1993. *The Irish Economy: Results and Prospects*, London, Pluto.

MUNCK, RONNIE and DOUGLAS HAMILTON, 'Alternative scenarios', in Munck, *The Irish Economy*, 1993, pp 135-60.

O'DOWD, LIAM, B. ROLSTON and M. TOMLINSON, 1980. *Northern Ireland: Between Civil Rights and Civil War*, London, CSE Books.

O'HEARN, DENIS, 1989. 'The Irish case of dependency: an exception to the exceptions?' *American Sociological Review* 54:4, August, pp. 578-96.

O'HEARN, DENIS, 1990. 'The road from import-substituting to export-led industrialisation in Ireland: who mixed the asphalt, who drove the machinery, and who kept making them change directions?, *Politics and Society*, 18:1, pp. 1-38.

O'HEARN, DENIS, 1993.

Putting Ireland in a Global Context, Occasional Paper Series No. 9, Cork, UCC Department of Sociology.

O'HEARN, DENIS, 1994. 'Innovation and the world-system hierarchy: British subjugation of the Irish cotton industry, 1780-1830', *American Journal of Sociology*, 100:3, November, pp. 587-621.

O'MALLEY, EOIN, 1980. *Industrial Policy and Development: A Survey of Literature from the Early 1960s to the Present*, Dublin, Economic and Social Research Institute.

O'MALLEY, EOIN, 1989. *Industry and Economic Development: the Challenge for the Latecomer*, Dublin, Gill & Macmillan.

O'MALLEY, EOIN, 1992a. 'Industrial structure and economies of scale in the context of 1992' in John Bradley, John Fitzgerald and Ide Kearney, *The Role of the Structural Funds*, Dublin, ESRI, pp. 203-49.

O'MALLEY, EOIN, 1992b. 'Problems of industrialisation in Ireland' in J.H. Goldthorpe and C.T. Whelan (eds.), *The Development of Industrial Society in Ireland*, Oxford, Oxford University Press, pp. 31-52.

OECD 1992. *Ireland: Country Report*, Paris, OECD.

O'MALLEY, EOIN, 1993. *Ireland: Country Report*, Paris, OECD.

O'TOOLE, FINTAN, 1994.

Black Hole, Green Card: the Disappearance of Ireland, Dublin, New Island Books.

POLANYI, KARL, 1957. 'The economy as instituted process', in Karl Polanyi, Conrad Arensberg and Harry Pearson (eds.), *Trade and Market in the Early Empires*, Chicago, Regnery, pp. 243-69.

PIORE, MICHAEL and CHARLES SABEL, 1985. *The Second Industrial Divide*, New York, Basic Books.

PORTER, MICHAEL, 1990. *The Competitive Advantage of Nations*, London.

PROBERT, BELINDA, 1978. *Beyond Orange and Green*, London, Zed.

SACHS, WOLFGANG (ed.), 1992. *The Development Dictionary: A Guide to Knowledge as Power*, London, Zed.

SCHUMPETER, JOSEPH, 1939. *Business Cycles*, New York, McGraw-Hill.

SENGHAAS, DIETER, 1985. *The European Experience: A Historical Critique of Development Theory*, Leamington Spa, Berg.

SO, ALVIN, 1990. *Social Change and Development: Modernization, Dependency, and World-Systems Theories*, London, Sage.

STEWART, J.C., 1976. 'Foreign direct investment and the emergence of a dual economy', *Economic and Social Review* 7:2, January), pp. 173-97.

SWEENEY, PAUL, 1992. 'A response to "A Time for Change"', unpublished paper delivered to the Statistical and Social Inquiry Society of Ireland, 22 March.

TELESIS CONSULTANCY GROUP, 1982. *A Review of Industrial Policy*, Report No. 64, Dublin, National Economic and Social Council.

TUCKER, VINCENT, 1993. *The Myth of Development*, Occasional Paper No. 6, Cork, UCC Department of Sociology.

WATERS, JOHN, 1992. *Jiving at the Crossroads*, Belfast, Blackstaff Press.

WICKHAM, JAMES, 1986. 'Industrialization, work and employment', in Pat Clancy *et al, Ireland: A Sociological Profile*, Dublin, Institute of Public Administration, pp. 70-96.

4
Development or Dependency? State, Economy and Society in Northern Ireland[1]

LIAM O'DOWD

Introduction: phases of development

Over the last one hundred years, the north-east of Ireland has been transformed from a core industrial area of the British empire to a peripheral region of the European Union. It has moved from being one of the most, to one of the least, industrialised regions of the UK. This change reflects not just developments within Northern Ireland and the UK, but in the wider restructuring and expansion of global capitalism. While this chapter concentrates on socio-economic development in the last twenty-five years, this period must be located within a longer timespan.

In the decades prior to 1920 the area centred on Belfast was a world leader in shipbuilding and linen manufacture and one of the main industrial areas of the United Kingdom, then the leading imperial power in the world. This regional economic complex provided necessary, if insufficient, conditions for partition and the creation of a distinct political unit within the UK, separate from the largely agricultural Free State. From its inception, however, Northern Ireland has struggled to combat mass unemployment, the contraction of its main industrial sectors and increasingly effective competition from other countries. In the immediate aftermath of partition, it was a net subscriber to the British exchequer and was expected to be financially self-sufficient. Mass unemployment between 1921 and 1939 put strains on this arrangement as did the rapid development of the British welfare state after 1948. De-industrialisation and the impact of the conflict over the last twenty-five years has dramatically increased dependency on the British exchequer, and by 1994, the British subvention to Northern Ireland was 3.4 billion pounds (over 2,000 pounds per capita per annum of the Northern Ireland population). In effect, Northern Ireland has become a dependent client of the British state (Rowthorn, 1993, p. ix).

Economic change in Northern Ireland can only be fully understood in the context of the particular kinds of political conditions and social relationships which have sustained it. The region's rise to industrial prominence was framed and stimulated, initially by the Ulster plantation settlement, and subsequently by British imperial expansion which provided markets and raw materials for its major industries. Northern Ireland has been a war-economy at key junctures in its history – economic activity benefited from war-time demand and post-war booms associated with the first and second world wars particularly (Johnson,1985, pp. 3-5; Kennedy 1989, pp. 6-8). Over the last twenty-five years another type of war-time economy has emerged – encouraging mass dependence on state expenditure, state employment and security-related jobs. The Northern Ireland economy has also been shaped by deeply intertwined local, class, sectarian and gender relationships, which have themselves altered as the basis of the economy has changed. These relationships have found local political expression over time in partition, in the long monopolisation of power by the Ulster Unionist Party, the sectarian and patriarchal character of society, and in the ultimate de-stablisation of devolved government and the form of centralised direct rule administration which succeeded it.

Viewed from the perspective of 1994, three distinctive, if overlapping phases in the socio-economic development of Northern Ireland can be identified:

- Between 1880 and the 1950s, the social economy of Northern Ireland rested on three major pillars: agriculture, shipbuilding/engineering and linen. Population and economic activity became concentrated in Belfast and the Lagan Valley. Even here, however, manufacturing was unevenly developed. By the 1950s, linen was a low wage sector marked by poor working conditions and high rates of female employment with a mixed Catholic and Protestant workforce. Shipbuilding and engineering, on the other hand, provided relatively high wages for a more skilled and largely Protestant male workforce. Production remained under the control of local, and mainly Protestant, capitalists. West of the Bann was heavily dependent on subsistence agriculture and the region as a whole continued to have a labour surplus with high emigration and unemployment rates. These varied with respect to locality, class and communal affiliation. Despite its industrialised and 'developed' profile, the Northern Ireland economy in this period was highly vulnerable to cycles of boom and recession – intensified employment and economic activity in wartime and periods of mass unemployment in the inter-war period. The most characteristic political expression of this period was the dominance of the Ulster Unionist Party and the Orange Order, linking landed gentry, the industrial and commercial bourgeoisie and a skilled working class in a class alliance which aimed to exclude and dominate a much weaker nationalist class alliance.
- The second period, between the 1950s and 1970s, witnessed the undermining of the economic and political edifice which comprised Northern Ireland. The British welfare state was extended to the province, to be managed successfully for a time by a Unionist Party

ideologically opposed to its principles. By the 1960s, however, employment in three indigenous sectors of the Northern Ireland economy was contracting dramatically, and Stormont, like the Dublin government, began to sponsor multi-national investment which for a time managed to compensate for declining employment in the traditional sectors. Belfast began to lose its industry and population to the surrounding areas. The new investment, the growth centre planning which accompanied it, and the impact of universalistic forms of welfare began to undermine the stability of both the majority and minority political blocs in Northern Ireland. The emergence of the Northern Ireland Civil Rights Association, the challenge to discriminatory and exclusivistic practices, the response of hard-line loyalists and the re-emergence of the IRA led to the collapse of Stormont and to direct rule from Westminster in 1972.

- After the early 1970s, a state-dependent economy quickly emerged under direct rule. The successive oil crises and cyclical downturns of the 1970s undermined employment even in the new multinational industries. Manufacturing employment declined and mass unemployment returned. New foreign investment dried up as the conflict escalated. Parts of west and north Belfast became industrial wastelands and cockpits of conflict. Even the new suburbs and growth centres of the late 1950s and 1960s suffered. Public service employment and public expenditure rose dramatically. There was large-scale growth in female full-time and part-time employment in the public sector and in security employment for Protestant males. Sectarian and gender employment practices came under closer scrutiny from newly-established regulatory bodies. Because of the special local circumstances the transition from Keynesianism to Thatcherism was not as marked in Northern Ireland as levels of public expenditure were to remain an indispensable means of managing the conflict.

Table 1:   **Percentage of employees in employment in the main industrial sectors in Northern Ireland, 1952-91**

	1952 (%)	1971 (%)	1981 (%)	1991 (%)
AFF*	6	3	2	1
Man & Con**	53	45	34	27
Services	41	52	64	72
Number	466,000	473,241	466,611	480,520

* Agriculture, Forestry and Fisheries
** Manufacturing and Construction.

Sources: Isles and Cuthbert (1957, p. 63); Department of Manpower Services (DMS) Gazettes; Census of Population 1981, 1987.

Table 1 indicates the scale of socio-economic change since 1952 in Northern Ireland, notably the proportionate shift of employees in employment from manufacturing and construction into the service sector, a pattern common to most industrialised countries over the same period.

Changes in civil employment (self-employed plus employees) are demonstrated in Table 2 which also indicates the remarkable convergence of the sectoral profile of Northern Ireland and the Republic.

Northern Ireland is more dependent on services and the Republic on agriculture but the gap continues to narrow. Sectoral convergence should not be confused with complementarity or high levels of interaction between both economies, however. For example, North-South trade remains limited – 5 per cent of the South's total exports going to the North while the latter supplies only 4 per cent of the South's imports (Government of Ireland, 1992, p. 26).

The relatively limited scale of interaction between both Irish economies is a reminder of the differential integration of both parts of Ireland into the global economy since the

Table 2:   **Civil employment in the main industrial sectors as a percentage of total employment in Northern Ireland and the Republic of Ireland 1973-91**

	1973 %		1991 %	
	NI	RoI	NI	RoI
Agriculture	8.5	24.6	4.3	13.7
Industry	38.5	30.7	27.2	28.6
Services	53.0	44.7	68.5	57.7
Total	100	100	100	100
Manufacture	29.4	20.5	19.8	21.7

Sources: Bradley and Dowling (1983, p. 40); NI Census of Population 1991; RoI Labour Force Survey 1991.

nineteenth century. Partition confirmed the status of Northern Ireland as a region within the UK, with limited power to affect its own development policy. It ensured that there were no attempts to develop complementarity between both economies as a means of maximising Ireland's capacity within the global economy (Kennedy *et al*, 1988, p. 110). It is only recently that a sustained campaign has emerged to create a unified and integrated all-Ireland economy to offset the potentially devastating effects of the Single European Market on both parts of Ireland (Anderson and Goodman, 1994).

Over the last 50 years, accounts of socio-economic change have been intimately bound up with the issue of 'development'. Since 1945, the latter has become the major policy objective of nation-states, trading blocs and international agencies such as the United Nations and the World Bank. It is worth asking therefore whether the experience of Northern Ireland, sketched in preliminary form above, can be construed as development. The answer to this question is far from simple given that development itself, despite its widespread currency, remains a highly contested term. There is wide disagreement over its measurement and its objectives. Nevertheless, it typically implies some quantitative notion of growth measured by national or regional economic indicators such as gross national product or income per capita. Technological expertise and the 'march through the sectors' evident in the shift in employment from agriculture to manufacturing to services are also frequently associated with advanced or 'developed' economies.

Development also involves a whole range of assessments of social and cultural change which aim to measure quality of life and standards of living. Examples range from such measurements as life expectancy, literacy rates, expenditure on consumer durables and income distribution, to rather less quantifiable factors like social differentiation and specialisation, citizenship rights, political participation and cultural freedom. Much of the debate over development concerns the nature of the relationship between economic growth and many of the non-economic factors listed above (e.g. see Mjoset, 1992).

No single interpretation of socio-economic change and development in Northern Ireland could hope to encompass the many dimensions of development. Yet, it is possible to identify three different styles or genres in the approach to the subject in Northern Ireland. These are by no means mutually exclusive in practice:

- overall assessments about progress or decline, i.e. about the direction or merits of change which involve explicit or implicit comparisons across time and place.
- specialised studies of a series of critical development issues aimed at informing government policy since the early 1970s. Three of the major themes addressed are discussed below: Northern Ireland's productive base, equality issues and the problem of state dependence and governance structures.

- attempts at explaining socio-economic development in
  Northern Ireland in terms of overarching theories of
  development.

Decline or progress?

Ideas of progress and decline are deeply embedded, not only
in the development literature, but also in the long history of
Western social philosophy. Decline is often predicated on
images of a more prosperous golden age – a world now lost
or disappearing, and frequently imagined in terms of (rural
or urban) community, kinship, and stability. Ideas of
progress, on the other hand, typically emphasise scientific
and technological advancement and improved material
circumstances. Overall, images of decline seem to
predominate in current assessments of socio-economic
change in Northern Ireland, notably those which trace its
path from being one of the centres of the industrial
revolution to being a peripheral, high unemployment region,
heavily dependent on state transfers. Images of Northern
Ireland's decline are frequently framed in the context of the
wider decline of the UK from its position as 'workshop of the
world' and dominant imperial power.

The golden age of Northern Ireland economic development in most accounts is the period between 1880-1920 when
Belfast and the Lagan Valley were core areas of global
industrial production. The creation of Northern Ireland in
1920 marked the political high water mark of this era, even if
by then the economic tide had begun to ebb. The devolved
administration was left the task of presiding over long-term
secular decline in key industries – a decline interrupted by
war-time boom and tempered initially by a sense that
Northern Ireland was increasing its economic advantage over
the Free State (Republic).

It appears that North-South differences did widen
dramatically between 1938 and 1947, opening up a major
economic gap in average incomes, perhaps for the first time

(Kennedy, 1989, p. 7). Whereas average income per head in both parts of Ireland were much the same in 1930 by the late 1940s they were 75 per cent higher in Northern Ireland (Johnson, 1985, p. 43). These differentials were to persist throughout the 1950s and early 1960s. Although Northern Ireland was only half the size of the Republic, the value of its merchandise exports exceeded those in the Republic by one fifth as late as 1974 (after reaching over three times the Republic's figure in 1946). By the 1980s, however, the Republic's exports were larger, and growing faster, than those of the North (Kennedy, *et al*, 1988, pp. 101-2), even if this was largely due to the multinational, rather than the indigenous, sector of its economy (see O'Hearn's chapter in this volume).

Since the late 1950s, the programmes of re-industrialisation in the North, and 'late industrialisation' in the South were based on the same strategy of promoting multinational investment. The result, however, was an historic shift in the balance of manufacturing employment (see Table 2) and output in favour of the South. Between 1973 and 1990 the volume of manufacturing production increased by over 160 per cent in the Republic, and remained almost unchanged in Northern Ireland (Government of Ireland, 1992, p. 26). More recently (since 1990), manufacturing output has begun to recover in Northern Ireland, but unemployment remains high (Northern Ireland Economic Council, Report 113, 1994, pp. 16-17). As the productive base of Northern Ireland stagnated, employment and income levels became more and more dependent on state transfers from Britain. From the early 1970s, therefore, to the extent that Northern Ireland measured its development against the rest of Ireland, the relative decline of the former was obvious. This image of decline was reinforced by the far more frequent comparisons made between Northern Ireland and other regions of the UK (e.g. see Harris, Jefferson and Spencer, 1990; Wilson, 1989).

The context of economic change had changed dramatically also. Northern Ireland was perceived as a peripheral region of a country which not only had lost an empire but also had failed to match the economic growth rates of other major EU partners. Prior to the signing of the Treaty of Rome, the UK's national income and foreign trade were greater than those of any EU country. Since 1957, UK national income has been vastly outdistanced by Germany, surpassed by France and is roughly equivalent to that of Italy (Millward, 1992, p. 436). More recently, the EU as a bloc is struggling to keep pace with other economic superpowers, the US, Japan and the newly-industrialised countries of the Pacific rim. Northern Ireland, therefore, can be seen as lagging behind much of the developed core of the global economic system. Yet, core countries as a whole have widened their advantage over the poorest underdeveloped countries of the world. In a more global context, therefore, conventional economic indicators (e.g. income per capita, gross domestic product, economic growth rates), suggest that Northern Ireland clearly remains a 'rich' region in its own right and the beneficiary of being part of a relatively large and 'rich' state.

Comparisons across time, utilising a broad range of development indicators, demonstrate that relative decline on some measures can co-exist with an absolute increase in the average standard of living of the population. The latter has risen substantially over the last seventy years. Higher incomes, better welfare services and housing, less onerous employment, better diet, increased longevity, and more widespread access to household appliances, cars, televisions, and other communications technology have enhanced the quality of life of the population. Unemployment levels have risen and declined over the whole period and remain relatively high at present. Yet, the depth of deprivation experienced by the unemployed today does not compare with that of the inter-war period. It is possible to present the current socio-economic structure of Northern Ireland as the culmination of a progressive modernisation, as well as an expression of long-term decline. Even the greater degree of state dependency, which has developed since 1970, can be portrayed as 'the normal' consequence of belonging to a wealthy country which ensures transfers between its richer and poorer parts. The existence of several, often contradictory assessments of development is an indication of the extent to which the term itself is contested by academics, politicians and government officials.

Critical development issues

Until the early 1970s, social science was poorly developed in Northern Ireland. Economic analysis and debate was limited and rested on one major book by Isles and Cuthbert (1957), supplemented by attempts at economic planning in the 1960s (Wilson, 1989). With the development of the social sciences generally, and particularly with the escalation of the conflict, more specialised social scientific analysis began to proliferate, much of it aimed at informing the direct rule administration. Three issues came to dominate the study of socio-economic development: the crisis of Northern Ireland's productive economy, a series of equality issues associated with class, gender, unemployment, sectarian division and locality, and finally, the problem of state dependency and governance structure.

The productive base: restructuring or collapse?

From the 1960s onwards two interrelated factors were emphasised in accounts of the productive base of Northern Ireland's economy. The first was the long-term contraction in traditional employment sectors such as agriculture, engineering, shipbuilding and linen manufacture. The numbers employed in manufacturing, for example, have almost halved since 1950 (Borooah, 1993, p. 6). The second factor stressed was structural reliance on declining industries which was frequently highlighted as the reason for Northern Ireland's loss of manufacturing employment and poor economic position *vis-à-vis* the rest of the UK. Official responses to these problems have been built around attempts to renew and diversify the region's industrial base. A measure

Table 3: **Percentage of overall manufacturing employment
in major industries in Northern Ireland, 1952-91**

	1952 (%)	1971 (%)	1991 (%)
Ship/Eng	26	22	12
Text/Clt	51	40	18
Total	77	62	30
N	161,480	104,940	40,724

Sources: Isles and Cuthbert (1957, p. 63); Department of Manpower
Services Gazettes 1978-9; Unpublished Department of Economic
Development statistics; 1971 & 1991 Census of Population

of diversification has occurred, if only by default, as
employment loss in traditional industries proceeds more
rapidly than in other forms of manufacturing. By 1991, the
shipbuilding/engineering and textiles/clothing industries
accounted for only 30 per cent of manufacturing industry
compared to 62 per cent in 1971 and 77 per cent in 1952.

The contraction and sectoral diversification of manufacturing employment are only part of the story, however.
Control of the major manufacturing sectors passed out of
local hands. For example, in the early 1950s, the linen
industry employed over 60,000 people in over 400 factories
dominated by small family concerns (Steed, 1974; Dohrs,
1950). By the 1960s, the local linen-complex had almost
disappeared to be replaced by short-lived multinational
investments in synthetic fibre production dominated by firms
such as ICI, Courtaulds and Enkalon. The recessions of the
1970s, the oil crises and cheap labour in the 'Third World'
put paid to this wave of investment. Meanwhile, major
shipbuilding and engineering firms such as Shorts, Harland
and Wolff, Sirocco, and Mackies, not only lost jobs on a large
scale but also changed their ownership and control, often
with massive state financial assistance.

Manufacturing decline, and the need to diversify, informed the central plank of state modernisation strategy, the sponsorship of multinational enterprise. This was relatively successful in the 1960s when employment in incoming industry largely replaced losses in the traditional sector. In the 1970s, however, promoting external investment became much more difficult and risky. A combination of international recession and the escalating conflict meant that new foreign investment dried up. Canning *et al* (1987) estimated that, between 1971-83, the 'troubles' prevented the creation of approximately 40,000 extra manufacturing jobs in Northern Ireland. This compares with an estimate of 46,000 by Rowthorn and Wayne (1988) for a slightly different period. The main difficulty was in attracting new multinationals to the region. Those which did come to Northern Ireland included several high profile and risky investments such as the De Lorean car company and Lear Fan aerospace company which failed spectacularly in the late 1970s and early 1980s. Moreover, many of the firms set up in the 1960s closed in response to the recessions of the 1970s with a particularly sharp contraction between 1979-82. Closures occurred, not because of the 'troubles', but because of the marginal role the Northern Ireland branch plants played within the overall multinational enterprise (Fothergill and Guy, 1990).

The overall result was that employment dependence on externally-owned firms actually declined between 1973 and 1990 against a background of decline of 36 per cent in overall manufacturing employment (the corresponding figure for the Republic was a decline of 11 per cent in the same period) (Northern Ireland Economic Council, Report 99, 1992, p. 36). In 1973, 53 per cent of jobs in manufacturing were in externally-owned plants, compared to only 39 per cent in 1990 (The corresponding figures for the Irish Republic were 31 per cent and 45 per cent respectively). The bulk of deindustrialisation in Northern Ireland occurred in externallyowned, mainly British plants. The latter's share of total manufacturing employment in externally-owned plants shrunk from 74 per cent in 1973 to 57 per cent in 1990, the US-owned proportion showed a small increase from 20 per cent to 23 per cent, while there was growth in the proportion owned in the Irish Republic (2 per cent to 7 per cent), the rest of the EC (3 per cent to 8 per cent) and the Far East (0 per cent to 4 per cent) (Northern Ireland Economic Council, Report 99, 1992, pp. 15, 34). Therefore, the pattern of manufacturing change in Northern Ireland is one of overall employment decline, heavy, if decreasing dependence on British-owned firms, and an increased reliance in the shrunken manufacturing sector on indigenous firms. A notable feature of both the multinational and indigenous sector is very low levels of expenditure on research and development (R & D) and an over-representation of firms in low-technology sectors (Northern Ireland Economic Council, Report 101, 1993; Hamilton, 1993).

Northern Ireland's experience of inward investment contrasts dramatically with that in the Republic, where employment dependence on external investment has increased. This reflects the much greater success of the Industrial Development Authority (IDA) in promoting 102,000 new overseas investment jobs between 1980-91 compared to the 8,835 jobs promoted by the Northern Ireland Industrial Development Board (IDB) over roughly the same period. Of course, jobs actually created are considerably less than those promoted (Northern Ireland Economic Council, Report 99, 1992, pp. 50-51) and, as O'Hearn indicates elsewhere in this volume, the 'development' effects of transnational investment in peripheral regions are debatable. The reduced dependence on this form of investment in Northern Ireland is more a product of circumstances (e.g. the negative effect of the 'troubles') than of deliberate policy choice. Furthermore, the remaining external manufacturing investment in Northern Ireland is in 'more traditional and declining' industries such as textiles and clothing, food, drink and tobacco. The contrast with the

Republic is stark where foreign investment has been dominated by US companies and is focused in 'modern' sectors such as electronics, chemicals, and pharmaceuticals (Northern Ireland Economic Council, Report 99, 1992, pp. 17-18, 35-37; Hamilton, 1993).

Continuing high unemployment, the difficulties of attracting inward investment and the Thatcherite project of generating a local enterprise culture have combined to shift the focus of industrial policy towards encouraging indigenous investment and small firm creation and encouraging competitiveness (Department of Economic Development, 1987, 1990). Overall employment in indigenous manufacturing employment declined by only 16.5 per cent between 1973-1990, compared to a 53 per cent decline in externally-owned firms (derived from Table 3.2, Northern Ireland Economic Council, Report 99, 1992, p. 15). However, these figures obscure a considerable turnover of firms through openings and closures, excessive reliance on the small local market and poor levels of productivity and competitiveness (Hart, 1993, pp. 230-232). Although there are indications of improvement in firm formation and employment growth since the mid-1980s, indigenous small firms have failed to offset the decline of employment in the non-indigenous sector, nor have they made many inroads into the unemployment problem.

Northern Ireland would appear to share with the Republic the lack of what Lee has termed a 'native entrepreneurial cadre of the requisite quality' (Lee, 1989, p. 535). The private sector in Northern Ireland is by far the most heavily subsidised in the UK, and possibly in the EU as a whole (Northern Ireland Economic Council, Report 82, 1990, p. 49). Private sector 'enterprise culture' has been heavily dependent on public sector promotion. The poor productivity and competitiveness of Northern Ireland industry in comparative terms, identified by Hitchens *et al* (1990), is one measure of the limits of this strategy. Where Northern Ireland firms do better in comparative terms (in comparison to Britain), as in the area of average profitability, this can be directly linked to larger government subsidies (Roper, 1993).

The poor record of manufacturing in Northern Ireland seems to have more to do with its structural role as part of the UK economy than with its location on the EU periphery. The UK, having accounted for 23 per cent of total EC manufacturing jobs in 1973, accounted for 43 per cent of the total job loss over the next eight years. Only Belgium fared worse proportionally, while the Irish Republic was the only country to show an increase in this period (Wabe, 1986, p. 29). An index of de-industrialisation constructed for the ninety-six regions of the nine-member EC (excluding Luxembourg) between 1973 and 1981 ranked Northern Ireland joint fourth with Picardie (France). Only the West Midlands (UK), Lorraine (France) and West Berlin fared worse. Many peripheral regions gained manufacturing jobs and as a whole they did not fare worse than central regions (Wabe, 1986). Walker and Keeble (1987) underline the poor employment performance of Northern Ireland in the EC between 1977-83 but note that it ranked better than the EC periphery on other indicators and had an income per capita growth not only higher than the EC periphery, but higher than that of the EC as a whole. Clearly the high point of manufacturing collapse was cushioned by state transfers to Northern Ireland and probably by the convergence of the regional and national wage rates resulting from the expansion of state employment.

By the 1990s, therefore, the Northern Ireland economy was in a much weakened state although its plight was obscured by state transfers to the region. The weakness of the productive base had created a massive trade deficit in the region, estimated as 17 per cent in 1970; 28 per cent in 1984 and 25 per cent in 1990 (Rowthorn, 1987; Smyth, 1993). The main root of its weakness was a manufacturing sector which now employed only 20 per cent of the workforce, and which was characterised by low levels of technological innovation, minimal investment in R & D and relatively poor productivity and competitiveness. Nor did service sector expansion compensate. Although the service sector had created many new jobs, for women in particular, it was weak in the area of private tradeable business or white-collar services (Teague, 1994, p. 276). The tenuous nature of the productive economy is further illustrated by its dependence on a narrow range of markets – 72 per cent of manufacturing exports go to the rest of the UK and Ireland. The three largest manufacturing firms account for 40 per cent of all exports and the ten largest for 54 per cent (Bradley and Wright, 1993, p. 22).

Viewed historically, the crisis of the productive sector in the last twenty-five years is the latest and most radical phase in the dismantling of what might be termed a regional system of innovation which linked agriculture (*via* flax growing) to linen production and also to engineering. In its place is an incoherent, disarticulated regional manufacturing economy, with poor linkages between indigenous and multinational industry, which is sustained only by massive state involvement in the local economy. If regional coherence exists today, it is mainly political and administrative, rather than economic, in form – a direct consequence of the British state's intensive management of Northern Irish society.

Equality issues
Socialists and social democrats have typically seen state intervention in the economy as moderating the social inequalities inevitably generated by capitalist development. Neo-liberals, on the other hand, accord much lower priority to reducing inequality, seeing it as an integral part of the human condition and the result of the system of rewards and incentives necessary to drive capitalist enterprise and competitiveness. Responding to this view, which has become increasingly influential since the mid-1970s, some social scientists began to argue that inequality and the divisions it engenders are themselves an obstacle to economic development and to development more broadly conceived to include political and cultural rights and freedoms.

In Northern Ireland, inequality, and the debates surrounding it, have been shaped by three interrelated factors: (1) the remarkably high level of state intervention in the Northern Ireland economy (discussed further below); (2) the imposition of direct rule by Westminster; and (3) the ongoing political conflict and argument over the constitutional future of the region. While this context does not necessarily diminish inequalities arising from class, gender and high unemployment, their political significance is heavily influenced by the primacy accorded to communal inequalities and their implications for the future of the state itself.

Class inequalities
One of the more remarkable aspects of research on Northern Ireland is the relative lack of attention paid to social class. Yet, class plays a crucial, if much understated, role underlying gender and sectarian inequalities. As Drudy points out elsewhere in this volume, there are considerable disagreements on the definition and interpretation of class in sociology. Local and ethnographic studies clearly show, however, that working-class areas have borne the brunt of the radical transformation of the Northern Ireland economy and the conflict of the last twenty-five years (e.g. Jenkins, 1983; McNamee and Lovett, 1987; Hamilton et al, 1990; Howe, 1990; Leonard, 1994). There are signs that middle-class occupations have benefited from high public expenditure and wage rates at British levels, while a core of deprived and long-term unemployed households have emerged in working-class areas.

Seldom represented politically in their own right, class inequalities find expression within unionist and nationalist politics and in various kinds of local community group activism. As there are no systematic analyses of class inequalities *per se*, it is necessary to rely on indirect evidence. Thus, for example, income inequality, which was stable in the UK and Northern Ireland in the 1970s, grew substantially in the 1980s. In Northern Ireland, the highest 10 per cent of male workers were paid 3.6 times as much as the bottom 10 per cent in 1993 compared to 2.7 times in 1979. The same pattern, albeit not as accentuated, emerges if the earnings of the top and bottom 25 per cent of male earners are considered (Northern Ireland Economic Council, Report 108, 1994, pp. 45-6, 114). The Family Expenditure Survey demonstrated that the average gross weekly household income in 1990 of those with mortgages were 2.29 per cent higher than for those in local authority housing. The corresponding figure for the UK was 1.98. It also appears that richer households in Northern Ireland can save more of their income because of lower costs of living than their counterparts in the UK as a whole (PPRU Monitor, 1992, pp. 7, 15). Miller's (1986) account of social mobility suggests that Northern Ireland occupies an intermediate position between England and Wales on the one hand, and the Irish Republic on the other. It shows more gross mobility than the Republic and less than England and Wales. The Republic is exceptional in the extent to which access to its 'elites' is closed.

Clearly, one of the distinguishing marks of class is relative vulnerability to unemployment. Smith and Chambers (1991, p. 184), for example, found that Protestant males' propensity to be unemployed ranged from 7.8 per cent for professional-managerial groups through 23.9 per cent for skilled manual workers to 38.8 per cent for semi-skilled manual workers and 53.5 per cent for unskilled manual workers. The corresponding figures for Catholics were 14.9 per cent, 39.4 per cent, 56.9 per cent and 70.4 per cent respectively. The effect of socio-economic group is found to be considerably larger than that of religion in explaining the Catholic-Protestant unemployment differential (discussed further below).

Gender, sectarian, locational and class inequalities interact in complex ways. What is striking, however, is the extent to which these inequalities have survived, and even strengthened in many cases, over the last twenty-five years. In its most violent manifcstations the conflict has been an 'intra-working class war'. Not only has the gulf widened between the Catholic and Protestant working class, it has also widened between them and their respective middle classes who have been the main beneficiaries of the heavily-subsidised economy which has emerged in the region. Yet, it could also be argued that the level of subsidy has moderated the scale of conflict and inequality that might have emerged otherwise.

Gender and differential access to paid work
Differential access to work, and the types of work available to different groups, are perhaps the most important measures of inequality in both the formal and informal economies. A number of researchers have shown the extent of inequality in the informal economy in terms of access to work and remuneration. They have demonstrated the disadvantages suffered by women and those with poor links to the world of paid work (Leonard, 1994; Howe, 1990; see also, relevant chapters in this volume). In this chapter discussion is confined to the formal economy. In common with old industrial regions elsewhere, the paid workforce in Northern Ireland has become more feminised.
    Table 4 shows the gendered nature of overall sectoral

Table 4: **Sectoral distribution of all female employees among the main industrial sectors (male figures in brackets)**

	1952 %	1971 %	1993 %
Manufacture	55 (39)	35 (37)	13 (26)
Services	44 (40)	63 (45)	85 (61)
Agric/Const	1 (21)	2 (18)	2 (13)
	100%	100%	100%

Sources: Isles and Cuthbert (1957, p. 63); Department of Manpower Services Gazettes; Regional Trends 1994.

change in employment in Northern Ireland. The much reduced manufacturing sector has become more of a male preserve while the expanding services sector has become more feminised.

Between 1952 and the 1990s the female proportion of employees has increased from 36 per cent to over 48 per cent in an expanded workforce. Two crucial qualifications need to be entered, however: firstly, women continue to be concentrated in a very limited number of sectors and in low-paid, frequently part-time jobs in the service sector (Trewsdale and Toman, 1993); secondly, although the participation of women in the labour force has increased, it remains below that of men. This serves to ensure that official male unemployment rates remain substantially above those for women. However, as McLaughlin (1993, pp. 139-40) observes, men's unemployment frequently becomes women's problem as female partners carry the burden of family poverty or leave paid work because their husbands are unemployed (in response to the way in which the benefit system works).

One of the more dramatic changes in female employment has been the increase in the numbers of married women in employment. In 1961, just under 30 per cent of married women had a paid job compared to 59 per cent by the 1980s (Montgomery, 1993, p. 15). This change is part of the wider

Table 5: **Part-time workers as a percentage of all workers in Northern Ireland, 1971-91**

	1971	1981	1991
	%	%	%
Male	4.8	7.5	12.0
Female	19.0	34.5	40.2
Total	10.3	19.6	25.8
N	48,623	95,127	139,832

Sources: Department of Manpower Gazettes; DED Statistics; 1991 Census of Employment and Farm Census.

restructuring of the labour market expressed in the growth in part-time and public-sector jobs mainly filled by women, declining jobs for men, and mass unemployment. Table 5 indicates the scale of expansion in female part-time work.

Related changes in public sector employment have had differential gender consequences also.

Table 6: **Public Sector Employment 1974-94**

	1974	1979	1994	% change 1974-94
Male	89,649	98,514	79,376	−11%
Female	83,420	108,660	114,271	37%
Total	173,069	207,174	193,647	12%

Sources: Northern Ireland Abstract of Statistics/DED (provisional data for 1994)

The decline in male public-sector jobs obscures some shifts in the type of male public-sector jobs available. There has been a massive growth in security-related jobs, whereas privatisation has moved many male jobs from the public to the private sector. Insofar, therefore, as there has been an expansion of job opportunities, it has benefited women.

Unemployment and Catholic-Protestant inequalities
Mass unemployment, however, rather than changing employment patterns, has remained the fulcrum of most academic and policy debates about inequality in Northern Ireland. Unemployment reached crisis proportions in the late inter-war period – a crisis briefly resolved by the near full employment engendered by the second world war. Thereafter, unemployment remained stubbornly high at a time when full employment existed in Britain. The unemployment rate reached a post-war low of 4.5 per cent in 1974, but this was short-lived. The numbers unemployed doubled between 1970 and 1979 and doubled again between 1979 and 1982.

Thereafter, the rate stabilised and shows signs of slow decline in the 1990s. The current unemployment figures have been greatly influenced, however, by the impact of some thirty definitional changes in the official claimant count instituted by the British Conservative government since 1979. Without these changes, the Unemployment Unit in Britain estimates that Northern Ireland unemployment rates would be currently 19 per cent rather than 13.2 per cent and UK rates would be 13.9 per cent compared with the official rate of 9.8 per cent (Northern Ireland Economic Council, Report 108, 1994, p. 36). Whatever measure is used Northern Ireland has retained its place among UK regions on top of the unemployment league, although its official rate is currently lower than that in the Republic of Ireland (15 per cent).

Long-term unemployment is now assuming major significance, with clear signs that it is not responsive to the recent cyclical upturn in the Northern Irish and British economies. The proportion of the unemployed out of work for more than one year has continued to increase, from 30 per cent in 1979 to over 53 per cent by July 1994. The corresponding figures for the UK as a whole were 25 per cent and 38 per cent. Eighteen per cent were unemployed for five years or more, compared to 4.4 per cent in the UK as a whole (Northern Ireland Economic Council, Report 113, 1994, p. 37; Scott, 1993, p. 87).

The high incidence of unemployment marks a fundamental and enduring aspect of social inequality in Northern Ireland. One of its most debated aspects has been its differential effects on Protestants and Catholics. The overall unemployment rate has varied from over 5 per cent to 21 per cent in the period 1971 to 1991, yet the inter-communal unemployment differential has remained relatively static. As Table 7 shows, in 1971, Catholic males were 2.6 times more likely, and Catholic females twice as likely, to be unemployed than their counterparts in 'Other Denominations'. The gap had declined relatively little twenty years later.

In a recent study of Labour Force and Continuous House-

Table 7: **Unemployment rates by religion*, 1971-1991 (percentages)**

	1971		1981		1991	
	ODs	*C*	*ODs*	*C*	*ODs*	*C*
	%	%	%	%	%	%
Males	6.6	17.3	12.0	30.0	11.2	25.1
Females	2.4	4.9	10.0	17.0	8.2	14.9

* ODs = Other Denominations; C = Catholics. Those in the 'No Religion' and 'Not Stated' groups have been distributed proportionately between Catholics and Other Denominations.

Sources: 1971, 1981, 1991 NI Census of Population

hold Survey (CHS) data between 1985 and 1991, Murphy and Armstrong (1994, p. 14) confirmed that the average differential is 2.5 for males. The unemployment rates even understate Catholic disadvantage in that Catholic males are over twice as likely to be on government schemes and to be inactive (retired, long-term sick or full-time students) as Protestants. Moreover, Catholics continue to have a higher propensity to emigrate than Protestants. The CHS sample also showed that only 61 per cent of Catholic males were employed compared to 81 per cent of their Protestant counterparts (1994, p. 17).

An intense academic debate has developed on the causes of the religious unemployment differential which influences, and is infused by, political debate on the issue. However, two most comprehensive academic studies on the subject broadly agree on their findings. They conclude that religious difference accounts for half the unemployment differential between Catholic and Protestant males once the models control, for age, number of children, housing tenure, educational and other qualifications, socio-economic group and area of residence (Smith and Chambers, 1991; Murphy and Armstrong, 1994).

Much of the debate centres around whether discrimination, direct or indirect, constitutes an explanation of the differential, and this leads to a discussion of the merits of the policies initiated to combat discrimination by the British government since the early 1970s. Whyte (1990, p. 64) in summarising the literature suggests that all authorities on the subject agree that it exists but disagree about its extent. Smith and Chambers (1991) distinguish between inequality of condition and inequality of opportunity. Their main concern is with inequality of opportunity and they demonstrate clearly that Catholics with similar abilities who make similar choices as Protestants, do less well economically. They also provide evidence of 'inequality of condition', e.g. socio-economic group, area of residence, and qualifications, for example, and recognise that this may be the result of past discrimination or continuing inequality of opportunity.

At the other end of the spectrum are those who question the prevalence of systematic discrimination as an explanation of the differential (e.g. Gudgin and Breen, 1994; Compton, 1991) and who see the latter as arising from the characteristics of the Catholic community and/or the nature of Northern Ireland's economy and labour market. These views oscillate between denying that evidence of systematic discrimination exists and pointing to the danger of 'reverse discrimination' were Catholics to gain at the expense of Protestants. Frequently, however, excessively restrictive definitions of discrimination, in terms of intent, ensures that no large-scale survey methods could ever be capable of generating such evidence anyway. Such approaches refuse to acknowledge the significance of indirect discrimination, i.e. actions which have the consequence, if not the intention, of reproducing unequal access to jobs in different social groups and which result in institutionalised discrimination over time. As anti-discrimination cases prove, intent is notoriously difficult to prove, even in court. Thus, it is possible both to define 'discrimination' out of existence and to render 'fair' employment largely irrelevant by restrictive definitions of 'fairness'.

Point of departure also shapes the nature of the debate. Smith and Chambers, for example, are primarily concerned with inequality and they conclude that the unemployment differential is the key to a wider pattern of substantial inter-communal inequalities in living standards which include four further factors: a higher proportion of Protestant families have two earners, a larger number of earners supports families of smaller size; on average Protestants (especially men) tend to have higher-level jobs than Catholics, and Protestants, especially at lower job levels, are more likely to work overtime than Catholics (1991, pp. 370-71).

An alternative point of departure is the Northern Ireland economy. Teague (1993; 1994), for example, points to the extent to which Northern Ireland wage rates are set by British rates, thereby closing off the option of higher employment and a more equitable wage structure. Others point to poor skill levels and chronic labour surplus brought about by high (Catholic) birth rates and lack of mobility brought about by insufficient emigration. Proposed solutions here are controversial as in Gudgin and Roper's (1990, p. 5) recommendation that the unemployed be trained to emigrate (for critique, see Dignan, Haase and Healy, n.d.). Here, it might be noted in passing, that had emigration constituted a sure way to economic development, the Irish Republic would probably be the wealthiest country in the world. Other proposals include a massive extension of government employment schemes for the long-term unemployed, most of whom are Catholic (Gudgin and Breen, 1994). Few have ventured to suggest a government plan to control births (in any case, Catholic birth rates have now fallen dramatically). These solutions are controversial to the extent that they locate the causes of unemployment among those most affected by it, and to the extent that they fuel the politics of sectarian headcounting which has been so politically central in Northern Ireland. In any case, they lean heavily towards the maintenance of the existing political and socio-economic system rather than contemplating any radical alternative to it.

There is a political dimension to the debate, however, which is not reducible to questions of evidence. Persisting communal inequality is evidence of how difficult it is to reform Northern Ireland as presently constituted. On the other hand, steps taken to alleviate communal inequality have produced 'alienation' among Protestants of all classes who see 'fair employment' strategies as reverse discrimination (*Observer*, 16.10.94). Doyle (1994) shows that the issue has united unionist defenders of the *status quo* around a three-stranded argument – denial, justification and community self-interest. Discrimination is either denied or, if admitted, is justified on the grounds that Catholics are not loyal citizens of the state. Finally, unionists argue that both communities prefer to employ their own and base their opposition to fair employment legislation on a zero-sum view that their community is losing out in the fight for jobs. As Doyle (1994, p. 59) observes, here the argument over discrimination, the unemployment differential and communal inequality is a proxy for the argument over the nature and existence of the state itself. Ruane and Todd (1991) argue that both communities are locked together in a fundamental conflict of interest – greater equality for nationalists undermines the security of unionists' link with Britain and this 'structural bind' is maintained by the wider relationships between Britain and Ireland. Ethno-national politics, therefore, provide a dimension to all forms of inequality which is missing in societies where state and ethnic boundaries are uncontested.

Unequal localities
The contesting of boundaries is not confined to the external border of Northern Ireland. The region is characterised by a sectarian geography, i.e. by a multiplicity of internal borders which mark off predominantly Protestant, Catholic and mixed areas from each other. Map 1 provides one indication of the way in which unemployment rates vary spatially in conjunction with unemployment differentials between both

communities at district council level. High unemployment rates are concentrated in parts of Belfast and in the border region. Areas with Catholic majorities are prone to have higher unemployment rates than other areas and generally these areas are also marked by relatively higher differentials between the Catholic unemployment rate and that of 'other denominations'. Furthermore, a recent study of the border region shows a combination of population increase, employment decline, lower rates of workforce participation, and high unemployment rates which distinguish it from the rest of Northern Ireland (O'Dowd, Moore and Corrigan 1994). The political significance of this spatial inequality is reflected in the fact that Catholics (who are overwhelmingly nationalist) have a two to one majority in the Border Region, the inverse of the situation in the rest of Northern Ireland where Protestants are in a two to one majority. Robson *et al* (1994) have demonstrated the existence of deep-rooted and complex patterns of social deprivation (using up to eighteen indicators) at various scales of disaggregation: district council areas, wards, and census enumeration districts throughout Northern Ireland. In this study too, the concentration of deprivation in parts of Belfast and in border areas is apparent.

Spatial analysis, spatial categories or administrative areas, however, fail to capture the full significance of locality or place in Northern Ireland. Underneath the network of administrative boundaries such as those indicated on Map 1 lies a complex of territorial boundaries etched in popular consciousness and collective memory where class, gender and sectarian relationships intermesh and are shaped by a long history of state-locality relationships. Whyte (1990, p. 259) underlines the extent of local diversity within Northern Ireland, noting how 'areas only a few miles apart differ enormously in terms of religious mix, economic circumstances, level of violence and political attitudes'. The political significance of local diversity is that there is a correlation between localities which are predominantly

Map 1:   **Unemployment rates/Catholic: Other Denominations Unemployment Differential by District Council Area, 1991 Northern Ireland Census of Population**

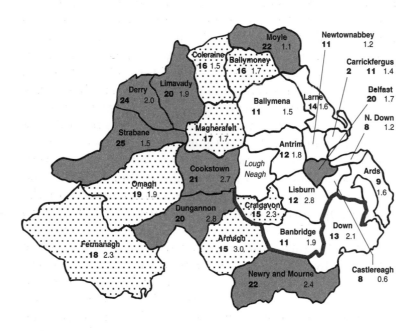

Unemployment Rates

- 20% and over
- 15-18%
- Under 15%

Border Region Boundary

Bold figure – Unemployment rate
Light figure – Catholic/Other Denominations
              Unemployment Differential

Catholic and most disaffected from the Northern Ireland state and those which suffer most from socio-economic disadvantage. The full impact of the conflict over the last twenty-five years is most visible at local level, manifesting itself in struggles over the control of territory, whether it be para-militaries and police in Belfast or the British army in Crossmaglen and other border districts. Here the role of coercion, official and unofficial, has been as central as it was in the original drawing of the Northern Ireland boundary in 1920-21 (Whyte, 1990, pp. 163-4; O'Dowd, 1994). 'Politics', even the very constitution of Northern Ireland itself, pervade questions of socio-economic advantage and disadvantage.

During fifty years of one-party unionist control, the Stormont government had the understandable imperative of prioritising the needs of its own supporters thereby consolidating the pro-union majority in Northern Ireland. The most obvious way of accomplishing this was to ensure the economic well-being and high employment levels of the area east of Bann where the vast majority of unionist supporters resided. Attempts at spatial and growth centre planning in the 1960s sought to reconcile this political imperative with the requirements of modernising the region's industrial base. For nationalists, key locational decisions such as the choice of sites for growth centres and the new university were seen as an updating of traditional policies of discrimination and exclusion against the minority community. This helped to fuel the conflict which erupted in the late 1960s (O'Dowd, 1985).

After over twenty years of direct rule many of the develop-ment strategies of the 1960s have been moderated or rescinded either by government policy or by changing economic circumstances. Fair employment legislation and monitoring of the communal effects of government decisions have increased the employment prospects of some, mainly middle-class, Catholics. A whole series of development programmes have been targeted on areas with high levels of socio-economic deprivation. Examples include the EU's INTERREG programme aimed at the border region, the various schemes of the International Fund for Ireland and the 'Making Belfast Work' initiative directed towards the high unemployment areas of west and north Belfast.

The belief that modernisation would lead to a 'homogenisation' of space and a convergence in the socio-economic profiles of regions and localities has proved to be untenable. A considerable body of international social research in the last two decades has suggested that the globalisation of economic life has been counterbalanced by associated patterns of localisation (e.g. Stohr, 1990; Harloe *et al*, 1990). Researchers have underlined the success of some localities (frequently in core regions), and the failure of others, in capturing and generating resources for development. In Northern Ireland, global processes of economic restructuring have interacted with state policy and the formation of localities in ways which have underlined the historical resilience of patterns of economic advantage and disadvantage (O'Dowd, 1991, 1993).

Space and place remain important in Northern Ireland, in an era of increasing globalisation. Given the region's relatively low levels of innovation and entrepreneurial activity, localisation frequently means the ability to capture state resources. But the economic significance of state-locality relationships are also infused with the political divisions around which Northern Ireland is built. Socio-economic inequalities at locality level are deeply rooted because they are so intertwined with a history of inter-communal relations, political domination and subordination, which proves resilient and adaptable in the face of global economic change and shifting government policies.

State dependency and governance structure

Fifty per cent of public expenditure in Northern Ireland is a subvention from Westminster, compared to levels of between 5 per cent and 10 per cent in the 1960s (Wilson, 1990, p. 11). In other words, approximately half the public expenditure in

Northern Ireland is raised from tax revenue collected in the region; the other half is a grant from Britain.

In a rather striking, if unflattering, metaphor, Rowthorn (1987, p. 118) compares Northern Ireland to 'a vast workhouse in which most of the inmates are engaged in servicing and controlling each other'. The gap between imports and exports is offset by 'taxes levied on an external population' (the British subvention) like a typical workhouse or prison. Rowthorn's metaphor is interesting in that it implies that the burden on the British taxpayer is carried unknowingly or perhaps reluctantly. The alternative metaphor of Britain as 'kind auntie' utilised by Smyth (1993) and Teague (1994) implies a rather more active benevolence. In either case, the scale of the subvention emphasises the underlying weakness of the Northern Ireland economy under direct rule. (Smyth 1993, pp. 138-9, concludes that the public sector is the 'dominant feature of the region's economy' and that it has been 'a surrogate for automonous growth' and 'a buttress against political instability'.)

At first glance, this degree of state dependence is curious in a period marked by the dominance of 'free-market' liberalism in North America, Britain and the rest of the EU. The economic ideology of the Reagan and Thatcher administrations and of the Single European Market urged less state intervention in the economy – a policy which recognised the decreasing capacity of national governments to control monetary policy, financial flows and the activities of multinational corporations. In Northern Ireland, however, high levels of government expenditure were driven by two main factors. Firstly, UK-wide welfare policies of support for the unemployed and the deprived meant a large automatic transfer of resources to Northern Ireland where levels of unemployment and social need were exceptionally high. Secondly, and perhaps more significantly, rising levels of public expenditure were a reaction to the conflict and its effects. State intervention in the economy, therefore, was more reactive than proactive, less driven by explicit models of development, than by the exigencies of managing a peripheral economy in an increasingly parlous state. What emerged was a peculiar hybrid of apparently social democratic and neo-liberal policies. Nevertheless, after 1979, the management of the Northern Ireland economy became infused with terms such as 'value for money', 'productivity', 'enterprise culture', 'competitiveness', while the practical exigencies of day-to-day policies continued to undermine such notions. For example, the huge investment in law and order was not easily subject to 'value for money' or productivity 'considerations'. Alternatively, the enterprise culture was so massively subsidised that the meaning of enterprise itself was redefined as to how best to access government grants, bringing with it what Teague (1994, p. 289) terms a 'mendicant entrepreneurial culture'. (This phenomenon might also be identified in the Republic of Ireland, in relation to EU transfers).

One consequence of a state-dependent economy is that it shatters the illusion that economic development, or the economy generally, can be treated somehow in abstraction from political, administrative and social institutions. Awareness of the way in which economic activities are embedded in 'non-economic' institutions is gradually gaining ground in Northern Ireland. This has led, in turn, to increased scrutiny of how governance structure, broadly defined, influences economic development. Firstly, the 'troubles' have initiated for the first time a debate on the relationship between Northern Ireland's governance structure and its development performance and prospects. For example, the economic effects of partition, various constitutional scenarios and the consequences of the British subvention have come in for increased scrutiny (New Ireland Forum, 1984; Rowthorn and Wayne, 1988; Cadogan Group, 1992; Teague, 1993; Munck, 1993). Secondly, the SEM has accelerated debate in Ireland about the relationship between economic and political integration (Government of Ireland, 1992; Anderson and Goodman, 1994). Thirdly, there is a growing interest in how physical and commercial infrastructure, inter-firm links and decision-making, and sectarian division affects economic development (Teague, 1994). Finally, the cease-fires announced since August 1994 have generated an interest in the 'economic consequences of peace' – how a 'war' economy has been created in Northern Ireland and how it might be dismantled with a 'peace dividend' (e.g. Tomlinson, 1994). While this literature is in its infancy, it is beginning to open up questions about the institutional dimensions to economic development and competitive advantage (raised by O'Hearn elsewhere in this volume).

The massive British subvention, and the resultant somewhat higher standard of living in Northern Ireland, continues to be used as proof of the self-evident merits of the union (see Whyte, 1990, p. 161 for summary). This case is conceded by many nationalists who question the economic viability of Irish unity in the short-run. Yet, the subvention has not prevented the crumbling of the productive base of the economy (it may even have contributed to it), nor has it fundamentally altered the socio-economic inequalities discussed above. Teague (1993) has argued that a British industrial relations regime may not deliver the optimum employment outcome in Northern Ireland. He has also argued that sectarian divisions limit the emergence of inter-firm linkages necessary for development. It may be argued further that, to the extent that the British state has supported the institutionalisation of sectarian division and antagonism, and failed to prevent the eruption of conflict over the last twenty-five years, it has undermined the conditions for socio-economic development.

Hutton (1994) points to an increasingly moribund governance structure in Britain which intersects fatally with Northern Ireland to ensure poor economic performance. He argues that this structure is characterised by a reluctance to innovate, invest, and concentrate on industrial production because of chronic 'short-termism' and a refusal to enter into 'relationships of commitment and co-operation' in industry akin to those prevalent in East Asia and Germany. He argues that the economic system takes its lead from an archaic political system which is excessively centralised, based on majoritarianism, and a 'pre-modern idea of sovereignty'. Britain has a 'winner-take-all economy and polity'; commitment, co-operation and consensus run a long way behind 'deal-making, competition and celebrated acts of individual executive heroism' (1994, p. 5).

Hutton argues that Northern Ireland suffers from a particularly acute version of the 'British disease' and argues that a suitable framework for economic development will emerge only with the radical overhaul of the governance system in the UK as a whole. Majoritarianism has to be ended because it has become a vehicle for rule by one community in Northern Ireland, and the ensuing violent conflict. Hutton concludes that the way forward is devolution within a reformed UK, and the creation of consensual political and economic institutions within Northern Ireland, and between the Republic and the North.

In Northern Ireland, however, the rooted nature of Rowthorn's 'servicing and controlling society' is clearly observable. Containment of the conflict has been a priority. State intervention in the economy has operated through an official culture of control and centralisation. Intensive state management has succeeded in preventing the disintegration of Northern Ireland as a political and administrative unit and in generating a large measure of acquiescence to the *status quo*. However, this success should not be confused with social consensus or active consent. In this environment, economic policy has been caught between the ideal of the 'free market' and practical imperatives of state management. Cutbacks in public expenditure in the wake of prolonged ceasefires risk leaving exposed the greatly weakened productive base of the Northern Ireland economy. The latter is now faced with freer competition within the EU and GATT and it is difficult to see where its comparative advantage will lie.

The changing global environment has contributed to an upsurge of support from the business sector for an integrated all-Ireland economy. In part this development is driven by the threat of the Single European Market to small-scale enterprises on each side of the border. It also marks an explicit recognition of the constraints placed on economic development by the existence of two small, separate, economies on one peripheral island and the lack of linkages with multinational companies on the island. Already there are clear signs of North-South corporate integration in banking, building materials, food processing and retailing (Kelleher in Bradley and Wright, 1993, p. 64). While there is less agreement on the political and administrative framework most conducive to an all-Ireland economy, the old governance structure associated with the partition settlement is no longer seen as adequate (Anderson and Goodman, 1994).

General theories of development

As this chapter has argued, assessments of development in Northern Ireland depend on the way in which the term is defined and on the temporal and geographical contexts in which the region is located. While there is much evidence of improvement in material conditions and standards of living, more recently maintained by state transfers, there is an almost overwhelming sense of relative economic decline in the social science literature. This decline is perceived as part of a wider British fate, a sense that Northern Ireland's 'golden age' is long past and that it is now even falling behind the Republic.

On the other hand, commitments to the constitutional and political *status quo* and a perceived lack of economic options have led many commentators to propose adjustments rather than radical alternatives to the state-dependent system which has emerged. This system, as described above, is characterised by a greatly weakened productive base, high levels of overall and long-term unemployment, contracting employment opportunities for males and the creation of a more feminised and casualised (part-time) workforce where many work in low-paid insecure jobs. At the other end of the spectrum are those in well-paid, secure, frequently public-sector jobs, benefiting from higher British wage rates and lower Northern Ireland costs of living. There is considerable evidence of enduring class, gender, and area-based inequal-ities encapsulated in persisting inequalities of power, wealth and opportunity between Catholics and Protestants. Clearly, the experience of 'development' depends *inter alia* on one's class, gender, locality and communal affiliation. Inter-communal inequality, and the conflict it generates, has produced a specific form of governance structure which may, in itself, limit the prospects for future socio-economic development.

What can general theories of social change and develop-ment tell us about long-term socio-economic transformation in Northern Ireland and vice versa? Three such theories may be identified: modernisation, dependency and world system approaches (So, 1990). Of these, modernisation theories are by far the most pervasive; they inform most of the academic and government analyses of Northern Ireland development issues. The strength of the modernisation theory may be gauged from the extent to which its assumptions are taken for granted as common sense by its adherents who frequently fail to realise or acknowledge that they are subscribing to a particular theory of social change. Modernisation theory assumes above all the superiority and efficacy of the 'western' or capitalist path to development, i.e. that path which leads from the first industrial revolution in western Europe to the mass-consumption, high-technology societies of the dominant economic powers of today. Entrepreneurs investing money in new productive technologies and in producing commodities for profit in the market place are seen as the driving forces of a staged developmental process. This process typically takes the form of a 'march through the sectors' beginning with the mechanisation and commercialisation of agriculture, then a period of industrialisation and urbanisation, and culminating in a post-industrial service economy.

Development in this view is rendered synonymous with modernisation and often with 'progress'. The path to development is seen to be via the diffusion of entrepreneurial skills, technology and capital to less-developed countries and regions. The latter are urged to subscribe to global 'free trade' principles and develop export-led strategies. There are 'strong' and 'weak' versions of the modernisation theory. The 'strong' thesis links modernisation with evolution and progress, often portraying it as natural and inevitable. This view has appeared in the 1980s in North America and western Europe in the guise of a renewed belief in the primacy and efficacy of 'market forces'. In its most extreme form the economic elements of the modernisation process are linked to the emergence of a much wider range of social changes such as nuclear families, the work ethic, secularisation, pluralism and representative democracy. The recent collapse of state socialist systems has served to confirm the identification of modernisation with capitalism, progress, and the alleged superiority of the western path to development.

'Weak' theories of modernisation, on the other hand, while accepting the primacy accorded to economic and technological change, avoid suggesting that this change has the wider political and cultural consequences mentioned above. These 'new modernisation theories' (So, 1990) are more circumspect and limited in their claims. They point out that capitalism is compatible with a wide variety of political and cultural forms, indeed that there are several types of capitalism ranging from the 'free-market' variety practised in the US to the more regulated version practised in Japan. Recent research within the modernisation framework pays more attention to the historical analysis of concrete case studies, acknowledges that there are several paths to development, and that 'traditional' practices may help as well as hinder development (So, 1990, p. 62; Webster, 1984). Although there is a greater focus on 'external' factors, the basic unit of analysis is still the nation-state. The underlying framework remains the transition from traditional to modern society and the *sine qua non* of this transition is economic growth.

In Northern Ireland and Ireland generally, discourse about development is dominated by economists and policy-makers, few of whom feel it necessary to either elucidate or justify their broad acceptance of the modernisation framework. The objective of development is typically considered to be economic growth as measured by conventional economic indicators although terms like 'dependency' and 'peripherality' have begun to seep into conventional economic discourse (e.g. NIEC, 1994, p. 111). The debate is about the conditions which help or hinder such growth. Even if the record of modernisation is decidedly patchy, few analyses or prescriptions envisage alternative options as realistic. Yet, the most prevalent views of economic development in Northern Ireland are closer to the 'weak' rather than 'strong' version of modernisation theory; the focus is mainly on internal obstacles to development and on problems of adapting to a global economy characterised by neo-liberal policies of free trade and export-led development.

Dependency and world system theories, on the other hand, argue that by its very nature, capitalist development generates socio-economic, political and spatial inequalities (for fuller discussion, see O'Hearn's account elsewhere in this volume). For these theories, such inequalities cannot be blamed on 'traditional' society, nor are they correctable side-effects of the process of modernisation. Rather they are endemic to capitalist development. The key process of change is seen as domination and exploitation rather than diffusion – a process rooted in the history of western imperialism, colonialism and the forms of neo-colonialism practised today by multinational corporations and their sponsoring states. Thus, the development of the core regions of the world economy is at the expense of peripheral regions which have become underdeveloped in the process. While these theories have gained more currency in so-called developing countries, they have been applied also to peripheral regions of the 'developed' world including Ireland (e.g. Crotty, 1986; Munck, 1993).

Clearly, as indicated above, Northern Ireland has manifested many of the characteristics of the modernising core of the world economy, including the shift to a post-industrial service economy and improved standards of living. Nevertheless, it also indicates many of the hallmarks of dependency and underdevelopment: the lack of a self-sustaining productive base, chronic unemployment, and enduring social and spatial inequalities. The relative decline of the UK as a whole seems to support some of the key tenets of world system theory about changing hegemony within the advanced core of the global economy.

The appeal of the modernisation approach lies in its perceived practicality under current conditions. Encouraging entrepreneurial activity and the diffusion of skills, technology and multinational investment to Northern Ireland seem feasible, i.e. within the ambit of policy-making. Moreover, participation in the EU and other international trading regimes seems to preclude radical options. The failures of economic development strategy, outlined above, have led to a concern to reduce dependency on state spending and to strengthen the indigenous industrial base within the North and within Ireland as a whole (Department of Economic Development, 1987, 1990). Multinational investment, for example, is no longer seen as a panacea (though it remains an important part of industrial policy), either in terms of restructuring the productive base or in solving the unemployment problem. The Northern Ireland experience has not only underlined the volatility of such investment, but also its sensitivity to conditions of political instability.

The growing interest in the impact of governance structure on socio-economic development echoes some of the central tenets of dependency and world system theories, e.g. the importance of politics in shaping economic development (Munck, 1993, p. 160; Mjoset, 1992). However, interest in economic and political governance structures also derives from 'new modernisation theories' which suggest that there are many paths to development and many forms of capitalism, of which the once dominant British type is currently among the least successful (see Hutton, 1994).

One of the merits of Northern Ireland as a case study in development is that it renders transparent the impact of political and administrative influence on development strategy. From this it is a short step to the proposition that the economy should serve social needs and democratic partici- pation, while helping to reduce inequalities of power, wealth and opportunity. These inequalities in themselves prevent the type of social consensus and popular mobilisation which might encourage economic development – that is, unless repressive and authoritarian paths to economic development such as some Latin American models are favoured. The Northern Ireland case shows the need for in-depth understanding of historically specific regions; it also underlines the need for a multi-institutional approach – what So (1990, pp. 266-8) terms the complex interplay of 'family, religion, ethnic groups, the state, social movements, trans- national corporations, the inter-state system and the world economy'. Neither this chapter, nor the Northern Ireland case as such, can illustrate all these dimensions. On the evidence examined above, however, the most distinctive lesson to be learned from Northern Ireland is the extent to which development theories need to register the significance of ethno-national divisions, and by extension, the importance of a democratically agreed state framework for development in the wider sense of that term.

Note

1 I would like to thank Tim Moore for his help and Douglas Hamilton for his comments on earlier versions of this paper.

References

ANDERSON, J. and J. GOODMAN, 1994. 'European and Irish Integration: Contradictions of Regionalism and Nationalism', *European Urban and Regional Studies*, 1 (1), pp. 49-62.

BOROOAH, V.K., 1993. 'Northern Ireland – Typology of a Regional Economy' in P. Teague (ed.), *op. cit.*, pp. 1-23.

BRADLEY, J. F. and B. DOWLING, 1983. *Industrial Development in Northern Ireland and in the Republic of Ireland*, Belfast & Dublin, Co-operation North.

BRADLEY, J. and J. WRIGHT, 1993. 'Two Regional Economies in Ireland', *Journal of Statistical and Social Inquiry Society of Ireland*, Vol. XVI, Part V, pp. 1-67.

CADOGAN GROUP, 1992. *Northern Limits: Boundaries of the Attainable in Northern Ireland Politics*, Belfast, Cadogan Group.

CANNING, D., B. MOORE and J. RHODES, 1987. 'Economic Growth in Northern Ireland: Problems and Prospects', in P. Teague (ed.), *Beyond the Rhetoric: Politics, Economy and Social Policy in Northern Ireland*, London, Lawrence and Wishart.

COMPTON, P.A., 1991. 'Employment Differentials in Northern Ireland and Job Discrimination' in P.J. Roche and B. Barton (eds.), *The Northern Ireland Question, Myth and Reality*, Aldershot, Avebury, pp. 40-75.

CROTTY, R., 1986. *Ireland in Crisis: A Study in Capitalist Colonial Undevelopment*, Tralee, Brandon Press.

DEPARTMENT OF ECONOMIC DEVELOPMENT, 1987. *Building a Stronger Economy: The Pathfinder Initiative*, Belfast, HMSO.

DEPARTMENT OF ECONOMIC DEVELOPMENT, 1990. *Competing in the 1990s – The Key to Growth*, Belfast, Department of Economic Development.

DIGNAN, T., T. HAASE and T. HEALY, n.d. *Planned Migration as Regional Policy: A Critique of Recent Proposals for Northern Ireland*, Working Paper No. 33, Belfast, NIERC.

DOHRS, F.E., 1950. *The Linen Industry in Northern Ireland*, Chicago, unpublished PhD dissertation, North-Western University.

DOYLE, J., 1994. 'Workers and Outlaws: Unionism and Fair Employment in Northern Ireland', *Irish Political Studies*, 9, pp. 41-60.

FOTHERGILL, S. and N. GUY, 1990. *Retreat from the Regions: Corporate Change and the Growth of Factories*, London, Jessica Kingsley.

GOVERNMENT OF IRELAND, 1992. *Ireland in Europe: A Shared Challenge,* Dublin, Stationery Office.

GUDGIN, G. and R. BREEN, 1994. 'Evaluation of the Ratio of Unemployment Rates as an Indicator of Fair Employment', paper presented to the Central Community Relations Unit Conference on Employment Equality Review, Belfast, 12 September.

GUDGIN, G. and S. ROPER, 1990. *The Northern Ireland Economy: Review and Forecasts to 1995,* Belfast, NIERC.

HAMILTON, A., C. McCARTNEY, T. ANDERSON, and A. FINN, 1990. *Violence and Communities: The Impact of Political Violence on Intra-Community, Inter-Community and Community-State Relationships,* Coleraine, University of Ulster, Centre for the Study of Conflict.

HAMILTON, D., 1993. 'Foreign Investment and Industrial Development in Northern Ireland', in P. Teague (ed.), *op. cit.,* pp. 190-216.

HARLOE, M., C. PICKVANCE and J. URRY, (eds.), 1990. *Place, Policy and Politics: Do Localities Matter?,* London, Unwin Hyman.

HARRIS, R.I.D., C.W. JEFFERSON and J.E. SPENCER (eds.), 1990. *The Northern Ireland Economy: A Comparative Study in the Economic Development of a*

Peripheral Region, London, Longman.

HART, M., 1993. 'The Labour Market Impact of New and Small Firms in Northern Ireland', in P. Teague (ed.), *op. cit.,* pp. 217-39.

HITCHENS, D., K. WAGNER and J.E. BIRNIE, 1990. *Closing the Productivity Gap: A Comparison of Northern Ireland, the Republic of Ireland and Germany,* Aldershot, Avebury.

HOWE, L., 1990. *Being Unemployed in Northern Ireland,* Cambridge, Cambridge University Press.

HUTTON, W., 1994. *Britain and Northern Ireland, The State We're in – Failure and Opportunity,* Annual Sir Charles Carter Lecture, Report 114, Belfast, NIEC.

ISLES, K.S. and N. CUTHBERT, 1957. *An Economic Survey of Northern Ireland,* Belfast, HMSO.

JENKINS, R., 1993. *Lads, Citizens and Ordinary Kids: Working Class Youth in Belfast,* London, Routledge and Kegan Paul.

JOHNSON, D., 1985. *The Interwar Economy in Ireland: Studies in Irish Economic and Social History,* 4, Dundalk, The Economic and Social History Society of Ireland.

KENNEDY, K., T. GIBLIN and D. McHUGH, 1988. *The Economic Development of Ireland in the Twentieth Century,* London, Routledge.

KENNEDY, L., 1989. *The Modern Industrialisation of Ireland, 1940-1988: Studies in Irish Economic and Social History*, 5, Dundalk, The Economic and Social History Society of Ireland.

KREMER, J., and P. MONTGOMERY (eds.), 1993. *Women's Working Lives*, Belfast: Equal Opportunities Commission/HMSO.

LEE, J., 1989. *Ireland, 1912-1985: Politics and Society*, Cambridge, Cambridge University Press.

LEONARD, M., 1994. *Informal Economic Activity in Belfast*, Aldershot, Avebury.

McLAUGHLIN, E., 1993. 'Unemployment', in J. Kremer and P. Montgomery (eds.), *op. cit.*, pp. 131-49.

McNAMEE, P. and T. LOVETT, 1987. Working Class Community in Northern Ireland, Belfast, Ulster People's College.

MILLER, R., 1986. 'Social Stratification and Mobility' in P. Clancy *et al* (eds.), *Ireland: A Sociological Profile*, Dublin, IPA, pp. 221-43.

MILLWARD, A.S., 1992. *The European Rescue of the Nation-State*, London, Routledge.

MJOSET, L., 1992. *The Irish Economy in a Comparative Institutional Perspective*, Report 93, Dublin, National Economic and Social Council.

MONTGOMERY, P., 1993. 'Paid and Unpaid Work' in

J. Kremer and P. Montgomery (eds.), *op. cit.*, pp. 15-42.

MUNCK, R., 1993. *The Irish Economy: Results and Prospects*, London, Pluto Press.

MURPHY, A. and D. ARMSTRONG, 1994. *A Picture of the Catholic and Protestant Male Unemployed*, Belfast, Central Community Relations Unit.

NEW IRELAND FORUM, 1984. *The Macroeconomic Consequences of Integrated Economic Policy, Planning and Coordination in Ireland*, Dublin, Stationery Office.

NORTHERN IRELAND ECONOMIC COUNCIL, 1990. *The Private Sector in the Northern Ireland Economy*, Report 82, Belfast, NIEC.

NORTHERN IRELAND ECONOMIC COUNCIL, 1992. *Inward Investment in Northern Ireland*, Report 99, Belfast, NIEC.

NORTHERN IRELAND ECONOMIC COUNCIL, 1993. *R & D Activity in Northern Ireland*, Report 101, Belfast, NIEC.

NORTHERN IRELAND ECONOMIC COUNCIL, 1994. *Economic Assessment*, April 1994. Report 108, Belfast, NIEC.

NORTHERN IRELAND ECONOMIC COUNCIL, 1994. *The Implications of Peripherality for Northern Ireland*, Report 111, Belfast, NIEC.

NORTHERN IRELAND
ECONOMIC COUNCIL,
1994. *Autumn Economic Review,*
Report 113, Belfast, NIEC.

O'DOWD, L., 1985. 'The Crisis
of Regional Strategy: Ideology
and the State in Northern
Ireland' in G. Rees *et al* (eds.),
*Political Action and Social
Identity,* London, Macmillan,
pp. 143-65.

O'DOWD, L., 1991. 'Local
Responses to Industrial
Change in Northern Ireland:
A Comparison of Newry and
Craigavon', Final Report to
the ESRC. (Ref. R000231161)

O'DOWD, L. 1993. 'Craigavon:
Locality, Economy and the
State in a Failed "New City"',
in C. Curtin, H. Donnan and
T. Wilson (eds.), *Irish Urban
Cultures,* Belfast, Institute of
Irish Studies, pp. 39-62.

O'DOWD, L., 1994. *Whither the
Irish Border?: Sovereignty,
Democracy and Economic
Integration in Ireland,* Belfast,
Centre for Research and
Documentation.

O'DOWD, L., T. MOORE and
J. CORRIGAN, 1994. *The Irish
Border Region: A Socio-Economic
Profile,* Belfast, Queen's
University.

PPRU MONITOR, 1992. *The
Family Expenditure Survey:
Report for 1987-1990,* Belfast,
Policy Planning Research
Unit.

ROBSON, B., M. BRADFORD
and I. DEAS, 1994. *Relative
Deprivation in Northern Ireland,*
Occasional Paper No. 28,
Belfast, Policy Planning
Research Unit.

ROPER, S., 1993. *Government
Grants and Manufacturing
Profitability in Northern Ireland,*
Belfast, Northern Ireland
Economic Research Centre.

ROWTHORN, B., 1987.
'Northern Ireland: An
Economy in Crisis', in
P. Teague (ed.), *Beyond the
Rhetoric: Politics, Economy and
Social Policy in Northern Ireland,*
London, Lawrence and
Wishart, pp. 111-135.

ROWTHORN, B., 1993.
'Foreword' in R. Munck,
op. cit., pp. viii-xii.

ROWTHORN, B. and N. WAYNE,
1988. *Northern Ireland: The
Political Economy of Conflict,*
Cambridge, Polity Press.

RUANE, J. and J. TODD, 1991.
'Why can't you get along with
each other?: Culture,
Structure and the Northern
Ireland Conflict' in E. Hughes
(ed.), *Culture and Politics in
Northern Ireland 1960-1990,*
Milton Keynes, Open
University Press, pp. 27-44.

SCOTT, R. 1993. 'Long-term
Unemployment and Policy
Response in Northern
Ireland', in G. Gudgin and
G. O'Shea (eds.),
*Unemployment Forever?: The
Northern Ireland Economy in
Recession and Beyond,* Belfast,
NIERC, pp. 84-98.

SMITH, D.J. and
G. CHAMBERS, 1991.

Inequality in Northern Ireland, Oxford, Clarendon Press.

SMYTH, M., 1993. 'The Public Sector and the Economy' in P. Teague (ed.), *op. cit.,* pp. 121-40.

SO, A., 1990. *Social Change and Development: Modernization, Dependency and World-System Theories,* London, Sage.

STEED, G.P.F., 1974. 'The Northern Ireland Linen Complex, 1950-1970', *Annals of the Association of American Geographers,* Vol. 64, pp. 397-408.

STOHR, W.B. (ed.), 1990. *Global Challenge and Local Response: Initiatives for Economic Regeneration in Contemporary Europe,* London, The United Nations University.

TEAGUE, P. (ed.), 1993. *The Economy of Northern Ireland,* London, Lawrence and Wishart.

TEAGUE, P., 1994. 'Governance Structures and Economic Performance: the Case of Northern Ireland', *International Journal of Urban and Regional Research,* Vol. 18, No. 2, pp. 275-92.

TOMLINSON, M., 1994. *25 Years On: The Costs of War and the Dividends of Peace,* Belfast, West Belfast Economic Forum.

TREWSDALE, J. and A. TOMAN, 1993. 'Employment' in J. Kremer and P. Montgomery (eds.), *op. cit.,* pp. 85-112.

WABE, J.S., 1986. 'The Regional Impact of De-Industrialization in the European Community', *Regional Studies,* Vol. 20, No. 1, pp. 27-36.

WALKER, S. and D. KEEBLE, 1987. 'The European Regions and the Twelve-Member European Community: An Overview', paper presented to the British Association for the Advancement of Science, Annual Meeting, Belfast, August.

WEBSTER, A., 1984. *Introduction to the Sociology of Development,* London, Macmillan.

WHYTE, J.H., 1990. *Interpreting Northern Ireland,* Oxford, Clarendon Press.

WILSON, T., 1989. *Ulster: Conflict and Consensus,* Oxford, Blackwell.

WILSON, T., 1990. 'Introduction' in R.I.D. Harris, C.W. Jefferson and J.E. Spencer (eds.), *op. cit.,* pp. 1-20.

5
The European Community and the Irish Rural Economy

PATRICK COMMINS

Introduction

The Republic of Ireland made its first bid to join the European Economic Community, as it then was, in 1961, simultaneously with the UK and Denmark. When France vetoed the British application, negotiations on Ireland's position were postponed and it took over ten years more for agreements to be reached on the enlargement of the Community. In 1972 when the Republic held a national referendum on the issue of membership 83 per cent of the votes cast were in favour. In fact all constituencies had substantial majorities voting for membership. The corresponding vote in the Danish referendum was 63.5 per cent. In the UK the decision to join was taken by Parliament with a 59 per cent majority.

The Republic's overwhelming support for accession to the European Community (EC) has to be seen in the context of the prevailing socio-economic and political circumstances. In the early 1960s agriculture was by far the country's biggest single industry, employing one-third of the labour force (compared to one-eighth now), accounting for one-quarter of Gross Domestic Product (one-tenth now), and earning almost two-thirds of its foreign exchange (two-fifths now).

About half of the sales from Irish farms were exported but most of these went to the UK which was among the lowest-priced food markets in the world. Growing surpluses in other agricultural exporting countries also meant limited opportunities for Ireland in wider world markets. Producers' incomes were depressed, and the decade of the 1960s was one of militancy by farmers as they protested their disadvantaged situation (Matthews, 1982, p. 244). The massive rural emigration of the 1950s had waned but not ceased and many areas continued to lose population.

Successive governments were obliged to support farm commodity prices in order to maintain a degree of stability in farm incomes. However, despite considerable increases in state support to agriculture, the average per capita income in farming deteriorated relative to industrial earnings (Sheehy, 1980). In addition, governments warned that the capacity of the Irish exchequer to support domestic farm prices was not comparable to that of other countries with greater financial resources and a relatively small agricultural sector. Accordingly, government statements pointed out that state expenditure in agriculture would be concentrated more on measures to improve agricultural productivity and competitiveness rather than on additional price supports.

Not surprisingly, then, the prospect of Irish membership of the EC was greeted with considerable relief; the burden of farm price support could now be shifted to Brussels (Matthews, 1982, p. 245). The Community's Common Agricultural Policy (CAP) guaranteed farm prices by controls on Third World imports, subsidisation of exports, and by buying up and storing surplus production. The enthusiasm of Irish governments for 'going into Europe' was surpassed only by the high expectations of the farming, rural and agribusiness organisations which formed a strong 'yes' lobby during the referendum campaign. In the public debate on the risks and benefits of EC membership it was recognised that Ireland's fisheries and some other non-agricultural industries would be adversely affected by the free trade inevitable in the

European 'Common Market'. On the other hand the prospective gains to agriculture seemed so decisive, any losses
elsewhere, the argument went, would be offset by benefits
available from other Community instruments, such as the
Regional Fund and the Social Fund.

This chapter reviews the experience of Irish membership
of the EC in relation to the country's rural economy, and with
particular reference to the influence of the CAP. The mid-
1980s are taken as marking a transition phase from a period
of liberal farm price supports to a period of CAP retrenchment and reforms, and of attempts to address agri-rural
problems through a more diversified set of Community
measures.

Our main conclusion is that despite substantial EC
monetary transfers to Ireland over almost two decades some
fundamental problems of the rural economy still remain
unsolved.

The first phase: 1973 to mid-1980s

The predominant significance of the CAP to Ireland can be
seen, first of all, in financial terms. The Republic is a
considerable net beneficiary of EC funds. Total payments
received during 1973-92 (about £2,000m annually in the early
1990s) have been over five times the sum Ireland contributed
to the Community. Of the monies received between 1973 and
1986 about 81 per cent were obtained under FEOGA – the
Agricultural Fund. In this same period the Social Fund and
the Regional Fund accounted for 9.9 per cent and 8.3 per
cent of payments respectively. FEOGA payments have not
retained this high level of dominance in recent years but they
still make up almost two-thirds of Community receipts. The
financial impact of the CAP can be gleaned from the fact that
in 1973 – the first year of EC membership – the Irish taxpayer
paid for 65 per cent of the cost of supporting the country's
agriculture but by the late 1980s the corresponding proportion had dropped to 12-15 per cent.

The second impact of the CAP is observable in the way the payments influence the economic conditions of the farm population. Before discussing this issue it is necessary to make two explanatory points, one concerning the aims of the CAP, the other relating to its operational mechanisms. The principal aims of the CAP are set out in Article 39 of the Treaty of Rome as follows:

- to increase agricultural productivity through technical progress and by ensuring the rational development of agricultural production
- to ensure a fair standard of living for the agricultural population, particularly by increasing the individual earnings of persons engaged in agriculture
- to stabilise markets, assure regular supplies of food and guarantee reasonable prices to consumers.

Closer consideration will show that the simultaneous attainment of these objectives may be in conflict; some can be achieved – at least beyond a certain point – only at the expense of others (CEC, 1987, p. 16). For example, 'rational' development through rapid technological progress might ensure a fair standard of living only for those who could survive in competitive conditions; or, increasing farmers' incomes might not guarantee reasonable consumer prices. Hence, in practice, the CAP became a series of political compromises reflecting the different capacities of organised interests to influence the policy agenda and the policy measures adopted.

With regard to its operational procedures, the benefits of the CAP flow in two streams. First, there are the budgetary transfers available under FEOGA and which ultimately come from EC *taxpayers;* secondly, there are the transfers from EC *consumers* as trade in agricultural produce takes place at prices above world levels (Agriculture and Food Policy Review Group, 1990, p. 5). FEOGA itself has two components. The 'Guarantee fund' finances the price supports to farmers and the market policies of the CAP while the 'Guidance fund' is used to finance structural policies in agriculture, e.g. farm development, training for farming, retirement schemes for older farmers, and improvement of processing facilities. We shall have occasion to refer repeatedly to this distinction between price support ('Guarantee') measures and structural policy ('Guidance') measures.

CAP price and market support policy

The original intention of the Community was that one-third of the CAP resources would be allocated to structural policies but, for reasons to be explained presently, this did not happen. Thus, by the time Ireland joined the Community, price and market policies dominated the CAP, accounting for some 95 per cent of its budget. This support system was fully in the tradition of the policies previously practised by member states (Tracy, 1982, p. 286). In Ireland the principal approach of governments to Community agricultural policy was to maximise money receipts from Brussels. Ministers for agriculture and the farm lobby were at one in the tactic of extracting the highest possible price supports for farmers from the EC bargaining table.

Adjustments to EC membership were not quite as immediately rewarding as farmers anticipated, with a collapse in cattle prices in 1974 bringing an early portent of the difficulties that would emerge later to plague the CAP (Lee, 1989, p. 474). In addition, the oil crisis in 1973 raised the costs of fuel and fertiliser. Nevertheless, because of common agricultural price increases and currency adjustments farmers, during the 1970s, enjoyed the most prosperous period in the history of Irish agriculture (O'Connor et al, 1983, p. 44). Between 1970 and 1978 the annual rate of increase in gross agricultural output was the highest ever achieved by the agricultural sector over a sustained period. By 1978, real incomes in farming had doubled compared to 1970. Income per person engaged in agriculture in 1978 was equivalent to 109 per cent of the average industrial earnings, compared to 80 per cent in 1970. However, the improvements in farmers' real incomes (i.e. adjusted for inflation) were not as great as officially projected because the decline in the farm labour force was much less than expected (O'Connor *et al*, 1983, p. 44).

Of course these trends did not serve the interests of the consumer. One estimate for 1978 suggested that for every extra £100 received by Irish farmers the Irish consumers paid about £30 in higher food prices, with foreign consumers paying the remaining £70 (Sheehy, 1984). Nevertheless, food price increases were lower than the levels of inflation. The other losers were those in industries such as car assembly, hit by free trade. On the other hand, however, there was an indirect gain to the Irish taxpayer who was spared the burden of paying for national price support policy. Moreover, CAP funds went to the benefit of suppliers of farm production materials and to the food processing industries (O'Connor *et al*, 1983, pp. 70-76). Indeed, it has been argued (Tovey, 1991, p. 334) that a disproportionate amount of EC income supports were siphoned off to the food industry, to the disadvantage of producers.

CAP structural policy

As already noted, CAP structural policies have always remained of much less significance than price policies in FEOGA expenditures. Farmers lobbied for prices first and foremost and national governments did likewise. Furthermore, unlike price support policies, structural measures were based on principles of co-financing. Member states had to carry portions of the costs involved and, in the case of Ireland, this was an important factor in determining the government's attitude towards CAP negotiations.

Yet, as far back as the late 1960s one of the inherent disadvantages of price policy – its encouragement of overproduction – was recognised. The 'Community of Six' was already self-sufficient in a number of products; the problems of funding support policies were becoming serious, and despite large agricultural expenditures, major structural problems – such as the high incidence of small farms – were not being addressed. The agricultural commissioner of the time, Sicco Mansholt, considered that more fundamental adjustments were needed if the aims of Article 39 of the Treaty of Rome were to be attained. Structural policy would have to be more closely linked to the common price policy. In the 'Mansholt Plan' of 1968 the aim was to create 'modern production units', through more selective farm investment supports. For dairy farms, for example, the target envisaged was 40-60 cows; most Irish dairy farms of the time would have fewer than 20 cows. Millions of people would be helped to leave agriculture during the 1970s by retraining or early retirement. Farms would be amalgamated, and since the creation of modern production units would also increase output, millions of hectares (5 million out of 70 million) would have to be taken out of production and used for other purposes, such as afforestation. Farm prices would find their own level and thus be restored to their true economic role of guiding the appropriate level of production.

Mansholt's attempt to break new ground must be seen not only against the background of farm problems but in the context of a post-World War Two boom in mid-Europe which gave rise to labour shortages in parts of the economy and the consequent recruitment of 'guest-workers' from outside the Community. Nevertheless, his 'rationalist' solution provoked violent opposition throughout the Community, especially in those countries, like Ireland, where there would be acute problems of transition from a small-scale farming pattern, depending considerably on family labour, to large-scale, mechanised and capital intensive units. After protracted negotiations and some violent farmer demonstrations the EC Council of Ministers agreed a package of 'guidelines for socio-structural policy' which were much less ambitious and less selective than those of the Mansholt Plan. In particular, agreement was reached on three common or 'horizontal'

measures: a farm modernisation scheme providing investment aids for farmers to develop their holdings (Directive
72/159); a retirement scheme offering pensions to farmers
aged over 55 years who released their land to modernising
farmers (Directive 72/160); and the promotion of socio-
economic guidance and training whereby farmers could
improve their farming skills or else retrain for work elsewhere
(Directive 72/161).

These 'horizontal' measures, so called because of their
applicability throughout the Community, were supplemented
in 1975 by measures which recognised the specific structural
adjustment problems of particular areas, such as mountain
areas, or less-favoured areas with low-yield land.

In Europe generally significant changes occurred in the
overall socio-economic climate after 1973 which reduced the
impact of the EC's structural policies. The opportunities for
labour to move out of agriculture declined as unemployment
in the non-farm economy increased. Investment costs for
farm development rose steadily because of inflation and the
increase in interest rates. The trend towards increasing surpluses on the markets for the main agricultural commodities
further discouraged heavy investment on farms.

In Ireland, the numbers of farmers applying for assistance
under the farm modernisation scheme were comparatively
high – equal to almost half of all farms (over one hectare) in
the state for the period 1975-83 (Cox, 1985, p. 15). However,
grants – mostly capital for investment – were paid on a
selective basis, with the most favourable allocations being
made to those farms capable of providing an income comparable with other occupations in the respective regions. As
these tended to be holdings with the better resources of land
and labour, only 26 per cent of all applicants qualified for the
preferential supports, while the proportion was as low as 14
per cent in western counties.

The retirement scheme offered special annuities to elderly
farmers on condition that they relinquished control (use or
ownership) of their holdings to 'developing' farmers. In

Ireland, however, this was a failure. During 1974–83 only 614 persons took up the idea. The annuities did not keep pace with inflation or with the increasing value of the regular old age pension. Another consideration was that those farmers who benefited from the rising agricultural commodity prices began to put the extra money into land purchases. Consequently, the price of land increased rapidly during the 1970s and it made little economic sense for any landholder to dispose of the family holding for a pension that seemed set to lose its value.

Ireland's major gains from CAP structural policies came not from the horizontal measures but via the series of schemes for designated regions – those for Less Favoured Areas (LFAs), a programme for western drainage and a Programme for Western Development ('the western package'). Between 1975 and 1983 these measures, combined, accounted for 54 per cent of Ireland's total receipts from the Guidance section of FEOGA, the LFA measures alone representing one-third of that total (Cox, 1985, p. 5). In this way these structural policies offset somewhat the tendency for price support policies to favour the larger, high production farms in the more fertile eastern counties.

However, even within the LFAs the larger farms received a disproportionately higher share of the transfers from structural policies. The really important schemes in the LFAs are the 'compensatory allowances', better known as 'headage payments'. These are not linked to prices received by farmers but are generally based on the numbers of livestock on the farm. As we shall see later, these direct (non-price) payments have become a significant component of incomes on western farms.

Overall, in Europe and in Ireland the outcomes of CAP structural policy have been quite limited, certainly if judged against the radical intentions of the Mansholt Plan, or even by comparison with the more modest ambitions of the 1970s' watered-down package itself (Tracy, 1982, p. 346). The funding was comparatively low; Guidance payments to

Ireland in the period 1975-83 were about 8 per cent of the country's receipts from FEOGA. While labour continued to leave the land, thus accomplishing – at least in part – one aim of structural adjustment, another aim, that of getting land into the control or ownership of the more productive farmers, was not solved. Although the numbers of *farmers* in the Republic declined by 34 per cent between 1971 and 1986 the number of *landholdings* remained relatively stable, decreasing by 5 per cent between 1975 and 1987. This indicates that farmers were turning in greater numbers to other occupations for their livelihood while retaining possession of their holdings and farming only on a part-time basis. In any event, the urgency for reforming land structures (i.e. to create larger holdings) receded in the 1980s as the aims and mechanisms of the CAP came to be increasingly questioned in a changed context.

The second phase: mid-1980s to 1990s

Already in the 1970s, the Commission of the EC had drawn attention to the problems the CAP might face if no corrective action were taken – though little heed was given to these warnings in Ireland. By the mid-1980s the problems became more pronounced and new difficulties emerged. High price policies, coupled with gains in productivity arising from technological improvements, resulted in surplus production which could not be profitably sold. The CAP, accounting for 70 per cent of the Community's budget, was stretching the limits of the finances available, and absorbing resources that could be used in other ways to further the development of the EC. Concerns were growing about the deleterious environmental consequences of intensive commercial farming. In its distributive impact the CAP militated against principles of equity as between different categories of farmers and different regions. This was because 20 per cent of Europe's farmers accounted for 80 per cent of production and the benefits of price supports, which were basically social transfers, went predominantly to the larger, high-volume producers on the better soils. Consumers became more vocal in arguing that they were paying artificially high prices for their food, while taxpayers were paying farmers to produce food that was not saleable at the cost of its production (Murray, 1991). The expectation of continued economic growth in Europe had not been realised and with growing urban unemployment the security of farming seemed to offer some compensation for its lower earnings (Tracy, 1982, p. 349). This slowed down the movement of labour from the land.

The CAP had succeeded in its economic aims of ensuring Europe's food supplies but this success did not square with its social aim of ensuring a fair income to farmers. How could this second aim be achieved, in an economic environment not conducive to facilitating structural adjustments in agriculture (e.g. by absorbing more redundant farm labour in other jobs), while at the same time curbing surplus production and avoiding excessive costs? This was the task facing successive EC Commissions from 1985 onwards. We review here the main responses and how they related to Ireland. The enormous variety of measures may be classified under four broad headings:

- reforming the CAP price and market policies
- adapting the CAP structural policies
- linking CAP structural policies with the re-organisation of the Regional Fund and the Social Fund in the context of the Single European Market
- supporting rural development.

Reforms of price and market policy

Since the late 1970s there has been a succession of increasingly restrictive measures designed to bring commodity supply and demand into greater balance, and to contain the costs of the CAP. A 'prudent price policy' was introduced in 1977 which had the effect of lowering the real (adjusted for inflation) prices paid to farmers. In the mid-1980s those who produced quantities of certain commodities above a specified limit became subject to levies charged on their surplus production, such levies being then used to pay for disposing of the surplus. Another production control was the 'stabiliser', a phasing down of Guarantee payments once production thresholds were reached. Quantitative restrictions – quotas – were introduced for some products, e.g. milk.

Yet the problems of market imbalance and budget excesses re-emerged. Although farm incomes were squeezed, production continued to rise because farmers reacted to price pressures by raising productivity. At the same time, in the wider international arena, the impending finalisation of GATT negotiations and the concern to allow market forces take their effect brought further pressure on the Community to adjust its internal price and market systems. In this context the most recent CAP reforms – the 'MacSharry' proposals – were adopted. These reforms reflect the principle that it is neither economically sensible nor financially feasible to guarantee prices for unlimited quantities produced. Put another way, ensuring a fair standard of living for farmers could no longer be pursued to the same extent through a food production policy, while farmland may serve other functions for society besides producing its food.

The main thrust of the CAP reforms has been to switch the emphasis away from price and market supports and towards direct ('compensatory') payments to producers. Taken together with a number of related measures the revised arrangement of market and non-market mechanisms includes: price reductions (mainly on commodities sold into storage); restrictions on production (principally a continuation of quotas on milk); increased incentives to diversify into non-conventional lines of production (such as forestry); incentives for producers who meet specific low-intensity farming criteria (mainly for conserving the environment); an enhanced scheme to encourage farmers over 55 years to retire from farming; and extra annual compensation payments to offset the effects of price reductions. In the case of large-scale cereal growers, compensation for price cuts is conditional on their setting aside a proportion of their land from arable production.

It is too early to assess the actual impact in Ireland of these more recent CAP reforms. One analysis of their likely effects suggests that compensation payments will more than offset income losses (Fingleton *et al*, 1992) but the issue is complicated by the GATT Agreement of 1993. The main outcome of the earlier reforms was a reduction – because of quota limits – in milk production, but this was countered by expansion in cattle and sheep production. The effect of quotas in dairying has been to speed up the exit of small producers out of milk production. With their prospects as dairy farmers curtailed these sold or leased their milk quotas and opted for other enterprises or left farming altogether. The movement of labour out of agriculture helps to maintain the real incomes of those remaining. Quota restrictions also give an impetus to efficiency in production in that profits which cannot be earned by expanding production can be made up by cutting production costs on the quota allowable. The renewed emphasis on competitiveness echoed the policy of Irish governments in the stringent national budgetary circumstances of the 1960s.

Adapting structural policies: the role of direct payments

Farm structural policies have also been adapted in the interests of controlling production. In 1986 the existing farm modernisation scheme was replaced by a Farm Improvement Programme (FIP), in which eligibility conditions were much more restrictive than for its predecessor – the farm modernisation scheme of the 1970s. For instance, no investment aid could be given where the farm plan would exacerbate the problem of surpluses. Furthermore, grant aid was weighted in support of farms in the Less Favoured Areas, thus giving the new programme a more distributive and less of a productionist orientation. The FIP benefited small-scale farmers mostly in western counties who undertook minor improvements which enhanced working conditions on their holdings (O'Hara, 1986).

As noted above CAP reforms strengthened the incentives to divert farm production from conventional commodities, but an early impetus to tree-planting by landholders was provided by the EC-financed 'western package' beginning in 1981. Similar incentives later became available nationally under the 1987 Programme for National Recovery. The outcome was that by the early 1990s private afforestation had expanded considerably, and of the area taken up by the private sector an increasing percentage was accounted for by farmers planting on their own lands – as distinct from forestry companies.

It will be apparent from the foregoing discussion that market and non-market agricultural policy measures have been brought into closer alignment, especially with the reform of the CAP. In particular, recurring direct payments have become increasingly important in reconciling the economic objective of achieving a better balance between supply and demand with the social objective of supporting farm incomes. In a more precise sense direct payments to producers, which may or may not be linked to the regulation of production, can be used to achieve a number of aims such as: altering the form of income support (e.g. to replace a price support policy), cushioning the transition to a lower level of income support, encouraging the provision of public goods (e.g. to conserve the landscape), and providing a minimum level of income (Sheehy, 1994).

In Ireland the most significant types of direct payments, as already noted, are the allowances payable to farmers on the basis of their livestock numbers. Under the CAP, livestock headage payments were introduced initially to compensate for the 'natural handicaps' of the economically disadvantaged areas. With more restrictive price and supply control policies on the horizon in the late 1980s, Irish farmers lobbied strongly for even higher headage payments and for an extension of the geographical area of the country classified as 'disadvantaged'.

When this was increased from 60 per cent to 72 per cent of the state's territory, 120,000 of the country's 170,000 farm holders received headage payments. In addition, certain livestock premium payments are available to farmers in all parts of the country. As noted already, these various compensatory measures have been augmented under the CAP reform.

The importance of direct subsidies in contemporary agriculture policy may be seen in their contribution to incomes on family farms. In 1992 such subsidies represented 30 per cent of the average farm income, although this proportion varied by farm size and farm system. For example it was approximately 5 per cent on the larger and more profitable dairy farms (16 per cent of all farms in the country), 60 per cent on the smaller and lower income cattle farms (47 per cent of all farms), and over 90 per cent on sheep farms (18 per cent of all farms). It is clear that large numbers of farmers – especially in western counties – would have serious difficulties were it not for direct payments, particularly where off-farm earnings are not part of household income (Power and Roche, 1990, p. 13).

The Single European Market and the reform of the Structural Funds

To an extent the structural measures of the CAP have been functioning in effect as a regional policy. On the other hand, the expectation that rural Ireland would benefit substantially from the EC Regional Fund was not realised. Compared to what Ireland obtained from FEOGA the country fared rather poorly from the Regional Fund. Moreover, as the government decided that all parts of the Republic were to be eligible for support from the Fund it was not used to improve any specific region but to help finance the public capital programme. Similarly, the EC Social Fund represented only a minor share of Ireland's EC receipts and, in any event, was not primarily designed for rural areas.

However, in the late 1980s two considerations brought the problem of adjustments in the agricultural sector within the influence of other policies and funds. The first was the establishment of the Single European Market (SEM). It was realised in Brussels that the SEM, which permitted the free movement of capital, labour and services within the Community, would pose problems for 'lagging regions' remote from the European hub and highly dependent on agriculture. At the same time the EC had to declare in favour of maintaining and fostering economic and social cohesion within an enlarged Community of pronounced regional diversity. The compromise was to be reached by re-organising what had come to be known as the 'three Structural Funds' – the EC Regional Fund, the Social Fund and the Guidance (non-market) component of FEOGA. The reform of these funds meant in effect:

- doubling their money value in real terms between 1989 and 1993
- concentrating on priority objectives, among which are the development and structural adjustment of less-favoured areas; in this context the Republic and Northern Ireland form one of the areas to be given priority status
- co-ordination and complementarity among the various development actions being supported by the three funds.

On this last point the Commission, together with the government and private investors, provides finance for developments on the basis of a *programme* of interventions – rather than single projects – submitted by member states. Under an agreed 'Community Support Framework' (CSF) twelve such 'operational programmes' were initiated in Ireland during 1989-93, the most relevant for present purposes being the following: (i) a programme for environmentally-friendly farming which provided grant aid to farmers for investments designed to control farm-based pollution; (ii) a farm improvement programme incorporating the existing FIP; (iii) a forestry programme which greatly increased existing financial incentives to landowners to plant commercial trees; and (iv) a programme for rural development which included a range of measures to encourage alternative lines of production (e.g. organic farming), promote farm-based tourism, assist small-scale or community-based enterprises, develop harbours and roads, and improve opportunities for vocational training.

Early indications are that these measures have evoked an enthusiastic response (Government Information Services, 1992) although it is too soon to assess their total or distributive impact on the rural economy. It may be said, however, that the amount expended annually on direct payments to farmers is equal to the total public expenditure on these programmes during 1989-93.

Operational programmes of a similar type will be submitted to Brussels for approval in a new CSF for 1994-99.

Changing institutional approaches to rural development

So far we have considered the influence of the EC on the Irish agricultural economy mostly in terms of production or financial impacts. However, another implication of EC membership, especially in the context of more recent attempts to find solutions to agri-rural problems, is that the Community has obliged Ireland to adopt new institutional arrangements in expending EC monies. A key principle underlying the reform of the Structural Funds is that of 'partnership', defined as close consultation between the Commission, national governments and relevant authorities or organisations at regional and local level, with each party acting as a partner in pursuit of a common goal (CEC, 1989, pp. 14-15). The practical application of this concept means not only some decentralisation of Community actions to local levels but also the participation of various non-governmental economic and social partners (e.g. co-operatives, local development associations, trade unions) in the design and implementation of operational and related programmes.

Given its highly centralised administrative system, compared to continental countries, the Republic did not have the ready-made structures to facilitate the kinds of partnership and sub-national participation envisaged by the Commission. In preparing plans for the Structural Funds seven regions were designated and ad hoc steering committees set up in each region. These were composed of personnel from local authorities, government departments, semi-state agencies, as well as representatives of the private sector. Provision was made for advisory groups as a means of giving a voice to non-statutory organisations. Even so, there have been many criticisms of this arrangement, mainly to the effect that it was a token gesture to the notion of partnership and devolution of authority, and that it deprived community-based groups of any real participation in decisions affecting their areas (Community Workers Co-operative, 1989). However, new regional structures were established in 1994 to monitor the implementation of programmes under the EC Structural and Cohesion Funds. The members of these authorities are city and county councillors.

There are two EC initiatives in local rural development in Ireland which give more concrete and visible expression to the concepts of partnership, popular participation and an integrated approach to development now being advocated in Brussels (see Curtin and Varley, this volume). One is the Community's Third Anti-Poverty Programme which includes a rural-based 'model action' project (in the Clifden Rural District of north-west Connemara). The purpose of model actions in this programme is to develop innovatory organisational structures for taking preventative action to deal with economic and social marginalisation (Combat Poverty Agency, 1994). This project has a number of features of relevance to the present discussion, including the following:

• it is financed directly from Brussels with co-financing by the Irish government (through the Combat Poverty Agency)

- it is being implemented not exclusively by a local non-statutory group or by a state agency – as in previous anti-poverty programmes – but by a local partnership formally constituted as a legal entity. This partnership brings together officials of the local authority and state agencies, as well as representatives of local communities
- it works to a strategic and multi-dimensional plan which integrates action across a number of economic and social sectors
- it advocates the participation of the 'target groups' in decision-making
- it employs its own professional staff.

This form of EC model action approach is now reflected in the Dublin government's 'response to long-term unemployment' which is based on similar local partnerships in twelve pilot areas, four of which are in rural areas.

The second exemplar of the principles governing current Community action in rural development is the LEADER programme (Liaison Entre Actions de Développement de l'Economie Rurale). In 1991 interested parties such as co-operatives, local development associations, state-sponsored bodies, and local authorities were invited by the Commission to form unified 'rural development groupings' and submit plans for the development of their areas (typically sub-county or county areas of up to 100,000 population). Out of some 200 such groups chosen by the Commission throughout the Community sixteen have been selected in the Republic, with one large grouping in Northern Ireland. These groups were chosen on the basis of their collective organisation, their plans for local development and their capacity to contribute a share of the costs of implementing actions. Total funding of the 1992-94 LEADER programme in the Republic is shared by the EC (30 per cent), the state (20 per cent), with approved groups ensuring that another 50 per cent is contributed by private sources. The private sources are those who come forward with projects for funding. About half of the value of total investments under the programme have been concerned with the provision of facilities for rural tourism.

Concluding comment

Benefits and limitations

Over its two decades of membership of the EC the Republic has been a substantial beneficiary of financial transfers within the Community. Because most of the EC budget has been absorbed by the CAP the more immediate gains of membership have gone to the agricultural sector, mainly through the system of financially supporting the prices of commodities produced on farms. However, it could be said that while Irish consumers have had to carry some of the costs of supporting farm prices they have also gained indirectly from EC membership in so far as they have benefited from the reallocation of the national exchequer resources that had previously been devoted to supporting agriculture before the burden was taken up by the EC.

This generally positive evaluation must be qualified in three important respects. First, because price supports dominated the CAP budget, the distribution of benefits within the agricultural sector has been highly skewed in favour of producers of particular commodities (such as milk), particular regions (mainly the more prosperous areas), and the high-volume producers. Thus the social goals of ensuring a fair standard of living for the farm population, but especially that of ensuring a better distribution of income, were negated by the price policy. For example, in the EC in general, in 1984-86, the level of price support to larger farms was 15 times the magnitude of support to smaller farms (Brown, 1989).

Second, and arising from what has just been said, the CAP did not address the structural problems of Irish agriculture, such as the need to achieve a greater degree of land mobility from older occupiers to younger farmers. There was little enthusiasm on the part of governments or farmers for policy measures other than price supports. It was only in the late 1980s that direct subsidies to farmers in disadvantaged areas (through livestock 'headage' payments) made a significant contribution to farm incomes in those areas. Such payments, however, are another form of income support and not a measure to alter land/labour relationships or other structural features of Irish agriculture.

The third disappointment of EC membership can be seen by comparing the high expectations of government for regional policy with what has actually transpired. In 1972 it was anticipated that Community policy would raise living standards in less-favoured areas and that the aids to regional development available from Brussels would help provide a wider range of economic and social opportunities and so minimise population dislocation (Department of Foreign Affairs, 1972; Government Information Bureau, 1972). But Ireland's receipts under the Regional Fund remained comparatively small – at about 8 per cent – during 1973-90, although the proportion has risen to almost 20 per cent in the 1990s.

So, some of the fundamental problems of the Irish rural economy remain unsolved. Despite EC financial transfers households headed by a farmer accounted for one-quarter of all households below the poverty line in 1987 (Callan *et al*, 1989). Much of the country's land resources remain under-utilised. Many farms are still small, unproductive and occupied by older people. The labour market in rural areas cannot absorb all those leaving school. Rural depopulation is again evident after a short period of stability and growth in the 1970s (Commins, 1992).

The policy-making process
Viewed in a wider perspective the Irish experience of EC membership – dominated as it was by agricultural issues – allows us an insight into the processes of public policy

formation and change. The CAP was designed in the context of an inefficient agrarian structure and in a Europe heavily dependent on food imports. Yet despite increasing self-sufficiency in food in the 1960s and the build-up of surpluses in the 1970s and 1980s there was great reluctance to reform the CAP. One reason for this, of course, is that it was intended not only to ensure food production but also to guarantee a fair level of living for those producing food. But, in addition, we must take account of the politically determined way in which public policies are designed and maintained. Policies are the outcomes of bargaining processes among diverse interests with unequal influence. Bowler (1985, p. 43) describes the network of lobbying and consultations in EC agricultural policy-making which allows close contact to be developed among government ministers, Commission officials and leaders of pressure groups. In this arena producers are better organised than consumers. Tracy (1989, p. 333) argues that the tardiness in dealing with the problems of the CAP during the 1970s and 1980s was due to the tendency of many agricultural ministers to be overly concerned with political survival and thus with the need to curry favour with the farm electorate.

To say that the public policy agenda tends to be appropriated by certain interest groups is not to exclude the influence of bureaucratic rationality, in this case by the leadership in the EC Commission (Commins, 1990, pp. 51-52). However, little by way of alternatives to price support policies had been put on the bargaining table until the problems of the CAP reached crisis proportions in the mid-1980s. Mansholt's implicit assumption of a buoyant non-farm economy to absorb redundant farm labour did not materialise and, understandably, the farm lobby clung to the price support mechanism. From the producers' standpoint, income transfers, 'concealed' in the prices obtained for their products and inherited from times of food scarcity, were the most politically defensible means of re-distributing income to them from consumers and taxpayers.

Economic and social elements of agricultural policy

Nevertheless, EU agricultural policy has moved on and now seeks to separate measures which encourage efficient food production from measures which support farm incomes and promote rural development and from schemes which acknowledge the social and public good functions of farming in modern society. Thus there is gradually emerging a set of distinct but complementary policies which (i) allow farm prices to reflect more truly the market realities, (ii) provide support for the production of non-surplus products (e.g. commercial timber), (iii) support farming activities designed to protect the environment and conserve natural amenities, and (iv) provide direct income subsidies to farmers and so help to maintain rural population numbers. However, the funds being provided for the diversification of production and the protection of the environment are very limited compared to the volume of direct income supports. Moreover, by European standards Ireland does not have intensive farming systems and Irish policy has been slow in designating environmentally sensitive areas where farmers would be compensated for environmentally-friendly production practices.

Recurrent non-market money transfers, paid directly to farmers, have become an important lever in achieving greater market liberalisation. Given their transparency as 'cheques in the post' – compared to price support – and hence their political vulnerability they have not been favoured enthusiastically by farmers' organisations *as compensations for lowering commodity prices* despite their important contribution to the incomes of smaller-scale farmers. In fact the possibility has been raised (Sheehy, 1994) that direct subsidies, as welfare payments to redundant farmers, may eventually be fused with welfare payments generally. In that case a major social element of agricultural policy, which has been strongly differentiated from general social policy, may cease to lose its uniqueness and become integrated with mainstream economic and social policy.

From a sectoral to a territorial emphasis

In addition to the above set of measures, the task of making adjustments in the agricultural sector in the face of longer-term macroeconomic forces is increasingly seen as one requiring a comprehensive policy framework reaching outside the agricultural sector itself. In fact the experience of the CAP shows a progression from a rationalist, economistic and *sectoral* approach (typified by Mansholt but weakly pursued in the scaling down of his proposals) to a more *territorial* strategy.

This is evident in the supplementation of horizontal or common measures by regionally-specific schemes and, more recently, by area-based rural development policies. Thus the answers to agriculture's problems are no longer seen mainly in terms of having fewer people living on the land, amalgamating holdings and building up bigger farm businesses. Desirable adjustments in the agricultural sector can also be facilitated by the diversified development of the whole rural economy, allowing landholders to remain on their holdings and support themselves through multiple sources of income. In this way the continuity of the household does not become overly dependent on the economic viability of the farm. In fact farming is but one of the economic activities undertaken by Irish farm households and, increasingly, on the under-50 acre holdings it is not even the most significant contributor to total household income.

A territorial or spatial – as distinct from a sectoral – orientation to development also dovetails with other stated concerns of the Single European Act to maintain economic and social cohesion among different regions of the Community. But now the critical question is: to what extent will official EU rhetoric be given practical effect through increasing other types of resource transfers besides farm price supports and social welfare forms of direct income subsidisation? The free movement of capital, labour and services in a common European market does not harmonise with aspirations to have more balanced distribution of economic activity and employment across Europe's regions. Commitments to regional policy and to the reduction of regional disparities normally involve special provision of regional supports for economic development but these conflict with the principles of competition policy and so tend to have a secondary status (Drudy, 1984, p. 97). Thus as regards the Structural Funds, even when their amounts are doubled, the resources available as a proportion of the total EU budget are still very small in relation to the grand objectives set. Additionally, for the immediate future the EU's concerns for eastern Europe must be balanced against the claims of the western periphery.

References

AGRICULTURE AND FOOD POLICY REVIEW GROUP, 1990. *Report,* Dublin, Stationery Office.

BOWLER, I.R., 1985. *Agriculture under the Common Agricultural Policy,* Manchester, Manchester University Press.

BROWN, C., 1989. *Distribution of CAP Price Support,* København, Jordbrugsøkonomiske Institut.

CALLAN, T., B. NOLAN, C. J. WHELAN, D. F. HANNAN, and S. CREIGHTON, 1989. *Poverty, Income and Welfare in Ireland,* Dublin, ESRI, Paper No. 146.

CEC (Commission of the European Communities), 1987. *The Common Agricultural Policy and Its Reform,* Brussels.

CEC (Commission of the European Communities), 1989. *Guide to the Reform of the Community's Structural Funds,* Brussels.

COMBAT POVERTY AGENCY, 1994. *Combating Exclusion,* Dublin CPA.

COMMINS, P., 1990. 'Restructuring Agriculture in Advanced Societies: Transformation, Crisis and Responses', in T. Marsden, P. Lowe and S. Whatmore (eds.), *Rural Restructuring: Global Processes and their Responses,* London, David Fulton Publishers.

COMMINS, P., 1992. 'Rural Development: Trends and Issues', in National Economic and Social Council, *The Impact of Reform of the Common Agricultural Policy,* Dublin,

NESC, No. 92, pp. 189-207.
COMMUNITY WORKERS CO-OPERATIVE, 1989. *Whose Plan?*, Dublin.
COX, P.G., 1985. 'The Impact of EC Structural Policy in Ireland', in *The Challenge Facing Agriculture in Difficult Times,* Dublin. An Foras Talúntais, pp. 1-30. Conference Proceedings.
DEPARTMENT OF FOREIGN AFFAIRS, 1972. *Ireland and the Common Market: Regional Development,* Dublin.
DRUDY, P. J., 1984. 'The Regional Implications of EEC Policies in Ireland', in P. J. Drudy and D. McAleese (eds.), *Ireland and the European Community,* Cambridge: Cambridge University Press.
FINGLETON, W. A., A. LEAVY, J. F. HEAVEY, and M. ROCHE, 1992. *Impact of Common Agricultural Policy Reforms 1992,* Dublin, Teagasc.
GOVERNMENT INFORMATION BUREAU, 1972. *Statement on Regional Policy,* Dublin.
GOVERNMENT INFORMATION SERVICES, 1992. 'Minister Hyland outlines progress under Structural Funds' Programmes', Dublin, No. 219/92, 1 October.
LEE, J. J., 1989. *Ireland 1912-1985: Politics and Society,* Cambridge: Cambridge University Press.
MATTHEWS, ALAN, 1982. 'The State and Irish

Agriculture, 1950-1980', in P. J. Drudy (ed.), *Ireland: Land, Politics and People,* Cambridge, Cambridge University Press, pp. 240-269.
MURRAY, J., 1991. Address to Seminar on the Reform of the Common Agricultural Policy, Dublin.
O'HARA, P., 1986. 'CAP Socio-Structural Policy – A New Approach to an Old Problem', in *The Changing CAP and Its Implications,* Dublin, An Foras Talúntais, pp. 34-69. Conference Proceedings
O'CONNOR, R., C. GUIOMARD, and J. DEVEREAUX, 1983. *A Review of the Common Agricultural Policy and the Implications of Modified Systems for Ireland,* Dublin, ESRI Broadsheet No. 21.
POWER, R. and M. ROCHE, 1990. *National Farm Survey 1989 – Provisional Estimates,* Dublin, Teagasc.
SHEEHY, S. J., 1980. 'The Impact of EEC Membership on Irish Agriculture', *Journal of the Agricultural Economics Society,* Vol. XXX1, No. 3, pp. 297-310.
SHEEHY, S. J., 1984. 'The Common Agricultural Policy and Ireland' in P. J. Drudy and D. McAleese (eds.), *Ireland and the European Community,* Cambridge, Cambridge University Press.
SHEEHY, S. J., 1994. 'The Future of Direct Payments to

Farmers', paper to Agricultural Economics Society of Ireland, 24 January.

TOVEY, HILARY, 1991. 'Of Cabbages and Kings: Restructuring in the Irish Food Industry', *Economic and Social Review,* Vol. 22, No. 4, July 1991, pp. 333-350.

TRACY, M., 1982. *Agriculture in Western Europe,* London, Granada, Second Edition.

TRACY, M., 1989. *Government and Agriculture in Western Europe, 1880-1988,* Hampstead, Harvester Wheatshop, Third edition.

6
Family and Household in Ireland

TONY FAHEY

Introduction

Sociologists studying the family have been preoccupied by
the changes in family life which have occurred during what
we might loosely call the 'modernisation' of western societies
– and by 'modernisation' here is meant generally the bundle
of economic, social and cultural transformations that have
overtaken the western world since the industrial revolution.
The family in Ireland is particularly interesting in this regard
since its evolution from the 1930s or so is often thought to
encapsulate in a short period many of the tendencies found
in other western countries over a much longer term. The
Irish case is thus worth examining both for its own inherent
interest and as a test case for the validity of more general
views of the relationship between family change and broader
social change in the recent history of western countries.

It must be kept in mind that the family, our main object of
interest, is not easy to define, in spite of the considerable
effort that has been expended in the attempt to do so. Some
have argued that the term 'family' should be avoided
altogether on the grounds that it has become too loaded with
ideological overtones to be of use as an analytical term.

Furthermore, it is strongly identified with traditional concepts of marriage and parenthood, to the neglect of increasingly common domestic arrangements such as unmarried parenthood, one-person households, homosexual relationships and so on (Elliot, 1986, pp. 4-8). The problem of definition is further complicated in that the family is sometimes defined in terms of kin and sometimes in terms of co-residence or households, alternatives which identify different, though overlapping, fields of reference for the study of the family. It is outside the scope of the present chapter to try to resolve these definitional questions, but it is well to remember the uncertain, multi-faceted nature of the basic concept of the family as we examine the way it has been dealt with in sociology.

Theoretical background

The major nineteenth-century pioneers of sociological study of the family were preoccupied by the disruptive effects of the new industrial capitalism on traditional family organisation. Frederic Le Play (1806-1882), a French mining engineer-cum-social analyst who carried out an extraordinarily extensive programme of empirical study of family patterns in Europe in the mid-nineteenth century, was the first to examine these effects in a systematic way and his work identified many of the themes that have persistently recurred in family studies since (see Le Play, 1982 for selected extracts from his work). For him, the principal and most worrying outcome of the new capitalist industrialisation was the rise of what he called the *unstable family* among the new, rootless urban working class, a family type which he compared unfavourably with the more cohesive *stem family* of European tradition.[1] The transformation, in his view, was caused partly by factors such as the decline in traditional religious belief and the increasing intervention by the state in family affairs, especially, in France at least, in the area of inheritance practices. But by far the most important cause was the declining importance of family property. The family holding, whether farm or small business, was the magnet at the heart of the traditional family which kept its members together and gave it a focus of identity, while the family in the new urban proletariat, which inevitably lacked substantial property, was subject to the individualising, disintegrative effects of impersonal wage labour. For Le Play, the shift in the economic base of the family from the jointly operated family enterprise to individualistic wage labour was the central (and largely negative) influence of industrialisation on the new patterns of family life.

Frederick Engels, Marx's collaborator, offered a different but equally seminal slant on the same issues in his *The Origins of the Family, Private Property and the State* (1884). He too felt that the changing relationship between family, property and wage labour was the central driving force in family change. In his view, marriage evolved in history as a device created by men to control women's sexuality, in order thereby to control the production of heirs for male property. Thus traditional marriage, and with it the entire system of sexual morality and family life familiar to western civilization, were not 'natural' forms of family life but social constructs designed to serve the needs of property – and of male property at that. Among the working class in capitalism, concepts of property and inheritance had lost their significance and, in consequence, according to Engels, traditional marriage was gradually losing its reason for existence. However, where Le Play bemoaned the new instability this gave rise to, Engels celebrated it as the harbinger of a new liberation where intimate human relationships would be created on the basis of emotional needs rather than the stultifying requirements of property.

Despite their many differences, Le Play and Engels both saw economic factors as the dominant influences on family organisation and in consequence they both saw the advent of industrial capitalism as causing a radical break with traditional family structures, especially among the new urban working class. This theme of the radical break between tradition and modernity as a consequence of industrialisation was carried over into the present century and dominated sociological thinking on the family until the 1960s (though Engels' focus on gender and class oppression as central aspects of family structure largely disappeared as a concern for most of this period). Oddly, much of the research which took this radical break as its starting point focussed very much on the 'modern' side of the divide, so that, until the 1960s at least, the pre-industrial 'traditional' family was conjured up by assumption and nostalgia as much as by concrete research.

One exception to the general neglect of the 'traditional' family in research was provided by the American anthropologists Arensberg and Kimball in their classic study, *Family and Community in Ireland* (first published in 1940). This consisted of a detailed account of family and community practices in the countryside around Ennis (and to some extent in Ennis itself) in Co Clare in the 1930s. Its concern was to show that, however antiquated and strange family practices in rural and small town Ireland might seem by the new standards then emerging in other western countries, they made sense and 'functioned' in their own terms, that is, by reference to the survival needs of the local economy and community. The label 'functionalism' was applied to the school of anthropological analysis to which Arensberg and Kimball belonged because of its emphasis on explaining social and cultural practices by identifying the functions they fulfilled for the communities in which they were found. They focussed on a number of characteristic features of rural Irish family life such as the patriarchal authority of the family head, the stem-family inheritance system, practices surrounding arranged marriages and dowries, the pre-occupation with 'keeping the name on the land' through inheritance in the male line and the role of kin networks and neighbourly co-operation in economic life. They tried to show how these characteristics worked together to form a distinctive, cohesive social system with quite a different logic from that of the modern industrialised world.[2]

The other side of the coin – the urban-industrial counter-
part of the traditional institution represented by the Irish
farm family – was also subject to functionalist analysis, particularly under the intellectual leadership of the American
social theorist, Talcott Parsons (see esp. Parsons and Bales,
1955). According to Parsons, the modern urban family was of
a distinctive 'nuclear' type which was recognisable by a
number of key features: it was small in size, normally consisting only of the married couple and a small number of
children; it was relatively isolated from kin and community,
partly because of an increased emphasis on family privacy
and partly because of increased social and geographical
mobility; its principal internal focus was on the nurture of
children and emotional fulfilment of spouses, rather than on
work or family enterprise; and its principal role-divisions
centred on a characteristic division of labour between the
breadwinner husband and the homemaker wife, with children
in the role of non-productive dependants. Parsons viewed this
assemblage of features as a viable, functional response to the
needs of the new industrial order. The smallness and
detachment of the nuclear family, in contrast with the
extended, socially embedded traditional family, facilitated
the kind of mobility required by the fluid social structures
and rapidly changing labour markets of industrial society.
The loss of the 'instrumental' functions of the family during
industrialisation – as production moved from the household
to the factory and as education and health care moved to
schools and hospitals – freed it to concentrate on the 'expres-
sive' functions so that the human warmth and intimacy of the
family actually increased and served as an essential counter-
weight to the increasing impersonality of the larger society.
    Since the 1960s, many of the tenets hitherto accepted as
basic by those concerned with the impact of industrialisation
on the family came in for sustained criticism and revision.
The re-think was inspired partly by new evidence (both
historical and contemporary) and partly by ideological
upheavals in family studies. New evidence from historical

sources indicated that the contrast between the traditional extended family and the modern nuclear family had been overdrawn. Small, nuclear households and a substantial degree of geographical mobility, it was found, had always been common in western Europe, at least since the late Middle Ages (Wall *et al*, 1983; for a somewhat different view of the same issue, see Flandrin, 1979). Another distinctive feature of western European family history, both before and after the industrial revolution, was the less-than-universal availability of marriage. Many never married at all (normally 10 to 15 per cent of the adult population). Those who married generally did so at an age which was quite late by the standards of most other societies in human history (early to mid-twenties for women, mid-twenties to early thirties for men) (Coale and Watkins, 1986). Restrictions on access to marriage acted as a form of birth control and led to lower birth rates in pre-industrial western Europe than in the rest of the pre-industrial world. The need to control the sexuality of relatively large populations of unmarried adults also affected approaches to sexuality in general and helps explain the pre-occupation with sexual morality in western Christianity both before and after the industrial revolution.

New evidence about family structures *after* industrialisation also tended to undermine the old dichotomies. Studies of the early industrial period in Britain and America showed that extended families and kin networks became more rather than less important in the new industrial cities, largely because poverty and economic instability turned kin networks into vital support systems for the new working class families (Anderson, 1971; Hareven, 1978). Research on urban communities in the 1950s also suggested that extended kin ties continued to be a common part of family life as industrial societies matured, in working class as well as middle class areas (Wilmott and Young, 1960; Young and Wilmott, 1962; Litwak, 1965). In Ireland, Hannan and Katsiaouni's (1977) study of farm families in the west of Ireland showed that those families with a modern commercial approach to farming were, paradoxically, likely to have stronger kin structures – i.e. to be more 'traditional' in their participation in extended family networks – than the families who were 'traditional' in their farming practices.

However, this new evidence about the factual inadequacy of the old tradition/modernity divide probably had less of an effect on family studies than the upheavals in ways of thinking about the family which emerged in the 1960s, most of which were associated with the growing intellectual influence of feminism. For feminists, the problem with the conventional wisdom on the family (and indeed on social issues generally) was not in what it said but in what it did not say – in the questions it did not ask and the aspects of reality it did not address. Feminists' focus on women's experience and on the oppressiveness to women of traditional social institutions opened a whole new dimension to enquiry about the family. From this perspective, the important concern was not any supposed radical break between traditional and modern forms of family life but the continued subordination of women, in the present as well as in the past. Some strands of feminism harked back to Engels and viewed women's subordination in the family as a consequence of capitalist economic organisation. This approach maintained a continuity of sorts with the tradition which saw economic imperatives as the dominant influences on family structures. Other variants of feminism traced male dominance to sources as diverse as cultural stereotyping, male physical strength and capacity for violence, and the male psychological need to dominate women (for an overview, see Lengermann and Niebrugge-Brantley, 1992). In spite of their diversity, the common focus on the position of women in these approaches has defined a new set of questions for family studies. These questions have focussed on such diverse issues as the role of the state in shaping women's position in the family through family law and social policy, the effects of education and the mass media on sex-role stereotyping in the home, the use of male sexual and physical violence to subjugate women within the family, and patterns of power and control within the family in matters of affection and emotion as well as money, work and other material resources.

Family and household in Ireland

Ireland in the twentieth century offers a good example of some of the basic transitions affecting families during indus-trialisation and also shows how a simple binary opposition between 'traditional' and 'modern' does not do justice to the complexity of what those transitions amounted to. As already mentioned, the small-farm, small-business family type prevail-ing in rural and small town Ireland in the first half of the twentieth century, especially as depicted by Arensberg and Kimball, has often been considered a late-surviving version of wider European patterns of 'traditional', pre-industrial family organisation. The push towards industrialisation in Ireland in the 1960s can be taken to provide an instance of how rapid modernisation can transform such a traditional survival, so intensifying the interest in processes represented by the Irish case.

We are now more aware than Arensberg and Kimball were that the dominant family type in Ireland in the 1930s was less traditional than it seemed. Its origins lay not in the distant past but in the land reforms, raised living standards and the decline of rural wage labour in post-famine Ireland. We are also aware of the many ways in which it is misleading to speak of this 'traditional' family type as pre-industrial since it was strongly influenced by forces rippling out from the centres of industrial expansion. Emigration, for example, provided a powerful link between 'traditional' Ireland and the inter-national industrial system and was one of the forces shaping the development of family patterns in Ireland since the early nineteenth century. It provided an outlet for surplus children (i.e. those who could not be placed through marriage or inheritance in the local economy) and so made large family sizes more feasible. It yielded an important source of additional family income in the form of emigrants' remittances and so made the small family farm more viable. Both these influences helped consolidate a certain pattern of life in the small farm system and enabled it to survive longer into the twentieth century than it otherwise might have done. At the same time, as living standards rose in other countries, emigration provided what young people – and especially young women – increasingly came to see as an escape from the bleak conditions of Irish rural life. It thus had a debilitating effect on family life in rural and small town areas, particularly by reducing the marriage chances of those (mainly men) who stayed behind. So it eventually hampered the ability of the 'traditional' family system to reproduce itself (Hannan, 1979). Thus some of the effects of emigration on the 'traditional' Irish family were supportive, others were destructive, and together they limit the sense in which that system can be considered fully pre-industrial.

The traditionalism of family patterns prior to the 1950s was also modified by the growing role of the state in family matters. Ireland in the first decades of the twentieth century had already acquired some early manifestations of the welfare state, such as schemes for old age pensions (1908), health insurance (1911) and child health services (1915-1919). The national primary school system, founded in 1831, gradually brought elementary schooling into the lives of all children and their families. This central plank of modernity had manifold effects on family life (Fahey, 1992a) and had become so pervasive by the mid-twentieth century that it had become subsumed into our conception of the traditional. Some forms of state intervention were designed not to transcend but to preserve the 'traditional'. This was true not only of prescriptive measures such as the banning of artificial contraceptives in 1935 or the prohibition of divorce in the 1937 constitution, but also of such positive measures as the children's allowances scheme introduced in 1944. This was inspired at least in part by the desire to maintain the tradition of large family size, especially in rural areas (Lee, 1989,

pp. 277-85, describes how some conservative critics interpreted the children's allowance scheme as anti-family; see
also Farrell, 1983, p. 62; Kennedy, 1989 provides a general
overview of the role of government in the family in Ireland
since the 1930s).

One of the most important state influences on the family
derived from the land reform programme of the 1870s to the
1920s, the most important element of which was the Land Act
of 1903. This state-directed, state-subsidised programme
transferred ownership of the bulk of Irish agricultural land
from the landlord class to the class of small and medium sized
farmers, thereby making small property owners into the
largest class in the Irish social structure. One aspect of the
mass political campaign which had led to this outcome was
the ideological glorification of the small family farm and the
promotion of 'rural fundamentalism' in Irish culture. This
worldview included a particular set of family values which
were linked to the interests and outlooks of small property
owners (mainly male) but which promoted certain attitudes
on marriage and sexuality, gender roles, patterns of fertility
and child-rearing as valid for all classes in Irish society. The
paradox is that this conservative and 'traditional' value
system won supremacy on the back of such 'modern'
elements in the political life of late nineteenth century
Ireland as the Parnellite parliamentary party and the Land
League.

It is clear, therefore, that many 'modern' influences lay
behind the dominant 'traditional' family type of the first half
of the twentieth century in Ireland. This family type, however,
undoubtedly possessed one key 'traditional' feature – its
economic base lay in the small-scale family enterprise (farm
or small business) worked by family members. A clear
instance of the transformative effect of industrialisation on
family patterns in recent decades has been the declining
significance of this family type in favour of the urban family
type founded on wage and salary earning. Breen *et al* (1990,
p. 56) illustrate the scale of this transformation by contrasting

the occupational outlook of new cohorts of young men (aged fifteen to nineteen) in the 1920s and the 1970s:

> Over half of the cohort remaining in Ireland in the 1920s could depend on family employment that would ultimately lead to direct inheritance of the family business. By the 1970s, this would be true for less than 15 per cent of a cohort.

This shift has had many important implications for the family. Among these are the effects it had on the nature of inheritance, which changed from a focus on property to education. This in turn had consequences for the nature of parent-child relationships. The decline of small property also had effects on the structure of the household economy and on relations between men and women within the family, though other factors apart from economic change also had effects in these areas.

Education and inheritance
In the 1920s in Ireland, parents typically secured their child's economic future by passing on a farm or a business (*material* capital) – or, in the case of daughters, by securing a marriage to a neighbouring inheritor. In the 1970s they achieved the same end by ensuring their child, whether male or female, got good educational credentials (*cultural* capital). This shift in the focus of inheritance was one consequence of the growth of white-collar and professional occupations and the decline of farming and unskilled occupations in the Irish labour market, especially since the 1960s. It coincided with the rapid expansion of the education system from the mid-1960s onwards which meant that second and third-level educational credentials became the principal route of entry into the new occupations. This development is often regarded as signalling a shift from inheritance to merit as a basis for social position – who you are becomes less important than what you can do in determining occupation and thus income (Erikson and Goldthorpe, 1992, p. 6). In fact, it

actually did little to change structures of social inequality in Ireland: those with good education in the 1970s were largely the descendants of those with family property in the 1950s, just as the uneducated of the 1970s were heirs to the propertyless of the 1950s (Breen *et al*, 1990, pp. 53-69). Family background continued one of the dominant influences on educational attainment. This shows how better-off families can use their resources to capture educational advantage for their children, thus converting the external resources of the educational system into an extension of the internal resources of the family, to be preserved and transmitted across generations in the manner of a family possession.

Though education today may be broadly comparable to family property of previous generations in its economic value (that is, in its long-term income-generating potential) and in its capacity to reproduce family advantage across generations, it has some quite distinctive implications for family organisation. Most fundamentally, it reflects a shift in the distribution of resources between parents and children. Property inheritance in the western European tradition was essentially parent-centred (usually, in fact, father-centred): it gave husbands/fathers a powerful instrument of authority over their children (and, in a somewhat different way, over their wives), enabling them to command the loyalty and the labour services of their heirs-in-waiting until well into their adult years. Furthermore, the economic demand made on fathers by property inheritance was minimised by the lifetime's usage they obtained from family property before they were obliged to pass it on to the next generation. In other words, traditional inheritance was part of a system where over a life-time, as far as material resources were concerned, children gave their parents more than they received in return (Caldwell, 1980).[3]

Education, by contrast, is more child-centred and reverses the life-time net flow of resources so that, in material terms, parents give more to children than they receive in return. Children receive education in childhood and adolescence, and parents bear the cost of it in the peak years of family formation, rather than (as is normally the case in property settlements) towards the end of their active days or after they die. It thus represents a more burdensome draw on parents' resources, since it directs resources away from the household and does so before parents have had the opportunity to extract much benefit from those resources themselves.[4] In addition, western educational thought now values child independence and self-development over parental interests and control and so discourages the expectation that parents' interests should dictate the pattern of children's education or that adult children should pay their parents back for the investment in them which their education represents (Fahey, 1992a).

Education also has important consequences for sibling equality. Traditional property inheritance normally favoured the child who inherited the main holding (usually a male unless no male offspring was available), though out of a concern for fairness between children, parents often made some compensation to non-inheritors out of the household's movable assets – for example, in the shape of dowries or funding for an education or for emigration (Ó Gráda, 1988, pp. 153-75). Despite these gestures towards fairness, the property inheritance system was inherently unequal since there could only be one principal heir. Girls were at a particular disadvantage: they became main heirs only in default of a suitable male sibling and because the type of transfers they did get, such as a portion or dowry, was usually intended to transfer to a prospective husband or his family rather than to remain the young woman's personal property (Curtin et al, 1992).

Education, by contrast, is more divisible between siblings: though selective acquisition of education for certain children may occur (particularly where property is given to one child and education is acquired for the others), it is more common for families (especially non-property owning middle class families) to aim for a certain standard of education for all

218 Irish Society: Sociological Perspectives

siblings rather than a very high standard for one. Furthermore, education is a personal, inalienable acquisition, so
that, unlike a dowry, a girl's educational credentials cannot
be transferred to a husband on marriage. The expansion of
second and third level education for girls thus has significant
underlying implications for gender equality within and
without the family. These implications are not always followed
through, since gender inequalities in education may persist
and since barriers in the labour market may hamper women
from reaping the full economic benefit of whatever
educational credentials they obtain (Hannan *et al*, 1983; Pyle,
1990). However, these obstacles are somewhat less deep-
seated and less immovable than the gross inequalities in
property ownership which characterised the 'traditional'
family economy, so that rising education in the long run
provides a significant impetus towards greater equality in
gender relations inside and outside the family.

Thus, the shift from family property to education as the
principal means of reproducing social status has a profound
effect on internal family relations. It transforms children into
consumers rather than producers of family income and
advances the interests of children relative to those of their
parents. The result is to greatly increase the cost of children
to parents, in terms of effort and commitment as well as in
money. This, in turn, is a major contributor to one of the
most striking features of modern family life: the typical desire
to avoid large families among both fathers and mothers,
leading to the sharp fall in average family size which is
familiar to all western countries in the present century. This
decline has occurred later and more slowly in Ireland than in
other countries but nonetheless has been in train here more
or less continuously since the 1880s (Ó Gráda, 1988,
pp. 163-4; Coale and Watkins, 1986). Resource disparities
between males and females in the family, that is, between
siblings and between husbands and wives, tend to reduce as
property declines and education increases in economic
significance, since women generally have shared more

equally in education than they traditionally did in property. That tendency can be inhibited in many ways – mainly by the pressure on women to confine themselves to domestic roles – but it has been reinforced in others – such as the decline in marital fertility which is part cause and part consequence of women's freedom to realise the income-earning potential of their education outside the home.

The household economy

These references to the resource-equalising effects of education on gender relations within the family lead us on to consider a second set of consequences of the shift from family property towards wage labour which we mentioned above, the transformation of the household economy. A three-stage development can be identified here (see Kennedy, 1989, pp. 52-60, for a more elaborate periodisation). The first stage is the pre-industrial household economy, of which the traditional Irish farm households beloved of ethnographic studies provide a good example. Here, households are work units as well as residential units and the viability of the unit depends on the work contribution of each member. Tasks are strictly segregated by sex, with men in the fields and women in the house and farmyard. Authority too is structured by sex: the husband/father owns the property, controls the income generated from it and is the dominant figure in the household, and even non-property owning sons, while subordinate to the father, usually have a higher status than their sisters (Kennedy, 1973, pp. 51-65; Shortall, 1991). However, women work hard, often harder than the men, and the work they do as part of the farm labour unit goes much beyond the domestic tasks common to modern urban housework (Shortall, 1991).

The second stage in the development of the household economy is the classic breadwinner-husband/stay-at-home housewife economy of the industrial era. Here, the unity of the family production system is broken: men (and many single women) increasingly move into wage labour away from the family home, while married women concentrate on housework and childcare within the home. The economy thus polarises between the non-household wage sector which is dominated by men (with single women having a transient, subordinate place) and the unpaid household sector which is defined as women's, and especially married women's, preserve. The unpaid household sector loses the connections with goods and commodity production which it had possessed in the pre-industrial household economy (in the form of farm work, for example) and is directed instead to the type of intensive household services production which we associate with modern housework. Because of the decline of paid domestic service, the unpaid, familial character of housework becomes even more pronounced than before and the contrast between the 'domestic' realm and the wage economy becomes sharper. This contrast is reflected in popular and academic discourse in the labelling of housework as non-productive work and as thus less important than 'real' wage work.

In some of the more advanced western countries, the development of this stage in the household economy has been linked to the maturation of the industrial economy and its peak has been located in the decades before World War II (for the US, see Goldin, 1990, p. 12; for Britain and France, see Tilly and Scott, 1987, pp. 176-213). In Ireland, its development was slower given the absence of significant industrial development at this time. However, state policy and cultural developments actively promoted the family patterns involved, so that many of the changes occurred even in the absence of industrialisation. Bourke (1991) has traced an increasing emphasis in public policy and in popular dis-course on the kind of domesticity or 'housewifery' associated with this stage in the development of household economy in the period between 1880 and World War I. Subsequently, the restriction of married women to domestic roles was intensified by the setting up of formal legal barriers to their participation in employment outside the home.[5] At the same time, public health services promoted stay-at-home motherhood by emphasising the role of the mother in the home in safeguarding children's health (Barrington, 1987, pp. 76-80). The introduction of compulsory schooling legislation in 1926 also extended and intensified state intervention in the way parents approached a number of central aspects of child-rearing (Fahey, 1992a). All of these aspects of domesticity were reinforced by Catholic teaching on the family, which presented the family structures involved as both morally and socially right (Inglis, 1987, pp. 198-214; Mahon, 1987; Coleman, 1992, pp. 75-77). Other cultural influences of a different kind which had an influence in the same direction included the psychology of childhood – for example, the psychological theories on the damage wrought by maternal deprivation on children gained currency internationally in the 1940s and 1950s and eventually affected thinking and public policy in Ireland (Goldthorpe, 1987, pp. 46-55; O'Sullivan, 1979).

The third stage in the development of the household economy is most often defined by reference to the large-scale entry of married women into the paid labour force, or, to put it another way, the decline of full-time housework as an occupation for married women. This stage is sometimes labelled the dual-earner household economy, and above all else implies greater equality in gender roles inside and outside the home. However, the 'dual-earner' term is somewhat misleading for a number of reasons. One is that fewer households contain two adults of working age. In the UK in 1992, for example, over one household in three contained only one adult, the great majority of them without children, while less than a quarter of households were of the 'nuclear' type containing man, woman and dependent children (Central Statistics Office, 1994). Thus an important element in the development of this stage of the household economy is the decline in the average size of household to the point where many households are not even dual-person, not to mind dual-earner, and where the remaining households become so small that a full-time unpaid houseworker is either unnecessary or difficult to sustain. Another reason the 'dual-earner' label is misleading is that many of the women who are the female half of dual-earner households work part-time or for very low pay, so that the dualism in earnings, and thus in economic power within the household, is far from balanced. Many feminists have argued that, as far as symmetry in gender relations are concerned, third-stage households are much less different from their second-stage predecessors than the surface appearances would suggest.

While most western countries are dominated by third-stage households, households in Ireland are still largely in the second stage, though with signs of movement towards the third. In 1986, average household size in Ireland was the largest in western Europe at 3.5 persons per household and almost eight out of ten households contained at least two adults (*Census of Population* 1986, Vol. 3; 'adults' here include persons aged sixteen or over). In the male workforce, 85 per cent were engaged outside household-based economic activity in 1986, though the 15 per cent still in the household sector (mainly family farming) reflected an exceptional durability in that economic form by international standards (Hannan and Commins, 1992). Unpaid work in the household sector was still the principal occupation for over 60 per cent of women (Fahey, 1992b), a higher than average proportion for western countries. Although married women's participation in paid work has increased since the 1960s, it still remains low by international standards (Pyle, 1990). As a result, inequality of economic power between husbands and wives is common in Irish households (but not, it seems, to the extent that there are substantial numbers of women and children living in poverty simply because their husbands/ fathers who control the economic resources refuse to give them an adequate share to live on – Rottman, 1994).

One area of change in the workings of households which has been little investigated in Ireland is the emergence of new styles of emotional relationship. Emotional minimalism was a striking feature of family life documented by Arensberg and Kimball, especially in the way patriarchal family heads related to the other members of the family. Marriages were pragmatic alliances arranged by families where the farms of prospective husbands could be matched with the dowries of prospective wives. Questions of love or sexual desire scarcely arose, and life-long marriages were often lived through in the same atmosphere of mutual emotional isolation that they started with. The cost in human frustration and loneliness is impossible to count. By the 1970s, as Hannan and Katsiaouni's (1977) study showed, a more companionate model of marriage and of family life had taken hold among younger, progressive farmers, and the roles of husband and wife were negotiated between partners, at least to some degree, rather than being adopted wholesale from cultural prescription.

In recent years, there has been little by way of systematic research in Ireland into the affective domain of family life. Everyday observation makes clear that the emotional quality of family life today is more open, communicative and affectionate, at least as an ideal. There is also a greater willingness to define as defective families where that emotional quality is lacking, even to the point where breakup of the family (through separation of spouses, for example) is socially accepted. Beyond that, however, we know little about the precise character of emotional and sexual relations within Irish families, about social class or regional differences in that character, or about differences in the way men and women, or parents and children, experience this aspect of family life.

Crisis in the family?

The 'crisis' theme has occupied a permanent place in sociological writing on the family, with the result that a substantial 'literature of anxiety' about the condition of the family has been built up in the social sciences. Debates within this literature have tended to fall into a standard pattern. Assertions are made that the family is in 'crisis' (or in decline, in danger of collapse etc.), and these are countered by claims either that the extent of change in the family is exaggerated (things were always as bad as they are now), or that the changes which have occurred are positive rather than negative. The contrasting viewpoints of Le Play and Engels on family crisis outlined earlier in this chapter is a good early example of this recurrent pattern, while there are multitudes of examples in more recent years (see, for example, the debate on the effects of divorce on children in the *Journal of Marriage and the Family*, Vol. 55, No. 1, Feb 1993).

The repetitive, inconclusive nature of debates on family crisis could be taken to indicate that the term 'crisis' is vague and value-laden, of little use in sociological analysis, and therefore to be avoided for research purposes. At the same time, the term is hard to dismiss, if only because 'crisis' is one of those evocative cross-over terms from everyday discourse which it is impossible to avoid even if one wanted to. Furthermore, it can be used in a neutral, non-rhetorical way to refer to moments of basic structural change (shift and instability) in social systems (cognate terms include revolution, turning point etc.) – i.e. as a term of analysis rather than of anxiety.

In Ireland, the crisis literature in sociology as far as the family is concerned has for a long time focussed more on the rural farm family than on the urban family. Even in the heyday of the farm family system early in this century, an ongoing crisis of sorts was reflected in the huge numbers who were denied the opportunity to marry and found a home (Fahey, 1993). Since the 1960s, the concern with crisis in the 'disillusioned, demoralised remnant' of the farm family class has continued to outweigh interest in the urban family (see, e.g. Brody, 1973; Scheper-Hughes, 1979; Hannan, 1979), though it has been argued more recently that this research has exaggerated the extent of crisis in the farm family to some extent (Hannan and Commins, 1992).

As far as the non-farm or urban family is concerned, social research in Ireland has had little to say. As a result, the crisis theme has found expression mainly in popular debate and the media rather than in research work. News reporting of criminal violence, rape and sexual abuse within families has repeatedly shocked public opinion in recent years and has shaken confidence in the general healthfulness of family and sexual life (the Kilkenny incest case and the 'X' abortion case are but the best-known of these cases).

Apart from overtly criminal and violent perversions of family life, a number of changes has occurred in family behaviour which are by no means criminal (and by many would be regarded as morally acceptable and normal) but which have become the focus of much of the crisis debates today. Two of these in particular have attracted attention – the increase in non-marital births and the increased incidence of marital breakdown. In 1961, 1.6 per cent of births in Ireland occurred outside of marriage. By 1981, this proportion had increased to 5.4 per cent, while by 1991 it had jumped dramatically to 16.6 per cent. More significantly, 32.5 per cent of *first births* in 1991 occurred outside of marriage, compared to 15.8 per cent in 1981. Since the birth of the first child is a crucial moment in family formation, the large proportion of first births occurring outside of marriage clearly signals a substantial departure from at least the family formation process of standard family patterns. However, while the incidence of non-marital parenthood has risen, a large proportion of it has lost the extreme 'crisis' character it possessed in former years as it has become increasingly normalised within new patterns of family life. A recent study has shown that over half of unmarried mothers in the late 1980s had a close relationship with the father of the child at time of birth (Flanagan and Richardson, 1992, pp. 29-33) and there is some evidence that over half marry within five years of giving birth (O'Grady, 1992; more generally, see McCashin, 1993). The vast majority of unmarried mothers also receive extensive support from their own parents, particularly their mothers: at time of birth, 57 per cent of all unmarried mothers, and almost three-quarters of teenage unmarried mothers, actually live in their parents' homes (Flanagan and Richardson, 1992, p. 37).

The very limited quantitative evidence that is available on the incidence of marital breakdown in Ireland suggests that it is still relatively rare but is increasing rapidly. In the 1986 Census, some 40,000 people reported that they had been involved in marital breakdown, which represented a quite low 2.6 per cent of the ever-married population.[6] Even among younger age-groups, the incidence of marital breakdown as measured in this way was generally not much over 3 per cent. By 1991, the number currently separated (i.e. excluding those in second unions) had increased by over one-fifth. While the total number was still small in relative terms, it indicated a substantial rate of increase. A rising trend in marital breakdown is also suggested by social welfare data: the numbers receiving payments under deserted wives' schemes rose from over 10,000 in 1986 to nearly 16,000 in 1990, an increase of over 50 per cent in four years (*Marital Breakdown*, 1992, p. 28; Millar *et al*, 1992, p. 20; McCashin, 1993).

If Ireland is distinctive in its low incidence of marital breakdown, it is also distinctive in its prohibition of divorce. However, while the absence of divorce makes Ireland quite exceptional internationally, related trends are very much in keeping with developments in family law in other countries. For example, the *Judicial Separation and Family Law Reform Act, 1989*, introduced what in effect is a liberal, no-fault regime regarding grounds for judicial separations. The grounds for separation recognised in Irish law are now broadly similar to liberal no-fault grounds for divorce in other countries – though of course re-marriage is not provided for and regulations regarding maintenance arrangements after separation are crude and ineffective (Ward, 1990, 1993). Reform of family law, however, has to cope with the very conservative nature of the articles in the Irish Constitution on the family. At time of writing, for example, the constitutionality of the

Judicial Separation and Family Law Reform Act is being challenged in a test case in the Supreme Court. In 1986, the Irish electorate rejected a constitutional amendment which would have permitted the introduction of divorce legislation. Even at that time, however, there was evidence of wavering and uncertainty in Irish public opinion on this question (Dillon, 1993), and a re-run of that referendum is planned by the government for 1995.

A further important shift away from traditional principles of family organisation was introduced by the *Status of Children Act, 1987,* which generally aimed to eliminate discrimination against non-marital children. It placed such children on the same legal footing as marital children in regard to guardianship, maintenance and property rights, in keeping with a broad international trend towards greater recognition of the rights of all children. One implication of this development was a certain downgrading of the legal significance of marriage, since a traditional important legal function of marriage was to distinguish between legitimate and illegitimate children.

Abortion was one issue on which there seemed to be an overwhelmingly hostile consensus in Ireland in the 1980s, especially given that the electorate had inserted an anti-abortion clause into the Constitution in 1983. However, even that certainty was shaken by the details of the famous 'X' case which came before the Supreme Court early in 1992. The court ruled in favour of a fourteen-year-old girl's right to have an abortion on the grounds that her life was threatened by the suicidal tendencies arising from her pregnancy. Given that the girl had been raped by an older man who was ostensibly a friend of the family, the court's decision was widely welcomed and led to a new openness to a pro-choice points of view in Irish public debate (Kennelly and Ward, 1993). In the three-part referendum held later that year to deal with the unsettled constitutional questions arising from the Supreme Court's ruling, the electorate showed a significant shift in a liberal direction: the rights to travel abroad for an abortion and to have information disseminated in Ireland on foreign abortion services were affirmed, while a proposed new and more restrictive wording for the 1983 anti-abortion clause in the Constitution was rejected. These sudden shifts on the abortion issue illustrate how a number of hitherto unquestioned tenets of Irish family and sexual values have lost their traditional fixity and have entered a period of flux from which no new consensus has yet emerged (Whelan and Fahey, 1994).

Conclusion

The Irish experience in the twentieth century indicates that certain key changes associated with industrialisation do have profound effects on family and household patterns. The main such effects looked at here centre on the shift in the economic base of the household from the jointly operated family enterprise to individual wage and salary earning, most of which has taken place in Ireland since the 1960s. The consequences of this shift can be traced in many aspects of parent-child and husband-wife relationships and in the general economic operation of the household. However, the Irish case has other lessons too. One is the importance of the external economic environment. British and American industrialisation has had manifold effects on the Irish family since the early nineteenth century, mainly through its influence on the structure of the Irish economy and the consequent rise in emigration. A second lesson is the importance of cultural influences, ranging from the emphasis in Catholicism on traditional family morality to the assault by feminists on the oppressiveness to women of that same morality. A third lesson is the important role of the state in moulding the family as part of the infrastructure of a modern society, particularly in regard to maintaining the physical and cultural 'quality' of children. In more recent times, Irish family law and social policy has retained strong support for many aspects of 'traditional' family principles, at least in principle and sometimes in practice as well (Pyle, 1990). At the same time, a number of decisive moves away from traditional legal concepts have occurred in order to accommodate to new patterns of behaviour in family life, and there is now much greater diversity in popular views on what healthy, acceptable family life should look like.

Notes

1. In the stem family, the main family holding is inherited by a single heir (usually a son, though not necessarily the oldest). Other children are either provided with the means to set themselves up elsewhere (for example, by funding their education for a career or, in the case of women, by providing a dowry for marriage) or remain on in the main family household as unmarried assistants in the family enterprise.
2. Since the 1970s, an extensive debate has occurred on the accuracy of Arensberg and Kimball's ethnography, with some advancing a vigorous criticism and others an equally vigorous defence (see Tovey, 1992 for a brief overview).
3. The control and exploitation by patriarchal household heads of the work of their children (and of their wives) is a common theme in ethnographic and literary accounts of the Irish farm family (for overviews, see Shortall, 1991; McCullagh, 1991).The dominance of parents' interests over those of children in Irish rural family life is also reflected in the traditional ideal of children as silent and passive and in the use of corporal punishment, ridicule and a sense of fear to instil that ideal (Curtin and Varley, 1984).
4. This is true not only in terms of what parents might spend on education, either directly (in the form of school materials, books or fees) or indirectly (to provide the good home backup which is necessary to enable children to function well in school), but also in terms of the loss in household income which arises because children go to school rather than to work and because mothers stay at home to look after them.
5. The 'marriage bar' instituted in teaching and the public service in the 1930s (and widely in force in a less formal way in private sector white collar employment such as banking) was the most obvious of these barriers. 'Protective' legislation designed to safeguard women from 'unsuitable' work practices such as

nightwork and heavy manual labour also had an effect in limiting women's work roles (International Labour Organisation, 1962; O'Leary, 1987; Pyle, 1990).

6. The measure of marital status used in the 1986 Census (which for the first time included categories for various kinds of marital breakdown) may understate the true incidence of martial breakdown, but there is no hard evidence on this possibility. The marital status categories used in the census do not include any reference to informal marriage or co-habitation. This may result in an undercount of separated persons who have entered second unions and who cannot formalise those unions because of the absence of legal divorce in Ireland.

References

ANDERSON, MICHAEL, 1971. *Family Structure in Nineteenth Century Lancashire.* Cambridge, Cambridge University Press.

ARENSBERG, CONRAD and SOLON T. KIMBALL, 1940/1968. *Family and Community in Ireland,* Cambridge, Mass., Harvard University Press.

BARRINGTON, RUTH, 1987. *Health, Medicine and Politics in Ireland 1900-1970,* Dublin, Institute of Public Administration.

BOURKE, JOANNA, 1991. 'Women, economics and power, Irish women 1880-1914', *Irish Home Economics Journal* 1, 2.

BREEN, RICHARD, DAMIAN F. HANNAN, DAVID B. ROTTMAN and CHRISTOPHER T. WHELAN, 1990. *Understanding Contemporary Ireland. State,* *Class and Development in the Republic of Ireland,* Dublin, Gill and Macmillan.

BRODY, HUGH, 1973. *Inishkillane – Change and Decline in the West of Ireland,* London, Penguin.

CALDWELL, JOHN C., 1980. 'Mass education as a determinant of the timing of the fertility decline', *Population and Development Review* 6, 2.

CENTRAL STATISTICS OFFICE, 1994. *Social Trends,* London, HMSO.

COALE, ANSLEY J. and SUSAN C. WATKINS (eds.), 1986. *The Decline of Fertility in Europe,* Princeton, Princeton University Press.

COLEMAN, DAVID, 1992. 'The demographic transition in Ireland in international context', in J. Goldthorpe and C.T. Whelan (eds.), *The Development of Industrial Society*

in Ireland, Oxford, Oxford
University Press.
CURTIN, CHRIS, EOIN
DEVEREUX and DAN
SHIELDS, 1992. 'Replaying
the "match": marriage
settlements in North Galway',
Irish Journal of Sociology, 2.
CURTIN, CHRIS and
ANTHONY VARLEY, 1984.
'Children and childhood in
rural Ireland: a consideration
of the ethnographic literature',
in C. Curtin, M. Kelly and
L. O'Dowd (eds.), *Culture
and Ideology in Ireland.* Galway,
Galway University Press.
DILLON, MICHELE, 1993.
*Debating Divorce. Moral Conflict
in Ireland,* Kentucky, Kentucky
University Press.
ELLIOT, FAITH ROBERTSON,
1986, *The Family: Change or
Continuity?,* London,
Macmillan Education.
ENGELS, FREDERICK, 1884/
1972. *The Origins of the Family,
Private Property and the State,*
London, Lawrence and
Wishart.
ERIKSON, R. and J.H.
GOLDTHORPE, 1992. *The
Constant Flux,* Oxford,
Clarendon Press.
FAHEY, TONY, 1992a. 'State,
family and compulsory
schooling in Ireland',
Economic and Social Review 23,
4, pp. 369-395.
FAHEY, TONY, 1992b.
'Housework, the household
economy and economic
development in Ireland since

the 1920s', *Irish Journal of
Sociology* 2, pp. 42-69.
FAHEY, TONY, 1993. 'Full
citizenship for the next
generation', in S. Healy and
B. Reynolds (eds.), *New
Frontiers for Full Citizenship,*
Dublin, Conference of Major
Religious Superiors.
FARRELL, BRIAN, 1983. *Seán
Lemass,* Dublin, Gill and
Macmillan.
FLANAGAN, NIAMH and
VALERIE RICHARDSON,
1992. *Unmarried Mothers. A
Social Profile,* Dublin,
University College Dublin.
FLANDRIN, JEAN LOUIS,
1976/1979. *Families in Former
Times: Kinship, Household and
Sexuality,* Cambridge,
Cambridge University Press.
GOLDIN, CLAUDIA, 1990.
*Understanding the Gender Gap.
An Economic History of
American Women,* New York,
Oxford University Press.
GOLDTHORPE, J.E., 1987.
Family Life in Western Societies.
Cambridge, Cambridge
University Press.
HANNAN, DAMIAN F., and
L. KATSIAOUNI. 1977.
*Traditional Families? From
Culturally Prescribed to
Negotiated Roles in Farm
Families,* Dublin, Economic
and Social Research Institute.
HANNAN, DAMIAN F., 1979.
*Displacement and Development:
Class, Kinship and Social
Change in Irish Rural
Communities,* Dublin,

232   Irish Society: Sociological Perspectives

Economic and Social Research Institute.

HANNAN, DAMIAN F. and PATRICK COMMINS, 1992. 'The significance of small-scale landholders in Ireland's socio-economic transformation', in J.H. Goldthorpe and C.T. Whelan, *The Development of Industrial Society in Ireland.*

HANNAN, DAMIAN F., RICHARD BREEN, BARBARA MURRAY, DOROTHY WATSON, NIAMH HARDIMAN and KATHLEEN O'HIGGINS, 1983. *Schooling and Sex Roles: Sex Differences in Subject Provision and Choice in Irish Post-Primary Schools,* Dublin, Economic and Social Research Institute.

HAREVEN, TAMARA K., 1978. 'The dynamics of kin in an industrial community', in J. Demos and S.S. Boocock (eds.), *Turning Points: Historical and Sociological Essays on the Family,* Chicago, Chicago University Press.

HUMPHREYS, ALEXANDER, 1966. *New Dubliners. Urbanisation and the Irish Family,* London, Routledge and Kegan Paul.

INGLIS, TOM, 1987. *Moral Monopoly. The Catholic Church in Modern Irish Society,* Dublin, Gill and Macmillan.

INTERNATIONAL LABOUR ORGANISATION, 1962. 'Discrimination in employment or occupation on the basis of marital status', *International Labour Review* 85, pp. 262-82, 368-389.

KENNEDY, FINOLA, 1989. *Family, Economy and Government in Ireland,* Dublin, Economic and Social Research Institute.

KENNEDY, ROBERT E., 1973. *The Irish – Emigration, Marriage and Fertility,* Berkeley, University of California Press.

KENNELLY, B. and E. WARD, 1993. 'The abortion referendums' in M. Gallagher and M. Laver (eds.), *How Ireland Voted, 1992,* Dublin, Folens and PSAI Press.

LEE, J.J., 1989. *Ireland 1912-1985. Politics and Society,* Cambridge, Cambridge University Press.

LENGERMANN, PATRICIA MADOO and JILL NIEBRUGGE-BRANTLEY, 1992. 'Contemporary Feminist Theory', in George Ritzer, *Sociological Theory,* New York, McGraw-Hill.

LE PLAY, FREDERIC, 1982. *On Family, Work and Social Change,* Edited, translated and with an introduction by Catherine Bodard Silver, Chicago, Chicago University Press.

LITWAK, EUGENE, 1965. 'Extended kin relations in an industrial democratic society' in E. Shanas and G.F. Streib (eds.), *Social Structure and the Family: Generational Relations,* Englewood Cliffs, NJ, Prentice Hall.

LYON, STANLEY, 1947-48.
'Natality in Dublin in the
Years 1943, 1944, 1945',
*Journal of the Statistical and
Social Inquiry Society of Ireland,*
Vol. 18.

McCASHIN, A., 1993. *Lone
Parents in the Republic of
Ireland. Enumeration,
Description and Implications for
Social Security,* Dublin, ESRI.

McCULLAGH, CIARAN, 1991.
'A tie that blinds: family and
ideology in Ireland', *Economic
and Social Review* 22, 3.

MAHON, EVELYN, 1987.
'Women's rights and
Catholicism in Ireland', *New
Left Review* 166, pp. 53-77.

*Marital Breakdown. A Review and
Proposed Changes,* 1992.
(Pl. 9104), Dublin, Stationery
Office.

MILLAR, JANE, SANDRA
LEEPER and CELIA DAVIES,
1992. *Lone Parents. Poverty and
Public Policy in Ireland,* Dublin,
Combat Poverty Agency.

Ó GRÁDA, CORMAC, 1988.
*Ireland Before and After the
Famine,* Manchester,
Manchester University Press.

O'GRADY, TONY, 1992.
'Married to the State. A Study
of Unmarried Mother's
Allowance Applicants',
Seminar paper presented to
the Federation of Services to
Unmarried Parents and their
Children, Dublin, September
1992.

O'LEARY, EOIN, 1987. 'The
Irish National Teachers'
Organisation and the
marriage bar for women
national teachers, 1933-1958',
Saothar, 12.

O'SULLIVAN, DENIS, 1979.
'Social definition in child-care
in the Irish Republic: Models
of the child and child-care
intervention', *Economic and
Social Review* 10, 3, pp. 209-29.

PARSONS, TALCOTT and
ROBERT F. BALES, 1955.
*Family Socialisation and
Interaction Process,* Glencoe,
Ill. Free Press.

PYLE, JEAN LARSON, 1990.
*The State and Women in the
Economy. Lessons from Sex
Discrimination in the Republic of
Ireland,* Albany, N.Y., State
University of New York Press.

ROTTMAN, DAVID, 1994.
'Allocating money within
households: better off
poorer?' in B. Nolan and
T. Callan (eds.), *Poverty and
Policy in Ireland,* Dublin, Gill
and Macmillan.

SHORTALL, SALLY, 1991. 'The
dearth of data on Irish farm
wives: a critical review of the
literature', *Economic and Social
Review* 22, 4.

TILLY, LOUISE A. and JOAN
W. SCOTT, 1987. *Women,
Work and Family,* London,
Routledge.

TOVEY, HILARY, 1992. 'Rural
sociology in Ireland – a
review', *Irish Journal of
Sociology* 2, pp. 96-121.

WALL, RICHARD, JEAN
ROBIN and PETER LASLETT

(eds.), 1983. *Family Forms in Historic Europe*, Cambridge, Cambridge University Press.

WARD, PETER, 1990. *Financial Consequences of Marital Breakdown*, Dublin, Combat Poverty Agency.

WARD, PETER, 1993. *Divorce in Ireland. Who Should Bear the Cost?*, Cork, Cork University Press.

WHELAN, C.T. and T. FAHEY, 1994. 'Marriage and family', in C.T. Whelan (ed.), *Values and Social Change in Ireland*, Dublin, Gill and Macmillan.

WILLMOTT, PETER and MICHAEL YOUNG, 1960. *Family and Class in a London Suburb*, London, Routledge and Kegan Paul.

YOUNG, MICHAEL and PETER WILLMOTT, 1962. *Family and Kinship in East London*, London, Routledge and Kegan Paul.

7
Women and Informal Economic Activity in Belfast

MADELEINE LEONARD

Introduction

The notion that work equals formal paid employment continues to hold sway among political, social and economic theorists in most modern industrial societies. Such an emphasis on formal employment reinforces the idea that paid employment is the only significant form of work. This leads to a misplaced focus on the male income earner rather than the household as the basic economic unit. This chapter aims to challenge this limited concept of work by examining the economic behaviour of women in an area of high long-term unemployment in Belfast. Statistics on the labour force participation of residents from the area (Field, 1958; Boal *et al*, 1974; Doherty, 1977; Doolan, 1982) have resulted in an under-estimation of the economic activities of males and females. This is because the area is one where the formal labour market has not penetrated many spheres of human activity. This neglect is more pronounced in relation to the females in the area because of their enormous contribution to domestic work, reproduction and other forms of hidden economic activity. The chapter will illustrate how conventional definitions of active labour bias the evaluation of women as economic agents.

Active and inactive labour

For orthodox economics, active labour is labour concerned with the production of goods and services for exchange in the formal market. A monetary value is attached to these activities and this monetary value denotes their economic worth. It follows that activities falling outside the formal market are considered peripheral to the economic system. Since much of women's work remains unpaid and generally takes place outside the formal market, it is obvious that the above definition of active labour promotes the obscurity and low value attached to women's work in most societies. In order to try and redress the ideological devaluation of women's work in society, feminist and marxist theorists have emphasised the economic importance of reproduction along with production, and use value along with exchange value. While Marx himself (1967) paid little attention to use value and reproduction, focusing mainly on analysing the capitalist mode of production and the dynamics of accumulation, his followers have highlighted the role of women in providing supportive domestic work for their husbands and in reproducing the next generation of healthy labourers through bearing children. In the process, women engage in use value production, that is, the production of goods and services for immediate consumption. These goods and services are rarely exchanged through the formal market system; hence the mistaken inclusion of women among the economically inactive groups in society.

This chapter will attempt to expand on these debates by focusing on the informal economic activity of women in a specifically disadvantaged economic setting. Informal economic activity refers to paid and unpaid economic trans-actions that occur outside the mainstream market economy and are not regulated or recognised by any official agency in their counting procedures. Four different aspects of women's economic activity will be addressed: self-provisioning within the household; reciprocal transactions among friends, neigh-bours and relatives outside the household; the informal provision of goods and services for money within the community and finally, the informal selling of one's labour power to formal employers who operate outside the community. The main thrust of the chapter is to point out that a full understanding of the economic significance of women's labour necessitates that we move beyond the narrow confines of definitions which link active labour with the formal production and exchange of goods and services.

Domestic work and self-provisioning

Until recently, the routine domestic activities performed by women in the household were not taken seriously as a form of labour. During the 1970s, the so-called 'domestic labour debate' emerged and by 1979 more than fifty articles on housework had been published in British and American journals alone (Molyneau, 1979). Much of this literature was concerned with rectifying the neglect of the economic value of women within the household and challenging the associated tendency to regard women's work as secondary and subordinate to men's. A further aspect of this debate was to highlight the dubious distinction between economic and non-economic activity and active and inactive labour. The ambiguity surrounding these divisions was symbolised by the fact that domestic activities such as cooking and cleaning were classified as economic and as performed by active labour when such activities were marketed (performed for money for other people outside the household), and non-economic and inactive when they were not (Beneria, 1988).

By the end of the 1970s, the narrow concern with housework and housewives gave way to a much broader analysis of the full range of women's economic activities and the social relations in which they were embedded (Pahl, 1988, pp. 350-351). The term self-provisioning emerged to encompass the wide range of activities that takes place within the household outside of the routine chores of cooking, cleaning and looking after children (Windebank, 1991).

In the estate where this research was carried out, a survey of one in four households carried out by the author in 1989, revealed that formal paid employment was a scarce resource for both males and females (Leonard, 1994). Only 26 per cent of males in the sample had any access to formal employment. Only 22 per cent of females worked in formal paid employment. Moreover, the majority of these females worked part-time. This meant that the females in the sample fell into the traditional path of working a double-day by combining paid employment with overall responsibility for housework and childcare. In unemployed households, male unemployment did not lead to any significant re-negotiation of the gendered division of labour within the household. Women in unemployed households remained responsible for domestic duties and childcare. Unemployment increased males' leisure time, although access to leisure pursuits was severely restricted by their meagre financial circumstances. For women, poverty plus the presence of an 'inactive' partner within the household heightened the stress associated with domestic work and childcare. Women were faced with a daily economic struggle of attempting to satisfy internal family needs on a limited budget.

Both men and women engaged in a number of self-provisioning tasks within the household. However, as in the domestic division of labour, participation in self-provisioning was gender specific. Males tended to take responsibility for the maintenance and repair of dwellings. These tasks included changing light bulbs, attaching plugs to electrical items, engaging in general do-it-yourself repairs and painting and decorating. Since these tasks were carried out infrequently, male participation in all forms of household work remained negligible.

Women also engaged in various forms of self-provisioning outside their everyday chores of cooking, cleaning and childcare. Often these activities were carried out with such frequency and were integrated so closely with domestic work that they were rendered invisible as market activities. This neglect is all the more pronounced since women's self-provisioning activities often feed into the surrounding wider community.

In order to illustrate the importance of women's role in self-provisioning, I intend to focus on knitting and dress-making within households to fulfil internal family members' clothing needs. This was by no means the only type of self-provisioning work undertaken by females but it serves as a useful illustrative example. It also formed the backbone of female reciprocal favours between households, as well as providing an income-generating activity for some females. Hence, knitting and dressmaking played a key role in the economic functioning of the household at an internal and external level. This section will deal with the internal economic value of knitting and dressmaking.

In just under one-third of households, the knitting of family garments was undertaken by female household members. While items were knitted for all household members, women were particularly active in knitting garments for young children. Knitting was aimed at satisfying young children's school and leisure needs. In just under one-tenth of households, women also engaged in a wide variety of dressmaking activities. These activities were not just restricted to family clothing needs but to supplying a wide variety of household furnishings such as curtains, bed and cushion covers. Providing for these needs internally meant that scarce income could be reserved for purchasing goods and services where substitution was more difficult to implement.

Reciprocal transactions outside the household

A significant proportion of women's economic activity takes place at the community level. The recent focus on the importance of community care highlights the over-representation of women in the role of looking after others. This has led many commentators (Finch and Groves, 1983; Ungerson, 1987) to acknowledge that the term 'community

care' really means care by females within the community,
since the burden of responsibility for looking after less able
groups falls disproportionately on the shoulders of women.
Looking after the sick, the disabled and the elderly within
local communities rarely counts as economic activity, yet if
these roles were not undertaken by caring females a substantial drain on formal welfare sources of provision would
result. Beneria (1988, p. 385) suggests that the concept of
active labour should be redefined in such a way as to relate it
to human welfare rather than to processes of growth and
accumulation. Such a redefinition would clearly result in
women being catapulted to the centre stage of active labour.

Within the community where the research was carried out,
a substantial proportion of the needs of the sick and elderly
were informally met by caring females. Activities here ranged
from making meals for the sick and elderly, fulfilling their
shopping needs, reducing feelings of isolation and loneliness
and occasionally extending financial support to those in
desperate need. While these informal support mechanisms
rarely replaced the need for formal welfare provision,
nonetheless they played an essential part in meeting the daily
needs of many less able members of the community.
However, some sick and elderly members of the community
were unable to plug into these informal support systems.
Participation depended on prior friendship and association
and there were instances where sick and elderly community
members were left outside the caring networks of more able
females.

Males also engaged in reciprocal favours for other
residents in the estate. However, often male motivation for
participating in helping others was tinged with economic
rationality. This resulted in males performing favours for
those most able to reciprocate and furthered the neglect of
those unable to pay back favours such as the sick or the
elderly. This contrasts starkly with the behaviour of females
described in the previous paragraph as females tended to
assist those least able to return such favours.

The knitting and dressmaking activities discussed in the previous section were also a prominent feature of the informal exchange of goods and services between households within the estate. Just under 19 per cent of households involved grandmothers knitting for grandchildren. This not only meant that grandchildren's clothing needs could be met informally but resulted in grandmothers strengthening their relationships with extended kin living in separate households within the estate. Married daughters and their mothers were able to keep in frequent contact with one another through the informal provision of clothing items. Knitting and dressmaking also provided a way of fulfilling the social obligations attached to birthdays and Christmas. Home-made presents enabled low income households to acknowledge their perceived social commitments. Relying on the internal talents of females in this way made rational economic sense as scarce income could be redirected to areas where substitution was more problematic.

Informal provision of goods and services for money

The final two activities to be discussed in this chapter concern work which has a monetary exchange value although this remains hidden from the state. Both men and women participate in the informal provision of goods and services for money within the estate. However, the activities males and females engage in are gender specific and mirror the pattern outlined earlier. Males tend to engage in household and car repair and maintenance while females engage in knitting, dressmaking, hairdressing and selling items from mail order catalogues.

Some of the women who engage in knitting and dressmaking to fulfil their families' internal needs have turned their talents into income-generating activities. In fifteen households, a female member engages in knitting/dressmaking for monetary payment. The most common dressmaking items are christening robes, first communion outfits, wedding dresses and household furnishings. Knitters receive three main types of orders. The first is for hand knitted or crocheted baby clothes, the second is for hand or machine knitted school jumpers and the third is for Aran cardigans or jumpers. Most orders are generated within the community itself and the payment received rarely compensates for the amount of labour time involved in providing these goods.

Two of the women have turned their knitting and dressmaking skills into viable business enterprises. One woman has converted her roof space into a workshop and supplies track suits to a city-centre store. The other woman has converted a pigeon shed in her back garden into a workshop. She informally employs her two sisters and another woman from the estate to help her fulfil orders. Her husband also helps out. She has her own designer label for knitwear and her customers come both from within and outside the estate.

Four other women engage in hairdressing either from their own homes or within the homes of customers. Most requests for their services come from friends, neighbours and relatives within the estate. A further thirteen women are involved in selling goods from mail order catalogues. Forty-three per cent of households in the sample regularly purchase items from catalogues. The availability of a whole range of goods on credit, for the residents in the estate, is the primary incentive for purchasing in this manner. Toys for Christmas and household appliances were the most popular items purchased.

In all of the above ways many women engage in the informal production and exchange of goods and services within the estate. In all cases, the economic value of these activities remained invisible. The two most successful women were married to unemployed males who continued to claim family welfare benefits. As a result, their wives' economic activities remained hidden activities as far as formal labour market statistics were concerned.

The remainder of the women did not classify themselves in terms of their income-generating activities. This was partly because such activities were often sporadic and in most cases did not generate a viable weekly income. Moreover, since often one's customers were also one's friends, neighbours and relatives, this often lessened the individual woman's awareness that what she was engaging in was 'work'. Such home-based activities are often omitted from government surveys as being far too minor and insignificant to be worth the effort of identifying and counting them as jobs (Hakim, 1989, p. 481). The Family Expenditure Survey initially identified people earning small amounts from casual work such as mail order selling as self employed, but from 1982 such people have been re-classified as unoccupied. This is a further illustration of the way in which official statistics on labour market participation minimise the economic value of women's work.

Informal wage labour

The last activity I want to concentrate on in this chapter is informal wage labour. This refers to the practice of selling one's labour power informally to others who operate in the formal labour market. The practice is commonly known as 'working-off-the-books' or 'doing-the-double'. The latter term is restricted to those who work informally while simultaneously collecting welfare benefits. Because of high levels of male unemployment in the area, many married women with unemployed husbands are deterred from entering the formal labour market and hence are open to exploitation by unscrupulous formal employers seeking cheap labour. This is because married women's earnings, if formally declared, would affect the family's benefit entitlements. Like most other claimants, the unemployed are able to earn a small amount of money without loss of benefit. Earnings above this 'disregarded' amount are deducted pound for pound from benefits and therefore leave the claimant no better off. In some cases, it may leave claimants worse off as extra declared income may affect entitlement to other benefits. Since April

1985, either spouse is allowed to earn up to £15 per week before it will affect benefits, provided that the male in the household has been unemployed for at least two years. Hence welfare benefits legislation acts as a disincentive against women entering the formal labour market and encourages them to seek 'off-the-books' employment where the opportunity arises.

Twenty-four women from the estate were engaged in informal wage labour. Eight of the respondents were informally employed as shop assistants, hairdressers or waitresses. The remaining sixteen women were employed informally as contract cleaners in the city centre of Belfast. There was evidence to indicate that the contract cleaning industry deliberately seeks to employ a mixture of formal and informal workers in order to cut down labour costs and secure contract cleaning tenders (Leonard, 1993). All of the women experienced poor working conditions and were paid very low wages. Some of the sample were paid as little as £1 per hour. Because of the informal nature of doing-the-double, the productive value of this work remains unrecognised yet the women's extra income is vital to the economic survival of their households. The practice is a further illustration of the marginalisation of women's economic contributions to their families' well being.

Work and female values

Some feminists see women's attitudes to informal work as representing an alternative value system. Hoyman (1987) suggests that women's motivations for participating in household and community work illustrates their rejection of the rationalist and materialist values that characterise success in the formal economy. Throughout this chapter, I have tried to emphasise women's specific economic contributions to society. The research indicated, however, that there were significant social aspects to the various economic activities described thus far. For example, knitting for internal household members was often accompanied by chatting to friends, neighbours and relatives. Tea would be made. Conversations would centre around knitting patterns and progress to local gossip. Knitting thus provided the background whereby some of the women could emphasise their common identity. Where knitting was done without payment for outside household members, the women's motivations for engaging in this activity were as much to do with enhancing social relationships between households as fulfilling the economic needs of other households. The significance of a female culture was also evident in motivations to participate in reciprocal favours for other households. Whereas male participation was influenced by economic rationality, females tended to derive satisfaction from helping others irrespective of whether such factors would be repaid at a future date.

Lenz and Mayerhoff (1985) argue that the values women experience in their unpaid work activity can humanise the employment experience and thereby reduce the conflict between work, household and community life. Some evidence to support this observation can be derived by focusing on the values associated with economic activity where money forms the medium of exchange. Like knitting, selecting and purchasing items from a sales catalogue was also predominately a social affair. Potential purchases were discussed between customers and the operator of the catalogue. Advice from other customers and the vendor was often sought as to the suitability of a particular item. These negotiations took place in a congenial setting, in the home of either the purchaser or vendor and since this trading usually took place among friends, neighbours and relatives, then other customers were often present. On the other hand, there was some evidence to indicate that this cordial atmosphere was deliberately orchestrated by the vendor as in this relaxed atmosphere many orders were generated. Hence catalogue operators had economic incentives in enhancing the social aspects of catalogue selling.

There were significant differences in the motivations of males and females who engaged in the production of goods and services within the community for money. Many of the females interviewed placed greater value on the intrinsic satisfaction they gained from their work rather than on profit maximisation. This is most clearly apparent in the pricing mechanisms implemented by males and females. Whereas males tended to charge fixed prices for the goods and services they supplied within the community, females tended to operate more flexible pricing systems. For the females in the sample, pricing was often influenced by the social relationship between customer and vendor. The more impersonal the relationship, the more market oriented the pricing procedure became. This resulted in females often operating a two-fold pricing procedure, with friends and relatives being charged the lower of the two prices and impersonal contacts being charged the higher of the two prices. Hence, in many instances, female labour was not subject to market calculations of the value of the service or commodity.

The females who worked as contract cleaners engaged in deliberate attempts to humanise the employment experience. Since the women came from the same community and in some instances worked together in the same building, employment presented an opportunity to enhance their social relationships with each other. Morgan (1972) found that whereas men are alienated at work and seek consolation outside the workplace, women suffer such alienation at home and find some measure of satisfaction and reward from social relationships at work. For the female contract cleaners in this study, work provided an avenue for catching up on local gossip. The social relationships created by the women permeated the workplace and when individual women had to take time off work due to sickness or some family crisis, the other women pulled together to fulfil the woman's workload. This meant that the woman still received her usual pay packet, her employment was not placed in jeopardy and the cleaning contract could be successfully completed. In these ways, the exploitative aspects of the women's work experiences were diluted through their attempts to humanise the work process.

The issue of choice

The question of whether women self-select the informal economy or are pushed into it by problems in the formal economy has not been specifically addressed in this chapter. Hence, the positive stance of the previous section has to be located in the wider context of possible lack of alternative avenues for economic activity. The informal economy may be thrust upon women as an economy of last resort rather than of choice. Therefore, women's participation in the informal economy cannot be assumed to reflect their preference for informal work. It is more than likely that women are forced by a combination of economics and gender bias in the formal economy and welfare benefits legislation to concentrate on informal economic activity. Many women engage in informal economic activity out of necessity rather than choice (Hoyman, 1987). Moreover, as the chapter illustrates, the informal economy reinforces the strong division of gender roles. Men and women engage in gender specific informal economic activities and these divisions generally reflected the gender specific nature of the formal economy.

Conclusion

This chapter has sought to illustrate the ways in which women's economic activities tend to be marginalised within social and economic theory. The issues raised reflect the difficulty of drawing a dividing line between economic and non-economic activity. The research suggests that the household cannot be viewed as being isolated in the private sphere distinct from the public sphere. Both spheres are highly interconnected and have an influence upon each other. Focusing on the economic value of women's work in the household and surrounding community forces us to challenge the artificial distinction between active and inactive labour and between use value and exchange value production. Beneria (1988, p. 386) suggests that we should focus on how households 'make' rather than 'earn' a living, while Pahl (1988, p. 354) suggests that we should concentrate on the question of livelihood, broadly conceived. Adopting such a position would enable us to include household and subsistence production along with other forms of 'invisible' work in our concept of active labour. Such an approach would enable us to view women's work as economically productive and essential for the functioning of the economic system. Until we dispense with simplistic notions of work being synonymous with formal employment, women's specific economic contributions to society will continue to be undervalued or ignored.

References

BENERIA, L., 1988. 'Conceptualizing the Labour Force: the underestimation of Women's Economic Activities, in R. Pahl (ed.), *On Work*, Oxford, Blackwell.

BOAL, F. W., P. DOHERTY and D. G. PRINGLE, 1974. *The Social Distribution of Some Social Problems in the Belfast Urban Area*, Belfast: Northern Ireland Community Relations Commission.

DOHERTY, P., 1977. 'A Geography of Unemployment in the Belfast Urban Area', Unpublished PhD Thesis, Queen's University, Belfast.

DOOLAN, L., 1982. 'Elements of the Sacred and Dramatic in some Belfast Urban Enclaves', Unpublished PhD Thesis, Queen's University, Belfast.

FIELD, D., 1958. *A Report on Unsatisfactory Tenants*, Belfast, Belfast Council of Social Welfare.

FINCH, J. and D. GROVES, 1983. *A Labour of Love*, Routledge and Kegan Paul.

HAKIM, C., 1989. 'Workforce Restructuring, Social Insurance Coverage and the Black Economy', *Journal of Social Policy*, Vol. 18, pp. 471-503.

HOYMAN, M., 1987. 'Female Participation in the Informal Economy: A Neglected Issue', in L. Ferman, S. Henry and M. Hoyman (eds.), *The Informal Economy: The Annals of the American Academy of Political and Social Science*, Beverly Hills, Sage Publication.

LENZ, E. and B. MYERHOFF, 1985. *The Feminization of America*, Los Angeles, Jeremy P. Tarcher.

LEONARD, M., 1994. *Informal Economic Activity in Belfast*, Aldershot, Avebury.

LEONARD, M., 1993. 'The Modern Cinderellas: Women and the Contract Cleaning Industry in Belfast', in S. Arber and N. Gilbert, *Women and Working Lives: Divisions and Change*, MacMillan.

MARX, K., 1967. *Capital*, Vol. 1. New York: International Publishers.

MOLYNEAU, M., 1979. 'Beyond the Domestic Labour Debate' *New Left Review*, No. 116, pp. 3-27.

MORGAN, D.H.J., 1972. 'The British Association Scandal: The Effect of Publicity on a sociological investigation', *Sociological Review*, Vol. 20, No. 2, pp. 185-206.

PAHL, R.E., 1988. *On Work*, Oxford, Blackwell.

UNGERSON, C., 1987. *Policy is Personal: Sex, Gender and Informal Care*, London, Tavistock Publications.

WINDEBANK, J., 1991. *The Informal Economy in France*, Aldershot, Avebury.

8
Caring Labour and Love Labour[1]

KATHLEEN LYNCH and EITHNE McLAUGHLIN

Introduction

It is widely recognised among feminists, sociologists and social policy analysts that, in its common usage, 'work' has a very masculine and materialist bias. In traditional sociological theory, and, to an even greater degree in economics, very little attention has been paid to the specific contribution made to society by various forms of caring and love labour. In this chapter we will examine the debates that exist about the nature of work, focusing especially on two interrelated forms of work, caring and love labour. The chapter will also review the extent and significance of these forms of work in contemporary Ireland, North and South. Taking these forms of labour together, it is clear that they represent the largest work activity in which people are engaged, and it is also clear that it has been, and continues to be, women who are disproportionately engaged in them, whether in an unpaid or paid capacity.

In both parts of Ireland, women's participation in paid employment has increased dramatically since the 1960s. Most of this employment is in the services sector and thus is continuous, rather than discontinuous, with women's disproportionate participation in, and responsibility for, people work in general. However, increases in paid employment also mean that there is greater uncertainty about who has responsibility for unpaid work, especially caring. In domestic work, and some areas of personal care work, such as personal care for young children, pressures are met by the transformation of unpaid work into paid work (albeit generally at low wage rates) or the transfer of the burden of unpaid work from younger generations of women to older women. Sometimes the answer is that less time is devoted to the care work *per se*.

While certain aspects of care work can be easily translated into paid work, pressure on love labour (the labour involved in developing solidary bonds) cannot be resolved in this way. Indeed love labour itself may be competing with the demands of domestic and personal care work. As a result, the only solution is for less love labour to be performed. The implications of this for quality of life within the household, the family, the community and society generally are enormous. If a concern with quality of life is to be taken seriously, then other resolutions to this dilemma must be found. These could include higher levels of statutory support to households at lifecycle points where levels of domestic and personal care work are high, a more equal distribution of domestic and personal care work between men and women within households, and a more equal distribution of love labour between men and women within and without the household.

More significantly, perhaps, what is required is a radical review of the relationship between caring, love labour and so-called productive work. The institutional structures of our society are heavily weighted in favour of the interests of materially productive labour. There is widespread recognition that constant conflict and tension exists between the demands of caring labour and the requirements of employment or paid labour (Pichault,1984; Hertz,1986; Hoschchild, 1989).

1 The nature of work

Whether in mainstream academic scholarship in the social sciences or in the public world of policy and politics, even a brief inspection of the ways in which 'the economy' and/or 'work' is measured shows a systematic devaluation and failure to count the productive contribution made to society by women. This occurs in two ways: first, through the straightforward and direct exclusion of certain productive activity from the label 'economic' and/or 'work'; and secondly, through what appears to be the 'gender-blind' collection and analysis of information. This results in under-measurement of women's, but not men's, 'economic' contribution to society.

Classical economists make a distinction between all productive activity and a subset of activity which is called 'economic', and it is this distinction which mainstream sociology has adopted. Measures such as Gross Domestic Product and Gross National Product are calculations of the value of a country's 'economic activity'. In deciding which parts of productive activity are economic, economists draw two basic distinctions. One distinction is between activities which produce goods, on the one hand, and those which produce services, on the other. The second distinction is between activities which will result in money changing hands and those which will not. When these two dimensions overlap, four kinds of activity can be identified:

1. the production of goods where the goods are then sold
2. the production of goods where the goods are not intended for sale
3. the production of services where the services are sold
4. the production of services where the services are not intended for sale.

Examples of these kinds of different productive activities are:

1. growing carrots, for sale to a wholesale distributor

2. growing carrots, for eating by the farmer or other people in the farm household, or for bartering with other local households

3. cooking and serving carrots, and then charging people to eat them, for example in a café

4. cooking and serving carrots, and not charging people for eating them, for example, in an ordinary household.

Economists have defined the first three types of activities as 'economic' but not the last. So for the purposes of national accounts (GDP, GNP), various attempts are made to measure the first three kinds of productive activities but not the last one. This last category is, of course, dominated by 'housework' and 'caring', i.e. services performed for others without payment. It also refers to personal servicing, such as personal hygiene, which, among adults, is most often carried out by the person concerned. Among children and among adults with certain kinds of disabilities, these tasks are often performed not by the person concerned, but by someone else (for example, a mother, a spouse, a grown-up daughter). As Tony Fahey (1991) says, the 'exclusion of [housework] from the definition of economic activity is a well-known feature of conventional economic measurement.'

The result is that a much 'looser' definition of what is economic is applied to the production of *goods* than is applied to *service* work. Unlike the production of goods, only those services which are paid for are defined as 'economic', while the same services which are not paid for, are labelled 'non-economic'. As a result, the level of national output is understated since a major form of productive activity is excluded from the calculations. Estimates of the size of what is excluded range from 25 per cent to 40 per cent of Gross Domestic Product, depending on the country being discussed and the method of measurement used. Since the bulk of this contribution to GDP is made by women, at the broadest level the result is a devaluation of the productive contribution of women compared with men. From this it follows that women's productive activity will be under-measured since what is commonly measured is not productive activity but rather that subset of it labelled 'economic activity'. In turn, the conflation of the label 'economic activity' with the label 'work', means that the 'non-economic' work commonly carried out by women is not defined as work at all.

In addition it becomes impossible to ascertain changes over time in the balance between 'paid-for' and 'not-paid-for' service activities since the 'not-for-paid' have been excluded from measurement in the first place. An example of both the effect of the exclusion of 'not-paid-for' service work as 'economic', and the related problem of not being able to measure trends over time, is given by Tony Fahey (1991). By the 1930s, in the Republic of Ireland, although the number of female domestic servants had already shrunk greatly (to 85,000 from 250,000 at the end of the nineteenth century), their work still accounted for 2.4 per cent of national income. As more of this work shifted from paid-for to not-paid-for contexts, this 2.4 per cent of national income effectively disappeared.

But there is another problem with traditional ways of counting and valuing the contributions made to society by women: 'productive activity' does not include the direct physical production of people (as opposed to activities intended to maintain or sustain people) – having babies. This is of special import in Ireland which has occupied a distinctive economic niche in the Western world as the major producer and exporter of people to other Western countries. Even with this unique place in the international economic order, the physical reproductive activity of Irish women has never been 'valued' economically. Yet there is an economic trade in people – immigration and emigration flows – as well as bits of people – the trade in blood and organs. The economic value of the trade of people between countries, and of the production of these people, remains to be counted.

'Work' and 'leisure'

Men's productive activities fit reasonably well with the two-dimensional model of time used in mainstream social science research. This conventional model sees individuals making decisions about only two kinds of uses of time – (paid) 'work' and 'leisure'. Although economists do not use the word 'leisure' in its common-sense meaning, nonetheless one (homogeneous) category of 'non-work' is conceptualised as the opposite of 'work'. Most of women's productive work (the unpaid service work) is placed in the category of non-work, that is, 'leisure'. As many feminist scholars have pointed out, the result is that the complex decisions women make about the allocation of their time between several kinds of productive activities are badly modelled by this two-dimensional approach. In the Italian feminist Laura Balbo's famous analogy, women's productive lives are a patchwork of 'crazy quilting' and at the very least need to be modelled in three dimensions – paid work, unpaid work and leisure.

These productive activities are usually characterised by feminist scholars (see for example, Delphy and Leonard, 1992, pp. 20-23) as involving physical work or labour of one kind or another and the definitions and categories are task-oriented. That is, housework, childcare and informal care are conceptualised as a series of specific and discrete tasks. Once these spheres of human activity are conceptualised as made up of a series of specific tasks, it becomes possible to analyse the extent to which they have become 'commodified' – that is, taken out of the unpaid work sector and into the market place or public sector – in which case the tasks are counted as 'work' and money is exchanged for labour. Then it becomes possible to place a 'value' (or more accurately 'cost') on them and, by extension, to estimate the value of these activities which have remained uncommodified. Thus, for example, it has been estimated that in Britain the provision of unpaid informal care has a value of £24 billion (the 'cost' of the 'work' involved if it were transferred to the public sector or market place and paid for at the same rate as public sector home-help services). This (materialist) approach has been immensely valuable in demonstrating the hugely productive value of the unpaid work provided mainly by women in contemporary societies and upon which modern welfare states have built partial public welfare systems and provisions. This materialist approach is used in the second half of this paper, when we describe and critique the extent to which the welfare state has acknowledged the value of women's labour in the field of long-term care provision in Ireland.

However, despite the value and importance of the materialist approach, there are a number of problems with it. Whilst women's (and some men's) productive activities have traditionally been excluded from mainstream social science research and theory, even the inclusion of housework, childcare and 'informal' care does not include all of the kinds of 'work' which contribute to society. If we think of 'work' as the application of effort to achieve a given end, we can begin to see how a narrow focus on sets of discrete tasks masks a great deal of the kinds of 'work' involved in any social, i.e. human, context. A great deal more 'work' than the production of goods and the physical provision of services goes on in any society. This 'extra' work is what we refer to as 'love labour' and is to be distinguished from the common sense meaning of the word 'leisure' though it often takes place in the same settings and involves the same people as (common sense) leisure (Lynch, 1989, 1994). This sphere of activity is close to what has been termed, 'caring about'. What exactly it is, how to theorise and conceptualise it, and how to conceptualise the relationship between it and 'caring for' tasks or 'unpaid work' in materialist terminologies, is emerging as a new field of scholarly thought (Ungerson, 1990; Leira, 1994).

Part of this involves an examination of the difference between people work such as 'caring for' (catering for the material and other general well-being of the one receiving care) and 'caring about' (having affection and concern for the other and working on the relationship between the self and the other to ensure the development of the bond). It involves an analysis of which of the various 'caring for' tasks can satisfactorily be, or should be (from the point of view of those receiving care), divided from 'caring about' (and hence suitable for commodification), and about the extent to which 'caring about' itself can be developed within commodified 'caring for' relations. Clearly there has been a considerable commodification of 'caring for', for example in the development of both public and market childcare services and residential care facilities. The implications of this for those at the receiving end of 'caring for' need to be given much more thought than has been evident in the materialist approach. In most of the analyses to date, the 'good will' and 'altruism' of the carer has been an unnamed assumption in the research. The carer is situated as the 'giver' and the person cared for as the 'receiver'; the level of reciprocity and the nature of the power differentials in the relationship have not been problematised, be it in a family situation or in public formal care.

And the question of the divisibility of 'caring for' and 'caring about' needs fresh attention. For example, many women express 'caring about' via 'caring for' tasks (e.g. cooking for one's child, making the effort to find the kinds of food which one's elderly father likes) and hence these tasks are not always 'burdens' which one wishes to be removed; on the other hand, commodified 'caring for' tasks may yet permit the development of 'caring about' at least sometimes and to some extent.

What is being suggested in the next section is that there is a form of work which is love labour which has not been systematically addressed in the materialist analysis of care work. It involves emotional work primarily (albeit not exclusively) including both *sentient activity*, i.e. planning, organising, deciding about or with another, and *active sensibility*, which is feeling a responsibility and commitment to someone as yours, not someone else's (Mason, 1994).

2 Love labour

Love labour and emotional work

Delphy and Leonard (1992) equate emotional work with the development of solidary relations. They define emotional work as 'work which establishes relations of solidarity, which maintains bonds of affection, which provides moral support, friendship and love, which gives people a sense of belonging, of ontological strength, of empowerment, and thereby makes them feel good' (1992, p. 21). However, while emotional work may involve solidary relations, not all emotional work is of a solidary nature. Indeed one cannot draw a neat distinction between emotional work and all other work. Teaching, counselling and social work are very clear examples of work which involve a considerable expenditure of emotional energy; they have emotional dimensions to them although they are not principally emotional forms of work. In other contexts, such as in sales and marketing, emotional work is engaged in to increase productivity; displaying annoyance with workers to improve performance or smiling at customers to increase business are clear examples of emotional work which is not solidary in the business context (Hochschild, 1983). Consequently, it is important not to label activities which are solidary in nature simply as 'emotional' work. Much emotional work may not be solidary, and indeed even materially productive labour, such as producing goods on an assembly line, is not devoid of emotional involvement. The context in which emotional labour takes place and the intention with which it is undertaken, therefore, determines whether it will be solidary or not. When the intersubjective relationship is mediated by profit, gain or some other occupational, professional or instrumental goal, a solidary relationship tends to be precluded (Lynch, 1989, 1994).

Love labour therefore only refers to that emotional work which has as its principal goal the development of solidary bonds in and of themselves. It refers not only to a set of tasks but to a set of perspectives and orientations integrated with tasks. It is a feeling and a way of regarding another while relating to that person. It denotes not just the activity of thinking about people or having them on one's mind, although this may be part of it. It also refers to the very real activities of looking out for, and looking after, the other; and that includes the management of the tensions and conflict which are an integral part of solidary relations.

Because of the indecipherability of its boundaries and because it operates primarily in the affective rather than the rational domain, there is a tendency for sociologists to ignore love labour or to equate it with romantic ideology. Yet love labour occupies mental and social space. It takes energy, presence and time to undertake it. Bonds of intimacy, affection and support are not imaginary; they are real, even though the bonds may be weak at times or fraught with all kinds of tensions and contradictions. For many it is the central energy force in life.

Sociologists have tended to ignore the reality of this social phenomenon. Love labour has been taken as a given – it has been the presumed food on the table of emotional life. Its place has been guaranteed at the table by the efforts of silent people, mostly women. It has not been systematically analysed as it has not been a generative force in the domain assumptions of predominantly male sociologists.

Domestic labour and love labour
Not only must love labour be differentiated from emotional labour, it must also be differentiated from domestic work. While domestic chores such as cleaning, cooking, washing, etc., can have solidary dimensions to them, such as when a person cooks a meal in a way that pleases a friend, or when a person buys food that their child likes etc., the reality is that domestic labour is distinct from love labour. One fundamental way in which the two differ is that domestic labour involves the transformation of nature, in the sense of making or doing something to the material world, while love labour involves the transformation of persons. In addition, domestic

labour is not based on the expenditure of emotional energy, although it may well be expended as a by-product of domestic work; by contrast, love labour does essentially involve emotional energy. Domestic tasks can be undertaken alone and for oneself; they are not necessarily or essentially social in nature. Love labour is by definition relational.

Caring and love labour
The activity of caring must also be distinguished from love labour *per se*. While all love labour involves caring, not all caring involves love labour. That is to say, there are many activities which could be defined as care in a logical sense that may not necessarily involve love labour at all. For example, Waerness (1984) has identified three different types of care – personal services, care-giving work and spontaneous care. As defined by Waerness, neither personal services nor spontaneous care involve any solidary intent except in the weakest sense. The intention in both cases is to provide a personal service, not to develop a solidary bond. The distinction made by Ungerson (1983) between 'caring about' and 'caring for' someone, further highlights the fact that caring can, but does not necessarily, involve love labour. Although it is intellectually awkward to draw distinctions between caring and love labour, the distinctions are real as caring takes many forms and some of these have little to do with the development of solidary bonds. Professional welfare workers are examples of people who are taught how to care but are trained not to become emotionally involved with 'clients'. Welfare workers, be they social workers, family therapists or counsellors, do 'care for' people but their contract often specifically excludes the development of solidary bonds between themselves and those for whom they care.

While certain aspects of caring can be commodified and commercialised, including practical domestic tasks such as cooking and cleaning, and emotional work such as listening, not all aspects of the caring relationship can. The intentions or feelings of others cannot be commodified; one cannot commodify the quality of a relationship. Undoubtedly it is true that there is a growing industry in certain societies around therapy, massage, counselling, etc., which would suggest that the commodification and commercialisation of even the most intimate forms of care is possible. While these services do exist, they do not necessarily replace love and intimacy in other relationships. Mostly they exist alongside and parallel to other more intimate relationships. This point has already been noted by Waerness (1990, pp. 122-3) in relation to the public care of older people. While public care services for older people are greater than they were 50 years ago, this does not necessarily mean that people receive less care from close kin or friends; public care most often supplements informal care rather than substitutes for it. Caring is not a zero-sum activity; there is no clear limit to the amount of it that people need. Indeed, it is probably true to say that most people get less care than they would wish for. So the existence of commodified care systems, be they in the form of public care institutions or private therapy for those who can pay for it, does not mean the end of intimacy or solidary relationships; it may indeed reflect the very opposite, a demand for greater satisfaction in personal lives by having basic caring needs provided for on a contractual basis or by developing one's emotional life via therapy to enable one to have more fulfilling personal relations. One can see easily, for example, how home help with routine caring tasks could supplement other caring in the lives of older people, thereby freeing relatives for more satisfying solidary tasks.

While commodified care is essential, it cannot substitute for love or solidary relations. The problem is that one cannot provide love on a rational contractual basis like one can provide other services. As Waerness (1984) has observed, the rationality of caring is different from, and to some degree contradicts, scientific and bureaucratic rationality. There is no hierarchy or career structure to solidary relations. They cannot be provided on a hire and fire basis. There is no clear identifiable project with boundaries illuminating the path to

the realisation of the goal. Indeed, as the goal is the relationship itself, there is no identifiable beginning, middle and
end. The goal or objective is often diffuse and indefinable.

What is being suggested is that the quality of the relationship between the carer and caree changes fundamentally
when it is commodified and commercialised. It is not the
tasks of caring which of themselves make up love labour.
There are many activities which can make up an act of caring,
e.g. washing, ironing, cooking and even talking with someone
and listening to their problems, which can be, and are, paid
for in society. Once commercialised, the quality of the
relationship is one of contract either directly between the
carer and caree or between the carer and someone on the
caree's behalf, such as a child minder. It is also a financial
contract; the carer being given a wage or payment for care.
Because the context for the tasks of caring changes, the
nature of the caring relationship changes. The focus of the
relationship from both the carer and caree's perspective is
not on the development of a bond; the carer is not primarily
interested or focused on the development of the social bond
per se. And while the caree may or may not need or want such
a bond to be the focus of the relationship, she/he is generally
aware (unless they are very young for example) that the carer
is on a care contract and is therefore working primarily to
obtain a wage or payment. This is not to say that bonds and
solidary dimensions may not develop in the contract caring
relationship, but these are incidental rather than integral
elements in the relations. Whether or not they develop
depends on the particularities of the care context and of the
personalities involved.

The reality of social life is that one cannot pay someone to
love someone else; one cannot pay someone to make love to
one's partner and claim that this is a substitute for oneself;
one cannot pay someone to hug one's children and pretend
that this is 'one's own hug'; one cannot pay someone to visit
or talk to a friend in hospital and pretend that the visit is from
oneself. If the solidary dimension of the relationship is

missing then the character of the relationship changes. Those aspects of the relationship which boost confidence, inspire strength and encouragement, give people a sense of belonging, and a sense of being wanted and needed and of being free – these cannot be commodified; they can only exist in a context where there is some choice or decision to care and commit oneself for the sake of the relationship and not for payment. This is not to deny the reality of the 'compulsory altruism' which has been a feature of so many women's lives, nor is it to suggest that those who care should not get paid for certain types of caring work. As Qureshi (1990) has pointed out, payment for caring often actually has a positive rather than a negative effect on the caring relationship, as it makes the relationship between the carer and the person being cared for more reciprocal and more equal.

In outlining the parameters of love labour, we are not trying to romanticise it. Furthermore, there are several aspects of caring activities which can be commodified and commercialised and without which solidary relationships will survive; indeed, it could be argued that there is more time for the core activities of the love relationship if certain activities related to caring are commodified, or even ignored, such as cleaning or washing to high standards of perfection. What is being suggested is that there is a clearly identifiable dimension of social behaviour which involves the production and reproduction of social bonds of a solidary nature, namely love labour. Because it involves a considerable expenditure of energy over time, and because it produces a commodity, namely a supportive, enhancing and empowering relationship, it is a form of work. 'Solidary labour occupies a similar structural role in relation to one's affectual life that material labour occupies in relation to the natural world. Just as use-value-creating-labour can be seen as "an eternal natural necessity" mediating between "man and nature" (Marx, 1976, p. 133) so love labour is also an eternal necessity mediating human beings' relations to each other as affectual entities' (Lynch, 1989, p. 8).

Love labour, passivity and power
When love labour is defined as work, there is a real danger that the person at the receiving end of the love labour is seen as a passive product to be moulded and serviced in a non-reciprocal relationship. The second danger, and the one which has been clearly identified by feminists, is that one eschews the question of power when one focuses on the solidary aspect of human relationships.

Love labour is not like materially productive labour as originally conceived. It is not about the moulding and mani-pulation of raw materials to create some desired end product. Indeed, even in the material sphere, raw materials cannot be seen as simple objects for human manipulation and use. They constitute life forms which have ontological and ecological functions irrespective of human intervention.

Love labour involves reciprocity in most cases, although there may be some rare cases where one or other party cannot respond or reciprocate. One of the key factors here is that the reciprocal character of the love labour relations may not be self-evident at any given moment, but it is evident over time. We know from socialisation theory in particular, that social relations are not one way: even though one party may contribute more to establishing, maintaining and influencing the flow and character of the relationship at any one time, they rarely control the relationship completely or indefinitely. So it is in love labour relations, even though one party may give more to the relationship at any given time, the formation and development of the bond means that there will be some contribution from both sides.

While friendships and solidary relationships can and do survive periods of separation and detachment, periods in which no time and energy is invested in them, they cannot survive like this indefinitely, especially if the time and energy invested in the development in the bond was limited prior to the separation or detachment in the first place. While we are not suggesting that reciprocity is perfect especially in highly unequal situations in terms of power and resources, what is being suggested is that there is a reciprocal dimension to solidary relations even in unequal power situations.

Women, love labour and equality
There is little doubt that the focus on 'love' as a phenomenon can serve as a distraction from the fact that women are the ones who do most of the loving and the caring, and that it is women's unpaid domestic and love labour which reproduces men's power, which men use in turn to further exploit women. However, there is a need, not only to focus on how women are exploited in loving and caring relations, as has been done by Pateman (1988) and Delphy and Leonard (1992) for example, but also to explore the subjectively situated meanings of these relations for women, men and children. It is important to understand how it is that the subjective understanding of a relationship can be one of love and care, while in structural terms the person who loves and cares is being exploited. Even to understand how exploitation continues, it is essential to examine how relationships are subjectively experienced. By not taking account of the view of the oppressed, one may well be ignoring the very reality that matters in terms of ending exploitation. To analyse love labour relations or caring is not to ignore inequality. In fact, the opposite is the case: if love relations are undertaken continuously in an exploitative context, then it is necessary to explore the ways in which this can be changed, and this means exploring the subjective reality of relationships and how intervention can occur at this level.

Although it is undoubtedly true that women do most of the caring in society, and it is very likely that they are also the people who exert most energy in love labour, men are involved in these relational activities too and the labour involved cannot be simply defined as women's work. It needs to be theorised, as it were, from all sides. Women do not have a monopoly on the creation of solidary bonds in society.

3 The sexual division of labour in Ireland

In this section we return to the more usual materialist analysis of women's unpaid work. The reason for this is because there has been no attempt to document and analyse the nature and extensiveness of love labour.

The differences between women's and men's productive work in Ireland are fourfold: (a) far more women than men spend time on housework and caring; (b) far fewer women than men are employed, especially full-time; (c) men and women in employment are segregated into very different kinds and levels of occupations; (d) employed men earn much more than employed women. There is insufficient space here to discuss all four of these fully and (b), (c) and (d) are well documented elsewhere (for example, see Callan and Wren (1993) and Morrissey (1991) on wage differentials South and North respectively, and Callan and Farrell (1991) and McWilliams (1991) on employment rates South and North respectively). In this section we focus on (a) above, namely gender differentials in caring and domestic work.

The majority (53 per cent) of adult women in the Republic of Ireland are homeworkers and therefore mostly unpaid. The comparable proportion of adult men who are home-workers is a meagre 0.5 per cent. More rigorous analysis of the nature of women's work within the household is not possible because the care work and domestic work under-taken in the household is not counted or documented in any official statistics or most survey data. The analysis of the household as a unit has meant that work within it is both analytically and statistically invisible. Moreover, there have been no major time-budget studies of domestic work, care work or love labour within the household. The result is that the analysis here has to be confined to those areas where research has been undertaken.

In the North, a study of women's working lives (Kremer and Montgomery 1992), provided some data on the 'caring for' tasks involved in childcare and housework. Among 71 per

cent of couples, the woman carried out all or most of the
housework, with only 26 per cent reporting equal sharing of
housework. Among 60 per cent of couples, childcare was, or
had been, the sole or main responsibility of the mother.
Between a quarter and a fifth of fathers had not carried out
the basic childcare tasks of washing or bathing their children,
changing a nappy, getting up at night to attend to a child, or
reading to their children, even once in their parental careers
(Montgomery 1992). Although sharing of both housework
and childcare was more likely when women were in full-time
employment (but not part-time), even so, among 40 per cent
of full-time working couples, childcare was solely or mainly
provided by the woman, and in 58 per cent, housework was
solely or mainly provided by the woman. In addition,
Montgomery notes that men's participation in housework
and childcare when the man is unemployed, though higher
than in couples where the man is the sole earner, is lower
than in couples where both are employed full-time, and tends
to decline as the duration of unemployment increases.
Leonard's (1992) research also confirms this finding.
Although there is no national study of the division and
allocation of tasks within the household in the Republic of
Ireland, studies such as those of Mahon (1991) and a small
study by Foley (1994), indicate that women still have primary
responsibility for the care of children even when they are in
full-time employment. There is little reason to believe therefore that the patterns of women's work in the household are
any different in the South compared with the North.

In addition to what is normally thought of as women's
unpaid 'domestic work' and 'caring for' tasks, women are also
more likely than men to be engaged in what has become
increasingly known as 'informal care'. This refers to the
unpaid labour involved in providing domestic and personal
care services to adults with impairments in need of assistance
to perform activities of daily living (ADL) such as shopping,
cooking, cleaning, personal hygiene, toileting and mobility.
The level of need for such assistance in any society tends to

rise when the proportion of older people in the population rises. Old age and need for personal assistance are by no means synonymous, since there are many adults of working age and children who have impairments which result in a need for personal assistance, but it is true that the incidence of such incapacities rises with age and becomes prevalent among the older elderly (that is, those over age 85).

There is a danger when writing about caring and care needs that those who are cared for are cast in the role of a 'social burden'. As O'Donoghue (1993, p. 16) points out in her study of severely disabled young adults: 'There is no absolute line between carer and cared for, and perhaps this is clearer to women than men. Everyone is dependent for some period of their lives; everyone therefore should have an interest in decent, non-exploitative care.' In the discussion of 'informal care', therefore, it must be remembered that caring and being cared for are fluid states and it is possible to occupy both roles at once. Fallon (1993, p. 62), for example, noted that older women with physical care needs, living with their daughters who provided assistance with these needs, nevertheless acted as carers for their grandchildren. Such double roles, of caring and being cared for, are much more likely for women than for men. In addition, while O'Donoghue is right to point out that everyone should have an interest in decent, non-exploitative care, in fact, non-exploitative care would be much more in women's interests than men's. Women are the majority of older people needing assistance with the activities of daily living and women are the majority of those who provide such assistance, often in addition to their childcare work, or very soon after their children have grown up.

Whenever and for whomever care needs occur, there are many ways in which such needs for personal assistance can be, and have been, met: through residential care facilities (old people's homes, nursing homes, etc) and through domiciliary services (home helps, meals-on-wheels, etc), either of which may be provided by central government, local authorities or voluntary organisations, as well as by unpaid individuals within family networks. In the South and North of Ireland, there has traditionally been a relatively high rate of residential/institutional care; for example, in the South, 8.5 per cent of the over 65s in 1986 were in residential care. At least part of this relatively high level of residential care is due to Ireland's traditionally low marriage rate (Glendinning and McLaughlin, 1993). About a quarter of men and women over 55 in Ireland have never married, compared with about a tenth in other EU countries. Single childless people are an important group because, they are the most likely to provide informal care to others (the single son or daughter in their 50s caring for one or both of their older parents) (see Qureshi and Walker, 1989, and Finch and Mason, 1990, for studies of the 'rules' by which individuals get 'selected' or 'select themselves' for care-giving). On the other hand, they are also the least likely to be provided with family care when they need it because they lack adult children of their own and/or a spouse.

High rates of residential care may also result from low levels of domiciliary services. In the Republic, meals-on-wheels, home help services, rehabilitation services and training centres for non-elderly physically disabled people, day centres and visiting schemes, clubs and holidays are all offered by the voluntary, not the public, sector. A National Council for the Elderly study showed that very few people with needs for assistance received any services: 'Domiciliary services ... are virtually non-existent being received by just 3 per cent of the elderly' (O'Connor and Ruddle, 1988, p. 129).

Most of those in the study who had requested either home-help or respite care did not receive either: 'In Ireland most of these domiciliary services are delivered by voluntary organisations and are not evenly distributed. As yet few relief or respite care services are available – only 9 per cent of carers received short-term relief/respite' (O'Connor, 1992, p. 31).

The only services which are widely available are medical –

for example, from the family doctor (80 per cent) or a public health nurse (47 per cent). In the absence of collective provision, either from the voluntary or statutory sectors, the labour involved in meeting care needs falls to families and, within families, to women.

The extent of care needs and care labour
One way of estimating how much of this kind of labour exists is to examine levels of need for personal and domestic assistance among relevant sub-populations and compare this with the public provision of such assistance. The gap between the two is, in most cases, filled by the informal or unpaid labour of individuals. It is precisely because this kind of labour is not recognised in official statistics of productive activity that indirect estimates of the amount of such work being performed are necessary.

In the North, an estimated 17.4 per cent of all adults have some level of disability (compared with 14 per cent in Britain, for example), though not all of these lead to a need for personal assistance. However, 5.4 per cent have extra personal needs, 11.3 per cent have mobility impairments, 3.8 per cent intellectual functioning and behavioural impairments (e.g. senile dementia), all of which will require some level of personal assistance. People aged 60 or more account for nearly two-thirds of disabled people. Among those aged 75 or over, the rates for the kinds of disabilities noted above rise to 39 per cent with personal care needs, 62 per cent with mobility impairments and 22 per cent with intellectual functioning impairments (McCoy and Smith, 1992). In the Republic, information is available on older disabled people only. O'Connor *et al* (1988) found that from a population of 341,500 older people (all 65 or over) not in residential care, an estimated 66,300 (19 per cent) had care needs of some kind. In rural areas, 24 per cent of older people were receiving some care while 13 per cent in urban areas were (national average 19 per cent). Subsequently, O'Connor (1992) has revised these estimations upwards. Taking physical and mental needs together, O'Connor (1992) estimates 17 per cent of older people to be very highly dependent and 22 per cent highly dependent. Six per cent of older people at home were permanently bed-ridden and 8 per cent temporarily bed-ridden; 41 per cent could not leave the house without help and 17 per cent were permanently housebound. Overall, 8 per cent were highly dependent in that they were both doubly incontinent and bedridden and a further 10 per cent exhibited two of these three impairments; 15 per cent showed symptoms of dementia continuously and another quarter to one third showed these symptoms occasionally. Six per cent of those cared-for at home no longer recognised family members (O'Connor, 1992, p. 16).

These levels of care needs both North and South are high relative to other European countries (especially with regard to whether a person is bed-ridden), perhaps reflecting generally lower health standards in Ireland compared with her better-off European neighbours. Given low levels of domiciliary services, this means a high volume of informal care labour is required if needs are to be met. The amount and nature of care labour varies greatly, from keeping an eye out for an older neighbour, cutting the grass and collecting the pension, to providing total care and supervision to a bedridden doubly-incontinent person with advanced senile dementia. The demands, emotionally and in terms of time, at the two ends of this continuum are very different and it is towards the 'total care' end of the continuum that informal care is likely to result in lower participation in employment, reduced incomes, and mental and physical health difficulties, for the carer.

The severe and adverse effects that a lifetime of unpaid caring can have on women's income has been recognised in the Second Commission on the Status of Women Report (1993, p. 83). It recommended, for example, that ideally: 'PRSI (Pay Related Social Insurance) contributions for retirement/old age/survivors pensions payable by married persons should provide pension cover for both spouses irrespective of whether the income is directly earned by one or both spouses.' As a minimum it recommended an 'amendment of the Social Welfare Code to allow home-makers to make voluntary contributions in respect of years spent caring for pre-school children, the elderly or disabled.'

Smaller-scale studies of informal caring *per se* offer further evidence on the extent and effects of informal caring among men and women, and confirm that informal care, especially where it conflicts with opportunities for earned income, is more likely to be provided by women than men. In the North of Ireland, 9 per cent of all men but 14 per cent of all women were providing some level of assistance to others in 1985 (McLaughlin, 1992). In the South, 70 per cent of older people receiving care were helped by members of the same household, and in the majority (78 per cent) of these households, the carers were women (O'Connor *et al*, 1988; O'Connor and Ruddle, 1988). Co-resident care (i.e. where the person needing help and the person providing informal care live together) is particularly important because high levels of informal care-giving usually necessitate living together and it is high levels of informal care labour which are likely to involve substantial material costs.

Co-resident carers, and other carers who provide high levels of care, are disproportionately female. Table 1 shows that in the Republic, nearly half (44 per cent) of co-resident carers of older people were daughters or daughters-in-law, while only 16 per cent were sons. Similarly in the North, the majority (65 per cent) of female carers care for their own or their husband's parents (McLaughlin, 1992). It is only where one spouse is caring for the other that sex imbalances begin to even out, and in these situations, usually both spouses are over pension age. The result is that women are likely to provide care to a range of people across the generations – parents, parents-in-law, siblings, as well as spouses – whereas men are likely to provide care to their own wives. This, in turn, means that women are more likely than men to provide care while they are of working age, and therefore that women are much more likely than men to forego earnings from paid employment in order to provide care.

Table 1:   **Relationship of co-resident carers to older cared-for people** (1985, Rep. of Ireland)

	%
Spouse	24
Son	16
Son-in-law	0
Daughter	30
Daughter-in-law	14
Other relative	14
Non-relative	2

Source: Tables, 3.2, 4.2, O'Connor *et al,* 1988

One interpretation of the evidence on sex imbalances among informal carers could be that intergenerational care (i.e. between parents and their grown-up children) rests upon patriarchal 'familiar exploitation' to use Delphy and Leonard's (1992) phrase. When an unmarried 'child' provides care to their elderly parent/s, there is little difference between the sexes (53 per cent of such carers were female and 47 per cent male in O'Connor and Ruddle's study, 1988). But when married 'children' are called upon to provide elderly care, sex imbalances are considerable. Married women are likely to provide care to their own parents and their husband's parents, whereas married men are unlikely to provide care to their own parents and virtually never provide care for their wife's parents (the sons providing co-resident care for elderly parents in Table 1 were almost all single men). Seventy per cent of all male carers in O'Connor and Ruddle's study (1988) were not married compared with 25 per cent of female carers, and male carers who are married are usually caring for their spouses, not their parents. The sex imbalance among married carers, and especially the prevalence of care for their husband's parents by married women, could then be viewed as reflecting the appropriation of married women's labour by their husbands upon marriage. This is, of course, a central theme in theoretical discourse on patriarchy (Delphy and Leonard 1992), though the way in which (married) brothers as well as husbands benefit from this appropriation of married women's labour has not yet been theorised adequately.

The extent to which some siblings benefit from the informal care provided by another is underlined by the absence of support and assistance provided by others in family networks to the main informal carer. Despite a certain national and cultural pride taken in the idea and vitality of extended family support in Ireland (McLaughlin, 1993a), support for carers from other people in family networks, particularly siblings, is not extensive. In O'Connor *et al*'s study, for instance, the majority of carers had siblings who lived in other households (81 per cent), but 30 per cent of them rarely or never had a visit from these sibling/s. Only 17 per cent were visited by their siblings more than once a week. In addition, 48 per cent of carers received no practical help from family, friends or neighbours and help with personal care tasks specifically was rarely or never given. (See St Ledger and Gillespie, 1991 and McLaughlin, 1993a, for similar findings in the North.)

Unpaid labour and incomes
Informal care for other adults, as with childcare, can have substantial material opportunity costs: loss or restriction of employment (for example, reduction of hours at work, fewer opportunities for overtime, restricted career development and promotion); loss of pension rights; reduced income and increased expenditure. There may also be non-material costs such as social isolation, psychological stress, and physical ill health, but in this section we are focusing on material costs. The extent of material costs will vary depending on how old

the carer was when they began caring, the intensity, nature and level of the care provided, and the extent to which care is shared with other informal carers and the welfare state (through domiciliary services or day-care for the disabled person needing care). The largest cost to individual carers will occur if they do not return to paid employment because of their caring responsibilities for a disabled or older person. In Britain, the 1985 General Household Survey showed that carers who provided high (20 to 49 hours a week) or very high (50 or more hours a week) levels of care were less likely than other carers, or the general population, to be in employment, particularly full-time employment (see Table 2).

Table 2:   **Employment status by amount of care provided**
(population under pension age, 1985, GHS, Britain)

Employment status	Carers				
	Total %	All Carers %	<20hrs %	20-49hrs %	50+hrs %
Employed full-time	52.0	44.0	48.0	36.0	21.0
Employed part-time	15.0	20.0	20.0	22.0	12.0
Not employed	33.0	36.0	32.0	42.0	67.0
Base		1827	1467	180	180

Sources: Table 2.9 Green, 1988 and Table 3.2 McLaughlin, 1991

Comparable data on hours of care provided and employment status for Ireland are not available. However, in the Republic, the National Council for the Elderly study found that only 16 per cent of all carers were employed (although 77 per cent had been at some time) and 39 per cent of employed carers were working part-time, a much higher proportion than in the general population (7 per cent). Similarly, in Northern Ireland, a smaller study of women's working lives (McLaughlin, 1992) showed that high levels of informal care among women are associated with both higher rates of part-time work and lower employment rates.

Although associations between caring and increases in part-time employment rates and lowered employment rates are reasonably clear from the data, direct causality cannot be inferred. It may be that it is women whose labour market attachment is already 'weak' (probably because they have previously been at home providing child care) who find themselves 'selected' or are self-selected from within the family circle to fulfil the role of carer. Qureshi and Simons (1987), Qureshi and Walker (1989) and Finch and Mason (1990) in Britain have all demonstrated the existence of 'a systematic set of rules for deciding who should care for older people between available network members' (Qureshi and Walker, 1989). The closeness of kinship ties, gender, marital status, proximity (in same house, in house close by, or in distant separate house), strength of labour market attachment and extent of other caring commitments, for example, for young children, all interact to produce a hierarchy of expectation and obligation within family circles. In relation to labour market attachment specifically, an unmarried son or daughter who is, and has been, in stable employment will not be likely to provide care for a dependent parent. In contrast, a married daughter, or even daughter-in-law, whose children are no longer highly dependent, and who has either not yet returned to the paid labour market or who has returned in a part-time capacity to a relatively low-status, low-paid job, is a likely candidate. On the other hand, an unmarried son or daughter who is unemployed is more likely to provide care than a married daughter who is in a full-time 'good' job or who has substantial childcare commitments. With regard to gender specifically, an unemployed son is less likely to provide care than his sister if she is also unemployed. A combination of marital status, previous labour market participation, and other 'family duties' leads to the scenario whereby married women are particularly likely to provide care for their own, their siblings, and their husband's, parents.

Although it may not be the case that the majority of carers actually give up a full-time well paid job in order to provide high levels of care, providing large amounts of unpaid care will inevitably lower opportunities for employment and hence earned income. For married women, informal care becomes intertwined with the previous employment and income effects of providing childcare, and is part of the reason why middle-aged and older women are disproportionately likely to have no or low personal incomes as well as low household incomes. Data on the personal incomes of married women is difficult to obtain because of the orientation of official surveys to 'household' or 'tax/benefit unit' incomes and thus the merging of couples' incomes. With respect to carers' household incomes in the Republic, O'Connor *et al* (1988) found that only a quarter of carers had household incomes of IR£200 or more gross per week, even though in 47 per cent of cases there were four or more people in the household. Clearly per capita income was very low in most cases. In the North, an analysis of household incomes, weighted for differences in the numbers of adults and children in each household, showed that, for example, in the category of households with between 1.5 and 2.5 (weighted) 'adults', only one out of fourteen informal carers, providing 30 or more hours of care a week, had above average household incomes, compared with 45 per cent of all informal carers and 40 per cent of non-informal-care-giving households (McLaughlin, 1992).

Care labour and social policy
In both the North and South of Ireland, the bulk of care labour is performed by women, in an unpaid capacity. This has negative effects on the employment and earned incomes of working-age women. At present, domiciliary services for disabled and older people, and publicly subsidised or provided childcare facilities, in both the North and South of Ireland, are at lower levels than in other European countries (see Glendinning and McLaughlin, 1993; Hinds, 1991; Moss,

1988). There are, however, other ways in which welfare regimes can share in the costs of this production of welfare. For example, employment policies could address the needs of women and, to a lesser extent those of men, who are seeking to combine care of severely disabled adults or young children with employment. And tax and social security systems can be used to provide income protection and maintenance for women or men who are out of the paid labour market altogether because of caring responsibilities. These, then, are other ways in which the costs of welfare production can be shared between individuals and the state.

Some debate on the kinds of measures necessary to bring about an increase in sharing between the state and individual women with regard to childcare has taken place (McKenna, 1988, and The Dept of Equality and Law Reform, 1994). However, these have been primarily concerned with examining childcare service provision for employed parents. Ireland's membership of the European Union has led to improvements in the provision of maternity rights and benefits, although little has been achieved in terms of longer 'protected' breaks (care leaves) from employment. In the North, women receiving child benefit can also apply for home responsibilities protection which reduces the number of years of national insurance contributions required to qualify for the state retirement pension. Neither the North nor the South, however, provide income maintenance to women who are out of employment because of childrearing. Taken together with low levels of publicly-provided or subsidised childcare services, the degree of sharing of the costs of raising children between the state and mothers remains low.

With respect to informal care for disabled and older adults, there has been no debate on the need to reform employment policy and law to allow protected care leaves from employment. Nothing comparable to maternity rights exist in other fields of care. In neither the UK's nor the Republic of Ireland's tax systems are there provisions for the financial consequences of informal care-giving, whether loss of earnings, the extra expense of providing a home to a disabled relative, or the costs of employing additional help, variations of which exist in a number of other European countries (see Glendinning and McLaughlin, 1993; Evers *et al*, 1994). On the other hand, both countries (i.e. the UK with respect to Northern Ireland, and the Republic of Ireland) have introduced limited social security provision for informal carers. The reasons behind the development of these social security provisions are complex and provision in the North differs greatly from that in the South. In the South, social security provision targeted at the costs of informal care was introduced in 1968, and pre-dated similar developments in other European, including Scandinavian countries (Glendinning and McLaughlin 1993; Evers *et al*, 1994). The prescribed relatives allowance (PRA) was introduced apparently in response to concern about high rates of residential care among elderly and disabled adults and was paid to the person needing care, rather than the relative providing it. This allowance therefore operated along a 'logic of the gift' (Joel and Martin 1994), in that it was assumed that if a person needing care had money attached to their care needs, they would be more 'attractive' to other family members, who might be motivated to form a joint household with them, and provide informal care in return for such money as the person with care needs gave them, either directly or through the household 'pot'. It was not assumed that the person with the disability or care needs could use this money to hire someone of their own choice as it was set at too low a level and named as a relatives allowance not a personal assistance allowance.

The PRA allowance was hedged around with substantial eligibility criteria, and it was available only to single women and male carers who could not work because they were caring for a disabled relative with whom they shared a household. The allowance was not paid for married women's services as it was assumed that 'they would not normally be in paid employment and could not, therefore, lose income by providing care' (O'Connor, 1992). It was also assumed that married women did not require an 'incentive' to provide care services to family members, since that was deemed to be the natural duty of married women. Such a view was and is still enshrined in the Constitution (see Connelly, 1993 for a more detailed commentary on this). The level of the allowance was much lower than benefits paid to all other categories of social security recipients and could not have provided basic income maintenance for informal carers. Not surprisingly, then, the number of people receiving a PRA was both small and in decline from its introduction until its end in the late 1980s (down, for instance from 4,169 in October 1976 to 2,067 in March 1983). Overall, only 4 per cent of the carers in O'Connor *et al*'s (1988) study benefited from this provision and more than half of those who applied were refused (Noonan, 1983).

In terms of sharing the costs of unpaid caring between individuals and the state, the PRA was inadequate owing to the low extent of coverage, mainly caused by the exclusion of married women from eligibility, and the low level of payment offered. Even if the allowance was received by the cared-for person, it was up to her/him to pass all or some of the allowance to the carer, and of course this did not always happen. While the payment of the allowance to the older/ dependent person could be seen as a recognition of their rights, it did not really give the person any choice about the person who would care for her/him as the rate of pay was too low and the carer had to be a specific co-resident relative. The PRA did little for the independence of the family-based carer either. It did not represent an attempt by the state to recognise the value of the productive welfare activity of informal carers. In sum, the majority of carers in Ireland had no incomes of their own, or relied on other social security benefits, despite the existence of the PRA.

If the carer and the person being cared for are living as part of a larger family unit, the carer is deemed to be

part of that unit and supported by it. She is not entitled
to any social welfare benefit even if without her care the
relative would have to be admitted to a home or a
hospital. She cannot claim unemployment benefit or
unemployment assistance because she is not 'available
for work'. Therefore unless she has private means
(highly unlikely) or is over 58 and can claim the social
assistance allowance for single women, she will not have
any income other than whatever other family members
are able or choose to give her. Most try to earn some
money by knitting, making jam, giving music lessons etc.
The amounts earned are small, often spasmodic, but 'to
have a few pounds of my own' is highly prized (Noonan
1983, p. 5).

Thus despite the efforts of the Single Women's Association
(set up in 1973 to represent the needs of single women
carers), and the existence of the PRA, the needs of carers in
Ireland remained largely unmet. In 1981 Irish carers were
described as a 'victimised and forgotten group in our society'
by the Council for the Status of Women. By the mid- to-late
1980s, however, the climate of public discussion had
changed. There was public discussion of the needs of carers
for income in their own right, and various cases where the
PRA was not passed on to the carer/helper were publicised,
and there was some public pressure for a better deal for
informal carers which contributed significantly to the
replacement of the prescribed relatives allowance by a carers
allowance. Although this informed the government's
decision to pay the carers allowance directly to the carer
rather than to the cared-for person, the carers allowance, like
the PRA, is primarily a measure intended to promote
informal care and lower residential care admissions among
low-income families (Glendinning and McLaughlin, 1993).
As such it is not seen by government as a benefit based on a
concept of social rights, as unemployment benefits or
retirement pensions are. The carers allowance was IR£53 a

week in 1992 but it is means tested. While the carers allowance is generally regarded as an improvement on the prescribed relatives allowance, problems remain with both the amount paid and the conditions of eligibility.

Just over half of the 10,000 claims for the carers allowance which had been made by May 1992 were unsuccessful (McLaughlin, 1993b). The most significant reason for unsuccessful claims from working-age carers is that (despite very low levels of employment among carers in Ireland), the carer has failed the couple-based means-test. The means-tested nature of the benefit has been under considerable public debate since the introduction of the carers allowance. Public, and to some extent civil service, expectations at the time the allowance was introduced were that generally non-employed married women carers would get the allowance, whereas they had been ineligible for the PRA. However, the government's decision to introduce the CA as a means-tested benefit has meant that this is so only if husbands are unemployed or on other benefits, or possibly on exceptionally low wages. The result has been that very small numbers of informal carers, and married women in particular, have proved to be eligible for the CA, contrary to public expectations. This has resulted in a much more critical political debate about the allowance than seems to have been anticipated by government, who clearly underestimated the extent of public opinion in favour of independent, as-of-right, incomes for married women engaged in substantial levels of informal care-giving.

Both the means-tested nature of the carers allowance and the level of the allowance are the result of the location of the benefit within the category of social assistance. The carers allowance is deemed not to be employment-related, and hence insurance-based, despite the research evidence that most carers (for example, 77 per cent in the National Council for the Elderly study) have been in paid work previously. The Irish social security system has three types of benefits: universal (e.g. child benefit); contributory (on the basis of

PRSI   pay related social insurance contributions); and the residual category of social assistance (all means-tested). As in other European countries, the system shows a preference in terms of level of benefits to contributory benefits. Contributory benefits are generally more likely to be received by men than women, because the kinds of 'risks' common among women, notably the risks associated with providing care, have not been accepted by European states as comparable to those more likely among men, such as the 'risks' of unemployment, sickness or old age. This reflects the origins of social insurance systems in the early to mid twentieth century, when social insurance was developed as part of the 'social wage' deal struck between working-class men and capital (see, for example, Epstein-Andersen, 1990), at a time when the needs and rights of married women to income and employment protection in their own right was not acknowledged or reflected in public provision. This enduring legacy means that probably no more than 6 or 7 per cent of even those informal carers who provide substantial levels of informal care in below-average-income households, are actually receiving financial support, despite the introduction of the carers allowance (McLaughlin, 1993b).

Although, then, the Republic of Ireland is relatively unusual in having some provision in its social security system for informal carers, the extent to which the costs of care are shared between carers, especially married women carers, and the state, remains very small. Public expenditure on the carers allowance is very small compared with either (a) opportunity costs to informal carers or (b) the 'replacement' costs to public expenditure if care was not provided informally. Blackwell *et al* (cited in O'Connor, 1992) have estimated the average weekly cost of 'community care' reckoned on the basis of opportunity costs to be IR£164.30 per person per week. Using a public expenditure 'replacement' cost, instead of an opportunity costs basis, Blackwell *et al* estimate that the cost of informal care is doubled. The vast majority of these costs are clearly borne by carers themselves, notwithstanding the availability of some financial support for a minority of informal carers. Finally, public expenditure on the carers allowance is also very small compared with public expenditure on other elements of the social security system. For example, expenditure in 1991 on the newly introduced pre-retirement allowance, mainly received by men (94 per cent), was 4.5 times greater (IR£27,047,000) than that on the carers allowance, mainly received by women (76 per cent) (Dept of Social Welfare, 1992).

In Northern Ireland, informal carers can apply for the invalid care allowance, which has had a very different history to the Republic's prescribed relatives allowance/carers allowance, but which suffers the same limitation as the carers allowance. That is, the invalid care allowance, too, is not part of the UK's social insurance system and as a result is set at a very low level (£33.70 a week in 1993/4). The invalid care allowance (ICA) was introduced in the UK in 1976 for men and single women carers of working age, and married women were excluded from eligibility for the same 'reasons' that married women were excluded from the prescribed relatives allowance in the Republic of Ireland, that is, that they 'would be at home anyway' (McLaughlin, 1991). The invalid care allowance was eventually extended to married women in 1986 following a ruling by the European Court that it contravened the equal treatment in statutory social security directive.

The ICA was introduced to protect the incomes of working-age single women and men who had given up or had to forego employment in order to care for their parents or spouses. It was introduced in a special category of non-contributory but insurance-like benefits, that is, eligibility was not based on past national insurance contributions but neither was it considered part of the residual social assistance category and hence means-tested. This anomalous position in the social security system resulted from the pragmatic recognition that many informal carers in 1975/6 had already been caring for many years and hence did not have recent national insurance contribution records. Rather than introducing a radical change to the insurance system in order to accommodate those with 'weak' insurance records because of caring responsibilities (which would have benefited married women, as informal carers and as mothers), instead the invalid care allowance (along with a couple of specific disability benefits) was left outside both the contributory and the social assistance systems. However, the non-contributory status of the benefit was also held to mean that it had to be set at a lower level than contributory benefits, specifically at 60 per cent of national insurance benefit levels in order to maintain a preference within the social security system for benefits based on contributions (benefits which are more likely to be received by men) (McLaughlin, 1991).

The reluctant extension of ICA in 1986 to married women resulted in a ten-fold increase in payments but, nevertheless, the proportions of informal carers who receive the benefit remains low. In 1991/92, 170,000 people in the UK received the benefit. In contrast, an estimated 50,000 carers were providing 50 hours or more care a week in 1985: 'Crude estimates may therefore be that one in ten carers providing around 35 hours per week receive ICA' (McLaughlin, 1991, p. 2). This is mainly the result of the requirement that the person receiving care must be in receipt of a specific disability benefit – the attendance allowance (over 65s) or disability living allowance (under 65s) – and because until recently it was difficult for informal carers who combined part-time work and informal caring to be eligible (McLaughlin, 1991). In addition, because the invalid care allowance is a basic income maintenance benefit, it cannot be received at the same time as other income maintenance benefits (such as the retirement pension or social assistance), all of which are paid at higher levels than ICA, and many informal carers are therefore better off on other benefits. The invalid care allowance, although it makes it possible for married women, as well as other carers, to receive some income in their own right while caring, remains a very partial measure in terms of sharing the material costs of the production of informal welfare between the state and individuals.

4 Conclusions

This paper has tried to untie some of the elements that make up the love and caring labour work of households. There are a number of limitations to this exercise: there is no empirical research in Ireland isolating out love and caring labours from domestic labour. Moreover, these are fluid categories within themselves; a task which might be defined as pure domestic labour in one context could in fact be an act of love and care in a different context. There is much work to be done both empirically and conceptually to understand the complex interrelationships between domestic labour, love labour and care labour, and to disaggregate the precise dimensions of labour that comprise each of these.

In addition, care must be examined from the perspective of the person in need of assistance and care. Most socio-logical and social policy analyses of care have been under-taken from the perspective of the carer and this, in itself, has led to a limited and one-sided perspective on care. The disability studies movement has much to contribute to the traditional analysis of care although it has not yet become part of mainstream social scientific analysis. The work of Barnes, 1990, and Oliver, 1991, for example, highlight the way in which traditional sociological and social policy analysis of care has been blind to the interests and perspectives of disabled people. Qvortrup *et al* (1994) and Nic Ghiolla Phádraig (1994) have raised similar questions with respect to the analysis of the care of children. Once one moves out of an adult-centred framework to analyse the relations between children and parents to take account of the perspective of the child, the notion that caring is a task 'done to children by adults' is itself highly problematic.

The area of care labour which has been subjected to most empirical analysis and research in recent years has been so-called 'informal care'. This refers to the largely unpaid labour involved in providing domestic and personal care services to adults who have impairments and need assistance with the activities of daily living. In addition, feminist scholarship has been instrumental in drawing attention to the effects of women's childrearing responsibilities on their employment histories. It has demonstrated the many ways in which welfare states fail to challenge, and even perpetuate, inequalities between men and women in society and within couples and families (see, for example, Pascall, 1986; Williams, 1989; Connelly, 1993). Feminist activism has succeeded in bringing case issues into the political and policy agenda, although this remains very much unfinished business. It remains the case that the productive activities of women are less likely to be recognised and valued than those of men, and the material costs of the provision of care in contemporary Ireland fall mostly on individual carers and people needing care, rather than on the state, and mostly on women rather than on men. Equality debates and employment and social security policies have not so far taken on board the issues raised by the varied caring responsibilities which women are likely to face in their lives. Nor have social welfare policies attempted to develop 'non-exploitative' care arrangements which would be in the interests of women (and men) needing care, and women (and men) providing care. Measures such as publicly-supported day-care provision for children; day-care provision, personal assistants and domiciliary services for disabled people; care leave entitlements for employed women or men caring for children or adults; appropriate safeguarding of carers' pension entitlements (occupational and statutory); and adequate social security protection for carers who give up paid work for substantial periods of time, all require much wider discussion if the labour of caring is to be recognised, rewarded, valued and equitably shared. Moreover, the rights and wishes of those cared for must also become central to the debate.

Whether viewed from the perspective of the carer, the child or the disabled and/or older person, the reality is that there is a world of labour out there which is primarily solidaristic in nature; it is oriented to the maintenance of relationships, rather than task-centred in the materialist sense. Such work cannot easily be accommodated within the language of debate on the material costs and conditions of unpaid 'caring for' labour. Throughout Europe and further afield, *ad hoc* responses to unpaid caring labour and care needs are developing (see, for instance Glendinning and McLaughlin, 1993; Evers *et al*, 1994), most of which address care as a task-oriented set of activities, and which often seek to commodify both care labour and care needs. This is true of both child-care, disability-related care and care of older people. The extent to which different aspects of care can be, and should be, commodified, and the consequences of this for society need to be the subject of much more analysis and research.

Note

1. We would like to express special thanks to Pat O'Connor of the University of Limerick for her insightful comments and suggestions on an earlier draft of this paper.

References

ARBER, S. and J. GINN, 1990. 'The Meaning of Informal Care: Gender and the Contribution of Elderly People', *Ageing and Society*, Vol. 11, 127-48.

BLACKWELL, J., 1986. *Women in the Labour Force: a statistical digest*, 1st ed., Dublin, Employment Equality Agency, Dublin.

BLACKWELL, J., 1989. *Women in the Labour Force: a statistical digest*, 2nd ed., Dublin, Employment Equality Agency.

BARNES, C., 1990. *Cabbage Syndrome*, Lewes, Falmer Press.

BRANNEN, J. and G. WILSON (eds.), 1987. *Give and Take in Families: Studies in Resource Distribution*, London, Allen & Unwin.

CALLAN, T. and B. FARRELL, 1991. *Women's Participation in the Irish Labour Market* (Report No. 91), Dublin, National Economic and Social Council.

CALLAN, T. and A. WREN, 1993. *Male-Female Wage Differentials: Analysis and Policy Issues* (General Research Series), Dublin, Economic and Social Research Institute.

CONNELLY, A., 1993. *Gender and the Law in Ireland.* Dublin, Oak Tree Press.

DELPHY, C. and D. LEONARD, 1992. *Familiar Exploitation: A New Analysis of Marriage in Contemporary Western Societies,* Cambridge, Polity.

DEPARTMENT OF EQUALITY AND LAW REFORM, 1994. *Report of Working Group on Child Care Facilities for Working Parents,* Dublin, Government Publications.

DEPARTMENT OF SOCIAL WELFARE, 1992. *Statistical Information on Social Welfare Services 1991,* Dublin, Government Stationary Office.

EPSTEIN-ANDERSEN, G., 1990. *The Three Worlds of Welfare Capitalism,* Princeton, Princeton University Press.

EVERS, A., M. PIJL and C. UNGERSON (eds.), 1994. *Paying for Care – An International Overview,* Aldershot, Avebury.

FAHEY, T., 1991. 'Measuring the Female Labour Supply: conceptual and procedural problems in the Irish official statistics', *The Economic and Social Review,* Vol. 21, No. 2, 163-91.

FALLON, M., 1993. *Older People and their Experience of the Health Services: An Egalitarian Issue.* Master of Equality Studies thesis (unpublished), University College Dublin, Equality Studies Centre.

FINCH, J. and J. MASON, 1990. 'Filial Obligations and Kin Support for Elderly People', *Ageing and Society,* Vol. 10, 151-75.

FOLEY, F., 1994. 'A Case Study of the Sexual Inequality of the Division and Distribution of Time Spent on Domestic Labour amongst Two-Job Families.' Master of Equality Studies thesis (unpublished), University College Dublin, Equality Studies Centre.

GLENDINNING, C. and E. McLAUGHLIN, 1993. *Paying for Care – Lessons from Europe,* HMSO, London.

GREEN, H., 1988. *Informal Carers OPCS,* London, HMSO.

HERTZ, R., 1986. *More Equal Than Others: women and men in dual career marriages,* Berkeley, University of California Press.

HINDS, B., 1991. 'Childcare provision and policy', in C. Davies and E. McLaughlin (eds.), 1991. *Women, Employment and Social Policy in Northern Ireland: a problem postponed?,* Belfast, PRI Publications.

HOCHSCHILD, A., 1989. *The Second Shift: working parents and the revolution at home,* Middlesex, Penguin.

HOCHSCHILD, A.R., 1983. *The Managed Heart,* Berkeley, University of California Press.

JOEL, M. and C. MARTIN, 1994. 'France' in A. Evers, M. Pijl, and C. Ungerson (eds.), *Paying For Care – An International Overview*, Aldershot, Avebury.

LEIRA, A., 1990. 'Coping with care: Mothers in a welfare state', in C. Ungerson (ed.), *Gender and Caring*, New York, Harvester Wheatsheaf.

LEIRA, A., 1994. 'Concepts of Caring: Loving, Thinking and Doing', *Social Service Review*, Vol. 68, No. 2, June, 185-201.

LEONARD, M., 1992. 'Ourselves Alone: Household Work Strategies in a Deprived Community', *Irish Journal of Sociology*, Vol. 2, 70-84.

LYNCH, K., 1989. 'Solidary Labour: its nature and marginalisation', *The Sociological Review*, Vol. 37, No. 1, 1-14.

LYNCH, K., 1994. 'Love Labour, Equality and Society', Paper presented to the XIII World Congress of Sociology, Bielefeld, Germany, July 18-23.

MAHON, E., 1991. *Motherhood, Work and Equal Opportunity, First Report of the Third Joint Oireachtais Committee on Women's Rights*, Dublin, Government Publications.

McCOY, D. and M. SMITH, 1992. *The Prevalence of Disability Among Adults in Northern Ireland, PPRU Surveys of Disability No. 1*, PPRU, Dept of Finance and Personnel, Stormont, Belfast.

McKENNA, A., 1988. *Child Care and Equal Opportunities*. Dublin, Employment Equality Agency.

McLAUGHLIN, E., 1991. *Social Security and Community Care: the case of the Invalid Care Allowance*, London, HMSO.

McLAUGHLIN, E., 1992. 'Informal Care' in J. Kremer and P. Montgomery (eds.), *Women's Working Lives*, Belfast, HMSO.

McLAUGHLIN, E., 1993a. 'Women and the Family in Northern Ireland: a review', *Women's Studies International Forum*, 16, 6, 553-68.

McLAUGHLIN, E., 1993b. 'The Republic of Ireland', in C. Glendinning and E. McLaughlin, 1993. *Paying for Care – Lessons from Europe*, London, HMSO.

McLAUGHLIN, E. and C. GLENDINNING, 1993. 'Hypertension and Hypotheses: Conflicting Perspectives on Paying for Care', paper presented at the SPA Annual conference, 15th July, 1993, Liverpool.

MARX, K., 1976 edition. *Capital*, Vol. 1, Harmondsworth: Penguin.

MASON, J., 1994. 'Reconceptualising Care: Gender, Sensibility and Moral Responsibility in Family and Kin Relationships', paper presented to the XIII World Congress of Sociology, Bielefeld, Germany, July 18-23.

MONTGOMERY, P., 1992. 'Paid and Unpaid Labour' in J. Kremer and P. Montgomery (eds.), *Women's Working Lives*, Belfast, HMSO.

MORRISSEY, H., 1991. 'Different Shares: women, employment and earnings', in C. Davies and E. McLaughlin (eds.), *Women, Employment and Social Policy in Northern Ireland: a problem postponed?*, Belfast, PRI Publications.

MOSS, P., 1988. *Childcare and Equality of Opportunity – Consolidated Report to the European Commission, Commission of the European Communities*, Brussels, Directorate General Employment, Social Affairs and Education.

NATIONAL COUNCIL FOR THE ELDERLY, 1991. *Fact Sheet on Ageing*, Dublin, National Council for the Elderly.

NESC, 1991. *Women's Participation in the Irish Labour Market*, Dublin.

NIC GHIOLLA PHÁDRAIG, M., 1994. 'Day Care – Adult Interest Versus Children's Needs? A Question of Compatibility', in J. Qvortrup *et al*, (eds.), *Childhood Matters*. Aldershot, Avebury.

NOONAN, M., 1983. *Who Cares About the Carers?*, Dublin, Council for the Status of Women.

O'CONNOR, J. *et al*, 1988. *Caring for the Elderly Part I*, National Council for the Aged.

O'CONNOR, J., 1992. 'Carers of the elderly in the community', *National Report for the Family Care of the Very Elderly Cross-national Study*, Shankill, Rep. of Ireland, European Foundation for Living and Working Conditions.

O'CONNOR, J. and H. RUDDLE, 1988. *Caring for the Elderly Part II – the caring process: a study of carers in the home*, Dublin, National Council for the Aged.

O'CONNOR, P., 1992. *Friendships Between Women, A Critical Review*, London, Harvester Wheatsheaf.

O'DONOGHUE, M., 1993. *Costing the Halo: The Effects of Compulsory Altruism on the Lives of Mothers with Severely Handicapped Adult Children*. Master of Equality Studies thesis (unpublished), University College Dublin, Equality Studies Centre.

OLIVER, M., 1991. *Social Work, Disabled People and Disabling Environments*, London, Kogan Page.

PARKER, G., 1990. *With Due Care and Attention: a review of research on informal care*, second edition, London, FPSC.

PASCALL, G., 1986. *Social Policy: a feminist analysis*, London, Tavistock.

PATEMAN, C., 1988. *The Sexual Contract*, London, Polity Press.

PICHAULT, C., 1984.
Day-Care Facilities and Services for Children under the Age of Three in the European Community. Luxembourg, Office for Official Publications for the EC.

QURESHI, H., 1990. 'Boundaries between formal and informal care-giving work", in C. Ungerson (ed.), *Gender and Caring,* New York, Harvester Wheatsheaf.

QURESHI, H. and K. SIMONS, 1987. 'Resources within families: caring for elderly people' in J. Brannen and G. Wilson (eds.), *Give and Take in Families: Studies in Resource Distribution,* London, Allen & Unwin.

QURESHI, H. and A. WALKER, 1989. *The Caring Relationship: elderly people and their families,* London, Macmillan.

QVORTRUP, J., *et al,* 1994. *Childhood Matters,* Aldershot, Avebury.

SECOND COMMISSION ON THE STATUS OF WOMEN, 1993. *Report to Government of the Second Commission on the Status of Women,* Dublin, Government Publications Office.

SEVENHUIJSEN, S., 1992. 'Paradoxes of Gender: ethical and epistemological perspectives on care in feminist political theory', paper given to the BSA/PSA Conference, 'The Politics of Care', LSE, 14 Feb. 1992, London.

ST. LEDGER, F. and N. GILLESPIE, 1991. *Informal Welfare in Belfast: Caring Communities?,* Aldershot, Avebury.

UNGERSON, C., 1990. 'Why do Women Care?', in J. Finch and D. Groves (eds.), *A Labour of Love: Women, Work and Caring,* London, Routledge and Kegan Paul.

WAERNESS, K., 1984. 'The Rationality of Caring', in *Economic and Industrial Democracy,* Vol. 5, 185-211.

WAERNESS, K., 1990. 'Informal and Formal Care in Old Age', in C. Ungerson (ed.), *Gender and Caring,* New York, Harvester Wheatsheaf.

WILLIAMS, F., 1989. *Social Policy: A Critical Introduction,* Cambridge, Polity.

PART TWO
Class, Politics and The State

9
Class Society, Inequality and the 'Declassed'

SHEELAGH DRUDY

'You're working class aren't you?'
'We would be if there was any work.' Jimmy Rabbitte to Dean Fay in
Roddy Doyle and Alan Parker's Commitments.

Introduction

Contemporary capitalist societies are class societies. This is one of the key propositions in sociology. Sociologists argue that class position is a major determinant of life conditions and resources, including access to property and income, to education, to housing, to good health and to power. Class is also a significant element in consciousness and behaviour. The concept of class is therefore central in social theory and analysis. Yet the categories used to describe the class structure are themselves social constructs. They are therefore subject to some of the same processes in their development as the very conditions they describe. These processes are ones of selection and definition. They involve the perceptions, the cultural and intellectual viewpoints and assumptions, the resources and the influence of those who are in the position to make such definitions. They are, in effect, the 'domain assumptions' of sociologists themselves (Gouldner, 1970;

Lynch, 1987) which serve to form part of the paradigm, or framework, of theories and concepts, within which social scientific enquiry is carried out (Kuhn, 1970).

One of the great achievements of the social sciences in the nineteenth and twentieth centuries has been the systematic enumeration, documentation and interpretation of the social and economic conditions of the populations of the so-called 'developed' societies. In particular, the social sciences have drawn attention to the predicament of the marginalised sections of these societies. However, it is argued in this chapter that a very central tool of social scientific analysis – that of class theory – has led to an incomplete understanding of the conditions of a number of important segments of contemporary societies. For convenience, these segments are referred to as the 'declassed'. The problem arises as the result of the concepts and methods used to construct class categories. The difficulty is to be found both in independent research and in the production of official statistics. This incomplete analysis leads in turn to a poorer understanding of systems of power and privilege, and to the danger that social and economic policies will be misdirected.

In order to examine these propositions, this chapter traces the development of the main concepts used in class theory, with particular emphasis on the period from the 1970s onwards. It presents the contrasting perspectives offered in a number of different 'schools' of sociological thought. It then focuses on a number of current debates, including those ranging round the impact of mass unemployment on the class structure, the question of the existence or otherwise of an 'underclass', and the relationship of women to the class structure.

Social theory and class analysis

Functionalism
Until the early 1970s functionalism was the dominant social

theory in sociology, in Ireland as elsewhere (Drudy, 1991a). Within functionalism, the emphasis in the analysis has been on 'stratification'. Although closely related to the concept of class, stratification is -conceptually distinct. Stratification theory suggests that individuals and groups in society are divided into a variety of layers or 'strata'. These different strata are presumed to be hierarchically arranged, pyramid fashion, based on a system of differential prestige and rewards.

The classic functionalist position on this was set out in the well-known paper by Davis and Moore (1945). In this they argued that stratification is both inevitable and 'positively functional' in modern societies. Functionalists have contended that the state must preserve a measure of economic inequality, which, it is suggested, is both legitimate and acceptable (Marshall, 1971, pp. 38-56). Discussions on stratification in functionalist sociology may be summarised as follows: the basic unit of analysis is the nuclear family; configurations of nuclear families comprise the strata of industrial societies; most families in advanced industrial societies tend to have positions in the economic hierarchy which are similar to their positions in the status hierarchy; such configurations of families are called 'social classes' and the strata in an industrial society are likely to be social classes; the best single index of the social class position of a family is the occupation of the head of household – usually a male (Hopper, 1971, pp. 13-37).

The influence of functionalist stratification theory is still to be seen in contemporary analyses. It is particularly evident in analyses which focus on the occupational hierarchy. It is also observable in debates on whether the household, or individuals, should be the unit of analysis (Nolan and Callan, 1994; see below for further discussion). Stratification theory also essentially underpins the social class distributions to be found in many official publications, such as the Census classifications of occupations in Ireland and Britain (Drudy, 1991b).

Neo-Weberian[1] theory

Another important influence in sociological analysis of the class and occupational structure is that of Weber. Weber's work, as well as recent work based upon it (e.g. Goldthorpe, 1980; Whelan and Whelan, 1984), is more properly referred to as 'class theory' than the work on stratification outlined above. Weber suggested that a 'class' arises when a number of people have in common a specific causal component of their life chances, insofar as this component is represented exclusively by economic interests in the possession of goods and opportunities for income, and is represented under the conditions of the commodity labour market. This is a 'class situation' (Weber, 1968 edition, Vol. 2, p. 927). Property and lack of property are, therefore, according to Weber, the basic categories of all class situations. Weber also recognised the existence of market and status situations, correlated with, but conceptually distinct from, class situation. He identified four principal 'social classes'. These are: (a) the working class as a whole; (b) the petty bourgeoisie; (c) the propertyless intelligentsia and specialists (technicians, white-collar employees, etc.); (d) the classes privileged through property and education (Weber, 1968 edition, Vol. 1, pp. 302-7).

Although Weber's theories on class have had an important influence on the development of class analysis as a whole, its impact has perhaps been greatest among those studying patterns of social mobility. The term 'social mobility' has been used to refer to the process by which individuals move from one position to another in society. What this movement almost invariably describes is movement from one occupational position to another. These positions are normally given specific hierarchical values (Lipset and Bendix, 1959, pp. 1-3). 'Mobility' may be used to describe three different things: individual movement, generational movement and occupational redefinition (Ibid).

In Britain, there has been a continuing interest in the question of social mobility since the end of the last war. The most notable of the early analyses was that carried out by

Glass and others (Glass, 1954). More recently the most comprehensive work is that carried out by Goldthorpe and his colleagues (Goldthorpe, 1980; Goldthorpe and Payne, 1986; Halsey *et al*, 1980). The main focus of concern in these studies is on male mobility trends and the degree of 'openness' of the class structure, measured according to the amount of movement in and out of seven principal class categories, based on groupings of occupations. Similar work has been carried out by Whelan and others in the Republic of Ireland, and by Millar (1986) in Northern Ireland. Whelan's work, and the theory and methodology used, is described in this volume. This is a detailed example of the application of neo-Weberian class theory to the Irish social structure.

Neo-Marxist[2] theory
The second great evolutionary strand in class theory emanates from the work of Marx. Since the 1970s neo-marxist theory has made significant contributions to the debates within sociology. The Marxist viewpoint on class starts from the premise that every kind of production system entails a definite set of social relationships existing between individuals involved in the productive process. Classes emerge, according to Marx, where the relations of production (i.e. the social relationships existing between individuals involved in the production process) involve a differentiated division of labour which allows for the accumulation of surplus production which can be appropriated by a minority grouping. This minority grouping (in the capitalist instance, the bourgeoisie) thus stands in an exploitative relationship to the mass of producers (Marx, 1976 edition, 1060-5). Marx specifies the 'owners merely of labour power, owners of capital, and land owners' whose respective sources of income are wages, profit and ground-rent respectively, as the three main classes of modern society. They live on the realisation of their labour-power, their capital and their landed property (Marx, 1962 edition, pp. 862-3).

According to Marxist theory, capitalist society is characterised by the simplification of class antagonisms. Society as a whole was described by Marx and Engels as progressively splitting up into two great classes directly facing each other – the bourgeoisie and the proletariat. The bourgeoisie is the class of modern capitalists, owners of the means of social production and employers of wage labour; the 'proletariat' is the class of modern wage-labourers who, having no means of production of their own, are reduced to selling their labour power in order to live (Marx and Engels, 1967 edition, pp. 48, 64). Marx connects the development of the class struggle between capital and labour with the production of surplus value,[3] since he sees the class struggle as originating in the process of production (Mandel, 1976, pp. 11-86).

Neo-Marxist writers have developed Marx's distinction of the basic groupings and have applied modified versions of his notions on class to modern capitalist economies. These take into account the changes in the occupational structures which have occurred in capitalist economies since the end of the nineteenth century, but like Marx, they suggest that the economic and political life of capitalist societies is primarily determined by the relationship, born of the capitalist mode of production, between two classes – the class which on the one hand owns and controls, and the working class on the other. These, it is argued, are still the social forces whose confrontation most powerfully shapes the social climate and the political system of advanced capitalism (Miliband, 1973, p. 17). Neo-Marxist research in the United States, for example, has indicated that class divisions between property holders and non-property holders is still very real, even when only small property holders are considered (Wright and Perrone, 1977). Thus, the political process in capitalist societies is mainly about the confrontation of these forces, and it is intended to sanction the terms of the relationship between them. This analysis, nevertheless, does not under-estimate the importance of other 'intervening' classes in capitalist societies. These classes are of considerable importance, not least because they significantly affect the relations between the two 'polar' classes (Miliband, 1973, p. 17).

It is precisely these intervening classes which often present a problem when Marxist analysis is applied in empirical studies. This problem is sometimes evaded by the lack of clear definitions. However, much of the difficulty arises from the problem of the definition and classification of the 'working class' *vis-à-vis* the intermediate classes. Indeed, in the literature on class theory there have been quite heated debates about exactly which groups compose the working class. As an example, let us consider the debate between the social theorist, Poulantzas, and his critics.

Poulantzas defined what he called 'social classes' as groupings of social agents (i.e. individuals), defined principally but not exclusively by their place in the production process, i.e. in the economic sphere. Economic place, however, is not necessarily sufficient to determine class: political and ideological criteria, he argued, also have an important role. Thus, a class may be defined by its place in the social division of labour as a whole, which includes political and ideological relations (Poulantzas, 1978, p. 14). Like Althusser (Althusser, 1972, pp. 242-80), who referred to the 'determination in the last instance by the economic base' of what happens in the 'superstructure' (ideological and political relations), Poulantzas also referred to the determining role of economic elements (Poulantzas, 1977, pp. 113-24). This was in spite of his view that economic place is insufficient to determine class position – that one must also use political and ideological criteria.

This was, of course, a deterministic view and has been described as 'profoundly economistic' (Hunt, 1977, pp. 81-111). In spite of this criticism, Poulantzas attached importance to the field of political and ideological relations. This led him to specify certain 'categories', 'fractions', or 'strata' of classes on the basis of differentiations in the economic, and also the political and ideological relations spheres. These may take up class positions which may or may not correspond to their interests (Poulantzas, 1978, p. 15), e.g. as in the matter of voting for particular political parties. In addition, he emphasised that any society involves more than two classes insofar as it is composed of various modes and forms of production. The two fundamental classes of any society are those of the dominant mode of production in that society. In capitalist societies, as has been pointed out, these are the bourgeoisie and the proletariat (or working class). The bourgeoisie are defined by ownership and control of the means of production. Poulantzas also spends some time (as does Wright, 1986) discussing the position of managers who exercise control over, but do not necessarily own, the means of production. Poulantzas concludes that, although they are not owners, they are nevertheless part of the *bourgeoisie* or capitalist class (Poulantzas, 1978, p. 181). Whether one is a member of the *working class* depends on one's involvement in 'productive labour' – i.e. labour that produces surplus value for capital and the accumulation of wealth (Ibid, p. 211). In short, only those who are manual workers in the production of material commodities are members of the working class. This definition would thus exclude manual workers in the services from the working class, although their skills, life-conditions and culture are very similar to those of other manual workers.

Between the bourgeoisie and the working class there are also to be found the *traditional petty bourgeoisie* (craftsmen, small traders), dependent on the form of simple commodity production, and the *'new' petty bourgeoisie* composed of 'non-productive' (i.e. not directly engaged in the production of physical commodities) wage earners, dependent on the monopoly form of capitalism. The 'new' petty bourgeoisie is composed of wage earners in commerce, advertising, marketing, accounting, banking and insurance and other services. These, it is claimed, do not produce surplus value and do not form part of the working class. They simply 'contribute towards redistributing the mass of surplus value among the various fractions of capital according to the average rate of profit' (Poulantzas, 1978, p. 212). However, these wage earners themselves are also exploited. Surplus labour[4] is extracted from them, but they are not directly exploited in the form of the 'dominant capitalist relation of exploitation', the creation of surplus value (Ibid). Thus, Poulantzas identified four different social classes. When subjected to scrutiny, these bear a remarkable resemblance to Weber's four social classes (Drudy, 1991b).

As a solution to difficulties presented by definitions of productive and unproductive labour, Hunt placed a greater emphasis than did Poulantzas on political and ideological practices. On the basis of these, he suggested, it would be possible to exclude, for example, military and police personnel from the working class, without having to rely on economic criteria. With political and ideological practices in mind, Hunt argued that the subjective orientations of various groups are important, not because they determine class location, but as evidence of the effects of politics and ideology (Hunt, 1977). However, Wright argues that cross-national comparisons indicate that the link between class structure and class consciousness varies considerably and is contingent on political and historical differences in different capitalist societies (Wright, 1986).

By contrast, the French neo-Marxist sociologist, Bourdieu, distinguishes two main groups throughout most of his writings – the dominant and subordinate classes. The dominant classes, according to Bourdieu, consist of: teachers, top civil servants, professionals, engineers, managers, heads of industry and heads of commerce (Bourdieu, 1973, pp. 71-112). This classification differs somewhat from the Marxist definitions of class discussed above. Poulantzas has queried his use of these categories saying that they are based on those of the Institut National des Statistiques et Etudes Nationales (INSEE) – the French equivalent of the Census and, as such, display several contradictions (Poulantzas, 1978, p. 177).

Bourdieu's analysis does, in fact, refer primarily to France and there might well be difficulties in applying this exact dichotomy in the Irish context – especially if teachers, and indeed some other professionals, e.g. nurses, were to be included among the 'dominant classes'. This criticism can also be applied to other Marxist empirical class definitions (Marsh, 1986).

Wright's work represents an attempt to resolve some of the problems outlined above. He argues that classes in capitalist society are based upon three forms of exploitation: exploitation based on the ownership of capital assets, the control of organisational assets and the possession of skill or credential assets (Wright, 1986). However, it has been suggested that even Wright's work introduces Weberian elements (Carter, 1986; Giddens, 1985). On the other hand, Giddens's work (1973 and 1982), represents an attempt to move beyond the categories generated in previous debates and to arrive at some form of theoretical synthesis, in particular one which would take account of human agency; yet his analysis also is primarily Weberian in character.

The neo-Marxist debate on class, although it contains some rather complex and difficult concepts, has one thing in common with both functionalist and Weberian approaches. When it comes to the empirical measurement of class, what is really at issue is the classification of occupations, since these are used as the prime indicator of the relationship to the system of production. This is as true of neo-Marxist analysts such as Poulantzas and Wright, whose theoretical approaches explicitly argue that the various dimensions of class are not purely defined by occupation, as it is of functionalists and Weberians, such as Goldthorpe. The reason for this is that occupation is usually seen (not without good reason) as the most reliable, shorthand indicator of relationship to the production process and the ability to command resources.

The similarities in the empirical operationalisation of neo-Marxist and Weberian class categories, outlined above, may have roots in the class analysis of Weber and Marx themselves.

Certain similarities in their treatment of class have been noted in the work of Marx and Weber. Firstly, Weber's own definition of 'class' was similar to Marx's, insofar as both saw class position as a matter of the place occupied by people in the system of production. Secondly, both saw shared class position as a potential basis for recognition of common interests and for collective class organisation and action in consequence (Westergaard and Resler, 1976, pp. 72-106).

As regards the production of official figures, these are based exclusively on a classification of occupations into a series of hierarchies or strata. The socio-economic groupings of the Irish Census have been based upon an assessment of the level of skill or educational attainment required by each occupation (CSO, 1986). For historical reasons, the Irish approach to the production of official statistics owes much to British empiricism. Consequently, there are many similarities in the way that figures are produced. For example, the basis for the British Census social class classification of occupations is very similar to that in Ireland. Occupations are ranked on the basis of social standing or prestige, and on the 'level of occupational skill' (Drudy, 1991b).

Occupations are less than perfect indicators of class. In spite of this, survey investigations, no matter what their theoretical origins, rely on them as a form of measurement because of the sheer operational difficulties attaching to other forms of class measurement. The outcome of this is that classifications based primarily on occupations will have broad similarities, irrespective of the theoretical orientation from which they are constructed, if they are used in sample surveys of the general population, as opposed to small-scale, specialised studies. In particular, there is evidence to suggest that in circumstances such as these, there are broad similarities in measures based on scales which derive from neo-Weberian and neo-Marxist theoretical orientations (Drudy, 1991b).

The fact that most analyses of the class structure make use of occupations to indicate class position gives rise to one

major difficulty. How can one classify the very large number
of people in society who do not have a job? The next section
of this chapter outlines some of the problems.

The labour force and the rest of the population

We have seen that the conceptualisation and measurement of
class has been translated, in empirical studies within all
theoretical approaches, into the analysis of the position of
individuals in relation to occupation. In this section we
consider the position of those who are not holders of
occupations, who are not in the paid labour force. In Ireland
this is the condition of a very large proportion of the adult
population. The broad pattern is indicated by the 'economic
status' of the population and is shown in Table 1.

Table 1: **Economic status of the population aged 15 and
over, Republic of Ireland, 1992**

Economic Status	Number (000s)*	Percentage
At work	1,139.3	43.5
Unemployed (including first job seekers)	221.0	8.4
Student	306.7	11.7
On home duties	653.4	25.0
Retired	212.8	8.1
Unable to work due to permanent sickness or disability	68.8	2.6
Other	16.2	0.6
Total	2,618.2	100.0

Source: Labour Force Survey 1992 (CSO, 1994a, p. 2)
*Estimates based on sample survey

This table is derived from the Central Statistics Office Labour
Force Survey and is an example of 'official figures'. Only the
population over the age of 15 is included here since this is the

official minimum school-leaving age. The Labour Force Survey defines the first two categories (those 'At work' and 'Unemployed') as being 'in the labour force'. All the other categories are 'not in the labour force'. However, while unemployed people may be 'in the labour force', they are not in occupations. Consequently, the table illustrates that a minority (43.5 per cent) of the 'adult' population (i.e. those above the minimum school-leaving age) are in an occupation. Even if we exclude those in full-time education, this still leaves a very sizeable proportion (50.7 per cent) who are outside the class structure, as conventionally measured in most existing class schema. These are the groups that are referred to here as the 'declassed'.

The largest proportion of these are those classified as on 'home duties', followed by 'people in retirement'. We further discuss these two groups below. However, those 'unable to work due to permanent sickness or disability' also form a significant element. People with disabilities are particularly disadvantaged in the labour market. It is generally agreed that there are four areas where people with disabilities fare worse than everybody else. One of these is in labour market participation. The others are that more disabled people have low earnings; more hours tend to be worked to secure the same earnings; and slightly fewer have good conditions of work (Oliver, 1991, p. 132).

Does this mean that class analysis cannot give an indication of the life conditions of these groups who are not 'at work', their ability to command resources and their access to power? Class theory does offer some insights. Social analysts have devised a number of strategies to classify and interpret the position of this very large grouping. A number of these strategies are examined below.

The 'declassed' as 'residual'

One strategy is to assume that one's present life conditions and circumstances are closely related to one's most recent employment. Obviously substantial proportions of the population who are not currently 'at work' have held occupations in the past. This applies to those on 'home duties', the unemployed, the retired and to some of the disabled. It is therefore possible to assess people on the basis of the social class position of their most recent occupation. Undoubtedly, this will give some indication of ability to command resources. For example, until July 1994, in the case of the short-term unemployed still in receipt of pay-related unemployment benefit, income was assessed on the basis of the income which attached to their previous employment. This payment was normally significantly below their income when working, except for those whose occupations were extremely low-paid (Callan and Nolan, 1994, pp. 105-6).[5] Similarly, the pensions of those in retirement relate to income and contributions made while in employment. Previous employment may also give an indication of the social attitudes and class consciousness typical of the relevant class position (Charles, 1990, p. 85).

A second strategy sometimes adopted by sociologists is to exclude altogether those groups not in occupations from the analysis of the class structure. They are then treated as a 'residual' category, on the grounds that they are not regular participants in any form of economic activity (Rottmann et al, 1982, p. 9). Some neo-Marxist theory (e.g. Braverman, 1974, p. 386; Morris, 1991, pp. 74, 77), while accepting that these groups are not regular participants in any form of paid economic activity, regards them as a more integral part of the class structure. Their position, it is argued, can be interpreted as a 'reserve army of labour' on which capitalist enterprise may call during times of economic expansion but which will leave the labour market, without precipitating too much structural crisis, during times of economic recession. This is not to suggest, of course, that unemployment does not cause severe personal and psychological crisis. There is now mounting evidence of the psychological distress and damage which is the result of the social exclusion experienced by 'residual' groups, such as the unemployed (Whelan, 1994a, p. 160).

The 'reserve army of labour' thesis is one which is based upon a notion that capitalist economies are both crisis-ridden and cyclical. However, what has characterised western economies, and Ireland in particular, since the end of the 1970s has been the steady and drastic increase in unemployment. Two digit levels of unemployment are now increasingly seen as normal (Korpi, 1991, p. 316).

It is not only in the allocation of people to class categories that definitions are important. Definitions are equally important when it comes to the issue of unemployment. Figures can vary quite significantly depending on the nature of the definition used. We have seen that the most recently published Labour Force Survey figure, based on mid-April estimates for 1992, resulting from a sample survey of *households*, put the number of people unemployed as 221,000. This figure normally differs significantly from that based on the monthly Live Register which gives details of those 'signing on' at local employment exchanges. The numbers on the Live Register fluctuate from month to month in response to changing employment opportunities (Drudy and MacLaran, 1994, p. 21). The figure for the total on the Live Register for April 1992 was 280,900 (CSO, 1994b, p. 4), almost 60,000 higher than that in the Labour Force Survey. Two years after the most recently published (at the time of writing) Labour Force Survey figures, the numbers on the Live Register stood at 284, 509 (CSO, 1994b). The method of calculating the unemployment *rate*, as a proportion of the labour force (defined as consisting of those at work plus the unemployed, and adjusted to take account of seasonal variations such as periodic influxes of students to the labour market), is known as the 'seasonally adjusted standardised unemployment rate'.[6] This figure was 15.5 per cent for the first quarter of 1994. This unemployment rate puts Ireland second from the top of a rather invidious league of high unemployment rates in the countries of the European Union. Spain leads with a figure of 23.9 per cent, while the EU average is 11.2 per cent (OECD, 1994).

In contrast to the debates of the 1970s and early 1980s when, as we saw earlier, the focus was on how membership of the working class might actually be best defined, persistently high levels of unemployment in Ireland and elsewhere have led to the question of whether we should now talk about an 'underclass' in western societies, and even whether the concept of a class structure is still of any relevance at all (Emmison and Western, 1990). There is also the argument that accepts that capitalist societies are based on an inherent conflict of interests between capital and labour, but suggests that the concept of class has been debased through inappropriate and uncritical usage (Pahl, 1989). In relation to the question of whether the concept of class is still relevant most analysts are agreed, not too surprisingly, that social class still has a powerful explanatory force in western societies (Marshall *et al*, 1988; Runciman, 1990). Recent research suggests that class solidarities retain an importance and that social class is to the fore among conceptions of collective identity (Marshall *et al*, p. 267). However, the question of the existence of an underclass is of particular value to consider in more detail. This is especially so in the context of the very high level of unemployment in the Irish Republic.

The underclass

The concept of an 'underclass' suggests that a relatively fixed, and more or less homogeneous, social grouping exists and is clearly differentiated from the working class (Rodger, 1992, p. 46). The concept was originally developed in the United States. In recent years attempts have been made to test its applicability in Britain, especially in relation to the position of Carribean and Asian immigrant workers (Rex, 1988, pp. 112-13). The focus in British research has been primarily upon the structural conditions and processes within which marginalised and 'problem' populations grow (Rodger, 1992). These conditions include record levels of unemployment; widening class differences; the exclusion of the very poorest from rising living standards; and a significant change in public attitudes towards those in poverty (Field, 1989, p. 2). However, in Britain the notion of an underclass has become controversial due to its association with the politics of the 'New Right'. This has arisen mainly as the result of the publication of an analysis by the American commentator, Murray, who focused on the behavioural characteristics of the so-called underclass and the 'moral hazard' caused by the latent functions of welfare policy (Murray, 1990). The debate surrounding this publication, and indeed around previous publications in the US, has led some to suggest that social commentators and policy makers would do well to avoid the term (Dean, 1991, p. 39). Nevertheless, because of its linkages to the structural conditions which give rise to marginalisation and social exclusion, the term continues to be used by social scientists.

In Ireland the question of whether this term is appropriate to describe the conditions of marginalised groups has been explored by Whelan (1994b). This work arises as a consequence of the increase in the proportion of the unemployed who were in receipt of long-term social welfare support (i.e. unemployment assistance). This rose from 48 per cent of those on the Live Register in 1980 to 58 per cent in 1987 (Ibid, p. 2). Indeed this increase in the proportion on the Live Register who are in receipt of long-term social welfare support has accelerated into the 1990s. In April 1994 the figures showed that 203,229 persons, or 71 per cent of all those registered, were receiving unemployment assistance (CSO, 1994b).

Whelan draws upon a definition of the underclass which involves three features: (i) prolonged labour market marginality; (ii) greater deprivation than is general for the manual working class; (iii) the possession of its own sub-culture. On the basis of his analysis, Whelan suggests that the 'marginalised working class' form 11-12 per cent of non-farm households (Whelan, 1994b, p. 9). On the basis of the evidence he argues that the marginalised working-class are not concentrated in public sector housing in major urban areas. Rather than being a consequence of location, pervasive marginalisation appears to be a hazard of lower working class origins, and includes the effects of educational failure. In Whelan's study it is contended that in the Republic of Ireland what confronts us is not the emergence of an underclass, but different types of working-class marginalisation. Nevertheless, it is argued that households from which the next generation of the marginalised working-class are most likely to be drawn are presently experiencing extreme deprivation. Consequently, it is not possible to rule out the emergence of a fraction of the working-class characterised by its own distinctive sub-culture (Ibid, pp. 21, 30-31).

It would thus appear that, on the basis of existing work in Ireland and Britain, the concept of an underclass does not advance us very much in the analysis of the position of the very substantial sections of the population who experience unemployment and deprivation. Indeed this work would suggest that it is inappropriate to exclude them from class analysis. However, the problem still remains that, because they do not have occupations, and because a very significant proportion are now long-term unemployed, they disappear from social surveys.

Women and the household

Women form another major category whose position poses problems for class analysis. Part of the problem here has been the assumption in many studies that the basic unit of class or stratification analysis is the household (Hopper, 1971; Nolan and Callan, 1994). This is the assumption that underlies the production of many official statistics also. For example, the target of the Labour Force Survey is the usually resident population of all private and non-private households in the state. The Labour Force Survey defines a private household as 'any person or group of persons (not necessarily related) with common living arrangements, separately occupying all or part of a private house, flat, apartment or private habitation of any kind' (CSO, 1994a, p. 66). For the purposes of the Labour Force Survey non-private households are also included, such as hospitals and other residential health care establishments. These are not usually included in other household surveys.

The most recent major survey of poverty, class, unemployment and social welfare in Ireland uses the household as the unit of analysis (Nolan and Callan, 1994). Although this research acknowledges the distinction between the individual, the family and the household (p. 20), on the whole it uses the terms 'household' and 'nuclear family' interchangeably (Rottman, 1994, p. 193). The difficulty with such an approach in this, or any other study, is that gender differences, and in particular the position of women, tend to be subsumed within the household or family. This problem is examined in the study mentioned above in relation to poverty. There the questions of the 'feminisation' of poverty and the unequal distribution of income within the household are explored (Callan, 1994, pp. 178-92; Rottman, 1994, pp. 193-213). The study indicates relatively little evidence in support of the former, and rather more in support of the latter.

To put the problems in relation to class position into context, let us turn again to the Labour Force Survey. Table 2 examines the economic status of the population, this time subdivided by sex.

The most salient elements of Table 2 are the low participation rate of females in the paid labour force compared to males, and the very low participation rate of males on 'home duties'.[7] In fact, if we break down the total number (653,400) on home duties by gender, we find that 99 per cent of them are female. As we saw earlier, only the first two categories are defined by the Labour Force Survey as 'in the labour force'. Consequently, the total labour force, so defined, is composed of 33.4 per cent women, whereas women form almost 70 per cent of the total *not* in the labour force.

Table 2:   **Economic status of the population aged 15 and over, Republic of Ireland, 1992, by sex**

Economic Status	Female %	Male %	Total %
At work	30.0	57.5	43.5
Unemployed (including first job seekers)	4.2	12.9	8.4
Student	11.5	11.9	11.7
On home duties	48.5	0.6	25.0
Retired	3.6	12.8	8.1
Unable to work due to permanent sickness or disability	1.6	3.7	2.6
Other	0.6	0.6	0.6
Total	100.0	100.0	100.0
N (000s)	1,331.1	1,287.1	2,618.2

Source: Labour Force Survey 1992 (CSO, 1994a, p. 2)
*Estimates based on sample survey

The arguments presented earlier in this paper are that class is a powerful explanatory tool in relation to access to resources, power and 'life chances'. Nevertheless, whatever the analytical constructs, occupation is almost invariably used as the primary indicator in all of the class schema when it comes to measurement. There is, of course, no doubt that access to a job is the most important transition that an individual can make in terms of being able to stake a claim to resources. It is a key element for all young people in the transition to adulthood (Hannan and Ó Riain, 1993).

Since occupational position is used as the main indicator of class position this automatically excludes a very high proportion of adult women from the analysis. The analysis of women's occupational experiences in the paid labour market is of course itself very useful, even if it refers to just a minority of adult women. For example, such studies have indicated substantial wage differentials between women and men (Blackwell, 1989; Callan and Wren, 1994). They have also shown the negative impact that women's caring roles have on their labour market experiences (Callan and Wren, 1994, pp. 56-64; see also Lynch and McLoughlin in this volume). However, this does not solve the ambiguities of women's relationship to the class structure.[8] The issue has been the subject of intense debates in the literature. Nevertheless, the problem is as yet unresolved.

Using the household as the unit of analysis is one way of addressing the issue. This can provide rich insights into the distribution of income and resources, as recent studies of poverty have shown (Nolan and Farrell, 1990; Nolan and Callan, 1994). Nevertheless, the culture of gender relations within which such analyses take place, and the evidence of unequal power relationships within a sizeable proportion of families, especially those where women are economically dependent (Rottman, 1994) has to be borne in mind. Thus, class analysis in which the household is assigned a class position on the basis of the position of the 'head' of household is almost certain to distort the interpretation of central processes such as social mobility (Hayes, 1987; Leiulfsrud and Woodward, 1987; Bonney, 1988; Hayes and Miller, 1993).

Studies which have included women in the paid labour force and those who work full-time as housewives have shown that the two groups did not appear to differ greatly from each other in terms of their perceptions of class. Nor do they experience their situation as marginal to the class structure (Charles, 1990). Such research offers little support for the view that members of families necessarily share a class position, or that the current occupation of either or both partners can tell the whole story about class identities. It further suggests that using a partner's occupation only, to define the class of married or cohabiting women is likely to cloud rather than clarify the processes which lead to class identity and class consciousness (Ibid, pp. 84-5).

To some extent, the method of measurement of class
position varies according to the aspect of class under scrutiny.
Attempts have been made to develop composite measures of
class, using a variety of indicators (e.g. Osborn and Morris,
1979; Wright, 1986; Duke and Edgell, 1987). However, these
involve complex procedures which would be difficult to
implement in most sample surveys. When the focus of
attention is on the cultural and attitudinal area, other
approaches have been used. For example, in a study of
second-level student performance Breen used the
qualifications of mothers and fathers as an indicator of
'cultural capital', i.e. the cultural goods transmitted by
different families (Drudy and Lynch, 1993, p. 155). Using
educational qualifications implied that parents' education
could be used as a referent for the skills, attitudes and
abilities of pupils 'that derive from their home environment'
(Breen, 1986, p. 89). While there are obvious difficulties in
relying totally upon qualifications as a referent for class
position, it at least avoids the difficulty of automatically
eliminating 70 per cent of the female population aged 15 and
over, and indeed more than 40 per cent of the male
population, from the analysis.

It is interesting to note that the debate on the class position
of women is one that has only developed since the 1980s. To
a large extent this is the result of a heightening of the
awareness among social scientists regarding the importance
of female experience of the class and occupational structure.
This has been the result of much feminist theory and analysis.
Until this time, the implications of the focus on mainly male
experiences of class and the labour force were not seen as
problematic by researchers, who themselves were
predominantly male. So it was not unusual that studies of
class mobility such as *Origins and Destinations* (Halsey *et al*,
1980) or *Social Mobility and Class Structure in Modern Britain*
(Goldthorpe, 1980) appear by their titles to be inclusive
studies of the entire population but are, in reality, studies of
male cohorts only. It is indeed as a result of critiques

(originating in feminist analysis) that there has been a movement away from mobility studies restricted to males.[9]

Conclusion

In this chapter, it has been argued that the heavy reliance on the use of occupation as the sole indicator of class position has been part of the dominant paradigm of class analysis in social science. Methods of class allocation based primarily upon the occupational structure, although they offer great insights, are also incomplete and fraught with difficulties. Nevertheless, most researchers make use of class schema based upon the classification of occupations because of the sheer complexity of alternative methods. In relation to the ability to command resources, there is little doubt that occupation is a good indicator. However, it must be remembered that the lack of an occupation is perhaps an even greater indicator.

The complex relationship of women to the occupational structure, and the condition of economic dependence of such a large proportion of them, gives rise to many problems of classification and interpretation. These are by no means solved through the mechanism of using the household as the unit of analysis.

If the focus of attention is on the cultural and attitudinal area, then it is possible that the more inclusive indicator of 'educational qualifications' may be useful. However, although there are very close linkages between education, occupation and the risk of marginalisation, qualifications in themselves are not an adequate indicator of levels of income or other resources.

While occupation (or the lack of one) may give an indication of one's relationship to the production process, and education may indicate one's level of cultural capital, neither tells us very much about one's relationship to property. After all, was it not Marx and Weber, those two great 'fathers' of class theory, who argued that property or the lack of property are the basic categories of all class situations?

Notes

1. The term 'neo-Weberian' refers to the work of contemporary sociologists whose fundamental concepts derive from the socio-economic analysis to be found in the writings of Max Weber.
2. 'Neo-Marxist' approaches are contemporary ones whose fundamental concepts derive from the socio-economic analysis in the work of Karl Marx. Generally speaking, the terms 'Weberian' and 'neo-Weberian', as well as 'Marxist' and 'neo-Marxist', are used interchangeably.
3. 'Surplus value' is the source of capitalist profit. It is the value created by the labourer but appropriated by the capitalist (Freedman, 1961).
4. 'Surplus labour' is extracted from wage earners who do not produce surplus value but who are themselves also exploited (Poulantzas, 1978).
5. This connection between former pay and current benefit for unemployed people no longer obtains. From 21 July 1994 pay-related unemployment benefit was abolished. A flat rate of unemployment benefit is now payable for a period of fifteen months, provided appropriate insurance payments have been made, while in employment. This rate differs only slightly from unemployment assistance. The chief difference between the two since July 1994 is that assistance is means-tested whereas benefit is not (information from Department of Social Welfare).
6. The seasonally adjusted standardised unemployment rate for a particular month is described as the ratio of the standardised unemployment level to the labour force. 'The standardised level is obtained by multiplying the seasonally adjusted Live Register figure by the ratio of the number of persons unemployed on an ILO basis (as measured by the most recent Labour Force Survey) to the number of persons on the Live Register for the corresponding April' (CSO, 1994b, p. 8). This quotation is taken from the methodology note appended to the monthly Live Register Statement issued by the Central Statistics Office on behalf of the government. It is obvious that this definition would not easily be understood by the general public.
7. The implications of the lack of involvement of males in caring labour is treated by Lynch and McLoughlin elsewhere in this volume.
8. Some of the ways in which sociologists attempt to deal with these ambiguities are outlined by Whelan elsewhere in this volume.
9. See also Whelan elsewhere in this volume.

References

ALTHUSSER, L., 1972. 'Ideology and Ideological State Apparatuses', in B. Cosin (ed.), *Education, Structure and Society*, Harmondsworth, Penguin Books, pp. 242-80.

BLACKWELL, J., 1989. *Women in the Labour Force*, Dublin, Employment Equality Agency.

BONNEY, N., 1988. 'Gender, Household and Social Class', *British Journal of Sociology*, Vol. 39, pp. 28-46.

BOURDIEU, P., 1973. 'Cultural Reproduction and Social Reproduction', in R. Brown (ed.), *Knowledge, Education and Cultural Change*, London, Tavistock, pp. 71-112.

BOURDIEU, P., and J. C. PASSERON, 1977. *Reproduction in Education, Society and Culture*, London, Sage.

BRAVERMAN, H., 1974. *Labor and Monopoly Capital*, New York, Monthly Review Press.

BREEN, R., 1986. *Subject Availability and Student Performance in the Senior Cycle of Irish Post-Primary Schools*, Dublin, Economic and Social Research Institute.

CALLAN, T., 1994. 'Poverty and Gender Inequality' in B. Nolan, and T. Callan (eds.), *Poverty and Policy in Ireland*, Dublin, Gill and Macmillan, pp. 178-92.

CALLAN, T. and B. NOLAN, 1994. 'Unemployment and Poverty', in B. Nolan, and T. Callan (eds.) *Poverty and Policy in Ireland*, Dublin, Gill and Macmillan, pp. 97-115.

CALLAN, T. and A. WREN, 1994. *Male-Female Wage Differentials: Analysis and Policy Issues*, Dublin, Economic and Social Research Institute.

CARTER, R., 1986. 'Review of E. O. Wright, "Classes"' *Sociological Review*, Vol. 34, pp. 686-88.

CENTRAL STATISTICS OFFICE, 1986. *Census of Population of Ireland*, Vol. 7, *Occupations*, Dublin, CSO.

CENTRAL STATISTICS OFFICE, 1994a. *Labour Force Survey 1992*, Dublin, Stationary Office.

CENTRAL STATISTICS OFFICE, 1994b. 'Live Register Statement, 29 April 1994', *CSO Statistical Release*, Government Information Services.

CHARLES, N., 1990. 'Women and Class – a Problematic Relationship?' *The Sociological Review*, Vol. 38, No. 1, pp. 43-89.

DAVIS, K. and W. E. MOORE, 1945. 'Some Principles of Stratification', *American Sociological Review*, Vol. 10, pp. 242-9.

DEAN, H., 1991. 'In search of the Underclass', in P. Brown and R. Scase (eds.), *Poor Work: Disadvantage and the Division of*

320   Irish Society: Sociological Perspectives

Labour, Milton Keynes, Open University Press, pp. 23-39.

DRUDY, S., 1991a. 'Developments in the Sociology of Education in Ireland 1966-1991', *Irish Journal of Sociology*, Vol. 1, pp. 107-27.

DRUDY, S. 1991b. 'The Classification of Social Class in Sociological Research', *British Journal of Sociology*, Vol. 42, No. 1, pp. 21-41.

DRUDY, S. and K. LYNCH, 1993. *Schools and Society in Ireland*, Dublin, Gill and Macmillan.

DRUDY, P. and A. MACLARAN, 1994. *Dublin: Economic and Social Trends*, Dublin, Centre for Urban and Regional Studies, Trinity College.

DUKE, V. and S. EDGELL, 1987. 'The Operationalisation of Class in British Sociology: Theoretical and Empirical Considerations', *British Journal of Sociology*, Vol. 38, pp. 445-63.

EMMISON, M. and M. WESTERN, 1990. 'Social Class and Social Identity: a Comment on Marshall *et al*', *Sociology*, Vol. 24, No. 2, pp. 241-53.

FIELD, F., 1989. *Losing Out: The Emergence of Britain's Underclass*, Oxford, Basil Blackwell.

FREEDMAN, R. (ed.), 1961. *Marx on Economics*, Harmondsworth, Penguin Books.

GIDDENS, A., 1973. *The Class Structure of the Advanced Societies*, London, Hutchinson.

GIDDENS, A., 1982. 'Power, the Dialectic of Control and Class Structuration', in A. Giddens and G. Mackenzie (eds.), *Social Class and the Division of Labour: Essays in Honour of Ilya Neustadt*, Cambridge University Press.

GIDDENS, A., 1985. 'Review of E. O. Wright, "Classes"', *New Society*, 29.11.85, pp. 383-384.

GOLDTHORPE, J. H., 1980, *Social Mobility and Class Structure in Modern Britain*, Oxford, Clarendon Press.

GOLDTHORPE J. and C. PAYNE, 1986. 'Trends in Intergenerational Class Mobility in England and Wales 1972-1983', *Sociology*, Vol. 20, pp. 1-24.

GLASS, D. V. (ed.), 1954. *Social Mobility in Britain*, London, Routledge and Kegan Paul.

GOULDNER, A. V., 1970. *The Coming Crisis of Western Sociology*, London, Heinemann.

HANNAN, D. and S. Ó RIAIN, 1993. *Pathways to Adulthood in Ireland: Causes and Consequences of Success and Failure in Transition Amongst Irish Youth*, Dublin, Economic and Social Research Institute.

HAYES, B. C., 1987. 'Female Intergenerational Occupational Mobility within Northern Ireland and the Republic of Ireland: the Importance of Maternal

Occupational Status', *British Journal of Sociology*, Vol. 38, pp. 66-76.

HAYES, B. and R. MILLER, 1993. 'The Silenced Voice: Female Social Mobility Patterns With Particular Reference to The British Isles', *British Journal of Sociology*, Vol. 44, No. 4, pp. 653-72.

HOPPER, E. (ed.), 1971. 'Notes on Stratification, Education and Mobility in Industrial Societies', in *Readings in the Theory of Educational Systems*, London, Hutchinson, pp. 13-37.

HUNT, A., 1977. 'Theory and Politics in the Identification of the Working Class', in A. Hunt (ed.), *Class and Class Structure*, London, Lawrence and Wishart.

KORPI, W., 1991. 'Political and Economic Explanations for Unemployment: a Cross-National and Long-Term Analysis', *British Journal of Political Science*, Vol. 21, pp. 315-48.

KUHN, T., 1970. *The Structure of Scientific Revolutions*, Chicago, University of Chicago Press.

LEIULFSRUD, H. and A. WOODWARD, 1987. 'Women at Class Crossroads Repudiating Conventional Theories of Family Class', *Sociology*, Vol. 21, pp. 393-412.

LIPSET, S. and R. BENDIX, 1959. *Social Mobility in Industrial Societies*, Berkeley, University of California Press.

LYNCH, K., 1987. 'Dominant Ideologies in Irish Educational Thought', *Economic and Social Review*, Vol. 18, No. 2, pp. 110-22.

MANDEL, E., 1976. 'Introduction to K. Marx', *Capital*, Vol. 1, Harmondsworth, Penguin Books, pp. 11-86.

MARSH, C., 1986. 'Social Class and Occupation', in R. G. Burgess (ed.), *Key Variables in Social Investigation*, London, Routledge and Kegan Paul, pp. 123-152.

MARSHALL, G. H. NEWBY, D. ROSE and C. VOGLER, 1988. *Social Class in Modern Britain*, London, Unwin Hyman.

MARSHALL, T., 1971. 'Social Selection in the Welfare State', in E. Hopper (ed.), *Readings in the Theory of Educational Systems*, London, Hutchinson.

MARX, K., 1962. *Capital*, Vol. 3, Moscow, Foreign Languages Publishing House.

MARX, K., 1976. *Capital*, Vol. 1, Harmondsworth, Penguin Books.

MARX, K. and F. ENGELS, 1967. *The Communist Manifesto*, Harmondsworth, Penguin Books.

MILIBAND, R., 1973. *The State in Capitalist Society*, London, Quartet Books.

MILLER, R., 1986. 'Social Stratification and Mobility', in

322   Irish Society: Sociological Perspectives

P. Clancy, S. Drudy, K. Lynch and L. O'Dowd (eds.), *Ireland: A Sociological Profile*, Dublin, Institute of Public Administration, pp. 221-243.

MORRIS, L., 1991. 'Women's Poor Work' in P. Brown and R. Scase (eds.), *Poor Work: Disadvantage and the Division of Labour*, Milton Keynes, Open University Press, pp. 71-87.

MURRAY, C. 1990. *The Emerging British Underclass*, London, Institute of Economic Affairs.

NOLAN, B. and T. CALLAN (eds.), 1994. *Poverty and Policy in Ireland*, Dublin, Gill and Macmillan.

NOLAN, B. and B. FARRELL, 1990. *Child Poverty in Ireland*, Dublin, Combat Poverty Agency.

OECD, 1994. 'Standardized Unemployment Rates', Press Release 24 June 1994, Paris, OECD.

OLIVER, M., 1991. 'Disability and Participation in the Labour Market', in P. Brown and R. Scase (eds.), *Poor Work: Disadvantage and the Division of Labour*, Milton Keynes: Open University Press, pp. 132-46.

OSBORN, A. F., 1987. 'Assessing the Socio-Economic Status of Families', *Sociology*, Vol. 21, pp. 429-48.

OSBORN, A. F. and T. C. MORRIS, 1979. 'The Rationale for a Composite Index of Social Class and its Evaluation', *British Journal of Sociology*, Vol. 30, pp. 39-60.

PAHL, R., 1989. 'Is the Emperor Naked? Some Questions on the Adequacy of Sociological Theory in Urban and Regional Research', *International Journal of Urban and Regional Research*, Vol. 13, No. 4, pp. 709-720.

POULANTZAS, N., 1977. 'The New Petty Bourgeoisie', in A. Hunt (ed.), *Class and Class Structure*, London, Lawrence and Wishart, pp. 113-24.

POULANTZAS, N., 1978. *Classes in Contemporary Capitalism*, London, Verso.

REX, J., 1988. *The Ghetto and the Underclass*, Aldershot, Avebury.

RODGER, J., 1992. 'The Welfare State and Social Closure: Social Division and the Underclass', *Critical Social Policy*, Vol. 12, No. 2, pp. 45-63.

ROTTMAN, D., 1994. 'Allocating Money Within Households: Better Off Poorer?' in B. Nolan and T. Callan (eds.), *Poverty and Policy in Ireland*, Dublin, Gill and Macmillan, pp. 193-213.

ROTTMAN, D. B., D. F. HANNAN, N. HARDIMAN and M. M. WILEY, 1972. *The Distribution of Income in the Republic of Ireland: a Study of Social Class and Family Cycle Inequalities*, Dublin, Economic and Social Research Institute.

RUNCIMAN, W., 1990. 'How Many Classes Are There in Contemporary British Society?', *Sociology*, Vol. 24, No. 3, pp. 377-96.

STANWORTH, M., 1984. 'Women and Class Analysis: a Reply to John Goldthorpe', *Sociology*, Vol. 18, pp. 159-70.

WEBER, M., 1968. *Economy and Society*, Vol. 1, New York, Bedminster Press.

WESTERGAARD, J. and H. RESLER, 1976. *Class in a Capitalist Society*, Harmondsworth, Pelican Books.

WHELAN, C., 1994a. 'Poverty, Social Class, Education and Intergenerational Mobility', in B. Nolan and T. Callan (eds.), *Poverty and Policy in Ireland*, Dublin, Gill and Macmillan, pp. 130-146.

WHELAN, C. 1994b. 'In Search of the Underclass: Marginalisation, Poverty and Fatalism in the Republic of Ireland', Working Paper 51, Dublin, Economic and Social Research Institute.

WRIGHT, E. O., 1986. *Classes*, London, Verso.

WRIGHT, E. O. and L. PERRONE, 1977. 'Marxist Class Categories and Income Inequality', *American Sociological Review*, Vol. 42, pp. 32-55.

10
Class Transformation and Social Mobility in the Republic of Ireland[1]

CHRISTOPHER T. WHELAN

Ní uasal ná íseal ach thuas seal agus thíos seal
— Irish proverb

Introduction

People have long been fascinated by the manner in which some attain position, power and wealth while others remain in obscurity. Popular explanations for the phenomenon of social mobility vary from the '*e deo rex*' of medieval philosophers to the wry cynicism of the Irish proverb with which this chapter is headed.[2]

A detailed study of prevailing patterns of social mobility is of critical importance to an understanding of modern Irish society. The social significance of issues of equality of opportunity is recognised in a variety of official sources. Indeed, the Proclamation of the Irish State guarantees to cherish 'all the children equally'. Yet a substantial body of research exists documenting the degree of inequality in the society. These range from studies of income inequalities, poverty and access to education, to health inequalities (Nolan and Callan, 1994).

Inequalities of mobility opportunities are not simply one additional inequality but are, in fact, the crucial mechanism by which resource differences become perpetuated across generations. It is through the operation of restrictions on social mobility that closed social groupings emerge which are characterised by disparities in material and cultural resources, contrasting employment experiences and residential segregation.

Approaches to the study of social mobility in industrial society[3]

A conducive ideological context for the study of mobility in industrial society emerged only after the end of the last century. Nineteenth-century liberalism neglected socio-cultural influences on industrial achievement because of beliefs rooted in social Darwinism which provided legitimation for the *de facto* distributions of positions of privilege and power in terms of the survival of the fittest. For marxism, on the other hand, individual advancement was a collective myth. In fact, such mobility, by impeding the development of class consciousness, would retard true advancement by collective means.

However, in the early twentieth century a new interest emerged in mobility as a value to be preserved and maximised. In particular, in the years following the Second World War

> ... it was the problems of liberal democracy rather than the achievement of socialism which provided the major socio-political context of mobility research (Goldthorpe, 1987, p. 13).

The discussion of mobility in industrial societies was linked with the question of whether American society was distinctive in the amount of social mobility that it displayed. The conclusion reached was that vertical mobility rates across the manual and non-manual divide in industrial societies were strikingly similar and, by any reckoning, high.

An explanation of these findings was sought in factors

universal throughout industrial societies. Among the most important processes were (i) changes in the number of available positions, and (ii) changes in the number of inheritable positions. Industrial societies are those with expanding economies which need increasing numbers of higher level workers. Furthermore, the family enterprise gives way to the bureaucratic organisation with its formal methods of selection, with education becoming a more significant determinant of occupation position than occupational inheritance. The central question for American researchers, operating from the perspective of 'status attainment', concerned the relative importance of ascription and achievement. A stable industrial society was seen to require that greater emphasis be placed on what one is rather than who one is or who one knows. Furthermore, what one is is to be judged by 'universalistic' criteria such as educational attainment.

>   Nepotism and the 'old school tie' must give way to publicly demonstrable merit (Heath, 1981, p. 44).

The existence of high mobility can then be seen as contributing to the legitimation of inequalities because of the incentives it offers for the development and application of abilities in a manner which is in the interest of the society as a whole.

This view contrasts with that underlying the attack which British socialists launched on classic liberalism: that of exposing the gap that existed between liberal ideology and social reality. Equality of opportunity and equality of condition were seen as essentially complementary. The greater the degree of equality of opportunity that could be obtained, the more market forces could be enabled to work to egalitarian effect. Furthermore, it was considered that maximum opportunity for mobility would ensure that elite positions were open to talent and guard against the formation of permanent elites. Thus the theme of equity occupies centre stage.

There are major contrasts between the foregoing

approaches to the study of social mobility. However, they share in common a preoccupation with questions of 'who gets ahead and why'. The focus tends to be on the manner in which individuals move up and down a series of continuous dimensions of stratification. For those who follow in this tradition, mobility refers to the movement of individuals as between social groupings, or aggregates, that are ranked according to such criteria as their members' prestige, status or economic resources, i.e. within some form of *social hierarchy*.[4] An alternative tradition envisages mobility as occurring within a *class structure* with movement occurring between social positions that are identified in terms of relationships within labour markets and production units.

From a class structural perspective, one of the limitations of analysing mobility in terms of movement up or down a prestige scale is that occupations as different as skilled industrial workers and small proprietors, or industrial labourers and farmers, may be attributed very similar scores. Thus major shifts, such as those arising from decline in the agricultural sector, involving the movement of small farmers and their offspring into the industrial working class, cannot be captured within this approach.

> ... where mobility is analysed in a hierarchical context as represented by occupational prestige or status scales, it becomes difficult for the structural influences that bear on mobility rates and patterns to be adequately isolated and displayed. Occupational groupings that are treated as equivalent will in fact often be ones that are affected in quite different ways by, for example, shifts in demand, technological innovation, or the policies of national governments, and that may thus be following within the overall course of economic development, quite divergent trajectories of expansion or decline (Erikson and Goldthorpe, 1992, p. 31).

While it remains possible to address questions relating to individual attainment within a class perspective other issues relating to the effects on mobility rates of patterns of economic development and political intervention and, in turn, the consequences of mobility for class formation and action are brought into focus.[5]

A class schema for the analysis of social mobility

In this section we provide an outline of the class schema, deriving from Goldthorpe's (1987) work, which has been employed in the most comprehensive comparative analysis of social mobility to date (Erikson and Goldthorpe, 1992). This schema is operationalised through a threefold procedure. First, occupations are placed in occupational groups according to the content of their jobs; second, they are given an employment status that reflects their social relationships and work. Finally, a social class position is obtained for each individual by cross-classifying the relevant occupational group and employment status (Marshall, 1991, p. 55).

The basic purpose of the class schema is to differentiate positions within labour markets and production units in terms of the employment relationships they entail. Employers, self-employed, and employees are distinguished but it is also recognised that employer/employee relationships are based on quite heterogeneous principles (Erikson and Goldthorpe, 1992; Evans, 1992). The classification is based on an understanding of the development of class relations within large-scale industrial capitalist organisations and the nature of control in such organisations. Employees may be differentiated in terms of their conditions of employment, degree of occupational security and promotional prospects. There is a basic difference in the way employers relate to higher-level employees and working-class employees. The key difference lies in the ways in which commitment is obtained from the workforce. A much greater degree of trust is reposed in higher-level white-collar employees than in working-class members of the organisation. There is a direct link between the nature of these employees' tasks and the typical form of their conditions of employment. Such conditions can be seen to reflect the need for creating and sustaining organisational commitment. The logic of high trust relationships centres on the significance of prospective rewards, as embodied in incremental salary arrangements, security and, most particularly, career opportunities.

Combining these distinctions between types of employment status and employer-employee relationships and adding a degree of differentiation in terms of acreage for farmers gives us a detailed fourteen-category class, as set out in Table 1. For most purposes, though, we will operate with the aggregated seven-class scheme also shown in this table which is the one most frequently employed in comparative analysis. In analysing women's mobility we make use of a slightly modified version of this schema in which lower grade routine white-collar work positions are combined with non-skilled manual ones.[6]

Consistent with their class analysis perspective, Erikson and Goldthorpe's class schema is not organised around a single hierarchical principle; any such ordering must be introduced by reference to criteria such as job rewards and entry requirements. The most frequently-used hierarchical grouping distinguishes between the service class (I & II) at the top and the lower working-class (VIIa, VIIb) at the bottom, while the remaining classes occupy an intermediate position.

Class transformation in the Republic of Ireland

In our discussion of class transformation and mobility in Ireland, we shall draw on two different sources of information. The first source is the official statistics from the Census and Labour Force Surveys. Here the class schema involved is necessarily somewhat different from that outlined earlier but our results will be interpreted within the same conceptual framework. The second source is the national surveys conducted in 1973 and 1987; although the 1973 survey provides information on men only (Hout, 1989;

Table 1   **The class schema**

	Full version		Seven-class
I	Higher-grade professionals, administrators and officials; managers in large industrial establishments; large proprietors	I + II	Service class; professionals, administrators and managers; higher-grade technicians; supervisors of non-manual workers
II	Lower-grade professionals, administrators and officials; higher-grade technicians; managers in small industrial establishments; supervisors of non-manual employees		
IIIa	Routine non-manual employees, higher grade (administration and commerce)	III	Routine non-manual workers; routine non-manual employees in administration and commerce; sales personnel; other rank-and-file service workers
IIIb	Routine non-manual employees, lower grade (sales and services)		
IVa	Small proprietors, artisans, etc., with employees	IV a+b	Petty bourgeoisie: small proprietors and artisans, etc., with and without employees
IVb	Small proprietors, artisans, etc., without employees		

Table 1   The class schema *(contd.)*

Full version		*Seven-class*
IVc	Farmers and smallholders; other self-employed workers in primary production (i) owning 100 acres or more (ii) owning 50-99 acres (iii) owning less than 50 acres	IVc	Farmers: farmers and small-holders and other self-employed workers in primary production
V	Lower-grade technicians, supervisors of manual workers	V + VI	Skilled workers: lower-grade technicians; supervisors of manual workers: skilled manual workers
VI	Skilled manual workers		
VIIa	(i) Semi-skilled manual workers (not in agriculture, etc.) (ii) Unskilled manual workers (not in agriculture, etc.)	VIIa	Non-skilled workers: semi- and unskilled manual workers (not in agriculture, etc.)
VIIb	Agricultural and other workers in primary production	VIIb	Agricultural labourers: agricultural and other workers in primary production

Whelan *et al*, 1992). In order to facilitate documentation of changes in mobility patterns over time and cross-national variation, our initial focus will be on men aged between twenty and sixty-five. In a later section we will consider the substantial literature which has emerged in recent years dealing with women and class mobility.

While the core processes that formed the change to the Republic of Ireland's class structure are typical, their sequencing was not. Late industrialisation in a peripheral economy does not transform the class structure in a fashion identical to that experienced previously in the core capitalist countries. Late and rapid industrialisation meant that in Ireland the massive decline in opportunities for agricultural employment could not be compensated for by alternative opportunities. Emigration filled the gap for the cohort of males born between 1936 and 1940; only 59 per cent were still resident in Ireland by 1981.

Prior to 1960, the main dynamic of class change was exodus from the land. Between 1926 and 1961 the percentage of gainfully occupied males in agriculture fell from 58 to 43 per cent. After 1960 the rate of change accelerated dramatically. Between 1961 and 1981 males in agriculture as a fraction of males at work fell from one in two to one in five. The professional and managerial group grew from 8 per cent of those at work to 18 per cent between 1961 and 1990. Skilled manual workers also grew from 12 per cent to 18 per cent. The 'lower' middle class experienced more marked increases, while semi-skilled and unskilled workers, who constituted more than one in five of males at work in 1961, contracted to less than one in eight of this group by 1990. Over the same period, the total unemployed as a percentage of the gainfully occupied rose from 7 per cent to 16 per cent (Breen *et al*, 1990; O'Connell and Rottman, 1991).

Changes in the class composition of the Irish workforce emerged from industrial development that was more rapid, occurred later, and was more state-inspired than in most western societies. State policies were instrumental in setting industrial development in motion and influential in shaping the class structure. The latter effects have been summarised by O'Connell and Rottman (1992, pp. 212-218):

- state policies fostered public employment; employment in the state sector grew from 118,000 in 1961 to 235,000 in 1981
- welfare state expansion created jobs not only for public sector employees but also for self-employed professionals and private sector employees
- state policies contributed to a situation in which Ireland's class structure appears distinctive in the degree to which it fostered an expansion of non-agricultural proprietors
- regional policies distributed industrial jobs from urban to rural areas.

The intensity of changes in the class structure in Ireland should not lead one to overlook their incompleteness. By 1990 a substantial share of the workforce was in residual classes stranded in the cause of industrial development, especially farmers on marginal holdings, and labourers without skills.

Absolute social mobility

Class composition: inflow patterns
The degree of mobility that is observed in any society depends on the number, size and character of the class categories distinguished. Employing the seven-class schema outlined earlier, we find that there was a rise in the level of mobility between 1973 and 1987 from 58 per cent to 63 per cent. In the 1970s, only Sweden displayed a substantially higher level.

It is absolute class mobility which determines the composition of current classes in terms of the class origins of the incumbents, i.e. the inflow to a particular class from the range of class origins. Whelan *et al* (1992) summarise the broad situation in Ireland in 1987 based on their analysis of men aged between twenty and sixty-five years.

- The service class is a heterogencous group. As a consequence of an expansion of this class, its members are drawn from across the range of class positions. Almost one in three originate in the working class and a further one in five have agricultural origins. This is not a closed elite group.
- The *petit bourgeoisie* has become a relatively more heterogeneous group. Its members are less likely to have been born into this class and are increasingly likely to have farming and working-class backgrounds.
- The working-class displays high levels of self-recruitment even when the substantial inflows from the agricultural classes are taken into account. Almost two in three of its members had been intergenerationally stable and a further quarter had agricultural backgrounds.

Class mobility: outflow patterns
The results available from the 1973 and 1987 surveys provide evidence of a remarkable degree of similarity in mobility chances at both points in time, i.e. the patterns of outflow from each class origin to the various destinations. Just over one half of those from service class origins were found in this class and just over one-fifth in the industrial working class. These figures are very close to those other western European countries in the early 1970s. Focusing on men from the industrial working class, we find that one in nine is located in the service class, while seven out of ten have remained in their class of origin. The Irish figure for immobility is comparatively high. However, what marks Ireland out as distinctive, in comparative terms, is the extremely low level of upward mobility from the industrial working class into the service class; the Swedish rate, for example, is twice the Irish one.

The picture of stability in mobility patterns at the top and the bottom of the class hierarchy contrasts with the substantial improvement in the mobility chances of those from *petit bourgeoisie* and farming origins. Between 1973 and 1987 a major improvement took place in the chances of mobility to the service class for sons of small employers and, more particularly, those of the self-employed. The percentage achieving such mobility rose from 30 per cent to 36 per cent for the former and 13 per cent to 36 per cent for the latter. This was associated with a sharp drop in the numbers remaining in their class of origin. Those from farming origins displayed lower levels of immobility over time and an increased tendency to move into both the service class and the skilled manual class.

The Irish pattern of class mobility chances displays the following distinctive features:

- Opportunities for long-range upward mobility from the industrial working class to the service class are substantially lower than in other European countries.
- The advantages enjoyed by property-owning groups are significantly greater.

While the changes in mobility rates were greatest for the *petit bourgeoisie*, the fact that the farming group was so much larger meant that the less dramatic improvement in mobility chances of the latter was a more significant contribution to the process by which the sons of the working-class were 'crowded out'.[7]

The sociological significance of absolute *versus* relative mobility

Absolute mobility rates refer to the proportion of individuals in some base category who are mobile. Such rates are easily expressed in the sort of percentage terms we have employed thus far. We have dealt with three kinds of absolute rates – total, inflow and outflow. Relative rates are produced by comparisons of absolute rates. Such comparisons may be across countries, time, or socio-demographic groups.

The observed pattern of mobility in a table has been considered by many mobility analysts to arise from two rather different processes which have frequently been labelled *structural* and *exchange* mobility. The basic idea underlying this distinction is the simple one that the extent of intergenerational mobility observed will depend to a significant extent upon the degree of change over time in the class structure. Those originating in contracting classes, such as farming, will be 'pushed' out of such classes. Similarly, as the service class expands dramatically many people from other class origins are 'pulled' into the class. The difference between the origin class and destination class distributions has sometimes been taken as an indicator of the extent of such mobility. Structural mobility was usually conceived to be independent of exchange mobility which reflected the relative advantages associated with different class origins in pursuing desirable destinations, i.e. inequalities of opportunity. In the absence of structural mobility changes in the pattern of exchange mobility would, necessarily, involve both winners and losers; with increased upward mobility for those from some class origins being compensated for by increased downward mobility for others.

However, attempts to disaggregate mobility in this fashion involve assumptions about what the extent and pattern of mobility might have been in the absence of structural change. In fact, it becomes implausible to assume that the factors which transform the class structure, such as the rate of economic growth, are unrelated to those which influence the pattern of exchange mobility, such as educational institutions. It thus seems better to avoid the notion that mobility in any particular table can be divided into two components. Instead, it seems preferable to proceed on the basis that where we have more than one mobility table involving different countries, different points in time, age groups or sexes, they can be compared under two different aspects, i.e. absolute and relative mobility.

In order to develop the concept of relative mobility, it is

necessary to deal with the notions of disparity and odds ratios. In Table 2 we display a section of the overall outflow or class mobility chances table showing the movement between the service class and the non-skilled manual class.

Table 2:   **Class mobility chances**

| | Present class | |
Class origins	Service class	Non-skilled manual
Service class	56.6%	10.6%
Non-skilled manual	11.7%	47.7%

A useful indicator of the advantage enjoyed by those from service class backgrounds over those with non-skilled manual origins in gaining access to the service class is provided by the disparity ratio found by dividing 56.6 by 11.7, giving us a *disparity ratio* of 4.85; meaning that those from service class backgrounds have 4.85 times better chance of ending up in the service class than those from non-skilled manual backgrounds. Similarly, an index of the disadvantages experienced by the non-skilled manual class relative to the service class with regard to current location in the former class is given by the *disparity ratio* 47.7/10.6, i.e. 4.50; meaning that those from non-skilled manual backgrounds have 4.5 times more chance of remaining in that class than those from service class backgrounds have of being downwardly mobile into it. Multiplying these disparity ratios gives us an *odds ratio* of 21.8.

An odds ratio can be calculated for every pair of origin and destination classes in a mobility table. The notion of odds is a familiar one to anyone with an interest in gambling; rather than saying that the probability of one team winning is .2, we say that the odds are four to one against their winning. Our odds ratio is constructed by comparing the odds of entering one destination rather than another for two classes of origin by taking the ratio of the two odds.[8] The set of odds ratio associated with a mobility table can be interpreted sociologically as showing the outcome of a series of 'competitions' between individuals of different class origins to achieve – or avoid – one rather than another location within the class structure. The closer the value of the odds ratio to unity the more equal or 'perfect' is the particular competition to which it refers. Odds ratios are usually set up so that they measure the odds of getting into a 'higher' or more desirable destination class relative to entering a lower or less desirable class. If the odds ratio is more than one, this reflects greater advantage to the class whose odds form the numerator of the ratio, while an odds ratio less than one indicates that the advantage accrues to the origin class whose odds form the denominator.

Odds ratios can be interpreted as expressing the pattern of *net* association between origins and destinations. Expressed somewhat differently, Erikson and Goldthorpe (1992, p. 56) suggest that odds ratios reflect the pattern of *social fluidity*. The crucial idea being captured here is that two or more mobility tables could have the same pattern of relative rates as expressed by odds ratios, even though they have different origins and destinations distributions and consequently different absolute mobility rates.

Recently, a number of British authors have argued that an emphasis on relative rates by sociologists such as Goldthorpe grossly overstates the extent to which Britain is a closed society (Payne, 1990; Saunders, 1990). Does the application of procedures based on odds ratios leave us vulnerable to a similar accusation with regard to Irish society? In fact, as Goldthorpe (1990, p. 421) emphasises, such critiques require that 'social fluidity' be equated with social mobility. It is clear, however, from Goldthorpe's writings that he understands increased openness as involving a reduction in the degree of inequality of relative rates; in other words, an enhancement of the *ability to compete* of those for whom the dice were unfavourably loaded (Gagliani, 1990, p. 90).

In answer to the question of whether relative or absolute mobility is more important, the only sensible response is that

It depends on the particular issue with which one is trying to grapple. Social mobility is a complex phenomenon and it is desirable that we should avoid 'true' number approaches. If the focus is on class formation and its implication for class consciousness and political mobilisation, then what is likely to be crucial is the *de facto* patterns of mobility as reflected in the current composition of each class, in other words, the outcomes that structural change and the underlying pattern of inequality produce. If, on the other hand, concern is with equality of opportunity, then mobility must be assessed in relative terms.

Much of the criticism of the analysis of relative mobility rates has involved an implicit distaste for the use of sophisticated statistical methods, such as log-linear modelling, to analyse the pattern of odds ratios. These criticisms frequently present themselves in the guise of the 'plain man' who cuts through the distracting technical detail in order to deal with the central issues. Here Goldthorpe's (1990, p. 414) response is unequivocal:

> This position ... is both mistaken and, so far as the future of the social sciences is concerned, a dangerous one. It is not in truth, that of the 'plain man' but rather, and, even if unintentionally, the academic Luddite. The fact is that in regard to the analysis of mobility rates log-linear mobility is not now something that one can simply take or leave ... it is quite integral to any worthwhile understanding of what certain major *substantive* issues are.

Analysing patterns of social fluidity

In recent years, sociologists have devoted a great deal of their attention to developing models of social fluidity, i.e. models which hypothesise a particular pattern of odds ratio which allow us to successfully predict the frequencies in the observed mobility. In developing such a model one is influenced by one's understanding of the resources that individuals can draw on and the attractiveness to them of particular destinations.

Goldthorpe (1987, p. 98), from his class structural perspective, identifies three general considerations:

- the relative desirability of different class positions, considered as destinations
- the relative advantages associated with different class origins, in the form of economic, cultural, and social resources
- the relative barriers that face individuals in gaining access to different class positions – which involve requirements corresponding to the resources identified above.

Given the perspective from which he approaches the study of mobility, it is hardly surprising that these factors are not conceptualised by Goldthorpe solely in hierarchical terms; although a vertical ordering of origins and destinations is one crucial element in the attempt by Erikson and Goldthorpe (1992) to develop a model of social fluidity in industrial nations. Other important effects relate to inheritance and sector. Inheritance effects cover all those that increase the likelihood of individuals being found in the same class from which they originated. A tendency towards such inheritance, over and above that which we might expect on the basis of the impact of hierarchical influences, could be expected to arise as a result of the particular attractiveness to individuals of positions within their own class of origin or as a consequence of opportunities and barriers being of a somewhat different sort for 'insiders' and 'outsiders'. Over and above this, we should expect some degree of immobility to result from inheritance; in the direct sense of transfer of ownership of a business. Finally, with regard to sectoral effects, tendencies towards movement within the agricultural and non-agricultural sectors are likely to be stronger than movement between the sectors, even when we allow for the influence of hierarchy and inheritance.

Breen and Whelan (1992; and 1994b), taking Goldthorpe's theoretical model as a base, provide a detailed account of the development of a model which is intended to account for the pattern of social fluidity or inequalities in competition which characterises mobility for men in the Republic of Ireland. The model which they refer to as the Agriculture, Hierarchy and Property (AHP) model involves the following three main dimensions.

Agriculture: the term reflecting the barrier to movement into agricultural destinations

Hierarchy: which captures the effect of generalised resources, desirability and barriers, of a hierarchical kind

Property: which involves a measure of ownership of the means of production for origins and destinations.

A model incorporating measures of these variables provides a satisfactory account of the pattern of social fluidity for men in the Republic of Ireland. By this it is meant that the cell frequencies in the mobility table predicted by the equation derived from this model came very close to matching the observed frequencies. When such a model is applied to the data for men in 1973 and 1987, no change can be detected along these dimensions. However, while ownership of the means of production continues to be associated with distinct mobility advantages, these advantaged have increasingly come to operate through education. At the same time, it appears that class background influences other than those mediated by education and property, such as use of social networks and specialised labour market knowledge, have become more important (Breen and Whelan, 1993).

A variety of such models has been applied to the Irish case and, while differences exist in terms of detailed interpretation, there is a consensus that among western European countries, for whom data are available, Sweden lies at one extreme in terms of openness and Ireland at the other (Erikson and Goldthorpe, 1987; Hout, 1989; Whelan and Whelan, 1984; Breen and Whelan, 1985).

Gender and class mobility

Theoretical issues

Gender has frequently been identified as the most contro-versial issue confronting present-day class analysis (Marshall *et al*, 1988; McRae, 1990). Hayes and Miller (1993) acknowledge that the debate has become increasingly acrimonious and offer a review of the evidence which is intended to promote discussion and reflection. However, their conclusion that the neglect of women 'has effectively distorted understanding of the central social processes of social mobility' is itself far from uncontroversial, as anyone familiar with Erikson and Goldthorpe's (1992a, 1992b) most recent contributions to the debate will recognise. The central issue relates to the appropriate unit of composition for class analysis. A number of options are available:

- One can proceed with analysis of men only.
- One can follow the 'conventional' approach whereby married women are allocated to a class position on the basis of their husband's position in the labour market.
- One can adopt an individual approach whereby individuals are assigned a position solely on the basis of their own participation in the labour market. In this case a married woman who is a shop assistant and married to a teacher will be allocated the same class position as a woman in the same occupation married to an unskilled manual worker. It also becomes necessary to decide whether one wishes to modify this approach for married women who are not currently in the labour market.
- One can assign the family unit a class position on the basis of the joint characteristics of the husband and wife members. However, this creates a great deal of artefactual mobility since the class position of the family changes as wives withdraw from, or re-enter, the labour market.
- The class position of the family may be determined by reference to the employment of either the husband or

the wife depending on which may be regarded as 'dominant' in their labour-market participation according to criteria of both employment status and level of employment.[9]

Those, such as Erikson and Goldthorpe, who seek to uphold, to a significant extent, the so-called 'conventional view', insist on continuing to regard the family as the appropriate unit of class analysis. Against this, many feminist sociologists (and others) argue that it is the individual who is the appropriate unit of class analysis (Abbot and Sapsford, 1987; Abbot and Payne, 1990; Stanworth, 1984).

Many of the controversies in this area have their roots in fundamental conceptual differences (Goldthorpe, 1983, 1984, 1990; Stanworth, 1984). Before proceeding to consideration of the available Irish evidence, it is necessary to make clear the position adopted here on a number of crucial issues. First, we are concerned with *class* rather than occupational mobility. Many legitimate questions relating to individual occupational attainment are not part of our brief. One example of such issues is the influence of mothers' occupation or labour market status on the corresponding outcomes for daughters and the potential impact of role models and socialisation (Hayes, 1990).

Secondly, class analysis focuses on the processes occurring within a given context. In this sense, the occupational order may be seen to form 'the backbone of the class structure' (Parkin, 1972, p. 18). However, the fact that a class categorisation is intended to apply to occupational positions does not involve a commitment to the view that 'the class of all individuals alike will be most validly determined by reference to their own employment' (Erikson and Goldthorpe, 1992a, p. 37). The rationale of class analysis requires that members of a class are associated with particular sets of positions over time and would be undermined if classes were to appear as highly unstable aggregates of such positions. The existence of such stability provides the basis for the key role of the family as a unit of strategic action in terms of consumption and production.

Thirdly, the implications of the employment relationship of that member of the family unit who may be regarded as 'dominant' in terms of labour market position extends beyond the work-place in terms of its consequences for

> ... experiences of affluence or hardship, of economic security or insecurity, of prospects of continuing material advance, or of unyielding material constraints (Erikson and Goldthorpe, 1992, p. 236).

This position does not involve a neglect of differences in resources and power among family members (Arber, 1989; Arber, 1993; Pahl, 1989, 1990). On the contrary, it is precisely the existence of such differences which typically sees the class position of other family members being 'derived' from the male 'head' in virtue of their degree of economic dependence on him.

Fourthly, gender differences in absolute mobility *per se* and, in particular, their intragenerational patterning, can hardly be held to undermine the argument for the family as the unit of analysis. The existence of such differences, arising from the disproportionate extent to which women bear the burden of family and domestic commitments, provides the major justification for this approach and, in particular, the need to identify the member of the household with the dominant relationship to the labour market.

Fifthly, acceptance of these points does not require that women be excluded from mobility analysis nor that in households with married or cohabiting couples it should be the male who determines the family's class position. Critics of the conventional approach have been successful in bringing about a movement away from the situation where mobility analysis was restricted to males (Dex, 1990; Roberts, 1993). This, however, does not resolve the empirical issue of the extent to which such restrictions have distorted our understanding of the mobility process.

Absolute mobility of women via employment[10]

Focusing on the Irish situation, we find that official statistics suggest that the most striking change for women is not their distribution across class categories but the increased numbers of married women at work and the continued concentration of women in a restricted set of occupational categories. In 1991, three of four women in employment were located in white-collar work compared to one in two males, although it is necessary to note that the percentage increase in the number of women in the service class equals that for men (O'Connell, 1993). Once again our survey evidence makes it possible to elaborate on the findings deriving from official statistics. Over one in four gainfully occupied women aged between twenty and sixty-five is located in the service class. A further one in five is engaged in higher level routine white-collar work and over two-fifths can be classified as lower white-collar or semi-skilled manual. A mere 12 per cent are distributed across the agricultural, *petit bourgeoisie* and skilled manual classes, compared to one in two men.

In examining the mobility of women, we employ a slightly modified version of the seven-class schema in which lower-grade routine non-manual occupations are combined with semi-skilled and unskilled manual occupations. Comparing the origin to destination mobility tables for men and women, we find that, while their origins differ little, their destination distributions reflect the operation of processes of gender segregation. Women are over-represented in the lower white-collar and non-skilled manual categories and underrepresented among the small proprietors, farmers and the skilled manual class. Associated with such segregation there is a significantly greater tendency for women in the service class to come from farm backgrounds than is the case for men; the respective figures being one-third and one-sixth. Correspondingly, women from non-skilled manual backgrounds make up a significantly lower percentage of the female service class than do their male counterparts. A similar pattern holds for both in higher white-collar work. Finally, a significantly greater percentage of women in the non-skilled manual and lower white-collar class came from non-working class backgrounds.

As a consequence of their exclusion from those class categories in which inheritance has its greatest influence, women experience greater mobility than men; with 70 per cent of women having changed their class position in comparison with 60 per cent of men. The difference was due, primarily, to differences in levels of vertical mobility (which had been experienced by 57 per cent of women and 44 per cent of men) and, within this, to differences in downward mobility, which had been experienced by 29 per cent of women but only 18 per cent of men.

Patterns of relative mobility of women via employment

When attention is directed to a comparison of male and female relative mobility rates, the major question which must be addressed is whether the sole source of variation in men's and women's mobility chances arises from differences in the objective opportunity structure as reflected in gender segregation of occupations. In order to test this hypothesis, Breen and Whelan (forthcoming a) sought to establish if it was possible to explain gender differences in mobility, simply by allowing for differences in origin and destination distribution while assuming that the underlying pattern of association or social fluidity was the same for women and men. In fact, this proves to be possible. The forces that make for inequalities in *relative* mobility chances among men, stemming from the advantages associated with one class origin rather than another, are not in any serious way modified for women (Erikson and Goldthorpe, 1992, p. 253).

Women's marital mobility

The pervasiveness of class effects is also shown when we examine marital mobility. The debate on the appropriate unit of class composition has led to agreement on all sides that women's mobility through marriage is an important and neglected topic. If married women are to be seen as tending to derive their class position from their husbands, then an understanding of their intergenerational class mobility requires that we direct our attention to the experience of women in 'marriage markets' as well as in labour markets; specifically, it is necessary to examine rates and patterns of marital mobility.

A recurring hypothesis in the literature is that women experience more mobility through marriage than do men through employment and their 'class fate is more loosely linked' to their social origins than is the case for men (Heath, 1981). The main argument underlying this hypothesis is that physical or personality attributes, which can make women more or less attractive as marriage partners, are less closely associated with social origins than are those that mainly influence men's achievements in their working lives. If this hypothesis is true, then focusing solely on men's mobility could lead to substantial underestimation of the extent of mobility opportunities within the society.

In fact, applying the AHP model, we find that it does a remarkably good job for women's marital mobility (Breen and Whelan, forthcoming). The results indicate that women are more likely to change class through marriage than men are to change class through employment mobility; and that it is easier (*ceteris paribus*) for women to marry farmers and farm workers than for men not born into agriculture to become farmers or farm workers themselves. Notwithstanding these differences, if we know how men of given class origin are distributed within the class structure, we can predict with no great inaccuracy how their 'sisters' have fared through marriage (Erikson and Goldthorpe, 1992a).

Breen and Whelan (1994b) also applied the AHP model to a 'complete' mobility table constructed on the basis of the dominance procedure where information on the class position, employment status and number of hours worked of both husband and wife are used to select the 'dominant' individual. The results of the analysis show that only modest differences exist in the pattern of social fluidity associated with complete and men-only tables. The findings in relation to both women's mobility, marital mobility and complete mobility tables support the argument of Erikson and Goldthorpe (1992, p. 235) that 'the lines of class division run between but not through families'.

Class mobility and unemployment

The discussion of social mobility up to this point has taken no account of unemployment. In Irish social mobility surveys the unemployed have been allocated to a class on the basis of their last job. Given current rates of unemployment and the prospect that relatively high rates will persist, the question arises whether the class structure can be adequately represented without denoting a distinctive position for the long-term unemployed.

One response to the challenge raised by long-term unemployment is to think of this group as part of an underclass who effectively fall outside the class system (Runciman, 1990). This approach appears to be based on the assumption that the class characteristics of the unemployed are distinct from those of the working class; although the available evidence provides little support for this view (Gallie, 1994; Heath, 1992). An alternative approach is to ask whether as a consequence of detachment from the labour market and social isolation we can identify a class which cannot be categorised simply as a fraction of the working class. In England, Goldthorpe and Payne (1986, pp. 17-18) concluded that mobility chances for manual workers polarised between 1972 and 1983, with more experiencing upward mobility, but more being downwardly mobile into unemployment. The return of mass unemployment 'has had the general effect of "raising the stakes"' in that the cost of intergenerational stability in the working class is now higher. In Ireland, low growth rates in the 1980s have been reflected, not in obvious changes in the class structure, but in a dramatic rise in the unemployment rate coupled with a process of 'trading down' for middle-class school leavers as they took up jobs which traditionally had been the preserve of the working class (Breen, 1984). No improvement in the prospects of upward mobility has occurred for those from manual backgrounds but, undoubtedly, their risk of unemployment has grown rapidly. In England, men from manual origins are twice as likely to appear in the service class as to be unemployed but in Ireland this probability is reversed. It is for the intermediate class in Ireland that such a polarisation can be observed with the probability of both upward mobility and unemployment increasing. At the top there has been relatively little change.

In order to bring out some of the distinctive aspects of the Irish mobility experience, it is necessary to distinguish, within the non-skilled manual class, between semi-skilled and unskilled workers. The unskilled male manual group, which forms 10 per cent of the destination class distribution, is particularly distinctive. In the first place, while one in four of the semi-skilled manual group is intragenerationally mobile, out of the working class, this is true of only one in seven of the unskilled manual group. An inflow perspective brings out the distinctive nature of this class more clearly. While over 80 per cent of the members of the semi-skilled manual group are drawn from working class or small farm origins, this holds true for 94 per cent of the unskilled manual group. Furthermore, the impact of current class and class origin is cumulative. The probability of being unemployed or permanently unable to work due to illness or disability rises to two out of three for men in the unskilled manual group from manual backgrounds.

Long-term unemployment presents serious difficulties for class analysis only if we adopt a static rather than a dynamic perspective; if we emphasise structure at the expense of process (Marshall *et al*, 1994). In the Irish case, Whelan (1994b) concludes from an examination of the evidence relating to the social and psychological consequences of a high level of long-term unemployment that what we are confronted with is not the emergence of an underclass but different types of working-class marginalisation. The costs of the most extreme form of working-class marginalisation has been disproportionately borne by those members of the younger cohorts originating in the lower working class rather than by those in particular geographic locations (Nolan *et al*, 1994; Whelan, 1994b). While intergenerational transmission of unemployment was not evident by 1987, it seems inevitable that it will become more common.

This analysis suggests that issues posed by long-term unemployment, rather than undermining class analysis, provide support for Goldthorpe and Marshall's (1992, p. 382) argument for the 'promising future of class analysis' understood as

> ... a specific way of investigating interconnections ... between historically formed macro social structures, on the one hand, and, on the other, the everyday experience of individuals within their partial social milieux.

Conclusions

Structural change in Ireland has been associated with large-scale mobility. As a consequence, the service class is not a closed *élite* but a relatively heterogeneous group in terms of their class origins. The creation of increased room at the top of the class hierarchy and a contraction of places at the bottom can lead to a general shift upward without, necessarily, reducing the relative advantages enjoyed by those families which experienced privileges in the old class structure. Economic change, no matter how deep, may not be associated with an alteration in relative advantages. This is what has occurred in the Irish situation where the strength of hierarchical and property influences in influencing equality of opportunity over time has remained unchanged.

Extension of mobility analysis to women serves to confirm the constancy of class influences on relative mobility opportunities. Differences in female mobility patterns are almost entirely a consequence of gender segregation in the labour market. Class influences on underlying patterns of inequality of opportunity operate in a 'gender blind' fashion. This finding should not be taken as providing justification for the exclusion of women from mobility analysis. It does suggest, however, as Erikson and Goldthorpe (1992a, p. 253) have argued, that any adequate explanation of the disadvantages suffered by women as a consequence of gendered labour market segmentation and the lack of continuity in their work histories is likely to be developed, for the most part, independently of class analysis.

Politicians in Ireland shared with many social scientists a sanguine view of the relationship between economic growth and mobility opportunities. In fact, the nature of Irish industrialisation has been such that the degree of disadvantage suffered by the working class has been greater than conventional mobility table analysis would suggest since it conceals the dramatic increase in the risk of unemployment for this group. The logic of Irish industrial development involving the dispersal of industrial location to rural areas in the 1960s and 1970s involved particular costs for the urban working class. The main beneficiaries, though, were not those from the rural working class but the sons and daughters of farmers and the *petit bourgeoisie*.

Furthermore, the available evidence suggests that emigration now reflects an extension of mobility differential. Economic 'push' factors dominate the migration decisions of the poorly educated working class while occupational status and 'pull' factors are more important factors for the better educated middle class. The available evidence on the composition of emigrants suggests that unlike the 1950s, few opportunities now exist for those without skills and qualifications to work outside Ireland (Sexton *et al*, 1991). Those without educational qualifications and work remain in Ireland and contribute to an expanding marginalised working class (Whelan, 1994b).

Acknowledgements
I would like to thank Tony Fahey and two anonymous referees for their helpful comments on an early version of this paper.

Notes

1. No attempt has been made to provide statistical support for the conclusions presented in this paper. Detailed accounts of the relevant analysis of the 1987 ESRI survey are provided in Breen and Whelan (1992; 1993, 1994b and forthcoming a and b) and in Whelan, Breen and Whelan (1992). Marshall, *et al* (1988) provide an evaluation of contemporary approaches to class analysis. Breen and Rottman (forthcoming) provide an overview of developments in relation to class analysis and social mobility which is both accessible and innovative.

2. Roughly translated, the proverb means:
   'Neither noble nor humble but up a while and down a while'.

3. The discussion in this section draws on reviews provided by Goldthorpe (1987) and Heath (1981).

4. For a discussion of the difficulties presented by certain undemonstrated assumptions about the social relationship of deference, acceptance or derogation implied in prestige or socio-economic scales and the methodological difficulties caused by the synthetic nature of the scales, see Goldthorpe and Hope (1972).

5. It is not possible to deal in any detail in this chapter with the consequences of social mobility. Breen and Whelan (1994), Hardiman and Whelan (1994) and Whelan (1994a) deal with some aspects of the social and psychological consequences of social mobility in the Republic of Ireland.

6. For men, the number of respondents in such positions is sufficiently small that it makes relatively little difference how they are allocated.

7. See Hannan and Commins (1992) for a discussion of the survival strategies of small farm households.

8. Thus, in our example, the odds on someone from the service class entering the service class rather than the non-skilled manual class is $56.6/10.6 = 5.34$. Similarly, the corresponding odds for a person from the non-skilled manual class is $11.7/47.7 = 0.245$. The odds ratio is therefore $5.34/.245 = 21.8$.

9. Erikson (1984) defines dominance in terms of two criteria: those of 'work time' and 'work position'. The first to which priority is given dictates that employment dominates non-employment and full-time employment dominates part-time employment. The second requires that higher-level employment dominates lower-level employment.
10. Women who were not in the labour force were excluded from the analysis.

References

ABBOT, P. and G. PAYNE, 1990. 'Women's Social Mobility: The Conventional Wisdom Reconsidered', in G. Payne and P. Abbot (eds.), *The Social Mobility of Women*, London, The Falmer Press.

ABBOT, P. and R. SAPSFORD, 1987. *Women and Social Class*, London, Tavistock.

ARBER, S., 1989. 'Gender and Class Inequalities in Health: Understanding the Differentials' in J. Fox (ed.), *Health Inequalities in European Countries*, Aldershot, Gower.

ARBER, S., 1993. 'Inequalities Within the Household' in D. Morgan and L. Stanley (eds.), *Debates in Sociology*, Manchester, Manchester University Press.

BREEN, R., 1984. *Education and the Labour Market: Work and Unemployment Among Recent Cohorts of Irish School Leavers*, Dublin, The Economic and Social Research Institute.

BREEN, R. and D. ROTTMAN (forthcoming). *Class Stratification: A Comparative*

Perspective, Harvester Wheatsheaff.

BREEN, R. and C. T. WHELAN, 1985. 'Vertical Mobility and Class Inheritance in the British Isles', *British Journal of Sociology*, Vol. 36, pp. 175-192.

BREEN, R. and C. T. WHELAN, 1992. 'Explaining the Irish Pattern of Social Fluidity: The Role of the Political', in J. H. Goldthorpe and C. T. Whelan (eds.), *The Development of Industrial Society in Ireland*, Oxford, Proceedings of the British Academy 79, Oxford University Press.

BREEN, R. and C. T. WHELAN, 1993. 'From Ascription to Achievement? Origins, Education and Entry to the Labour Force in the Republic of Ireland During the Twentieth Century', *Acta Sociologica*, Vol. 36, No. 1, pp. 3-17.

BREEN, R. and C. T. WHELAN, 1994. 'Social Class, Class Origins and Political Partisanship in the Republic of Ireland', *European Journal of*

Political Research, Vol. 26,
No. 2.
BREEN, R. and C. T. WHELAN
(forthcoming, a). 'Gender
and Class Mobility: Evidence
from the Republic of Ireland',
Sociology.
BREEN, R. and C. T. WHELAN,
1994 b. 'Modelling Trends in
Social Fluidity: The Core
Model and a Measured
Variable Approach', *European
Sociological Review,* Vol. 10,
No. 3.
BREEN, R. and C. T. WHELAN
(forthcoming, b). *Social Class
and Social Mobility in the
Republic of Ireland,* Dublin, Gill
and Macmillan.
BREEN, R., D. F. HANNAN,
D. B. ROTTMAN, and C. T.
WHELAN, 1990.
*Understanding Contemporary
Ireland: State Class and
Development in the Republic of
Ireland,* London, Macmillan.
DEX, S., 1990. 'Goldthorpe
on Class and Gender' in
J. Clarke, C. Modgill and
S. Modgill (eds.), *John H.
Goldthorpe: Consensus and
Controversy,* London, The
Falmer Press.
ERIKSON, R., 1984. 'Social
Class of Men, Women and
Families', *Sociology,* Vol. 18,
No. 4, pp. 500-514.
ERIKSON, R. and J. H.
GOLDTHORPE, 1987a.
'Commonality and Variation
in Social Fluidity in
Industrial Nations, Part I: A
Model for Evaluating the

"FJH Hypothesis"', *European
Sociological Review,* Vol. 33,
pp. 56-77.
ERIKSON, R. and J. H.
GOLDTHORPE, 1987b.
'Commonality and Variation
in Social Fluidity in Industrial
Nations, Part II: The Model of
Core Social Fluidity Applied',
European Sociological Review,
Vol. 3, pp. 145-166.
ERIKSON, R. and J. H.
GOLDTHORPE, 1992a. *The
Constant Flux: A Study of Class
Mobility in Industrial Societies,*
Oxford, Clarendon Press.
ERIKSON, R. and J. H.
GOLDTHORPE, 1992b.
'Individual or Family? Results
from Two Approaches to Class
Assignment', *Acta Sociologica,*
Vol. 335, pp. 95-106.
EVANS, G., 1992. 'Testing the
Validity of the Goldthorpe
Class Schema', *European
Sociological Review,* 1992, Vol. 8,
No. 3, pp. 211-232.
GAGLIANI, G., 1990. 'Class and
Economic Development: A
Critique of Marxist Theories'
in J. Clarke, C. Modgill and
S. Modgill (eds.), *John H.
Goldthorpe: Consensus and
Controversy,* London, The
Falmer Press.
GALLIE, D., 1994. 'Are the
Unemployed an Underclass?
Some Evidence from the
Social Change and Economic
Life Initiative', *Sociology,*
Vol. 28, No. 3, pp. 737-757.
GOLDTHORPE, J. H., 1983.
'Women and Class Analysis: In

Defence of the Conventional View', *Sociology*, Vol. 17.

GOLDTHORPE, J. H., 1984. 'Women and Class Analysis: A Reply to the Replies', *Sociology*, Vol. 18, No. 4, pp. 491-500.

GOLDTHORPE, J. H. (with CATRIONA LLEWELLYN and CLIVE PAYNE), 1987. *Social Mobility and Class Structure in Modern Britain*, Oxford, Clarendon Press.

GOLDTHORPE, J. H., 1990. 'A Response', in J. Clarke, C. Modgill (eds.), *John H. Goldthorpe: Consensus and Controversy*, London, The Falmer Press.

GOLDTHORPE, J. H. and K. HOPE, 1972. 'Occupational Grading and Occupational Prestige' in K. Hope (ed.), *The Analysis of Social Mobility*, Oxford, Clarendon Press.

GOLDTHORPE, J. H. and G. PAYNE, 1986. 'Trends in Intergenerational Class Mobility in England and Wales 1972-1983', *Sociology*, Vol. 20, pp. 1-24.

GOLDTHORPE, J. H. and G. MARSHALL, 1992. 'The Promising Future of Class Analysis: A Response to Recent Critiques', *Sociology*, Vol. 26, No. 3, pp. 381-400.

HANNAN, D.F. and P. COMMINS, 1992. 'The Significance of Small Scale Landholders in Ireland's Socio-Economic Transformation', in J. H. Goldthorpe and C. T. Whelan (eds.), *The Development of Industrial Society in Ireland*, Oxford, Proceedings of the British Academy 79, Oxford University Press.

HARDIMAN, N. and C. T. WHELAN, 1994. 'Values and Political Partisanship' in C. T. Whelan (ed.), *Values and Social Change in Ireland*, Dublin, Gill and Macmillan.

HAYES, B. C., 1990. 'Inter-generational Mobility Among Employed and Non-Employed Women: The Australian Case', *Australian and New Zealand Journal of Sociology*, Vol. 26, pp. 368-388.

HAYES, B. C. and R. L. MILLER, 1993. 'The Silenced Voice: Female Social Mobility Patterns with Particular Reference to the British Isles', *British Journal of Sociology*, Vol. 44, No. 4, pp. 653-672.

HEATH, A., 1981. *Social Mobility*, London, Fontana.

HEATH, A., 1992. 'The Attitudes of the Underclass', in D. Smith (ed.), *Understanding the Underclass*, London, Policy Studies Institute.

HOUT, M., 1989. *Following in Father's Footsteps: Social Mobility in Ireland*, London, Harvard University Press.

McRAE, 1990. 'Women and Class Analysis', in J. Clarke, C. Modgill and S. Modgill (eds.), *John H. Goldthorpe: Consensus and Controversy*, London, The Falmer Press.

MARSHALL, G., 1990. 'John Goldthorpe and Class Analysis' in J. Clarke, C. Modgill and S. Modgill (eds.), *op. cit.*

MARSHALL, G., H. NEWBY, D. ROSE, and C. VOGLER, 1988. *Social Class in Modern Britain*, London, Unwin Hyman.

MARSHALL, G., S. ROBERTS, C. BURGOYNE, and D. ROUTH, 1994. *Social Class and Underclass in Britain and the United States*, Oxford, Nuffield College.

NOLAN, B. and T. CALLAN (eds.), 1994. *Poverty and Policy in Ireland*, Dublin, Gill and Macmillan.

NOLAN, B., C. T. WHELAN, and J. WILLIAMS, 1994. 'Spatial Aspects of Poverty and Disadvantage' in B. Nolan and T. Callan (eds.), *Poverty and Policy in Ireland*, Dublin, Gill and Macmillan.

O'CONNELL, P., 1993. *Economic Development and the Transformation of Class Positions of Males and Females at Work in the Republic of Ireland, 1961-1991*, Dublin, The Economic and Social Research Institute.

O'CONNELL, P. and D. ROTTMAN, 1992. 'The Irish Welfare State in Comparative Perspective' in J. H. Goldthorpe and C. T. Whelan (eds.), *The Development of Industrial Society in Ireland*, Oxford, Proceedings of the British Academy 79, Oxford

University Press.

PAHL, J., 1989. *Money and Marriage*, Basingstoke, Macmillan Educational.

PAHL, J., 1990. 'Household Spending, Personal Spending and the Control of Money in Marriage', *Sociology*, Vol. 24, pp. 119-138.

PARKIN, F., 1972. *Class Inequality and Political Order*, London, Paladin.

ROBERTS, H., 1992. 'The Women and Class Debate' in D. Morgan and L. Stanley (eds.), *Debates in Sociology*, Manchester, Manchester University Press.

RUNCIMAN, W.G., 1990. 'How Many Classes are there in Contemporary British Society', *Sociology*, Vol. 24, No. 3, pp. 377-396.

SAUNDERS, P., 1990. *Social Class and Stratification*, London, Routledge.

SEXTON, J. J., B. M. WALSH, D. F. HANNAN, and D. McMAHON, 1991. *The Economic and Social Implications of Emigration*, Dublin, National Economic and Social Council.

STANWORTH, M., 1984. 'Women and Class Analysis: A Reply to John Goldthorpe', *Sociology*, Vol. 18, No. 2, pp. 159-170.

WHELAN, C. T., 1994a. 'Social Class, Unemployment and Psychological Distress', *European Sociological Review*, Vol. 10, No. 1, pp. 49-61.

WHELAN, C. T., 1994b.

'Marginalisation, Deprivation and Fatalism in the Republic of Ireland: Class and Underclass Perspectives', paper presented at European Research Conference on European Society or European Societies? Changes in the Labour Markets and European Integration, Espinho, Portugal.

WHELAN, C. T. and B. J. WHELAN, 1984. *Social Mobility in the Republic of Ireland: A Comparative Perspective*, Dublin, The Economic and Social Research Institute.

WHELAN, C. T., R. BREEN and B. J. WHELAN, 1992. 'Industrialisation, Class Formation and Social Mobility in Ireland', in J. H. Goldthorpe and C. T. Whelan (eds.), *The Development of Industrial Society in Ireland*, Oxford: Proceedings of the British Academy 79, Oxford University Press.

11
Interest Groups and the State in the Republic of Ireland

MICHEL PEILLON

German philosophers, up to Hegel, used to make a clear distinction between the state and what they called civil society. Civil society was the economic society, which was composed of particular groups with particular interests each competing with the other. The state, on the other hand, referred to the collectivity which was organised politically, that is to say according to universal values. This kind of distinction immediately raised the question of the nature of the links between state and society. In this context, the state meant the whole population which is politically organised through a constitution or a legal framework. Nowadays the state is more likely to indicate the institution which exercises central power. It refers to the individuals and agencies which make and implement decisions for the collectivity as a whole. They form the apparatus of central authority. The state is then associated with such attributes as centralisation of power, territorial sovereignty, a monopoly of the legitimate use of force. There remains some debate about the exact composition or boundaries of this specialised apparatus of central power. It includes the legislators, who set the rules according to which the group operates; the governmental ministers who pursue policies; the administrators who conduct public affairs on a day-to-day basis and implement the decisions of the rulers; the judges who decide on the right application of rules; the police which enforces the rules; the army which protects the territory, etc. Others include in the state apparatus schools, media, local government.

The very fact of a differentiation between state and society raises the question of the kind of rapport which has developed between them. How is the state inserted within society, what impact has it on society and what impact do the diverse forces active in society have on the state? In this chapter, we consider how the link between the state and society has been analysed in the Republic of Ireland. The state has been presented as ruling society on behalf of a particular group; it is said to participate to a structure of class domination. For others, the activity of the state manifests the balance which develops between the major organised forces in society. Such a balance fluctuates according to the changing relations between interest groups. This balance may even become institutionalised in a corporatist framework. But the state has also been viewed as a source of autonomous power, as a force in its own right. In this case, the state does not simply represent the product of forces weighing upon it, but acts on society.

State and class
A possible point of departure in the analysis of the relations between state and society is given by the image of society one relies upon. It may be viewed in terms of socio-economic categories which are hierarchically arranged and form a class-structure. Admittedly, what is meant by social class and class-structure will vary, but it tends to refer to different categories of people, who are diversely located in the occupational structure of society and enjoy an unequal access to social goods. They form clusters of social inequality, and possibly develop a collective identity around common interests.

The state has been presented by many as the upholder of the collective interest, of the common good. But what is the common interest of a society divided into classes, and who defines it? The state can hardly be above the contradictions and conflicts of such society, and its activity reveals biases in the way it operates. The policies it pursues benefit some categories and disadvantage others. A study of the redistributive impact of the state in the Republic of Ireland, through direct taxation and public financial transfers, has revealed quite an extraordinary pattern (Rottman, 1982). Redistribution implies that the state extracts a greater proportion of the income of the wealthier groups, and distributes this wealth, in the form of allowances and services, to the worse-off social categories. Such redistribution occurs in the Republic of Ireland, and marginal social classes, such as small farmers or semi-skilled and unskilled manual workers, depend on the state for their existence. Some of the wealthier categories, such as professional workers, are heavily taxed and lose a great deal of their income this way. On the other hand, some high income categories (such as large proprietors and farmers) give little away or even actually profit from their relation to the state. Finally, some categories which enjoy a good share of the national income benefit further from their relation to the state. Redistribution occurs, but in a distorted way: it takes place within the non-property classes, while all property classes lose very little and more frequently gain by relating to the state. A definite bias exists in favour of the propertied class in the way taxation operates. Similar state biases could be identified in a range of areas.

The existence of such biases shows that the state cannot remain aloof from social conflicts, and that it defines its policy within these conflicts of interests. Such biases become regular and systematic: the activity of the state consistently favours some social categories and disadvantages others. The question is why? Such biases may reflect the goals it wants to achieve. For instance, the state promotes the development of an indigenous capitalist class, in order to sustain economic development, and it provides incentives to this end. In contrast to this benign interpretation, the observed biases can be said to result from the unequal access social groups enjoy to the state. In this case, the state participates in a structure of domination, and upholds the interests of some social classes over those of others. It defends the interests of particular groups within society, and even becomes the instrument of domination for a particular class.

R. Miliband (1977, pp. 68-74) has given three main reasons to explain why the state apparatus acts in favour of particular groups. Firstly, he contends that the personnel in the more responsible positions of the state apparatus are recruited within the economically dominant classes, thus making the state of a capitalist society dependent on the capitalist class. The second reason put forward concerns the control that a particular group exercises over strategic resources for capitalist development. Finally, with the role of guaranteeing the continuity and smooth functioning of society as a whole, the state of a capitalist society would have no choice but to reproduce this society.

The argument of the social background of state personnel does not carry much weight in the Irish context. The social origin of parliamentarians and ministers in the Republic reveals a clear pattern in this respect, but not the expected one (Chubb, 1982; Gallagher, 1984). A professional and a small business background is more conducive to membership in the political elite; the economic elite, although not altogether absent, does not figure prominently. At the same time, one observes a nearly exclusive middle-class background for both political and administrative elite. But the middle-class contains a diversity of social categories, and the business element constitutes only a minority within it.

The view that the state responds to the needs and interests of the capitalist class, because the latter possesses a strategic and scarce resource, applies better to the Irish situation. The state would enter into a close alliance with the capitalist class, in order to foster capital investment and promote a particular type of economic development. In so doing, its policies favour capital investment and satisfy the needs of the capitalist class.

The view that the state defends the interests of a particular group within society creates a rather simplified picture of a complex reality. It also raises the question of empirical validation: what kind of evidence can substantiate this close association? The question was investigated in *Contemporary Irish society: an introduction* (Peillon, 1982). It started with a picture of society as composed of diverse social forces, of collective agents whose activity shapes Irish society. Such forces are rooted in a particular position in society and, on this objective basis, they elaborate a project, meaning a coherent orientation for the future. Projects do not so much embody the ideas shared by the members of such groups, but the principles of their practice. In the light of such projects, which are objectively grounded but allow for a range of possible orientations of action, social forces define what their interests are.

The state should be seen as a social force, itself upholding a project, manifesting and anticipating through its activity the kind of society it endeavours to establish. Such a project is not of course arbitrary, and it is articulated with those of the major forces in Irish society. One of the central characteristics of the state project remains its complexity, in that it seeks to encompass a diversity of orientations of action which may appear contradictory. How the state is linked with Irish society can be read in the state project: how its practical orientation of action emerges on the basis of the respective projects of the major forces in Irish society. The analysis concluded that the state project corresponds quite closely to the project of the bourgeoisie, which promotes economic development based on private enterprise. But the state orientation of action also overlaps with the project of industrialisation associated with organised labour. Furthermore, it succeeds in rallying support from the Catholic Church, by containing it within particular areas of influence, and from the nationalist movement by ritualising it.

The attempt of the state to integrate in its orientation of action a diversity of social forces does not imply that all these forces enjoy the same position within the framework of state action. Some projects have acquired a dominant position in that they constitute pillars of state action, while others are placed in a secondary or subordinate position. In other words, the project of the state is structured, and this structure reveals the differential relation of social forces to the state. That the state places the project of the bourgeoisie at the core of its own orientation of action does not necessarily transform it into an instrument of this particular class. The conflicts of interest which erupt from time to time between state and bourgeoisie simply rule out such a possibility. The state itself constitutes a force and cannot be reduced to a class or coalition of them. Its autonomy is manifested by the fact that it manages to take on board diverse orientations of action and orchestrate them. It plays one force against the other, and uses the orientations of action of diverse forces to construct its own. It may even build its own basis in society, independently of all organised forces. It does that by mobilising social categories without definite interests or organisational capacity, and consequently without a clear orientation of action. Its own organisational dynamic also plays a role, as does the fact that it extracts more and more resources from society. It may also use the capital of legitimacy which it has accumulated in the past. In that sense, the extent and the modalities of such autonomy are not given: they are themselves socially produced.

The study of the autonomous action of the state on society should not lead to a neglect of the study of the processes through which society produces an autonomous (but not arbitrary) state. Theda Skocpol (1985) contends that the social sciences have of late rediscovered the significance of the state in accounting for many aspects of modern industrial societies. She asserts that the focus has shifted from the internal dynamic of societies to the impact of state activity on society. The state ceases to be seen as a mere manifestation of society, but is considered as a force in its own right, capable of shaping society. An interpretation of contemporary

Ireland has been recently attempted with such a framework in mind. The study investigates how the state participates in the formation of Irish class structure (Breen, 1990, p. 98; also see Whelan in this volume). In such a perspective, the state is perceived as an agent in its own right, whose action has a definite impact on society. This renewed emphasis on the autonomous action of the state raises some difficulties if taken too literally. First of all, society can hardly be presented as the mere object or outcome of state action: society acts on the state. More essentially, what kind of agency is the state? What is it trying to achieve? Which goals is it aiming at? Unless one attributes a particular dynamic to the state, by reducing it to its bureaucratic organisation, one has to identify the social processes which fashion its autonomy. The state is produced by the society in which it operates. If it is contended that the Irish state endeavours to achieve such goals as economic development, welfare, equality of opportunities, etc., how does one explain that the state possesses such goals? The question of the impact of the state on society must be asked in connection with the question of the impact of society on the state.

Social differentiation and pluralism

In the previous pages, a particular image of advanced industrial societies has been given: that of a society structured into social classes, competing for scarce resources and possibly locked in antagonism. But another tradition in social thinking has put a different light on the development of modern societies. It emphasises the long process of social differentiation through which a complex and diverse society emerges. Ireland at the beginning of the twentieth century could be portrayed as a traditional society, with a low level of social differentiation. Most people were engaged in agriculture and cultivated the land in a rather similar way. They lived in numerous villages which resembled each other. Social differentiation occurs when a widespread specialisation of tasks takes place. Society contains a wide range of people involved in very different types of activity, developing their own views and interests. And this would correspond to the situation we can nowadays observe in Ireland.

The process of social differentiation leads to the emergence of a multiplicity of occupations and groups, with their respective outlooks and interests. Most of them manage to organise themselves into pressure groups in order to defend their interests. The growth of social differentiation is measured, in a rough way, by the increase in the number of organised interests. The Institute of Public Administration's *Yearbook and Diary* lists all the significant associations which are registered in Ireland. The list has grown quite considerably over the last twenty years, and more than eight hundred organisations were included in 1987. One gets a picture of society made up of a great variety of pressure groups, representing particular interests or values, and jostling one another in their attempt to influence the state. This is more or less what is meant by pluralism, and how it derives from the process of differentiation and modernisation. The pluralist play of interests actually takes two major forms; it operates through the competition which exists between political parties, and also more directly, through the action of pressure groups directed at the political centre.

Ireland, from the start, has organised its political life on the model of a liberal democracy. The exercise of authority is granted to those who obtain the majority of votes in parliament, and political life is centred on the effort of different parties to attract votes for their candidates. Respective parties seek the support of a range of social categories by upholding their grievances and defending their interests. In this way, diverse socio-economic categories influence those competing for central power: political competition makes parties responsive to the needs and claims of as wide a range of interests as possible. In fact, political competition in Ireland may not have such an effect, and the extent to which the political parties take on board socio-

economic interests remains a matter for discussion. The Irish
political system enjoys a particularly high level of autonomy
in relation to social differences. Political divisions developed
around issues which were of a purely political character, in
that they concerned the conditions of accession to independence from Britain. The autonomy of political life in relation
to socio-economic issues manifests itself in the very diversified social basis of the major political parties. Irish political
parties hardly reflect social cleavages. Such a statement
applies more particularly to the larger party, Fianna Fáil,
which is electorally supported by a significant proportion of
farmers, manual workers, white-collar workers, businessmen,
etc.; it gets the support of nearly half of each socio-economic
category.

The extent to which such a 'politics without social basis'
characterises Ireland has been much debated, and such an
idea has now been revised. The two major parties are not
separated by different philosophies concerning the running
of the economy or the way Irish society should be structured.
Nevertheless, social and economic issues dominate the
political agenda nowadays. Elections are won or lost according to electoral fluctuations which have a great deal to do
with socio-economic issues. Furthermore, the parties on the
left have always received a distinctive support. For instance, in
1989, the Labour Party attracted little support from the
farmers (5 per cent of them voted for this party) and only
limited support from the middle classes (10 per cent of the
professional and managerial categories) (Laver, 1992, table 1).
Its electoral basis remains the working class, with 27-28 per
cent of manual workers voting for its candidates. Even
political parties which, like Fine Gael, were in the past widely
based in social terms, now receive a more selective electoral
support: in 1989, it attracted 35 per cent of the votes of the
professional and managerial categories and only 15 per cent
of unskilled manual workers' votes.

In that sense, a social patterning of political life is not
entirely absent and is probably increasing. However, it

remains that political life seems to enjoy a dynamic of its own, and that it does not directly reflect social divisions. For this reason, obtaining electoral support by upholding the interests of particular socio-economic groups does not constitute an essential part of the strategy of the parties, even if they avoid alienating large categories of voters. Political pluralism in Ireland hardly allows for the play of interests to develop, and for diverse organisations to put pressure on the political centre.

Pluralism represents the conventional picture of the relations between state and major groups in society. Society is seen in terms of numerous groups of people who organise themselves in order to defend their particular interests or who are concerned with the particular causes and values they wish to promote. These organisations retain their autonomy, in the sense that they define their goals in an independent manner and decide on the best strategy to achieve these goals. Invariably, they turn to the political centre in order to influence diverse agencies and advance their interests or preferences. The state is then perceived as the target of the activity of all these groups; they ensure that their views are not ignored at the political centre. A sort of balance is reached between all these forces, but a fleeting one: the state is placed at the apex of these pressures, a sort of resultant of all the forces within society.

A pluralist play of interest groups can certainly be observed in the Republic of Ireland. These organisations enjoy autonomy, for they define their own goals and freely decide on the way to go about achieving them. Their action is usually directed at the political centre, either to influence the legislators, or else to exercise pressure on those who implement central policies. Clearly defined and organised interests do not alone put pressure on the state. Broad movements, which involve a wide range of associations, also exercise influence on the state. They may not always engage in the kind of strategic activities which go with pressure-groups; nonetheless, they constitute significant forces.

Very few studies of the activity of pressure groups, more particularly of their strategies of influence, have been conducted in Ireland. Even less is known about the effects of such pressures on state agencies, or the effectiveness of such activity. Finally, the view that the policies of the central state represent the point of equilibrium of all the forces is not easily validated. The political centre certainly responds to some or even most of the influences which are directed at it, but in its own way. The efficiency of the pressures is determined only with difficulty.

Corporatism

The pluralist play of interest groups does not necessarily provide the best key to understanding the state orientation of action in Ireland. One must also take into consideration the corporatist tendencies which have developed. The idea of corporatism has a long history. It was first an ideology which offered a third way of organising industrial societies, half-way between capitalism and socialism. It entered history in the respectable form of Catholic social thinking, but was dramatically discredited by the experience of Italian fascism. It has been reactivated, more recently, to indicate an institutional form of advanced capitalism. J. Winkler equates corporatism with an economic system which is neither a market economy nor a planned economy. Corporatism corresponds to a market economy in which the state directs and controls private enterprise. 'Directive state intervention is the principal defining characteristic of corporatism,' he declared (Winkler, 1976, p. 105), but he also suggested that such a trend radically transforms capitalism and leads to a new type of society.

More modestly, corporatism nowadays is perceived as an institutional system of a political rather than an economic character. Philippe Schmitter (1979) has proposed the term 'interest intermediation' to characterise it. Corporatism and pluralism would then represent two institutional ways of arranging the participation of organised socio-economic groups into the process of public decision-making. In the pluralist play of interests, pressure groups organise themselves and act independently from the state. They defend their particular interests and seek to influence legislators or civil servants. In the corporatist system, some organised groups are granted a special and even official status, and they are treated as privileged partners by the central powers. They participate directly in the process of public decision making, not from outside through external influences, but from inside.

Several conditions are said to facilitate the emergence and development of corporatism. First of all, one organisation only speaks for a particular socio-economic sector, and defines its interests. Such peak associations enjoy what amounts to a monopoly of representation. They are granted a privileged position, and often a special formal status; they are incorporated into the state, they are made part of the 'corpus' of the state. In doing so, they cease to promote systematically their own, particular interests, and have to take into consideration the demands of the other social partners and the interest of the collectivity as a whole. They must negotiate, accept compromises, and even co-operate with each other. The restraint that the central powers expect from their social partners is compensated for by the access that such groups enjoy to the political centre.

The idea that advanced capitalism is progressing towards a corporatist system has been much debated. It remains difficult to identify any contemporary society as being corporatist. This does not mean that a phenomenon of incorporation is not taking place. Rather than a structure, corporatism should be seen as a process. To follow the lead of Claus Offe (1985, p. 237): 'Corporatism is a concept that does not describe a situation, but rather an axis of development. In other words, political systems can be more or less corporatist, more or less advanced in the process of corporatisation, depending on the extent to which public status is attributed to organised interest groups.' Such a statement emphasises the variable extent to which particular interest-groups are integrated into the process of public decision-making. Every case of consensual or concertative policy tends nowadays to attract the label of corporatism (or neo-corporatism): it simply indicates that the economic policy pursued by the government is more or less agreed on by the major partners, through a process of consultation and negotiation. But a consensual policy does not necessarily imply the formal integration of particular interest groups in the state apparatus. And this latter situation only corresponds to the strict meaning of corporatism.

We are not concerned, in relation to Ireland, with the question of deciding if the pluralist play of interests has been replaced by a corporatist system of interest intermediation. The issue becomes, rather, the extent to which particular interest groups participate in a stable and formal way in the institutions of central power. A dialogue has certainly developed between central powers and organised groups, since the premiership of Seán Lemass. It has done so, originally, in association with planning exercises which were undertaken in the Republic from the late 1950s. At about the same time, several tripartite institutions were created. The so-called dialogue between state and major socio-economic groups has quickly acquired a regular and institutional character. At the beginning of the 1960s, seventy-three consultative agencies had been counted in ministerial departments (Leon, 1963). Twenty-four of them included representatives of interest groups, while sixteen other such agencies in which representatives of private interests participated, were in fact performing a public service. Nowadays, the number of such consultative agencies, committees or commissions listed in the Yearbook of the Institute of Public Administration (1988) is about sixty. They provide a framework for consultation between interest groups and the ministerial departments.

Irish peak associations also belong to institutional bodies, in a more formal capacity. The National Economic and Social Council (NESC) has been given the task of advising the government on matters of economic and social policy. The latter must consult the NESC and take note of its advice, although it is not obliged to follow it. The main interest groups are represented in many public agencies or semi-state bodies, in a quasi-statutory manner. The Irish Congress of Trade Unions nominates or recommends delegates to numerous committees associated with ministerial departments (just to give an example, it sent representatives to twenty seven such committees in 1987). Half of these agencies were consultative, while three such agencies played a regulatory or supervisory function. Five other agencies performed public services, while six others had been bestowed with the responsibility of applying some aspects of public policy. Such organisms deal with issues, such as fire prevention or road safety, which do not raise many controversies. But other agencies are involved in more central and more controversial matters. The trade unions, for instance, participate in the management of youth training agencies. The National Health Service Council is required to promote cooperation between official health services and charitable associations, and this concerns directly the mode of provision of social services in Ireland. Agencies such as the National Prices Commission and the Irish National Productivity Committee have a regulatory function, which they perform for the state.

National wage agreements, which dominated the field of industrial relations from the early 1970s, have progressively involved tripartite negotiations (O'Brien, 1981; Roche, 1989). Between 1970 and 1975, the state participated in these negotiations as an employer, and tended to follow the trend. In 1976, the state intervened more directly and threatened to impose a statutory wage policy in order to obtain wage moderation. In 1977, the government offered tax concessions in exchange for moderate wage increases. In 1979, it went one step further by linking wage negotiations to measures concerned with employment, social services, social security and youth training. In so doing, the government was linking its whole budgetary policy to wage negotiations, and in the process was granting to the employers and trade unions the possibility of influencing from the inside the budgetary policy of the country. It was also relying on a trade-off between economic and social policy, which has emerged as another element of the corporatist framework (Mishra, 1984).

From consultative committees to agencies of regulation, the representatives of peak associations contribute to the elaboration and the implementation of some aspects of public policy. Does all this add up to the emergence of a corporatist type of socio-politico-economic system? The practice of integrating representatives of major interest groups into the process of public decision-making is certainly widespread, and trade union leaders have for long complained that ... 'it is surely well known to ministers of the government that most of the time of the officials of the ITCU is spent working on various committees set up by the government' (quoted in Bew and Patterson, 1982, p. 159). But the significance of the incorporation of such interest groups into the state structure is easily exaggerated. More essentially, does such an incorporation signal the changing nature of the relations between central powers and particular interest groups? Do such practices add up to a corporatist system?

> ... trade unions and employers' associations have been party to a variety of consultative bodies. And even in the controversial area of income policy, an array of employer-labour structures, with varying links back to government, have existed in this country of a sort which might be expected to facilitate a neo-corporatist concer-tation of interests. Yet these structures have not developed significantly as sub-systems of the polity: they have not functioned as the principal instruments

whereby private interests engage in bargaining with direct or indirect state input, to reach agreement concerning the formulation and implementation of aspects of public policy (Hardiman, 1984, p. 84).

A similar conclusion about the weakness and instability of corporatist institutions in Ireland has been reached by commentators such as W. K. Roche (1989), while Breen *et al* (1990, p. 124) attribute this failure to the divisiveness of interest groups, and to their inability to find some kind of common ground on the major socio-economic issues of the time. But as soon as the end of corporatism in Ireland is announced, another corporatist framework is set up. However unstable and contingent such arrangements have proven to be, they show a remarkable tendency to recur. One observes a growing reliance by central powers and by major interest groups on corporatist solutions. The Programme for Economic and Social Progress (1991-1993), negotiated and agreed by the main functional interest groups, was immediately followed by another three-year corporatist programme (Programme for Competitiveness and Work).

Ireland may not have developed into a corporatist system, but it certainly has had recourse to corporatist practices. The incorporation of socio-economic interests into the process of political decision-making has largely been realised in Ireland, and the co-operation between government, trade unions and employers' representatives is generally considered successful. But such incorporation remains voluntary, and has not become part of the formal institutions of the state. This incorporation of particular interest groups does not threaten or deny the autonomy of interest groups. The latter organise themselves as they see fit, although the state has encouraged a policy of union amalgamation and provided financial incentives to this end. The contingent character of corporatist arrangements has been emphasised by Niamh Hardiman in her book *Pay, politics, and economic performance in Ireland 1970-1987*. In it she shows why the government, employers and employees consider it beneficial, at particular times, to enter into corporatist agreements. Such a convergence of interests remains flecting, and the instability of the corporatist framework derives from the fact that participants withdraw when they cease to benefit from it.

Leo Panitch (1980) has played down the significance of corporatism. He refuses to present it as a new socio-economic organisation, and simply treats it as a way of managing class conflicts in an advanced capitalist society. In fact, corporatism does not guarantee social peace, for it only displaces conflicts: from the relations between groups and state to the relations between the leadership and the rank-and-file of major groups. It is also accompanied by the emergence of uncontrolled collective action. Finally, corporatism excludes many groups from the process, and for this reason enjoys little legitimacy.

Corporatism allows for some control by the state over the activities of major socio-economic forces in society. It also formalises the access of these interest groups to the political centre. But equality of power between social partners should not be assumed. Corporatist arrangements do not equalise power between organised groups; they simply open access to the centre to a selected range of players which respond to each other's needs. The game is still played within a framework of differential power between interest groups, but in a streamlined and organised manner. Nonetheless, it remains a struggle. Corporatist agreements and institutions have developed in the context of wage policies, and they were adopted as a procedure for ensuring wage moderation and industrial peace. They continue to be used as a tool in what constitutes the main distributive conflict in advanced capitalist societies. Improvement in the provision of social services, which nowadays are included in corporatist transactions, can be explained in a similar way. Corporatism is eminently concerned with the conflict between the two major social categories of advanced capitalism: employees and employers. It reaches right to the core of the play of class interests. The compromise which is reached between the major groups does not transcend the structure of domination which exists between them. It simply builds on it.

Conclusion

In this chapter, two main ways of analysing the links between state and society have been investigated. In the first one, the state is rooted in the class structure of society; it is defined in terms of the pattern of class domination. The second mode of analysis places the state as the point of equilibrium between many pressure groups. But the play of interest groups does not always develop freely. The state often intervenes to decide which group will enjoy access to the political centre and participate directly in the process of policy-making. In this way, political pluralism turns into corporatism. But, as already stated, the corporatist framework does not imply that the participants exercise equal power. Trade unions and employer organisations do not bargain from an equivalent position. They put pressure unequally on the state, or on each other, because of their class position. One is back to the insertion of the state into a structure of class domination. But this does not mean that the state can be reduced to the social determinations which constrain or even shape it. For the state defines its own set of preferences and policy orientations, and it acts on society. Both the social determination of the state and the action of the state on society must be taken into consideration, although one need not assume their equal significance.

This chapter has focused on the relations which exist between the state and particular interests in the Republic of Ireland. But what about the relations between the state and external interests? Relevant agencies of the state apparatus take them into account when elaborating their policy. They form external constraints which become part of the strategic assessment of the situation within which they act. If the state wants to attract foreign companies to Ireland, it must take into consideration whatever will attract such large companies to invest in this country. The real issue emerges about deciding to what extent can external interests and forces determine or shape the kind of agency (or arena) the state is. A policy of providing tax incentives for the implantation of foreign firms, after a while, may produce high sensitivity by the state apparatus to the needs of such forces. Close and privileged links may even develop in this context between some segments of the state and external interests. In which cases, such interests are shaping the state apparatus itself.

Kay Lawson (1980) has made the comment that control, in general terms, can be exercised through two different kinds of process. Linkage by reaction consists in making sure the other agent responds to your demands and complies with your wishes. Linkage by penetration involves the direct intervention of one agency into the other. Penetration of the state by external forces is difficult: their direct participation in the process of public decision-making is always considered illegitimate, and penetration by elite overlap (between a political elite and an external economic elite) rarely occurs to any significant extent. But external forces also exercise their action from the inside, by becoming part of the internal set-up. For instance, the interests of multinational companies operating in Ireland are represented by organisations of employers. They influence the policies of such organisations, which in turn deal with the state within the structure of domination which has been internally produced. In that sense, such forces operate more effectively by integrating the internal dynamics of Irish society. Once within Irish society, the range of mechanisms of linkage which they can use becomes much wider.

References

BEW, PAUL and HENRY PATTERSON, 1982. *Seán Lemass and the making of modern Ireland, 1945-66*, Dublin, Gill and Macmillan.

BREEN, RICHARD, DAMIAN F. HANNAN, DAVID B. ROTTMAN and CHRISTOPHER T. WHELAN, 1990. *Understanding contemporary Ireland: state, class and development*, Dublin, Gill and Macmillan.

CHUBB, BASIL, 1982. *The government and politics of Ireland*, London, Longman.

GALLAGHER, MICHAEL, 1984. '166 who rule: the Dáil Deputies of November 1982', *The Economic and Social Review*, Vol. 15, No. 4, pp. 241-264.

HARDIMAN, NIAMH and STEPHEN LALOR, 1984. 'Corporatism in Ireland: an exchange of views', *Administration*, Vol. 32, No. 1, pp. 76-87.

HARDIMAN, NIAMH, 1988. *Pay, politics and economic performance in Ireland, 1970-87*, Oxford, Clarendon Press.

LAVER, MICHAEL, 1992. 'Are Irish parties peculiar?', in J. H. Goldthorpe and C. T. Whelan (eds.), *The development of industrial society in Ireland*, Oxford, Oxford University Press.

LAWSON, KAY, 1980. 'Political parties and linkage', in K. Lawson (ed.), *Political parties and linkage, a comparative perspective*, New Haven/London, Yale University Press.

LEON, DONALD E., 1963. *Advisory bodies in Irish government*, Dublin, Institute of Public Administration.

MILIBAND, RALPH, 1977. *Marxism and politics*, Oxford, Oxford University Press.

MISHRA, RAMESH, 1984. *The welfare state in crisis: social thought and social change*, Brighton, Wheatsheaf.

O'BRIEN, JAMES F., 1981. *A study of national wage agreements in Ireland*, Dublin, The Economic and Social Research Institute.

OFFE, CLAUS, 1985. *Disorganized capitalism. Contemporary transformations of work and politics*, Cambridge, Polity Press.

PANITCH, LEO, 1980. 'Recent theorizations of corporatism: reflections on a growth industry', *The British Journal of Sociology*, Vol. 31, No. 2, pp. 159-187.

PEILLON, MICHEL, 1982. *Contemporary Irish society*, Dublin, Gill and Macmillan.

ROCHE, WILLIAM K., 1989. 'State strategies and the politics of industrial relations in Ireland', in Department of Industrial Relations (ed.), *Industrial Relations in Ireland (contemporary issues and development)*, 2nd edition,

Dublin, University College
Dublin.
ROTTMAN, DAVID B.,
DAMIAN F. HANNAN,
NIAMH HARDIMAN and
MIRIAM WILEY, 1982. *The
distribution of income in the
Republic of Ireland: a study in
social class and family-cycle
inequalities,* Dublin, Economic
and Social Research Institute.
SCHMITTER PHILIPPE C. and
G. LEHMBRUCH (eds.),
1979. *Trends towards corporatist
intermediation,* London, Sage
Publications.

SKOCPOL, THEDA, 1985.
'Bringing the state back in:
strategies of analysis in
current research', in P. Evans,
D. Rueschemeyer and
T. Skocpol (eds.), *Bringing the
state back in,* Oxford,
Clarendon Press.
WINKLER, J. T., 1977. 'The
corporate economy, theory
and administration', in
R. Scase (ed.), *Industrial
society: class, cleavage and
control,* London, George Allen
and Unwin.

12
Community Action and the State

CHRIS CURTIN and TONY VARLEY

Community action in Ireland has assumed a multiplicity of forms and any discussion of relations between community groups and the state must begin from the reality of this diversity. At the same time this complexity does not defy classification. Ultimately the eight modes of 'community development' that Commins (1985) identifies can be reduced to 'conflict' and 'consensus' approaches. Similarly, the two broad tendencies of community action, based on the predominance of either 'integrationist' or 'oppositional' views and tactics that feature in Varley's (1991) discussion and that will help frame our discussion here, can be said to correspond broadly to 'consensus' and 'conflict' perspectives.

Epitomised in Ireland by the representative community councils of Muintir na Tíre, the integrationist tendency is remarkable for an 'all-together' ideology that projects itself as concerned with the common good and as capable of transcending class, party, gender, religious and even spatial divisions within localities. As well as seeking to build 'partnership' ties with the state, the two characteristic claims of these community councils is that they can speak for the locality as a whole and that all locals stand to benefit from their activities.

The oppositional tendency in Ireland, in contrast, as classically found in the 'social action' elements of the first EC anti-poverty programme in the 1970s, adopted a view of community that focused not on whole localities but on certain disadvantaged categories such as low-income farmers or unwaged women. The structural analysis elaborated by 'social action' activists revealed that the state played an important role in underpinning patterns of disadvantage and that a redistribution of wealth and power in favour of the weak and excluded would not be conceded without struggle, consciousness-raising and the use of confrontation tactics (Varley, 1988).

The dominant integrationist tendency has received a powerful boost over the past decade or so as the state in Ireland, faced with a complex of crisis conditions, has sought to mobilise 'communities' and community groups for certain purposes: job-creating economic activity, social service delivery, or as a means of conferring legitimacy on a range of new area-based special interventions. Inevitably, this spate of state activity has had major implications for what community groups do and how they do it, and for their ability to reproduce themselves over time.

On the basis of a very different analysis, however, other groups (also claiming to represent communities) have come to see the state more as the problem rather than the solution to their difficulties. These are the groups that protest about state action or inaction and seek to defend localities against the loss of employment, cuts in public services, long-term neglect, community-destroying urban renewal proposals and decisions to site toxic dumps or controversial industries in particular localities. The very presence of such an opposi-tional strand of community action alongside the dominant integrationist tendency that thinks in terms of 'partnership', draws our attention to the complexity of 'community action' in Ireland today.

So far we have discussed the state as if it was a unitary entity; the reality, of course, is that the state in a liberal

democracy encompasses a whole set of institutions, each with
its own organisational culture and operational rules. Recent
state-centred literature in the social sciences has taken state
'autonomy' and 'capacity' as major themes. Autonomy can be
said to refer to the state's ability to formulate its own interests
'independent of or against the will of divergent societal
interests'; 'capacity' is used to denote 'the state's ability to
implement strategies to achieve economic, political, or social
goals in society' (Barkey and Parikh, 1991, pp. 525-6).

A number of recent studies have sought to specify the
relationship between autonomy and capacity in Ireland
(Breen *et al*, 1990; Bew *et al*, 1989; Girvin, 1989). The
suggestion of Breen *et al* (1990, p. 20), for instance, is that the
Irish state has for most of its existence 'retained substantial
autonomy but exercised only a limited capacity'. Certainly
such key indicators as emigration rates, unemployment and
poverty levels provide substantial evidence of the extent to
which development outcomes have fallen short of official
expectations (O'Dowd, 1991, pp. 101-2). The most striking
illustration of the state's weak capacity in present-day Ireland
is found in the tendency for unemployment rates to reach
historically high and ever greater 'crisis' proportions.

One approach to conceptualising 'crisis' phenomena is to
see the state as a set of institutions that, in upholding the
general interests of capitalism, finds itself faced with two
central problems: legitimation and rationality/accumulation.
Crisis in legitimation results from a failure to maintain 'the
necessary level of mass loyalty' (Habermas, 1976, p. 375). The
state's inability to fulfil 'the imperatives of control which it
has taken over from the economic system' is what makes for
crises in economic 'rationality' or accumulation (Habermas,
1976, p. 375). Both these forms of crisis can be intimately
connected. Solutions to a crisis of accumulation that impact
negatively on certain groups may provoke a withdrawal of
legitimacy, for instance (O'Connor, 1973, p. 6).

How applicable is all this to the Irish case? What seems
clear is that the crisis in contemporary Ireland has resulted

not from inability of the dynamic export sector to achieve profitable accumulation but from the failure to 'translate' this into adequate levels of employment creation. A host of other factors, especially the crisis of the public finances, has added to the state's difficulties here and set limits on its room to manoeuvre. Failure to deliver jobs in a situation where the public at large can see the evidence of economic growth while the state is falling down in discharging its responsibility to create employment, threatens to provoke a crisis in legitimation, particularly in the most disadvantaged rural and urban areas where conditions have worsened steadily.

Up to recently the state had seen 'communities' to be largely irrelevant to the process of accumulation and to have but a very marginal contribution to make to social service provision.[1] Accumulation was seen to be in the hands of the private and public sectors in the first instance. Some state officials, it is true, did see an indirect role for community groups in hosting manufacturing industry and making it feel welcome in those localities where it chose to locate (Killeen, 1973). As a very minor element of Gaeltacht regional policy, community-based co-operatives had begun to appear in the 1960s. Nor did community groups, thin on the ground, weakly organised and overshadowed by a political culture dominated by parties, clientelist practices and national sectionally-organised interest groups pose any danger of provoking a crisis in legitimation.

In the crisis-ridden circumstances of the 1980s, however, things began to change rapidly. Partly in response to demands from below as local groups appeared on the scene and partly as a result of an official desire to exploit all possible avenues of job creation, the 'community' has come to be constituted as a significant actor in its own right in policy discourse if not in the development process itself. The creation of a new state body, the Youth Employment Agency and the community enterprise programme it launched in 1983, were obviously very important here. At the level of EU-inspired interventions, the anti-poverty programmes have

recognised since the 1970s the potential for mass unemploy
ment and attendant social marginalisation and exclusion to
generate deep-seated crises in legitimation.

The recent emergence of 'partnership' and 'participation'
as key elements in development discourse in Ireland has
coincided with the commencement in the late 1980s of a
whole series of mainly EU-inspired area-based development
programmes.[2] These initiatives, based on a sharing of
responsibility and resources over a specified period of time,
have sought to institute a formal structure of co-operation
between the state and local actors. Central to the entire
approach is that a consensus of interests about local development can be achieved and that rapid advances are possible
over a relatively short time period on the strength of local
and state interests operating in tandem.

What distinguishes the third EU anti-poverty programme
(Poverty 3) (1989-1994) in Ireland is its explicit concern with
equity considerations, the channelling of benefits to the most
disadvantaged and deprived and the central role ascribed to
the community 'sector'. We propose to illustrate the entire
area-based approach by drawing on the experience of the
rural and urban area-based initiatives of Poverty 3. That
tendency in Ireland for community groups to aspire to
partnership with the state pre-dates, of course, the recent
spate of area-based development programmes. Before
looking at Poverty 3, therefore, two other important strands
of the integrationist tendency that extend farther back in
time – the work of Muintir and the experience of community
enterprise groups in the 1980s – will be examined.

As far as its goals are concerned, the oppositional tendency
can be found expressed in two basic forms. The first of these
is seen in the essentially single-issue groups that take
exception to some facet of state policy or to some instance of
development perceived to impact negatively on a given
locality. In the second form, the focus is broadened to a
concern with the decline of a locality or a whole region, a
decline typically attributed to the actions or inactions of the

state. In practice, these two forms may be strung together, or the second form may emerge from the first.

We find examples of the first form in the attempts to use community-based collective action to counter the degradation of infrastructure and service provision and the threat of environmental pollution. Examples of the second form can be found in rural areas in the 'Save the West' movement of the 1960s and the Gaeltacht Civil Rights Movement of the 1960s and 1970s, and in the campaigns organised to resist urban renewal proposals in Dublin since the 1970s.

The integrationist tendency

Community councils

The movement known as Muintir na Tíre is now made up of a national office and a collection of about 120 affiliated community councils. Since the early 1970s Muintir, setting aside its earlier suspiciousness of the interventionist state, has sought to win acceptance for a model of community action that rests on the community council. Muintir community councils claim to represent the locality, pursue a broad programme of self-help activities and proceed on the basis of establishing 'partnership' relations with the state. Acceptance of partnership is seen to rule out community councils resorting to confrontation tactics in their dealings with statutory agencies (Muintir na Tíre n.d., pp. 4-5).

A statutory basis for the creation of partnership-type ties between local authorities and approved voluntary local councils has existed since the 1941 Local Government Act provided local authorities with permissive power to 'approve' local voluntary groups and to assist and delegate functions to them. This provision, however, is largely a dead letter today, partly it would seem because of the low opinion local authority officials and elected councillors have of voluntary councils of the type associated with Muintir (Roche, 1982, p. 98; Ó Cearbhaill and Varley, 1988), and partly because of the absence of pressure from below. Rather than exploiting the potential of the 'approved' council legislation, Muintir as a national movement has chosen since the 1970s to put its energy into the much larger undertaking of securing local government reform.

The approach taken to 'partnership' by individual community councils has been dominated by pragmatic considerations and has been very much geared to the availability of resources and the creation of networks of official contacts. Those community councils that have prospered have tended to rely heavily on the cultivation and maintenance of good working relations with sets of individual officials (Ó Cearbhaill and Varley, 1988, p. 282). In recognition of their value as intermediaries, close relationships have been cultivated with well-disposed politicians.

In the face of deteriorating state services and physical infrastructure in the 1980s, some individual community councils have come to look much more coldly at the ideal of partnership. It would be wrong to say, however, that even these community councils have in principle abandoned the ideal of partnership with the state. The use of confrontation tactics has been adopted only when forced to extremities and then against certain arms of the state and in relation to specific issues – the effects of local authority financial retrenchment in particular (Ó Cearbhaill and Varley, 1988, p. 290).

At national office level Muintir's attempt to establish a stable partnership with the state was severely set back in the late 1980s when its annual state subvention of £30,000 was halved as part of the 1987 programme of public spending retrenchment. Traumatic consequences were to follow this cut in funding; the national organisation's small complement of paid staff was virtually all laid off and ability to service affiliated community councils was reduced drastically.

That Muintir's ventures in promoting 'community enterprise' have not been crowned with success has added to the national movement's difficulties. The view senior figures in the organisation now take is that job creation lies beyond the competence of resource-starved disadvantaged groups

(Ó Cearbhaill and Varley, 1991, p. 354). In an effort to fight back and based on reasoning that it is wiser in the current climate to look for a contract rather than a handout, Muintir has recently sought to establish a new niche for itself in the area of community policing where, on the strength of its national lottery-funded community-based crime prevention programme, Community Alert, it is endeavouring to build partnership ties with the Gardaí and the Department of Justice.

The fact that Muintir's attempts to forge partnership ties with several branches of the state have often been poorly reciprocated has not meant that faith in partnership with the state has been irretrievably shattered at national office level. It is only when the whole community is opposed to government policy, or when things reach such a pass as to require drastic action, that this position is likely to be overturned. The threatened closure of many sub-post offices in 1991, which provoked the Muintir national chairman to add his voice to the opponents of closure and even to join protest demonstrations, is a telling case in point.

Community enterprise

There appeared in the 1980s an array of temporary employment, training and enterprise development schemes, many of them sponsored and administered by community groups. Frequently found in local authority housing estates and in deprived rural localities, community enterprise groups increased from about 70 at the start of the 1980s to about 500 a decade later (Donnison et al, 1991, p. 48; Ó Cinnéide and Walsh, 1990, p. 330).

In principle community enterprise can have 'an educative aspect which may be of enduring benefit in helping to improve the levels of skill as well as the self-image and self-confidence of those experiencing urban deprivation' (Donnison et al, 1990, p. 59). In practice, however, in a situation where expectations have been raised the 'sense of failure and frustration generated by CEP (Community

Enterprise Programme) at individual, group and community level can be demoralising' (Kelleher and Whelan, 1992, p. 115). Certainly the obstacles facing the long-term unemployed without capital, skills or business expertise and saddled with 'the difficulty of securing a living income while developing the enterprise' are indeed formidable (Donnison *et al*, 1990, p. 56; Kelleher and Whelan, 1992).

A good deal of ambivalence tends to characterise the attitude of the state to community enterprise. On the one hand, community enterprise has been attractive to some politicians as a source of possibly large-scale job creation and as a cost-effective means of job creation.[3] Some state agents, on the other hand, seeing community groups as frequently 'weighed down by internal dissensions and external apathy' would sooner deal with private enterprise (Ó Cinnéide and Keane, 1987, p. 5). A possibly more serious impediment is that the payment of decent wages and the successful accumulation of profit tends to be precluded by the marginal products and services that predominate in Irish community enterprise (Ó Cinnéide and Keane, 1987, p. 33).

The most recent analysis suggests that the FÁS community enterprise programme 'as at present constituted has little impact on local economic regeneration in disadvantaged areas' (Kelleher and Whelan, 1992, p. 172). These writers suggest that 'economic viability' be dropped by FÁS as its sole funding criterion and that greater weight be placed on community enterprise's capacity to generate 'part-time work and supplementary income' (Kelleher and Whelan, 1992, p. 117).

The new area-based partnerships
Among the fundamental aspirations and organising principles that underlie Poverty 3, the creation of 'partnerships' between statutory bodies, community groups and the private sector at local level takes pride of place. The Republic's two model action projects, selected from a field of seventeen applicants, are sited in two very contrasting areas. The Forum project in north and west Connemara operates in an area dis-

advantaged by its remote rural location and by the nature and structure of the local economy. The People Action against Unemployment Limited (PAUL) project area in Limerick city, on the other hand, has as its site an urban location marked by very high (up to 60 per cent) unemployment levels. The focus in each case in these area-based schemes is to attempt a comprehensive assault on disadvantage and exclusion. To this end both have operational plans which select key target groups, identify the causes of impoverishment and exclusion and set out concrete strategies to remedy matters. Each model action project is managed by a steering committee, made up of the different interests that form the anti-poverty partnership, and whose responsibility is to agree and oversee the implementation of a programme of work.

Within the catchment areas of the nine community groups participating in the Forum anti-poverty partnership, this project (which also has as statutory partners FÁS, City of Galway VEC, County of Galway VEC, the Western Health Board and Galway County Council) is focusing its efforts on the elderly, the unemployed and underemployed, women and young people. Initially consisting of Limerick Corporation, FÁS, the Mid-Western Health Board, Shannon Development, two voluntary associations and four community groups, the PAUL partnership in 1991 absorbed the PESP Area-based Response to Long-term Unemployment and the expanded entity, with its 25-member board of management, is now known as the 'PAUL Partnership Limerick'.[4]

Partnerships can be seen as having the potential to be both enabling and constraining. They can provide almost endless scope for conflict and disagreement, may become cumbersome and bureaucratic in their styles of operation, and may come to be viewed with suspicion both by established agencies that see their jurisdictions being infringed and by politicians who see their role as local representatives being undermined. They also have to somehow bridge the quite formidable gap between senior state officials and those without employment or prospects, at least to the point where both parties can converse and deal with one another as 'partners' for purposes of Poverty 3 project work.

How committed are community groups to the ideals of partnership? The 'all together' ideology of many community groups does fit well with the unifying ideology of partnership and participation that dominates the official thinking behind Poverty 3. However, as the anti-poverty partnerships emerged not organically but in response to specific funding opportunities, the commitment would seem to be strongly instrumentalist on all sides. Cash-starved local groups see schemes such as Poverty 3 as a lifeline; in fact, the advent of the programme has breathed new life into old groups in some cases. To be involved in state-of-the-art EU projects can enhance the public image of state agencies and departments as well as the career prospects of individual officials.

Involvement in partnerships obviously imposes burdens that weak community groups find hard to shoulder. The experience of very different organisational cultures has acted as an impediment to full participation. Lacking experience of the administrative style of large bureaucratically-run state agencies, of managing large budgets and paid staff, many community organisations have found the responsibilities imposed by partnership burdensome. If community groups are to become seriously involved, they therefore come under pressure to adopt a more formalised and professional approach to what they do. The response here has been to allocate resources to run training workshops in management techniques and organisational development.

The difficulties here should not be underestimated, however; one of Webster's (1991, p. 58) interviewees graphically illustrates the imbalance by suggesting that 'they (the statutory sector) are taking the leading roles across the board. If it's to do with social matters it's the Health Board ... if it's to do with education matters, it's the VEC ... training, it's FÁS ... enterprise, it's Shannon Development'. To counter such imbalance special measures have been taken in some instances to give the community representatives a greater voice and so counterbalance the superior power (in organi- sational, decision-making and resource terms) of the statutory sector and allow the 'partners' to deal with one another on more equal terms.

How effective have the projects been in realising their aims? It is clear that the anti-poverty partnerships are indeed innovative in the context of the strongly centralist and bureaucratic structures that dominate the Irish public administration system. Both the strength of centralised decision-making and political clientelism in Ireland has, at the same time, created an unfriendly environment for the sort of participatory democracy to which these projects aspire. Dark shadows can be cast by the wider environment on the work of the anti-poverty partnerships. Attempts by Forum to expand the scope of state interventionism in Connemara, for instance, are taking place in a context in which other arms of the state have been reducing welfare state and other services in the area (Byrne, 1991).

Pilot schemes can bring about changes in structures, services and attitudes. What is learned from the schemes may be more important than what the projects themselves achieve during their lifetimes. What chance is there this time that the lessons may become the basis of long-term policy? Reflecting the dearth of strategic thinking about combating poverty across the state sector (the Combat Poverty Agency (CPA) being an illustrious exception here), it is not clear how the anti-poverty partnerships are to be integrated into regional or national planning. For all the talk of inclusion, therefore, the long-term fate of these partnerships may be one of continued exclusion for community groups.

The oppositional tendency

Single issue campaigns
Recent years have seen the emergence of a welter of 'pot hole', 'post office' and 'hospital' groups seeking to mobilise

local support to fight the degradation of local services and physical infrastructure. What has come to be called the Roscommon Hospital Campaign provides a good illustration of community-based collective action built around infrastructure and service provision issues. The background in this case is found in the 1968 Fitzgerald Commission proposals to rationalise the hospital system in Ireland by instituting regional health boards and concentrating facilities in a small number of regional hospitals. This would mean, of course, that county hospitals would effectively be downgraded with a direct loss of staff, beds and functions. A related effect would be the longer distances to be travelled to avail of certain hospital services. Initial opposition to the Fitzgerald proposals in Roscommon came from aggrieved county councillors who claimed that the whole community stood to lose should the county hospital lose its 'acute' status and be relegated to 'community health centre' status. The county council, in fact, wanted to see Roscommon County Hospital upgraded to being a 'general hospital'. (At first the county council, fearing that its position would be outvoted, refused to nominate representatives to the new regional health board; before long, however, it found itself compelled to abandon this opposition.)

From the mid-1970s Roscommon Town Community Council took an active interest in the hospital issue. Effectiveness, it quickly came to see, depended on all shades of political opinion being combined in a united and powerful spatial coalition. Over time it succeeded in putting together a broad county-wide alliance of voluntary groups, politicians, health service professionals and hospital workers and their dependents – the County Hospital Action Committee – in opposition to the implementation of the Fitzgerald proposals in the county.

To make a convincing case, the campaign adopted a series of tactics: sending deputations to the Minister for Health and the Western Health Board; holding public meetings and rallies and using the local media to keep the issue alive. While publicly backing the campaign and its aims it was noticeable that local members of the party in power were lacklustre in their support. In these circumstances and in the absence of any notable progress, the Roscommon campaign decided to enter politics directly, first by contesting the local, and then the Dáil, elections. At its second attempt to secure Dáil representation the campaign won a seat in 1989 when its candidate, Tom Foxe, unseated Seán Doherty.

Out of this election was to come the so-called 'Foxe deal'. The precise details of this deal have never been made public, but Foxe and the Action Committee did hold an unofficial reception to celebrate the opening of a new 30-bed in-patient psychiatric unit at the county hospital in February 1992. In his successful bid for re-election in November 1992, Foxe's election literature highlighted his role in saving the hospital from closure. The Hospital Action Committee again endorsed him as its candidate and many of its members and supporters were active workers in his campaign.[5] The image Foxe was eager to present in 1992, however, indicated his desire to be seen as not only concerned with the local hospital and extra jobs in the health services but with a wider set of issues that encompassed the preservation of rural sub-post offices, road improvements and the 'overall welfare and preservation of rural communities'.[6]

Environmental campaigning
Although neither their ideology nor actions amount to a generalised attack on state development policy, the groups (frequently rural) that organise campaigns against the environmental pollution associated with dirty or potentially dangerous industries, are hardly likely to be susceptible to the sort of social control which partnership with the state implies. In defence of the environmental integrity of specific localities, such groups have cast themselves in a custodial role and spearheaded opposition to developments in the mining, pharmaceutical and petro-chemical sectors of the economy, developments viewed ultimately as the product of misguided

state policy. Especially in County Cork and in Dublin where local groups have resisted attempts to open dumping sites, the question of toxic waste disposal has emerged as a very live issue (Allen and Jones, 1990, pp. 208-28). The search for a site for a national toxic waste incinerator has given rise to a proposal to install a toxic waste incinerator at the Du Pont plant in Derry. Over fifty groups participated in the campaign this proposal attracted before the project was abandoned in 1991, ostensibly because it was judged uneconomic.

By its very nature environmental activism is geographically unevenly spread; in Ireland, campaigning has been especially pronounced in County Cork, the leading centre of the Irish chemical industry. A full investigation of the social composition of the different groups that participate in environmental campaigns has yet to be undertaken. One initial characterisation stresses that this strand of the oppositional tendency 'crosses class boundaries and unites an often highly divergent set of interests' (Allen and Jones, 1990, p. 273).

Recruiting their own technical expertise, making use of the planning and legal machinery, lobbying and relying on direct action to 'block drilling, construction and dumping' are among the tactics used in Irish environmental campaigns (Allen and Jones, 1990, p. 274). The 'most successful struggles', Allen and Jones (1990, p. 275) suggest, are those that have mixed 'legal/administrative and political/direct action tactics'.

As environmental campaigns typically oppose particular instances of development or call for more rigorous impact assessments and tighter regulation, they have frequently been viewed by state officials as unhelpful at best, and downright subversive of the efforts of state agencies to stimulate development at worst. In the wake of the Merrell Dow planning appeal, which went against the pharmaceutical company, Pádraic White of the IDA, for instance, described the local opposition as composed of 'small undemocratic groups' intent on 'blocking industrial development' (Allen and Jones, 1990, p. 1). Yet, in a clear change of tactics in the wake of the Merrell Dow pull-out, Sandoz and the IDA sought to build a climate of trust and secure a 'public mandate' before applying for planning permission (Allen and Jones, 1990, p. 183).[7]

Similarly the tendency is for other pro-development voices (management personnel, trade union officials, local politicians and business leaders especially) to marginalise environmental campaigns, accusing them of scaremongering tactics, of being motivated by selfish interests (e.g. the protection of property values), or of being masterminded either by 'blow-ins' with no proper local standing or by political extremists (Allen and Jones, 1990, p. 275).

How have community-based campaigns fared in pursuing their goals? Unofficial industrial action to highlight hazardous working conditions was evidently as weighty a factor in Raybestos Manhatten's decision to pull out of Ireland as was the considerable pressure exerted by a collection of eighteen 'political groups' and 'residents' associations' (Allen and Jones, 1990, p. 116). It similarly remains a matter of debate whether Merrell Dow abandoned their Killeagh project in County Cork primarily for 'business' reasons, because of high-level political intervention or on account of the relatively large-scale protest campaign the company encountered (Allen and Jones, 1990, p. 156).

The strength of the 'mobilisation of east Cork and west Waterford against Merrell Dow' shows that environmental campaigns can attract significant popular support (Allen and Jones, 1990, p. 276). Powerful local interests may lend crucial weight to environmental campaigns. The success of the campaign to stop gold mining in the environs of Croagh Patrick in west Mayo, for instance, owed much to the strength of tourist interests and the stances taken by the local Catholic church authorities and the county council. What is also clear is that while different environmental campaigns do not comprise a movement in any centrally-co-ordinated sense and that their fate may be to fizzle out and disappear, they do not always vanish without trace. The legacy of experience and self-assurance which can follow even minor successes, and the willingness to assist and learn from each other, attests to the learning-process nature of environmental campaigning. 'Communities', of course, may frequently be divided on environmental issues, as the Mullaghmore interpretative centre controversy well illustrates. In such circumstances environmental disputes are capable of causing immense difficulties for those groups that purport to represent the 'community' as a whole.

Area-based protest movements
The economic planning of the late 1950s and 1960s is often regarded as having ushered in a period of national economic expansion. But for some community activists in the west the new development strategy was perceived as leading only to further concentration of economic growth and accelerated rural decline in the remotest, most disadvantaged counties of Ireland. Their response was to organise protest movements to challenge government policies. The campaigns put together by the 'Charlestown Committee' and the 'Save the West' movement favoured an alternative development strategy which emphasised 'the right of local community groups to choose and implement their own development plans' (Tucker, 1989, p. 287).

The leading public figure associated with these protests, Fr James McDyer of Glencolumbkille, who was partly freed from his parochial duties in the mid-1960s to devote himself more fully to campaigning, held up the experience and the predicament of his own parish, then attempting to get an ambitious experiment in communal farming underway, as a model to be emulated by other communities. An insight into the nature of the demands made by these protest movements is captured in McDyer's (1982, p. 84) statement that 'people must not wait on governments and bureaucrats or strangers to come and improve their lot. They must do it the hard way and that was to unite into community co-operatives and embark on a job creation spree.' The tactics employed to achieve change, however, were in important respects centred on the state. Primarily they involved seeking to mobilise public support at mass meetings so as to pressure government officials and politicians to make concessions and release resources for genuine community-based development.

Inevitably the movement became 'politicised' in the sense that the popular support for these campaigns came to be seen as a threat to the Fianna Fáil government and to the party's local standing (Tucker, 1987, pp. 297-8). So as to capitalise on this the possibility of forming a western political party was even considered, but McDyer opposed the idea on the grounds that a priest could have no truck with 'divisive' party politics (McDyer, 1982, p. 85).

Personal health reasons and the necessity to pay closer attention to Glencolumbkille forced McDyer to disengage from the campaign in 1968. Thereafter the movement quickly disintegrated, though Fr McDyer (1982, pp. 84-5) admits himself that it was ever 'too dissipated to be a success'. Many of its activists and ideas were to resurface during the western campaign to oppose the Republic's entry to the EC in the early 1970s. Even before the EC, of course, foreign industrialists, induced in part by state regional incentives, were seeking out greenfield sites in the west in increasing numbers. In time this development, at least in official circles, was to virtually eclipse the whole McDyer approach.

In a very real sense, of course, it was the failure of this strategy to deliver sufficient jobs and sustained economic development, combined with the increasingly adverse conditions experienced by the smallholder population, that lies behind the recent 'Developing the West Together' initiative of the western Catholic bishops. The central aim of the bishops' campaign has been to transform local anger and fear into the basis of a popular movement capable of exerting moral force and convincing state/EU elites in Dublin and Brussels that only drastic measures will now suffice to combat the causes of accelerating rural decline.

In comparison to the 'Save the West' movement, the Gaeltacht civil rights campaign of the early 1970s achieved more tangible results in that its demands for an Irish language radio service and a restructured and more locally accountable Gaeltacht development authority were ultimately conceded. Its use of confrontation tactics and direct action (such as setting up a pirate radio station) were complemented by carrying the struggle into the realm of party politics so as to embarrass and pressure Fianna Fáil governments (the campaign ran candidates in Galway West in the 1969 and 1973 general elections) (Akutugawa, 1987).

Urban renewal protests
What was to become the North Centre City Community Action Project (NCCCAP) came into being in Dublin in 1975 when representatives from twelve local tenant groups joined forces to resist rising unemployment and the local authority's policy of detenanting the inner city. This project was built up on the basis of using 'a broad based, participative, community development model to mobilise around issues of local concern' (Kelleher and Whelan, 1992, p. 119). Issues especially contentious were housing maintenance and control of summer project grants paid by Dublin Corporation but administered by the Catholic Youth Council (Kelleher and Whelan, 1992, p. 27). Blame for many of the difficulties confronting local communities was laid at the state's door and the conclusion drawn was that 'state agencies were making critical decisions about the future of the area without recourse to local people' (Kelleher and Whelan, 1992, p. 27).

The NCCCAP was to play a leading role in opposing Dublin Corporation's 1978 development plans that sought to free up space for car parks, office blocks, shops and a new motorway by clearing public housing tenants and relocating them in the suburbs. Tenant associations in those areas where the plan would have greatest impact were assisted by the NCCCAP to pool their effort in a joint Housing Action Committee, distribute leaflets and organise marches against the proposals. The NCCCAP went on the offensive by commissioning a firm of architects to produce an alternative development plan which took as its starting point the preservation of housing and communities in the inner city.

When the NCCCAP's secretary, Tony Gregory, was elected as a community candidate to the city council this at once 'endorsed the legitimacy of NCCCAP' and opened 'access to senior officials of Dublin Corporation and to information and decisions being made at city council level' (Kelleher and Whelan, 1992, p. 120). After Dublin Corporation had failed to present local groups with a revised plan by mid-March 1979, however, a series of street protests and occupations was organised. At one street protest in May 1979, traffic was disrupted and six arrests were made. The revised corporation plan, published on 29 October 1979, allowed for 127 houses (as compared with thirty in the original plan) and was deemed a victory of sorts by community activists (Kelleher and Whelan, 1992, p. 121).

The election of Gregory to Dáil Éireann in 1982 marked a further success. Fortuitously finding himself holding the balance of power after the first election of that year, the 'Gregory deal' negotiated with the Taoiseach had as a central element the building of 440 public authority houses in the inner city. Another element was the establishment of an Inner City Development Authority, the chairperson and five members of which were to be nominated by Gregory (Browne, 1982, p. 82). Very little of the 'Gregory deal' was implemented, however, before the Fianna Fáil government's defeat in the November 1982 election.

The 'citizen mobilisation of the 1970s', in Kelleher and Whelan's (1992, p. 11) view, 'had a certain autonomy from the state and was not dependent on the state for funding'. Since then NCCCAP has drifted away from broadly-based campaigning and has become increasingly consumed by the burdens of administering state-funded training and enterprise and development schemes; through its hands have gone more than 600 trainees (Kelleher and Whelan 1992, pp. 94-5, 169-5). More recently, however, the Alliance for Work Forum has begun to rekindle the earlier campaigning tendency in the north inner city (Kelleher and Whelan, 1992, p. 102; Rafferty, 1992).

Conclusion

For all their differences, there are certain underlying resemblances between the 'integrationist' and 'oppositional' tendencies we have been discussing. Each accepts that change is desirable and that collective action can be effective both in getting things done and in realising empowerment goals. Nor are these two tendencies mutually exclusive in another important sense; integrationist groups can adopt oppositional tactics and vice versa. We have seen, for instance, how the scale of rural decline is pushing Muintir to question its traditional commitment to integrationism. That version of the oppositional view associated with environmental campaigning rests on an all-embracing view of community while desiring to mobilise oppositional energy on a locality-wide basis. Heavy reliance on an administration and management grant, paid annually by the Department for the Gaeltacht, has not stopped the Gaeltacht community development co-operatives from opting in large numbers to boycott the community development competition run by Údarás na Gaeltachta, so as to highlight dissatisfaction with the 'lack of a comprehensive policy for co-operative development in the Gaeltacht' (Ó Conghaile and Ó Cinnéide, 1991, p. 221).

The case of women's groups presents another instance where 'integrationist' and 'oppositional' tendencies can be found linked together in complicated ways.[8] While many women's groups have chosen to project themselves as community-based,[9] an underlying oppositional tendency can be detected when community action is built upon feminist principles and the critical perspective these imply.[10] Mainstream community action in Ireland, one central feminist-inspired argument maintains, can never live up to its own ideals until women are admitted on an equal basis to men. Conventional community action (certainly in rural Ireland), despite its rhetoric of participation and representation, has been characterised as yet another arena of male domination in which women are 'acutely under-represented', if not wholly excluded from public life (Byrne *et al*, 1993, p. 1; *Women and Rural Development*, 1994, p. 83).[11] To eliminate this pervasive and deep-rooted gender bias, women have been urged to see to it that community action be reformed to make it more sensitive to the realities of women's lives and to deliver equality to women.

The weak capacity of the state to provide for anything like full employment and the enormity of the crises it now faces has opened up new possibilities for community groups in Ireland. These possibilities are being pursued in two contrasting ways by groups that choose either to work with or against the state. For those that have taken the well-trodden integrationist path, the case for proper state support hinges on a belief that 'participation in community development can be a valuable education and morale-boosting experience for poor people, and that community development can revive a whole area and make public services more relevant and accessible to the local population' (Ó Cinnéide and Walsh, 1990, p. 332). The reality of community group dealings with the state, as has been seen, has tended to fall far short of these ideals.

Rather than promoting genuine empowerment or changing conditions for the better, one general view sees state interventions directed at community groups as a means of social control and the maintenance of existing power relations in society (Gilbert and Ward, 1984, p. 770). This same theme of control looms large in discussions of the state's relations with community groups in Ireland, north and south (Crowley and Watt, 1992; Rolston, 1991), and at once reflects the high degree of dependence on public funding and experience of a centralised and highly bureaucratic state. The concrete issues that have made relations between statutory bodies and community groups 'more fraught than ever', in Ó Cinnéide and Walsh's (1990, p. 333) view, are funding as well as manipulation. Typically the state can set its own priorities which community groups must accept to secure funding, provided on an ad hoc and piecemeal basis as a rule. Funding may be delayed or even withdrawn from groups whose actions the state disapproves of, as is vividly illustrated by the political vetting phenomenon in Northern Ireland and the denial of funds to groups *suspected* of paramilitary links (Glynn, 1992). Those who enter into partnerships or come to depend on the state for funding in whatever form may find it hard, out of fear of the consequences, to exercise an advocacy or critical role.[12]

Feelings of manipulation are perhaps inevitable when 'communities' are constituted as actors in the development process at a rhetorical level, yet where there is a reluctance to elaborate 'a comprehensive official policy in relation to community development overall' (Ó Cinnéide and Walsh, 1990, p. 334). What there is instead at once reflects the fragmentation of the state and its excessive centralisation. That several branches of the state – such as some health boards and local authorities – now have their own community workers, whose responsibilities include servicing community groups, attests to the reality of fragmentation. Fragmentation, of course, has been greatly added to by the proliferation of area-based and other schemes. Many of the community enterprise activists interviewed by Kelleher (1986, p. 16) registered some of the effects in their complaints of protracted negotiations, lack of co-ordination between state schemes and the mismatch between official requirements and the needs of local groups. The fragmentation of the state and of the community 'sector' itself might seem to rule out any overarching 'partnership', but hopes have been raised that the long awaited charter for the voluntary sector may put relationships on a more formal and stable basis.[13]

Control is frequently seen as almost synonymous with centralisation. Even before the area-based programmes had appeared on the scene, the clash between the 'technocratic or managerialist ethos' that pervades public administration and the democratic and participative ideals of community groups had been noted by Commins (1985, p. 172). Pervasive as the element of centralisation may be, contradictory tendencies are also in evidence, as when we find the CPA lobbying government for a proper policy framework and adequate funding for community groups while the Department of Finance turns down an EU offer to provide £8.5 million in direct funding to community groups in 1989 (Tucker, 1990, p. 46; Lynch, 1990, p. 122).

Can community group involvement in area-based programmes result in policy change? Policy-making is clearly a complex process and is the subject of much debate between the proponents of corporatist, pluralist and policy network models of the policy formulation process (Marsh and Rhodes, 1992). Whatever 'partnership' status community groups possess within relatively short-term area-based schemes, they are not recognised as a social partner at national level and are thus excluded from a major policy-making arena. Unlike farmers, employers and unionised workers, community groups are not represented by the 'peak associations' characteristic of liberal corporatism (see Dunleavy and O'Leary, 1987, pp. 194-5), despite the efforts of various alliances to establish themselves in such a role.

While community groups may be excluded from the process of policy formulation, evidence from the Poverty 3 model action projects does suggest that community groups can influence the *implementation* of policies, at least for the duration of special area-based interventions. In Forum, for example, the Western Health Board has been co-operating with community groups in providing new services for the elderly, and the project has persuaded BIM to test out new ways of supporting shellfish farmers.

There can be little doubt but that the standing and bargaining position of community groups has been weakened as a result of community enterprise falling short of that commercial viability state agencies take to be central to the 'market-led' model of development.[14] That the strengths community groups possess are more 'social' than 'economic' in character, however, may not be a liability in a situation where the state is increasingly keen to contract out social services and so hive off some of its welfare state obligations to the private and voluntary sectors. To the extent that all this is occurring at a time when services are being cut, there is a distinct danger that increased reliance on community provision may become 'a means of tempering the worst effects of present policies while pre-empting more radical structural change' (Tucker, 1990, p. 36).

Groups that mobilise against the state can expect to be ignored (as happened to the groups that sought to influence the National Development Plan in the late 1980s (Fay, 1989, pp. 48-9)), belittled (as we have seen with environmental campaigns) and most of all, as the cases of NCCCAP (Kelleher and Whelan, 1992, pp. 94-5) and the Gaeltacht civil rights movement (Akutagawa, 1987, p. 138) make clear, co-opted. Some token concessions – such as agreeing to fund a study of the problem or to institute a pilot scheme – may involve an attempt by the state to buy time, to throw a sop to its critics or 'to block the communal farming plan without losing broad political support in the west', in the case of McDyer's Glencolumbkille (Tucker, 1987, pp. 294-5). Even when important changes are conceded, as was the case for instance with the Gaeltacht radio station and development authority, the principle of central control is unlikely to be relinquished (Akutagawa, 1987, pp. 138-9).

A number of the oppositional movements we have considered, however, have politicised their struggles by competing with the mainstream parties for votes at local or general elections. They have scored some notable successes, especially when they find themselves holding the balance of power and can exact major concessions in return for crucial support. Protest movements flare up and burn out, though the politicians they produce, like Gregory and Foxe, may end up with 'safe' seats in Leinster House. The energy these campaigns generate can be formidable and it is possible to conceive of these politicised protest campaigns becoming more numerous as success encourages others and conditions worsen further.

For their part, growing dissatisfaction with short-term schemes is evident among groups constituted according to integrationist principles. One of the chief ironies of the whole area-based 'partnership' approach is that far from being empowered in the longer term, their temporary nature can leave community partners dangerously exposed once projects are wound up. Having been encouraged to take seriously the ideals of participatory rights and 'partnership' status, there may come a day when community groups insist that the state take these elements equally seriously.

Notes

1. The same cannot be said of the voluntary sector more generally, of course, as the case of church-controlled education makes clear (Breen *et al*, 1990, 33).
2. Leading examples have been the Department of Agriculture and Food's Pilot Programme for Integrated Rural Development (1988-90), the Third EU Programme to Combat Poverty, the PESP Area-based Response to Long-term Unemployment and the new generation of EU area-based rural development programmes – such as LEADER and INTERREG.
3. The Minister for Labour went so far to predict in 1989 that community enterprise in Ireland could be expected to generate as many as 10,000 new jobs each year (*The Irish Times*, 31 March, 1989).
4. The problems of developing a common vision independent of sectional interests is, if anything, a more difficult task in the PAUL project where employers and trade unions have been admitted as additional partners (PAUL *Midway Report*, 1992, p. 87).
5. *Roscommon Herald*, 20 November, 1992.
6. *Roscommon Herald*, 4 December, 1992.
7. Allen and Jones (1990, pp. 183-89) interpret this as mainly a PR exercise designed to paper over fundamental conflicts of interest.

8. 'Women's groups', a recent report concludes, 'are flourishing in rural areas throughout the country' (*Women and Rural Development*, 1994, p. 82). McEllin (1991) succeeded in identifying forty women's groups active in the west region (Galway and Mayo) in 1991; ten new women's groups were formed in north-west Connemara alone in the lifetime of the Forum project (1990-94).

9. It is possible that this orientation will be strenthened by the Department of Social Welfare scheme (initiated in 1990) which provides grant assistance to 'locally based women's groups'. A mere fourteen of the 180 group participants in the scheme examined by Mulvey, however, 'were involved in work which trained women for active participation in the development of their own communities'. At the same time, these fourteen groups did absorb 20 per cent of the scheme's total funding in 1990 (Mulvey, 1991, pp. 8, 25).

10. Coulter (1993, p. 48) suggests that the 'mushrooming of locally-based women's groups over the past few years has been the result of a marriage between the influence of modern feminism and tradition'. Very little in detail is known, however, about the different strains of feminist ideology and their distribution among the memberships of Irish women's groups. Mulvey (1991, p. 14) documents the central involvement of religious sisters in 44 per cent of 157 of the women's groups she examined.

11. The situation in practice is not always so clear cut. The central part played by women activists in environmental campaigning has been noted by Allen and Jones (1990, p. 273). D'Arcy's (1990, p. 108) study of the Inishmaan Community Co-operative presents a case in which most of the leadership roles were occupied by women. A recent survey by UCG Diploma in Community Development students of ninety-one community and voluntary groups in north-west Connemara, indicates that women held 27 per cent of officer positions.

12. The Dublin Travellers Education and Development Group (DTEDG), an 'innovatory initiative' project of Poverty 3, is an interesting exception in that it has chosen formally to shun full partnership in light of the degree of victimisation suffered by Irish Travellers (Varley, 1992, pp. 47-8).

13. Since this document was mooted as far back as 1981 (Commins, 1985, p. 175), however, it is hard to be too optimistic.

14. The reality, of course, is that private enterprise is typically also the beneficiary of a wide array of ongoing state assistance.

References

AKUTAGAWA, MICHIE, 1987. 'A Linguistic Minority Under the Protection of its Own Ethnic State: A Case Study in an Irish Gaeltacht'. In Gearóid Mac Eoin, Anders Ahlqvist and Donncha Ó hAodha, (eds.), *Third International Conference on Minority Languages: Celtic Papers*, London, Multilingual Matters.

BARKEY, KAREN and SUNITA PARIKH, 1991. 'Comparative Perspectives on the State', *Annual Review of Sociology*, 17, pp. 523-49.

BEW, PAUL, ELLEN HAZELKORN and HENRY PATTERSON, 1989. *The Dynamics of Irish Politics*, London, Lawrence and Wishart.

BREEN, RICHARD, DAMIAN F. HANNAN, DAVID B. ROTTMAN and CHRISTOPHER T. WHELAN, 1990. *Understanding Contemporary Ireland: State Class and Developemnt in the Republic of Ireland*, Dublin, Gill and Macmillan.

BROWNE, VINCENT, (ed.), 1982. *The Magill Guide to Election '82*, Dublin, Magill Publications.

BYRNE, ANNE, 1991. *North-West Connemara: A Baseline Study of Poverty*. Letterfrack, FORUM (North and West Connemara Rural Project Ltd).

BYRNE, ANNE, BREDA LYMER and MARY OWENS, 1993. Women in the Rural World, ESRC Workshop on Agriculture and Rural Development, Queen's University, Belfast, February 3.

COMMINS, PATRICK, 1985. 'Rural Community Development – Approaches and Issues', *Social Studies*, 8, pp. 165-178.

COULTER, CAROL, 1993. *The Hidden Tradition: Feminism, Women and Nationalism in Ireland*, Cork, Cork University Press.

CROWLEY, NIALL and PHILIP WATT, 1992. Local Communities and Power. In Thérèse Caherty *et al* (eds.), *Is Ireland a Third World Country?* Belfast, Beyond the Pale Publications.

D'ARCY, DIARMUID P., 1990. Cooperating Communities? A Study of the Inishmaan Community Cooperative. MA thesis, Department of Political Science and Sociology, University College, Galway.

DONNISON, DAVID, DAVID BELL, JOHN BENINGTON, JOHN BLACKWELL, CHRIS ELPHICK, ANDREW McARTHUR, KIERAN McKEOWN and EAMON O'SHEA, 1991. *Urban Poverty, The Economy and Public Policy: Options for Ireland in the 1990s*, Dublin, Combat Poverty Agency.

DUNLEAVY, PATRICK and
BRENDAN O'LEARY, 1987.
*Theories of the State: the Politics
of Liberal Democracy*, London,
Macmillan.
FAY, RONNIE, 1989.
'Campaigning Issues', in
*Whose Plan? Community Groups
and the National Development
Plan*, Dublin, Community
Workers Co-operative.
GILBERT, ALAN and PETER
WARD, 1984. 'Community
Action by the Urban Poor:
Democratic Involvement,
Community Self-help or a
Means of Social Control?'
World Development, 12,
pp. 769-782.
GIRVIN, BRIAN, 1989. *Between
Two Worlds: Politics and
Economy in Independent Ireland*,
Dublin, Gill and Macmillan.
GLYNN, EVELYN, 1992.
Strategies of Control: the
Political Vetting of
Community Work in Northern
Ireland. Unpublished MA
thesis, University College,
Galway.
HABERMAS, JURGEN, 1976.
'Problems of Legitimation in
Late Capitalism', in Paul
Connerton (ed.), *Critical
Sociology*, Harmondsworth,
Penguin.
KEANE, JOHN, 1984. 'Civil
Society and the Peace
Movement in Britain'. *Thesis
Eleven*, 8, pp. 5-22.
KELLEHER, PATRICIA, 1986.
*To Scheme ... Or Not to Scheme?
Community Groups and State*

Employment Schemes, Dublin,
Independent Poverty Action
Movement.
KELLEHER, PATRICIA and
MARY WHELAN, 1992. *Dublin
Communities in Action: A Study
of Six Projects*, Dublin,
Community Action Network
and Combat Poverty Agency.
KILLEEN, MICHAEL J, 1973.
'Industry'. In Michael Viney
(ed.), *Western Alliance: Report
of the Western Development
Conference October 1972*, Tralee,
Anvil Books.
LYNCH, FERGUS, 1990. 'State
Agencies and Community
Development', in *Community
Work in Ireland. Trends in the
80's Options for the 90's*, Dublin,
Combat Poverty Agency.
McDYER, JAMES, 1982.
*Fr. McDyer of Glencolumbkille.
An Autobiography*, Dingle,
Brandon.
McELLIN, VENETIN, 1991.
Networking Women's Groups
in the West of Ireland,
Unpublished report.
MARSH, DAVID and R. A. W.
RHODES (eds.), 1992. *Policy
Networks in British Government*,
Oxford, Clarendon Press.
MUINTIR NA TÍRE, n.d.
*Community Development and the
Representative Community
Council*, Tipperary, Muintir na
Tíre.
MULVEY, CRIS, 1991. *Report on
the Department of Social Welfare's
Grants Scheme for Locally based
Women's Groups (1990)*, Dublin,
Combat Poverty Agency.

408   Irish Society: Sociological Perspectives

Ó CEARBHAILL, DIARMUID and TONY VARLEY, 1988. 'Community Group/State Relationships: The Case of West of Ireland Community Councils', in Reginald Byron (ed.), *Public Policy and the Periphery: Problems and Prospects in Marginal Regions*, Belfast, International Society for the Study of Marginal Regions.

Ó CEARBHAILL, DIARMUID and TONY VARLEY, 1991. 'Muintir na Tíre and the Crisis of Community Development in Ireland', in Marcel Leroy (ed.), *Regional Development Around the North Atlantic Rim*, Vol. 1, Nova Scotia, International Society for the Study of Marginal Regions.

Ó CINNÉIDE, M. S. and M. J. KEANE, 1987. *Community Self-Help Economic Initiatives and Development Agency Responses in the Midwest of Ireland*, Galway, Social Sciences Research Centre, University College Galway.

Ó CINNÉIDE, SÉAMUS and JIM WALSH, 1990. 'Multiplication and Divisions: Trends in Community Development in Ireland since the 1960s'. *Community Development Journal*, 24, pp. 326-336.

Ó CONGHAILE, MAIRTÍN and MICHEÁL Ó CINNÉIDE, 1991. 'Competition as a Means of Promoting Local Development: An Assessment of a Community Development Scheme in the Irish Gaeltacht', in Tony Varley, Thomas A. Boylan and Michael P. Cuddy (eds.), *Rural Crisis: Perspectives on Irish Rural Development*, Galway, Centre for Development Studies, University College, Galway.

O'CONNOR, JAMES, 1973. *The Fiscal Crisis of the State*, New York, St. Martin's.

O'DOWD, LIAM, 1991. 'The States of Ireland: Some Reflections on Research'. *Irish Journal of Sociology*, 1, pp. 96-106.

PAUL Partnership Limerick, 1992. *Mid-Way Report*, Limerick, PAUL Partnership Limerick.

ROCHE, DESMOND, 1982. *Local Government in Ireland*, Dublin, Institute of Public Administration.

ROLSTON, BILL, 1991. 'Voluntary Sector Funding'. *Scope*, 130, pp. 10-12.

RAFFERTY, MICK, 1992. 'The Colour of the Cat'. *Co-options: Journal of the Community Workers Co-operative*, Spring.

TUCKER, VINCENT, 1987. 'State and Community: A Case Study of Glencolumbkille', in Chris Curtin and Thomas M. Wilson (eds.), *Ireland From Below: Social Change and Local Communities*, Galway, Galway University Press.

TUCKER, VINCENT, 1990. 'Community Work and Social Change', in *Community Work in Ireland. Trends in the 80's Options for the 90's*, Dublin, Combat Poverty Agency.

VARLEY, TONY, 1988. *Rural Development and Combating Poverty: The Rural Projects of the Second European Combat Poverty Programme (1985-9) in Historical and Comparative Context*, Galway, Social Sciences Research Centre, University College Galway. Research Report No 2.

VARLEY, TONY, 1991. 'On the Fringes: Community Groups in Rural Ireland', in Tony Varley, Thomas A. Boylan and Michael P. Cuddy (eds.), *Rural Crisis: Perspectives on Irish Rural Development*, Galway, Centre for Development Studies, University College Galway.

VARLEY, TONY, 1992. 'Partnership in Poverty 3'. *Co-options: Journal of the Community Workers Co-operative*, Spring.

WEBSTER, CATHERINE M., 1991. How Far Can You Go? The Role of the Statutory Sector in Developing Community Partnership. Unpublished MA thesis, University College Galway.

WOMEN AND RURAL DEVELOPMENT (First Report of the Fourth Joint Oireachtas Committee on Women's Rights), 1994. Dublin, Stationery Office (Pn. 0445).

13
Getting The Criminals We Want: The social production of the criminal population

CIARAN McCULLAGH

Introduction

One of the major changes in Irish society over the past thirty years has been the growth in the level of recorded crime and in the accompanying perception that there is now a significant crime problem in that society. The problem is seen as one of increasing levels of violent crime, such as murder and assault, and of property crimes such as burglary and car-theft, many of which are felt to be drug-related. Closely allied to this concern is the public image of the typical criminal. It tends to be one of a young, tough, closely cropped, denim-clad man. Liberal images of him would add the features of unemployment and social deprivation. Less liberal ones would emphasise the danger that he represents.

This view of the crime problem tends to be reinforced in the limited research that has been done on crime in Ireland. Analysis of the backgrounds of those involved in crime tends to confirm aspects of the public image. A survey of the backgrounds of those arrested in Dublin in 1981, for example, found the majority to be young, unemployed and under-educated young males (see Rottman, 1984). Paul O'Mahony's recent research (1993) on prisoners in Mountjoy

Prison supported much of this. The typical prisoner was male, had left school before the legal minimum age, had limited experience of the world of work and was likely to have serious emotional and personal problems, such as a history of drug abuse or of psychiatric difficulties.

This view of the criminal has also shaped the agenda of academic criminology which sees the uncovering of the nature of the link between social deprivation and criminal behaviour as a major task. Unemployment, educational failure and inadequate cultural controls have, for example, either together or separately been seen as possible factors in motivating deprived people to get involved in crime (see for example, Mc Cullagh, 1996). These concerns have also shaped proposals to reduce or alleviate the crime problem. Thus David Rottman (1984) has suggested that dealing with crime in Ireland requires, among other things, addressing the structured inequalities that exist in Irish society, particularly in education and employment. The Committee of Inquiry into the Penal System (1985, p. 30) is in agreement with this. It talked of the need 'to correct the deprivation and social disadvantage which play so large a part in creating dissidents and criminals'.

However the argument of this chapter is that these perspectives while relevant only tell one side of the story. It may be the case that deprivation plays a part in the creation of the criminal population, but there is more to it than that. The criminal population that we have is also a product of the means through which society responds to the socially harmful behaviour of different sections of the community. Some of these means enable the powerful and socially respectable in Irish society to escape criminal sanction when they engage in socially harmful behaviour. The purpose of this chapter is to describe some of these means and processes, show how they work and discuss their results.

Three of these are of central significance. The most important is the process of law-making. This is the means through which the criminal label is distributed in society. As it operates in Ireland, the process of law-making distributes this label in an uneven manner. It sanctions some kinds of socially harmful behaviour and ignores others. It is aided and abetted by an enforcement system that devotes more resources to the pursuit of some kinds of law-breaking than to others. The final element is a court system in which some people and some offences are treated more harshly than others. The end product of this system is a criminal population which contains 'a disproportionate number of those who are poor, uneducated and unskilled' (Council for Social Welfare, 1983, pp. 14-15).

The Role of the Legal System

'Killing, injuring or molesting others, or stealing from them', the Committee of Inquiry into the Penal System tells us (1985, p.28), 'are ... unacceptable infringements of personal and property rights. Such injustices and offences society must seek to eliminate or prevent and when they occur, must penalise as a mark of its disapproval and as a warning against repetition'. It is the law that designates these infringements of rights as illegal but it must be recognised that the reach of the criminal law is uneven.

All infringements of personal and property rights are not treated as criminal and so are not subject to criminal sanction. Moreover decisions as to what to treat as crime and as criminal are not necessarily a direct reflection of the objective dangers of particular kinds of behaviour. In Ireland the law has been written in such a way that the anti-social behaviour of those in business, corporate and commercial positions is inadequately regulated or, where it is regulated, it is generally not done so through the criminal law. Consider the following examples.

Bantry Bay
Just after 12.30 am on the morning of 8 January 1979, a small fire started on a tanker, the *Betelgeuse*, which was discharging

fuel at the Gulf Oil Terminal in Bantry Bay. Within a period of about fifteen minutes the fire became a major one and culminated in a huge explosion which killed fifty people. This is the largest number of people to be killed in a single incident in the history of the state. It was, for example, more than were killed in the loyalist bombing of Dublin in 1974. These deaths are not recorded in crime statistics for 1979 but they are recorded in Department of the Marine accident statistics as shipping casualties (Statistical Abstracts, 1979/80, p. 309).

The evidence presented at the Tribunal of Inquiry set up by the Irish government suggested however that the case may not have been that simple. Undoubtedly the elements of coincidence and of operator error were factors in the explosion. But the evidence also suggested that the attitudes and behaviour of the state and the companies involved were very important elements in what happened.

The state, it would seem from the evidence of the tribunal, may have failed to provide for the effective regulation of the activities of the companies working with oil in Bantry Bay. Gulf Oil, the corporation running the oil terminal, was, according to Chris Eipper (1989, p. 158) 'subjected to no coherent regulatory framework'. A Dangerous Substances Act had been passed by the Dáil in 1972, seven years before the incident. This gave the Minister for Labour extensive powers to control the storage of petroleum products and to regulate for safety standards. But the necessary regulations to bring the law into effect were not brought in until nine months after the disaster. The Tribunal of Inquiry concluded that the statutory obligations placed on Gulf Oil in relation to safety and fire fighting 'were wholly inadequate' (Costello, 1980, p. 24).

A key reason for the fire turning into an explosion was the fact that the ship split in two when its back broke. This was partly caused by a ballasting error. This error would not have happened if the ship had been fitted with a loadicator to calculate stress levels in the ship. The tribunal said that this 'is now virtually standard practice for large tankers'. Its installation would have cost a few thousand pounds. The tribunal records that it was given no adequate explanation for this omission. 'It had most serious consequences' (Costello, 1980, p. 212).

If the ship had been properly maintained the error would not have been as significant or as fatal. The ship had, what the tribunal described as, 'a seriously weakened hull' (Costello, 1980, p. 23), something of which the crew could not have been aware. A ship's inspector told the tribunal that on the day of the explosion, the *Betelgeuse* was 'a bloody awful-looking ship' (Costello, 1980, p. 210). It was in 'a seriously corroded and wasted condition' (Costello, 1980, p. 20). Repairs to the ship which in 1977 would have cost $311,000 were never carried out, because the ship's owners had been considering selling it. All of these decisions were taken by Total, the ship's owners, 'in the interests of economy' (Costello, 1980, p. 212). The tribunal concluded that 'The major share of the responsibility for the loss of the ship must, therefore, lie on the management of Total' (Costello, 1980, p. 321).

Gulf Oil, the owners of the terminal, had also been less than responsible in the area of safety regulations. Their own procedures said that if a tanker was unloading oil there should be a tug in the vicinity on fire-watch duties. Instead the tug was almost three miles away and out of sight of the jetty where the oil was being discharged. Gulf had also failed to provide 'suitable escape craft at the jetty' (Costello, 1980, p. 23). An automatically pressurised fire-main had been decommissioned in 1970. If it had been under pressure the fire could have been contained. There had been a decline in the quality of the training given to the jetty workers and 'there was no training or drill of any sort in the evacuation of the jetty' (Costello, 1980, p. 145). If many of these conditions had been met, the tribunal concluded that 'the lives of the jetty crew and those on board the vessel would have been saved' (Costello, 1980, p. 23).

The companies involved eventually paid compensation to the victims' families. The conduct resulted, in what Steven Box (1983, p.25) has called, 'avoidable death'. Yet there were no criminal prosecutions directly concerned with the circumstances of these deaths.

The Process of Law Enforcement

The composition of the criminal population reflects the way in which the law includes and excludes certain kinds of behaviour from its remit, but it also reflects the way in which the existing laws are enforced. If all law-breakers were pursued with the same level of thoroughness and efficiency, the prison population would be more representative of law-breakers generally. However the available evidence suggests that this is not the case. Where law-breaking is concerned there appears to be selective enforcement. As the Council for Social Welfare (1983, p.15) puts it, 'the forms of theft more likely to be committed by the better-off, the educated, the employed ... are much less likely to be reported as crimes and even where they have been and are detected, the perpetrators may not be charged'. Consider the following:

Corporate Fraud
The most common offence recorded in Garda crime statistics is larceny. The range of crimes covered by the term includes larceny from the person, car-theft, and what is perhaps the most frequently recorded offence in Garda statistics, larceny from unattended vehicles. In 1993, for example, just over 47,000 larcenies were recorded. About 45 per cent of these involved amounts of less than £100. Sixty-three per cent involved amounts of £200 or less. Only 8 per cent of larcenies involve amounts of £1,000 and over. The average amount taken in these larcenies in which property was stolen was £446.

Let us look at a case involving £500,000, or over 1,000 times the size of the average larceny. It first came to light in the

Goodman organisation in December 1986. The irregularities involved claims for EC subsidies on meat which did not exist. The Investigations Section of the Revenue Commissioners, having investigated the matter, were concerned that serious criminal offences may have been committed.

Their report was completed in September 1987. It recommended that the Goodman company Anglo-Irish Beef Processors be sanctioned and that the Garda Fraud Squad be called in. The report reached the Department of Agriculture on 5 October 1987. Five months later, on 4 February 1988, the Fraud Squad was called in, though the Beef Tribunal concluded that this delay was not inordinate 'having regard to the complexity of the matter' (Report of the Beef Tribunal, 1994, p. 402). To begin their investigation they had to get a copy of the report of the Revenue officer involved. They went to the Department of Agriculture and were advised to contact the author of the report. A police officer contacted him on 2 May. He was told there was no problem in getting access to the report if the request was put in writing. This was done on 16 May but, according to the Report of the Beef Tribunal (1994, p. 402) 'the letter containing the written request does not appear to have reached the Revenue Commissioners'. On 18 October a copy of the letter was delivered by hand. The report was received by the Gardaí seven weeks later on 2 December. While the Beef Tribunal report concluded that 'there was nothing sinister in the delay of the Customs & Excise authorities making the file available to the Garda Fraud Squad' (Report of the Beef Tribunal, 1994, p. 403), there appeared to be little evidence of a sense of urgency.

The result of the delay had the effect that the Garda investigation of the alleged fraud did not begin until two years after the fraud was discovered. The Fraud Squad spent a further two years investigating. The fraud was alleged to have taken place in two locations, Waterford and Ballymun, but the Waterford plant was never investigated. The Ballymun plant was. The reasons given were that the complexity of the matter and the resources available to the Gardaí suggested that one factory should be investigated in detail (Report of the Beef Tribunal, 1994, p. 403). Ballymun was chosen, according to the police officer involved, because of its proximity to the Fraud Squad offices in Dublin. The Director of Public Prosecutions decided in May 1991 not to prosecute. In the course of a letter written on 16th May 1991 the senior legal assistant in the Office of the Director of Public Prosecutions said that '[W]hatever hope there might have been of bringing home criminal responsibility for such activities was effectively eliminated by the inordinate delays in completing the investigations and in particular in referring the matter to the Gardaí' (Report of the Beef Tribunal, 1994, p. 398).

It has been suggested that fraud such as this which comes to public attention is only the tip of the iceberg (see Magee, 1988). Up to 1988 there had been only eight investigations of irregularities in the meat industry. Only one prosecution resulted. A German businessman, who was charged in Germany with defrauding the EC, said that Ireland was the easiest country in Europe where one could get away with such fraud (quoted in Magee, 1988). The problem is compounded by the unwillingness of many companies to involve the Fraud Squad in the first place. A security organisation which specialises in the detection of corporate fraud claims to deal with up to 500 cases a year and only 8 per cent of these end up in court (see Magee, 1988). Many companies opt to avoid the publicity by simply sacking the individuals involved and 'one or two were actually given golden handshakes to terminate their contracts' (Magee, 1988, p. 15).

Moreover, if the seriousness with which a particular kind of crime is considered in a society can be gauged from the resources that it is willing to put into its detection, then on this basis fraud and white collar crime generally have a fairly low status. The Garda Fraud Squad, for example, would seem to be considerably understaffed and under-resourced. In 1992 it had forty-five staff, and while it had little professional expertise itself, it had access to a panel of accountants. But as the Advisory Committee on Fraud (1992) discovered, this arrangement is of limited value. As a result businessmen, according to Magee (1988, p.15), say that the Fraud Squad does not have the ability to get down to the 'nitty gritty' of fraud cases.

This is in contrast to the Serious Fraud Squad in England and Wales. It has a staff of 130, two-fifths of whom are lawyers and law clerks and one-fifth accountants. They are investigating up to sixty cases at any one time, with a minimum value of £2 million, half of which involve direct fraud on investors and creditors and 16 per cent of which involve fraudulent manipulation of financial markets (*Observer*, 16 February, 1992, p. 21). Even this level of staffing is not adequate for the Fraud Squad and the recent collapse of a number of their more serious cases would suggest that their current level of resources might not be sufficient.

The Advisory Committee on Fraud (1992) proposed the setting up in Ireland of a National Bureau of Fraud Investigation with an adequate level of staffing, a number of accountants and access to information technology. It remains to be seen if the proposals are acted upon. However, the key measure of the seriousness of political intention here will not simply be the decision to set up such a bureau, but the decision to provide it with a level of resources commensurate with the size of the problem with which it is dealing.

Tax Evasion

Tax evasion is a criminal offence in Ireland. This has been the situation for over forty-five years, since a Supreme Court ruling in the *State* v *Fawsitt* in 1945 (Irish Reports, 1945, 183). According to the Collector General, it is not a victimless crime. 'The victims', he is quoted as saying (*Cork Examiner*, 25 September 1990), 'are the complying public'. It also has what are, by Irish standards, severe penalties attached to it. Under the 1983 Finance Act the maximum sentence, if convicted on indictment, is five years in prison, a fine of

£10,000, or both. As a crime it would seem to be fairly widespread. In May 1992, for example, it was alleged by the tax officers union that the state was owed £2.5 billion in unpaid tax (*Cork Examiner*, 10 October 1992). Despite this it is not always perceived as a crime. An accountant, quoted in Magee (1988, p. 16), said that as many as one in ten company liquidations in Ireland are the result of declining moral standards in the business community. But the quote from him shows some subtle differentiation in this area. 'Immoral management practices in business seem to be increasing. Even if it is only the non-payment of PAYE and PRSI'.

As a crime it has tended to be under-policed. According to the tax officials union, a major cause of the high level of evasion is the virtual non-policing of the corporate tax sector (*Irish Times*, 10 October 1992). In 1990, for example, there were seven tax inspectors auditing the returns of the self-employed. At that speed, Greg Maxwell, general secretary of the then Union of Professional and Technical Civil Servants, said 'it will take 300 years to audit all of those making returns' (*Irish Independent*, 12 September 1990, p. 3). It should be noted that this is an area where the commitment of resources can have an immediate impact. Recent changes in staffing levels, for example, have increased the percentage of the self-employed who make tax returns.

A more significant issue in dealing with tax evasion is the political one. The government for instance declared a tax amnesty on 26 May 1993 under which tax evaders could agree to pay a tax of 15 per cent of their undeclared money. Not surprisingly the amnesty proved somewhat unpopular among the general public and in response to that the Minister for Finance threatened that anyone who gave false information to the Revenue Commissioners would run the risk of a prison sentence. Indeed he was quoted as saying that he looked forward to seeing tax evaders going to prison (*Irish Times*, 7 July 1993). However when the Tax Amnesty Bill became law the proposals for prison sentences had been replaced by a system of fines.

Thus, while tax evaders may now have more fear of detection, they are still fairly secure from the criminal sanctions available in the law. Criminal proceedings are seldom used against them. In the rare cases that end up in court a conviction has never 'led to a sentence of imprisonment' (Rottman and Tormey, 1986, p. 43). The situation with tax evasion can be summarised as being a common activity where the chances of non-detection are still significant and the risks of being criminally adjudicated are relatively minor.

Insider Dealing

Insider dealing is where people in the financial world take advantage of privileged information that becomes available to them in the course of their work. It is generally information on the likely future movements of share prices of a company. It is also information that can be used to make substantial profits. If, for example, you have access to information that will, when it is made public, increase the share price of a company, you can use this information to buy company shares and then sell them when the price rises. The outcome is substantial profits with no risk. A judge in Singapore, quoted by Anthony Collins (1990, p. 32), said that essentially it was stealing information 'because, as in the case of theft of goods, the person using the information had no right to it'.

In the 1980s public concern about this practice led to its being made a criminal offence in Britain and in the United States. It also produced a number of highly publicised cases where large amounts of money were made using insider information, and where the individuals involved ended up being prosecuted for the offences and in some cases serving substantial prison sentences. The case of Dennis Levine and Ivan Boesky illustrates this. Levine worked for a number of stock-brokers where he had access to information on business take-overs. He passed this on to Boesky who used it to turn an inheritance of $700,000 into a fortune of $200 million dollars. He gave Levine 5 per cent of his profits for the use of the information (Box, 1983).

In Ireland, however, it was up until recently a perfectly legal practice. Senator Shane Ross told the Senate 'it is happening all the time and it is just a historical fact on the Dublin Stock Exchange' (Report on Debates in Seanad Éireann, Vol 116, No. 9, 16 July, 1994, p. 2545). It is now an offence under the new Companies Act 1990, but the way in which it is made illegal is interesting. Under section 110 a person who is charged with insider dealing will, on summary conviction, be liable to a maximum sentence of twelve months or a maximum fine of £1,000. If convicted on indictment, the maximum sentence is ten years in prison or a fine of up to £200,000. Initially the provision will be enforced by the Stock Exchange. 'Substantial duties are imposed on recognised stock exchanges who have an obligation to provide a report to the DPP if it appears to the relevant authority that any person has committed an offence under section 107' (Collins, 1990, p. 35). So in the end it can be enforced by the courts. The reality however is that these procedures are not particularly effective.

Public Buildings
It is, of course, difficult to separate the issue of law-making and law-enforcement. This can be illustrated by examining the legal regulation of public safety in places of entertainment. The importance of this was highlighted in a horrific manner by the fire in the Stardust in Coolock, Dublin on 14 February 1981. The incident and the response to it illustrate that the legal framework by itself is insufficient unless the law is enforced. There are indications that it might not be.

There were over 750 people in the ballroom when a small fire was noticed at 1.41 a.m. Within two minutes the fire had reached the false ceiling of the main room. It collapsed onto the dancers. In another five minutes it had burned through the entire ballroom. The fire brigade arrived at 1.51 a.m. just ten minutes after the fire was noticed. By then it was already on the decline. Forty-four people died in the fire, four died later in hospital and over 120 people were injured, some with appalling burns to the body and the face. Seven of the dead were burned beyond recognition and it was not possible to formally identify them. A Tribunal of Inquiry (1982) was set up by the government. It concluded that there was not sufficient evidence to say whether the fire was started deliberately or not. Seven weeks after its publication the Director of Public Prosecutions announced that there were insufficient grounds to bring charges against anyone.

One would anticipate that following the disaster the necessary legal changes would be made to ensure such a disaster did not happen again.[1] But this does not appear to have been the case. Legislative changes were made in some areas. The tribunal had, for example, found that fire exits were blocked and that this may have contributed to avoidable deaths and injuries. The government acted on this. The Fire Services Act 1981 was passed quickly after the disaster. This led in turn to the Ease of Escape Regulation (1985). In theory these are strict. They allow for fines of up to £10,000 and prison sentences of up to two years for anyone found guilty of breaching these regulations. But in practice it would seem that it is very difficult to enforce. The secretary of the Chief Fire Officers Association told *The Irish Times* (14 February 1991) that 'the staff are not there to implement them on a regular basis ... There is nothing to stop somebody locking exits and not getting caught for some time'.

In other areas the changes do not appear to have been made. There is, for example, no legal requirement to count the number of people in a public building at any particular point in time. This is despite a recommendation from the tribunal and the expressed desire of fire personnel (see *Irish Times*, 14 February, 1991). The absence of the power makes it difficult for fire officers to know if a building is overcrowded or not. There is also no legal power available to fire officers to empty a building that they believe to be overcrowded. A fireman told *The Irish Times* (14 February 1991) that public places can be places of potential disaster. 'The only way you can prevent a disaster is to bring in legislation – and enforce it'.

The Process of Court Decision Making

As we have seen, it is difficult for corporate misbehaviour in Ireland to achieve the status of a crime. It is either not regulated, is treated as an administrative matter, or does not come to the attention of the police because those involved choose to deal with it in alternative and non-public ways. There are however some kinds of corporate misbehaviour that are covered by Irish law. The main one is embezzlement, the 'classic Irish white-collar crime' (Rottman and Tormey, 1986, p. 48). What happens when such offences lead to criminal prosecution? The research of Rottman and Tormey (1986) answers this question.

They looked at all the indictments for six different offences brought before the Dublin Circuit Court between 1980 and 1984. The offences they covered were: obtaining goods by false pretences, fraudulent conversion, embezzlement, customs violations, forgery and receiving offences. This gave them 272 individuals who were involved in either professional crime – where criminal activity was their livelihood, or occupational crime – where the offences were carried out while involved in legitimate activities. Where occupational crime was concerned, they found that of every hundred defendants charged with such offences, fifty-nine were convicted by the court. This was considerably less than the rate of seventy out of every hundred for professional offences and, on the basis of 1981 cases, the sixty-eight out of every one hundred individuals found guilty of what might be termed more 'conventional' crimes.

There also a major difference when it comes to sanctioning. 'Imprisonment', they conclude (1986, p. 50), 'is used sparingly'. Only 20 per cent of all such convictions resulted in a prison sentence compared to 50 per cent of 'conventional' crimes and 40 per cent of 'professional' crime.

When a prison sentence is given it tends to be severe but the typical sentence is a suspended one with a compensation order attached to it. This was applied in almost half the cases. The researchers concluded that 'for those offences reaching the Circuit Criminal Court, the probability of conviction is low for occupational offences. Similarly, the prospect of imprisonment if convicted is low' (Rottman and Tormey, 1986 p. 52).

Concluding Considerations

This chapter has suggested that there is some fairly compelling evidence that corporate and white-collar mis-behaviour is a significant problem in Irish society. It is however an under-appreciated one. The main reason for this is that the way we respond to such behaviour does not mobilise the stigma of criminality. We either ignore it through the absence of an adequate regulatory framework, use civil or administrative procedures to deal with it or, in those few cases that come to the attention of the courts, offenders are 'let off' with a fine. This is in some contrast to the way in which the criminality of the working class is dealt with. At the most basic level there is a somewhat greater willingness to use prison as the sanction for the offences they commit.

A number of issues arise from this. One is the argument that, as the kind of corporate behaviour outlined here is generally of a relatively trivial and low cost nature, it does not deserve the stigma of criminality. On this basis some criminologists have argued that it is far more important for a society to protect itself against crime on the streets than against crime in the suites. James Q. Wilson (1975, p. xx), for example, has argued that predatory street crime is far more serious than white-collar crime because 'it makes difficult the maintenance of meaningful human communities'. This position however ignores two important aspects of white-collar crime. The first is that, as two criminologists in the realistic tradition have pointed out, 'minor violations can and do have major consequences in terms of death and destruction' (Pearce and Tombs, 1991, p. 423). The wrong combination of a range of 'minor' violations can lead to tragedy on the scale of Bantry Bay.[2] The second is that this argument ignores the financial cost of white-collar crime. We have seen how significant the amount lost in fraud is when compared to the amount lost in more conventional crime. Another way of making the same point is to compare the latter figure with the estimate given in the Report of the Committee of Inquiry into the Penal System (1985, p. 55) for white-collar crime. It put the combined cost of offences such as tax evasion, evasion of the payment of debts, worker's tax liability and social welfare entitlements, business sharp practices, company frauds, abuses of the social welfare system and a wide range of other such evasions at between £300 million and £1,000 million a year, that is between eight and twenty-eight times the amount taken in conventional crime in 1984.

A second argument in this area acknowledges the seriousness of such crime but says that the criminal label and, more particularly, the penal sanction is not the most effective and appropriate one for corporate offenders. Michael Clarke (1990, p. 20) has argued that 'the criminal justice approach is largely inappropriate and ineffective' for business crime. The imposition of fines and the payment of compensation are more suitable sanctions for such offences and have more deterrent effect than a prison sentence. This kind of argument is part of the overall retreat from the justice model in dealing with corporate crime. Its relevance can be disputed. Edwin Sutherland (1961), for example, has shown that the use of administrative procedures against large corporations was not particularly efficient. Just over 97 per cent of the corporations he studied had two or more offences recorded against them. On the other hand, Francis Cullen *et al* (1983, p. 490) have suggested that there are cases where 'the imposition of criminal penalties have had demonstrable deterrent effect on

upper-world illegality'. It can also be argued that penal
sanction is not the most appropriate or effective sanction for
what are conventionally considered to be criminal offences
either. There are a number of difficulties in calculating the
rate of recidivism in the Irish prison system, but David
Rottman (1984, p. 160) has suggested that it is very
substantial. The Annual Report on Prisons and Places of
Detention for 1991 (p. 110) shows that 51 per cent of the
prison population in that year had served a previous prison
sentence and 17 per cent had been in prison on six or more
previous occasions. This would suggest that prison is probably
not appropriate or efficient for any kind of offender, but that
does not detract from the point that it is only the law-
breaking of the working class that is punished by
imprisonment.

It is also relevant to point out that the argument that these
matters are more appropriately dealt with as breaches of
contract or as torts, to be sorted out by civil litigation between
the various parties involved, is a somewhat idealistic point of
view. It suggests that, because the law guarantees formal
equality between the parties involved, this kind of legal
process will always be fair. However this divorces the law from
its social context. Cases proceed on the basis that all parties
are equal, but they are not. At a very basic level the risks in
litigation are not evenly distributed. The costs of litigation are
high and they rise significantly the further up the legal
pyramid that one goes. The effect, as Curtin and Shields
(1988, 123) put it, is that 'where the resources of wealth,
information and possession belong to one group while the
other group (although it may be in the right) has none of
these advantages, there can be no real contest'.

The cases that are successfully concluded often require
extraordinary commitment and exceptionally determined
people to pursue them. The examples of John Hanrahan, the
Tipperary farmer who pursued Merck, Sharpe and Dohme
(*Hanrahan* v *Merck, Sharpe and Dohme (Ireland) Ltd*, 1988,
ILRM, 629) and Margaret Best who pursued a pharmaceutical

company through a long and involved court process are cases in point. Hanrahan believed that the discharge from the plant had killed his cattle and damaged both his health and that of his family. He initiated a civil case against the company and ended up being involved in the longest civil action in Irish legal history. He lost the case in the High Court. He finally won a judgement in the Supreme Court and despite this fact it still took two and a half years for the financial settlement to be paid over to them (O'Callaghan, 1992). Margaret Best took on a company with annual profits of £200 million from a situation of little money and no access to free legal aid. She lost a High Court case and only won on appeal to the Supreme Court (*Best* v *Wellcome Foundation Ltd*, 1992, ILRM, 12). In the end the case turned on a piece of evidence that was discovered by Ms Best among the over 50,000 sheets of paper she had accumulated during the case. This was a memo between two of the company's scientists saying that a particular batch of a vaccine had failed routine tests and was particularly toxic but nevertheless had been released on to the market. Her lawyer described it as a 'stunning admission' (see *Sunday Tribune*, 7 June 1992, p. A7)

We need also to consider the argument that the weaknesses of the law, and of the mechanisms for the regulation of corporate behaviour, are simply problems created by the speed of development in the Irish economy. It could be argued that the industrial and financial structure has developed faster than the legal system thus creating a problem of 'institutional lag'. Now, however, the gaps are being closed as the law is updated to match the complexity of the behaviour it is designed to regulate. The new Companies Act 1990 would be a case in point. Against this it needs to be noted that while at a legal level gaps in the law are closing, the problem of enforcing the legislation remains a major one. There is no credible incentive to enforce corporate regulations, and those charged with the relevant responsibility do not have the resources to adequately discharge their role or function. An example of this is the way the task of enforcing many of the laws on pollution has been delegated to the local authorities. Because they are major polluters themselves they may lack the moral energy to enforce the law (see Leonard, 1988, p. 212). Also, they may be unable to do so because of a lack of personnel and resources. Under the recent Air Pollution Act 1989 local authorities are the enforcing agency. Yet the testing for dioxin levels – which is essential to see if regulations are being broken – has to be contracted out to the private sector where a single test costs £10,000. At a time when such authorities are under financial pressures this may seem like an unnecessary luxury.

An alternative argument would see these issues as problems of the form of development rather than of its speed (this argument is more fully developed in Keohane, 1987). The broad outline of the argument is that the exploitation of labour, of nature and of natural resources has created major problems in the core industrial societies of the world. These are manifested in class conflict and environmental depletion. The state in these societies has been forced to place limits on the economic system, thus creating the potential for further crisis pressures. The form of development initiated in the late 1950s and early 1960s in many peripheral countries offered a potential solution to these problems. The attempts by peripheral countries to attract external investment opened up the possibility of crisis transfer. It allowed the displacement of the crises of developed countries and the transfer of the problems they were experiencing to peripheral societies. An example here would be the pressures that polluting industries came under in the developed world and their subsequent search for peripheral societies that would allow them 'the right to pollute'. The administrative systems of peripheral countries then had to take on the problems that this kind of industry and this kind of crisis displacement created. But these systems were themselves caught in a bind; the industries that were coming were required for job creation and the societies they were coming into did not have the capacity to control them. The solution was to ignore the misbehaviour of these corporations or, if placed under pressure to regulate it, to do so through legislative structures which create the illusion of control but, because they are inadequately resourced, do not interfere unduly with the activities of anyone concerned. When this is superimposed on a society that has already had problems of regulating the behaviour of native capital, the way is open for the kind of pattern of corporate misbehaviour outlined here. The major point is that these problems will not be alleviated by further development along these lines but will be further complicated by it.

Finally, the existence and extent of this kind of crime has important consequences for our view of the causes of crime in Irish society. As we have seen, liberal interpretations typically stress the centrality of unemployment and poor living conditions and, arising from this, the need to eliminate such conditions if crime is to be reduced or eradicated. The argument of this chapter is that it is not that clear-cut. The majority of people involved in the behaviours outlined here are not poor, unemployed or powerless. They also do not come from 'culturally' deprived backgrounds. This means that we need to rethink our views on crime causation, on crime control and on the control of socially harmful behaviour. We need to take fuller account of the notion that if poverty and the absence of power makes it difficult to adhere to the normative standards of a society so also does the possession of significant amounts of wealth and power.

Notes

1. This paragraph and the next one are drawn from the account in the *Irish Times* newspaper of 14 February 1991.
2. On the central importance of series of minor errors in producing major accidents in modern high-tech industry, see Perrow (1984).

430 Irish Society: Sociological Perspectives

References

ADVISORY COMMITTEE ON FRAUD, 1992. Report, Dublin, Stationery Office.

BOX, STEVEN, 1983. *Power, Crime and Mystification*, London, Tavistock.

CLARKE, MICHAEL, 1990. *Business Crime*, Oxford, Polity Press.

COLLINS, ANTHONY, 1990. 'The Irish Dimension – the Companies (No. 2) Bill, 1987' in Irish Centre for European Law (eds.), *Insider Dealing*, Dublin, Trinity College, pp. 31-38.

COMMITTEE OF INQUIRY INTO THE PENAL SYSTEM, 1985. Report, Dublin, Government Publications.

COMMISSION ON TAXATION, 1985. Fourth Report, Dublin, Stationery Office.

COSTELLO, JUDGE, 1980. *Report of Tribunal of Inquiry into Disaster at Whiddy Island*, Dublin, Government Publications.

COUNCIL FOR SOCIAL WELFARE, 1983. *The Prison System*, Dublin, Council for Social Welfare.

CULLEN, FRANCIS *et al*, 1983. 'Public Support for Punishing White-Collar Crime', *Journal of Criminal Justice*, Vol. 11, pp. 481-493.

CURTIN, CHRIS and DAN SHIELDS, 1988. 'The Legal Process and the Control of Mining Development in the West of Ireland', in M. TOMLINSON, T. VARLEY and C. Mc CULLAGH (eds), *Whose Law and Order*, Belfast, Sociological Association of Ireland.

EIPPER, CHRIS, 1989. *Hostage to Fortune*, Newfoundland, Institute of Social and Economic Research.

KEOHANE, KIERAN, 1987. *Dependent Industrialisation, Crisis and Displacement*, unpublished masters thesis, U.C.C.

LEONARD, H. JEFFREY, 1988. *Pollution and the Struggle for the World Market*, Cambridge, University Press.

MAGEE, JOHN, 1988. 'Fraud: Why the war is being Lost', *Business and Finance*, 11 August.

Mc CULLAGH, CIARAN, 1996. *Crime in Ireland: A Sociological Introduction*, Cork, University Press (forthcoming).

O'CALLAGHAN, JERRY, 1992. *The Red Book: the Hanrahan Case against Merck, Sharp and Dohme*, Dublin, Poolbeg.

O'MAHONY, PAUL, 1993. *Crime and Punishment in Ireland*, Dublin, Round Hall Press.

PEARCE, FRANK and STEVE TOMBS, 1991. 'Policing Corporate "Skid Rows"', *British Journal of Criminology*, Vol. 31, No. 4, pp. 415-426.

PERROW, CHARLES, 1984.
Normal Accidents, New York,
Basic Books.
REPORT OF THE TRIBUNAL
OF INQUIRY INTO THE
BEEF PROCESSING
INDUSTRY, 1994. Report,
Dublin, Stationery Office.
REPORT OF THE TRIBUNAL
OF INQUIRY ON THE FIRE
AT THE STARDUST,
ARTANE, DUBLIN ON THE
14TH FEBRUARY, 1981.
Report, Dublin, Stationery
Office, 1982.
ROTTMAN, DAVID, 1984. *The
Criminal Justice System: Policy*

and Performance, Dublin,
National Economic and Social
Council.
ROTTMAN, DAVID and
PHILIP F. TORMEY, , 1986.
'Respectable Crime:
Occupational and
Professional Crime in the
Republic of Ireland', *Studies*,
Vol. 75, No. 297, pp. 43-55.
SUTHERLAND, EDWIN, 1961.
White Collar Crime, New York,
Holt, Rinehart and Winston.
WILSON, JAMES Q., 1975.
Thinking About Crime, New
York, Basic Books.

14
Fortress Northern Ireland:
a Model for the New Europe?

MIKE TOMLINSON

Introduction

The purpose of this chapter is to examine some of the key
features of the Northern Ireland conflict and its management
in the context of the emergence of pan-European structures
of inter-state co-operation and regulation, and debates over
the nature of the European Union (EU). The process of
'Europeanisation' has stimulated considerable discussion
within the social sciences, much of which centres on how
national sovereignty, citizenship and the sense of nationality
is being shaped by the development of international goals for
economic policy, social policy and human rights (Roche,
1992; Room, 1992; Simpson and Walker, 1993; Wistrich, 1989).
This discussion in turn reflects a profound ambivalence in
popular attitudes towards Europe as shown by the marginal
majorities in referenda on the Maastricht Treaty and in
countries voting to join the expanding EU.

One pole of the debate on Europeanisation focuses on the
development of a single market based on the free movement
of capital, goods, services and labour, a single market underpinned by a 'level playing field' of labour costs, welfare
provision and rules of competition. It also involves paying

attention to European policies concerned with 'cohesion' and compensating peripheral regions and countries which are predicted to lose out from the concentrations of production and wealth creation at Europe's core. These are the concerns, in other words, which form the 'first pillar' of the EU, as the Maastricht Treaty calls it.

The other pole of debate concerns the 'second and third pillars', covering foreign affairs and defence, and justice and home affairs respectively – the external and internal security of the new Europe. Here, the discussion is less about the freedoms of the EU than about the threat to democracy and human rights posed by the development of 'fortress Europe' (Spencer, 1990). This is the term used to describe a whole series of measures designed to police the external borders of Europe under the guise of the control of terrorism, refugees, immigration and organised crime and drug trafficking (See Title VI, Article K1 of the Maastricht Treaty). Fekete and Webber (1994) see fortress Europe as part of the shift in Western Europe's concern with an 'external' Soviet threat towards a post-cold war focus on internal threats. In particular, they argue that Europe's policing is increasingly organised around 'the non-citizen within Europe's borders'. They suggest that the single market is founded on an essentially Eurocentric and racist notion, namely that 'Europe is for Europeans' and has to be fortified to stop 'third country nationals' from Asia, Africa, the Middle East and elsewhere being included in the labour market. Fortress Europe involves both the expulsion of persons already settled in Europe as well as procedures for preventing people entering Europe. This is a Europe of exclusion, expulsion and the denial of citizenship and human rights – a 'racist Europe' in which border and internal policing strategies seem to be reinforcing xenophobia and the rise of far-right political movements.

A key problem with fortress Europe is the lack of account-ability in the emerging structures of police co-operation (Benyon, 1994). Working groups established by the Council of

Ministers to further liaise between military, intelligence and police structures, were, until recently, largely unknown to the public. The TREVI Group[1] (covering terrorism and other matters) and the Ad Hoc Working Group on Immigration, for example, form part of an embryonic secret European state, argues Bunyan (1993a; 1993b), which lies beyond the scope of the European Parliament and the Commission, and hence is outside existing democratic mechanisms of accountability. This remains the case with the K4 Committee under which the ad hoc groups were subsumed after the implementation of Maastricht from 1 November 1993. For O'Dowd (1995, forthcoming), the issue is not so much one of a secret European state but more the way that European co-operation enhances state power at the national level, especially regarding those state structures furthest removed from public scrutiny.

In Ireland, and in the North in particular, interest in Europeanisation has for the most part been confined to questions of economic and social policy, and to the prospects for cross-border economic co-operation (Matthews, 1989; Government of Ireland, 1992; Irish Social and Economic Research Unit, 1992; Laffan, 1989; Taillon, 1993). The deployment of structural funds and the application of special initiatives such as INTERREG (targeted specifically on border areas) or the LEADER programme (rural development), provide fairly visible manifestations of EU policy at work.

There is also growing interest in how EU economic integration might provide a new context for resolving the conflict in the North (Bew and Meehan, 1994). To some Irish nationalists, north/south economic co-operation will eventually erode the border as a political divide. This view has its echoes in unionist opinion insofar as there is a good deal of nervousness about cross-border co-operation because it might, in some shape or form, constitute a breach of British sovereignty (Tomlinson, 1994, p. 10). This is why the Cadogan Group, for example, argues that limited forms of cross-border co-operation would only be welcome if the constitutional position of Northern Ireland is settled once and for all in favour of the union with Britain (Cadogan Group, 1992). O'Leary and McGarry (1993, p. 300) argue, however, that 'the removal of tariff barriers and increased cross-border co-operation between the Republic of Ireland and Northern Ireland, if they materialise, will not resolve a conflict centred on national identity and ethnicity'. Economic co-operation, in other words, should be seen as just that – an opportunity to substantially increase cross-border trade, not as a political threat. In any event, economists seem to be at odds over the benefits to the island of Ireland of a single market (Hutton, 1994; Birnie and Hitchens, 1994).

The discussion of Europeanisation in the Irish context, therefore, has thus far avoided scrutiny of the other side of European integration, the co-ordination of external and internal security, notwithstanding the sizeable 'security economy' in the North (Rowthorn and Wayne, 1989; Tomlinson, 1994) and arguments over its sustainability (Hutton, 1994). This chapter seeks to show that while Northern Ireland might be peripheral and insignificant in terms of the European economy, it assumes a much greater importance in shaping Europe's emerging security policies. Until the IRA ceasefire (from 1 September 1994), Northern Ireland was the foremost source of armed conflict within the EU, often with consequences for mainland European countries. In particular, the chapter indicates how the conflict has produced the most developed counter-terrorist policies of anywhere in Europe, whatever might be said about the weakness of their intellectual and political foundations (Rolston 1991). Above all, the chapter is concerned with the implications of the institutionalisation of the conflict for questions of state power and accountability, human rights and for the emerging shape of EU integration. Northern Ireland provides a model of forms of conflict and policing which have both tested the boundaries of the permissible within Europe and which have contributed to the construction of fortress Europe.

It is important to recognise that there are methodological

difficulties associated with studying matters which are generally shielded from public scrutiny and surrounded by controversy. These difficulties are not an excuse to avoid a sociological analysis of contested and covert aspects of state power, but should become a part of that analysis. Because the representation of events and agencies are so much a part of the overt propaganda of the protagonists, particularly the state agencies (Miller, 1994), it is necessary to approach some of the sources used in this article with more than the usual degree of sociological scepticism. It remains essential, however, to examine what emerges in the public domain from the entire range of sources, from parliamentary records through to popular expressions of opposition to state power. The chapter does not, however, address the institutionalisation of the conflict at the level of republican and loyalist armed groups which has been covered extensively elsewhere (see Boulton, 1973; Bruce, 1992; Coogan, 1980; Dillon, 1989, 1990; Holland and McDonald, 1994).

The first section examines the build up of armed forces, gathering together the available information on the security agencies, their size, cost, and changes over the last two decades. The second section is on the role of intelligence agencies and undercover units, in particular, the rise of the British security service, otherwise known as MI5. Counter-terrorist policy has been at the centre of the restructuring of intelligence and police work, and has given rise to a growing concern over the relations between loyalist groups and official forces, also examined in the second section.

The closer the date for the removal of all border controls in Europe, the more fortified the border has become, and the more pressing has been the issue of north/south collaboration on security policy. This is the subject of the third section. The fourth section takes up the question of the accountability of state power and considers the efficacy of the European Convention on Human Rights and the extent to which the Convention acts as a restraint on military and police practices in the North.[2]

Armed Forces

In his evidence to the British House of Commons Defence Committee in November 1992, General Sir Martin Farndale drew a distinction between the army's primary function – the ability to engage in the 'high intensity operations' of general warfare – and the secondary function which he described as 'short term low intensity tasks' (Defence Committee, 1993, p. 32). Included in the latter is the British army's role in Northern Ireland where it has had an active presence on the streets for twenty-five years.

At the start of the current conflict, in the summer of 1969, there was an active deployment of just over 5,700 troops and police officers. By the time direct rule from London was instituted in 1972, the British army had over 17,000 troops committed in Northern Ireland. From the mid-1970s these numbers began to decline as part of an official policy of 'police primacy' designed to give the Royal Ulster Constabulary (RUC) the primary role in managing the conflict. 'Ulsterisation' is a better description of the policy at this time because the main objective was to replace or downgrade the role of the British army with forces recruited from within Northern Ireland itself. This meant building up not only the RUC but also the Ulster Defence Regiment (UDR) which, although formally a regiment of the British army, was entirely dependent on local recruits and had no military role outside of Northern Ireland. By 1979, the army had reduced its numbers to just over 13,000, UDR full-time numbers stood at 2,400 and the RUC at 7,300 – a total of 22,700.

The decline of army numbers, matched by the build up of the RUC and UDR, continued in the early 1980s but the pattern changed in the late 1980s and early 1990s. In more recent years, there has been a continuing commitment to the expansion of the RUC and UDR, but army numbers have been increasing as well. In 1992, as part of the 'Options for Change' restructuring of the British army, the UDR was merged with the Royal Irish Rangers to become the Royal

Irish Regiment (RIR) (see *Statewatch* 1991). At the time the UDR was 6,200 strong, of whom 700 were women and about half full-timers. When the merger was announced the commander of the British army in Northern Ireland, Lt General Sir John Wilsey admitted that the UDR had a serious image problem. The regiment, he said, 'has not sought to be sectarian, one-sided or filled its ranks with Protestants, but that's the way it turned out'. More than a dozen members/ex-members of the UDR are in prison for murder and an estimated 120 are in prison for other serious offences related to conflict. Members of the regiment are twice as likely to commit a crime than the general public, on the basis of recorded crimes (Ryder 1991, p. 184). The Rangers numbered 1,300 but were to lose a battalion in the merger. The RIR has a target size of 6,750. Two extra battalions were committed to Northern Ireland early in 1991, one of which was to reinforce border garrisons to ensure the continuation of the building programme of new checkpoints and bases (see below).

Army and RUC numbers at December 1993 are given below (*New Internationalist* 1994, p. 19).

Table 1: **Numbers of uniformed police and military personnel**

Full-time RUC	8,464
RUC Reserve*	4,573
Army	12,079
RIR	5,427
RAF & Navy	1,340
TOTAL RUC and Army	31,883

*Two-thirds of the reserve is full-time.

These figures exclude the RUC's and army's civilian backup workforce of 3,250 and 2,600 respectively. The total uniformed RUC numbers are projected to rise to 13,460 by 1995 or a total of 16,840 including civilian workers. On this basis, by 1995 there will be one army/RUC member for every 3.7 Catholic males aged sixteen to forty-four. This compares with a Garda/population ratio of approximately 1 to 400.

The actual number of troops involved in the Northern Ireland commitment is much higher than the above figures suggest because of the cycle of preparation, training and re-training. As the deputy director of the International Institute for Strategic Studies stated recently: 'the British army in particular is overstretched. With 12,000 troops, mostly infantry, stationed in Northern Ireland and as many again caught up in the Northern Ireland cycle, that is either training for an emergency tour there or having just completed a tour in the province, there is little spare capacity to most additional commitments. Moreover, the degree of overstretch is particularly acute at present while commitments remain inflated' (Dewar, 1993). Hence a lobby within the Conservative Party and the military has been arguing for the cancellation of all cuts in the infantry, as well as for an expansion of the RIR to take on less specialised roles such as guarding prisons.

This kind of lobbying has less purchase after the loyalist and republican ceasefires. The problem of the financial sustainability of counter-terrorist policies also begins to look very different in conditions of peace. Relatively little infor-mation is available on the full costs of security policies. For example, it is not possible to compare the costs of different operations or the policing of the border as compared to Belfast. Capital expenditure on border checkpoints, watch-towers and bases is not visible in the defence estimates, although the Northern Ireland Office has admitted that border checkpoints are 'very costly to operate' (Northern Ireland Office, 1990).

The Defence Budget for 1993/4 put the cost of the Northern Ireland commitment at £477m (Ministry of Defence, 1993). The MoD does not publish a breakdown of how it spends its money in Northern Ireland, but it appears that about £450m goes on the pay of civilian personnel and special allowances, while a further £43m is spent annually on construction, surveillance equipment, and computers. Assuming the army cost at £500m, and adding the 1993/4 planned spending on prisons of £147m, what amounts to a weekly cost per prisoner of £1,600, and the cost of the RUC for the same year of £602m, the identifiable 'law and order' budget comes to £1,249 million per year (Treasury, 1993). It is estimated that the additional cost to the Irish government of the conflict in the North totals IR£2.5 billion, and is now running at IR£250 million per year (Dáil Debates, 1.4.93).

Such figures give an indication of what the conflict in the North has cost British and Irish governments over the years. Remarkably, these costs have escalated in real terms more in the period 1984-94 than between 1974 and 1984.

Army costs have more than doubled in the last decade while Northern Ireland Office costs have gone up by 60 per cent (in real terms) (Tomlinson, 1994, pp. 18-29). If the peace process continues, this vast resource devoted to policing in all its forms may be used by the British Treasury to reduce the budget deficit, or it may be redistributed in other forms of public expenditure in the North. Either way, the economic restructuring involved is considerable.

Intelligence and covert operations

> Be clear on one point above all else. The intelligence world is not answerable to secretaries of state. It is accountable to nobody – not the Prime Minister, not Parliament, not the courts.
>
> Colin Wallace (*The Irish Times*, 24.4.80)

Even more invisible than army costs is expenditure on intelligence agencies and undercover operations. This aspect of British policy on Ireland is, of course, the least accountable of all, both politically and in terms of the law. Covert operations have become the central feature of British security policy and ensuring that personnel, informers, and techniques remain secret has in itself become a key objective. As Urban (1992, p. 245) concludes, 'attempts to protect intelligence sources and techniques have frequently resulted in the deception of the courts in Northern Ireland. It is also apparent that deception has been used to allow soldiers or police officers who have acted mistakenly to escape criminal charges. The powers of the courts, in particular those dealing with inquests, have been modified in such a way as to make it extremely unlikely that they will ever uncover dishonesty on the part of the security forces.' Deception and censorship of the media has been another important ingredient (Miller, 1994).

In his review of the period 1976 to 1987, Urban (1992, p. 247) identifies the emergence of a pattern of aggressive covert operations 'with the acquiescence of politicians and senior officers'. Covert units have become more autonomous and powerful so that supervision and knowledge of what they are up to has lessened even within the Army and RUC themselves. Latterly, there has been less political compulsion to justify 'shoot-to-kill' operations.

During the earliest years of the current conflict, the British government favoured the use of the Secret Intelligence Service (MI6) in Northern Ireland (and in the Republic). On the basis of countering IRA bombing campaigns in Britain, MI5 pushed for a presence in the North and from 1973 onwards began to build itself organisationally. It was during this period, the mid-1970s, that intense rivalry and conflict arose between MI5 and MI6, as well as between the British military and the RUC (Foot, 1990). From this period onwards, the co-ordination of intelligence agencies and covert police and army units became a policy objective. In the late 1970s, the first of three Tasking and Co-ordination Groups was established, combining the intelligence of RUC special branch, MI5 and the army, allowing the linking together of informer-based intelligence and the surveillance and ambush activities of undercover units. The senior MI6 officer, Maurice Oldfield, was appointed as security co-ordinator for Northern Ireland in October 1979.

By this stage, most MI6 agents had been taken over by RUC special branch or MI5 and MI6 itself had withdrawn from RUC and Army headquarters, although it retained an office at Stormont. In contrast, MI5 installed itself to the extent that its operational head, the Director and Co-ordinator of Intelligence (DCI) at Stormont, is now a key adviser to the Secretary of State. This relationship is formally recognised under the Security Service Act (1989) which gave legal recognition to MI5 for the first time.

From the mid-1980s, counter-terrorist work became much more important to MI5. 'High flyers' in the service were often sent to Northern Ireland: Patrick Walker, appointed director general of MI5 in 1989 and current director Stella Rimington's immediate predecessor, served in Northern Ireland in the late 1970s. Eventually, counter-terrorism became a branch on its own and the director of counter-terrorism acquired the same status as director of counter-espionage. As such, the director of counter-terrorism sits on MI5's board, as does Northern Ireland's MI5 head, the director and co-ordinator of intelligence.[3] Rimington herself worked on Northern Ireland matters prior to her move to F branch ('internal subversion'). She was director of counter-terrorism before taking over as director general.

In May 1992 the home secretary, Kenneth Clarke, announced that MI5 was to be given the lead responsibility for intelligence work against the IRA in Britain. The change followed two reviews of the role of intelligence services undertaken by the former head of the Secret Intelligence Service (MI6), Sir Christopher Curwen, in 1990 and 1991. Curwen argued for a strictly limited and subordinate role for MI5 but the home secretary rejected this advice. MI5 already had primary responsibility for intelligence work in relation to loyalist and international terrorism, as well as IRA activity in Europe and elsewhere.

Curwen's reviews, and opposition within the police itself, were not enough to dissuade the home secretary from the

promotion of MI5. As he made clear in the House of
Commons, the ending of the cold war meant, 'we simply have
the opportunity to switch more resource within the security
services into this key area of Irish republican terrorism in this
country . . . As a result of political changes, there is greater
opportunity for the security service to put more of its
resources into that activity.' Clarke went on to state, 'it is
important that all the work on the mainland of Britain, in
Ulster and in the Republic of Ireland is co-ordinated to a
certain extent and that all the authorities co-operate as they
properly should in action against the joint threat which they
all face from the Provisional IRA. I am sure that proper
contacts will be maintained and will not be affected in any
way by the announcement today' (Hansard, 8.5.92, col. 302).

The rise of MI5, which ends police primacy in Britain in
relation to anti-IRA operations after 109 years of special
branch responsibility, raises the question of MI5's role in
Ireland on both sides of the border. The response to the
announcement by senior Garda officers was reported to be
'angry'. They had not been forewarned of the change and, as
one officer put it, 'we are very worried about this latest
development in Britain. We believe there are a large number
of MI5 agents now working here, particularly in Dublin and
along the border, but we've not been officially notified of
their presence. The (British) special branch would notify us
of any activities it carried out in the Republic. But since the
changeover, MI5 has not been in contact with us. For obvious
reasons we don't want an army of agents operating here and
carrying out dirty tricks' (*Police Review*, 5.6.92, p. 1028).

In the North the RUC officially retains primacy in intelligence and operational matters through its 660-strong special
branch, so the formal position is that MI5 is subordinate in
operational terms. But its influence has clearly expanded
over the years even if its role is confined primarily to securing
intelligence on potential IRA activity outside of Northern
Ireland, and on providing briefings to the secretary of state
for NI, the Cabinet Committee on NI and the Joint

Intelligence Committee. MI5 has an estimated one hundred full-time operatives in Ireland (*Intelligence Newsletter*, 5.11.92).

It is unlikely that the restructuring of relationships between MI5 and police forces in Britain and Ireland will resolve the tensions and rivalries between these agencies, given recent operational experiences and proposed developments. The peace process may even exacerbate the tensions. The RUC chief constable, Sir Hugh Annesley, has proposed two new operational units for Britain, a national crime squad and a national anti-terrorist unit. This unit, Annesley suggests, would incorporate the security service, the metropolitan police special branch and anti-terrorist unit, with a significant input from provincial CID and special branches. It would also include military and customs personnel with the capacity to co-opt specific skills from other agencies or departments as appropriate. The national anti-terrorist unit would provide 'a single police and intelligence focal point for liaison with the RUC, the Garda and the police forces and intelligence services of Europe and North America' (*Police Journal*, October, 1992). A national anti-terrorist unit of the kind envisaged by Annesley would involve MI5 as a partner, not as the lead authority. The head of MI5 has publicly opposed Annesley's plan.

Although inter-agency competition was particularly rife in the 1970s, there is evidence that it continued into the late 1980s, even though efforts have been made to co-ordinate operations, share intelligence and build teams especially at senior levels. This emerged from the prosecution of Brian Nelson who was an intelligence officer for a loyalist group but who was also working for military intelligence (see Tomlinson, 1993). Following the Nelson trial and a review of Army/RUC relations, carried out by a retired MI5 agent, a Provincial Executive Committee was established which includes the army's commander of land forces, the head of RUC special branch, a deputy chief constable with special responsibility for police/army liaison, and MI5's director and co-ordinator of intelligence.

Covert units have been responsible for an estimated sixty killings. Urban (1992, pp. 248-253) claims that the SAS killed twenty-five IRA volunteers between 1976 and 1987, and another five since then. The SAS was first sent to Northern Ireland in 1969, although its presence was not publicly admitted for several years. Between twenty and twenty-five SAS men are kept in Northern Ireland most of the time, but these numbers are reinforced for shoot-to-kill operations. Operation Judy, the Loughgall ambush which resulted in the killing of eight IRA members and one civilian, involved thirty-nine SAS men as well as fifty of the army and RUC's most experienced undercover operatives (Philip and Taylor, 1992). Urban's figures suggest that up to 1987, the SAS had killed six innocent civilians. As he recognises, however, many of the killings of IRA volunteers have been in disputed circumstances in that they were unarmed or were not arrested when they could have been. Murray (1990) lists forty-two SAS killings up to 1989 (see also Sutton, 1994). Whatever the true figures, it is evident that the SAS has killed considerably more people than 14th Intelligence Company or the RUC's E4A.

The extent of the intelligence effort, the use of informers and the involvement of official forces in loyalist paramilitary activities over the years has strengthened the view that there is co-operation of some sort and at some level between loyalist groups, the army and RUC, otherwise known as 'collusion'. Critics of this view, while accepting that 'rogue' members of the security forces have assisted loyalist groups, usually deny that collusion exists by saying that they have found no evidence of an official or stated policy, or of solid links between loyalists and senior army/RUC personnel (Bruce, 1992; Dillon, 1990) This judgement needs to be put alongside the following. Firstly, central to current security policy is the widespread recruitment of informers. There is nothing accidental about this; it is a systematic part of counter-terrorist policy. At any one time, as events have shown on many occasions, RUC special branch (and less often army intelligence and MI5) will have informers placed at some level within the IRA and loyalist groups. On grounds of protecting their sources, handlers will turn a blind eye to the participation of informers in operations. The Nelson case illustrates this very clearly although whether or not there are major differences between RUC special branch and military intelligence in terms of what they are prepared to tolerate is less clear. In terms of collusion, the use of informers allows the authorities the choice of what to do with the information they acquire. The informer system creates relationships with proscribed organisations through which the authorities can encourage, modify, ignore, intercept or prevent operations.

Secondly, there does not need to be a conspiracy or direct order for groups to know that a particular strategy or action has been signalled in high places – even if perpetrators still risk being caught in the act.

Thirdly, the social composition of the RIR and RUC is such that one in ten of all Protestant men works in the security services in some capacity. This means that, 'Protestants can be said to have a vested interest in the continuing emergency . . . (and) the policy of Ulsterisation has effectively created an armed Protestant force of considerable magnitude' (Hillyard, 1988, p. 200). An estimated 45,000 people passed through the ranks of the UDR during its 21-year history. There is a further implication which is that the social background of those in the security industry means that some are likely to have a degree of identification with, and local knowledge of, loyalist groups, both of which may be used at an informal level to facilitate such groups. One study of the RUC has concluded that 'the RUC is not selective or partisan' in its law enforcement and that most rank-and-file officers are able 'to divorce their opinions from their conduct'. It acknowledges, however, that the conflict 'introduces features that are core characteristics of RUC occupational culture . . . most notably Protestantism and sectarianism', even if 'both are less prominent than might be imagined from the social composition of the force' (Brewer, 1991). In addition, police resources and strategies differ according to Catholic and

Protestant areas – obviously the simple absence of police can assist a loyalist attack.

The strongest evidence that social composition translates into practical assistance for loyalist groups, however, comes from UDR involvement in killings and other activities. Regarding the 1970s, a Sinn Féin (n.d.) study suggests that, 'over the first ten years of the UDR's existence nearly 200 members were convicted in the courts'. The same study goes on to give a detailed examination of 113 killings by loyalist groups in the 1980s, concluding that in seventy of these 'collusion was a likely factor'.

A fourth factor which needs to be looked at in the collusion debate is related to the last point. Information from RUC and army intelligence files regularly finds its way to loyalist groups. This is not disputed. The RUC frequently approaches individuals to warn them that their personal details are in the hands of loyalist groups. The most dramatic illustration of this process occurred in the late 1980s when the Ulster Freedom Fighters started to publicise information it had secured from the RUC and UDR. The group did this because it wanted to prove that its killings were not random or 'sectarian' but well-targeted on the basis of lists of republican suspects held by the security forces. The information leaks mainly took the form of photomontages of these 'suspects'. It was during the Stevens' Inquiry into the leaks, that Brian Nelson (mentioned above) was arrested. The Stevens' Inquiry resulted in fifty-one people being convicted. Ten of these were members of the UDR, eight of whom were charged with having extra ammunition and two of whom were accused of taking photomontages from a police station. One British soldier was charged with leaking a photomontage which ended up on the front page of *The Sun*, but no RUC officers were charged.

Nelson was the only person to be charged with conspiracy to murder as a result of the Stevens inquiry and his trial presented a major opportunity for investigating collusion. But just before the trial, the most serious charges against him, including two murder charges, were dropped; he then pleaded guilty to the remaining charges. This led to a trial in which, as Amnesty International (1994) put it, 'only fragments of the truth bearing on allegations of collusion emerged'.

A final point is that some forms of collusion need not be extensive in order to have great impact. Following the Nelson trial, it has been alleged that British intelligence had full knowledge of Nelson's trip to South Africa to organise a substantial arms shipment which included 200 AK47 rifles, a dozen rocket launchers, ninety pistols and 500 fragmentation grenades. The RUC seized about a third of the shipment but the remainder has never come to light, other than from its usage in subsequent loyalist killings.

Fortifying the border

Northern Ireland, though heavily militarised for many years, became more so in the late 1980s and early 1990s. In the 1980s, a major programme of new RUC and army base building was implemented. To some extent, this was accelerated by IRA attacks on police stations and army installations, especially border checkpoints. Some thirty-five attacks on RUC stations, for instance, were recorded for 1980 but these had risen to over 200 by 1991 (RUC Chief Constable, 1991).

Since the mid-1980s, the army has been fortifying the border with a mixture of road closures, new permanent bases, watchtowers and checkpoints, including all the usual paraphernalia of cameras and telecommunications. The new border post at Killeen on the main Belfast to Dublin road, for example, now consists of a steel-clad military base, an inspection shed with X-ray equipment, and a system of traffic lights, cameras and barriers, including hydraulic pistons sunk in the road which can be triggered to stop vehicles which attempt to drive through the other barriers.

Many border communities have been disrupted by road closures, particularly in the Fermanagh and Tyrone areas.

The army closed border roads by means of trenches, craters and huge concrete blocks into which steel posts are embedded – known locally as 'dragon's teeth'. Of fifty-nine border roads in Fermanagh, only ten remained open until the post-ceasefire decision to open all border crossings over a three-year period. The Lackey bridge crossing, near Clones in County Monaghan, has been the focus of conflict between local people and the authorities for decades. It was first closed in 1922, reopened in 1925, spiked in the 1950s, reopened again in the 1960s until closure in the early 1970s. In the last few years, local people using heavy earth moving equipment have reopened the crossing on several occasions, including New Year's day 1993, the day on which border controls between EU member states were supposed to disappear. Under the Emergency Provisions Act, it remains an offence to use a crossing which the authorities have closed and an offence to build a by-pass around a closed road within 200yds of the blockade. The Act also introduced new powers to seize equipment such as tractors and JCBs which may be used to reopen roads.

Not all border crossing closures have been instituted by the British army. After the IRA killed a UDR man and his wife in 1972, Aghalane bridge was blown up by a loyalist group. A temporary bridge was put in place but this too was blown up. The bridge has not been re-built even though much investment has gone into dredging and landscaping the Woodford river, which it once crossed, as part of a major tourist development scheme to link the Erne waterway in the North with the Shannon.

In addition to campaigns to reopen roads, residents in the south Armagh area have been concerned for some years about the health effects of military equipment in use in border areas. They believe that the army may have established a 'microwave fence' along parts of the border and is using electronic grids for navigational and communications purposes (Porter, 1993). Although the army claims there are no health hazards relating to its equipment and has even invited selected people to view some of the equipment in use at the Bessbrook base, the secretary of state for Defence has declined to give details of the make, model and emission levels of each type of equipment in use by the military in border areas of NI which emits electromagnetic radiation (Hansard, Written Answers 17.2.93).

The border was relatively open in the 1960s and 1970s. Ireland north and south had an interchangeable currency and, apart from RUC and army patrols, travel was unrestricted between the two jurisdictions. In 1979, the South joined the EMS and currency and consumer tax differences began to emphasise the day-to-day economic differences either side of the border. With the signing of the Hillsborough Agreement (Anglo-Irish Agreement) in 1985, the British and Irish governments began to co-operate much more actively than they had in the past on security matters.

In the early 1970s, British troops regularly crossed the border, generating much local hostility and general political embarrassment. Between 1973 and 1976, 304 border incursions were recorded by the Irish government – an average of two per week (Murray, 1990, pp. 175-192). These incidents were prior to the introduction of the policy of police primacy and prior to any meaningful cross-border police co-operation on the ground. As Mark Urban (1992, p. 29) writes, 'the advent of police primacy in 1976 was a positive step for Dublin since it removed the army, with whom the Gardaí would not deal, from control of operations.'

High level contacts between RUC Chief Constable Flanaghan and Garda Commissioner Malone began in 1974. These meetings gave rise to a series of study groups called the 'Baldonnel panels' which were designed to facilitate intelligence exchanges as well as co-ordinated border patrolling (Ryder, 1989, p. 133). Around the same time, European-wide co-operation was being established by London's metropolitan police special branch, specifically with a view to responding to anti-terrorist matters, and in 1977 the TREVI Working Group I on terrorism began work. TREVI-I has been cited as proving 'valuable in relation to the United Kingdom's response to the Provisional Irish Republican Army' when the latter mounted a series of operations in Europe in the late 1980s (Home Affairs Select Committee, 1990). In the early 1980s, however, a rift between Chief Constable Hermon and Garda Commissioner Wrenn meant that the two had no meetings for three years. Relationships were further soured by Hermon's public criticisms of Garda inefficiency and policy with respect to border security and extradition (Brewer 1991, pp. 78-9).

The Hillsborough Agreement established an Intergovernmental Conference as the framework for regular North/South meetings of government ministers, officials, police and security personnel. The goals mentioned under security policy include the discussion of policy issues, serious incidents and forthcoming events, as well as improving relations between the security forces and the community.

The agreement resulted in the setting up of three joint RUC/Garda working groups on operational and technical co-operation. Groups of officials also began meeting on extradition and other legal matters. Progress on implementing recommendations on RUC/Garda operational co-operation were considered at a special meeting of the conference held in London in October 1986. By the end of 1989, the conference had held thirty-two meetings, with many more meetings of officials and police personnel taking place behind the scenes. Most of the intergovernmental meetings were (and are) attended by the garda commissioner and the RUC chief constable. At the April 1990 meeting, it was agreed to set up a working party on how to deal with 'fugitive offenders'. By February 1993, the Northern Ireland Office was referring to the 'high level of security co-operation' between North and South, but very few details have emerged as to what this amounts to (Press Release, 3.2.93).

Clearly, intelligence and operational information is regularly exchanged, and co-ordinated operations are routinely mounted either side of the border. In its 1989 memorandum to the Home Affairs Select Committee (1990, p. 176) on police co-operation, the Northern Ireland Office describes the border as 'a major strategic resource for terrorists' although it was unable to put a figure on the actual number of 'terrorist-related crimes which have a cross-border element'. Accordingly, it had developed a border policy with three elements: (i) road closures, (ii) permanent and selective vehicle check points (PSVCPs), and (iii) mobile patrols. The eighteen PSVCPs in existence in 1989 were all permanently occupied by the military, with an RUC presence at most of them.

Major Garda and Irish army reinforcements were deployed to assist the British army with road closures and the building of permanent checkpoints during 1991, but it appears that these operations are organised through RUC/Garda channels: according to the Irish army, 'there is no army-to-army communication' (*Sunday Tribune*, 10.1.93). When questioned about the role of intelligence services in October 1992, security minister Michael Mates replied, 'co-operation between the intelligence services of the Republic and ourselves has never been as good as it is now' (Hansard, 29.10.92, col. 1118). Ryder (1989, p. 370) claims that arrangements have existed for some time for bomb disposal teams to cross the border and for helicopter 'overflights'.

Nevertheless, there has been much debate as to how to increase further the effectiveness of cross-border security co-operation. It has been suggested at Westminster, for example, that for border security purposes Garda patrols should be armed or the Irish army put in the front line (Hansard 10.5.90 col. 390). Another idea is that joint RUC/Garda mobile units should be established along with common radio communications, and procedures for 'hot pursuit' have been proposed on a number of occasions.

Monitoring state power

At first sight, there would appear to be no shortage of official monitoring of the exercise of state power in Northern Ireland.

For example there is an Independent Assessor of Military Complaints Procedures, an Independent Commissioner for Holding Centres (interrogation centres), a judge who reviews emergency powers, an Independent Commission for Police Complaints and the Standing Advisory Commission on Human Rights. The presence of such monitoring, however, has not prevented the growth of a human rights lobby or the expanding influence of non-governmental organisations such as the Committee on the Administration of Justice (CAJ), the Centre for Research and Documentation, and Amnesty International. The human rights lobby has pursued individual cases through domestic and international law, sponsored citizens' inquiries and conducted major reviews of policing practices and human rights abuses. The Council of Europe's European Convention on Human Rights has been an important backdrop to much of this activity.

Approaches to the Northern Ireland conflict from a human rights perspective have gathered considerable momentum lately, both in non-governmental organisations and within state bodies such as the Standing Advisory Commission on Human Rights (SACHR). The rhetoric of human rights also pervades a government circular on Policy Appraisal and Fair Treatment in which emergency law is included among measures adopted to promote human rights.

SACHR advocates that the European Convention on Human Rights be incorporated into domestic law. This would have the advantage that those with serious human rights grievances would have a swifter remedy than that available through the various European mechanisms. The problem for the government is that it may have to drop certain powers and practices if it were to do so, such as the seven day detention power under the Prevention of Terrorism Act. But it has little incentive to speed up the legal processes which test its powers against international human rights standards. CAJ, on the other hand, has produced its own Bill of Rights which goes beyond the Convention.

Britain is a signatory to the UN Covenant on Human and

Political Rights which it ratified in 1976. At the time, the government entered a derogation with respect to Northern Ireland which it withdrew in 1984. It derogated from the European Convention as long ago as 1957 with respect to Northern Ireland. This was also withdrawn in 1984 and, as a result, 'Northern Ireland is no longer officially designated under the international instruments as a territory where "a public emergency threatening the life of the nation" exists' (Hadden, Boyle and Campbell 1988; p. 22). But after the Brogan case in 1988, in which the European Court of Human Rights had judged that the emergency power of seven-day detention was in breach of the convention, a further derogation was entered, leaving the question of whether Britain is justified in doing this with reference to the circumstances pertaining in Northern Ireland at the time. The convention allows states to derogate from certain articles (but not all) in time of war or if the 'life of the nation' is threatened. Clearly, the original drafters, Britain being foremost among them, used the convention to institutionalise national boundaries as they existed in the 1950s. In 1993, the court decided that Britain was indeed justified in derogating from the convention in respect of seven-day detention. It further argued that national authorities, not international judges, should be given wide discretion in deciding upon their own need to derogate, a judgment that some commentators have seen as reflecting a growing conservatism in the interpretation of the convention (McEvoy, 1993).

Notwithstanding rhetoric to the contrary, there is some evidence that British ministers have a cavalier attitude towards international human rights processes and standards. Take for example the way in which Amnesty International's report on political killings was treated by the secretary of state for Northern Ireland, the RUC, and senior Ulster Unionist politicians. Referring to the evidence of collusion between loyalists and official forces, Amnesty (1994) had argued that 'whenever clandestine groups claim they are supporting a government's security forces and a governmental system through political killings, the governments in question have a special obligation'. It therefore called for a wide-ranging investigation into the human rights implications of covert intelligence operations, urging the British government to establish a thorough and impartial investigation into collusion. Ken Maginnis, MP, responded to this call by accusing 'this self-appointed jury' (Amnesty) of setting out to discredit the security service. Similarly, Deputy Chief Constable Blair Wallace, attacked the Amnesty report by saying, 'it is unjust and insulting to these brave men and women to infer that they are anything other than even-handed' (*Statewatch*, 1994).

A broader indictment of Britain's human rights record is that, between 1983 and 1991, it has had more cases taken against it under the European Convention of Human Rights than any other country, and has had more adverse judgments made against it than any other country. It accounts for 17 per cent of all cases taken (1983-1991), 73 per cent of all adverse judgments by the Committee of Ministers (up to 1987) and 25 per cent of all adverse judgments by the European Court of Human Rights (up to 1987) (Council of Europe, Annual Survey of Activities and Statistics).

Pursuing cases under the European Convention on Human Rights, while providing an international mechanism for addressing human rights grievances, has limitations. The process of taking cases to Europe is time-consuming and costly. More importantly, several important judgments have been delivered over the years in support of the British government's position. Internment, for example, was judged to be acceptable in the circumstances. The notorious five techniques developed by the British army in Malaya, Kenya and Aden, which involved prolonged interrogation alongside sleep deprivation, no food, white noise, wall-standing and the use of hoods over suspects' heads, and which were used in Northern Ireland in the early 1970s, did not amount to torture according to the commission (they amounted to 'inhuman and degrading treatment'). It was also found that

neither the refusal of special category status nor the treatment of prisoners on the no-wash protest in the late 1970s was
in breach of the convention.

Some local groups within Northern Ireland have taken up
the government rhetoric regarding the real abusers of
human rights, and have sought to persuade civil liberties
lobbies and human rights bodies to examine and monitor the
conduct of paramilitary organisations. Civil liberties organisations explicitly condemn terrorism and so are not morally
at odds with such a stance. They do, however, face the
practical difficulty of the problems surrounding international
law when it comes to human rights abuses by paramilitary
groups. International humanitarian law, such as the Hague
Convention and the 1949 Geneva Convention (and subsequent protocols which sought to define the nature of conflicts
within countries as opposed to between them) has no
enforcement machinery. Besides, the British government has
refused to sign the protocols under which it might be possible
to define Northern Ireland as an 'armed conflict'. As
Campbell (1991) writes, 'before anyone rushes into applying
humanitarian law to Northern Ireland, some markers must
be put down: (a) it must apply across the board, to all paramilitary organisations and emanations of the state; (b) it
must not be used to divert resources or attention from abuses
by the state; and (c) it must be applied by independent
competent organisations, without political axes to grind –
preferably established international groups who can bring
sufficient clout to bear.'

Northern Ireland and the New Europe

This article has tackled several aspects of the Northern
Ireland conflict which have significance for the development
of Europe's internal and external policing policies. In its
management of Northern Ireland over the past quarter
century, Britain has built up a wealth of experience in
'emergency' law, intelligence gathering, surveillance, media

influence, covert operations and militaristic forms of policing. Such experience has already been influential in the construction of social control strategies for the new Europe. Arguably, Britain's justification of its general role in Northern Ireland, as well as its defence of a range of state practices, serves to tilt the political culture of Europeanisation towards technologies, strategies and structures which are non-accountable, secret and militaristic. We can expect to see, for instance, an increasing deployment of military-style and intelligence-based policing at Europe's external borders and associated 'buffer states', as well as internally in relation to the conflicts arising from Europe's increased xenophobia and racism. Britain has already shown Spanish interior ministry officials around its border installations, presumably to offer practical advice on how to keep Moroccans out of Spain (*Statewatch*, 1993a). Morocco, under an agreement with the Spanish government, deploys 2,000 troops along the coast to stop boats carrying refugees crossing to Spain. Similarly, Austria deploys 2,000 military personnel as border police who turned away 77,000 refugees in the first half of 1993 (Fekete and Webber, 1994, p. 31).

British government perceptions of the changing European threat are also important for the restructuring of the intelligence agencies. The conflict in Ireland, and specifically the countering of the IRA, has been an important factor for MI5 in forging its role in Europe. This ranges from the surveillance of Irish communities in Germany, the Netherlands, France and elsewhere (de Laval, 1994), to developing mechanisms of co-operation between European intelligence agencies geared towards the British agenda in relation to the Northern Ireland conflict. TREVI Group I, for example, agreed in 1990 to intensify regular exchanges of detailed information on terrorist groups, their techniques, logistic supports, financing and the incidents they provoke. Member states must communicate without delay any information they have about groups or suspects in which another state is interested. It was also agreed to examine the legal means required to allow police investigations into the financing of terrorist activities and, no doubt, the powers under the Prevention of Terrorism Act will be the model.[4] The TREVI Group established the co-ordination of counter-terrorist measures through a network of liaison officers who enjoy 'diplomatic immunity'. The supposed fruits of such co-operation were celebrated by Stella Rimington in her 1994 Dimbleby Lecture when she cited the example of the massive arms shipment from Poland, seized by police at Teesport (England). The shipment was reportedly destined for loyalists (see *Statewatch*, 1994b).

Another example of British influence in Europe is the proposed EU Council Regulation on security procedures – the UK-style European Official Secrets measure which was withdrawn at the Edinburgh summit in December 1992. Should this ever be introduced, Article 12 allows for the political vetting of appointments in relation to the commission's work along the lines of practices which have become all too familiar in Northern Ireland (Political Vetting of Community Work Group, 1990). It appears that the political vetting of Irish appointees to the commission by MI5 may already be in train with or without the proposed regulation (*Statewatch*, 1993b).

One of the most revealing aspects of Europeanisation is the physical fortification of the border. The fortification of the border has become the basis around which cross-border policing and intelligence liaison has been developed. At times the relationships at the level of policing and between the British and Irish governments have been difficult, especially when proposals or actions seem to threaten Irish sovereignty, or when the British appear to ignore Irish representations on the North. Border security policy in the early 1990s was of some comfort to unionists, who welcomed both the restrictions on cross-border traffic and the mobilisation of the Irish authorities in increasing levels of counter-terrorist work. They remain nervous, however, about the post-ceasefire opening of border crossings and more generally that British/Irish co-operation may further weaken the prospects of Northern Ireland remaining part of the UK. In the past unionists were more likely to make calls for the sealing of the border than to go along with the Social Democratic and Labour Party's idea of an all-Ireland anti-terrorist force. As we have seen, even self-styled 'realists' who advocate North/South co-operation on security, industrial development, tourism, transport, energy and so on, find it necessary to settle the constitutional question once and for all in favour of the union, with the border firmly intact (Cadogan Group 1992, p. 26).

The physical build-up of the border, however, directly contradicts Article 8a of the Single European Act which defines the single market as an area without frontiers and which allows the free movement of goods, services, capital and persons. Although the Act is qualified by the declaration permitting member states to take necessary measures against terrorism, the fortification of the North/South border is of dubious legality and certainly contradicts the spirit of EU integration. As a counter-terrorist measure, however, the fortified border suits Britain's opposition to the general relaxation of border controls. Whatever happens to the North/South border in Ireland, Hillyard's (1993) prediction is that British Prevention of Terrorism Act type powers, coupled with the introduction of compulsory ID cards, will form the core of a new system of surveillance and monitoring throughout the EU.

Conclusion

This article has sought to show that the promise of Europeanisation for Ireland in forging greater co-operation between North and South, and even in re-casting the question of national sovereignty, needs to be treated with caution. The capacity of 'first pillar' European programmes and institutions to break down North/South barriers needs to be weighed against the largely secret agendas of the second and third

pillars. The militaristic and intelligence-based management of
Northern Ireland looms large in the way Britain contributes to
the development of the K4 Co-ordinating Committee policies
on border controls, policing, information systems, counter-
terrorism, asylum and immigration.

In this direct sense, the type of Europe which is emerging
rests in part on how the conflict in Northern Ireland has
been managed over the last twenty-five years. It was argued
that human rights instruments such as the European
Convention have proved ineffective in preventing human
rights abuses and powerless in providing a basis for de-
escalating the military aspects of the conflict. Unless there is
some way of enforcing humanitarian law, or getting all parties
to a conflict to recognise the force of the Geneva Convention
and UN protocols, then moral invective against the
combatants, both official and unofficial, achieves little.

Notes

1. There is a dispute over the origins of 'TREVI' but most
   commentators accept that it is an acronym for 'terrorism,
   radicalism, extremism and violence'.
2. The Council of Europe's European Convention on Human
   Rights and its associated Commission and Court, are of course
   quite separate from EU law which is adjudicated by the
   European Court of Justice. It should be noted, however, that the
   European Court of Justice is considering the possibility of incorporating the convention into EU law.
3. The head of MI5 in Northern Ireland until June 1994 was John
   Deverell. On 2 June he was killed while travelling from the
   North of Ireland to a conference at Fort George, Scotland.
   Twenty-five intelligence personnel and four RAF crew were
   killed when their Chinook helicopter crashed on the Mull of
   Kintyre. Among the dead were ten members of RUC SB,
   including the head of SB, 2 regional heads and the divisional
   heads of E1, E2, E3, E3A, E3B, and E4. Five MI5 agents also
   perished in the crash along with a British army colonel, three
   intelligence corps lieutenant colonels, and five majors. It is
   widely acknowledged that the crash killed the upper echelons of

the intelligence agencies in the North, including key members of the Provincial Executive Committee.

4. Under Section 17 of the 1989 Act, there are powers to enable the police to obtain warrants to secure such information they need, for example from banks and building societies, for the general purpose of investigating terrorism. The Emergency Provisions Act 1991 allows for the seizure of documents and computer disks to find out if they are 'of use to terrorists'.

References

AMNESTY INTERNATIONAL, 1994. *Political Killings in Northern Ireland*, London, Amnesty International.

BENYON, J., 1994. 'Policing the European Union: the changing basis of cooperation on law enforcement', *International Affairs*, Vol. 70 (3), pp. 497-517.

BEW, P. and E. MEEHAN, 1994. 'Regions and Borders: controversies in Northern Ireland about the European Union', *Journal of European Public Policy*, Vol. 1 (1), pp. 95-113.

BIRNIE, J.E. and D. HITCHENS, 1994. *The Road to Prosperity or a Road to Nowhere? The Potential for a Belfast-Dublin Economic Corridor*, QUB Papers in Economics, Working Paper No. 46.

BOULTON, D., 1973. *The UVF 1966-73: an anatomy of loyalist rebellion*, Dublin, Torc Books.

BREWER, J., 1991. *Inside the RUC: Routine Policing in a Divided Society*, Oxford, Clarendon Press.

BRUCE, S., 1992. *The Red Hand: Protestant Paramilitaries in Northern Ireland*, Oxford, Oxford University Press.

BUNYAN, T., 1993a. 'Trevi, Europol and the European State' in T. Bunyan (ed.), *Statewatching the New Europe: A Handbook on the European State*, London, Statewatch.

BUNYAN, T., 1993b. 'Secret Europe', in T. Bunyan (ed.), *Statewatching the New Europe: A Handbook on the European State*, London, Statewatch.

CADOGAN GROUP, 1992. *Northern Limits*, Belfast, Codogan Group.

CAMPBELL, C., 1991. 'Humanitarian Law: Not as Simple as it Seems', *Just News*, Vol. 6, No. 11, December.

COOGAN, T.P., 1980. *The IRA*, London, Fontana.

DE LAVAL, W., 1994. 'Policing the Diaspora', *Irish Reporter*, No. 13, pp. 26-27.

DEFENCE COMMITTEE, 1993. *Britain's Army for the 90s: Commitments and Resources*, Defence Committee, Second

Report, HC 1992/93: 306. London, HMSO, 1993.

DEWAR, M., 1993. 'The Military Overdraft', *The Guardian*, 29.1.93.

DILLON, M., 1989. *The Shankill Butchers: A Case Study of Mass Murder*, London, Hutchinson.

DILLON, M., 1990. *The Dirty War*, London, Hutchinson.

FEKETE, L. and F. WEBBER, 1994. *Inside Racist Europe*, London, Institute of Race Relations

FOOT, P., 1990. *Who Framed Colin Wallace?* London, Pan Books.

GOVERNMENT OF IRELAND, 1992. *Ireland in Europe, A Shared Challenge*, Dublin, Stationery Office.

HADDEN, T., K. BOYLE and C. CAMPBELL, 1988. 'Emergency Law in Northern Ireland, The Context', in A. Jennings (ed.), *Justice Under Fire, The Abuse of Civil Liberties in Northern Ireland*, London, Pluto Press.

HILLYARD, P., 1988. 'Political and Social Dimensions of Emergency Law in Northern Ireland' in A. Jennings (ed.), *Justice Under Fire, The Abuse of Civil Liberties in Northern Ireland*, London, Pluto Press.

HILLYARD, P., 1993. 'The Prevention of Terrorism Acts and the new European State', in T. Bunyan (ed.), *Statewatching the New Europe, a handbook on the European State*, London, Statewatch, pp. 115-120.

HOLLAND, J. and H. McDONALD, 1994. *INLA, Deadly Divisions*, Dublin, Torc Books.

HOME AFFAIRS SELECT COMMITTEE, 1990. *Practical Police Co-operation in the European Community*, HC 1989/90, 363-I.

HUTTON, W., 1994. *Britain and Northern Ireland, The State We're In – Failure and Opportunity*, Northern Ireland Economic Council, Report No. 114.

IRISH SOCIAL AND ECONOMIC RESEARCH UNIT, 1990, 1992. *What it Means for Ireland*, Belfast, ISERU.

JENNINGS, A. (ed.), 1988. *Justice Under Fire, The Abuse of Civil Liberties in Northern Ireland*, London, Pluto Press.

LAFFAN, B., 1989. '"While You're over there in Brussels, Get us a Grant", the Management of the Structural Funds in Ireland', *Irish Political Studies 4*, pp. 43-57.

MATTHEWS, A., 1989. *Ireland in the European Community, Towards Economic and Social Cohesion*, Belfast, Policy Research Institute.

McEVOY, K., 1993. 'The Fox Guarding the Hen-house', *Just News*, Vol. 8, No. 6, June.

MILLER, D., 1994. *Don't Mention the War, Northern Ireland, Propaganda and the Media*, London, Pluto Press.

MINISTRY OF DEFENCE,
1993. *UK Defence Statistics
1993*, London, HMSO.
MURRAY, R., 1990. *The SAS in
Ireland*, Cork, Mercier Press.
NEW INTERNATIONALIST,
1994. Special Issue on
Northern Ireland, No. 255,
May.
NORTHERN IRELAND
OFFICE, 1990. *Memorandum
to the Home Affairs Select
Committee on Practical Police
Co-operation in the European
Community*, HC 1989/90,
363-II.
O'DOWD, L., 1995. 'Borders,
Security and the "free
market", Nation-States and
European Integration with
Special Reference to Ireland',
International Sociology,
forthcoming.
O'LEARY, B. and J. McGARRY,
1993. *The Politics of
Antagonism, Understanding
Northern Ireland*, London,
Athlone Press.
PHILIP, C. and A. TAYLOR,
1992. *Inside the SAS*, London,
Bloomsbury.
POLITICAL VETTING OF
COMMUNITY WORK
GROUP, 1990. *The Political
Vetting of Community Work in
Northern Ireland*, Belfast,
Northern Ireland Council for
Voluntary Action.
PORTER, S., 1993. 'Unhealthy
Surveillance, Investigating the
Public Health in South
Armagh', *Critical Public Health*.
ROCHE, M., 1992. *Rethinking

Citizenship*, Cambridge, Polity
Press.
ROLSTON, B., 1991.
'Containment and its Failure:
The British State and the
Control of Conflict in
Northern Ireland' and
A. George, 'The Discipline of
Terrorology', chapters 7 and 4
of A. George (ed.), *Western
State Terrorism*, Cambridge,
Polity Press.
ROOM, G. (ed.), 1992. *Towards
a European Welfare State?*
Bristol, SAUS Publications.
ROWTHORN, B. and
N. WAYNE, 1989. Northern
Ireland, *The Political Economy
of Conflict*, Cambridge,
Polity Press.
RUC CHIEF CONSTABLE,
Annual Report 1991.
RYDER, C., 1989. *The RUC,
A Force Under Fire*, London,
Methuen.
RYDER, C., 1991. *The Ulster
Defence Regiment, An Instrument
of Peace?* London, Methuen.
SIMPSON, R. and R. WALKER
(eds.), 1993. *Europe, For Richer
or Poorer?* London, Child
Poverty Action Group.
SINN FÉIN, n.d., *The Ulster
Defence Regiment, the Loyalist
Militia*, Dublin, Sinn Féin
Publicity Department.
SPENCER, M., 1990. '1992 and
all that', *Civil Liberties in the
Balance*, London, Civil
Liberties Trust.
STATEWATCH, 1991.
'Reforming the UDR?',
Statewatch No. 4,

September/October 1991,
pp. 3-4.

STATEWATCH, 1993a. 'Border
Tour', *Statewatch* Vol. 3, (3),
May/June.

STATEWATCH, 1993b. 'The
Mary Reid Story', *Statewatch*
Vol. 3, (2), March/April.

STATEWATCH, 1994a. Vol. 4,
(3), May/June, p. 18.

STATEWATCH, 1994b. 'MI5/
MI6 – Trick or Treat?',
Statewatch, Vol. 4 (1), Jan/Feb,
pp. 7-8.

SUTTON, M., 1994. *Bear in
Mind these Dead, An Index of
Deaths from the Conflict in
Ireland 1969-1993*, Belfast,
Beyond the Pale Publications.

TAILLON, R., 1993. *Chasing the
EC Rainbow, The Impact of
European Funding on Women in
Northern Ireland*, Belfast,
Women's Committee,
Northern Ireland Committee
of the Irish Congress of Trade
Unions.

TOMLINSON, M., 1993.
'Policing the New Europe,
The Northern Ireland Factor',
in T. Bunyan (ed.), *State-
watching the New Europe, A
Handbook on the European State*,
London, Statewatch.

TOMLINSON, M., 1994, *25
Years On, The Costs of the War
and the Dividends of Peace*,
Belfast, West Belfast Economic
Forum.

TREASURY, 1993. *Public
Expenditure Plans*, Cm. 1908,
London, HMSO.

URBAN, M., 1992. *Big Boys'
Rules: The SAS and the Secret
Struggle against the IRA*,
London, Faber and Faber.

WISTRICH, E., 1989. *After
1992, The United States of
Europe*, London, Routledge.

PART THREE
Education, Culture and Social Movements

15
Education in the Republic of Ireland: the Project of Modernity?

PATRICK CLANCY

In a recent review of developments within the sociology of education Dale (1992) has pointed to the way in which education as an institution has held a central place in what has come to be called the project of modernity. On the one hand, he argues, it has come to be seen as both the prevailing symbol and dominant strategy for that mastery of nature and society through rationality which has characterised the project of modernity from its origins in the Enlightenment. On the other hand, he suggests, education has been a keystone of attempts to extend the benefits of progress to whole populations, indeed to the whole of humanity. It has come to stand for the possibility of individual and collective improvement, individual and collective emancipation.

The centrality of education is exemplified by the rapid and continuing expansion of educational systems in all advanced societies. A forthcoming OECD (1995) report argues that the expansion of education and training systems has been so general and sustained over the whole post-war period that it stands out as perhaps *the* trend of OECD countries that historians in this field will chronicle and debate in future years. In the Republic of Ireland in 1992-3 a total of 976,181 students (28 per cent of the total population) were receiving full-time education. Of these, 529,811 were attending primary schools, 362,230 were attending post-primary schools, while 84,140 were attending third-level colleges. Second- and third-level enrolments have increased dramatically in recent years. For example in 1963-4 full-time enrolments in second- and third-level education were 129,365 and 16,819 respectively (*Investment in Education*, 1966). Schooling is compulsory up to the age of fifteen. However, in 1992-3, it is estimated that 73 per cent of the fifteen to nineteen age cohort and 17 per cent of the twenty to twenty-four age cohort were receiving full-time education (Department of Education, 1994).

In addition to considerations of increasing scale and the associated financial contribution by the state, representing almost 19 per cent of total expenditure by government on supply services and 6.5 per cent of GNP in 1993 (Department of Education, 1993), the importance of education is also reflected in its centrality in public debate. Almost 1,000 written submissions were made in response to the government *Green Paper, Education for a changing world*, 1992. In October 1993 a high profile National Education Convention was held in Dublin Castle involving representatives from forty-two organisations in discussions on key issues of educational policy in Ireland. While this extensive national debate has occurred as a prelude to the forthcoming *White Paper on Education* it reflects the importance of education in Irish national life.

This paper provides a sociological perspective on the educational system in the Republic of Ireland. The paper is divided into three sections. The first section examines briefly a number of theoretical approaches to education. The second section examines socialisation and the production of consciousness, and shows how this aspect of education is linked to the control and governance of education. The third section examines the process of selection and social reproduction.

Theoretical approaches

Most of the sociological research and analysis within the field of education has been carried out within a structuralist perspective, and this approach is followed here. Traditionally, sociologists have taken the total society as their unit of analysis and have sought to understand the contribution of the educational system to the maintenance and development of that society. This macro approach tended to leave the social processes and internal dynamics of the school unexamined. More recently, sociologists, using interpretative approaches, have turned their attention to the functioning of the school organisation and have examined the pattern of interaction within the classroom, and the nature of the curriculum through which the explicit goals of schooling are realised (see, for example, Woods, 1983).

An assertion that most sociological analysis of education can be located within a structuralist perspective should not be taken to imply that all sociologists using this approach share a common view on the role of education in society. In reality, two groups of scholars, functionalists and marxists, hold antithetical views about the functions of education in contemporary society. However, in spite of fundamentally contrary views, their approaches towards an understanding of education reveal a remarkable similarity.

Talcott Parsons, the leading exponent of structural functionalist sociology, set the agenda for many sociologists of education when he identified the 'dual problem' with which schools have to contend. Schools are simultaneously agencies of socialisation and selection. As a socialisation agency, the school is responsible for the development in individuals of the commitments and capacities which are prerequisites for their future role performance. This socialisation has both a technical and a moral component. At a technical level, schools teach the capacities and skills required for adult role performance. In an age of increasing technological sophistication society is becoming more dependent on the educational system to equip people with the range of skills necessary for the occupational world. For Parsons, the role of the school as an agency of moral socialisation is even more crucial. As a normative functionalist he insists that value consensus is essential if society is to operate effectively. Hence the significance of schooling where young people are socialised into the basic values of society (Parsons, 1959).

A key value which schools teach and which is of strategic importance to society is that of achievement. Within the family the child's status is ascribed; it is fixed by birth. However, status in adult life is largely achieved; for example, an individual achieves his or her occupational role. At school, students are encouraged to strive for high levels of academic attainment and, by rewarding those who do strive, the school fosters the value of achievement. The functionalist analysis suggests that the school's commitment to meritocratic principles (i.e. rewarding ability and effort) becomes the essential mechanism by which our society accepts the principle of differential rewards. Both the winners – the high achievers – and the losers – the low achievers – will see the system as equitable since status is achieved in a situation where all seem to have an equal chance.

This discussion of the way in which the norm of achievement is internalised leads us to an analysis of the school's selection function, the second element of Parsons' dual problem. The school functions as a crucial mechanism for the selection of individuals for their future occupational role in society. An important dimension of schooling is the on-going process of evaluation. Schools differentiate between pupils on the basis of their achievement. The differentiation which teachers make between students within the school prepares students for differential allocation in the labour market.

On the face of it, the strident critique of schooling which is contained in the marxist approach to education would seem to have little in common with the functionalist approach. While functionalists consider education to be an equalising force in society, marxist-oriented scholars argue that education merely serves the interest of the capitalist class. The meritocratic hypothesis, with its assumption that schools are efficient ways of selecting talented people, is emphatically rejected. Instead it is argued that schools work to convince people that selection is meritocratic. It is essential for the legitimacy of the capitalist order that the population be convinced that people in high status positions deserve their positions, that they are more talented and work harder than others. Schools are an essential prop of this legitimacy. The essentially optimistic functionalist view that education is intrinsically good, that it leads to individual emancipation and self-realisation, is countered by the marxists who stress its repressive features. They view the educational system as an instrument of cultural domination; its real function is best understood in terms of the need for social control in an unequal and rapidly changing social order. However, in spite of these antithetical views, and in spite of the use of very different terminology, both approaches to the analysis of education are strikingly similar. This similarity in approach is evident from an examination of the work of the American neo-marxists, Bowles and Gintis (1976).

Bowles and Gintis's analysis of the educational system begins with an assessment of the labour force requirement of capitalism. Education functions as an agency to supply appropriately educated labour power to the economy. Two modes of appropriateness are identified: firstly, the release of young men and women from the educational system at different ages and with different technical capacities and qualifications, and secondly, the production of personalities, attitudes and orientations which facilitate integration into the wage labour system with its attendant hierarchical division of labour. This latter objective is achieved through the operation of the 'correspondence principle'. Bowles and Gintis argue that major aspects of educational organisation replicate the relationships of dominance and subordinacy in the economic sphere. Thus, the social relations of schooling reproduce the social relations of production.

Not withstanding the fundamental ideological difference between the functionalist and marxist perspectives, their broad agreement on an approach towards understanding the function of education in contemporary society provides us with an orientation which can be used to explore the working of the Irish educational system. Its role as a socialising agency concerned with the reproduction of labour power with the appropriate skills and consciousness will first be examined. Then the school's function as a mechanism of role allocation, and its contribution towards the reproduction of existing social hierarchies will be explored. In examining both of these processes, it is contended that the situation in Ireland broadly parallels that found in other capitalist countries. Hence, the main concern of the paper will be to point towards any special nuances in the Irish experience.

Before turning to this analysis it is appropriate to note that while considerations of space allow us to discuss only two theoretical perspectives, a variety of other positions are to be found in the literature. For example Drudy and Lynch (1993) identify three further perspectives which have been influential; symbolic interactionism, feminist theory and the neo-Weberian perspective. The latter perspective has gained in popularity and is particularly valuable for its attempt to bridge the gap between micro and macro social processes. Weberian sociology seeks to 'interpret' the behaviour of human beings to understand the subjective meaning of their actions. But it also attempts to locate individual behaviour in its social context, accepting that all action takes place within a social and economic structure which, to some extent, limits what the individual can do. From this perspective Collins (1979) has examined the ways in which education is used by individuals and groups in the struggle for economic advantage, status and domination. Education, he argues, can be seen as a 'positional' good in the sense that it is a screening device for selecting and allocating individuals to the labour market. However, he points out that it is not because of the technical skills they certify that credentials are used increasingly for occupational selection. Rather he suggests that the lengthy course of study required by business and professional schools exist in good part to raise the status of the profession and to form the barrier of socialisation between practitioners and the lay public.

Socialisation and the production of consciousness

In nineteenth-century Ireland, the struggle to gain control of the national school system was explicitly a struggle to mould the consciousness of the Irish population. The British government pursued a policy of anglicisation by operating constraints on the language and culture transmitted in the curriculum. The religious denominations sought and attained the development of a religiously segregated system. This ensured the perpetuation of their particular ideologies. Social control was the main concern of those who sought to shape the system; issues of moral socialisation took precedence over issues of technical socialisation, although the latter was catered for by the inclusion on the curriculum of such subjects as needlework, cookery and laundry, manual instruction and rural science (see Coolahan, 1981). This technical socialisation was highly differentiated by gender (see Chapter 17 of this volume for a discussion of the gender dimension of education).

The development of the national system in the Republic of Ireland since independence illustrates further the close links between education and value systems. The curriculum changes which were introduced after independence were inspired by the ideology of cultural nationalism. It was felt that schools ought to be the prime agents in the revival of the Irish language and Gaelic culture. The work of the infant school was to be entirely in Irish; no teaching of English as a school subject was to be permitted. For senior classes, Irish was to be the medium of instruction for history, geography, drill and singing, and all songs in the singing class were to be Irish language songs. The programme in history was to deal exclusively with the history of Ireland, the chief aim being to develop the best traits of the national character and to inculcate national pride and self-respect.

The institutionalisation of the ideology of cultural nationalism was complemented by the special position accorded to the churches in the control of education. After independence, the *de facto* denominational status of the school system was quickly recognised and became institutionalised. Successive ministers of education adopted the view that the role of the state in education was a subsidiary one, aiding agencies such as the churches in the provision of educational facilities. The acceptance of this principle of subsidiarity is reflected in the structure of education in the Republic of Ireland, where the degree of control exercised by the religious personnel is almost without parallel.

The extent of church control in Irish education is described by Nic Ghiolla Phádraig elsewhere in this volume and in greater detail in Drudy and Lynch (1993; chs. 1 and 4). The essence of this control is rooted in the ownership and management of schools. At primary level more than 96 per cent of children of primary school-going age (4-12) attend state-supported national schools, although the term 'national' is somewhat misleading since the schools are not owned by the state. Almost all of these schools are denominational with 93 per cent under the patronage of the Catholic church. At second level 62 per cent attend secondary schools, 89 per cent of which are owned and controlled by Catholic religious communities; the remainder are divided between those which belong to other religious denominations, and those which are either privately or corporately owned by lay Catholics. Thus, the primary sector and the major part of the second-level sector consist of privately owned state-aided schools, with the state now paying over 80 per cent of capital costs of buildings and facilities and over 90 per cent of current expenditure. In their discussion of the policy issues on school governance the secretariat of the National Education Convention capture this distinctive feature of Irish education:

The different religious authorities, and indeed other
ethically or culturally motivated groups such as the
multi-denominational schools or Gaelscoileanna, who
set up or operate schools, do so because they wish to
ensure that certain fundamental beliefs, values and
culturally valuable practices are effectively taught and
learned/internalised within the schools they set up.
These fundamental beliefs, values and cultural practices
are to be expressed not only in explicit curricular
programmes, such as religious instruction classes, but
also clearly incorporated into the overall organisational
character and enlivening ethos of the school. The
patron/trustee in this sense stands for, or acts on behalf
of, a body (usually organised) of people who wish their
children to be educated within a particular religious,
ethical tradition (Report on the National Education
Convention, 1994, p. 24).

Traditionally the patron (usually the bishop of the diocese)
appointed the manager who administered the school in
accordance with the regulations laid down by the government
Department of Education. Typically the manager was the
parish priest or in the case of the schools operated by religious
congregations the superior of the religious community. More
recently (from 1975 in the case of primary schools and 1985
in the case of secondary schools) the single manager has been
replaced by a board of management. This change has not
significantly altered the power structure, since the patron's
nominees constitute a majority of the board. The other
members are elected parents and teacher representatives.

In recent years there has been a demand for more
democratic participation by parents and teachers whose
representatives have called for equal representation with the
nominees of the patron or trustees. In respect of parents this
demand reflects an unease with the traditional model
whereby the patron was deemed to 'act on behalf of parents'.
In responding to these demands for greater democratisation

and to the continuing insistence by the patrons and trustees on their need to appoint majorities on the boards so as to safeguard the ethos of their schools the secretariat of the National Education Convention suggested that both concerns might be accommodated by a clearer specification of the functions of patronage and management. It was suggested that the interests of patrons and trustees could be safeguarded by the drawing up of agreed deeds of trust and articles of management, within the ambit of which a board of management could operate and departures from which could lead to its being called to account. In this context it was suggested that boards could be equally representative of patrons, teachers and parents (Report on the National Education Convention, 1994, p. 29). It seems unlikely that this proposed compromise will be acceptable to the churches. In a press release after the March 1994 meeting of the Irish Bishops Conference Bishop Flynn reported that the Bishops' Education Commission is not convinced that either a charter or a deed of trust on its own would be capable of guaranteeing the Catholic character of the school into the future. He reported that 'the bishops have been unable to find a more effective way of ensuring the future of Catholic schools than through a majority of active and committed Catholics on boards of management' (Flynn, 1994).

The pressure for changes in school governance is also influenced by growing pluralism. One expression of this is in the establishment of a number of multi-denominational schools, eleven of which existed at primary level in 1993. There is also a minority of parents who seek a secular form of education for their children and who are unhappy with the current situation whereby almost all schools are denominational. While such parents are free to withdraw their children from religious instruction a civil liberties difficulty arises from the fact that denominational education implies that religion is fully integrated into the rest of the curriculum and that the ethos and 'hidden curriculum' fully reflect the religious ideals of the school.

Recent developments suggest that the second level sector may provide the most likely site for explicit conflict about church control in education. For several decades the main alternative to church-controlled secondary schools was the vocational school established following the 1930 Vocational Education Act and representing the first attempt to establish publicly-owned schools. Vocational schools were designed to provide a qualitatively different education from that offered by the academic, and mainly middle-class, secondary schools. The curricular pattern of secondary schools was firmly fixed within the humanist grammar school tradition where language and literary studies predominated. In contrast, the vocational school emphasised practical training in preparation for skilled and semi-skilled manual occupations for boys, and commercial courses and domestic economy for girls.

The binary or bipartite system of post-primary education reflected in the secondary-vocational distinction was not unique to the Republic of Ireland. However, the relative size of those two sectors was the inverse of that found in most other western European countries, where the grammar-type school catered for the minority of the post-primary school population. By the 1960s there was a growing realisation that the structure of the post-primary system in the Republic was unsatisfactory. The new policy adopted was designed to erode the academic/technical distinction, to raise the status of the vocational school and to encourage the provision of a more comprehensive-type curriculum in both secondary and vocational schools. In addition, a new form of post-primary school, initially comprehensive (1963), and subsequently community (1970), was to be established. These schools were to be co-educational, open to all classes and levels of ability, and offering a wide curriculum to match the full range of pupil aptitudes and aspirations. The desire to move away from a binary towards a more comprehensive system involved considerations of labour market needs, optimum utilisation of resources and egalitarianism. However, predictably in the

situation in the Republic, the aspect which attracted most
interest and considerable conflict was the question of control.
This conflict was most evident with respect to the community
schools which is the fastest growing sector. The community
school represents a partnership between religious authorities
and vocational education committees, each of which has
three representatives on the board of management in addition
to two elected parents and two teacher representatives. The
debate over the deeds of trust, which serve as the legal
instruments of partnership, lasted for many years before
agreement was reached.

The growth of the community school sector has given the
Catholic church considerable influence in what might be
considered 'public sector' education (Drudy and Lynch,
1993). Apart from their involvement on boards of management the religious orders involved in community schools also
have a number of teaching posts reserved for them. As
evidenced from the controversy in 1994 in relation to the
establishment of a new second-level school in Dunboyne, Co.
Meath, it is clear that this form of school is favoured by the
church over community colleges, which are under the
control of vocational education committees.[1] The designa-
tion of some VEC schools as community colleges arose as a
response to the impact of community schools. In some
instances the change involved little more than a change in
nomenclature designed to achieve greater public accept-
ability, although in many instances the community colleges
have arisen as a result of a merger of existing secondary and
vocational schools. In all cases the VECs have been prepared
to enter into agreements with religious authorities in relation
to guaranteed places on boards of management which are
broadly similar in structure to those of community schools.
Concessions have also been made in relation to selection
procedures for the appointment of teachers. However, these
boards are ultimately under the control of the VECs, being in
effect subcommittees of the VECs. While the development of
community colleges has allowed the Catholic church to gain

a considerable amount of control without cost (O'Flaherty, 1992, p. 75) the statutory basis for such influence is much weaker than in the case of community schools supported by deeds of trust.

The continuing significance of issues relating to values and the moral curriculum as reflected in the concern with religious control in education should not obscure the very high level of instrumentalism which permeates Irish education, especially since the 1960s. The publication of *Investment in Education* in 1966 marks a distinct reorientation in Irish education. In the wake of the adoption of a programme for economic development, with its commitment to economic growth and export-oriented industrialisation, the educational system would henceforth be assessed by its capacity to facilitate the achievement of these new economic objectives. It is noteworthy that the *Investment in Education* report was jointly funded by the OECD and the Irish government. This formal involvement of an influential international organisation in a major fact-finding and analytic report helped to reformulate objectives in education. A major preoccupation of the report was with labour market needs; it was suggested that there would be shortages of technically qualified personnel unless remedial action was taken. Concern was expressed that the post-primary curriculum was unsuited to the needs of a rapidly changing society. This strong instrumentalism has been an abiding emphasis in most subsequent official pronouncements on education. For example, one of the most persistent criticisms of the 1992 *Green Paper* has been its overemphasis on utilitarian and individualistic values, its overstress on enterprise, technology and economic concerns and its underemphasis on cultural, moral, artistic and civic elements (Report on the National Education Convention, 1994, p. 149). Even more emphatically, the Culliton Report (1992, 53) had concluded, largely on the basis of a background paper by Roche and Tansey (1992), that there is not enough emphasis in Irish second level education on technical and vocational training. (For a contrary view see Lynch, 1992.) Support for a stronger technical/vocational element at second-level was also voiced in the OECD (1991) report which commented on the enormous weight of the classical humanist tradition in Irish education.

Since the publication of *Investment in Education* there has been a notable shift in curricular provision and take-up in Irish post-primary schools. There has been a significant growth in the percentage of students taking science, business and technical subjects (Drudy and Lynch, 1993, chs. 8 and 10). It has been suggested that of all the interest groups who are seeking to redefine the purpose of post-primary schooling, it is the business and scientific sectors which have succeeded most in defining what is appropriate educational knowledge (Lynch, 1982). However, the pattern of curricular change reflects more than the success of a particular interest group. The growth in the provision and take-up of economically utilisable subjects on the post-primary school curriculum reflects the centrality of economic self-interest as a cultural value.

In addition to changes in the take-up of Leaving Certificate subjects other developments at second level also reflect a growing concern with vocational training. With effect from September 1995 a new Leaving Certificate Applied Programme (LCAP) is being introduced at senior cycle as an alternative to the traditionally more academic Leaving Certificate. The LCAP will replace the existing Senior Certificate and the Vocational Preparation and Training (VTP 1) programmes and is intended to cater for those students whose needs are not being adequately provided for by the existing Leaving Certificate programme (NCCA, 1993). It is envisaged that students on the LCAP will spend a minimum of 55 per cent of their time on vocational preparation and vocational education compared to a minimum of 30 per cent on general education. In addition the dramatic increase in the number of students who, having completed second level, embark on Post Leaving Certificate

(PLCs) programmes should be noted. In 1992/1993 a total of 16,514 students were enrolled in such courses, where vocational studies and work experience constitute the main elements.

The relationship between education and economic utility is perhaps best illustrated by changes in the pattern of third-level education in the Republic of Ireland. Developments over the past twenty-five years have effected a radical transformation of the system of higher education (Clancy, 1989). The major growth area has been the technological sector. Traditionally third level education was synonymous with university education; as recently as 1968-69, 78 per cent of total enrolments in higher education were in the university sector. However, by 1992/93 only 51 per cent of new entrants enrolled in the university sector. Almost all of the new third-level institutions which have been developed are in the technological sector. The establishment of eleven Regional Technical Colleges and two National Institutes of Higher Education (which subsequently became universities), where almost all course offerings are in the fields of applied science, engineering and business studies, testify to the trend towards vocationalism in higher education. This same trend is also evident within the universities, where the most highly valued places (as reflected in competition) are in the professional faculties. This predominantly utilitarian conception of higher education is enthusiastically endorsed by government, as evidenced by the chapters on higher education in the *White Paper on Educational Development* (1980) and the *Green Paper* (1992) although the latter publication does also give some recognition to the importance of broader cultural objectives.

In summary, it is evident that the educational system has been designed as a socialising agency producing citizens and workers with the appropriate moral and cultural orientations, skills and capacities. While there has been a notable absence of research which seeks to specify the detailed working of this socialisation process, it would appear that developments in education in the Republic since the 1960s have oriented the system to make it more responsive to the needs of the economy. The recent prominence given to utilitarian considerations must be viewed in the context of earlier preoccupations with more 'spiritual' values, whether they be religious or nationalistic. However, the apparent reorientation in the values which are given greatest visibility in the educational system signifies only a partial change. The educational system under colonial rule, the system after independence, and the present system fulfilled and continue to fulfil essentially similar functions. This continuity is most evident when we examine the second major function of schooling.

Selection and social reproduction

Most sociologists are keenly interested in the school's selection function. The increased significance of the school as a determinant of future status is linked to changes in the occupational structure of our society. Several indicators help to pinpoint the magnitude of this change in the Republic of Ireland over the past seventy-five years. For example, in 1926, 53 per cent of the workforce were employed in agriculture; by 1991 this percentage had dropped to 14. Within the non-agricultural workforce the main growth areas have been in the professional, semi-professional, managerial, administrative and other white-collar occupations; the number of skilled manual workers has also increased significantly while the percentage of the workforce categorised as semi-skilled or unskilled manual has decreased. When the employment status of the workforce is examined the increase in the percentage classified as 'employees' is notable. This has grown from 45 per cent in 1926 to an estimated 77 per cent in 1991. In reviewing these and other changes Rottman and Hannan (1982) concluded that during this century in the Republic of Ireland the basic structuring principle of the stratification system has changed: the determining role of family property and inheritance has been replaced by that of wage bargaining. In the early part of this century education was not a major determinant of adult life chances; its decisive impact was confined to a small section of the middle class who could afford private secondary and university education. By contrast, in recent years educational skills and credentials have differentiated between skilled and unskilled manual workers and between professional, managerial and other routine service workers. More fundamentally, in a society with high rates of unemployment (15.5 per cent of the labour force in 1994 – see Chapter 9 of this volume for further discussion), the possession of educational credentials is the best guarantee of avoiding unemployment. Comparative data from twenty OECD countries reveal that education is a more crucial determinant of employability in Ireland than in other countries. While the overall rate of unemployment of persons aged twenty-five to sixty-four in Ireland is twice the average for the twenty countries, the unemployment rate for those with university education in Ireland is actually below average; unemployment in Ireland is disproportionately concentrated among those with lowest levels of educational attainment (OECD, 1993).

Having identified the close relationship between the possession of educational credentials and the attainment of high status in the occupational world, we now turn our attention towards an examination of differential educational attainment. Research findings on this issue in the Republic have replicated the findings of sociologists in other countries. Since the issue was first examined in *Investment in Education,* a succession of studies demonstrated a close relationship between social class position and educational attainment. The process of social reproduction is complete; education mediates the relationship between origins and destinations. Future occupational status (destinations) is determined by educational attainment which in turn is determined by social class of origin.

There is evidence of clear class differences in the level of educational achievement, both at the primary and post-primary stage. For example, at primary level Fontes and

Kellaghan (1977) found that children from lower socio-economic groups were more likely to have problems related to literacy. At the post-primary level Swan (1978) found that 30 per cent of children of unskilled manual workers were retarded in reading compared with less than 5 per cent of children from upper middle-class groups.

Research data on class differentials in educational participation are considerably more extensive. In the late 1960s Rudd (1972) examined the social origin of national school terminal leavers, i.e. children leaving primary school without availing themselves of post-primary education. This group, which constituted about 15 per cent of the age cohort in 1966/67 came predominantly from the semi-skilled and unskilled manual and other agricultural social groups. Following the introduction of free post-primary education in 1967 and the raising of the school leaving age in 1972, there has been a dramatic rise in participation rates. By the early 1990s the percentage of the age cohort completing second-level education was approaching 80 per cent. In spite of this dramatic transformation which involved all social groups, class differentials in participation persisted. In a comparison of participation rates by social group for the fifteen to nineteen age group Breen *et al* (1990) compared findings from 1960/61 from *Investment in Education* with estimates for 1980/81. While the 1980/81 estimates show a near doubling of overall participation rates, from 30 to 56 per cent, they document the continuing marked class differences, concluding that, at worst, overall class differences have remained unchanged; at best, they may have been reduced by up to one fifth.

Comparing the respective participation rates of the professional, employers and managers and salaried employees group with that of the semi-skilled, unskilled manual and other agricultural groups, they found that the rate of increase of the latter groups (from 10 per cent to 31 per cent) was greater than the former (from 47 per cent to 76 per cent), while the absolute difference between these social groups had actually widened over the period.[2] One interpretation of this finding (which is not unique to the Republic of Ireland) might be to suggest that the real beneficiaries of the introduction of free post-primary education in 1967 were the middle classes. Post-primary education was made free in order to enable the poor to take more advantage of it but the paradoxical consequence was to increase subsidies to the affluent.

More recent data from the annual School Leavers Survey demonstrate the persistence of major class disparities in educational attainment at second level. An aggregate analysis of the three most recent surveys reveals that while 22 per cent of students left school without reaching the Leaving Certificate stage, only 3 per cent of the higher professional group failed to make this transition by comparison with almost half (47 per cent) of the unskilled manual group. Furthermore, for those who stay to complete the Leaving Certificate the level of achievement varies strikingly by socioeconomic group. For example, more than half of the school-leavers from the semi-skilled and unskilled manual group who sat the Leaving Certificate failed to attain 'honours' (grade C or higher on a higher level paper); this was true of less than 7 and 10 per cent, respectively, of those from higher and lower professional groups (Technical Working Group, 1995).

Social inequalities in educational participation are most apparent at third level. In spite of an approximately three-fold increase in total enrolments in higher education over the past two decades, substantial inequalities remain in the proportionate representation of the different social groups. In 1963 the *Investment in Education* team found that 8 per cent of university students were from the families of manual workers; twenty three years later the proportion had increased to only 11 per cent (Clancy, 1988); by 1992 the percentage had increased to 19 per cent. Over the past three decades the main progress made in increasing access to higher education has been in the non-university sector. While there continue to be large disparities between social groups in access to higher education in the RTCs and the Dublin Institute of Technology the degree of inequality is significantly less than in the university sector.

Table 1 gives an indication of the degree of progress which has been made in reducing equalities in access to higher education (all sectors) over a twelve-year period (1980-92). It presents estimates of the proportion of the relevant age cohort from the four highest (professionals, employers, managers and salaried employees) and the four lowest (skilled, semi-skilled, unskilled manual and other agricultural occupations) socio-economic groups who went on to higher education in 1980 and 1992. It is estimated that in a period when the overall rate of admission to higher education increased from 20 to 36 per cent of the age cohort, the rate for the four higher groups increased from 58 to 66 per cent compared with an increase from 7 to 22 per cent from the four lower groups. It is of interest to consider this finding on the relationship between expanded provision and inequality in the context of the Maximally Maintained Inequality (MMI) hypothesis developed by Raftery and Hout (1993). The essence of the MMI hypothesis is that while expansion allows a greater absolute number of persons to pass through the educational system, relative inequalities between classes are likely to change only when demand for advanced schooling from the privileged classes is saturated. While the estimates reported in Table 1 reveal that by 1992 two-thirds of the four higher socio-economic groups progressed on to higher education, in the case of the higher professional group this was approaching 90 per cent, which might be considered saturation point given ability and motivational thresholds (Clancy, 1995). Thus it would seem that, because access by competition to a scarce resource always tends to favour the privileged, increasing access is a precondition for wider access (Reid, 1991).

In spite of some evidence of a lessening of inequalities in recent years the persistence of marked differences in the

Table 1:   **Estimated proportion of college entry age cohort
from selected social groups entering higher
education in 1980 and 1992**

	1980	*1992*
Professionals, employers, managers and salaried employees	.58	.66
Skilled, semi-skilled, unskilled manual and other agricultural occupations	.07	.22
All social groups	.20	.36

Source: adapted from Clancy (1995)

participation rate of different social classes had led many
Irish social scientists to question the conclusions of an
important longitudinal study which suggested that 'the
meritocratic ideal is being approached if not quite being
attained' (Greaney and Kellaghan, 1984). The interpretation
of the findings of this study have become the focus of
academic debate (see *Economic and Social Review*, 1985).
Whatever the merits of the respective positions it would
appear that, since social destinations are so closely related to
social origins, the middle classes have perfected the process
of passing on their 'achieved status' from one generation to
the next. The reproduction of achieved status in an
apparently meritocratic society seems to have replaced the
inherited privileges of an ascriptive society.

Because of the persistence of the close relationship
between social class and educational achievement, much
research has been devoted to finding an explanation for this
relationship. Most attention has focussed on the differences
in home background of students. Initially the focus was on
differences in material circumstances of the home, such as
income, family size and housing conditions. Subsequently
much of the search for correlates of differential educational
achievement shifted towards an analysis of cultural features of

488   Irish Society: Sociological Perspectives

the family which were found to have greater explanatory power. Parental attitudes towards education and differences in more fundamental value orientations were found to be important. A Dublin study which highlighted the importance of future-orientation (especially mothers) as a determinant of the propensity of adolescents to stay in school beyond the minimum school-leaving age provides an example of this approach (Craft, 1974). Bernstein's research on the existence of two linguistic codes (restricted and elaborated) has also been invoked as providing a possible explanation for differential educational attainment (Bernstein, 1971). Bernstein suggested that in contrast to the middle class who have access to both codes many working class families will be limited to the restricted code and thus will be at a serious disadvantage in the school where the elaborated code is in use. While the applicability of Bernstein's work has been challenged, especially in so far as the restricted code is deemed to be inferior (Labov, 1973), it is of interest to note how the theory of linguistic codes parallels in some ways Bourdieu's concept of 'cultural capital'. Bourdieu's analysis suggests that the socially acquired capacities of one group (the middle class) are transformed into intrinsic virtues; the symbolic violence of schooling involves the imposition of a 'cultural arbitrary' (Bourdieu and Passeron, 1977).

This research on class-linked cultural differences between families raises a number of important questions. The first concerns the relative autonomy of the cultural domain. While it is clear that cultural orientations and dispositions are not entirely determined by material and structural conditions they are strongly conditioned by such factors. Thus the kind of familial cultural orientation which facilitates high educational achievement is partly a function of secure economic and material circumstances (Lane, 1972; Lareau, 1987). The second question concerns the relative autonomy of the school. Because of the cultural differences between families it is clear that the experience of schooling is qualitatively different for working-class and middle-class children. In the case of the latter the transition to school is facilitated by the essential continuity of experience, whereas in the case of many working-class children the transition is characterised by an essential discontinuity. However, posing the issue in these terms suggests the possibility of an alternative analytic approach. Instead of focussing on the class characteristics of those who succeed and those who fail it is appropriate to examine the class characteristics of the educational experience at which they succeed or fail. This reorientation in approach represents an important development within the sociology of education.

Although there is a substantial ethnographic literature which seeks to assess the independent effect on attainment of social processes within the school (see, for example, Hargreaves, 1967 and Willis, 1977), it has proved difficult to identify the school characteristics and processes which are associated with overall effectiveness or with effectiveness among different types of students. A succession of large-scale empirical studies concluded that schools had very little independent effect on attainment (Jencks, 1972). By implication it did not seem to matter what type of school a child attended since educational outcomes were almost entirely determined by individual and family background characteristics. While more recent research has suggested that schools do matter and that some schools are clearly more effective than others (see, for example, Rutter *et al*, 1979; Mortimore *et al*, 1988), it has proved difficult to identify the essential characteristics of the effective school. More significantly, not withstanding the burgeoning 'school improvement' industry in many countries, the design and implementation of successful change strategies remains problematic.

An important theoretical and substantive finding to emerge from the literature on school effectiveness is that differences in the socio-economic composition, academic balance and value climate of the student body represent important contextual variables which influence individual outcomes. This is especially relevant in the Republic of Ireland at the post-primary level. The present system of post-primary education is a highly differentiated one where variations in social selectivity, prestige and academic emphasis range from those found in fee-paying secondary schools, through non-fee paying secondary, comprehensive, community schools, community colleges and vocational schools. These different school types have different retention rates and different transfer rates to higher education (Clancy, 1982, 1995). While it is clear that the differential performance of the various types of schools reflects differences in individual pupil characteristics at intake, it would also appear that the social class composition of the schools has a significant effect on student aspirations and achievement, independent of the social class background of any individual student. The institutionalisation, within a system of publicly-funded education, of invidious status hierarchies between different post-primary schools serves to reproduce existing status hierarchies. The willing co-operation by the state with those religious communities which operate fee-paying secondary schools demonstrates a distinct lack of commitment to meritocratic principles.

Many of the analytical issues which arise in respect of differentiation between schools also arise in the case of within-school grouping. Here the main choices lie between mixed-ability grouping and streaming although a variety of less rigid forms of streaming such as banding and setting are also prevalent in Irish post-primary schools. While the effects of streaming have long been the subject of controversy in the research literature, it is interesting to note that the findings of the principal Irish study of this issue (Hannan and Boyle, 1987) replicate the main findings in the international literature. Streaming and other forms of homogeneous grouping had no significant effect on average attainment levels in Irish post-primary schools. However, increased differentiation was found to have pronounced polarisation effect; it increased the inequality (variance) in outcomes.

Conclusion

This paper has described some features of the educational system in the Republic of Ireland. The evidence reviewed points to the centrality of education in Irish life. Education is perceived as having a crucial role to play in the modernisation of Irish society. This perception is most explicit in relation to its potential contribution to the development of the economy. There is also considerable support for the view that education can be an important instrument in the achievement of personal emancipation and greater equality. However, in respect of the latter claim there is a large body of evidence which discredits any utopian view of the possibilities of education. While education has the potential to foster individual emancipation and development it can also function as a vehicle for social control and the pursuit of class interest.

Notes

1. A proposal to seek government support for the establishment of a voluntary secondary school had been made prior to the announcement of the decision to establish a community college. Following the government announcement the Bishop of Meath, Dr Smith expressed his support for the local committee's campaign to establish a community school rather than a community college.

2. This comparison has become the subject of academic debate in the correspondence pages of *The Irish Times* with Brendan Walsh (6/9/93) claiming that these data indicate a reduction in inequalities. However, Damian Hannan and Chris Whelan (8/9/93) pointed out that such a conclusion is warranted only if one focuses on class disparities relating to post-primary participation (success). If one examines class disparities in non-participation (failure) there has been a substantial increase in inequality. If information relating both to success and failure is used to calculate an 'odds ratio' the value of the index fell from 8.0 in 1961 to 7.3 in 1981, showing a reduction in inequality of opportunity of 9 per cent over the period.

References

BERNSTEIN, B., 1971. *Class, Codes and Control*, Vol. 1, London, Routledge and Kegan Paul.

BOURDIEU, P. and J.C. PASSERON, 1977. *Reproduction in Education, Society and Culture*, London, Sage.

BOWLES, S. and H. GINTIS, 1976. *Schooling in Capitalist America*, London, Routledge and Kegan Paul.

BREEN, R., D.F. HANNAN, D.B. ROTTMAN and C.T. WHELAN, 1990. *Understanding Contemporary Ireland*, Dublin, Gill and Macmillan.

CLANCY, P., 1982. *Participation in Higher Education: A National Survey*, Dublin, Higher Education Authority.

CLANCY, P., 1988. *Who Goes to College?*, Dublin, Higher Education Authority.

CLANCY, P., 1989. 'The Evolution of Policy in Third-Level Education' in D.G. Mulcahy and D. O'Sullivan (eds.), *Irish Educational Policy: Process and Substance*, Dublin, Institute of Public Administration.

CLANCY, P., 1995. *Access to Higher Education: A Third National Survey*, Dublin, Higher Education Authority.

COLLINS, R., 1979. *The Credential Society*, New York, Academic Press.

COOLAHAN, J., 1981. *Irish Education: History and Structure*, Dublin, Institute of Public Administration.

CRAFT, M., 1974. 'Talent, Family Values and Education in Ireland', in J. Eggleston (ed.), *Contemporary Research in the Sociology of Education*, London, Methuen.

CULLITON REPORT, 1992. *A Time for Change: Industrial Policy in the 1990s*, Dublin, Stationery Office.

DALE, R., 1992. 'Recovering from a Pyrric Victory? Quality Relevance and Impact in the Sociology of Education', in M. Arnot and L. Barton (eds.), *Voicing Concerns; Sociological Perspectives on Contemporary Reforms*, Wallingford, Triangle Books.

DEPARTMENT OF EDUCATION, 1980. *White Paper on Educational Development*, Dublin, Stationery Office.

DEPARTMENT OF EDUCATION, 1992. *Education for a Changing World: Green Paper on Education*, Dublin, Stationery Office.

DEPARTMENT OF EDUCATION, 1993. *Presentation to the National Convention*, 18 October 1993.

DEPARTMENT OF EDUCATION, 1994. *Tuarascail Staitistiúil 1992/93*, Dublin, Stationery Office.

DRUDY, S. and K. LYNCH, 1993.
Schools and Society in Ireland,
Dublin, Gill and Macmillan.

THE ECONOMIC AND
SOCIAL REVIEW, 1985.
'Symposium on Equality of
Opportunity in Irish Schools',
The Economic and Social Review,
Vol. 2, pp. 77-156.

FLYNN, T., (Bishop) 1994.
Press Release 9 March, after
March Meeting of the Irish
Bishops' Conference.

FONTES, P. and
T. KELLAGHAN, 1977,
'Incidence and Correlates of
Illiteracy in Irish Primary
Schools', *The Irish Journal of
Education,* Vol. 11, pp. 5-20.

GREANEY, V. and
T. KELLAGHAN, 1984.
*Equality of Opportunity in Irish
Schools,* Dublin, The
Educational Company.

HANNAN, D. and M. BOYLE,
1987. *Schooling Decisions: The
Origins and Consequences of
Selection and Streaming in Irish
Post-Primary Schools,* Dublin,
Economic and Social
Research Institute.

HARGREAVES, D.H., 1967.
*Social Relations in a Secondary
School,* London, Routledge
and Kegan Paul.

INVESTMENT IN
EDUCATION, 1966. Report of
the Survey Team appointed by
the Minister for Education,
Dublin, Stationery Office.

JENCKS, C. *et al,* 1972.
*Inequality: A Reassessment of the
Effects of Family and Schooling
in America,* New York, Basic
Books.

LABOV, W., 1973. 'The Logic
of Non-Standard English', in
N. Keddie (ed.), *Tinker Tailor
... The Myth of Cultural
Deprivation,* Harmondsworth,
Penguin.

LANE, M., 1972. 'Explaining
Educational Choice', *Sociology,*
Vol. 6, pp. 255-66.

LAREAU, A., 1987. 'Social Class
Differences in Family-School
Relationships: The
Importance of Cultural
Capital', *Sociology of Education,*
Vol. 60, pp. 73-85.

LYNCH, K., 1982. 'A
Sociological Analysis of the
Functions of Second Level
Schooling', *Irish Educational
Studies,* 2, pp. 32-58.

LYNCH, K., 1992. 'Education
and the Paid Labour Market',
Irish Educational Studies,
Vol. 11, pp. 13-33.

MORTIMORE, P. *et al,* 1988.
School Matters: The Junior Years,
Salisbury, Open Books.

NCCA, 1993, *The Applied
Leaving Certificate,* Dublin, The
National Council for
Curriculum and Assessment.

OECD, 1991. *Review of National
Policies for Education: Ireland,*
Paris, OECD.

OECD, 1993. *Education at a
Glance 2,* Paris, OECD.

OECD, 1995. *Access,
Participation and Equity,* Paris,
OECD (in press).

O'FLAHERTY, L., 1992.
Management and Control in

Irish Education: The Post-Primary Experience, Dublin, Drumcondra Teachers' Centre.

PARSONS, T., 1959. 'The School Class as a Social System: Some of its Functions in American Society', *Harvard Educational Review,* Vol. 29, No. 4, pp. 297-318.

RAFTERY, A.E. and M. HOUT, 1993. 'Maximally Maintained Inequality: Expansion, Reform and Opportunity in Irish Education', *Sociology of Education,* Vol. 66, pp. 41-62.

REID, E., 1991. 'Access and Institutional Change', in T. Schuller (ed.), *The Future of Higher Education,* Buckingham, SRHE/Open University Press.

ROCHE, F. and P. TANSEY, 1992. *Industrial Training in Ireland,* Dublin, The Stationery Office.

ROTTMAN, D.B. and D.F. HANNAN, 1982. *The Distribution of Income in the Republic of Ireland: A Study of Social Class and Family-Cycle Inequalities,* Dublin, Economic and Social Research Institute.

RUDD, J., 1972. 'A Survey of National School Terminal Leavers', *Social Studies,* Vol. 1, pp. 61-73.

RUTTER, M., *et al,* 1979. *Fifteen Thousand Hours: Secondary Schools and their Effects on Children,* London, Open Books.

SWAN, T.D., 1978. *Reading Standards in Irish Schools,* Dublin, The Educational Company.

TECHNICAL WORKING GROUP, 1995. *Interim Report of the Steering Committee's Technical Working Group,* Dublin, Higher Education Authority.

WILLIS, P., 1977. *Learning to Labour,* London, Saxon Books.

WOODS, P., 1983. *Sociology and the School: An Interactionist Viewpoint,* London, Routledge and Kegan Paul.

16
Education in Northern Ireland: the Struggle for Equality

BOB CORMACK and BOB OSBORNE

Introduction

In the last decade, ministers of state with responsibility for education have constantly pointed to the excellence of education in Northern Ireland as evidenced by high 'O', GCSE and 'A' level results. In this they have followed the lead given by a group of educational researchers (the 'Black Papers') in the early 1980s. For example, Marks and Cox (1984, p. 29) compared the proportions of leavers in England and Wales with those in Northern Ireland on the basis of obtaining five or more 'O' levels and one or more 'A' levels and concluded:

> For England and Wales, these proportions rose during the 1950s and 1960s but since 1970 have been fairly static. The proportions for Northern Ireland show a very different pattern – the rise there during the 1950s and 1960s continued throughout the 1970s and the figures there are now well above those for England and Wales. Two relevant factors here may be that Northern Ireland has retained a fully selective system of grammar and secondary modern (sic) schools and that many more schools are religious schools.

The imputation is that education in Northern Ireland avoided the comprehensivisation of secondary schools that swept Britain in the 1960s and 1970s, that 'fashionable' educational experiments were eschewed, and that the religious influence in schools helped maintain traditional standards.

This chapter will deal with the historical development of the system, its present structure and funding, and the patterns of achievement and attainment in schools. In addition, we will consider post-school destinations: the Youth Training Programme, the role of Further Education Colleges, and the patterns of higher education participation and subsequent labour market experiences of graduates. The focus throughout will be on the provision of equality of educational opportunities. This enduring theme in the sociology of education and social policy analyses of education has an edge in Northern Ireland that has perhaps been blunted elsewhere (although in the Republic of Ireland the work of Breen, Clancy and Hannan has often offered a parallel to Northern studies – see Drudy, 1991). Drudy (1991, p. 118) rightly recognises the 'extremely politically contentious issues of unequal participation and achievement of different groups' in Northern Ireland. It is fair to say that other, more recent, perspectives have not been applied to education in Northern Ireland with the same enthusiasm as elsewhere. There is, for example, a need for qualitative studies of schools, and of teachers' and pupils' cultures. There are honourable exceptions, notably Dominic Murray's study of the Catholic ethos in schools in *Worlds Apart* (1985) and Richard Jenkins' study of 'lads' in *Lads, Citizens and Everyday Kids* (1983). The principal focus, however, has been on fair provision and fair participation in educational institutions. To our minds, these 'bread-and-butter' issues should remain central, especially to policy-oriented social scientists working on educational issues in Northern Ireland.

Historical development of education in Northern Ireland
The historical development of educational provision in

Britain and Ireland differs significantly. In nineteenth century Britain 'laissez faire' ruled. Laissez faire is the policy based on a minimum of governmental interference in the affairs of individuals and society. Translated to the provision of education in nineteenth century Britain, this policy led to the view that if individuals or groups wished to provide education for young people that was their right. It was not thought a duty of the state to make such provision (Musgrave, 1968). The Churches clearly thought it in their best interests to provide an education in order to ensure the continuity of the faith. As Musgrave (1968, p. 11) describes it:

> The various religious bodies, who provided most of the formal education available for the working class, were quite explicit on what kind of education should be provided because they had a very clear goal at which to aim. Their schools were provided for religious purposes. Their aim was that the next generation should believe in the Christian religion. Children must, therefore, learn to read the Bible. The ability to write was less important than the ability to read, and some even held that it might be dangerous to teach writing since he who could write might write criticisms of the faith and of the established political order.

Elementary schools were established throughout Britain by Churches and charitable organisations. As the century progressed, the state increasingly made grants available to charities to support schools. However, provision was patchy and standards were often low.

Economic forces dictated a change of policy. The Great Exhibition of 1851 and a similar exhibition in Paris in 1867 symbolically demonstrated the degree to which Britain was falling behind in industrial and technological development. In particular, the rapid progress of German industry was noted. Much of this progress was attributed to a very well developed system of state elementary schools (Musgrave, 1968, pp. 28-29).

The Education Act of 1870 established compulsory, state elementary schools. From that point on laissez faire policies receded to be replaced by policies which increasingly involved the state in the central direction, funding and administration of education. This process continues to this day with the recent attempts in the Education Reform Act 1988 and other legislation to erode the powers of Local Education Authorities (LEAs) and to direct the system in England and Wales from the then Department of Education and Science (DES) in London (Ball, 1990).

The pattern of development in Ireland was different. A national school system was established in Ireland in 1831. The obvious question here is: why was a national system established in Ireland some forty years before England and Wales? The point alluded to by Musgrave above is taken-up by Coolahan (1981, p. 4) in *Irish Education*:

> In the context of post-Union politics the government felt that the schools could serve politicising and socialising goals, cultivating attitudes of political loyalty and cultural assimilation. The danger of separate school systems operating without official supervision needed to be countered.

In essence, social control would appear to have been a key factor in this early development of national schools.

Just as Lord Londonderry was to attempt after partition in the 1920s, Lord Stanley, the instigator of national schools in 1831, attempted to make the state system non-denominational. National schools were originally intended to provide an acceptable form of education for all denominations (Dunn, 1990). Seven 'commissioners of national education' were to be appointed: three from the Established Church (the Church of Ireland), two Catholics and two Presbyterians.

Reaction was swift. Ulster Presbyterians were the first to challenge the system insisting on state support for 'non-vested' denominational schools. Shortly after, the Established Church set-up its own school system in 1839 in opposition to the national system. They, too, demanded state support for these schools. Finally, the new Catholic archbishop, Dr Paul Cullen, in 1849, influenced by Pope Pius IX's concern over increasing secularisation and liberalism in Europe, committed the Church to building up a separate Catholic education system. By the 1870s the education system in Ireland had become firmly denominational (Coolahan, 1981).

In post-partition Northern Ireland the arguments for denominational education provide a strong sense of *dejà vu*. Cardinal Logue refused to participate in the work of the Lynn Committee which Lord Londonderry had set-up to advise him on the future structure of education in Northern Ireland. Akenson (1973, p. 52) argues:

> In all probability the refusal of the Roman Catholic authorities to join the Lynn Committee was the single most important determinant of the educational history of Northern Ireland from 1920 to the present day.

It is difficult not to agree with Akenson, although Cardinal Logue's decision should be placed in the context of Catholic fears and suspicions of the new Stormont regime and its various branches and committees, and the belief that the new partitioned Northern Ireland would not last long – a belief held by many both within Ireland and elsewhere. However, the way was left clear for Protestant leaders to demand and gain 'Bible teaching in schools' and 'Protestant teachers for Protestant pupils' (Buckland, 1979, p. 251). From 1930 state-provided schools were *de facto* Protestant schools, while Catholic schools were firmly outside the system enjoying initially modest but increasing support from state funds (Dunn, 1993).

Substantial inequalities in provision, and hence in participation and attainment, stemmed from these particular decisions. We will come back to these issues later in the chapter. On the other hand, state intervention was increasing general educational provision and most of it was geared to providing greater educational opportunities for all (Silver, 1973).

The landmarks in the expansion of educational opportunities might be laid out as follows:

- 1831 (Ireland), 1870 (England and Wales): the establishment of a state supported system of education providing universal elementary schooling.
- 1947 (Northern Ireland), 1944 (England and Wales): the establishment of a state supported universal secondary education.
- 1963 (England and Wales), 1965 (Northern Ireland): respectively the Robbins and Lockwood Committees were concerned with the 'wastage of ability' in terms of students from manual backgrounds (notably Robbins also included women in this wastage) entering higher education. A dramatic expansion of higher education provision followed; much fuelled by the availability of student maintenance grants following the recommendation of the Anderson Committee in 1962 (Kogan and Kogan, 1983, pp. 18-24).
- 1960s (England, Wales and Scotland): the expansion of comprehensive schools throughout England, Scotland and Wales. The attempt in 1976 by the Labour Minister of State for Education to introduce comprehensive schools in Northern Ireland failed because of the opposition of the middle classes, both Protestant and Catholic and, with the return of a conservative administration to Stormont in 1979, disappeared from the policy agenda.

These initiatives, and others, can be read as a steady attempt to expand equality of educational opportunities: from universal elementary education, to universal secondary education, to the expansion of higher education, to the attempt to introduce a common school for all the pupils in a community (comprehensives). For over a century the pursuit of equality of opportunity has led to a significant opening-up of opportunities for Catholic students, female students and students from manual backgrounds. To take but one example: the civil rights demands of the 1960s were led, in part, by a new and much larger cohort of Catholic students entering Queen's University (Arthur, 1974).

On the other hand, the present structure of education in Northern Ireland also displays the legacy of the past. As Patrick Shea, a permanent secretary to the Ministry (later Department) of Education, observed in his autobiography:

> The law which governs education in Northern Ireland is full of provisions which were the outcome of campaigns and compromises and deals and pledges wrung from our predecessors over a century and a half of government intervention in education and are still cherished by teachers or churchmen or whatever other interests promoted them (Shea, 1981, p. 186).

Over the years, educational opportunities have expanded but inequalities in provision, participation and attainment remain. Many of these inequalities can be laid at the door of the convoluted structure produced as the result of 'campaigns, compromises, deals and pledges' of the past. It is to this structure we now turn.

The structure of present-day educational provision

Up to 1993 schools in Northern Ireland could be described as follows:

Controlled Schools (primary, grammar and secondary intermediate; Protestant):
- provided by the Education and Library Boards (ELBs) and managed through boards of governors with built-in representation of the Protestant Churches
- running costs are provided through formula funding by the ELBs
- education is free.

Voluntary Maintained Schools (primary, secondary intermediate; Catholic):
- provided by voluntary school authorities and managed by Boards of Governors
- running costs are provided through formula funding by ELBs
- approved capital building costs are grant-aided up to 85 per cent by the DENI
- education is free.

Voluntary Grammar Schools (Protestant and Catholic):
- provided by voluntary school authorities and managed by boards of governors
- running costs met through formula funding from DENI
- up to 85 per cent of approved capital expenditure met by DENI
- education is free for pupils awarded a place through the transfer procedure. (A number of grammar schools have primary preparatory departments whose pupils are, in some limited circumstances, given a preference in the admission procedures to grammar school; some grammar schools also have fee-paying boarding departments where a pupil may enter grammar school with a transfer procedure ('eleven plus') grade that would not otherwise qualify them for a place. All these schools are Protestant schools.)

Integrated Schools (primary and secondary comprehensive/mixed ability; religiously mixed):
The aggregate enrolment of these schools (primary and secondary) is still small representing just under 2 per cent of all pupils. These schools began as independent schools and qualified for funding on the same basis as other non-state schools once they had established their viability. The Education Reform (NI) Order 1989 introduced new measures whereby these schools can be fully funded from their inception and where the DENI has a duty to 'encourage

and facilitate the development of integrated education' (HMSO, 1989, p. 67). An early indication of how this will be implemented is demonstrated by the DENI giving £150,000 and the EU £1.5m to the main charity supporting integrated schools. In addition, under the order, existing schools can opt for integrated status through a parental vote.

Following research sponsored by the Standing Advisory Commission on Human Rights (SACHR) government announced the creation of a new category of school. This enables all maintained schools to receive 100 per cent capital funding in return for a change in the composition of the boards of governors. Most maintained and Catholic voluntary grammar schools have at the time of writing (May 1994) begun the process of changing to this new status. The SACHR research is discussed below.

Table 1: **Social class by type of school attended**
          Northern Ireland (1986/87)

Social Class	Grammar	Secondary Intermediate
Non-Manual	69.8	34.3
Manual	31.1	65.7
Total	100	100

Source: A. M. Gallagher, Transfer Pupils at Sixteen (NICER, Belfast)

Table 1 suggests that Northern Irish grammar schools are largely middle class establishments. Gallagher (1988) shows that of entrants to post-primary schools in 1981, 69 per cent of grammar school entrants were from non-manual backgrounds, while 66 per cent of entrants to secondary intermediate schools were from manual backgrounds. This study also illustrated the particular advantage of preparatory schools to middle class pupils. Pupils take a test at the age of ten and eleven. On the basis of this test roughly 30 per cent of children, over the years, have been assigned a grammar school place (Wilson, 1987). The middle class have been able to maintain their grip on grammar school places through a number of means. Until the 1989 Education Reform Order it was possible to enter certain grammar schools on a fee-paying basis despite an 'eleven plus' result that did not entitle the child to a non-fee paying place. The 'Review Procedure' conducted one to two years later usually resulted in such children being given a non-fee paying place (Livingstone, 1987). This pathway has now been closed. However, in recent years, the increase in private tutoring for the 'eleven plus' has been noticeable. Anecdotal evidence from parents suggests that in some middle class schools very few members of the 'eleven plus' class are not tutored.

Government policy of 'open enrolment' has allowed schools to expand up to physical capacity. Although 'parental choice' of school is now official policy, grammar schools alone can use academic admissions criteria (performance in the transfer test). The decline in pupil numbers in recent years has meant that grammar schools have taken an increasing proportion of the eleven-year-old cohorts, leaving secondary schools to adjust to the demographic decline. In 1993 only about 70 per cent of eleven-year-olds transferring to post-primary schools (excluding special schools) sat the transfer test. While some of those not taking the test are in the Craigavon area, where a non-selective system exists, a substantial minority do not sit the transfer test. Those entering grammar schools in 1993 represented 49 per cent of those taking the transfer test and 34 per cent of the total cohort moving from primary to post-primary schools.

Children are divided by religion. Integrated schools currently educate less than 2 per cent of the school population. While it is likely, given the provisions of the Education Reform Order, that integrated schools will grow in number, it remains the case that, for the foreseeable future, the substantial majority of pupils in Northern Ireland will be educated in Protestant or Catholic schools.

In 1992, 47 per cent of grammar schools and 28 per cent of secondary intermediate schools are single sex schools. This is more prevalent on the Catholic side where 67 per cent of grammar schools and 40 per cent of secondary intermediate schools are single sex.

Access to grammar schools

Access to grammar schools was identified by research for the SACHR as being substantially greater for those transferring into Protestant grammar schools than Catholic schools (Cormack *et al*, 1992; Gallagher *et al*, 1994). There is some evidence, from West Belfast, that the difference in the numbers in grammar schools results to a limited extent from choice, i.e. parents and pupils selecting a secondary intermediate rather than a grammar school despite having the transfer grade to secure a grammar place (Armstrong, 1989). These decisions are based on financial circumstances and evaluations of school quality. However, there was a clear and major structural difference in the capacities of Protestant and Catholic grammar schools. It was calculated that if, for example, grammar schools in 1990 had been operating at full capacity, the grammar enrolment of the Catholic sector would have been 35.8 per cent of post-primary provision while the Protestant sector would have been 45.6 per cent (Gallagher *et al*, 1994). This research, published originally by the SACHR, prompted government to respond by announcing the funding for new Catholic grammar school provision in Belfast and Derry.

Levels of attainment in schools

The evidence suggests significantly better results in Northern Ireland schools compared to those in England and Wales at the upper echelons of attainment. Northern Ireland schools perform more poorly however at the lower levels of attainment.

Table 2:   **Qualifications of school leavers in 1992
            Northern Ireland, England and Wales**

	Northern Ireland %	England %	Wales %
2 or more 'A' levels	29.0	24.4	21.0
1 'A' level	3.2	3.9	4.0
5+ GCSEs (A-C)	13.3	16.2	14.0
1-4 GCSEs (A-C)	25.9	24.4	23.0
1+ GCSEs (D-G)	16.8	25.5	26.0
Leavers with no 'A' or GCSE qualifications	11.7	5.6	12.0
Total	100	100	100

Source: DENI Statistics Branch

From Table 2 there can be no doubt that, at the upper levels, pupils in Northern Irish schools do exceptionally well, as the 'Black Paper' authors noted. However, at the lower end of the scale the pattern is much less comforting, as the 'Black Paper' authors failed to remark upon. Over one in ten, of Northern Irish pupils leave school with no 'A' level or GCSE qualifications. Compared to England in particular this pattern is high.

There are significant differences in attainment by religion and gender. Table 3 reveals that Protestants do better than Catholics,[1] and that females do better than males in both communities. The Catholic male figure of 13 per cent leaving with no qualifications, almost twice that of Protestant males, although a lower figure than in the past, suggests a problem of considerable magnitude with continuing major implications for fair participation in the labour market.

Further gender and religion differences are visible in subjects studied (Table 4). Males are much more likely to take science 'A' levels than females. Protestants are much more likely than Catholics to take science subjects. All groups show a decline in the proportions taking all-science 'A' levels since the

Table 3:   **Qualifications of leavers by religion and sex 1990-91**

	Males	Females
Protestants		
3+ 'A' levels	22.0	26.9
2 'A' levels	5.1	7.0
1 'A' level	2.6	3.6
5+ GCSEs (A-C)	12.8	14.9
1-4 GCSEs (A-C)	26.3	25.1
1+ GCSEs (D-G)	19.1	14.4
Other qualifications	5.1	4.0
Leavers with no qualifications	7.1	4.4
Total Leavers	100	100

	Males	Females
Catholics		
3+ 'A' levels	17.7	23.8
2 'A' levels	5.8	8.2
1 'A' level	2.8	3.9
5+ GCSEs (A-C)	10.7	15.0
1-4 GCSEs (A-C)	25.9	26.4
1+ GCSEs (D-G)	19.6	13.9
Other qualifications	4.5	3.7
Leavers with no qualifications	13.0	5.0
Total Leavers	100	100

Source: DENI, Statistics Branch

late 1980s but all show an increase in those taking a 'mix' of 'A' levels. The figure of 10.8 per cent of Catholic females taking all-science 'A' levels however, is very low and, again, there are possible labour market consequences which in the midst of the government's commitment to fair employment in the labour

Table 4: **Subjects combinations of 'A' level students by religion 1991 (Percentages)**

Religion and Gender	Science	Arts	Mix	N
Protestant	22.0	39.5	38.6	2,862
Catholic	16.3	44.3	39.4	3,272
Protestant Male	35.0	26.3	38.8	1,935
Protestant Female	19.1	43.8	37.1	2,217
Catholic Male	23.5	38.0	38.5	1,407
Catholic Female	10.8	49.1	40.1	1,865

Source: DENI, Statistics Branch

market are likely to be unhelpful (Cormack and Osborne, 1991).

The key issues in secondary or, to use a less ambiguous Southern term, 'second level' education in Northern Ireland are: the continuing underachievement of children from working class backgrounds, particularly males and particularly Catholic males; the continuing but lessening over-representation of females, particularly Catholic females (but an issue for Catholic males also), in arts and humanities subjects; the selective system of second level education which relegates mainly working class pupils to an education which demonstrably fails to bring them up to a level of achievement now being gained by their class peers in Wales, England and most notably in Scotland (McPherson and Rabbe, 1988). These continuing inequalities in educational opportunities require to be addressed.

The Education Reform Order

The 1989 Education Reform (Northern Ireland) Order (ERO) has inaugurated some of the most far-reaching changes in Northern Ireland's education system for forty years. The ERO establishes a compulsory common curriculum in grant-aided schools. As well as core subjects, certain 'cross-curricular' themes, such as Cultural Heritage and Education for Mutual Understanding, are specified. Under the ERO, tests of performance at the ages of eight, eleven, fourteen and sixteen are to be conducted with associated attainment targets. Test results are to be published together with examination performance for each school which have already been published (DENI, 1994). These results are designed to enable informed parental choice of school, which is a major theme of the ERO. Parents can choose the school for their children and schools must establish and publish the criteria for entry. Schools perceived to be good, it is believed, will attract more pupils and will expand up to capacity, whereas schools perceived to be poor will lose pupils, will be unable to deliver the curriculum and may close.

The 'empowering' of parents and local communities is reflected in the provision for the local management of schools. Each school is given responsibility for its own budget. Budgets are calculated using formulae which are substantially based on pupil numbers in the school but have minor weightings for social deprivation and rural isolation. Each school will have an incentive to maximise its pupil numbers and to do this will have to make itself as attractive as possible to parents (McKeown, 1993).

While many of these measures mirrored the 1988 Education Reform Act of England and Wales, the ERO does concern itself with some issues specific to Northern Ireland, most notably in the provision for integrated education. New integrated schools can now receive full funding from inception and the DENI has indicated that capital projects in integrated schools will be given priority. In addition, any existing controlled or voluntary school can now apply for integrated status. A simple majority of parents voting in a secret ballot is now sufficient to initiate this process. The ERO, therefore, uses the 'opting out' procedures, which were developed in the Education Reform Act for England and Wales, to allow schools to break away from local authority control, in order to promote integrated education. The Catholic education authorities were sufficiently concerned that aspects of the ERO discriminated against Catholic schools that they mounted a legal challenge. In the event this was dismissed by the High Court but the legal proceedings revealed the poor state of church-state relationships in education at the end of the 1980s.

Many of the long-standing issues and problems in education remain on the agenda. The issue of selection at eleven will continue as only grammar schools will be allowed to select on academic criteria. The problems of underachievement in secondary schools, and especially in those which prove less popular, will increase. Parents may well find that choice is a chimera when constrained by imposed entry quotas. The common curriculum should enhance girls' access to a full curriculum but in general the ERO's emphasis on a market-based approach to educational reform is unlikely to reduce social inequalities.

However, extra resources for schools in 'deprived areas' would appear to be part of the spending priorities within the recently announced 'Targeting Social Need' programme of public expenditure particularly under the 'Making Belfast Work' initiative. Depending on how this new initiative develops, it may introduce an important *caveat* to the policy of equality of educational opportunities; a *caveat* reminiscent of the early work of Halsey (1972) and the recommendations of the Plowden Report in 1967. As Silver (1973, p. xxiii) puts it:

> In an unequal society, it was argued, equality of opportunity could only have meaning if those who began with unequal chances had unequal support from the educational system.

Plowden recommended the underprivileged required more money spent on their education, better primary schools, and a larger number of teachers than other pupils.

The underachievement of mainly working-class pupils has much, if not most to do, with provision and resourcing –

hence our commitment to what has been called the 'political arithmetic' tradition in the sociology of education (Karabel and Halsey, 1977). Measuring the origins (class, religion and gender) of pupils and locating their eventual destinations, both educational and occupational, is, to our minds, the nub of the matter (Halsey, Heath and Ridge, 1980). But, contrary to some critics, that does not make researchers blind to the value of other perspectives on education (Drudy, 1991). There can be no doubt that, especially in such a divided society, we need to know more, much more, about what goes on in schools. Moreover, the role of the state, again of particular importance in Northern Ireland, needs to be closely examined. The ERO demonstrates the growing interventionist nature of the DENI, albeit under the guise of 'empowering' parents and devolving budgets to schools.[2]

The funding of schools in Northern Ireland: the transition

The funding of schools in Northern Ireland has come on to the policy agenda as the result of research sponsored by the Standing Advisory Commission on Human Rights (SACHR). The SACHR was concerned with attainment differences between Protestants and Catholics (Osborne, Gallagher and Cormack, 1989) and the implications these differentials would appear to have for employment prospects, or, what in Northern Ireland is called fair employment (Osborne and Cormack, 1989).

Educational differences, it was believed, could be related to disparities in the funding available to Protestant and Catholic schools. The research (Cormack, Gallagher and Osborne, 1991) revealed:

- that the 15 per cent voluntary contribution for capital projects sought by the state, from all Catholic and other voluntary schools, resulted in a substantial financial burden on the Catholic community, a community already experiencing high levels of social deprivation

- that a likely consequence of the voluntary contribution was the smaller, on average, size of Catholic schools when compared with Protestant schools of the same enrolment
- that Catholic and other church schools in England and Wales, after the 1988 Education Reform (NI) Act, could, by 'opting out' of local authority control, maintain managerial rights and guarantees concerning the preservation of the religious 'ethos' of the school. By 'opting out' they also secured access to 100 per cent capital funding. This route to full funding was, under the Education Reform Order, only given to integrated schools. It appeared, therefore, that Catholic schools in Northern Ireland were treated less favourably than those in England and Wales
- that figures analysed for the 1980s revealed that per capita recurrent expenditure in Catholic primary, secondary and grammar schools was, on average, lower than in comparable Protestant schools (Table 5).

Although part of this differential could be accounted for by the, on average, smaller size of Catholic schools, this only served to raise further questions; notably the potential impact of lower per capita spending levels and smaller schools on the delivery of education to pupils.

The ERO has instituted a new basis for funding schools: Local Management of Schools (LMS). In the past, schools were funded on a historical basis – crudely: a school would receive what it received in the previous year plus an addition to take account of inflation. Over the years this historical basis for funding schools gathered and accumulated all kinds of anomalies. From the introduction of LMS all schools are funded on the basis of a formula. Each of the five ELBs and the DENI have developed formulae for funding the schools for which they are responsible. The expectation is that after the period of transition these formulae will begin to smooth out the unfair inequalities in the funding of schools.

Table 5:   **Recurrent expenditure in schools**

Voluntary Grammar Schools
Median Costs in £s per pupil

| | 1984/85 | | 1985/86 | |
	Protestant	Catholic	Protestant	Catholic
Teaching Costs	775	739	1218	1170
Other Costs	298	232	434	387

Secondary Schools
in £s per pupil

| | 1981/82 | | 1985/86 | |
	Protestant	Catholic	Protestant	Catholic
	279	239	350	312

Primary Schools
in £s per pupil

| | 1981/82 | | 1985/86 | |
	Protestant	Catholic	Protestant	Catholic
	146	120	178	143

Note: The data bases for calculating primary/secondary, and grammar schools costs were different – hence no direct comparisons between these figures should be made.

Source: Cormack *et al,* 1991

The publishing of how each school's budget is derived under the relevant formula has greatly increased the 'transparency' of funding. The 1993/94 budget statements reveal that nineteen voluntary grammar schools (all Protestant) plus six controlled grammar schools (all Protestant) received a total of £1.65m subsidy for private, fee-paying preparatory departments. The largest single payment was over £0.25 m. This payment of public money to private sector education directly subsidises the better-off, since fee levels charged are reduced accordingly. It is strange indeed that government should skew schools' funding on the basis of social *advantage* as well as social *disadvantage*.

The report to the SACHR concluded by recommending that the DENI reconsider the level of support for the capital funding of voluntary schools and that it conduct an annual and public monitoring of its treatment of Protestant and Catholic schools. The DENI accepted the latter recommendation and published a detailed outline of the matters relating especially to recurrent funding of schools. These are now monitored on an annual basis in the reports of the DENI and the ELB. In relation to the funding of capital projects in voluntary schools, government announced in November 1992 the creation of a new type of voluntary school which, in return for adjustments in the composition of the board of governors, will receive 100 per cent funding for capital projects. This proposal emerged after extensive discussion with the Catholic education authorities who pronounced themselves satisfied with the proposals. In having the right to appoint only four governors the Catholic authorities will lose their automatic majority on a new nine-member Board of Governors. However, the DENI appointee will be made 'only after consultation with the Council for Catholic Maintained Schools (CCMS)'. There seems little likelihood that the Catholic authorities will lose effective control of this new type of voluntary school.

Post-school destinations

We concluded the section on second level education by noting the divided nature of provision at that level. Moving from second to third level provision brings these divisions even more clearly to the fore. While university students enjoy halls of residence, students' unions, extensive sports facilities, course fees paid and means-tested maintenance grants, students on sub-degree courses in further education colleges and youth training programmes are exposed to a much inferior set of provisions. The scale of the differential is demonstrated by the fact that in 1991/92 public expenditure was £5,275 per university student in Northern Ireland compared with £2,607 per student in further education. The comparisons North and South are revealing. Higher (degree level) education and the students who enter universities in the South are less well treated than universities and students in the North. Northern Irish universities have been better funded and their students have their fees paid together with a universal entitlement to a means-tested maintenance grant (Osborne and Cormack, 1985). The latter is being steadily eroded with the introduction of the students' loans scheme (Cormack *et al*, 1989). Nevertheless, provision in the North remains markedly higher than that for students entering universities in the South where the majority are liable for course fees and their own maintenance. However, Southern students entering non-degree third level education (which, in the North, would be described as further and advanced further education) are much better treated. The regional technical colleges in the Republic of Ireland currently have a clearer mission, and through the European Social Fund, much better financial support for the majority of students (Osborne and Fisher, 1992).

Youth Training Programmes (YTP)

Conceived originally as a short-term measure to respond to rising youth unemployment, the YTP is designed:

> to enable young people to make the transition from school to adult working life; to enable them to secure a sound base of competence, self-confidence and knowledge through which they may achieve personal fulfilment; and in due course to play their part in enabling Northern Ireland to be economically competitive (Training and Employment Agency, 1991, p. 14).

The reality is that the YTP is still seen as the destination for those who leave school with no qualifications and are unemployed. Considerable research on YTP has been reported and in particular the results of a cohort study of trainees' experiences (McWhirter *et al*, 1987; McWhirter *et al*, 1991).

Table 6:   **Proportion of young people on each type of YTP scheme at ages 16 and 17 (Percentages)**

Scheme Entered	Age 16			Age 17		
	All	Prot.	Cath.	All	Prot.	Cath.
Workscheme	—	—	—	32	36	27
College-based	29	38	22	7	6	7
Training centre	28	28	29	14	16	13
Work preparation Unit/community workshop	19	15	22	20	13	26
Employer-based	9	8	9	8	8	7
Youthways	7	6	9	3	2	4
Young help	2	2	1	3	2	4
Enterprise Ulster	2	2	3	3	3	4
Youth community projects	—	—	—	6	8	4
Other	3	1	6	6	7	5
Total	100	100	100	100	100	100
N 688	371	302	263	122	140	

Source: McWhirter *et al*, 1991

What is clear from Table 6 is that Protestants are more likely to be on courses which offer rigorous training and which are more likely to lead to jobs. Workscheme is a real job where young people are employees rather than trainees; 36 per cent of Protestants were on Workscheme at age seventeen compared to 27 per cent of Catholic young people. On the other hand, work preparation units/community workshops, while often providing valuable training and work in communities, do not have the same reputation of providing an avenue into full-time paid employment; 26 per cent of Catholics were to be found in these schemes compared to 13 per cent of Protestant young people.

Further education

In terms of research, the further education sector in Northern Ireland has received very little attention. The House of Commons Select Committee report (HMSO, 1983) provides some information and this together with other information has been examined by Eversley (1989, pp. 182-190). Eversley comments on the small proportion of further education students undertaking advanced level courses, the domination of the Belfast area in terms of the provision of places and the importance of part-time enrolments in this sector of educational provision.

Due to the inadequacies of official statistics, however, no analysis of participation in these courses can be made in terms of religion.

Some light has been cast on the characteristics of entrants to a major set of courses run mainly in further education colleges. A postal survey of the 1991 entry cohort to BTEC higher courses reveals that entry patterns in terms of social characteristics are broadly similar to degree entrants.[3] The BTEC cohort, however, is slightly more male, slightly more Catholic and drawn significantly more from those from manual backgrounds (45.5 per cent compared with 34.8 per cent).

Higher education

Participation: The expansion of degree level higher education in Northern Ireland over the past thirty years has been considerable. In the mid-1960s there were 4,000 undergraduates in total while by the early 1990s there were twice

Table 7:   **Social class and higher education entry (1991)**

		1991 Census*	Higher Education Entrants**
Social Class	I	4.1	13.2
	II	20.4	44.9
	IIInm	9.7	7.3
	IIIm	27.9	25.4
	IV	13.0	7.1
	V	24.9	2.3
N		467867	5253

Notes: *   derived from the 1991 population census based on economically active males; those in the armed services and inadequately described occupations omitted; those recorded as 'no paid job in previous 10 years' and those recorded as 'on a government training scheme/ government employment' included in Social Class V.

      **   entrants to degree courses; based on occupation of father.

Source: unpublished 1991 census data; higher education survey.

that number of new entrants. Expansion in participation has given Northern Ireland a higher age participation index,[4] of almost 40 per cent higher than that for England and Wales and similar to the Scottish level. Expansion has also led to increasing participation by Catholics, women and those from manual backgrounds (Cormack *et al*, 1994). By the end of the 1980s, women represented half of new entrants and Catholics had increased their representation from 32 per cent of entrants in the early 1970s to half by the early 1990s. Similarly, entrants to degree courses from manual backgrounds went from representing about a quarter of entrants in the early 1970s to just over a third in the early 1990s. Relating the social class background to the social class profile of the population reveals the extent to which 'middle class' entrants, especially Social Classes I and II are over-represented. Table 7 also reveals, however, the high representation of those from Social Class IIIm – the skilled working class – which is represented amongst entrants almost in line with the population.

Another major change during this period related to the destinations of students to study (see Figure 1). In the mid-1960s, approximately 20 per cent of new entrants left Northern Ireland and about two-thirds of these went to institutions in the Irish Republic (mainly Protestant students attending Trinity College, Dublin). At the end of the 1960s, however, these patterns changed as a result of the extension of the UCCA scheme to Northern Ireland, the introduction of student grants and the outbreak of civil disturbances. In the early 1970s, 40 per cent of new entrants left Northern Ireland with the majority of these attending institutions in Britain and the proportion going to the Irish Republic declining substantially. During most of the 1970s and early 1980s the proportion of entrants leaving Northern Ireland settled at approximately one-third. From the mid-1980s, however, the proportion of leavers began to increase and reached 45 per cent at the end of the decade. The characteristics of leavers is distinctive: Protestants are twice as likely to be leavers as Catholics. Leavers also split between those attending universities (approximately one-third), who tend to be particularly well qualified, and the remainder who enter polytechnics (now the 'new' universities) who are less well qualified.

The growth in the out-migration of students has given rise to fears of a 'brain drain'. However, many students have always sought to leave home to study and it would have required a major expansion of provision in Northern Ireland to cater for the additional students if migration levels had been maintained at their 1960s' levels. Notably the proportion of Northern Irish higher education entrants going to British universities has stayed at the same level for the last decade or more. It is in the proportion going to the former polytechnics that a large increase in recent years is to be found.

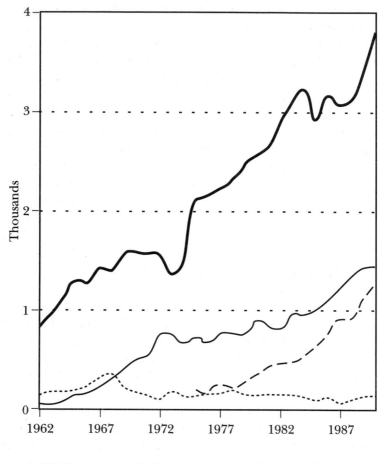

Note: Derived from data supplied by the DENI and based
on returns from ELBs. UP figures added to NI universities

Figure 1:   **Higher education destinations of Northern Irish
students**

A further dimension to this debate has come from the rise
in the numbers of new entrants from the Irish Republic.
Under an EU ruling, which enables EU students studying in
the UK to have their fees paid by the state, applications to UK

universities dramatically increased towards the end of the 1980s. Both the universities in Northern Ireland (especially the University of Ulster) began to accept larger numbers of entrants from the Irish Republic. At the end of the 1980s approximately 15 per cent of new undergraduate entrants to the University of Ulster were from the Irish Republic with most of these at the Coleraine and Magee campuses of the university. This in turn has led to political accusations that these students were 'displacing' Northern Ireland students. Careful scrutiny of the evidence suggests, however, that rising entry grades sought by the University of Ulster were forcing those with weaker 'A' levels to seek places in polytechnics while Southern entrants with very good Leaving Certificate results took places in Northern Ireland. Of course, if well qualified Southern students had not been available, then UU may have let more less well qualified Northern Irish entrants into the university.

Graduates: Studies of higher education have also examined the early labour market experiences of graduates and in particular the experiences of Protestants and Catholics and those of males and females. Overall Protestant graduates are more likely to have secured a job commensurate with having a degree. Catholics are more likely to be unemployed or not working or to be employed in non-graduate type jobs. More detailed breakdowns of economic activity demonstrated that there were significant differences in the types of work pursued by Protestant and Catholic graduates. However, these differences were significantly related to courses undertaken in higher education. Religion *per se* did not exert a significant effect upon economic activity when such factors were taken into account. There was little to suggest the existence of active discrimination against Catholic graduates in Northern Ireland. Protestant graduates who had the same educational characteristics as Catholics experienced similar disadvantages in the labour market (Miller *et al*, 1993).

The labour market experiences of male and female

graduates has also been assessed. In general, women do less well on all indicators of job reward. They are less likely to be in graduate level work and are more likely to be in non-graduate or routine non-manual work. For those in work, women are on average paid less regardless of the level of work, level of higher education attainment, subject of degree course, marital status or religion. There are some exceptions to these trends, most markedly in the medical and legal professions and in the traditionally 'female' semi-professions. Overall, female disadvantage can be partially accounted for by subject orientation at 'A' level and in higher education. Taking 'arts' subjects at 'A' level predisposes female students towards arts and social science courses. Possessing an arts or social science degree, in turn, effectively rules out the taking-up of certain types of occupation and makes the broadly less well rewarded types of occupation more likely (Miller *et al*, 1991).

The institution of the common curriculum in Northern Ireland should eventually ensure greater equality in gender access to the curriculum which may eventually pay dividends in terms of greater labour market equality between men and women. However, existing research demonstrates that women do worse than men in the labour market despite the significance of subject choice and other variables. Even if female graduates matched males in their subject choices and academic attainment they would still find themselves less likely to be in graduate level jobs and, even if in them, less well paid. The effect of gender remains significant even when other factors are taken into account.

The expansion of higher education based on a system of substantial state financial support to individuals has resulted in the increased representation of women, Catholics and those from manual backgrounds. These levels of participation may be reduced as the policy of shifting the cost of higher education towards individuals, for example, through 'top-up' loans, gathers pace (Cormack *et al*, 1989).

Graduate experiences during the 1980s suggest particular disadvantages for women, whereas Catholic graduate

disadvantage seemed mui link to subject of degree than
to discrimination.

Conclusion

Whether or not one believes in meritocracy as a credible social
value, whether or not one believes in competitive
individualism or that equality of opportunity is an achievable
policy goal, modern democracies still hold out the ideal of
equal chances for all to make their way in life unhindered by
disadvantages associated with gender, religion, class or
disability. As we have argued above, the question of equal
opportunities continues to have a particular edge in Northern
Ireland.

The work we have reported in this chapter is good at
answering the question of 'who gets where?' It is less good at
answering the question 'why?' What are the social processes
which operate to reproduce inequalities in opportunity
generation by generation? There remains, in Northern
Ireland, much for the student of education and education
policy to explore.

But, to return to the origins and destinations balance
sheet, our conclusion is that great gains have been made,
especially taking a century-long perspective. The working
class have gained least and the problem of the underachievement of students from working-class backgrounds remains as
pertinent as it was to Douglas (1964) in the 1960s, Glass
(1954) in the 1950s, Hogden (1938) in the 1930s and the
trades union movement and others at the turn of the century
(Silver, 1973). Catholics have made great gains. They are now
on a par with their representation in the age specific cohort
in higher education. The major remaining problems are the
disproportionate levels of underachievement at second level,
particularly of Catholic males; the continuing, but declining,
bias towards arts and humanities subjects; and the implications of formula funding and competition between schools in
disadvantaged areas. Likewise for females the story is one of

continuing improvement. Females in Northern Ireland now significantly outperform males at 'A' level and in GCSEs. A considerable problem remains with the arts and humanities bias in subjects studied. The 'gendering' of subjects may be addressed by the introduction of the common curriculum. However, studies of girls and science suggest the resolution of this problem will require more than merely forcing girls to study the sciences (Kelly, 1981; Whyte, 1986). However, for both Catholics and females, primarily from non-manual backgrounds, the problem of equality of opportunity lies less with education and now more clearly than ever in the labour market.

Notes

1. In Tables 3 and 4 the data are based on schools. There is some degree of 'cross-over', mainly Catholic pupils attending Protestant schools. Data on the extent of 'cross-over' is not available at this time.
2. Many working-class parents are unlikely to be 'empowered' by recent changes since choices in the education 'market' will only be available to those parents whose children achieve transfer procedure grades likely to gain them entry to grammar school.
3. These data are drawn from a survey undertaken by the authors and Tony Gallagher, Norrie Fisher and Maureen Poland. The data are currently being analysed for publication.
4. The age participation index is defined as all full-time entrants to higher education in the UK aged under twenty-one years as a percentage of the eighteen-year-old population.

References

AKENSON, D.H., 1973. *Education and Enmity: The Control of Schooling in Northern Ireland 1920-1950,* Newton Abbott, David and Charles.
ARMSTRONG, D., 1989. 'An Analysis of the Failure to Accept Grammar School Places in West Belfast: 1985-1988', MSSc Dissertation, Queen's University, Belfast.
ARTHUR, P., 1974. *The People's*

Democracy 1968-1973, Belfast, Blackstaff Press.

BALL, S. J., 1990. 'Education, Inequality and School Reform: Values in Crisis!', Inaugural Lecture, King's College, London.

BUCKLAND, P., 1979. *Factory of Grievances: Devolved Government in Northern Ireland 1921-1939*, Dublin, Gill and Macmillan.

COOLAHAN, J., 1981. *Irish Education*, Dublin, Institute of Public Administration.

CORMACK, R. J. and R. D. OSBORNE (eds.), 1991. *Discrimination and Public Policy in Northern Ireland.* Oxford, Clarendon Press.

CORMACK, R. J., R. D. OSBORNE and R. L. MILLER, 1989. 'Student Loans: A Northern Ireland Perspective', *Higher Education Quarterly*, 44, 4.

CORMACK, R. J., A. M. GALLAGHER, R. D. OSBORNE, 1991. 'Religious Affiliation and Educational Attainment in Northern Ireland' in Sixteenth Report of the Standing Advisory Commission on Human Rights, London, HMSO, pp. 117-212.

CORMACK, R. J., R. D. OSBORNE, and A. M. GALLAGHER, 1994. Higher Education Participation of Northern Irish Students, *Higher Education Quarterly*, in press.

CORMACK, R. J., A. M. GALLAGHER and R. D. OSBORNE, 1992a. 'Access to Grammar Schools', in Seventeenth Report of the Standing Advisory Commission for Human Rights, London, HMSO.

CORMACK, R. J., A. M. GALLAGHER, R. D. OSBORNE and N. A. FISHER, 1992b. 'Secondary Analysis of the School Leavers Survey (1989)', in Seventeenth Report of the Standing Advisory Commission for Human Rights, London, HMSO.

DENI, 1994. *School Performance Information 1992/1993*, Bangor, DENI.

DOUGLAS, J. W. B., 1964. *The Home and the School*, London, McGibbon and Kee.

DUNN, S., 1990. 'A Short History of Education in Northern Ireland, 1920-1990', in Fifteenth Report of the Standing Advisory Commission on Human Rights, London, HMSO.

DUNN, S., 1993. 'A historical context to church-state relations in Northern Ireland' in R. D. Osborne, R. J. Cormack and A. M. Gallagher (eds.), *After the Reforms: Education and Policy in Northern Ireland*, Aldershot, Avebury.

DRUDY, S., 1991. 'The Sociology of Education in Ireland, 1966-1991', *Irish Journal of Sociology*, Vol. 1.

EVERSLEY, D., 1989. *Religion and Employment in Northern Ireland*, London, Sage.

GALLAGHER, A. M., 1988. *Transfer pupils at sixteen*, Belfast, Northern Ireland Council for Educational Research.

GALLAGHER, A. M., R. J. CORMACK and R. OSBORNE, 1994. 'Religion and access to grammar schools in Northern Ireland', *Research in Education*, 51, pp. 51-58.

GLASS, D. V., 1954. *Social Mobility in Britain*, London, Routledge and Kegan Paul.

HALSEY, A. H. (ed.), 1972. *Educational Priority*, Vols. 1-5, London, HMSO.

HALSEY, A. H., A. F. HEATH and J. M. RIDGE, 1980. *Origins and Destinations: Family, Class and Education in Modern Britain*, Oxford, Clarendon Press.

HMSO, 1983. House of Commons Education, Science and Arts Committee, *Further and Higher Education in Northern Ireland*, London, HMSO.

HMSO, 1989. Education Reform (Northern Ireland) Order, Belfast, HMSO.

HOGDEN, L. (ed.), 1938. *Political Arithmetic*, London, Allen and Unwin.

JENKINS, R., 1983. *Lads, Citizens and Ordinary Kids*, London, Routledge and Kegan Paul.

KARABEL, J. and A. H. HALSEY (eds.), 1977. *Power and Ideology in Education*, New York, Oxford University Press.

KELLY, A., 1981. *The Missing Half: Girls and Science Education*, Manchester, Manchester University Press.

LIVINGSTONE, J., 1987. 'Equality of Opportunity in Education in Northern Ireland', in R. D. Osborne, R. J. Cormack and R. L. Miller (eds.), *Education and Policy in Northern Ireland*, Belfast, Policy Research Institute.

McKEOWN, P., 1993. 'The introduction of formula funding and local management of schools in Northern Ireland', in R. D. Osborne, R. J. Cormack and A. M. Gallagher (eds.), *After the Reforms: Education and Policy in Northern Ireland*, Aldershot, Avebury.

McPHERSON, A., and C. D. RABBE, 1988. *Governing Education: A Sociology of Policy since 1945*, Edinburgh, Edinburgh University Press.

McWHIRTER, L., U. DUFFY, R. BARRY and G. McGUINNESS, 1987. 'Transition from School to Work' in R. D. Osborne, R. J. Cormack and R. L. Miller (eds.), *Education and Policy in Northern Ireland*, Belfast, Policy Research Institute.

McWHIRTER, L., J. GILLIAN, U. DUFFY and D. THOMPSON, 1991. 'Religious

Affiliation and the Youth Training Programme' in R. J. Cormack and R. D. Osborne (eds.), *Discrimination and Public Policy in Northern Ireland*, Oxford, Clarendon Press.

MARKS, J. and C. COX, 1984. 'Educational Attainment in Secondary Schools', *Oxford Review of Education*, Vol. 10, No. 1, pp. 7-31.

MILLER, R. L., R. D. OSBORNE, R. J. CORMACK and A. P. WILLIAMSON, 1993. 'Higher Education and Labour Market Entry: The Differing Experiences of Northern Irish Protestants and Catholics' in R. D. Osborne, R. J. Cormack and A. M. Gallagher (eds.), *After the Reforms: Education and Policy in Northern Ireland*.

MILLER, R. L., C. A. CURRY, R. D. OSBORNE and R. J. CORMACK, 1991. 'The Labour Market Experiences of an Educational Elite: A Continuous Time Analysis of Recent Higher Education Graduates', Research Paper No. 2, Centre for Policy Research, University of Ulster.

MURRAY, D., 1985. *Worlds Apart: Segregated Schools in Northern Ireland*, Belfast, Appletree Press.

MURRAY, D., 1992. 'Science and Funding in Northern Ireland Grammar Schools: A Case Study Approach', in Seventeenth Report of the Standing Advisory Commission for Human Rights, London, HMSO.

MUSGRAVE, P. W., 1968. *Society and Education in England since 1900*, London, Methuen.

OSBORNE, R. D. and R. J. CORMACK, 1985. 'Higher Education: North and South', *Administration*, Vol. 33, No. 3.

OSBORNE, R. D. and R. J. CORMACK, 1989. 'Gender and Religion as Issues in Education, Training and Entry to Work', in J. Harbison (ed.), *Growing Up in Northern Ireland*, Belfast, Stranmillis College.

OSBORNE, R. D. and N. A. FISHER, 1992. 'Recent Developments in Third Level Education in the Republic of Ireland', Centre for Policy Research, Research Paper 4, University of Ulster.

OSBORNE, R. D., R. L. MILLER, R. J. CORMACK and A. P. WILLIAMSON, 1988. 'Trends in Higher Education Participation in Northern Ireland', *The Economic and Social Review*, Vol. 19, No. 4.

OSBORNE, R. D., A. M. GALLAGHER and R. J. CORMACK, 1989. 'Review of Aspects of Education in Northern Ireland', in Fourteenth Report of the Standing Advisory Commission on Human Rights, London, HMSO.

OSBORNE, R. D., R. J. CORMACK and A. M. GALLAGHER, 1991. 'Educational Qualifications and

the Labour Market', in R. J.
Cormack and R. D. Osborne
(eds.), *Discrimination and Public
Policy in Northern Ireland,*
Oxford, Clarendon Press.
SHEA, P., 1981. *Voices and the
Sound of Drums: An Irish
Autobiography,* Belfast,
Blackstaff.
SILVER, H., 1973. *Equal
Opportunity in Education,*
London, Methuen.
TRAINING AND
EMPLOYMENT AGENCY,
1991. Corporate Plan:
Strategy, Belfast, TEA.

WHYTE, J., 1986. *Getting the
GIST,* Henley-on-Thames,
Routledge and Regan Paul
WILSON, J. A., 1985. *Secondary
School Organisation and Pupil
Progress,* Belfast, The Northern
Ireland Centre for
Educational Research.
WILSON, J. A., 1987. 'Selection
for Secondary Education' in
R. D. Osborne, R. J. Cormack
and R. L. Miller (eds.),
*Education and Policy in
Northern Ireland,* Belfast, Policy
Research Institute.

17
Gender and Education: North and South

VALERIE MORGAN and KATHLEEN LYNCH

Introduction

The experiences of women in education in both the Republic and Northern Ireland are fraught with contradictions. In both systems girls attain higher aggregate grades than boys in major public examinations (Clancy, 1987; Gallagher, 1989; NCCA, 1992) and are more likely to remain in school after the age of sixteen. At the same time males slightly outnumber females in third-level education and greatly outnumber them in most physical science and technology courses. (Clancy, 1988; Osborne *et al*, 1988). And in the administration of education and the development of education policy, and in the highest levels of staffing in educational institutions, men dominate (Drudy and Lynch, 1993; Trewsdale and Toman, 1993). Throughout Ireland this pattern must be understood against the background of women's overall position in the social institutions of the two parts of Ireland. Traditionally women's place has been clearly defined as being in the home (McKenna, 1988; Davies and McLaughlin, 1991), and although patterns are changing the pace of change has been slow. Thus, less than 30 per cent of married women are in the paid labour force in the Republic of Ireland compared with

over 40 per cent in the other EU countries (Blackwell, 1989).
Northern Ireland also exhibits many of the characteristics of
a conservative, rural society in its treatment of women,
though 56 per cent of married or co-habiting women under
sixty were in paid employment by 1990 (Montgomery, 1993).

The churches have had a powerful influence on education
in Ireland, but religion acts as a particular complicating
factor in Northern Ireland where the education system is
dominated by the religious division between the two communities (Dunn, 1986). A dual system of schools has existed
in Northern Ireland since the inception of the state, with the
'controlled' schools effectively catering for the Protestant
community whilst the 'maintained' schools meet the needs of
the Catholic population. In spite of the growth of a number
of 'planned integrated schools' since the early 1980s, the
overwhelming majority of pupils attend schools which are
almost totally segregated on religious lines. Only in further
and higher education is there any large scale integration
(although primary teacher education is still largely under
denominational control) and by this stage friendship and
interest patterns have often already crystallised along
community lines. The experience of the last twenty years of
conflict also means that issues relating to the contribution of
education to community relations have dominated thinking
and research in the north (Gallagher, 1989; Dunn, 1986,
1991).

In the Republic all but ten of the primary schools are
denominationally controlled. The ten 'project or multi-
denominational schools', as they are known, mirror the
development of integrated schools in the North. At second
level, secondary schools predominate (60 per cent of all
schools are secondary) and these are also run on denominational lines. Most secondary schools (67 per cent) are
single sex, although a number have gone co-educational in
the last ten years. All but four of the sixty-eight community
and comprehensive schools are co-educational (Department
of Education, 1993, p. 38). As the latter have specific religious

representation on their boards of management, they are effectively denominational, albeit under greater public control than secondary schools. Vocational schools are also co-educational; they are the only non-denominational second-level schools in the Republic, but they cater for a minority of students at second level (a little over one-fifth).

Against this background of traditional and religious influence, there have, however, been major changes in many aspects of education in both North and South over the last ten years. In particular there has been a strong emphasis on the interface between education and employment and the need to train a skilled workforce. This has resulted in changes in both curriculum content and organisational structures. Within such a context, where education is defined in increasingly instrumental terms, it is perhaps hardly surprising that direct concern about differences between the educational experiences provided for girls and boys has not been a high priority (Lynch, 1991; Collins, 1989). Equality of opportunity between the sexes is strongly supported in official documentation (for example in the North the remit given to the working parties drawing up the Programmes of Study and Attainment Targets for the new Curriculum stressed gender equality, and in 1992 the Green Paper in the Republic put forward a number of proposals for promoting greater equality of opportunity for girls and women). The role of both the Equal Opportunities Commission for Northern Ireland (EOCNI) and the Council for the Status of Women in the Republic has been significant. Over many years these groups have sought to highlight gender issues in the education system and campaigned actively for change in several areas. In the North in particular the EOCNI has been central to what gains have been achieved over the past ten years, often against the grain of right-wing UK Government policies (Montgomery, 1991). However, the lack of resources and legislative backing has made the realisation of equality very difficult. The inability of the Minister for Education in the Republic of Ireland to achieve a fair gender balance (40 per cent is the stated ideal for all public boards) on the boards of the Dublin Institute of Technology Colleges in 1993/94 shows that mere exhortation and goodwill will not produce equality.

Types of schooling

As already indicated, religion has always had a powerful impact on educational provision throughout Ireland. Indeed, the history of the development of mass education in nineteenth century and early twentieth century Ireland is dominated by the struggles of the various denominations to gain control of educational provision for their own members. One effect of the strong tradition of religious involvement has been the persistence of a significant measure of single sex education in comparison to other European countries. In the Republic almost 22 per cent of primary schools are either totally or mostly single sex (with co-education in infant classes only) (Department of Education, 1993, p. 16). Whilst the majority of primary schools, in both the controlled and maintained sectors, in the North are mixed sex, especially in rural areas where schools are small, there was a tradition of single sex primary schools in the maintained (Catholic) sector in the larger towns, but this is now breaking down. Many amalgamations between maintained girls' and boys' primary schools have occurred or are planned, with the result that single-sex primary schools will probably have almost disappeared from the North within ten years (Curry, 1993). The same will probably be the pattern in the Republic of Ireland, but since a considerable number of single-sex primary schools are in urban areas it will not be quite as marked.

At secondary level the pattern of single- and mixed-sex schools is far from clear-cut. Both systems are fragmented, on the basis of school type, social class, denomination and sex, with measured academic ability playing an important part in the stratification of the North's education system. In Northern Ireland, grammar and secondary schools are provided in both the Protestant and Catholic sectors with selection currently based on a qualifying procedure at eleven plus (though the format has changed under the new curriculum, a selection process will continue to operate). There are single- and mixed-sex schools amongst both grammar and secondary schools and also in both Protestant and Catholic sectors (Gallagher, 1989). In the Republic, although there is no formal national selection test for pupils moving from first to second level education, differentiation by social class, sex and denomination operates. There are four different school types in the Republic (secondary, community, comprehensive and vocational/community colleges). Secondary schools tend to have a greater middle-class intake while vocational schools and community colleges have traditionally been more working-class in intake. Sixty-seven per cent of girls (compared with 57 per cent of boys) attend secondary schools, which are the least technically orientated schools in terms of curricula (Drudy and Lynch, 1993). In rural areas throughout Ireland, but particularly in the North, many secondary schools have traditionally been co-educational since the catchment areas could not sustain separate girls' and boys' schools. The urban areas, however, have always had many single sex schools, especially for Catholic pupils, but this has begun to change over the past ten years both in the North and in the South. In particular, many Catholic girls' grammar schools in the North, run by religious orders, have begun to enrol boys. This was partly designed to offset the shortfall in grammar school places for Catholic boys, but it has had a significant effect on the level of gender segregation (Gallagher, 1989). In the South girls' and boys' secondary schools have amalgamated in a number of areas, principally due to declining pupil numbers; demographic trends suggest that further amalgamations are likely.

Fifty-eight (7 per cent) of the 792 second-level schools in the Republic are fee-paying, thirty-six being Catholic and the majority of the remaining twenty-two being Protestant. These schools are state-aided as they receive capital grants and have salaries paid by the Department of Education. There are very few private schools of any sort in Northern Ireland. This is probably because until recently fee-paying pupils could be admitted to any of the grammar schools and their fees were set at a subsidised rate. Fee-paying pupils in grammar schools now have to pay full economic fees and there is much more regulation by the Department of Education of the number permitted and the conditions under which they can be accepted. It seems unlikely that the presence or absence of a private sector has contributed significantly to the pattern of gender differences *per se*. However, private schools do reproduce elite cultures and social networks, to which there is an inevitable gender dimension.

Gender differences in participation

The statutory requirement for full-time first- and second-level education for all children throughout Ireland provides a basic level of equality. In the Republic females have a higher participation rate than males at second level in spite of constituting slightly less than half of the total cohort, but this is lost at third level where males slightly outnumber females (Clancy, 1989). Clancy's research suggests, however, that if present growth rates continue, women will shortly constitute a majority of new entrants to higher education.

A similar pattern exists in the North, although with the split between grammar school and secondary school provision at age eleven some differences between the sexes begin to emerge. Until 1986-7 as near as possible equal numbers of girls and boys were admitted to the grammar schools and the marking of the qualifying examination was structured to ensure this. Since the successful legal challenge to this system on the grounds of gender bias, more girls than boys have gained entry to grammar schools each year. It is too early yet to say what effects this may have in terms of achievement patterns and the ethos of the schools but it does mean that more girls than boys now have access to the

Table 1:   **Female/male participation rates at the three major education levels in the Republic of Ireland, 1989-90**

	Females		Males	
	No.	%	No.	%
First level 4-12 years (approx)	272,592	48.6	288,278	51.4
Second level 12-17/18 years (approx)	174,872	51.1	167,492	48.9
Third level over 18 years	30,738	46.6	35,211	53.4
Total	478,202		490,981	

Source: Department of Education (1991)

traditional academic education provided by Northern Irish grammar schools (Collins, 1989) and by contrast increasing proportions of boys are likely to be found in the less well resourced secondary schools.

The participation rates for women and men in further and higher education throughout Ireland have tended to converge over the recent past, so that whilst women constituted only 27 per cent of full-time university students in Northern Ireland in 1966-67, by 1989 they accounted for 49 per cent of full-time undergraduates and 43 per cent of full-time postgraduate students. Over the twenty-year period from 1966/67 to 1986/87 the proportion of women amongst those gaining first or upper second class honours degrees rose from 14 per cent to 50 per cent (Osborne, 1992). In the Republic the pattern is extremely similar with women comprising just over 29 per cent of full-time students in higher education in 1965-66 and 47 per cent in 1989-90 (Clancy, 1989; Department of Education, 1991; Osborne *et al*, 1988). The changes in other sectors of post-compulsory education have been less marked. Women form over half the students on full-time vocational courses and just under half the students on part-time further education courses in Northern Ireland, and in both cases these are patterns which have remained almost steady over the past twenty years. In all sectors of higher and further education, both North and South, the main contrasts are not in the overall participation rates but in the types of courses which women and men take (Montgomery, 1991; Drudy and Lynch, 1993).

This is brought out by 1988-89 data for the North on proportions of women taking various types of courses of training in colleges of further education.

Table 2:   **Proportion of women in various forms of further education and vocational training in Northern Ireland, 1989-90**

Courses	Full-time			Part-time			Total		
	Total	Females		Total	Females		Total	Females	
	No.	No.	%	No.	No.	%	No.	No.	%
City and Guilds	2338	1521	65.0	9685	2708	28.0	12023	4229	35.2
B-Tec	4408	1867	42.4	1767	620	35.1	6175	2487	40.3
GCE 'A' Level	1799	1014	56.4	2377	1323	55.7	4176	2337	56.0
GCSE	3435	1851	53.3	7439	4682	63.0	10874	6513	59.9
Other	4228	2706	64.0	17764	11069	62.3	21992	13775	62.6

Source: EOCNI, 1993

The full-time City and Guilds courses where women form almost two-thirds of the students are mainly secretarial and office skills courses, whilst the part-time B-Tec courses on which they form about a third of the students are mainly day-release technical and engineering courses.

The curricular options

Differences in types of courses undertaken by women and men relate directly to the central issue of stereotyping in subject choice. The primary level curriculum in the Republic provides a common basis of Irish, English, mathematics, social and environmental studies, arts and crafts, music, physical education and religion for both girls and boys. Similarly the Northern Ireland curriculum provides a core of English, mathematics and science and technology, plus history, geography, music, art, physical education and religious education for all pupils in primary schools. This does not of course mean that girls and boys have identical educational experiences at primary level. The limited amount of research which has been done reinforces evidence from other countries in suggesting that gender differences are frequently found in areas such as teacher-pupil inter-action patterns, access to equipment and management strategies (Morgan and Dunn, 1990; Wilson, 1991). Even some elements of the official guidelines given to teachers provide evidence of sexism although these are now being revised. With regard to the teaching of music, the Teachers' Handbook for Primary Teachers issued by the Department of Education suggests:

> While a large number of songs are suited to both girls and boys, some songs are particularly suited to boys, e.g. martial, gay, humorous, rhythmic airs. Others are more suited to girls, e.g. lullabies, spinning songs, songs tender in content and expression.
>
> (Department of Education, 1971)

At second level, a common curriculum for all pupils operates up to the age of fifteen in the Republic of Ireland and sixteen in Northern Ireland. However, in both cases there are slight but significant variations which may have gender implications. In the Republic, the pattern of subjects studied varies between schools of different types. Thus, for example, although mathematics is compulsory, science is not a core subject and one finds that in single sex schools only 65 per cent of girls took the main science A course for Intermediate Certificate in 1989-90, as against 93 per cent of boys. Interestingly, however, more girls (72 per cent) than boys (66 per cent) took Science A in co-educational schools that year. By contrast, less than 1 per cent of boys in single sex schools and only 9 per cent of those in co-educational schools studied home economics for Intermediate Certificate in 1989-90. The comparable rates for girls were 53 per cent and 75 per cent respectively (Department of Education, 1991, Table 15.5).

In Northern Ireland there is choice over the level or format in which several subjects are studied. In particular three different levels of mathematical study are provided in the GCSE examinations and science can be provided by single GCSE or double award or study of three separate science subjects (Morgan, 1991). The result of these differences is to initiate a separation in terms of subject level along traditional lines, with girls moving away from the sciences, and boys away from arts and modern languages. Although the problem has been partially mitigated over the past twenty years, clear differences remain as the data for Northern Ireland on proportions of girls passing in various subjects illustrates (Table 3).

Table 3:   **Females as a percentage of those passing in various subjects in 16+ examinations in Northern Ireland**

GCE 'O' Level/GCSE	1970	1980	1991
Biology	55.7	56.8	60.8
Chemistry	27.1	40.4	49.7
Computer Studies		36.3	47.6
English	54.3	56.9	58.3
French	60.3	58.5	60.9
History	58.9	54.7	57.2
Home Economics	99.9	99.3	96.0
Mathematics	44.0	47.1	49.3
Physics	20.4	28.6	35.9
Technology			12.5

Source: EOCNI, 1993

Table 4: Changes in subject participation in the senior cycle between 1972/73 and 1989/90: proportion of the Leaving Certificate cohort taking each subject (Republic of Ireland)

Subjects	1972/73* Girls %	1972/73* Boys %		1989/90** Girls %	1989/90** Boys %
Language Subjects					
Irish	97.9	96.5	Irish (H.C.)***	34.0	28.4
			Irish (L.C.)	54.7	60.2
			Irish (C.C.)	8.7	7.3
			(total)	*97.4*	*95.7*
English	99.6	97.8	English (H.C.)	48.8	44.4
			English (L.C.)	40.0	44.6
			English (C.C.)	9.6	8.6
			(total)	*98.4*	*97.6*
French	58.6	33.0		73.0	57.0
Spanish	10.7	4.4		2.4	1.2
German	3.1	1.4		9.5	4.4
Italian	0.6	0.3		0.1	0.1
Greek	0.0	0.7		<0.01	<0.01
Hebrew	0.03	0.02		<0.02	<0.01
Arts, Humanities					
History	42.1	45.3		22.5	27.6
Geography	73.7	70.0		30.1	40.6
Art	29.1	14.9		22.5	13.7

Table 4:   Changes in subject participation in the senior cycle between 1972/73 and 1989/90: proportion of the Leaving Certificate cohort taking each subject (Republic of Ireland) (contd.)

Subjects	1972/73*		1989/90**	
	Girls %	Boys %	Girls %	Boys %
Arts, Humanities (contd.)				
Music and Musicianship	3.8	0.5	3.8	1.2
Classical Studies	not offered		0.2	0.5
Practical/Technological				
Home Economics (gen.)	51.4	0.2	5.9	0.5
Engineering	0.0	5.1	0.4	16.4
Technical Drawing	0.001	8.6	0.9	29.1
Construction Studies	0.0	5.5	0.4	19.1
Sciences/Applied Sciences				
Mathematics	78.2	97.1		
Maths (H.C.)			15.0 ⎫	26.1 ⎫
Maths (L.C.)			77.1 ⎬ 98.4	65.3 ⎬ 98.1
Maths (C.C.)			6.3 ⎭	6.7 ⎭
Applied Mathematics	0.05	4.4	0.4	3.5
Physics	1.9	22.3	9.6	31.0
Chemistry	7.6	30.5	13.4	18.8
Biology	28.6	21.1	60.1	35.7
Physics and Chemistry	2.0	7.4	2.2	4.9

Subjects	1972/73*		1989/90**	
	Girls %	Boys %	Girls %	Boys %
Sciences/Applied Sciences (*contd.*)				
Agricultural Science	0.1	4.3	1.2	7.6
Home Economics (Scientific & Social)	3.8	0.1	49.9	5.8
Business Subjects				
Accounting	21.0	17.6	26.3	28.3
Business Organisation	23.0	19.1	35.0	41.7
Economics	12.3	21.9	17.5	9.0
Economic History	1.0	1.2	0.1	<0.01
Agricultural Economics	0.0	0.9	0.7	0.0

Notes

* 1972/73 figures are based on the number who sat the Leaving Cert. examination in 1973. They refer, therefore, to *one year's* cohort. In 1973, 13,449 girls and 11,831 boys sat the Leaving Cert. examination.

** 1989/90 figures are based on the entire senior cycle student body studying for the Leaving Certificate. They refer, therefore, to the entire two-year Leaving Cert. cohort. In 1989/90, 59,450 girls and 54,619 boys were studying for the Leaving Certificate.

*** The distinctions between those taking higher (H.C.), lower (L.C.), common (C.C.) courses in Irish, English and mathematics for 1989/90 are presented for interest. Virtually all students sit examinations in these three subjects.

Source: Department of Education (1974, 1991).

The majority of those pupils who remain at school beyond sixteen in Northern Ireland embark on two-year GCE 'A' Level courses as a preparation for entry to higher education. Here choices become even narrower as most pupils study only two or three subjects and opt for a clear arts or science route, so that although the number of girls taking individual science subjects at 'A' level has increased over the past twenty years, the gender gap remains, with twice as many boys as girls taking three 'A' level science subjects (McEwen et al, 1986).

The situation is similar but not identical in the Republic. There has been a significant increase in women's participation in the sciences in the last fifteen years, although girls remain under-represented in the physical sciences and practical technological subjects (Table 4).

While girls are moving into the traditional boys' areas, there is less sign of a movement in the other direction. Overall, both boys and girls are moving out of the arts, humanities and certain languages into the sciences and business studies. It may become increasingly important to ask what boys lose by not studying languages and literature as well as looking at the problems girls face if they have a limited science background, although this question is rarely addressed in current educational research.

Differences in subject take-up rates between girls and boys were formerly explicable, at least in part, in structural terms. Many second-level schools, in both parts of Ireland, did not provide a full range of subject choices and girls' schools in particular often had limited provision for the teaching of science, while boys' schools had poor provision for art, music and home economics (Hannan et al, 1983; McEwen and Curry, 1987). Changes have occurred, however, over the past ten years, as data relating to the Republic illustrates (Table 5).

The main barriers which discourage pupils from choosing non-traditional subjects are now probably cultural and eliminating these is likely to remain a major task for many years. As Hannan et al (1983, p. 154) observed:

Although there are differences between the sexes in provision and allocation in the subjects we analysed, these differences are ... less than sex differences in the true rate of choice. In other words, the sex differences in pupils' own choices was greater than in either the provision or allocation of subjects to them. This finding suggests that simply increasing the provision or allocation of a subject to whichever sex ... will not automatically lead to a substantial reduction in the sex differences in take up.

This has considerable implications in terms of educational policy and suggests that models of equality such as those proposed in the new Northern Ireland Curriculum may be inadequate. The new Curriculum aims to give all pupils 'equal access to a broad and balanced curriculum' and in this way to provide 'equality of opportunity for boys and girls' (Department of Education for Northern Ireland, 1988). The

Table 5: **Proportion of single sex schools offering particular subjects to Leaving Certificate pupils in 1980/81 and in 1989/90 in the Republic of Ireland**

Subjects	Girls' schools		Boys' schools	
	1980/81 %	1989/90 %	1980/81 %	1989/90 %
Mathematics (higher)	73.9	89.4	91.7	90.7
Physics	34.8	78.8	79.2	92.6
Chemistry	73.9	88.9	83.3	87.0
Biology	100.0	97.9	75.0	87.7
History	95.7	97.4	84.0	92.0
Technical Drawing	0.0	3.2	33.3	62.3
Home Economics (Scientific and Social)	95.7	97.4	4.2	19.1

Sources: 1980/81 figures: Hannan *et al* (1983), Table 5.7
           1989/90 figures: Department of Education (1991).

actual model of equality which appears to underlie such measures is one in which the provision of the 'same' curriculum is equated with the provision of equality. This appears to ignore all the problems about whether all groups of pupils can take equal advantage of the 'same' curricular content and all the evidence about the importance of the social context of the classroom, the home and the peer group (Lynch, 1989b; Curry, 1989). Creating equality in education does not mean treating all people the same way.

Indeed, one fundamental problem with the debate about equality and the curriculum is that it tends to assume that equality will be attained when women adhere to the male norm. While it is undoubtedly true that women do not have the same career options as men if they fail to study science and technology, little consideration is given to the fact that the content of science and the context in which it is taught are frequently alienating for women (Kelly, 1985). The debate about curricular options often ignores the fact that much of the knowledge presented in schools has ethnic, class and gender connotations. This is equally true for the literature and language subjects (in which women excel) and for science and technology (Whyld, 1983). Achieving equality between the sexes in the curricular sphere is not merely a matter of getting women into science and technology, but of questioning the nature of the curriculum itself.

Differences in level of attainment

The evidence relating to levels of attainment suggests that gender differentials in performance are neither consistent nor clear-cut. In primary schools, girls appear to do better academically than boys. Their language development is more advanced than that of boys during the early phases of primary education and the proportion of girls who require remedial help in reading is considerably lower. In mathematics, the area where girls are frequently reported to have problems, there appears to be very little difference in attainment between the sexes at the end of the primary stage (IAEP, 1992). The higher level of achievement by girls in this first stage of education was highlighted by the litigation over the Northern Ireland transfer procedure in 1988 (Collins, 1989). Pupils were allocated to grammar or secondary schools on the results of two fifty-minute verbal reasoning tests taken in the first term of the final year of primary education. Until the successful legal challenge in 1988, the papers for girls and boys were marked separately, on the grounds that the sexes are 'inherently different from each other in terms of intellectual development (girls are more developed intellectually than boys at eleven years of age)' (Johnson and Rooney, 1987). The effect of differential marking up to 1987/88 was that girls needed marks of 71 on each of the two papers to gain a grammar school place whilst boys received a place if they got 69 and 66. It is interesting to note that the first sets of data from tests based on the new curriculum also suggest girls are out-performing boys at primary level.

Moving on to secondary schooling the pattern is complex and direct comparisons of overall achievement between girls and boys are not straight-forward. In terms of aggregate performance in public examinations, research in the Republic indicates that girls tend to do better overall (Lynch, 1991; NCCA, 1992). Analysis of the Leaving Certificate results for 1980 suggested that a higher proportion of girls obtained Grade C or higher in sixteen of the twenty-nine subjects taken by both sexes (Clancy, 1989) and this has been confirmed by later studies (Lynch, 1991; NCCA, 1992).

In Northern Ireland the picture is similar, although complicated by the selective secondary system which segregates pupils by ability as measured in the eleven plus and provides quite different opportunities for those in grammar and secondary schools. Within this pattern the most academically 'able'[1] girls achieve results comparable with those of the most academically 'able' boys and fewer girls than boys leave school with no qualifications at all. Throughout Ireland, however, there are considerable contrasts between

Table 6:   **Gender differences in Leaving Certificate performance among school regular candidates (i.e. taking the full Leaving Certificate for the first time at the end of second-level education) for the year 1991 in the Republic of Ireland**

| | *Proportion obtaining various grades* | | | | | | | |
| | *All examinations combined* | | | | | | | |
	% A	% B	% C	% D	% E	% F	% NG	% A+B
Higher Level Papers								
Girls	5.0	21.0	39.0	29.0	5.0	1.0	0	27.0
Boys	5.0	20.0	36.0	31.0	6.0	1.0	0	26.0
Ordinary Level Papers								
Girls	4.0	17.0	33.0	32.0	9.0	4.0	1.0	21.0
Boys	4.0	15.0	30.0	33.0	11.0	6.0	2.0	18.0

Source: National Council for Curriculum and Assessment (1992), Tables 34 and 48.

the performance of girls and boys in different areas of the curriculum. These are clearly related to the differences in the patterns of subject choice already noted. Two national studies of thirteen-year-olds' achievement in mathematics and science carried out in the Republic (IAEP, 1989, 1991) appear to provide conflicting evidence about gender differences in mathematics, although their methodology has been the subject of some criticism (Oldham, 1991). The 1989 study suggested no significant overall differences between thirteen-year-old girls and boys in mathematics whilst the 1992 findings do suggests boys were achieving better results than girls. In science boys performed significantly better than girls in both the 1989 and 1992 studies, but since virtually no science is taught in schools prior to age thirteen these tests seem likely to be demonstrating not the effects of the formal curriculum, but boys' superior socialisation into scientific culture by early adolescence. In addition, all these tests used a high proportion of multiple choice items and there is considerable

Table 7: **Gender differences in selected subjects at GCSE
and 'A' level in 1991 (Northern Ireland)**

GCSE	Entries	Males Awards	%	Entries	Females Awards	%
Biology	2959	1932	65.3	4980	2998	60.2
Chemistry	2788	1876	67.3	2657	1861	70.0
Computer Studies	2723	1569	57.6	2256	1428	63.3
English	10257	5150	50.2	11371	7222	63.5
French	3781	2069	54.7	5120	3233	63.1
History	2791	1376	49.3	2900	1839	63.4
Home Economics	308	112	36.4	4642	2725	58.7
Mathematics A & B	10948	6353	58.0	11334	6200	54.7
Physics	4374	2832	64.7	1982	1591	80.3
Technology	1286	707	55.0	163	101	62.0

GCE 'A' Level	Entries	Males Awards	%	Entries	Females Awards	%
Biology	632	540	85.4	827	701	84.8
Chemistry	1023	841	82.2	812	689	84.9
Computer Studies	389	302	77.6	183	144	78.7
English Literature	788	649	82.4	2102	1808	86.0
Mathematics	1043	834	80.0	556	462	83.1
Physics	1283	1003	78.2	454	384	84.6

Source: EOCNI, 1993

evidence that girls perform less well in this form of assessment (Bolger and Kellaghan, 1990; Meader and Dekker, 1992).

Research based on the results from public examinations in the Republic suggests that girls outperform boys in languages at both Intermediate and Leaving Certificate levels, whilst a higher percentage of boys than girls passed Intermediate and Leaving Certificate mathematics each year between 1975 and 1983, although the differential narrowed over the period (Carey, 1990). Recent evidence also suggests that gender differences in mathematical performance are continuing to decline (Lynch, Close and Oldham, 1992). In Northern

Ireland, at GCSE level, girls achieve better results than boys in almost all areas except biology and mathematics (Gallagher, 1988).

The better performance of girls in physics and technology, arguably the two most 'masculine' areas of the curriculum, provides an interesting twist to the pattern. While it is possible that girls' superior performance arises from the considerable degree of self-selection and high motivation amongst the limited number of female candidates, it is also possible that it is a function of improved pedagogical practices and changing educational attitudes. When success rates at GCE 'A' Level, the normal criteria for entry to higher education in the Northern Ireland system, are examined there is very little difference in the attainment of girls and boys. By this stage pupils are usually studying only those subjects which interest them and in which they think they are likely to do well, so the similarity in results is perhaps hardly surprising. The contrast is not in the level of success but in the numbers of boys and girls studying different subjects (Barry, 1992). Certainly, the fact that girls in the Republic of Ireland perform as well as boys in most science subjects in recent years (even though they outnumber boys in fields such as biology) suggests that educational attitudes and practices are changing (Department of Education, 1991, Table 24). When the scientific and technological education of girls is treated with the same seriousness as that of boys, and when it is given comparable resources, there is no reason why gender differences in performance should persist.

In further and higher education overall comparison of levels of attainment between the sexes is again difficult because of the continuing divergence in patterns of subject choice and type of qualification gained. But there is certainly no evidence that women's attainment is significantly lower than that of men.

One of the most interesting features in the debate about educational attainment is the absence of either serious analysis or concern about boys' inferior performance in the

language areas. One must ask the question, is this an indication of the superior status of science and mathematics-related
disciplines in our society or does it signify some type of bias
in educational thinking? Or perhaps it is a combination of
both? Certainly, it seems that when girls lack some skill which
boys possess they are deemed deprived, but when girls
succeed where boys fail a similar view is not taken. Maybe
there are shades here of the type of cultural deficit/cultural
deprivation thinking which constrained educational writing
about social class inequality in education for many years, with
differences in working-class attitudes and values interpreted
as deprivations and inadequacies. The same seems to be
happening with women at present. Languages and the arts
are defined as 'feminine', and the implication is that boys do
not have to aspire or achieve in these areas.

The ethos of schools

There is considerable evidence to suggest that the 'hidden
curriculum' has a powerful and differential impact on the
educational experience of girls and boys (Lynch, 1989b).
Research carried out in nursery and infant classrooms
suggests that even before children begin school their gender
identity is clearly established and moreover that schools tend
to reinforce differences from the outset (Whyte, 1983;
Morgan and Dunn, 1988).

Whilst nursery and infant teachers do not intentionally
differentiate between girls and boys there is evidence that they
do hold stereotypes about male and female characteristics and
that these affect their classroom management strategies and
their interaction patterns. Characteristics attributed to males
often appear to be valued more than those judged to be
female. In practical terms, young boys appear, on average, to
get more opportunities than girls to interact with the teacher
and also seem to get more access to some types of classroom
equipment and resources. This may more than compensate
for their slightly slower progress in areas of the formal

curriculum such as reading and language development (Morgan and Dunn, 1990; Dunn and Morgan, 1987).

Studies which have attempted to explain the difference in subject choice at second level have also highlighted the importance of the hidden curriculum and the ethos of schools (Rodgers and Mahon, 1987; McEwen *et al*, 1986; Agnew *et al*, 1989; Lynch, 1989a, 1989b). The attitudes of parents, teachers and members of the peer group appear to be very important in developing pupils' perceptions of 'appropriate' subject choices and career ambitions. Whilst teachers seem aware of the need to encourage pupils of both sexes to consider non-traditional choices, the home and the peer group appear to have a stronger influence and this frequently operates to reinforce stereotypes.

At a more specific level, many Northern Irish grammar schools have a strongly masculine ethos in areas such as sports. In the Protestant grammar schools for example, rugby is taken very seriously and even in co-educational schools the performance of the 'first XV' is regarded as an important measure of the school's standing. The progress of the girls' hockey team is not likely to be regarded as having anything like the same significance and girls themselves are well aware of the difference (Morgan, 1993). Similarly Lynch's work on the ethos of second level schools in the Republic revealed that boys' and girls' schools differ considerably in their 'social climates' (Lynch, 1989a, 1989b). While girls' schools did have strong academic climates, they also appeared to be emphasising the development of qualities such as 'caring, sincerity, gentleness and refinement'. Boys' schools, on the other hand, placed less emphasis on personal and social development and concentrated on progress and achievement either in the sporting or academic fields. In addition, the girls were subject to more strict controls on dress and behaviour than boys. The model which emerges of girls' schools continuing to seek to replicate 'traditional' Irish women is borne out by an analysis of school prospectuses. Those for girls' schools frequently state that they aim to develop self-discipline and

self-control, objectives which are absent from the equivalent
publications from boys' schools; by contrast, boys' schools
place a high priority on the development of physical prowess
and motor skills (Lynch 1989a, 1989b). Some quantitative
evidence for these differences can be found in data relating
to differences in the pattern of extra-curricular activities in
girls' and boys' schools (Table 8).

Table 8: **Differences between boys' and girls'* second-level
schools in extra-curricular provision in the arts and
in religious-related societies and activities
(Republic of Ireland)**

Type of Statistical Activity Significance	Name of Activity	Girls' Schools N = 21 %	Boys' Schools N = 20 %	
Religious-related	Temperance Society	76.2	40.0	P < .05
	Legion of Mary	28.4	5.0	–
	Vincent de Paul	19.0	25.0	–
	Charitable events	33.0	15.0	–
Arts	Debating/public speaking	100.0	75.0	P < .05
	Drama	85.7	40.0	P < .01
	Arts/crafts	71.4	25.0	P < .01
	Dancing	14.3	0.0	–
	Musical activities	100.0	55.0	P < .01
	School magazine	57.1	50.0	–
	Board games (esp. chess)	33.3	60.0	–
	Irish Club (cultural club)	23.8	10.0	–
	Photography	19.0	20.0	–

Note
* All the girls' schools and all but two of the boys' schools were
managed by Catholic authorities. Both girls' and boys' schools
were relatively similar in social class intake. The schools were part
of a stratified random sample (n = 90) of second-level schools.

Source: Lynch, 1989a

At the same time girls' schools also promote a strong achievement ethos with emphasis on high grades in public examinations. Indeed it seems that there is an underlying contradiction in the expectations being made of girls. Whilst boys are expected to see education as a basis for planning employment and career paths, girls, on the one hand, are expected to compete and succeed in academic terms but, on the other, to retain their role as unselfish and non-assertive bearers and transmitters of culture and tradition within the family and the community. For boys it is made clear that they will be expected to be in paid employment throughout most of their adult lives and that education is the preparation for this. Girls are also expected to use education in this instrumental fashion but in addition they receive strong messages about the other roles and responsibilities they will be expected to undertake as women (Lynch, 1989a, 1990; Morgan 1988, 1990). Whilst many of these messages are communicated outside school through parents, peers and the media, they also appear to affect, often subconsciously, the expectations and interactions of teachers and the patterns of activity within classrooms from nursery level right through the education system. Some of these messages clearly conflict but our education systems currently do little to examine the nature and implications of these conflicts for both women and men, or to support adolescent girls as they attempt to resolve their confusions.

The management of the education system and of schools

Professions related to education, welfare and health represent a major area of employment in both the Republic and Northern Ireland. Indeed, they are the third largest sector of female employment in Northern Ireland. For example, in 1988, 18.4 per cent of the female workforce were employed in these areas. Only clerical occupations (25.4 per cent) and personal services, including cleaning and catering (23.0 per cent) employ more women (EOCNI, 1989). In both

parts of Ireland women outnumber men in most areas of the
education system. In Northern Ireland 76 per cent of primary
school teachers and 49 per cent of secondary school teachers
are women, and during the academic year 1987-88 over 78
per cent of those training to be teachers in Northern Ireland
were women. In the Republic, 77 per cent of primary
teachers are women, while women comprise 55 per cent of
those on incremental scales in secondary schools. However,
men are in the majority in incremental posts in the community and comprehensive sector (54 per cent) and in
vocational schools (57 per cent) (Drudy and Lynch, 1993). As
in Northern Ireland, the great majority (over 80 per cent) of
those entering primary teaching are women. It is only in
further and higher education that men clearly predominate.
Research by the Higher Education Authority in Dublin
(1987) found that women comprised only 15 per cent of staff
in third-level colleges. In the universities only 3 per cent of
professorial posts were held by women, while only 7 per cent
of all senior lectureships were held by women. This contrast
provides a clue to the whole pattern of gender differentiation
in employment within the education sector.

Overall, it is true to say that 'women teach and men
manage' in schools. In Northern Ireland for example,
women form the bulk of the workforce in the primary sector,
yet the majority of women are on the main or basic salary
grades whilst a considerable proportion of the men are in
promoted positions and a clear majority of the principals are
men. In 1989, of 96 primary principals in the area covered by
the Belfast Education and Library Board, 59 were men. When
single-sex schools are discounted (since these all had a
principal of the 'appropriate' sex) the pattern is even more
pronounced. There were 68 co-educational primary schools
of which only 21 had a female principal. What remains clear
is that where women do become primary principals it is
usually in smaller schools, as the 1989 data for the North
Eastern Education and Library Board illustrates (Table 9).
Yet it is the small schools which are declining in number as

rural depopulation forces amalgamations and rationalisations throughout Ireland.

Table 9:   **Numbers of principals of co-educational primary schools in the North Eastern Board, 1989, by size of school**

Number of pupils	0-50	51-100	101-150	151-200	201+
Male principal	5	13	12	12	41
Female principal	14	7	2	0	2

In the Republic, 77 per cent of primary teachers are women but only 48 per cent of principalships are held by women at this level. While there is evidence that women are applying for and getting more principalships than men in recent years, they are still significantly under-represented at principalship level. Neither is it entirely clear whether women are getting principalships in large co-educational primary schools (Lynch, 1994).

At secondary level the picture is slightly complicated by the considerable number of single-sex schools and by the fact that many principalships in secondary girls' schools in the Republic are still held by nuns who did not compete for these posts in open competition: in fact 81 per cent of all female secondary principals are religious (Drudy and Lynch, 1993). In general, girls' schools have female principals and boys' schools male principals. But whilst there are a small but increasing number of girls' schools with male heads, there are virtually no boys' second level schools with female heads (only one at the time of writing, in the Republic). Amongst mixed sex schools, male principals predominate and it appears that women only become principals in exceptional cases. In the Republic, for example, only 9 per cent of principalships in community/comprehensive schools and 5 per cent of those in vocational schools are held by women (Lynch, 1994). While there are a number of women religious as heads of convent schools which have begun to take boys, there is also evidence that with the decline in the number of all-girls' schools and the move by some of the religious orders to relinquish direct control of their schools, the proportion of female principals in the secondary sector is declining. Between 1986 and 1991 (inclusive) 74 lay appointments were made in secondary schools, of which 61 (82 per cent) went to men. Twenty-four of the 26 principalships in co-educational secondary schools went to men, and six of the 16 principalships in girls' schools. Only one of the 32 principalships in boys' schools went to a woman (Lynch, 1994).

The changes in the management structure of the education systems and of individual schools may also have an impact on the position of women in the employment structure of education. As a distinct career path in school management begins to be identified, and the role of principal is seen more and more as requiring qualifications in administration and financial management, there is a danger that the separation of men and women may become even more pronounced. Women have traditionally expressed a preference for work in the classroom and with children, and it remains to be seen whether they will strive to compete in the management track and whether appointing panels will overcome traditional prejudices against women in management. Although there is considerable evidence from research on educational management that women are as good or better managers than men, there is also considerable prejudice against them (Shakeshaft, 1989). Part of the problem seems to be that a very hierarchical and patriarchal concept of educational management dominates thinking at present. The 'controlling chief-executive' concept of school principal has gained ground (see Green Paper, 1992) as the ideal role model although there is little evidence to show that such a management style is either desirable or effective in schools. In fact there is evidence to the contrary; contemporary management theory emphasises the importance of a consensual rather than an hierarchical approach to management, and collaborative rather than authoritarian responses to conflict resolution, both of which are styles women tend to adopt more than men (Fairholm and Fairholm, 1984; Pitner, 1981).

Currently there are very few women in the higher levels of educational administration in either the Republic or Northern Ireland; for example, none of the Northern Education and Library Boards has ever had a female chief officer. In the Republic, almost all the senior administrative posts in the Department of Education are held by men; in 1991, for example, the five assistant secretaries and the departmental secretary were male; and only 10 per cent of principal officers and 16 per cent of assistant principals were female. Within the inspectorate only 4 per cent of posts from senior inspector upwards were held by women (Drudy and Lynch, 1993).

Conclusion

In most societies the education system reflects social structures, and in Ireland the systems, both in the Republic and in Northern Ireland, mirror the essential conservatism of attitudes to gender equality and the role of women. Furthermore, gender equality has frequently aroused active opposition. It is often regarded with suspicion because of alleged links between feminism, socialism, materialism and even atheism (Morgan and Fraser, 1994). In Northern Ireland it is seen as a distraction from the issue of national identity which both communities believe must be successfully resolved before other social or economic problems can be tackled, whilst in the Republic the debates over divorce and abortion highlight the high levels of opposition to the changing role of women (Smyth, 1992).

Looking specifically at education, there has been the further problem that much of the most active concern has focused on other issues, the possible relationship between the segregated education system and community conflict, the links between education and employment and the roles of church and state in educational provision. Topics such as these have attracted the limited research and development funding available, to the neglect of many other areas, including gender equality.

The traditionally very conservative education systems in Ireland are bound to be deeply affected by social and economic forces operating at a European and even a global level over the next five or ten years, but many of the under-lying features may, as in the past, prove very resistant to fundamental change. Gender inequality is one such area; thus initiatives such as the new common curriculum and the educational recommendations of the Second Commission on the Status of Women may have only a limited impact on gender stereotyping and patriarchal structures. New patterns of educational management may even disadvantage the career prospects of women working in the education system. Formal equality may be increasingly written into legislation but the model of equality being used is a liberal passive rather than an egalitarian active one. Thus, its impact may be less than had been expected. Gender differentiation in education is often subtle and complex and yet paradoxically it may require more direct policy initiatives and interventions if it is to be tackled effectively. It also requires some imaginative and innovative thinking including research on issues which have not been addressed to date. One issue which has been subjected to neither policy analysis nor intervention is the type of male (often macho) culture which develops in all-male schools and which, at times, is the dominant culture in co-educational schools (Hanafin, 1992). While some atten-tion has been focused on how women learn to be sub-ordinate, insufficient attention has been given to the analysis of how boys learn to dominate and the ways in which schools perpetuate the culture of male domination.

Note

1. When talking of ability or 'able' pupils one needs to remember that tests such as the eleven plus assess a very narrow range of abilities. They measure principally linguistic and logical-mathematical skills. They do not measure all intellectual abilities and therefore one must not label pupils who do not succeed in such tests as lacking ability. See Gardner (1983) for a critique of traditional views of ability.

References

AGNEW, U., S. MALCOLM and A. McEWEN, 1989. *Gender and Careers Education*, Belfast, Equal Opportunities Commission for Northern Ireland.

BARRY, U., 1992. 'Females in Education: The Statistical Picture', paper presented at the British Psychological Society (Northern Ireland Branch) Conference, Girls and Women in Education, Stranmillis College, Belfast.

BLACKWELL, J., 1989. *Women and the Labour Force*, Dublin, Employment Equality Agency.

BOLGER, N. and T. KELLAGHAN, 1990. 'Method of measurement and gender differences in scholastic achievement', *Journal of Educational Measurement*, No. 27, pp. 165-174.

CAREY, M., 1990. 'Gender Differences in Attitudes and Achievement in Mathematics – A Study of First Year Students in Irish Post-Primary Schools'. Unpublished M.Ed.

thesis, School of Education, Trinity College, Dublin.

CLANCY, P., 1987. 'Does School Type Matter – the unresolved questions', *Sociological Association of Ireland Bulletin*, No. 45, April, pp. 12-14.

CLANCY, P., 1988. *Who Goes to College? A Second National Survey of Participation in Higher Education*, Dublin, The Higher Education Authority.

CLANCY, P., 1989. 'Gender Differences in Student Participation at Third Level'. In C. Hussey (ed.), *Equal Opportunities for Women in Higher Education*, Dublin, University College Dublin.

COLLINS, E., 1989. *Girls in Education. NICER Summary Series No. 8*, Belfast, Northern Ireland Council for Educational Research.

CURRY, C. A. and A. McEWEN, 1989. 'The "Wendy House" Syndrome: A teenage version', *Research in Education*, Vol. 41, pp. 53-60.

CURRY, C., 1993. 'Education and Training', in J. Kremer and P. Montgomery (eds.), *Women's Working Lives*, Belfast, HMSO and Equal Opportunities Commission for Northern Ireland.

DAVIES, C. and E. McLAUGHLIN (eds.), 1991. *Women, Employment and Social Policy in Northern Ireland: A Problem Postponed*, Belfast, Policy Research Institute.

DEPARTMENT OF EDUCATION, 1971. *Primary School Curriculum: Teacher's Handbook*, Dublin, Government Publications Office.

DEPARTMENT OF EDUCATION, 1974. *Statistical Report 1972/73*, Dublin, Government Publications Office.

DEPARTMENT OF EDUCATION, 1991. *Statistical Report 1989/90*, Dublin, Government Publications Office.

DEPARTMENT OF EDUCATION, 1992. *Statistical Report 1990/91*, Dublin, Government Publications Office.

DEPARTMENT OF EDUCATION FOR NORTHERN IRELAND, 1988. *The Way Forward*, Bangor, Department of Education for Northern Ireland.

DRUDY, S. and K. LYNCH, 1993. *Schools and Society in Ireland*, Dublin, Gill and Macmillan.

DUNN, S., 1986. 'The Role of Education in the Northern Ireland Conflict', *Oxford Review of Education*, Vol. 12, No. 2, pp. 233-242.

DUNN, S. and V. MORGAN, 1987. 'Nursery and Infant School Play Patterns: Sex-Related Differences', *British Educational Research Journal*, Vol. 3, No. 3.

DUNN, S. and V. MORGAN, 1991. 'The Social Context of Education in Northern Ireland', *European Journal of Education*, Vol. 26, No. 2, pp. 179-189.

EOCNI (Equal Opportunities Commission for Northern Ireland) (1993). *Where do Women Figure?*, Belfast, EOCNI.

FAIRHOLM, G. and B. C. FAIRHOLM, 1984. 'Sixteen power tactics principals can use to improve management effectiveness', *NASSP Bulletin*, Vol. 68, No. 472, pp. 68-75.

GALLAGHER, A. M., 1988. *Transfer Pupils at 16*, Belfast, Northern Ireland Council for Educational Research.

GALLAGHER, A. M., 1989. *The Majority-Minority Review, No. 1, Education and Religion in Northern Ireland*, Coleraine, Centre for the Study of Conflict, University of Ulster.

GARDNER, H., 1983. *Frames of Mind: The Theory of Multiple Intelligences*, London, Paladin.

HANAFIN, J., 1992. 'Co-education and attainment:

a study of the gender effects of mixed and single sex schooling on examination performance'. PhD thesis, University of Limerick.

HANNAN, D. *et al*, 1983. *Schooling and Sex Roles*, Dublin, Economic and Social Research Institute.

HIGHER EDUCATION AUTHORITY, 1987. *Women Academics in Ireland*, Dublin, HEA.

INTERNATIONAL ASSOCIATION OF EDUCATIONAL PROGRESS, 1989. *Learning Mathematics*, New Jersey, Educational Testing Service.

INTERNATIONAL ASSOCIATION OF EDUCATIONAL PROGRESS, 1991. *Learning Science*, New Jersey, Educational Testing Service.

INTERNATIONAL ASSOCIATION OF EDUCATIONAL PROGRESS, 1992. *A World of Differences: An International Assessment of Mathematics and Science*, New Jersey, Educational Testing Service.

JOHNSON, J. and E. ROONEY, 1987. 'Gender Differences in Education' in R. D. Osborne, R. J. Cormack and R. L. Miller (eds.), *Education and Policy in Northern Ireland*, Belfast, Policy Research Institute.

KELLY, A., 1985. 'The construction of masculine science', *British Journal of Sociology of Education*, Vol. 6, No. 2, pp. 133-154.

LYNCH, K., 1989a. 'The Ethos of Girls' Schools: An Analysis of Differences between Male and Female Schools', *Social Studies*, Vol. 10, Nos. 1/2, pp. 11-31.

LYNCH, K., 1989b. *The Hidden Curriculum: Reproduction in Education, A Reappraisal*, Lewes, Falmer Press.

LYNCH, K., 1991. 'Girls and Young Women in Education: Ireland', in M. Wilson (ed.), *Girls and Young Women in Education: A European Perspective*, London, Pergamon.

LYNCH, K., 1994. 'Women teach and men manage: why men dominate senior posts in Irish education', in *Women for Leadership in Education: Conference of Religious in Ireland*, Dublin, Milltown Park.

LYNCH, K., S. CLOSE and E. OLDHAM, 1992. 'Gender differences in mathematics in the Republic of Ireland'. Paper presented at the European Colloquium on Differential Performances in Assessment of Mathematics, University of Birmingham, 15-18 May.

McEWEN, A., C. A. CURRY and J. WATSON, 1986. 'Subject preference at A-Level in Northern Ireland', *European Journal of Science Education*, Vol. 8, No. 1, pp. 39-50.

McEWEN, A. and C. CURRY, 1987. 'Access to Science. single-sex versus co-educational schools', in R. D. Osborne, R. J. Cormack and R. L. Miller (eds.), *Education and Policy in Northern Ireland*, Belfast, Policy Research Institute.

McKENNA, A., 1988. *Child Care and Equal Opportunities*, Dublin, Employment Equality Agency.

MAHON, E., 1991. *Motherhood, Work and Equal Opportunity*, Dublin, First Report of the Third Joint Oireachtais Committee on Women's Rights.

MEADER, M. and T. DEKKER, 1992. 'Differential Performance in Assessment of Mathematics at the end of Compulsory Schooling: The Netherlands'. Paper presented at European Colloquium on Differential Performance in Assessment of Mathematics at the End of Compulsory Schooling, University of Birmingham, 15-18 May.

MONTGOMERY, P., 1991. 'Gender and Opportunity in Youth Training', in C. Davies and E. McLaughlin (eds.), *Women, Employment and Social Policy in Northern Ireland: A Problem Postponed*, Belfast, Policy Research Institute.

MONTGOMERY, P., 1993. 'Paid and Unpaid Work', in J. Kremer and P. Montgomery (eds.), *Women's Working Lives*, Belfast, HMSO and Equal Opportunities Commission for Northern Ireland.

MONTGOMERY, P. and C. DAVIES, 1990. *Sex Equality in the Youth Training Programme*, Belfast, Equal Opportunities Commission for Northern Ireland.

MORGAN, V., 1991. *Common Curriculum – Equal Curriculum: Girls and Boys and the Northern Ireland Common Curriculum: Mathematics, Science and English*, Belfast, Equal Opportunities Commission for Northern Ireland.

MORGAN, V., 1993. 'Gender and the Common Curriculum', in R. Osborne, R. Cormack and A. Gallagher (eds.), *After the Reforms: Education and Policy in Northern Ireland*, Aldershot, Avebury.

MORGAN, V. and S. DUNN, 1988. 'Chameleons in the Classroom: Visible and Invisible Children in Nursery and Infant Classrooms', *Educational Review*, Vol. 40, No. 1, pp. 2-12.

MORGAN, V. and S. DUNN, 1990. 'Management Strategies and Gender Differences in Nursery and Infant Classrooms', *Research in Education*, Vol. 8, No. 2, pp. 23-28.

MORGAN, V. and G. FRASER, 1994. 'Women and the Northern Ireland Conflict', in S. Dunn (ed.), *Facets of the Conflict in Northern Ireland*, London, Macmillan.

NATIONAL COUNCIL FOR CURRICULUM AND

562   Irish Society: Sociological Perspectives

ASSESSMENT, 1992. *The 1991 Leaving Certificate Examination: A Review of Results*, Dublin, NCCA.

OLDHAM, E., 1991. 'Second Level Mathematics Curricula: The Republic of Ireland in International Perspective', *Irish Educational Studies*, Vol. 10, No. 1, Spring, pp. 122-139.

OSBORNE, R. D., R. L. MILLER, R. J. CORMACK and A. P. WILLIAMSON, 1988. 'Trends in Higher Education Participation in Northern Ireland', *Economic and Social Review*, Vol. 19, No. 4, pp. 283-301.

OSBORNE, R. D., 1992. 'Higher Education in Northern Ireland: Participation, the Graduate Labour Market and Community Equity', Research Paper No. 5, Coleraine, University of Ulster, Centre for Policy Research.

PITNER, M. J., 1981. 'Hormones and harems: are the activities of superintending different for a woman?', in R. A. Schmuck *et al* (eds.), *Educational Policy and Management*, New York, Academic Press.

RODGERS, M. and

M. MAHON, 1987. *Opting In: Girls' Choice of 'A' Level Mathematics – A Case Study*, Coleraine, University of Ulster.

SHAKESHAFT, C., 1989. *Women in Educational Administration*, London, Sage.

SMYTH, A., 1984. *Breaking the Circle: The Position of Women Academics in Third-Level Education*, Dublin, EC Action Programme on the Promotion of Equal Opportunities for Women.

SMYTH, A. (ed.), 1992. *The Abortion Papers*, Dublin, Attic Press.

TREWSDALE, J. and A. TOMAN, 1993. 'Employment' in J. Kremer and P. Montgomery (eds.), *Women's Working Lives*, Belfast, HMSO and Equal Opportunities Commission for Northern Ireland.

WHYLD, J. (ed.), 1983. *Sexism in the Secondary Curriculum*, London, Harper and Row.

WHYTE, J., 1983. *Beyond the Wendy House: sex role stereotyping in primary schools*, London, Longman.

WILSON, M. (ed.), 1991. *Girls and Young Women in Education: A European Perspective*, London, Pergamon.

18
Broadcasting in Ireland: Issues of National Identity and Censorship

MARY KELLY and BILL ROLSTON

Two of the central questions asked by sociologists about the relationship between the media and society are: to what extent does it contribute to maintaining order in that society, and in whose interest is order being maintained? These questions can be examined either in terms of the extent to which the media is directed and controlled as it were 'from above' in the interest of maintaining social order – for example, through state censorship – or by observing how the media seeks to represent the existing socio–cultural worlds which exist within that society. In this latter way the media may contribute to maintaining order by articulating a sense of social and cultural identity and solidarity. Both of these questions will be raised in this chapter, the first section of which examines how the Irish broadcasting system has sought to represent national cultural identities, the second examining censorship practices.

National identity

Sociologists analyse the role of the media in representing a sense of national identity at two main socio–structural levels. The first is at the level of the state, the second at the level of the diverse range of social groups – including, for example those based on religious, class, or gender differences – which constitute that society. At each of these levels central questions regarding culture and national identity can be asked. At the level of the state, the question is: to what extent do the media contribute to elaborating a sense of national identity which contributes to maintaining the legitimacy of that state and consensus within it? At the level of social groups, the question is: in what way does the media's elaboration of a sense of national identity mesh with the cultural diversity of these groups? Do all social groups share the media's definition of national identity, and if not, whose definition is it elaborating?

Examining and comparing broadcasting in Northern Ireland and in the Irish Republic enables us to ask these questions, and in particular to ask questions regarding the extent to which a broadcasting system can contribute to constructing a sense of national identity in a society characterised by deep divisions. Or is its role more limited, confined to confirming an existing consensus if such exists? Before beginning to examine these questions it is important to differentiate between two elements within the concept of national identity – cultural identity and political identity. These may become fused when the culturally defined 'national' and the politically defined 'state' become one, as for many of those living in the Irish Republic. In Northern Ireland however, Catholic nationalists, drawing on a sense of cultural and political nationalism which transcends the boundaries of the Northern Ireland state itself, use this to question their membership of that state. Protestant unionists and loyalists, while politically committed to Ulster and to continued citizenship of the United Kingdom, often display a varying sense of national identity, which includes being British, Ulster and Irish (Whyte, 1990, p. 67 *seq*).

The early days of Radio Éireann
From the beginning, the Irish Free State prescribed a cultural and political role for its broadcasting service. When Radio

Éireann was established in 1926 its remit was to contribute to the project of building the Irish state and nation. Radio Éireann was placed under the direct responsibility of the Minister for Posts and Telegraphs. For him the progress of the nation and of the state should be synonymous, as he noted to the Dáil Committee investigating the establishment of radio in Ireland: 'We claim that this nation has set out on a separate existence. That existence not only covers its political life, but also its social and cultural life' (quoted in Gorham, 1967, p. 12). Irish radio should contribute to developing the country 'as an independent, self–thinking, self–supporting nation'; its separate identity would be confirmed by having broadcasts in the Irish language, and its educational programmes would contribute to agricultural, industrial and commercial development (Gorham, 1967, pp. 12–15).

The overlapping worlds of cultural and political nationalism, which had been gaining legitimacy since the 1890s, provided the cultural sphere from which both the programmes and staff of Radio Éireann were immediately drawn. Despite inadequate funding, the staff tapped readily and enthusiastically into this cultural world – its language, literature, music and drama – to fill its limited broadcasting transmission time.

A further cultural source of national identity was the Catholic Church. The audience for radio in Ireland was initially miniscule, confined mainly to Dublin and Cork. Contributing to the creation of a national radio audience was Radio Éireann's extensive and ambitious coverage of the Eucharistic Congress of 1932. In 1948, regular Sunday Mass broadcasts began. Services from Protestant denominations were also broadcast but irregularly. In 1960 at the suggestion of the Catholic archbishop of Dublin, Radio Éireann began broadcasting the Angelus at 6 o'clock.

BBC Radio: Northern Ireland
In contrast to the 'national' nature of Radio Éireann, BBC Northern Ireland was a regional station, adding a minority of

regionally based programmes to those nationally networked
and coming mainly from London. Its first director described
its role as not only requiring the transmission of regionally
derived programmes of 'Irish music, Irish drama and Irish
life', but as being:

> An Ulster Broadcasting Station, situated in Belfast,
> (radiating) to its listeners most of the important London
> programmes, and on occasions programmes ... from
> Scotland, Wales and the North of England. Thus the
> broadcasting service reflects the sentiments of the
> people, who have thus retained a lively sympathy with,
> and an unswerving loyalty to, British ideals and British
> culture. The chimes of Big Ben are heard in County
> Tyrone as they are in the County of Middlesex, and the
> news of the day emanating from the London Studio is
> received simultaneously in Balham as Ballymacaratt
> (quoted in Cathcart, 1984, p. 39).

London, Big Ben and the BBC lay at the metropolitan centre.
Until 1966, regional directors were appointed from outside
Northern Ireland, being either English or Scottish, and
having had experience of the BBC on 'the mainland'.
Indeed, almost all the programme staff and announcers
came from outside the region until after the Second World
War. Early regional directors identified closely with the
unionist government – although with its more liberal wing
rather than with its more populist and loyalist party political
element (Todd, 1987), and were easily incorporated into the
Unionist establishment (Cathcart, 1984, p. 36 *seq*).

   Northern Ireland regional directors had no readily acceptable and consensual cultural sphere on which to draw for
programming material – unlike Radio Éireann in the South.
The complex and conflictual sources of national, cultural,
political and religious identity in the North, and the mode in
which each of these was inflected in popular culture, made
the development of a regional broadcasting policy which
would be acceptable to a majority and across the political

divide extremely difficult. The primary political and religious fissure between Protestant-unionism and Catholic-nationalism was expressed and reproduced at almost all institutional and cultural levels – that of kinship, education and the economy, as well as in different recreational and cultural practices (Harris, 1972). Furthermore there were tensions and divisions within the two communities; these related particularly to class and, especially among the Protestant majority, divisions due to the lack of a clear sense of whether they were 'British', 'Ulster' or 'Irish'.

Within this socio-cultural context, BBC Northern Ireland failed to find a consensually based cultural sphere. An example lies in the difficulties it faced in finding acceptable programming for St Patrick's Day. The regional director in 1939 noted the 'extreme difficulty' in this regard, 'owing to controversies which are apt to start around the figure of the saint himself, or the songs or other matter chosen for the occasion' (Cathcart, 1984, p. 92). Even St Patrick's Day programmes taken from London or elsewhere frequently proved an affront to unionists, due, for example, to their playing of the Irish national anthem. After one such occasion, the regional director complained to BBC London that this was essentially a 'rebel' song and that playing it 'raises the acutest indignation in the six counties of Northern Ireland, where the Irish have remained loyal. Naturally, there has been an outcry in the press and the most violent protests' (Cathcart, 1984, p. 91). In the South no similar difficulties arose; here the day was celebrated on radio with, inter alia, a special broadcast by the Taoiseach, two Gaelic games from Croke Park – one commented upon in English the other in Irish – and programmes of popular Irish music.

In response to the political and cultural divisions in Northern Ireland, the BBC aligned itself, at least until the 1950s, with the unionist government. In its news and talks programmes, discussions on the most basic political division in Northern Ireland and its constitutional position were simply placed outside its agenda. Also avoided was any discussion of discrimination or news from the South. In the 1950s, the BBC began, very cautiously, to edge towards more open discussion and attempted to enlarge a presumed area of consensus by including some Catholic nationalists in talks' programmes on local and community issues. But these nationalists were of the distinctly 'safe' variety. They could be relied upon not to confuse 'local, social, economic and industrial issues with constitutional red herrings', as the Regional Director noted approvingly (Cathcart, 1984, p. 162).

Cultural contrasts: sports and music
The precise boundary between what was acceptable and unacceptable was often defined not by BBC Northern Ireland itself but by the unionist government responding to popular Protestant criticism of the BBC. Thus, for example, when the BBC decided in 1934 to include the results of GAA games in its Sunday evening news bulletin, the Protestant reaction was immediate and ferocious, not only on the basis of strong Sabbatarian commitments but because, as one complainant to the press stated, 'We do not want to hear of exploits in the realm of a sport which holds no interest for most of us – loyal citizens of a mighty empire to whom the Gaelic mind, speech and pastimes mean nothing' (Cathcart, 1984, p. 67). Lord Craigavon, the Northern Ireland prime minister, intervened with the BBC. The outcome was that the broadcasting of Gaelic sports results on Sundays was excluded. (In 1946 it was decided, after the BBC had discussed the matter with a Protestant clergyman, to include them again – but only in the Monday news broadcast.)

This may be contrasted with the symbiotic relationship between Radio Éireann and the GAA in the South, where both contributed to establishing and securing for Gaelic games a national role. No less than Radio Éireann's coverage of the Eucharistic Congress, the coverage of All-Ireland finals created an audience for radio on the one hand and a national audience for Gaelic games on the other. In its first year of operation Radio Éireann reported live on the

All-Ireland hurling final, one of the first radio stations in Europe to initiate live sports coverage. Coverage of All-Ireland finals was to become a major national and populist broadcasting ritual for radio and later for television, and its presenter was to become a national figure. It emphasised the linkages between the state (represented by the attendance of the President and Taoiseach), the Catholic Church (represented by leading members of the hierarchy) and the heroism of the ordinary Irish people (represented by the contending county teams, the band playing before the match, the singing of the national anthem and the great cheer of the spectators). Given the scarcity of receivers, listeners gathered in the few wireless households and small town centres to hear the match. Thus, together, Radio Éireann and the GAA built and fostered popular, if predominantly masculinist, cultural identities and loyalties, linking households, local parish, county, state and nation (Boyle, 1992).

A second area of Radio Éireann's programming which linked popular culture and national identity was traditional Irish music. Here again, as with Gaelic games, Radio Éireann contributed to its development and change, and indeed even to the creation of some of its forms (Gibbons, 1988, p. 224). Céilí dance music on radio was found to be highly popular in both urban and rural areas by audience research undertaken in the early 1950s (Fitzgerald, n.d.). In the longer term, Radio Éireann's efforts in researching and broadcasting traditional music was to foster a revival of interest and to create an audience for it, both on radio and elsewhere. Irish language programmes were provided from the outset, as were lessons in the Irish language, if only for small audiences. Nevertheless, Irish language groups continued a highly vocal campaign for more.

The limited amount of Irish traditional music broadcast by BBC Northern Ireland was non-contentious. However, a request by the Gaelic League, in 1936, that a comparable amount of time be given to Irish speakers as to Gaelic speakers on BBC Scotland, and particularly to initiate lessons in Irish, was refused, as it was in the 1950s and again in the 1960s (Cathcart, 1984, pp. 85, 249). It was not until 1981 that a regular Irish language programme was introduced on BBC.

Another area of programming which caused conflict for the BBC, though on different grounds, was the early emphasis placed on orchestral music and the very limited airplay given to local pipe bands. This was part of a larger conflict between middle class 'highbrow' interests and those of the working class, small farmers or 'lowbrows'. The highbrows favoured orchestral music, cosmopolitan plays and announcers with South of England accents, while expressing a distaste for local accents, rural life portrayed in local drama, and some local humour (Cathcart, 1984, pp. 46, 182 *seq*). Lowbrows frequently saw highbrows as too oriented to London and to metropolitan culture, and criticised them for being too elitist and imperial, and lacking in knowledge of, or interest in, Ulster Protestant working class popular culture.

These attitudes were seen to underlie the small amount of airtime given to local pipe and flute bands. In 1937, conflict between the Bands' Association and the BBC was considered sufficiently serious for the Northern Ireland prime minister to intervene and gain concessions on behalf of the bands. There was also criticism from unionists and loyalists of the lack of coverage of the Twelfth of July celebrations. The BBC refused coverage on the basis that this was a party political event, drawing criticism of the 'overlordship of imperial authorities ... The time has come for Ulster People to assert themselves to maintain their just rights and privileges' (Cathcart, 1984, p. 86).

In the South there was less perceptible class-based criticism of Radio Éireann programmes. The united phalanx of nation, state and church, reproduced on radio, did not encourage the development of alternative cultural practices or of a class-based cultural critique. On the contrary, the all encompassing concept of nation functioned to hide class differences, as well as those based on gender. Undoubtedly Radio Éireann programmes reflected upper middle class interests and biases more than those of the working class – for example the very expensive development and maintenance of its symphony orchestra, despite little evidence of its widespread popularity, and its emphasis on talks programmes. In the late 1930s when the first audience research was carried out, these two types of programmes were found to be the least popular. The most popular included any form of competitions, including the general knowledge programme 'Question Time', news and gramophone records (Gorham, 1967, p. 116).

A factor which contributed to Radio Éireann's need to foster as large an audience as possible and hence to provide more popular programmes was its dependence on advertising as well as licence fees. Advertising based on 'sponsored programmes' was offered, usually in quarter hour slots, at midday. These frequently included forms of popular music not offered elsewhere on Radio Éireann. This led to criticism of the 'jazz and crooning' on these programmes, their 'low quality' and their 'unnational' content (Gorham, 1967, p. 66). It was also on a sponsored programme that the first Irish radio soap opera, 'The Kennedys of Castleross', was developed in 1955. Despite criticism, sponsored programmes were found to be highly popular in the 1950s, indeed far more popular than evening programmes (Fitzgerald, n.d., p. 229).

Listeners who were dissatisfied with Radio Éireann could switch to foreign stations. In the 1950s, listeners frequently did so: each listener, on average, listened to two stations in the day – 85 per cent to Radio Éireann, 53 per cent to Radio Luxembourg, and 49 per cent to BBC Light Programme. Listening to foreign stations was particularly popular between 7 pm and 10 pm; of the 60 per cent of radio sets turned on during this time, somewhat less than 10 per cent were turned to Radio Éireann (Fitzgerald, n.d., p. 43).

The introduction of television in Northern Ireland and its response to violence
A major change in the late 1950s and 1960s was the introduction of television. BBC Television began to be received in

the North in 1953. However, it was not until 1959 when UTV, the locally based commercial station, came on air and offered serious competition, that both stations began to tap into local interests for weekly programme material. Ulster Television was owned predominantly by unionist press and entertainment-based interests and identified with the modernising and 'bridge-building' unionist rhetoric of the time (Butler, 1991, p. 107). It contributed to reinforcing the prevailing attempt by the BBC to foster consensus and to broaden the middle ground by opening up 'safe' debate between those at the centre of both communities. Thus by the mid–1960s the issue of discrimination was slowly beginning to receive a very tentative airing, although any analysis of its political and sectarian nature was still ignored. Furthermore those considered to be at the extremes, for example Paisley, tended to be excluded (Cathcart, 1984, p. 196 *seq* and Butler, 1991, p. 107 *seq*).

However, while the broadcast media in Northern Ireland attempted to represent itself as progressive and consensus oriented, the view of film crews from outside could differ. Vigorous unionist criticism of nationally networked programmes on the BBC about Northern Ireland, but made by outsiders, led to the cancellation of further programmes. Also, UTV prevented a 'This Week' film about virulent Protestants being shown locally. Thus Northern viewers were protected from seeing how others saw them, as were those in Britain from knowing what was going on in Northern Ireland. The extent to which censorship since the 1970s has continued to contribute to these patterns of ignorance is the subject of analysis in the second part of this chapter.

The limits to the policy of fostering a middle ground were indicated by the outbreak of violent conflict in 1969. Many would argue that it is not within the power of the media to foster such a consensually oriented middle ground, lacking as it did real institutional support from either the state, whether in Westminster or in Stormont, or from the majority Protestant community.

In response to the violence both the BBC and UTV developed a policy of what has been called, perhaps not always quite accurately, 'balanced sectarianism' (Butler, 1991, p. 112). This emphasised impartiality in coverage of both sides, yet also avoidance of what were seen as the violent extremes, especially any coverage that might be seen to legitimate the 'men of violence'.

As the violence continued, the two communities, especially in urban working class areas and in rural border communities, were increasingly polarised. Identification with one's own community and one's own territory became central and exclusive, imagined outwards to an idealised united Ireland by one group, or to a loyal Ulster by the other. In this situation the reporting on both communities from an 'objective', 'reasonable' and 'responsible' middle ground could not hope to please either, or indeed those in the middle. Thus, for example, the extent of the daily reporting of the hunger strikes of 1980 and 1981 was bitterly criticised by unionists, while the uncritical and frequent reporting of the activities of the Ulster Workers' Council which overthrew the legitimate power-sharing government in 1974, was thought to have aided this local *coup d'état* (Miller, 1993). Furthermore, the aligning of the broadcast media with the security forces' definition of events and their lack of criticism of some army and police activities, especially when people had direct knowledge of such activities, has undermined confidence in reporting (Butler, 1991, p. 118).

The broadcast media do not represent political violence in as balanced a manner as the characterisation 'balanced sectarianism' might suggest: Protestant violence has over the years been consistently under-reported and the repre-sentation of the actions of the security forces as 'violent', and hence open to question, has been consistently avoided. Violence, and in particular that of the IRA, has tended to be represented as an irrational evil against which the forces of good – the 'ordinary people', often represented by the victims of violence, representatives of church and state, and the security forces – must mobilise (Curtis, 1984). This is especially so on national rather than local news programmes. Casting violence in demonological terms means that it does not have to be examined, particularly in relation to its roots in the political, economic and social structure of the society.

Telefís Éireann comes on air and fights for audience share
An analysis of the development of programming policies in Radio Telefís Éireann (RTÉ) over the past thirty years indicates how far apart North and South have become. While the North's broadcasters ponder the fundamental question of the responsibilities of a broadcasting organisation in a society characterised by dissensus and violence, in the South, broadcasters, especially in the last fifteen years, have been more concerned with how to keep their viewers on all fronts. The national question – when it is discussed at all – tends to focus on cultural and arts issues rather than political ones. Events in Northern Ireland are reported in the news, but seldom examined in any depth.

In the 1960s the newly inaugurated RTÉ still carried its 'national' tasks up front, reinforced by the celebration of the fiftieth anniversary of the 1916 Rising in 1966. However, censorship between the early 1970s and 1993 effectively removed one of the central representatives of this tradition, the IRA and Sinn Féin, from Southern screens. This censorship also substantially inhibited investigation of the Northern conflict and encouraged marginalisation of, and indeed embarrassment with, this particular nationalist tradition.

Of greater importance to the Southern media than the national question – particularly in its more exclusivist and political guise – are economic questions and the liberalisation of family law. The media discussion of economic development, unemployment and Irish membership of the EU and ERM relies on a less exclusivist definition of national identity: the assumption is that economic survival requires more than national navel gazing, and a clearer strategy regarding Ireland's place in the EU and in the wider global system

Furthermore, 'liberal' issues such as contraception, divorce and abortion have forced a wedge into the earlier monolithic linkage of church and state. On radio, no one particular channel can claim a nation-wide audience. Audiences have become fragmented in at least five ways, the first three of which are reinforced by the interests of advertisers. Housewives and those at home during the day form one group, with RTÉ Radio 1 serving this daytime audience. Young adults between the ages of fifteen and thirty-five constitute a second audience segment and are catered for by 2FM. Both of these audiences however are also competed for by local commercial radio which gets roughly a third of the radio audience (Fahy, 1992, p. 4). RTÉ's FM3, which concentrates on classical music, and Radio 1 in the evenings serve a mainly middle class audience. The final audience segment is that of Irish language speakers served by Raidió na Gaeltachta. Speaking the Irish language is no longer idealised as being at the core of Irish identity; gaeilgeoirí are seen as a group with special minority rights, and as constituting a specialist listenership group. The differentiation of radio services to meet varying audience demands has been highly successful in terms of what has sometimes been called the 'repatriation' of the Irish audience: very few now listen to foreign radio stations, even if the content of programmes – especially music programmes – is often non-Irish.

The economics of television are such that RTÉ cannot afford to be so specialised in the number of channels and programme services it offers. Furthermore, RTÉ television competes with the far richer British channels in two-thirds of all homes with television. In this context RTÉ television has come increasingly to identify 'the family audience' as its core target audience on RTÉ1. At peak viewing time the increased number of home-produced magazine programmes, chat shows, competitions and soaps is evidence of this. Network 2 offers children's programmes, sports and a greater number of imported programmes (on RTÉ television as a whole, 50 per cent of programmes are imported). In multichannel homes, RTÉ holds just under 50 per cent of the audience in peak viewing hours, with this percentage declining further when satellite channels are available (Fahy, 1992, p. 5). Despite the overall pattern of a fragmented national audience due to the attractions of foreign channels and of some foreign programmes on RTÉ, certain programmes still generate national audiences and provide a source of shared interests, integration and celebration across generations, classes and regions. These programmes include the news, chat shows, soaps, competitions and international sports when Ireland is competing.

Consensus and national identity
It has been argued above that broadcasting in the South has both drawn upon and contributed to elaborating and confirming an existing sense of national identity, as well as responding to certain changing definitions of that identity. It has hence contributed to maintaining solidarity and integration – if perhaps within relatively narrow confines. These confines are defined by class, gender and élite interests within Irish society, and by the existing consensus which favours these groups. Broadcasting, especially if commercially dependent on advertising and thus on drawing as large an audience as possible, is not encouraged to expand beyond the boundaries of the existing consensus for fear of alienating and losing its audience.

Broadcasters in Northern Ireland have had no one existing source of cohesion and national identity on which to draw, and perhaps it is not within the power of broadcasters, of themselves, to generate such a consensus when major and powerful groups within society do not support it. The following section will examine the precise role of the state, in particular through its censorship practices, in enforcing limits and controls on broadcasters in an attempt to maintain order and build consensus in Britain, Northern Ireland and the Republic.

Censorship

Writing of BBC coverage of the Northern Ireland conflict, Schlesinger (1978, p. 243) draws the following conclusion:

> Ministerial intervention has been elusive, and there was nothing in the BBC's approach to editorial control which approximated to the popular imagery of classic totalitarian censorship, with its directives and specially planted supervisory personnel.

However, it would be wrong to take Schlesinger's point out of context and to conclude that the term 'censorship' can only be used when this classic totalitarian form of censorship exists. There are more subtle and often more efficient forms of censorship in democratic societies, as the case of broadcasting in Britain and Ireland shows.

Legal restraints on broadcasting

The states in Ireland and Britain have enough legal instruments at their disposal to ensure that something approximating classic totalitarian censorship of broadcasting could exist.[1] To begin with, there is direct legal regulation of broadcasting. In the UK the BBC is governed by its Licence and Agreement and commercial television and radio by the Broadcasting Act 1981. In the Republic of Ireland the equivalent acts are the Broadcasting Act 1960, amended 1976, which governs RTÉ, and the Wireless and Telegraphy Act and the Radio and Television Act, both 1988, in relation to commercial broadcasting. All these acts allow the relevant government ministers to forbid the broadcasting of certain items. In the UK between 1988 and 1994 the reporting of the direct speech of spokespersons from specified republican and loyalist organisations, in particular Sinn Féin, or words soliciting support for them, were banned. And in the South of Ireland between 1971 and 1994, Section 31 of the Broadcasting Act allowed the banning of interviews or reports of interviews with spokespersons of a number of organisations, in particular, Sinn Féin.

There is, in addition, legislation not directly designed to control broadcasters but which can affect them. The British Official Secrets Act 1911 (updated most recently in 1989) and its Irish equivalent dating from 1963, in effect make it a crime for a journalist or broadcaster to possess any piece of government information deemed classified. Broadcasters in the UK are constrained by the Contempt of Court Act 1981 and those in the South of Ireland by the Defamation Act 1961 and by the force of common law. Documents and film can be seized in Britain under the Police and Criminal Evidence Act 1984 and in Northern Ireland under the Northern Ireland Criminal Law Act 1967.

Finally, there is emergency legislation in relation to the conflict in Northern Ireland which requires all citizens, including broadcasters, to refrain from collecting or publishing subversive information or to pass on any such information to the police. In the UK overall there is the Prevention of Terrorism (Temporary Provisions) Act 1989 (PTA). In the North there is also the Emergency Provisions (NI) Act 1978. And in the South there is the Offences Against the State Act 1939.

A number of the laws cited above have been used to control publication or broadcasting in the UK. In May 1971 BBC broadcaster Bernard Falk was jailed in Belfast for four days under contempt of court legislation for refusing to identify a defendant as an IRA spokesperson he had previously interviewed. The Official Secrets Act was used against journalist Duncan Campbell and others in 1979 in relation to the disclosure of defence information. Emergency legislation, particularly the PTA, has been used to detain photographers in the North. And the PTA was successfully used to bring Channel 4 to court in 1992 over a programme alleging collusion between the police and loyalist paramilitaries.

Similarly, in the South, Section 31 allowed for the dismissal of the entire RTÉ Authority in 1972 over the reporting of an interview with IRA chief of staff Seán Mac Stiofáin. RTÉ journalist Jenny McGeever was sacked in 1988 for using some words spoken by Sinn Féin's Martin McGuinness during a broadcast. And in 1972 RTÉ reportér Kevin O'Kelly was sentenced to three months in prison for refusing to identify the voice on a taped interview he had conducted as that of Seán Mac Stiofáin.

Despite these examples, it is evident that the amount of direct state control of broadcasters has been relatively slight. Only one broadcaster in the North and one in the South have been jailed in more than two decades of coverage of the Northern troubles. Only two broadcasters in the South have been sacked and none in the North. Broadcasting law does not operate through the the continuous axing of completed programmes or the involvement of state-imposed officials in daily decision-making in the broadcasting organisations. This is not the stuff of classic totalitarian censorship. Yet, to conclude the story at this point would be a grave mistake. The laws work at a number of levels to control broadcasters and journalists.

First, the laws provide a constant backdrop, influencing, consciously or otherwise, decision-making and distorting professional practice. Their potential use is often threat enough. Second, even though their actual use has been infrequent, there have been some spectacular outcomes. There are frequently differences between broadcasters and governments on a whole range of issues, but as Purcell (1991, p. 55) puts it in relation to RTÉ:

> '... in the atmosphere of daily controversy ... managers learn that most conflicts blow over. Only on the sensitive subject of NI have heads rolled. And they were the most important heads in the organisation, those of the RTÉ Authority itself.

Meehan (1991) confirms this:

> No other law or internal regulation within RTÉ has functioned as a so-called 'sacking offence' – not even the

stealing of records for use by the then illegal pirate radio stations or the breach of the rule on membership of political parties.

Such cases act as exemplars and become part of the folk memory in the broadcasting organisations. It only takes one such case every decade or so to convince everyone to be cautious. Finally, the main control of broadcasters is through directives which are relatively imprecise in both content and threatened sanctions. The broadcasting bans in both societies operate not by involving the state directly in the day-to-day running of organisations. Rather they issue a blanket warning and leave both the implementation and the policing to the organisations themselves. For example, the directive under Section 31 issued in 1971 was imprecise. The RTÉ Authority asked for further clarification and did not get it. It is only when they carried a report of an interview, not the interview itself, with an IRA spokesperson, that the state announced that they had overstepped the invisible threshold. The message was: we'll not tell you what the limits are, but we'll let you know forcefully if and when you transgress them.

Similarly, as regards the British ban, the Home Office quickly made clear that it was up to the broadcasting organisations 'to decide whether the context in which elected Sinn Féin councillors speak on non-violent issues breached the ban' (cited in *Belfast Telegraph*, 3-11-1988). And Secretary of State Peter Brooke made the same point concisely in a reply to a complaint from Official Unionist MP Ken Maginnis: 'The interpretation of the notices [i.e. the ban] is a matter for the broadcasting authorities themselves' (cited in *Irish News* 8-12-1992).

The organisation Article 19 (1989, p. 25) refers to the type of censorship imposed by Section 31 and the British broadcasting ban as 'prior restraint' censorship; it threatens action if the ban is broken rather than responding to specific broadcasts. This is a powerful control mechanism for it works by imposing caution on the broadcasting organisations themselves.

Self-censorship: RTÉ

Even before the censorship directives were issued, there was already a high level of caution as regards the Northern conflict within the broadcasting organisations in Britain and Ireland. In RTÉ that caution was formalised and institutionalised early on as a result of Section 31. A government directive issued in October 1971 ordered RTÉ 'to refrain from broadcasting any matter that could be calculated to promote the aims and activities of any organisation which engages in, promotes, encourages or advocates the attaining of any particular objective by violent means'. Although this directive was aimed at a number of organisations, republican and loyalist, in reality the effect of the directive was to remove the voice of republicans, in particular Sinn Féin, from the airwaves.

One key effect of such directives was to prevent candidates for Sinn Féin, a legal political party, having access to broadcasts in the run-up to an election. This was challenged in 1982 by one such candidate, Seán Lynch. The Supreme Court upheld the ban, failing to judge it either unconstitutional or undemocratic, on the grounds that Sinn Féin was 'an integral and dependent part of the apparatus of the Provisional IRA, an illegal terrorist organisation which, by both its avowed aims and its record of criminal violence, is shown to be committed to, amongst other things, the dismantling by violent and unlawful means of the organs of the state' (cited in *European Commission on Human Rights,* 1992, p. 5).

As stated above, Section 31 is in some respects open to interpretation, but challenges to the state's interpretation came from outside the top management of RTÉ. Moreover, those challenges often related to the fact that RTÉ management interpreted Section 31 more strictly than was intended by the lawmakers. A case in point was that of Larry O'Toole, a trade union activist. During a strike at a bakery in Dublin in 1990, O'Toole was interviewed as spokesperson for the strikers by RTÉ. After this interview was broadcast, RTÉ discovered that O'Toole was also a member of Sinn Féin; further interviews were conducted but not broadcast. O'Toole challenged RTÉ's interpretation of Section 31 on the grounds that the Broadcasting Act forbade interviews or reports of interviews with spokespersons, not members, of Sinn Féin. In fact, it was RTÉ policy for many years to prohibit members of Sinn Féin from broadcasting, irrespective of the issue under consideration. This led to ludicrous incidents, such as the failure to broadcast an eye-witness account of a fire in Bundoran because the interviewee was a member of Sinn Féin, or the cutting short of a caller to a gardening phone-in who claimed to be a member of Sinn Féin.

The Dublin High Court found for O'Toole, pointing out that the ministerial directive did not prohibit 'all access to the airwaves at all times by a person who was a member of Sinn Féin' (Judgment of Justice O'Hanlon, July 1992, p. 7), and that had it done so, such a directive would probably have been invalid. Amazingly, RTÉ appealed the High Court judgment to the Supreme Court, arguing that:

> As an admitted member of Sinn Féin, the Respondent [O'Toole] was personally committed to the support of the Provisional IRA, an illegal terrorist organisation, and was accordingly committed personally to the dismantling by violent and unlawful means of the organs of the State established by the Constitution (RTÉ Notice of Appeal, August 1992: 2).

As staff at RTÉ concluded (Staff Information Bulletin, 31, September 1992, p. 2):

> It is probably the only broadcasting organisation in the world, outside of totalitarian countries, to invite censorship and a curtailment of editorial freedom in this way.

In March 1993, the Supreme Court upheld the High Court judgment. RTÉ's initial response was to agree to abide by the Supreme Court decision. However, there was no sign of any urgency on RTÉ's part between the Supreme Court decision

and the subsequent lifting of the Section 31 directive nine
months later.

One further challenge to Section 31 was a case brought by
the unions to the European Commission on Human Rights.
The commission drew heavily on the judgment in relation to
Seán Lynch, cited above, and rejected the broadcasters'
application.

> Given the limited scope of the restrictions imposed on
> the applicants and the overriding interests they were
> designed to protect, the commission finds that they can
> reasonably be considered 'necessary in a democratic
> society' ... It follows that the complaints ... are manifestly
> ill-founded and must be rejected ... (European
> Commission on Human Rights, 1992, p. 17).

The end result was that there was little scope for challenge or
subversion within RTÉ. As Purcell (1991, p. 61) points out,
the question automatically asked within RTÉ was not 'Who is
in Sinn Féin?', but 'Who is definitely not in Sinn Féin?' To
challenge this ritual was to run the risk of being labelled a
fellow traveller of subversives.

In January 1994, Michael D. Higgins, Minister for Arts,
Culture and the Gaeltacht in the Fianna Fáil-Labour coalition
government, decided not to renew the directive under
Section 31. The decision resulted not just from the strong
Labour presence in government, but also from the recognition of widespread opposition, in particular from journalists and human rights activists, to the continuing
censorship. Finally, the lapsing of the directive was viewed in
some quarters as an incentive to republicans in the North to
become further involved in the process of attaining a settlement of the conflict. To date, though, RTÉ has had the last
word. The caution that it has revealed in the past in relation
to interpreting government policy continues to express itself.
It decreed that live interviews with members of organisations
such as Sinn Féin are possible only with the express

permission of the director general, meaning that, in effect, the vast majority of such interviews are pre-recorded.

Self-censorship: broadcasting in the UK

The case is somewhat different as regards broadcasting in the UK. The British broadcasting ban was only formalised in 1988. But it served to emphasise, in fact worked by emphasising, a caution which had already been built into the British broadcasting system over a period of two decades.

The British broadcasters' initial enthusiasm over the major story of civil rights in Northern Ireland quickly led them into confrontations with the Right both inside and outside government. A number of run-ins, most spectacularly over a programme called 'The Question of Ulster' at the end of 1971, led to caution. Thus Lord Hill, chair of the BBC board of governors, stated in 1971: '... as between the British army and the gunmen, the BBC is not and cannot be impartial' (Curtis, 1984, p. 10). Nor were such sentiments confined to the upper echelons; Schlesinger (1978, p. 225) quotes a BBC television sub-editor: 'I've always assumed the official line is we put the army's version first and then any other.' Eventually this caution was institutionalised in the form of the reference up system. All items on the North were to be referred up to high levels of management in BBC and ITV, on occasions even to the director general himself. As Curtis (1984, p. 173) puts it:

> On virtually every other topic, programme editors, producers and journalists are trusted to make appropriate decisions about what subjects to select and how to present them. They are expected to 'refer up' to their superiors for guidance only in cases of real doubt or difficulty. On Ireland, however, no one was to be trusted.

Bolton (1990, p. 99) adds a nuance to Curtis' general conclusion:

> Such a massive amount of output meant delegation was inevitable, with reference up only when necessary ... this system did allow senior management a way out. If there

was no trouble, reference up had worked perfectly. If there was – then they had not been sufficiently put in the picture. Assistant heads must roll.

The last point is entirely autobiographical. A producer with the BBC, Bolton was sacked after the Carrickmore incident mentioned below.

Guidelines were produced which spelt out required behaviour and even covered language to be used. For example:

> 'The Irish Republican Army ... it is acceptable to call them "The Provisionals" – but *never* "The Provos" nor "PIRA". Don't give pet names to terrorists'

> 'DON'T speak of "IRA" volunteers – we don't know why they joined'
> (cited in typed internal document of the BBC, 'Northern Ireland: A Guide', no date).

Despite such caution, run-ins with the state continued – the interview with an INLA spokesperson about the killing of Airey Neave, MP on 'Tonight' in 1979; 'Panorama's' involvement in filming an IRA roadblock in Carrickmore in 1979; the centrality of Sinn Féin's Martin McGuinness in the 'Real Lives' programme in 1984, the banning of which led to the first ever journalists' strike in the BBC; and Thames Television's examination of the killing of three IRA members in Gibraltar in 1988, 'Death on the Rock' (Bolton, 1990; Windlesham and Rampton, 1989).

The official broadcasting line is that they won some of these battles and lost others, but that they maintained their independence throughout. However, this argument misses the point. Whether there was success or failure, each skirmish has led to increased caution and made it more difficult to make the next programme which might lead to confrontation with the state.

The end result is that there was a level of censorship within British broadcasting even prior to the 1988 ban not unlike that in RTÉ. One measure of this is that the appearances of republicans on network news and current affairs were few. On BBC there were five interviews with IRA spokespersons between 1971 and 1974, and none thereafter. There were two interviews with INLA spokespersons in 1977 and 1979, and none thereafter. On ITV there were probably six interviews with IRA spokespersons in 1973 and 1974, and none thereafter. And as regards Sinn Féin, John Conway, then Head of News with BBC Northern Ireland, summed up the broadcasters' reticence: 'We use sparingly the opportunity we have to interview Sinn Féin members and never forget their links to violence' (cited in Doornaert and Larson, 1987, p. 13). In fact, this reticence was one of the key arguments broadcasters used, when the ban was imposed, to prove their responsible credentials (Moloney 1991, p. 34).

Also, republicans were subjected to increasingly hostile questioning, especially as the 1980s progressed.

> 'How does it feel to be branded one of the guilty men, Mr Corrigan? ... You're very silent, Mr Corrigan' (BBC1 9-11-1987).

> 'Do you feel that you have a better line to God and God's wishes than the bishops and clergy do?' (BBC2 Newsnight, 31-3-1988) (both cited in Henderson et al, 1990, p. 42).

Again, this was a key point in the broadcasters' opposition to the ban, that they would no longer be able to harass republicans (Moloney, 1991, p. 35).

Richard Francis, controller BBC Northern Ireland, summed up the pre-ban broadcasting position:

> We do not deal impartially with those who step outside the bounds of the law and decent social behaviour. Not only do they get very much less coverage than those who pursue their aims legitimately, but the very manner and tone that our reporters adopt makes our moral position quite plain (quoted in Curtis, 1984, p. 148).

Given that mentality before the ban, it is no surprise that the initial reaction of top management to the broadcasting ban was one of supreme caution. They called in the lawyers and went far beyond what the directive demanded. Channel 4 said the ban applied to works of fiction, including feature films. The BBC banned songs.

Interestingly the Home Office stated that broadcasters were going too far. They pointed out that 'genuine works of fiction' were not banned. They also stated that 'a member of an organisation cannot be held to represent that organisation in all his (sic) daily activities' (Henderson, *et al*, 1990, pp. 14-15).

In short, there is more scope for interpretation, indeed for challenging the limits of the ban in the British system than in RTÉ. Reports of interviews are not ruled out. Interview footage with voiceovers can be used. Subtitles are allowed. On 'Dispatches' in 1991 Mary Holland conducted a lengthy interview with Sinn Féin president Gerry Adams. The electronically synchronised voiceover of Adams served to show up the ridiculousness of the ban – that it only forbids us hearing the actual words as actually spoken – in ways which the feeble challenge to censorship of RTÉ's top management never did.

Despite that, the legal challenges mounted by the unions and by Sinn Féin have petered out, in some cases because of lack of finance, in other cases because of the lack of enthusiasm on the part of official trade unionists to challenge the state on this issue and leave themselves open to the accusation of siding with terrorism.

As a result of union reticence, management caution and broadcasters' wariness, programmes on the North are increasingly seen to be too difficult, too time consuming, too dangerous. If confrontation was always a possibility before, it is more of a certainty now. The North never was the arena in which one could climb the promotional ladder easily; it is even less so now. It is easier to ignore the issue altogether, as Paul Hamann, a prominent producer, among whose programmes has been 'Real Lives', states:

Too many people in broadcasting have their eye on the next rung of the career ladder and not on the programmes. They would rather not have the bother and prefer to make a film on a safer topic (cited in *Sunday Life*, 15-10-89).

The effects of such increased caution have been obvious. Danny Morrison (1989, p. 10), then Sinn Féin's director of publicity stated that British media enquiries to Belfast's Republican Press Centre fell from 471 in the four months before the ban to 110 in the four months after. Research done by Henderson *et al* (1990, pp. 30, 37) confirms this. In the year before the ban there were ninety-three appearances by Sinn Féin, but only thirty-four in the year following the ban. Before the ban most Sinn Féin interviews were slight, with more than one question being asked on only seven occasions. After the ban there were no occasions when more than one question was asked.

In addition, the scope of the ban has frequently been interpreted very widely. Thus, non-members of Sinn Féin have been banned or subtitled: Brighton Labour councillor Richard Stanton, Errol Smalley, a campaigner for the release of the Guildford Four, and Bernadette McAliskey. Songs have been banned, in particular, the Pogues' 'Streets of Sorrow/ Birmingham Six'. And the Belfast Office of Visnews, the world's largest television news agency, revealed that it makes two versions of any story involving Sinn Féin, one for British consumption, and one for the rest of the world. (For this and other examples of the effects of the ban, see *Information on Ireland*, 1989.)

In short, despite the scope for challenging or subverting the ban, broadcasters have erred on the side of caution. Peter Taylor, who has been involved in some of the most incisive current affairs investigations on the North since the mid-1970s, states:

It has worked much better than the government would ever have hoped. And we have helped it to work by being unnecessarily cautious. Far more can be done within the framework of the restriction ... (cited in *Sunday Life*, 15-10-1989).[2]

The reality of censorship
There are a number of conclusions to be drawn in relation to broadcasting in Britain and Ireland. First, as was mentioned earlier, this may not be classic totalitarian censorship, especially in as far as it relies on self-policing. But it is censorship none the less, a peculiarly democratic form of censorship.

Second, it is important to remember the centrality of the conflict in the North in relation to censorship in these islands. Two out of three cases of the use of the law to control broadcasters have been about the North. And, despite the number of issues over which, to take the British example, there have been major confrontations between the state and broadcasters – the Zircon spy satellite, the bombing of Libya, etc. – most of the confrontations have been on one issue only, the North.

Third, the attempts to control broadcasters derive from and enhance an unhealthy censorship culture in Ireland. Such a culture leads to the disenfranchisement of whole sections of Irish society and to the demonisation of individuals from those communities. To take one example: in 1992 RTÉ refused an advertisement for a book of short stories by Gerry Adams, *The Street*. (The Independent Radio and Television Commission quickly followed suit, forbidding broadcast of the advertisement on the South's twenty-one commercial stations.) The editor of the North's main nationalist daily paper, the *Irish News*, commented thus:

> By depicting him [Adams] solely as a beast, RTÉ is denying him his humanity and contributing to a climate of opinion whereby his murder would be welcomed (26-10-92).

Conclusion

The censorship ethos discussed above which has characterised the state's approach to broadcasting in both the United Kingdom and Ireland is underpinned by a deep and authoritarian fear of the audience – that is, of its own citizens – and a denial of their right to know: to see, hear and judge for themselves what is happening in Northern Ireland. Both states seek to use broadcasting to reinforce identification with, and support for, the state – frequently through the symbolic meshing of images of the state, nation, national forces of law and order, and certain aspects of popular culture, e.g. music, sport and news. The biggest loser on all counts is Northern Ireland itself. Not only is a significant sector of the population demonised, but in a society lacking consensus regarding national identity, and hence without this source of state legitimisation, it needs above all to be able to draw on that other major legitimating resource – democratic and pluralist communication between all sides. This can begin to provide the foundation on which to build sufficient solidarity, consensus and trust to underpin a peaceful state. The communication model made available to it by both the Republic and the United Kingdom, however, is both authoritarian and anti-democratic, with little apparent commitment to open and pluralist communication practices.

The first section of the chapter demonstrated the historical attempts by broadcasting authorities in both parts of Ireland to construct a consensus about national identity and thereby to encourage integration and solidarity. The limits of this exercise were made clear. The consensus which the media hoped to foster was shaped by powerful elites including political, class and commercial interests. When a high level of consensus already existed – as was the case with regard to national identity in the Republic of Ireland – the media were successful in reproducing and celebrating this. When little consensus existed, as in Northern Ireland, its attempts to foster this – as in the 1960s – failed. Again it would appear that an open communication model which offers access to diverse voices and cultures is more appropriate in attempting to resolve conflict in a democratic manner than authoritarian and elitist communication media.

Notes

1. Thanks to Liz Curtis, Marie McGonagle, Niall Meehan and David Miller for help in compiling the section on censorship in this chapter.
2. In September 1994, in response to the IRA ceasefire, the British government lifted the broadcasting ban.

References

ARTICLE 19, 1989, *No Comment: Censorship, Secrecy and the Irish Troubles*, London, Article 19.

BOLTON, R., 1990. *Death on the Rock and Other Stories*, London, W.H. Allen.

BOYLE, R., 1990. 'From Our Gaelic Fields: Radio, Sport and Nation in Post-Partition Ireland', *Media, Culture and Society*, 14, pp. 623-636.

BUTLER, D., 1991. 'Ulster Unionism and British Broadcasting Journalism, 1924-89', in B. Rolston (ed.), *The Media and Northern Ireland: Covering the Troubles*, London, Macmillan, pp. 99-121.

CATHCART, R., 1984. *The Most Contrary Region: the BBC in Northern Ireland 1924-1984*, Belfast, Blackstaff Press.

CURTIS, L., 1984. *Ireland: the Propaganda War*, London, Pluto.

DOORNAERT, M. and H. LARSEN, 1987. *Censoring 'The Troubles': an Irish Solution to an Irish Problem?* Brussels, International Federation of Journalists.

European Commission on Human Rights, Decision of the Commission as to the Admissibility of Application No. 15404/889 by Betty Purcell et al against Ireland, 1992.

FAHY, T., 1992. 'Audience Research in RTE', *Irish Communications Review*, 2, pp. 1-7.

FITZGERALD, G., n.d., 'Radio Listenership and the TV Problem', *University Review*, 2, pp. 38-45.

GIBBONS, L., 1988. 'From Megalith to Megastore: Broadcasting and Irish Culture', in T. Bartlett *et al* (eds.), *Irish Studies: a General Introduction*, Dublin, Gill and

592   Irish Society: Sociological Perspectives

Macmillan, pp. 221-234.
GORHAM, M., 1967. *Forty Years of Irish Broadcasting*, Dublin, Talbot Press.
HARRIS, R., 1972. *Prejudice and Tolerance in Ulster*, Manchester, Manchester University Press.
HENDERSON, L., D. Miller and J. REILLY, 1990. *Speak No Evil: the British Broadcasting Ban, the Media and the Conflict in Ireland*, Glasgow, Glasgow University Media Group.
INFORMATION ON IRELAND, 1989. *Briefing Paper*, London, Information on Ireland.
McGEEVER, J., 1989. *Journalist*, January.
MEEHAN, N., 1991. 'Ireland's Censorship Culture', *Film Ireland*, p. 31.
MILLER, D., 1993. 'Official Sources and "Primary Definition": the Case of Northern Ireland', *Media, Culture and Society*, 15, pp. 385-406.
MOLONEY, E., 1991. 'Closing Down the Airwaves: the Story of the Broadcasting Ban', in B. Rolston (ed.), *The Media and Northern Ireland: Covering the Troubles*, London, Macmillan, pp. 8-50.
MORRISON, D., 1989. *Ireland: the Censored Subject*, Dublin, Sinn Féin Publicity Department.
PURCELL, P., 1991. 'The Silence in Irish Broadcasting', in B. Rolston (ed.), *The Media and Northern Ireland: Covering the Troubles*, London, Macmillan, pp. 51-68.
ROBERTSON, G. and A. NICOL, 1990. *Media Law: the Rights of Journalists and Broadcasters*, London, Longman.
SCHLESINGER, P., 1978. *Putting 'Reality' Together: BBC News*, London, Constable.
TODD, J., 1987. 'Two Traditions in Ulster Political Culture', *Irish Political Studies*, 2, pp. 1-26.
WHYTE, J., 1990. *Interpreting Northern Ireland*, Oxford, Oxford University Press.
WINDLESHAM, LORD AND R. RAMPTON, 1989. *The Windlesham/Rampton Report: Death on the Rock*, London, Faber and Faber.

19
The Power of the Catholic Church in the Republic of Ireland

MÁIRE NIC GHIOLLA PHÁDRAIG

Power has different aspects. Weber defined it as the 'chance of a man or a number of men to realize their own will in a social action even against the resistance of others who are participating in the action' (1982, p. 60). The exercise of power can take place not alone through coercive physical force but also through ideological control and through control of resources. These two aspects of the power of the Catholic Church in Ireland will be addressed here when the context of the discussion has been outlined.

Context

Ireland's religious profile is unusual in a number of respects. It is the only country in the English-speaking world which has a Catholic majority (93 per cent of the population in 1981). It is unique among western countries in not permitting divorce and abortion. Ireland is also unusual as a country with a Catholic majority in that the main proportion of the population regularly practise religion (82 per cent of Catholics in 1989 attended Mass each Sunday). Although unusual, Ireland is not unique in this respect. In Poland, until recently at least, the Catholic majority maintained high levels of religious practice. Significantly, perhaps, both countries were dominated historically by imperial powers with state religions other than Catholicism. In both cases religion became a powerful cthno-national marker (Martin, 1978; Nic Ghiolla Phádraig, 1988).

It is the continuing strength of Catholicism, more than seven decades after the attainment of independence that produces the greatest puzzle facing sociologists examining religion in Ireland. It is true that there has been some evidence of decline – Sunday Mass attendance dropped from 91 per cent in 1973 to 82 per cent in 1989 (Mac Gréil, 1991) – but with nothing like the rate of change in matters such as the decline in the birth-rate. Nor indeed did the decline reach the dramatic proportion of declines in practice in other countries and regions with a Catholic majority, such as the Netherlands and French Canada, which occurred after the Second Vatican Council. Continued high levels of practice do not merely reflect a certain inertia. The results of referenda prohibiting abortion and rejecting an opportunity to introduce divorce legislation point to the extent to which a significant number of Irish Catholics wish to prescribe church teaching in controversial issues. It is findings such as these which prompt the inquiry as to what is the power of the Catholic Church in the Republic of Ireland.

To examine this question we need to place contemporary Irish Catholicism in an appropriate historical context. This chapter does not engage with the major contemporary debate on secularisation (Martin, 1969); rather it focuses primarily on the power position of the Catholic Church in Ireland. It is worth noting in passing, however, that notions of secularisation are of little help in this exercise. Indeed in more general respects, a recent careful examination of the evidence led to the conclusion that 'in spite of considerable social turmoil and the religious transformations over the past three decades, it is clear that modernisation processes in Ireland have not been accompanied unambiguously by secularisation'(Hornsby-Smith, 1992, p. 289). Furthermore, signs of revitalisation can be traced to the impact of the Second Vatican Council (Ibid, p. 285).

Secularisation posits the notion of an early traditional sacred society which evolves into a modern secular society. Our images of the traditional Irish Catholic are of docile, devout, faithful Mass-goers with rosaries in pockets, respectful of clergy and religious, taking in the Parish Mission and a few novenas every year. This indeed is the prototype of the good Catholic familiar to the oldest members of the population and the dominant type in the first six decades of this century; but it does not extend equally far back into the nineteenth century. The pre-famine Irish had a very different relationship to the Catholic Church. Mass attendance was a minority observance, mainly concentrated in towns and among the better-off sections of the population. Instead there was a very rich folk culture of prayers during everyday activities and of religious patterns and shrines which took place largely without the assistance of clergy who were not very numerous in any case. It has been estimated that given the shortage of church buildings, even if each priest said two Sunday Masses, a maximum of 40 per cent of the Catholic population could have attended on a Sunday in 1842 (Larkin, 1976). Post-famine trauma, the death or emigration of mainly the unchurched poor and increased vocations to the priesthood turned this situation around. Not only did the quantity change, but also the quality. The style of religious worship adopted a pantheon of Italian and French saints and sacramentals and devotions. Churches became more numerous, larger and more ornate. The ceremonies became more diverse and spectacular: benediction, Corpus Christi processions – activities which were both uplifting and enter-taining in those pre-audiovisual days. Along with this 'devotional revolution' went a new emphasis in moral theology on sexual restraint and a higher value on celibacy which contributed towards both an increase in vocations and a disciplining of that sizeable section of the population who lacked the means to marry. The extent to which sexual restraint was adopted has been attributed to its utility (elective affinity) to the farming community in preserving the viability of the holding that could only be inherited by one heir (Inglis, 1987, Chap. 5). But this does not account for its adoption by non-farming and urban sections of the population also. It must not be forgotten that this strict sexual code was very much a part of Victorian morality in general.

Ideological control

Larkin (1976) argued that the Irish suffered a collective psychological trauma resulting from the famine and also the loss of an ethnic marker with the decline of the Irish language. These combined to motivate Catholics to accept the ideological leadership of the church in order to ensure their salvation in the next world and to provide a substitute badge of ethnicity to distinguish them from the colonial establishment. The use of parish missions with their sermons on hellfire and the individual counselling sessions in the confessional helped to reinforce this ideological control (Inglis, 1987, pp. 148-150). This process began at an early age through catechesis in the national schools which were managed by parish priests and staffed by the teachers they recruited who were trained by the religious orders. The affluent and those able to avail of scholarships continued to second-level education provided by religious orders and these produced the elite of government, public service and to some degree business and finance. It is argued by Inglis (1987, pp. 90-93) that the media – in particular television – posed the first real threat to ideological control by the Catholic Church in Ireland. It is true that chat shows provide a forum for challenging the church's position on various previously taboo issues and even trivialise them by the inter-spersal of commercial breaks and the inclusion of other items on diverse topics – so reducing everything to entertainment. The presentation of alternative lifestyles on television, from soaps to documentary to discussion, has opened minds to greater cultural relativism and liberalism in relation to sexual conduct as compared with the prescriptive approach which formerly characterised the lives of Catholics. To the extent that the media focus attention on church-state tension and on challenging church stands on matters of sexuality or education they distract from inquiry into the much greater power exercised by the wealthy. The liberal critique of the church diverts attention from the paradox of a country with economic growth on the one hand, and spiralling unemployment on the other.

A further indication of the erosion of ideological power in the Irish church is the decline in attendance at confession. In 1989 11 per cent of Catholics said they never attend confession. Monthly confession could be said to be the norm for good Catholics established by sodalities and the First Friday devotion – it was practised by 47 per cent in 1973-4, by 26 per cent in 1984 and by only 18 per cent in 1988/89 (Mac Gréil, 1991, Table 12). The 29 per cent decline in Confession is much greater than that for Mass attendance (9 per cent over the same 15 year period) and contrasts with the increase of 15 per cent in the reception of Communion weekly or more often. While sacramental confession has greatly declined a new phenomenon of public 'confession' grows and flourishes on the airwaves since the introduction of phone-in/write-in chat-shows. There is no way of knowing whether the people who 'phone-in' might formerly have approached their problems via the Confessional. The radio 'confessional' differs from the sacramental in its public exposure of problems and has played a role in drawing attention to the prevalence of matters such as child sexual abuse. The radio 'confession' also extends the counsellor role to that of adjudicator presenting and commenting on listeners' reaction to the problem or 'confession' offered on the air. At a time of less certainty regarding beliefs, values and norms of behaviour (Breslin, A. and Weafer, 1985) the extensive use of 'phone-ins' represents the search for new norms by consensus rather than the continued acceptance of church teaching.

In seeking to understand the ideological power of the church today and the extent to which it controls important resources in society, we must again take a historical perspective. The church and the state were developed simultaneously and gestated in mutual interdependence during most of the nineteenth century and into the twentieth century. Up to seventy years ago Irish Catholics were a minority in the context of the United Kingdom. The neo-colonial legacy of unfinished business with Protestant England has given Ireland a defensive, siege mentality, reflected in high levels of religious practice and belief. The Catholic Church has benefited at a social-psychological level from partition (by its minimising of the Protestant minority) and from the 'National Question' (by keeping alive the 'minority' feeling *vis-à-vis* Britain); religious observance has been promoted, while, up to recently, issues such as church control of education have conveniently been kept out of the arena of public debate. The legalism which pervades the Irish approach to religious practice owes much to this siege mentality (Nic Ghiolla Phádraig, 1988).

Catholic Church teaching was associated with a contraction in the opportunities for women in the newly independent state. Although feminism had played a role in the national movements which preceded the struggle for independence and several women achieved national prominence during this period, they were marginalised in the new state. The Marian cult pointed to a domestic, silent role for Irish Catholic women. 'Not only did the churches strongly project a predominantly private and familial role for women, they provided exemplary models of patriarchy in their own organisational arrangements' (O'Dowd, 1987, p. 12). Feminists point to the Catholic Church as one of the last bastions of exclusively male privilege. Indeed, feminism has offered one of the major coherent challenges in Ireland to traditional church teaching on women's economic and domestic roles and control over their bodies.

While the two national aims of reunification and the

restoration of the Irish language were the official rhetoric of the state and of political discourse, the main ideology of the Irish state was Catholicism. This was taken for granted rather than planned and hence all the more potent for this. The church was important in legitimating the new state in the eyes of citizens in the aftermath of the civil war and in providing a channel for external recognition. This was evident from the great diplomatic effort which the government invested in persuading the Vatican to hold the 1932 Eucharistic Congress in Ireland. From then on the mutual support of church and state and their shared vision of a society of rural families went unchallenged until the state abandoned its former economic policies in the 1960s and attempted to solve the unemployment-emigration crises by attracting in multinationals to provide industrial employment. In doing so the state abandoned the project of the church and 'adopted the project of the bourgeoisie' ... 'modernisation understood as industrialisation, economic growth under the aegis of private enterprise, confidence in the profit motive as a stimulus for development' (Peillon, 1982, p. 182). The Church now was faced with blatant acquisitive individualism and conspicuous consumption which has alienated the working class and unemployed from political, social and religious participation.

Many writers have dealt at length with the relationship between church and state in Ireland. The identification of the church as a potential or actual rival power base to the state is useful but to treat the church as if it were the sole body influencing state policy is inadequate. Eipper (1986) is one of the exceptions in pointing to the importance of the bourgeoisie in relation to power. 'It can be argued that the church, state and business came to function as a ruling bloc in Éire in the post-independence period ... the church, state and business became the major supports of a new class field of force in Éire ... the reproduction of the bloc itself became central to ... the maintenance of class power' (Eipper, C., 1986, pp. 18-19). While Eipper's study is confined to Bantry he claims this offers a microcosm of power relations in Irish society.

Structural aspects of power

Control of significant resources
Health and welfare
The Victorian solution to social problems was to gather persons in each category into large residential institutions. The main growth period for the Irish church occurred during this period and the church became heavily involved in establishing such institutions – from borstals to elite boarding schools to old people's homes; religious orders were imported from the continent or homegrown to respond to needs in that fashion. Vocations were plentiful, ensuring free well disciplined labour which provided for the cheap, efficient running of these institutions; dowries brought by aspirants to religious life together with bequests and donations provided the necessary capital to purchase or build large premises. These ventures were partly motivated by the fear of what was termed proselytisation which went on, particularly with regard to children, in certain Protestant-funded establishments – schools, orphanages, homes for the disabled. It is hard to see what other motivation might have prompted the involvement of religious brothers in juvenile prisons – Artane, Daingean, Letterfrack (many of the boys there had simply been poor school attenders). Having a baby out of wedlock often resulted in young women being placed for life in 'Magdalen Asylums' where they provided free labour in laundries and lived in prison-like conditions.

Religious-run institutions imposed on their inmates a monastic lifestyle of ascetic frugality, frequent devotions and emotional and physical control which however valid when freely adopted by committed mature adults was most unsuitable to the growth of children's personalities (Arnold and Laskey, 1985). The children frequently grew up as 'institutionalised' personalities, unable to cope with independent living and sometimes following an institutional 'career path' through prisons and mental hospitals or perhaps adapting to live-in work of various kinds as domestics, in the army, in hospitals or boarding-houses. There was little questioning of such institutions. Belief in the altruism of the religious running them and the fear of challenging the church together with ignorance of conditions and the inmates' lack of powerful connections isolated them from public scrutiny. It must be said that there is no evidence that conditions were any better in non-Catholic institutions – the Workhouse was viewed as a last resort by most.

A variety of factors combined to prompt withdrawal of religious from such institutions. These factors included: economic changes which greatly increased running costs; changes in the religious orders themselves, both from the decline in vocations, the post-Vatican II reassessment of their mission, and the greater inclusiveness of state welfare provisions. It is interesting to note that church views on welfare as only a subsidiary to voluntary charity were also transformed and the rhetoric of church teaching stressed instead the importance of principles of justice and equity and the role of the state in providing resources for the dis-advantaged (Peillon, 1982, p. 190).

Hospitals were established for the sick poor by some religious orders in the last century. Fear of losing members to the Established Church and a wish to provide the sick and dying and their families with spiritual comfort combined with humanitarian motives in the foundation of such hospitals. Another consideration was the desire to provide employment for Catholic doctors who were largely debarred from positions in the Protestant voluntary hospitals. (The Dublin Hospitals Commission in 1867 quoted in Inglis, 1987, p. 127).

Religious thus acted as gatekeepers for advancement among the Catholic medical profession and could ensure that Catholic medical ethics were enforced. Private hospitals or private wings attached to the charity/voluntary hospitals helped to subsidise the latter and also provided additional income for consultants. State funding for hospital care has eliminated the need for cross-subsidisation but today we find that of twelve private hospitals in Dublin listed by the

Voluntary Health Insurance Board six are run by religious orders (including some of recent development). The continuation of such private hospitals is probably mainly as a source of extra income to consultants but they also offer a service to members of the clergy and religious orders who require treatment. Such hospitals are an example of how religious orders may be utilised in the reproduction of inequality.

Apart from religious-run hospitals there are also examples of church influence on medical ethics in other hospitals. The Catholic archbishop of Dublin is on the board of the National Maternity Hospital which prohibits sterilisation. Catholic priests teach medical ethics to student nurses in other hospitals. The one remaining voluntary hospital which has an overtly Protestant ethos and restricts nursing intake to Protestants is the Adelaide, which has now gained effective control of the new hospital at Tallaght into which it will be incorporated.

A further example of significant resources controlled by the church is the extent of parochial land and buildings all over the country. Frequently the parish hall (where there is one) is the only meeting place in the community and access to this facility is in the hands of the parish clergy who may veto its use by groups of which they disapprove for whatever reason. There is very little secular use made of churches as such. For a long time respect for the Blessed Sacrament precluded this consideration and daily usage for liturgical purposes made it impractical. The design of new churches also tends to ignore the possibility of secular use.

Educational resources

The primary and secondary schools are by far the most important resources controlled by the Catholic Church. The Irish situation is quite unique in that the state provides the funding for schools whose running is in the hands of parish clergy and religious orders. This system dates from 1831 when the British authorities set up a universal national school system and invited existing church-run schemes to be part of it. Lack of agreement on management of schools resulted in the system being organised on denominational lines. In practice nowadays this means the vast majority are run by parish clergy (effectively, despite the introduction of management committees) both Catholic (and with a virtual monopoly of the other religious schools) the Church of Ireland. There are also ten multi-denominational schools and eighty Gaelscoileanna (Irish-medium national schools which are Catholic but not parochial and which are run by parents' committees). While most Catholic national schools are managed by parish clergy, some are managed by religious orders staffing them. Though the state pays the bulk of capital costs, the schools are the property of church bodies, although the Department of Education intends to amend this situation in the title of future schools.

The national schools operate a timetable and curriculum laid down by the Department of Education. Religious instruction is permitted as a subject as are prayers, devotional aids and a 'religious ethos'. It is through the schools that Catholic children are prepared for reception of the Sacraments of Penance (Confession), the Eucharist (Holy Communion) and Confirmation, which are major landmarks in a child's life. Catholic schools close on holy days to enable pupils to attend Mass. Parish clergy have access to the schools and use the opportunity to evangelise. There are diocesan advisors on religious education. Schools, therefore, are important tools of religious socialisation.

An important feature of the national school system is the extent to which opportunities for appointments and promotion to teaching positions are in the hands of parish clergy. (The establishment of boards of management still gives the majority of seats to the church.) National school teachers' education is entirely a church-run affair with intake on a denominational basis. One college of education is run by the Church of Ireland and the remaining colleges are run by religious orders. The Catholic Church regards this system as an extremely vital part of its overall pastoral strategy. Catholic schools are found in other countries which have sufficiently large Catholic populations but these required major funding by the parishes in most cases. The Irish system is unusual in providing Church schools with state finance (often supplemented by parents and/or the parish). There has been increasing criticism of denominational schools particularly because of the 'religious ethos' which extends beyond the period for formal religious instruction. Parents may request that their children be exempt from religious instruction but not all are satisfied with the arrangement and there are demands for total elimination of any reference to religion by groups such as the Campaign to Separate Church and State (Alvey, 1991). A less extreme position is taken by the multi-denominational schooling movement who provide access to pupils for instruction in their various individual faiths and also, in an effort to promote mutual understanding, give classes in comparative religions. The main ally of the Catholic Church in seeking to retain the present system is the Church of Ireland who regard their own schools not only as of pastoral importance but also as a significant means of maintaining the cohesion of their communities. Consequently, while their schools receive a significant number of Catholic pupils they are careful to limit their intake.

At second-level the picture is somewhat different. The state inherited a system of academic secondary schools catering only for a minority of teenagers and run on denominational lines. Catholic secondary schools were mainly run by religious orders although there were some diocesan colleges which were intended as junior seminaries to recruit candidates for the priesthood. The introduction of vocational schools in the 1930s was of little interest to the Church except to ensure that an academic curriculum would not be taught there and to provide priests as teachers of religion and in many cases as chairmen of vocational educational committees (Titley, 1983, p. 121). The introduction of free secondary education in the 1960s changed this situation with a greatly enlarged intake, the provision of academic curricula and leaving certificate in vocational schools, the introduction of community schools in new residential areas and the amalgamation of non-viable schools in small towns. The latter gave rise to lengthy conflict with both religious orders and bishops and resulted in the church gaining effective control in most cases. A feature of religious-run secondary schools has been the provision of elite schools for children of the bourgeoisie and upper classes. These schools were established in the last century as a counter-attraction to the Protestant public schools in England which drew pupils from the affluent Catholic classes in Ireland. Such schools were given the option to remain outside the free education scheme while still retaining substantial state funding. A number of these schools were closed down by religious orders who felt they were no longer an appropriate part of their apostolate in the wake of the Second Vatican Council renewal. But a significant number remain to reproduce a high proportion of the front-runners in the independent professions, the judiciary, business and finance. This is the major way in which the church contributes to the reproduction of inequality.

The division of labour between religious orders themselves in relation to provision of education is itself fascinating. While some orders run schools in a variety of categories, other congregations such as the Mercy and Presentation orders for girls and the Christian Brothers for boys cater mainly for lower socio-economic groups – working-class and lower middle class. Gaelic games are prominent among the main sports played in these schools. The Sacred Heart sisters teach girls from elite backgrounds whose brothers are taught by Jesuits or Holy Ghost Fathers. The main sports in these schools are elite English games – hockey and rugby – and this has ongoing utility for the 'networking' of past pupils (Lynch, 1989, Tables A35 and A36). School is frequently used as a symbol of status and a shorthand basis for the development of friendships at university (Hannan and Tovey, 1978).

The state has benefitted from the involvement of religious

orders in schools by their efficiency and relative cheapness in comparison with the vocational sector. There was a long period during which teaching religious did not draw salaries. Apart from ensuring the continued teaching of religion and the 'religious' ethos of the school, the religious have acquiesced in the curriculum and overall school system. There is some lip-service paid to holistic education but by and large religious have collaborated with the points-system and it is this ethos, rather than the religious ethos, which is most pervasive in their schools (Lynch, 1989, pp. 130-131). The points system has contributed to the marginalisation of the teaching of religion itself at second-level to the point where specialists are now advocating that religious studies be a part of the Leaving Certificate programme.

Once more we find that religious orders and bishops' representatives on school boards act as gatekeepers in recruitment to and promotion within the teaching profession at second-level. The 1994 conflict regarding a new second-level school between the Bishop of Meath who wished to provide a site for a community school (which would retain church influence) and the Minister for Education who wished instead to establish a community college on this site (under the control of the vocational education committee) illustrates the continuing church-state struggle for control in the post-religious order situation.

Third level education is largely devoid of church involvement. With the exception of the colleges of education, the Mater Dei Institute (for teachers of religion) and St Patrick's College, Maynooth, third level colleges are formally non-denominational. The attempt to set up a Catholic university in the nineteenth century was unsuccessful. The philosophy departments of NUI (National University of Ireland) colleges were once dominated by Thomism and staffed by Catholic priests but are now decidedly more pluralist. A condition for the Catholic bishops' support of the foundation of the NUI in 1909 was the prohibition of a theology faculty. This was indicative of the episcopal view of theology as a clerical preserve and so it is not surprising that Catholic intellectual laypersons have been very scarce in Ireland by comparison with France. The bishops were wary of intellectualism and its possible negative impact on the faith of university students and so a heavy commitment to university chaplaincies has been maintained.

We may conclude therefore that the main institutional power base of the church lies in its control over primary and second-level education. This power base was largely laid down during the colonial period and was extended and consolidated in the decades following independence.

What are the prospects for the continuation of this control? Levels of support for denominational schooling seem reasonably good. A study in the 1970s posed questions regarding a hypothetical choice of schools at both primary and secondary level between schools run by religious and schools run by lay people. A large majority in each case opted for schools run by religious but when asked why, the majority did not cite religious reasons but instead alleged that religious-run schools were better-disciplined or provided better education (Unpublished data from study reported in Nic Ghiolla Phádraig, 1976). This portrays a pragmatic and utilitarian approach rather than a confessional approach and is probably close to politicians' view of the system – it works.

Although the church's role in education is not under major threat from public opinion its days are numbered in its present form. The drop in vocations in progress since the late 1960s was particularly marked in the case of teaching orders. Between 1970 and 1981 the number of sisters in primary teaching declined by one third and in secondary by one quarter. Teaching brothers declined by a few percentages more (Weafer and Breslin, 1981). The contraction in numbers of religious occurred at precisely the time that numbers of pupils were expanding rapidly – at primary level through a higher birthrate and at second level because of free education. Hence the ratio of religious to lay teachers dropped steeply from 18.9 per cent of trained national school

teachers in 1965-6 to just 4.6 per cent in 1992. Worse still, on
1 November 1991 there was only one religious as a student in
a college of education for primary teachers. The proportion
of religious as full-time teachers on incremental salary in
secondary schools declined from 47.8 per cent in 1965-6 to
9.2 per cent in 1991-2 (Department of Education Statistical
Reports 1965-66; 1991-2). Henceforth, the church will be
forced to rely on lay teachers and already many schools have
appointed lay heads/principals – some being totally staffed
by lay teachers. Although such schools remain under the
management of religious who can still act as gatekeepers to
appointments and promotions, their day-to-day input into the
religious ethos has largely disappeared.

Church and politics

'The Irish Republic is a clerical state ... [which]
combines the continental and medieval ecclesiastical
monarchy of Rome with a modern, streamlined
parliamentary system in a unique mixture, and the two
organisations live in genuine amity most of the time
because the state does not venture to challenge clerical
authority directly and because the church is usually
discreet enough to assert its power unobtrusively'
(Blanshard, 1954, pp. 67-8).

'The British tradition of the partial union of church and
state was carried over into the life of Ireland' (Ibid,
p. 64).

Blanshard was writing from the perspective of the 1950s at
a time when the political power of the Catholic Church had
peaked with the success of its opposition to the Mother and
Child Bill. This episode and indeed the entire history of the
relationship of the church to the Irish state has been carefully
described in Whyte's classic *Church and State in Modern Ireland*
(2nd edition, 1980). Whyte argued that of 1800 measures
which were considered by the Oireachtas, on only sixteen

occasions was there evidence of episcopal interference and this hardly constitutes a clerical state. However, he does concede that politicians shared the values of the church and hence were unlikely to propose any policies which would repudiate these.

It could scarcely be expected that the fledgling Irish Free State which had been established with the support of the bishops for the Pro-Treaty side during the civil war would divest the church of the spheres of influence it had acquired during British rule. The willingness to concede further influence can be attributed to the lack of a realisable national goal by the state and a requirement for legitimation and cohesion. The church offered the state continuity and stability and in return sought its support for continuity and stability in its own work. The 'twenties and 'thirties were times when the Vatican actively pursued concordats with other Catholic countries and so the 'Catholic flavour' of some articles in the 1937 Bunreacht na hÉireann were a relatively mild innoculation by comparison and for that reason have lasted longer. Church and state were formally separate, but as the state lacked civic ceremonial there was a reliance on Catholic ceremonial, e.g. a special Mass for the opening of the Oireachtas each autumn.

> 'A significant aspect of the religious hegemonic role can be seen in the translation of religious preoccupations into law via the concept of natural law' (Fulton, 1991, p. 135).

The main application of arguments from natural law has been in relation to laws and policies bearing on sex and family life. In the first few decades after independence the Protestant churches had a very similar approach to such matters (O'Dowd, 1987). But since the 1960s the Catholic Church has fought a lone rearguard action over liberalisation of laws regarding contraception. The hierarchy is caught in a dilemma, under renewed pressure from Pope John Paul II to proclaim the official church position on such matters. They are nevertheless aware of the alienating impact of such statements and the tendency to see the Church exclusively as an enforcer of the sixth and ninth commandments – the only aspect of their teaching to receive detailed media attention. Whyte points to the first sign of departure from a dogmatic stance in a 1973 joint statement of the hierarchy regarding Mary Robinson's Bill on contraception when they stated that the state was not obliged to defend by legislation the moral teaching of the Catholic Church (Whyte, 1985, p. 7). Awareness of this dilemma was no doubt the reason for the reluctance of the bishops to express support for the lobby groups of lay Catholics who persuaded the main political parties prior to a general election to hold a referendum to insert a clause into the constitution prohibiting abortion. Abortion had not been on the 'liberal agenda' and was a matter about which the public in general were not very aware (despite the numbers of Irish women availing of it in Britain). Although achieving the desired result, the extent of support (66 per cent of a poll of only 54 per cent) was much lower than might have been expected and planted sufficient doubt in people's minds to engender widespread popular support for 'X' (a fourteen-year-old girl, pregnant as a result of rape) in the Supreme Court decision that she should be permitted to travel to Britain to avail of abortion facilities there. The case led to another referendum in 1992 to amend the Constitution to consolidate the right to travel and the right to information; but the proposed amendment which would have permitted abortion if the woman's life was endangered by the pregnancy failed.

The true 'core values' of the Irish hierarchy were revealed in relation to the Maastricht Treaty referendum, however. These are to preserve the stability and continuity of the Irish state as a means to their own stability and continuity. 'The church does not exist independently of the Irish political system, but it is one of the basic elements in that system' (Larkin, 1975, p. 1244). Despite the fact that European unity could lead to the Irish constitutional prohibition on abortion being over-ruled, the bishops offered broad support for Maastricht while adding muted cautions regarding abortion. Their willingness to trust the government to 'do the right thing' may indicate some kind of contact on the matter. Because of the ambiguity in the wording of the amendment proposed by the government to reduce the consequences of the Supreme Court's decision on the X case both pro-life and pro-choice lobbies campaigned against the referendum, making it impossible to draw any conclusions on its negative outcome regarding trends in public opinion. The bishops' initial statement indicating that Catholics could vote either *Yes* or *No* (because the wording was not totally acceptable) was dissented from by a number of bishops who supported a pro-life *No*. This indicates that such issues are as divisive of the hierarchy as they are of the Irish people as a whole.

The defeat of the amendment of the constitution to permit divorce legislation was assisted by the bishops' support for opposition groups and its several joint and individual statements. Pulpits were used in many places to reinforce this message at Sunday Mass. Dillon has argued that the hierarchy's stance on the 1986 Divorce Referendum involved for the first time the extensive use of sociological/empirical arguments, alongside theological arguments. The statement, while condemning divorce as morally wrong, recognised the right in conscience of Catholics to vote in favour of its introduction. However, a number of bishops adopted a 'harder' line in their own dioceses and urged a *No* vote (Dillon, 1993, Chap. 5). Yet again the size of the *Yes* vote indicated that a significant minority of Catholics dissented from Church teaching. However, the lack of clarity regarding the nature of legislation which might be introduced and in particular fears about the implications for income, pension rights, social welfare entitlements and property, especially farms, played a large part in securing the defeat.

Accompanying these campaigns has been a growing coolness between the governments and the hierarchy. The advance consultation with the hierarchy on policies or legislation impinging on sex, family life, or education gave way to informing them in advance, and then to the 1992 statement by An Taoiseach that he had no intention of talking to the bishops about the wording of an abortion referendum, and the 1993 permission for condom-vending machines again without notice to the bishops. The state, of course, has had a new external referrent since joining the European Community and looks to Brussels rather than Rome for approval of policies as well as for financial support.

The Catholic Church and the reproduction of inequality

Power is a tool in the creation and maintenance of inequality in society and is itself unequally distributed. Having described the power resources of the Catholic Church in both ideological and structural terms we shall now consider what the overall effect of the church is with regard to the reproduction of inequality.

The picture that emerges is neither white nor black. Peillon describes the church in Ireland as speaking with a plurality of languages (1982, p. 90) and this is nowhere better illustrated than in the case of inequality. At the pastoral/ teaching/ideological level the church is constrained by the papal encyclicals – *Rerum Novarum* and *Quadragesimo Anno* and the more recent *Centisimus Annus*. These support the right to private property and while stressing the duty of the wealthy to use their resources responsibly do not offer a legitimation of expropriation should they fail to do so. However, the former emphasis on Christian charity has given way to a highlighting of justice and equality, and the impact of liberation theology has brought renewed commitment to work for the elimination of poverty and the promotion of human rights – particularly among members of religious orders. The work of the justice office of the Conference of Religious of Ireland has been outstanding in this respect and offers a coherent challenge to the assumptions and construction of the annual government budget. The renewal movement among religious orders has also brought some of their members to live among local authority tenants and engage in community work with the most marginalised. There has been a shift in emphasis from working for the poor to working with the poor and empowerment is a guiding principle here.

Some diocesan clergy have also responded to this movement by leading simpler lives (cycling, doing their own housework), and by supporting community-building initiatives and working with the most marginalised groups.

There is therefore, a very clear radical movement within the Catholic Church in Ireland, which acts as 'the conscience of society' (Ryan, 1979) and which is critical of the institutional church itself. In some cases this has led to the alienation of the priests and religious themselves and has provoked controversy within religious communities. However, mutual tolerance and a capacity for self-criticism unrivalled by secular organisations has led to peaceful coexistence to an extent which has muffled the overall impact of the radical wing.

Unless this radical voice becomes louder the church may entirely lose the support of the urban working classes whose level of sacramental participation has slumped steeply by comparison with their own former involvement and with the current rates of middle class and rural Catholics. However, by moving to the left the church would risk alienating the support of the affluent, a risk the hierarchy avoided taking in their 1992 pastoral 'Work is the Key' which dealt with unemployment in a purely reformist and exhortative fashion in contrast with the prescriptive approach to the sexual code. The gospel message has been described as ambivalent, at once a comfort and a challenge; in seeking to achieve one goal the other may be weakened.

It is worth looking at the example presented by the church itself regarding inequality. The organisation is hierarchical with the papacy at the summit. The present pope has reasserted the Vatican's power to select bishops and recent appointments have often been at variance with the expressed preference of the priests of the diocese. Bishops, in turn, have the power to move and promote priests without consultation. The priesthood itself is open only to male candidates. Despite the rhetoric of Vatican II, 'The People of God' are outside any significant decision-making. Within many religious orders there was formerly a distinction between, on the one hand, lay sisters or brothers who were recruited from among the manual working classes to provide domestic, grounds maintenance and agricultural labour within the monastery and, on the other, the choir sisters or priests who were mainly of middle to upper class background, who brought dowries and were deployed in professional positions or pastoral work. The difference was underlined by in some cases different titles, and by eating apart; the lay religious were debarred from holding office in the community and received a shorter and separate formation in religious life (Clear, 1987). These distinctions were formally abolished in most orders after the Second Vatican Council and there is no longer a twofold recruitment but the effects have not been totally erased among the cohort who predate these changes. There was widespread perception of social distinctions between religious congregations also, often linked to the socio-economic groups which they served with the elite schools staffed by religious of elite background (generally recruited from their own school leavers). Aspirants to the priesthood whose parents could not afford the fees for Maynooth or the diocesan seminary were often accommodated in missionary orders or sponsored by short-staffed bishops from foreign dioceses to attend All-Hallows Seminary in return for a commitment to work for them. This meant that Irish parishes were staffed by priests of middle class/strong farmer background which added weight to their superiority over their parishioners and drew them to associate with better-off sections. Juniorates, in some orders, took in aspirants as young as twelve years – to the financial relief of their parents. In those days of plentiful vocations, the minute socio-economic distinctions of society were faithfully reproduced in the intake of aspirants to the priesthood and religious life. In this way inequality in society was legitimated. We have seen that Catholic control of education contributes to the reproduction of inequality through operating private fee-paying schools and a range of voluntary contributions to non-fee-paying schools. Inequality is also reproduced within schools and Catholic schools are no exception, particularly in the use of entrance examinations and ability streaming. The rise of credentialism and the declining importance of inherited family wealth as the basis of the reproduction of social class (Breen, *et al*, 1989, p. 133) means that schools have become even more important channels of social inequality in Irish society in the past twenty-five years. It should also be mentioned that some religious, notably the Christian Brothers, provide very cheap education to enable working-class children to become upwardly mobile.

Those who have been educated in elite Catholic schools are over-represented among the judiciary, financiers, business and independent professions. Past pupils who chose medicine might receive further assistance in their careers by appointments in the substantial proportion of voluntary hospitals run by religious. There is also a tendency to recruit teachers from among past pupils. In these ways religious have contributed directly to the reproduction of inequality. During the mid-nineteenth century the creation of a Catholic middle class was seen as a means of advancement for Catholics as a whole and as a defence against oppression and exclusion by the Protestant ascendancy – this argument now lacks validity.

If, as I have argued, the main goal of the Catholic Church in relation to Irish society is the maintenance of its stability, then the church's contribution to the reproduction of inequality may be understood in this light. Eipper describes this process concisely: 'the class character of the church's position in Irish society lay in the fact that ... it functioned as an ambivalent ideological auxiliary of the state. The church provided the state with independent legitimation and cast itself as the guardian of the common interests and values of both rulers and ruled. The state in turn protected the church's position and pursued policies compatible with its social teaching. This was not a static, functionalist relationship, but an evolving one ...' (1986, p. 108).

Conclusion

We have seen that the power of the Catholic Church has begun to wane in certain respects. Vocations have declined sharply for religious sisters and brothers but there has been a sufficient flow of students for the diocesan priesthood (Weafer, 1988). The pruning away of devotional ceremonial since the Second Vatican Council and the new focus on the Eucharist has given increased importance to the role of the priest which counteracts secular trends and attracts male vocations away from the brotherhoods. The holding of Mass in a variety of settings and times has also fostered a new dependency on the priesthood. The Eucharist is also celebrated at major rites of passage which are essentially family occasions. Secular funerals are very rare events. While regular Sunday attendance has grown smaller there would seem to be an ongoing demand for priestly service.

The vocations deficit has forced the withdrawal of religious from many of the institutions they established and a retreat to token presence in others. Parochial clergy and religious, however, still retain control of the major part of educational resources and are a significant minority in health and welfare services.

The gap left by the decline of religious could be filled by greater lay Catholic involvement and some steps have been taken to achieve this by, for example, Mater Dei college for teachers of education. Opus Dei have been active in setting up schools and a third-level college. The charismatic renewal movement offers new opportunities for spiritual development of lay people (Szuchewycz, 1988). The biggest impact made by lay Catholics has been in taking the lead on political matters such as the campaigns against divorce and abortion.

There are many spheres of Irish life over which the church has little or no influence. The mass media are the church's main competitors in the interpretation of Irish society. Public administration is outside the church's influence. The leading sector in Irish society and the one to which state policies are increasingly moulded is that of business and finance and transnational capitalism. Here again the Church is inexpert and a nonplayer. There has been a growing distance between bishops and politicians with regard to social policy and family law.

In the final analysis, the surrender of sovereignty by joining the European Community has interposed a set of institutions and higher courts which can repulse attempts to retain a traditional Catholic approach to legislation. The direct sphere of influence of the church is, therefore, limited. Its indirect influence is also limited in many respects, to a declining constituency of orthodox Catholics.

References

ALVEY, D., 1991. *Irish Education, the Case for Secular Reform*, Dublin, Church and State Books and Athol.

ARNOLD, M. and H. LASKEY, 1985. *Children of the Poor Clares: the Story of an Orphanage*, Belfast, Appletree.

BLANSHARD, P., 1954. *The Irish and Catholic Power: An American Interpretation*, London, Verschoyle.

BREEN, R. *et al*, 1989. *Understanding Contemporary Ireland*, Dublin, Gill and Macmillan.

BRESLIN, A. and J. WEAFER, 1985. *Religious Beliefs, Practice and Moral Attitudes: A Comparison of Two Irish Surveys 1974-1984*, Maynooth, Council for Research and Development Report No. 21.

CLEAR, C., 1987. 'Walls within Walls: Nuns in Nineteenth-Century Ireland' in C. Curtin *et al* (eds.), *Gender in Irish Society*, Galway University Press.

DEPARTMENT OF EDUCATION. Statistical Reports, 1965-6, 1991-2.

DILLON, M., 1993. *Debating Divorce: Moral Conflict in Ireland*, The University Press of Kentucky.

EIPPER, C., 1986. *The Ruling Trinity: A Community Study of Church, State and Business in Ireland,* Aldershot, Gower.

FULTON, J., 1991. *The Tragedy of Belief,* Oxford, Clarendon Press.

HANNAN, D. and H. TOVEY, 1978. 'Dependency, Status Group Claims and Ethnic identity'. Proceedings of the Fifth Annual Conference of the Sociological Association of Ireland.

HORNSBY-SMITH, M.P., 1992. 'Social and Religious Transformations in Ireland: a Case of Secularisation.' Proceedings of the British Academy, Vol. 79, pp. 265-290.

INGLIS, T., 1987. *Moral Monopoly: The Catholic Church in Modern Irish Society,* Dublin, Gill and Macmillan.

LARKIN, E., 1975. 'Church, State and Nation in Modern Ireland', *American Historical Review,* Vol. 80, No. 5.

LARKIN, E., 1976. 'The Devotional Revolution in Ireland, 1850-1875' in *Historical Dimensions of Irish Catholicism,* New York, Arno.

LYNCH, K., 1989. *The Hidden Curriculum: Reproduction in Education, An Appraisal,* London, Falmer.

MAC GRÉIL, M., 1991. *Religious Practice and Attitudes in Ireland: Report of a Survey 1988-89.* St. Patrick's College, Maynooth.

MARTIN, D., 1969. *The Religious and the Secular: studies in Secularization,* London, Routledge and Kegan Paul.

MARTIN, D., 1978. *A General Theory of Secularization,* New York, Harper and Row.

NIC GHIOLLA PHÁDRAIG, M., 1976. 'Religion in Ireland', *Social Studies,* Vol. 5.

NIC GHIOLLA PHÁDRAIG, M., 1988. 'Ireland: The Exception that Proves Two Rules' in T. Gannon (ed.), *World Catholicism in Transition,* London, Macmillan.

O'DOWD, L., 1987. 'Church, State and Women: The Aftermath of Partition', in C. Curtin *et al* (op. cit.).

PEILLON, M., 1982. *Contemporary Irish Society: An Introduction.* Dublin, Gill and Macmillan.

RYAN, L., 1979. 'Church and Politics: the last twenty-five years', *Furrow,* Vol. 30, No. 1.

SZUCHEWYCZ, B., 1988. 'The Meanings of Silence in the Irish Catholic Charismatic Movement', in C. Curtin and T.M. Wilson (eds.), *Ireland from Below,* Galway University Press.

TITLEY, E.B., 1983. *Church, State and the Control of Schooling in Ireland, 1900-1944,* Kingston, McGill-Queen's University Press.

WEAFER, J. and A. BRESLIN, 1983. *A Survey of Irish Catholic Clergy and Religious, 1970-1981,* Maynooth, Council for Research and Development, Report No. 17.

WEAFER, J., 1988. 'Vocations: a

Review of National and International Trends', *Furrow*, Vol. 39.

WEBER, M., 1982. 'The Distribution of Power: Class, Status, Party', in A. Giddens and D. Held (eds.), *Classes, Power and Conflict*, London, Macmillan.

WHYTE, J.H., 1980. *Church and State in Modern Ireland, 1923-79*, 2nd edition, Dublin, Gill and Macmillan.

WHYTE, J.H., 1985. 'Recent Developments in Church-State Relations', *Seirbhís Phoiblí*, Vol. 6, No. 3, pp. 4-10.

20
Cherishing the Children of the Nation Unequally: Sectarianism in Ireland

ROBBIE McVEIGH

The republic guarantees religious and civil liberty, equal rights and equal opportunities to all its citizens, and declares its resolve to pursue the happiness and prosperity of the whole nation and of all its parts, cherishing all the children of the nation equally, and oblivious of the differences carefully fostered by an alien government, which have divided a minority from the majority in the past (Proclamation of the Irish Republic, 1916)

Introduction

On the night of 14 August 1994, Seán Monaghan, a young Catholic man, was abducted in West Belfast by members of a Loyalist paramilitary organisation, the Ulster Freedom Fighters. He was taken to a house on the Shankill Road and tortured. He managed to escape through a window and appealed for help to a woman in a house across the street. The woman phoned her daughter who came with her boyfriend and took him to her home. 'Others then took possession of Mr Monaghan who was bound and gagged with black tape. He was taken out of the house and murdered a short distance away' (*Irish News*, 27/8/1994). The killing attracted a great deal of publicity. It was a particularly brutal

murder which revived fears of the 'Shankill Butchers'.[1] The
horror was compounded by the fact that Mr Monaghan had
so nearly escaped before being handed back to his killers.
Many people searched for an explanation for this killing.
In admitting the murder, the UFF claimed Mr Monaghan had
been 'picked up scouting loyalist areas' (*The Irish Times,*
15/8/1994). The RUC dismissed this claim: 'This was really a
horrendous sectarian murder of a quiet, timid, unassuming
20-year-old who only lived for his girlfriend, Noelle, and their
15-month-old twin girls.' The victim's father said: 'There was
no reason whatsoever for Seán's murder. He was not political
in any way. Any of his friends, Protestant or Catholic, will tell
you, he was never in anything at all. He worked in Protestant
areas cutting grass.' The *Irish News* (16/8/1994) wrote: 'It is
difficult to comprehend what must have been running
through the minds of those who slaughtered Seán Monaghan
... The history of sectarianism in Northern Ireland has been
punctuated by savage acts of unbelievable barbarity. There
appears to be no rational reason for such behaviour.'

Given the particular horror of Seán Monaghan's murder, this
popular incomprehension was understandable. Sociologists
however cannot be satisfied with explanations limited to
calling the perpetrators 'irrational' or 'evil'. They should
distrust the analysis of complex social phenomena in terms of
individual pathology. Sociologists have to search for themes
and patterns in acts of violence which begin to explain the
context in which they occur. The one thing that everyone –
apart from the killers – agreed was that this murder was
sectarian. There was nothing unusual in this in Northern
Ireland. About one third of all deaths in the last phase of the
'troubles' – from the murder of Catholic barperson Peter
Ward in 1966 to the Republican and Loyalist cease-fires of
1994 – were directly 'sectarian' in that people were killed
simply because they were perceived to be either Protestant or
Catholic (Sutton, 1994, pp. 195-203).[2] Some 750 Loyalist
killings (or around 80 per cent of all Loyalist killings) and
some 150 Republican killings (or around 10 per cent of all

Republican killings) were sectarian in this sense. Most other deaths were *sectarianised* in the sense that the sectarian identity of the victim lent some degree of meaning to her or his death. The adjective 'sectarian' is also routinely used by politicians and the media to explain a whole range of other events in Northern Ireland – from violent assault through cases of discrimination to incidents of name calling. However, if we want to go beyond this, there is less help available: people rarely tell us what it means to say something is sectarian; they rarely explain how individual sectarian acts connect to the wider phenomenon of sectarianism; indeed, they rarely tell us what sectarianism is.

This is not just the fault of politicians or the media. People who look to academia to explain what it means to say something is a 'sectarian act' will find little assistance. For example, when I started comparative research on racism and sectarianism in 1987, I went to the library of Queen's University, Belfast to obtain the list of references under 'sectarianism' in the subject catalogue.[3] There was one book listed in this category. The dearth of material on sectarianism contrasted starkly with the profusion of literature on racism in Britain. How could such a silence exist in a country which had been in the thrall of 'sectarian bloodshed' since 1966? How was it possible that sectarianism had – apparently – not been addressed at all?

The undertheorisation of sectarianism

In fact there are a number of works which have made the first steps towards a 'sociology of sectarianism'. Liechty's *Roots of Sectarianism in Ireland* (1993) is a concise overview of the historical development of sectarianism. Burton's *The Politics of Legitimacy* (1978) and Bell's *Acts of Union* (1990) stand out as fine examples of grounded theory based, respectively, on the experiences of Belfast Catholics and Derry Protestants. *Northern Ireland: Between Civil Rights and Civil War* (O'Dowd *et al*, 1980) was an important attempt to theorise the connection between sectarianism and the state. There is a substantial amount of work which makes points about sectarianism in the course of analysing something else. Discussion of the 'Northern Ireland conflict' inevitably touches on sectarianism (Bew *et al*, 1979; Boal and Douglas, 1982; Harris, 1986). There have been recent attempts at a more direct discussion and theorisation of sectarianism (Fulton, 1991; Jenkins, 1986; Logue, 1992; McVeigh, 1990; O'Dowd, 1989; Working Party on Sectarianism, 1993). We have also seen the beginnings of a 'micro-sociology of sectarianism' focused on the operation of sectarianism in different areas of social life in Northern Ireland (Bairner and Sugden, 1993; Counteract, 1994; Finlay, 1993; Smyth, 1990). However none of these analyses – important though they are – obscures the fact that the historical absence of theoretical and empirical work on sectarianism is much more remarkable than the contributions that have been made. For a long time there was more work on Irish-related sectarianism in Britain than in Ireland, north or south (Murray, 1984; Neal, 1988; Phillips, 1982; Waller, 1981). Sectarianism remains not just 'untheorised' but 'undertheorised' (McVeigh, 1992a). The failure of academics and intellectuals to explicate the concept of sectarianism is part of a process of silence on the subject.

This silence has occurred because analysing sectarianism has never been a neutral enterprise – it has always been laden with political implications. None of the main political and intellectual traditions in Ireland – British/colonial, Unionist/Loyalist or Nationalist/Republican – has wanted to engage with sectarianism (McVeigh, 1992a). British/colonial intellectuals have found it difficult to free themselves from the accumulated weight of 800 years of racist and sectarian stereotyping of Irish behaviour; nationalist and unionist intellectuals have resisted addressing their own responsibility for the perpetuation of sectarianism. Most academics work explicitly or implicitly within one of these frameworks and inherit the aversion to analysing sectarianism attendant to each. The underdevelopment of academia in the Republic of Ireland and the academic ghettoisation of Northern Ireland means there are relatively few people around wanting to sponsor, or undertake, or read, research on sectarianism. Those who exact government money for sectarianism-related research are tied very firmly to the British state's non-definition of sectarianism. Sectarianism becomes mistakenly or disingenuously identified with sectarian discrimination or equated with the actions of bigoted individuals. This approach allows for little more than exercises in sectarian head-counting – a kind of apolitical arithmetic. Sociologists, as well as other academics, have colluded in the under-theorisation of sectarianism.

The undertheorisation of sectarianism begs the question of what a comprehensive 'sociology of sectarianism' might involve. How should the concept of sectarianism be developed as an analytical tool? Certainly, any analysis must locate contemporary sectarianism in terms of the colonial history of Ireland. It must also move away from the view of sectarianism as 'nasty ideas' towards holistic, structural analysis. It must look at inequalities of power and at structures which reproduce these inequalities. The sociology of sectarianism must also be able to make sense of the key role of the state in structuring sectarian relations. It also needs to address the specificity of sectarianism as an explanatory concept: What is the connection between sectarianism and religion? And how does sectarianism connect with other social structures and processes like gender and ethnicity? This suggests that we need to address at least four key aspects of sectarianism before we arrive at a working definition:

- sectarianism and the colonial process in Ireland
- sectarianism as a structure
- sectarianism and the state
- sectarianism and other social structures and processes.

Much of our analysis will necessarily focus on Northern Ireland since sectarianism affects almost every aspect of life there. We should remember, however, that sectarianism played a crucial historical role over the whole of Ireland, and its contemporary importance in the south – while obviously less pervasive than in the north – is more than vestigial. We should also remember that sectarianism continues to be a feature of social relations in every country with a significant Irish emigrant bloc.

Sectarianism and the colonial process in Ireland

An analysis of the specificity of the British colonisation of Ireland is central to making sense of sectarianism. Contemporary sectarianism is rooted in the particular forms that colonisation assumed in Ireland. There are two ideal-typical forms of British colonial government: administrative and settler. Administrative colonialism leaves the indigenous social formation much as it is. Settler colonialism attempts to destroy the indigenous social formation and replace it with a colon, a newly planted social formation.[4] Ireland fell somewhere between these models. It suffered a complex combination of administrative and settler colonialism over a uniquely long period of time. This history accounts for much of the specificity of contemporary sectarianism.

Even before the Reformation religious difference was a key aspect of colonial discourse in Ireland. There is a kind of 'proto-sectarianism' in the writings of Giraldus Cambrensis and other intellectuals of colonialism who saw Irish religious practice as a prominent manifestation of Irish otherness as well as a justification for the Anglo-Norman colonisation of Ireland (Curtis, 1991, p. 10). However while religious difference – and an inchoate sectarianism – was part of anti-Irish discourse from the first, it was not fundamental to it. Early colonial legislation makes it clear that *Irishness* – not Irish *Catholicity* – was the threat and the problem for English colonists.

Plantation and the sectarianisation of the settler/native encounter
Settler/native relations only became inevitably sectarianised in the plantation period of British colonialism in Ireland

(Brady and Gillespie, 1986). At first the settler/indigenous difference was measured more in terms of nationality or 'race' than religion. The profusion of 'Irish' and 'Scotch' and 'English' streets in plantation towns shows that the early distinction was made between Scots and English who happened to be Protestant and Irish who happened to be Catholic. But the triumph of the Protestant Reformation in Britain and its failure in Ireland meant that religion became the key signifier of difference between settler and native – especially as second and third generation English and Scots planters became increasingly 'Irish'. Contemporary texts offer some evidence of how and when this transformation took place. Petty's groundbreaking *Political Anatomy of Ireland* (1691) classifies the inhabitants of Ireland thus:

There are of people, men, women, and children	1,100,000
Of the people, there are English	200,000
Scots	100,000
Irish	800,000
Of Papists	800,000
Of Non-Papists	300,000

The Scots are Presbyterian, and the Irish, Papists. But the English are above 100,000 legal Protestants, or Conformists and the rest are Presbyterians, Independents, Anabaptists, and Quakers.

Thus Petty uses both sectarian and national ascriptions for the different elements of the population of Ireland as early as the seventeenth century. More importantly, he is already conflating the two: all Irish are Papists and all Papists are Irish. In fact, elsewhere in his text he shows he is well aware of complicating examples such as the Catholic 'Old English' and Irish converts to Protestantism. But these examples prevent a simplistic analysis which supports an identity between nationality and religion and are therefore discarded. From this point on it is clear that sectarian labels are about more than religion in Ireland. They approximate more to notions of ethnicity – involving nationality, politics, culture, 'race', and boundary maintenance as much as faith and religious organisation (Barth, 1969). Religious identity had become – and remains – the main signifier of ethnic difference in Ireland.

The 'Protestantisation' of colonial rule proceeded through the seventeenth century as the sectarian politics of the British state assumed particular forms in Ireland (Foster 1988, pp. 51-9). The 'Glorious Revolution' of 1688 and the post-Limerick settlement in Ireland saw the sectarianisation of government in Britain in general, and in a specific form in Ireland, with the establishment of the Protestant ascendancy.[5] The penal laws were the most notorious aspects of this settlement. They assumed the form of religious apartheid in which Catholics were stripped of almost all their civil and political rights (Connolly, 1992). These laws were, however, more concerned with controlling indigenous Irish resistance than with instituting theocracy. Religion and nationality were becoming more intertwined in Ireland all the time. For example, by 1801, in the wake of the United Irish rising, Musgrave in his *Memoirs of the different rebellions in Ireland* makes clear his belief in the connection between the racial and religious inadequacies of the Irish:

> The country, as described by Giraldus Cambrensis, in the twelfth century, an eye witness of it, was overrun with forests, or cankered with bogs, and in all the arts of civil life, the inhabitants were little superior to the Indians of North America. Their Brehon laws were calculated to make them savage, and to keep them so; as they rendered the enjoyment of life and property insecure. Their kings or princes did not succeed each other by hereditary descent, or any fixed principles of succession, but by force and arms. It was a peculiar favour from heaven to send a civilized people [the English] among them ...

Speaking a different language, and obedient to different laws, it is not to be wondered at, that the English and Irish did not cordially unite, and coalesce into one people ... The introduction of the reformed religion, by increasing the antipathy of the native Irish to the English, was a new source of calamities; for, as the Irish ecclesiastics, to whom the ignorant and bigoted people were blindly devoted, received their education in foreign seminaries, particularly in those of France and Spain, they returned to their native country, bound solemnly to the pope, in an unlimited submission, without any bond of allegiance to the king, and full fraught with those absurd and pestilent doctrines, which the moderate of their own communion, at least, professed to abominate; of the universal dominion of the pope, as well spiritual as temporal; of his authority to excommunicate and depose princes; to absolve subjects from their oaths of allegiance, and to dispense with every law of God and man; to sanctify rebellion and murder, and even to change the very nature and essential difference of vice and virtue (1801, pp. 5-6).

Thus, by the start of the nineteenth century religion was inseparable from ethnicity and politics in Ireland. As Ireland industrialised, urbanised and democratised through the century, sectarian relations were transformed but not reduced. The north-east of Ulster – which already had a Protestant majority as a result of the plantation – became the focus of industrialisation. A new Protestant industrial elite developed alongside the existing Protestant aristocracy. Protestant and Catholic people moved from the country to the cities reproducing rural sectarian relations among the new industrial working class. Democratisation meant that unionists were increasingly vulnerable to popular opposition to the link between Ireland and Britain. The notion of there being 'two nations' in Ireland – a 'Protestant' north-east and a 'Catholic' south – began to gather support among unionists in Ulster who saw separation from the rest of Ireland as the only way of protecting their political and economic privilege (Buckland, 1973). Increasing political polarisation between unionists based in the north-east and nationalists dominant everywhere else eventually led to the British Parliament partitioning Ireland in 1920. Two states emerged from partition. The southern 'Irish Free State' gradually evolved towards independence from Britain; Northern Ireland emerged as a peculiar form of 'statelet' with *de facto* autonomy over internal affairs but ultimately subordinate to the British Parliament at Westminster. James Connolly had anticipated that partition would facilitate a 'carnival of reaction' on both sides of the Irish border (1973, p. 275). In the event, both states used sectarianism and religious identity to undermine radical social and political movements and secure a form of conservative populist hegemony – one 'Protestant', the other 'Catholic'.

The 'carnival of reaction': two sectarian states?

Northern Ireland (also known as 'Stormont' from its seat of government) lasted from 1921 to 1972 and institutionalised sectarianism in new forms. The state was sectarian in conception – it was constructed to provide the largest land area that could be safely governed by Unionists. The 'Six Counties' excluded the three Ulster counties which had large Catholic majorities but included two others – Tyrone and Fermanagh – which had Catholic majorities as well as Antrim, Armagh, Derry and Down which had Protestant majorities (Mitchell, *et al*, 1985, pp. 72-6). It was also sectarian in practice (Farrell, 1980). Most importantly it mobilised a huge proportion of the Protestant community to repress and police the Catholic community (Farrell, 1983). The sectarianisation of policing through the overwhelmingly Protestant RUC and 'B' Specials set the seeds of future conflict. It also routinely gerrymandered political con-stituencies to the advantage of Unionists. It discriminated against Catholics in public employment, public housing and in the development of the infrastructure of Northern Ireland (Hepburn, 1980, pp. 150-78). As the movement for civil rights and reform gathered momentum in the 1960s, Stormont became increasingly vulnerable. Sustained popular resistance to the security forces in 1969 brought the administration to the verge of collapse and the British state was forced to send in troops to support it. The British became increasingly reluctant to leave security policy – especially control of the British army – to the unambiguously sectarian Northern Ireland government. Stormont was prorogued in 1972 and replaced by Direct Rule from Westminster.

The focus on the sectarianism of the Northern Ireland state at Stormont has masked the profound changes in the nature of the state since the imposition of Direct Rule. Before 1972 the British state was more concerned to 'insulate' the Northern Ireland 'problem' than resolve it (O'Dowd, *et al*, 1980, pp. 16-21). When it could no longer do this, it was forced to blame the Stormont regime. The British intervention was justified in terms of 'keeping the peace' and addressing the existing unfairness of Northern Ireland. The suggestion that the state itself continued to be sectarian became increasingly embarrassing to successive British administrations. There was a basic acceptance that the state-let had been sectarian in concept and practice between 1920 and 1972 but that Direct Rule ushered in a brave new world of non-sectarianism. The state apparatus – which had been clearly and organically linked to 'one side' – was now neutral arbiter in an atavistic sectarian struggle between Protestants and Catholics.

Analysis of the Northern Ireland state in terms of 'British neutrality' is palpably misguided (O'Dowd, *et al*, 1980). Nevertheless, there is a need to theorise changes in the nature of the state and its relationship to sectarianism since 1972. The weakening of the links between the state and Orangeism/Unionism has forced enormous changes in cultural and political identity within the Protestant/

Unionist/Loyalist community. Equally the increased opportunity to work with and for the state has encouraged changes
in the Catholic/Nationalist/Republican bloc, particularly
within the Catholic middle class and the Catholic Church. Of
course sectarianism continues to structure almost every
aspect of life within the six counties – if anything it has
intensified since Direct Rule. This period has been characterised by 'more repression and more reform' (O'Dowd *et al*,
1980, pp. 1-27). The state has intervened to reform some of
the more blatant instances of sectarian discrimination. But it
has simultaneously vastly increased the capacity of the repressive state apparatus and done nothing to change the sectarian
nature of that apparatus.

The *raison d'être* of Northern Ireland was sectarian. In
contrast, the Irish Free State was established with the promise
of national independence transcending sectarian difference.
The proclamation of 1916 had made this explicit in its
aspiration to 'cherish all the children of the nation equally';
the constitution of the Free State and later the Republic
reaffirmed this commitment. So the new state was supposed
to transcend the sectarian division that had been imposed by
imperialism. However, the Catholic Church was also crucial
to securing political hegemony. Some key events – the
prohibition of divorce in 1925, the Censorship Act of 1929,
the Mayo County Library case in 1931, the Criminal Law
Amendment Act of 1935 which outlawed contraception, the
failure of the 'Mother and Child' health care scheme of 1951
and the 'Fethard on Sea boycott' in 1957 – illustrated the
power of the Catholic Church and the political capital that
could be made out of anti-Protestant sectarianism. In this
period the state and the major political parties – including,
crucially, Fianna Fáil – moved away from formal anti-
sectarianism towards Catholic populism (Hepburn, 1980,
pp. 133-49). However, the endowment of Catholicism in the
south was very different from the totalising sectarianism of
the north. The Catholic Church was given a 'special position'
– but other religions were also recognised and supported by

the state.[6] A form of pluralist theocracy developed which
established the Catholic Church but also incorporated other
religious blocs and ensured that they would not be
particularly critical of the state. Protestant spokespeople in
the Republic of Ireland have never felt the need to echo the
strident anti-Catholicism of their northern counterparts
(Bowen, 1983; White, 1975).

The institutionalised power of the Catholic Church in the
Republic of Ireland began to dissolve only recently. The
Church is now less powerful and has been subjected to a
degree of liberalisation from within. The state has begun
tentatively to withdraw some of the power and influence it
ceded to the Catholic Church. The recent political consensus
on equality for gay men was one indication of the relative rise
of secularist influence. However, the power of populist
Catholicism should not be underestimated – groups like
Youth Defence, Solidarity, and SPUC are testament to the
continued vibrancy of populist Catholicism and its ability to
mobilise politically. While this mobilisation has moved away
from   populist   anti-Protestantism   towards   populist
Catholicism which is sectarian by default rather than intent,
its power persists. The state in the Republic of Ireland is still
sectarian, albeit in very different ways to the Northern
Ireland statelet. Sectarianism has diminished in importance
in the Republic of Ireland but it continues to exist.

Sectarianism as a structure

Our historical overview makes it clear that sectarianism in
Ireland has involved much more than the actions of
individuals. Yet many analyses have made the mistake of
atomising sectarianism, seeing it as something involving the
actions of individual Protestants and Catholics. In consequence, explanation is couched at the level of individual
pathology and there is no analysis of structural sectarianism.
However, sectarianism has never been simply an aggregate of
the deeds of unpleasant or deviant 'sectarians' – although

these are an intrinsic part of sectarianism. Sectarianism is also a structure – the whole has properties not possessed by the individuals involved alone and the individuals involved can change without necessarily altering the properties of the whole.

One example of this is the way that sectarian cues have been transferred and changed across generations. Burton shows how everybody in Northern Ireland is involved in 'telling the difference' (Burton, 1978, pp. 37-67). People may or may not be sectarian – in the sense of being prejudiced – but they are all sectarianised. They draw on a complex system of signifiers to 'tell', with varying degrees of accuracy – whether someone is Protestant or Catholic. A whole range of cues – such as first name, surname, school attended, area lived in, football team supported, the way that someone says 'h' – are used in combination to establish sectarian identity.[7] 'Telling' happens because the information is crucial – not because people have some peculiar fetish for knowing religious identity. Sectarian identity always sets the parameters for conversation; it is sometimes a matter of life or death. So, even at an interpersonal level, sectarian relations involve a complex semiology which goes well beyond individual bigotry.

Sectarianism is even more clearly a structure when it is institutionalised across large areas of life in Ireland. This institutionalisation manifests itself in very different ways for Protestants and Catholics. While the marginalisation of Protestants in the Republic may still be very real, there is little evidence of Protestant disadvantage in consequence of this. In fact the Protestant population in the south always constituted a relatively privileged minority and it has managed to retain this status. In contrast, the disadvantage of Catholics in Northern Ireland across a whole range of indices is undoubted – unemployment, housing, education and so on (Hepburn, 1982; PSI, 1987, 1989; SACHR, 1987, 1990). Moreover, in the absence of alternative explanations, historical and contemporary discrimination is the most obvious cause of this disadvantage (Eversley, 1989; Jenkins, 1988). So sectarianism involves a whole system of inequality and disadvantage – institutional as well as individual discrimination.

Sectarianism structures every aspect of life in Northern Ireland: people live class, gender, sexuality, and so on through sectarianism. It structures people's lives at every stage: where they are born, where they go to school, where they work, where they socialise, where they live, where they die and where they are buried. It is more than an ideology or a set of practices or an amalgam of individual actions: sectarianism dominates every aspect of life. In a sense sectarianism is the modality in which life is lived in the six counties. It is less pervasive in the Republic of Ireland but it continues to influence social relations in areas with substantial numbers of Protestants and Catholics.

Sectarianism and the state

The state has to be a focus of any analysis of sectarianism because it has more power to be sectarian than any other social actor. Since both states in Ireland have been described as sectarian, there is clearly a need to investigate the role of the state in reproducing sectarianism.[8] We need to pose the question: is the state in Ireland – north and south – sectarian? It is clear that at one level both states are 'sectarian' simply because they have Protestant and Catholic citizens who stand in different relations to their respective states. The two states in Ireland involve quite different numbers and proportions of Protestants and Catholics (see table). In Ireland as a whole about three quarters of the population is Catholic, one fifth is Protestant and one tenth is 'other religion' or 'no religion'. In the south of Ireland the number of Protestants continues to decline. They form a tiny minority of the population. In Northern Ireland the proportion of Catholics continues to increase. The Six Counties will soon be fairly evenly divided between Protestants and Catholics.

	Total	Catholic	Protestant	Other/no religion
Ireland – 32 counties	5,101,237	3,890,111 (76.3%)	913,547 (17.9%)	297,579 (5.8%)
Republic of Ireland (69.1% of the Irish population)	3,523,401	3,284,472 (93%)	115,411 (3%)	123,518 (4%)
Northern Ireland (30.9% of the Irish population)	1,577,836	605,639 (38.4%)	798,136 (50.6%)	174,061 (11%)

Source: CSO 1991, NI Census 1991.

Each of these proportions is significant. In the south, the smallness of the Protestant minority makes it difficult for Protestants to challenge aspects of sectarianism that they might not like, e.g. legislation on divorce or the endowment of the Catholic Church. In the north, sectarian demography means that the state is increasingly unstable. Northern Ireland was brought into existence to perpetuate Protestant supremacy through formal democracy – the Protestant 'majority' upon which this was founded appears increasingly vulnerable. Elements of the state apparatus and civil society – including the security forces – that continue to have an over-representation of Protestants are increasingly problematised. The 32-county proportion makes it clear that Protestant 'fears' of a united Ireland have a basis in reality – Protestants are a minority. Equally it suggests that the north cannot be incorporated into the south without significant changes. The unproblematised Catholic ethos of the contemporary state in the Republic of Ireland will be impossible with a regionally-focused 20 per cent Protestant minority. So a simple demographic profile makes clear some of the nuances of sectarian relations in both states in Ireland.

There is also substantive work on the sectarianism of both

states. The relationship between church and state in the Republic of Ireland was usefully analysed by Whyte (1980). Farrell provided a similarly detailed analysis of the Northern Ireland state and sectarianism between 1921 and 1972 (1980). The relationship between sectarianism and Northern Ireland post-Direct Rule was addressed by O'Dowd *et al* when they demonstrated that the state is not 'above' the 'Northern Ireland problem' (1980). Neither is the state 'above' sectarianism – north or south of the Irish border. This is especially true in the north – sectarianism assumes a particular form because the British state is in Northern Ireland. Sectarianism has a specifically Irish dynamic but this does not preclude sectarianism being crucially affected by different British arrangements for the government of Northern Ireland. The telling example of this has been the changing character of sectarianism since 1972. Many people, not least British politicians and civil servants, anticipated that Direct Rule would remove the stigma of sectarianism from Northern Ireland. It was assumed that the new state formation – controlled as it was by 'non-sectarian' British people who replaced 'sectarian' Northern Ireland Unionists – could be unproblematically reformed.

Unfortunately, sectarianism could not be exorcised by such an act of the will. Since 1972 the British state has been managing rather than dismantling sectarianism. In many respects it is no less sectarian than the Stormont regime although the process is different. The state implicitly recognises the reality of sectarian social relations and works within those relationships. It is dependent on a sectarian security apparatus; it continues to tolerate segregation in employment and housing and education. It is constantly managing, reworking, and responding to social forces that are structured by sectarianism. We have already seen how the state worked and reworked sectarian relations in the south of Ireland. Both states – albeit in very different ways – have fundamentally affected the way in which sectarianism has manifested itself.

Sectarianism and religion

The relationship between sectarianism and religious faith and religious institutions continues to be crucial to understanding sectarianism. Contemporary sectarianism is sometimes regarded as being simply the negative face of religion. As we have already seen, however, the development of a settler/native dichotomy in Ireland lent sectarianism a significance beyond theological difference and dispute. The contemporary relationship between religion and sectarianism is just as complex. For example, there is no easy answer to the question, What makes someone an 'Ulster Protestant' or an 'Irish Catholic'? Many people are reluctant to surrender the notion that – at base – what makes them Protestant or Catholic is their religiosity. This suggests that it is impossible to be simultaneously Protestant or Catholic and agnostic or atheist. At one level this is entirely logical since the meaning of 'Protestant' and 'Catholic' is inseparable from their theological origins but, at another level, it is simply wrong. For instance, if we define 'Protestants' as those who attend a 'Protestant' church once a week, we exclude a large section of the Ulster Protestant community. In contrast, if we define 'Protestants' as those people opposed to the political machinations of the Catholic Church hierarchy, we include a fair number of 'Catholics'. The Church of Ireland (after the Roman Catholic Church, the largest denomination in Ireland) is – as part of the Anglican communion – more correctly 'reformed Catholic' than Protestant. In most theological and structural matters the Church of Ireland is closer to Roman Catholicism than to Presbyterianism and Methodism and other smaller Protestant churches.

Both despite and because of these differences, theological anti-Catholicism or anti-'Romanism' remains an important part of Irish Protestant identity. Theological anti-Catholicism, institutionalised through the Orange Order, becomes an integrative mechanism which constructs Irish Protestants as an ethnic and political community across class and denominational lines.[9] But this community is more about politics and ethnicity than theology. Likewise the Catholic Church helps to construct the notion of a 'Catholic community' which transcends political and social differences; but the community so formed includes many people who have no religious faith. Religious conviction and organisation is a part of what makes up Protestantness and Catholicness but it is not definitive.

However, the idea that politics or national identity defines Protestants and Catholics in Ireland is no more satisfactory. Sectarian identities do not form a continuum from 'pure Protestant' at the Loyalist end to 'pure Catholic' at the Republican end. While many Protestants are Unionists and Loyalists and many Catholics are Republicans and Nationalists, there are many counter examples of Protestant Republicans and Catholic Unionists (Campbell, 1991; Biggs-Davidson et al, 1984). If we take the example of Protestant identity, it becomes clear that simplistic definitions will not work. Many religious Protestants actively repudiate Loyalism; and many Loyalist Protestants actively repudiate religion. Furthermore many people who are neither Loyalist nor religious continue to see themselves as 'Protestants' in some way. This may be the strong assertion that being a Protestant is an ethnic identity which is independent of both religious belief and politics; or it may be the weak assertion that what makes someone Protestant in Ireland is simply not being Catholic.[10] Either way these Protestants remain as much part of the matrix of Irish Protestantism as the most committed Loyalist or Evangelical. There is nothing peculiarly 'Protestant' about this – the complexity is mirrored by the different political and national identities within the Catholic community in Ireland.

So there is no essence of 'Protestantness' or 'Catholicness'; they cannot be defined in terms of religious or political affiliation. Rather, in Ireland at least, what makes a Protestant a Protestant and a Catholic a Catholic is the interaction of a number of factors: historical, religious, social, cultural, and political. Protestant and Catholic are identities whose boundaries are both self-defined and other-defined.[11] Moreover, sectarian identity is defined by its relationship to its Protestant or Catholic *other*: a crucial element of being a Protestant is not being a Catholic, a crucial element of being a Catholic is not being a Protestant. Sectarian identity emerges and is reproduced in the midst of this complex matrix of self and other definitions. Religious belief and religious institutions are part of, but only part of, sectarian identity and sectarianism in Ireland.

Sectarianism and other social structures and processes

Sectarianism cannot be theorised in isolation from other social phenomena. Its connection to race, gender and class has to be central to any analysis. Racism is the most immediately important since many people have focused on the similarity of racism and sectarianism. Some have argued that sectarianism is definitely racism (Moore, 1972), while others have argued that it is definitely not racism (Nelson, 1975). Others have attempted to theorise both in comparative context (Brewer, 1991, 1992; McVeigh, 1990). It is easy to identify the commonalties between racism and sectarianism. Most importantly, violence is a defining part of the experience of both (Darby, 1986; GLC, 1984). Neither racist nor sectarian violence has received adequate attention from researchers but a complex combination of harassment and intimidation is central to the way in which both racism and sectarianism function (McVeigh, 1990). More specifically, both involve a problematic relationship between the policing and criminal justice system and communities in minority situations – whether minority status is based on numbers or power or both (McVeigh, 1994; Solomos, 1988). Discrimination is also common to both racism and sectarianism (Jenkins 1988). While there are contrasts between Catholic and Black disadvantage measured on a number of different indices – especially access to employment, housing and education –

there are equally significant differences within both groups.[12] The key element in racist and sectarian discrimination is the existence of relative disadvantage rather than some calculus of absolute disadvantage around the world. There is also a similarity in terms of racist and sectarian otherness. Both racism and sectarianism define who 'we' are and who 'we' are not. While the crucial signifier of difference is characteristically 'visible' with racism and 'invisible' with sectarianism, this point does not take us very far.[13] Unless we argue that racism is caused by differences in skin pigmentation, we have to accept that race is a social construct. If racism is essentially about socially constructed differences and sectarianism is undeniably so, then the issue of 'visible' or 'invisible' otherness is hardly crucial.[14] Finally, unequal power relationships are a defining feature of both racism and sectarianism. Any racialised or sectarianised situation involves a combination of the desire and the capacity to be racist or sectarian. It involves prejudice between social groups but it also involves differential access to power. Racism and sectarianism both involve an asymmetrical power relationship between different ethnic groups.

Despite all the similarities, however, it is not appropriate to collapse racism and sectarianism. The simplest reason for this is that people do not routinely use the term racism to describe sectarianism. People have sometimes attempted to identify the two but this has never been adopted in popular discourse. Another reason is that white Irish people, Catholic and Protestant, are very capable of being racist to minority ethnic people (Crowley, 1993; McVeigh, 1992b). In practice racism and sectarianism have separate – if related – dynamics in Ireland. A further reason is that with sectarian labels people can 'convert' – at least theoretically. A Protestant can become a Catholic and a Catholic can become a Protestant. A Black person cannot convert to being white and a white person cannot convert to being Black.[15] However, the principal reason for not collapsing sectarianism and racism is the current power location of the Protestant/Unionist/

Loyalist bloc in Ireland. This contrasts starkly with the position of white people in racist situations. However much members of the Protestant/Unionist/Loyalist bloc believe or wish themselves to be British, they have been constructed as Irish by the British. In consequence, they can experience just as much anti-Irish racism as the Catholic/Nationalist/Republican bloc in Northern Ireland.[16]

The British state stands in an antagonistic relationship with both the Catholic/Nationalist/Republican and Protestant/Unionist/Loyalist blocs in Northern Ireland. While it has historically empowered Protestants to be sectarian, this does not mean that the interests of Protestants and the British state in Northern Ireland are the same. The empowerment of Protestants was always based on an alliance rather than an identity of interest. This continues to be the case; only now the strain on the alliance is more marked, the divergence of interest is more obvious, and the increasing dissatisfaction of the British state less and less disguised. The ambiguity of the relationship between the British state and Protestants is crucial to understanding Protestant/Unionist/Loyalist dis-empowerment – Protestants feel that they may be abandoned in their minority status at any time by the British state. In many ways. Protestant sectarianism is a function of powerless-ness, while the racism of white people is a function of their power. This is the crucial substantive difference between sectarianism in Ireland and racism.

A more general point is that racism is a subset of a much wider group of conflicts involving ethnicity and different combinations of racial, religious, cultural and political factors. Racism involves huge power imbalances, such as those between white Americans and Native Americans or white and Black British people or Irish Travellers and settled people. Racism also usually involves a history of institu-tionalised violence of the most profound kind, e.g. colonial domination, slavery and genocide. While sectarianism involves differences in power between Catholics and Protestants, these are not of the same magnitude as those

involved in situations of racism. Sectarian conflict is more
akin to situations of ethno-religious conflict that are not
explained in terms of racism – like the war in the former
Yugoslavia or 'communalism' in India. In this sense relations
between Protestants and Catholics in Ireland are properly
described as sectarianised while those between Irish people
(Protestant and Catholic) and British people are properly
described as racialised.

Just as racism and sectarianism overlap and yet remain
separate, so other structures connect in particular ways with
sectarianism. O'Dowd *et al* throw useful light on the
relationship between sectarianism and class:

> Sectarianism is not a superstructural phenomenon
> floating free of an abstracted economic base which in
> turn is divided into classes. In NI sectarian division is a
> material reality which has been constituted and re-
> constituted throughout the history of capital
> accumulation and class struggle in Ireland as a whole. It
> is not merely an overlay on class division to be seen as
> something which is either more or less important than
> class ... Class relations in NI were only experienced as
> *sectarian* class relations. Sectarian division is itself a
> particular historical division of class, or more precisely of
> class fractions, cemented together in Protestant and
> Catholic class alliance. In other words sectarian division
> is a class phenomenon and *vice versa* (1980, p. 25).

There is no simple opposition of class identity and sectarianism.
Sometimes class heightened class consciousness combines with
and reinforces heightened sectarian consciousness (Patterson,
1980).

Equally sectarian division is a gendered phenomenon. The
construction of gender identity in Ireland is inseparable from
sectarian identity. Most analyses of sectarianism have
completely disregarded the issue of gender. Worse still they
have written about sectarian relations between Protestant and

Catholic men as if they were sectarian relations between Protestant and Catholic people. The experience of sectarianism by women and the gendered aspects of sectarianism remain crucial to any sociology of sectarianism and yet they remain largely unaddressed (Finlay, 1993; Moore, 1993). For example violence against women in Northern Ireland can be quite specifically sectarianised but this has never been given detailed attention (McWilliams, 1994). The relationship between gender and sectarianism requires much further theoretical and empirical work. This illustrates the wider point that sectarianism is not separate from other social structures and processes. Racism, sexism and class each structure sectarianism in specific ways and yet these often remain 'separated discourses' in academic discussion (Allen, 1987). Any analysis of sectarianism should seek to integrate these discourses and make sense of the way in which they intersect and structure each other.

Defining sectarianism

Definitions of complex social phenomena are never entirely satisfactory. Sectarianism, like racism or sexism, traverses centuries and continents and no definition can ever capture its full complexity. Nevertheless, the process of defining is useful because the limitations of any definition encourage further debate and refinement. And definition can at least highlight some of the constituent elements of a social phenomenon. It is useful, therefore, for us to develop a working definition of sectarianism:

> Sectarianism in Ireland is that changing set of ideas and practices, including, crucially, acts of violence, which serves to construct and reproduce the difference between, and unequal status of, Irish Protestants and Catholics.

This definition points to several of the key aspects of sectarianism. Firstly, sectarianism is connected to Ireland. Of course the term 'sectarianism' is used to explain inter-Christian conflicts that have nothing to do with Ireland; and sectarianism is akin to other ethno-religious phenomena like 'communalism' and 'fundamentalism'. But, in Ireland, sectarianism is not a theological dispute that can be abstracted from the wider society; it is a constituent part of Irishness. Secondly, sectarianism is a process – it has changed profoundly over time. Although there is a continuity between the two, the sectarian violence which took place in 1795 between rural labourers in Armagh is not the same as the sectarian violence which takes place in 1995 between urban working-class people in Belfast. Thirdly, sectarianism is about ideas and actions in combination. Sectarianism is institutionalised in different ways; it is about structures as well as individual behaviours. Fourthly, sectarianism is about difference – it provides one of the key categories of identity (who 'we' are) and otherness (who 'we' are not). Moreover, it is about unequal difference; sectarianism involves an asymmetrical power relationship. Fifthly, sectarianism involves groups that have formally religious labels, 'Protestant' and 'Catholic', but these labels are not theologically exact. These social identities are more about ethnicity than religion.

Conclusion

Sectarianism should be a key concept in Irish sociology. Without an appropriate theorisation of sectarianism it is impossible to achieve a full understanding of most aspects of contemporary Irish society. We should be suspicious of any analysis of aspects of Irishness that ignores the structuring effects of sectarianism. Despite this sectarianism has been undertheorised and under-researched by sociologists and other academics. We have looked at some of the necessary conditions for a satisfactory sociology of sectarianism: an understanding of the connection between sectarianism and colonialism in Ireland; a recognition that sectarianism is a structure; a focus on the role of the state in reproducing sectarianism; and close attention to the relationship between sectarianism and other structures like racism and sexism. We have looked at some of the key ways in which sectarianism manifests itself: through violence and discrimination and otherness. We have also developed a tentative definition of sectarianism that pulls some of these key elements together. It must be emphasised that there is a need for much further theoretical and empirical work on sectarianism. A comprehensive theorisation of sectarianism, grounded in extensive and properly resourced research, remains one of the fundamental challenges for Irish sociology.

Notes

1. See Bruce's *The Red Hand* (1992) for a detailed account of the operation of the Shankill Butchers and other Loyalist sectarian groups.
2. The point about 'perceived' sectarian identity is important. People have often been murdered by 'mistake' when they have been perceived incorrectly to belong to a particular sectarian category. For example, Margaret Wright, a young Protestant women was beaten and then shot several times in the head in a Loyalist club in April 1994 because she was believed to be Catholic and was unable to persuade her captors otherwise (McWilliams, 1994). Deaths such as this one are no less 'sectarian' than deaths in which the murderers get the sectarian identity of their victim 'right'.
3. It turned out that even this book made no reference to sectarianism in Northern Ireland; it looked at religious sectarianism in Britain. A whole sociology of sectarianism has developed outside the Irish context to research and theorise religious and political 'sects' (Wallis, 1975).
4. British India is a model of the first administrative colonialism; the British introduced a temporary political/military elite which 'taxed' the existing social system. British Australia is a model of the second settler colonialism; the British attempted to exterminate the indigenous people and replace them with a new social formation.
5. It important to remember that the United Kingdom remains a formally sectarian state – sectarianism is institutionalised in its

constitution and through an established church in a much more direct way than it ever was in Northern Ireland or the Republic of Ireland (Robilliard, 1984).

6. For example, the 1937 constitution recognised the role of all the major Protestant denominations in Ireland. It was also the first anywhere to recognise the role of Jewish people within the nation. The 'special position' of the Catholic Church was removed from the constitution by referendum in 1972.

7. Robert McLiam Wilson's novel *Ripley Bogle* (1989) illustrates the terrible importance of 'telling the difference'. It also captures the essence of sectarianism as it is lived in Northern Ireland better than most academic texts on the subject.

8. The absence of work on sectarianism and the state confirms the need for broader state research in Ireland (O'Dowd, 1991).

9. For example, the Loyal Orange Institution of Ireland defines itself thus: 'The Institution is composed of Protestants, united and resolved to the utmost of their power to support and defend the rightful Sovereign, the Protestant Religion, the laws of the realm, and the Succession to the Throne in the House of Windsor, BEING PROTESTANT; and united further for the defence of their own Persons and Properties, and the maintenance of the Public Peace. It is exclusively an Association of those who are attached to the religion of the Reformation, and will not admit into its brotherhood persons whom an intolerant spirit leads to persecute, injure, or upbraid any man on account of his religious opinions. They associate also in honour of KING WILLIAM II, Prince of Orange, whose name they bear, as supporters of his glorious memory.' (Constitution, Laws and Ordinances of the Loyal Orange Lodge of Ireland, no date, original emphasis).

10. The complexity of the religious/political interface in Northern Ireland is illustrated by the 12,386 people who insisted on recording their religious denomination as 'Protestant' in the 1991 census. This constitutes the seventh largest 'religious denomination' even though respondents were expressly instructed that 'Protestant' was an inappropriate response to the religious question. In the Republic of Ireland, where 'Protestant' was accepted as a legitimate discrete religious category for the first time in 1991, 6,347 people so identified.

11. For example, someone might define herself as a Catholic given her family background and yet have her Catholicness denied by other Catholics because she has no religious faith. In contrast, her brother might define himself as Irish (neither Protestant nor Catholic) and yet have his Catholicness confirmed by

Protestants who define him as a Catholic (or a 'Fenian' or a 'Taig') given that same family background. Indeed, the very names used in pejorative sectarian abuse confirm the complexity of the dynamics of sectarianism. While Protestant and Catholic are formally religious labels, anti-Catholic names like 'Fenian' and 'Taig' and anti-Protestant names like 'Orangie' or 'Black' more obviously involve a complex combination of different references. 'Fenian' (from the nineteenth century Irish revolutionary movement) is a formally political label; 'Taig' (from the Irish family name 'Teague') is a formally ethnic label first used in anti-Irish jokes in Britain; 'Orangie' is a reference to the Orange Order – an institution which consciously combines religious, ethnic and political identities; 'Black' combines allusion to the Royal Black Institute (the elite branch of the Orange Order) and the 'Black North' (the supposedly industrial and bleak character of Protestant Ulster) with a ready-made association between blackness and pejorative racial stereotypes.

12. For example, the disadvantage suffered by East African Asians and Bengalis in Britain is very different, yet both groups clearly experience racism (Modood, 1994).

13. This point also begs the question of 'racisms' where visible differences are much less obvious than in the Black/white interface in Britain. The racialisation of, and racism experienced by, Irish people, particularly Irish Travellers, is a case in point (Curtis, 1991; McVeigh, 1992c).

14. Sectarianism and religious stereotyping is sometimes a function of the decline of unproblematic racialisation. This is certainly true of the rise in anti-Islamic prejudice in Britain. As the obvious otherness of first generation Black immigrants was replaced by a more confusing interface with second generation Black Britishness, the importance of 'Islam' as a signifier of difference increased, so that Hindus, Sikhs and Christians of Asian origin all became 'Muslim' as post-Rushdie pejorative shorthand for 'British Asian'.

15. Racial categorisations are themselves by no means absolute: throughout history people have 'passed' in racial categories to which they have not belonged; and in apartheid South Africa, the government introduced the category of 'honorary white' for Black people who they needed to exempt from racist restrictions. The limited nature of the possibility of 'conversion' within Irish sectarianism is illustrated by the fact that the Orange Order, while committed to theological Protestantism, asks that it members be born Protestant.

16. In fact, given the perceived 'reasonableness' of many 'Catholic' demands, anti-Irish racist stereotypes may sometimes be more commonly applied to Irish Protestants, notably Ian Paisley, than Irish Catholics.

References

ALLEN, S., 1987. 'Gender, Race and Class in the 1980s', in C. Husband (ed.), *'Race' in Britain: Continuity and change*, London, Hutchinson.

BAIRNER, A. and J. SUGDEN, 1993. *Sport, Sectarianism and Society in divided Ireland*, Leicester University Press.

BARTH, F., 1969. *Ethnic Groups and Boundaries*, London, Allen and Unwin.

BELL, D. 1990. *Acts of Union: Youth Culture and Sectarianism in Northern Ireland*, London, Macmillan.

BEW, P., P. GIBBON and H. PATTERSON, 1979. *The State in Northern Ireland*, Manchester University Press.

BIGGS-DAVIDSON, J. and G. CHOWDHARAY-BEST, 1984. *The Cross of Saint Patrick: The Catholic Unionist Tradition in Ireland*, Buckinghamshire: Kensal.

BOAL, F.W. and J.N. DOUGLAS, 1982. *Integration and Division: geographical perspectives on the Northern Ireland problem*, London, Academic Press.

BOWEN, K., 1983. *Protestants in a Catholic State, Ireland's privileged minority*, Dublin, Gill and Macmillan.

BRADY, C. and R. GILLESPIE, 1986. *Natives and Newcomers: The making of Irish Colonial Society 1534-1641*, Dublin, Irish Academic Press.

BREWER, J.D., 1991. 'The Parallels between Sectarianism and Racism: the Northern Ireland Experience', *One Small Step Towards Racial Justice: The Teaching of Antiracism in Diploma in Social Work Programmes*, CCETSW, Education and Training Paper no. 8.

BREWER, J.D., 1992. 'Sectarianism and Racism and their parallels and differences', *Ethnic and Racial Studies* 15 (3), pp. 352-364.

BRUCE, S., 1992. *The Red Hand: Protestant Paramilitaries in Northern Ireland*, Oxford University Press.

BUCKLAND, P., 1973. *Ulster Unionism and the Origins of Northern Ireland 1886-1922*, Dublin, Gill and Macmillan.

BURTON, F., 1978. *The Politics of Legitimacy*, London, RKP.

CAMPBELL, F., 1991. *The Dissenting Voice, Protestant Democracy in Ulster from plantation to partition*, Belfast, Blackstaff.

CONNOLLY, J., 1973. *James Connolly: Selected Writings* (edited by P. Berresford Ellis), New York, Monthly Review Press.

CONNOLLY, S.J., 1992. *Religion, Law and Power, the making of Protestant Ireland 1660-1760*, Oxford, Clarendon.

COUNTERACT, 1994. *Dealing with Sectarian Harassment in the Workplace*, Belfast, ICTU.

CROWLEY, N., 1993. 'Racism and the Travellers', *Anti-Racist Law and the Travellers*, Dublin, DTEDG, ICCL and ITM.

CURTIS, L., 1991. *Nothing but the Same Old Story: The Roots of Anti-Irish Racism*, London, Information on Ireland.

DARBY, J., 1986. *Intimidation and the Control of Conflict*, Dublin, Gill and Macmillan.

EVERSLEY, D., 1989. *Religion and Employment in Northern Ireland*, London, Sage.

FARRELL, M., 1980. *The Orange State*, London, Pluto.

FARRELL, M., 1983. *Arming the Protestants*, London, Pluto.

FEA, 1983. *Report of an Investigation by the Fair Employment Agency for Northern Ireland into the Non-industrial Northern Ireland Civil Service*, Belfast, FEA.

FINLAY, A., 1993. 'Sectarianism in the Workplace: The Case of the Derry Shirt Industry 1868-1968'; *Irish Journal of Sociology* 3.

FOSTER, R., 1988. *Modern Ireland 1600-1972*, London, Penguin.

FULTON, J., 1991. *The Tragedy of belief, division, politics and religion in Ireland*, Oxford, Clarendon.

GLC (Greater London Council), 1984. *Racial Harassment in London: Report of a Panel of Inquiry set up by the Greater London Council Police Committee*, London, GLC.

HARRIS, R., 1986. *Prejudice and Tolerance in Ulster*, Manchester, Manchester University Press.

HEPBURN, A.C., 1980. *The Conflict of Nationality in Modern Ireland*, London, Edward Arnold.

HEPBURN, A.C., 1982. *Employment and Religion in Belfast 1901-1971*, Belfast, Fair Employment Agency.

HICKEY, J., 1986. 'Religion in a Divided Society' in P. Clancy, S. Drudy, K. Lynch, and L. O'Dowd (eds.), *Ireland: a Sociological Profile*, Dublin, IPA.

JENKINS, R., 1983. *Lads, Citizens and Ordinary Kids*, London, RKP.

JENKINS, R., 1984. 'Understanding Northern Ireland', *Sociology*, Vol. 18, No. 2.

JENKINS, R., 1986. 'Northern Ireland: in what sense 'religions' in conflict?', in *The Sectarian Divide in Northern Ireland Today*, Royal Anthropological Institute of Great Britain and Ireland, Occasional Paper No. 41.

JENKINS, R., 1988. 'Discrimination and Equal Opportunity in Employment:

650   Irish Society: Sociological Perspectives

Ethnicity and Race in the
United Kingdom' in Gallie
(ed.), *Employment in Britain*,
London, Blackwell.
LIECHTY, J., 1993. *Roots of
Sectarianism in Ireland:
Chronology and Reflections*,
Belfast, Working Party on
Sectarianism.
McVEIGH, R., 1990. *Racism
and Sectarianism: A
Tottenham/West Belfast
Comparison*, unpublished PhD
thesis, Department of Social
Studies, Queen's University,
Belfast.
McVEIGH, R., 1992a. 'The
Undertheorisation of
Sectarianism', *Canadian
Journal of Irish Studies* 16.
McVEIGH, R., 1992b. 'The
Specificity of Irish Racism',
Race and Class 33, no. 4.
McVEIGH, R., 1992c. 'Racism
and Travelling People in
Northern Ireland', *SACHR
17th Annual Report*, London,
HMSO.
McVEIGH, R., 1994. *The
Security Forces and Harassment
in Northern Ireland*, Belfast,
Committee on the
Administration of Justice.
McWILLIAMS, M., 1994. 'The
woman "other"', *Fortnight* 328.
MITCHELL, A. and
P. Ó SNODAIGH, 1985. *Irish
Political Documents 1916-1949*,
Dublin, Irish Academic Press.
MODOOD, T., 1994. *Racial
Equality: Colour, Culture and
Justice*, London, IPPR.
MOORE, R., 1972. 'Race
Relations in the Six Counties:

colonialism, industrialisation,
and stratification in Ireland'
Race, 14.
MOORE, R., 1993. 'Proper
Wives, Orange Maidens or
Disloyal Subjects? Situating
the Equality Concerns of
Protestant Women in
Northern Ireland',
unpublished MEq thesis,
Equality Studies, University
College, Dublin.
MURRAY, B., 1984. *The Old
Firm. Sectarianism, sport and
society in Scotland*, Edinburgh,
Donald.
MUSGRAVE, R., 1801. *Memoirs
of the Different Rebellions in
Ireland, from the Arrival of the
English*, Dublin, Milliken and
Stockdale.
NEAL, F., 1988. *Sectarian
Violence, the Liverpool Experience
1819-1914, an aspect of
Anglo-Irish history*, Manchester
University Press.
NELSON, S., 1975. 'Protestant
"Ideology" considered: The
Case of Discrimination', in
I. Crewe (ed.), *The Politics of
Race*, London, Croom Helm.
O'DOWD, L., 1989a. 'Ignoring
the Communal Divide: The
Implications for Social
Research' in R. Jenkins (ed.),
*Northern Ireland, Studies in
Social and Economic Life*,
Aldershot, Avebury.
O'DOWD, L., 1989b. 'Analysing
Sectarianism'. Paper delivered
to the Sociological Association
of Ireland Conference,
University College Galway,
1989.

O'DOWD, L., 1991. 'The States of Ireland: Some Reflections on Research', *Irish Journal of Sociology* 1.

O'DOWD, L., B. ROLSTON and M. TOMLINSON, 1980. *Northern Ireland: Between Civil Rights and Civil War*, London, Conference of Socialist Economists.

PATTERSON, H., 1980. *Class Conflict and Sectarianism: the Protestant Working Class and the Belfast Labour Movement 1868-1920*, Belfast, Blackstaff.

PHILLIPS, P.T., 1982. *The Sectarian Spirit: Sectarianism, society and politics in Victorian Cotton Towns*, London, Toronto University Press.

PSI (Policy Studies Institute), 1987. *Equality and Inequality in Northern Ireland*, PSI Occasional Paper 39. Part 1: Employment and Unemployment by D. J. Smith. Part 2: The Workplace by G. Chambers. Part 3: Perceptions and Views by D.J. Smith.

PSI, 1989. Equality and Inequality in Northern Ireland, PSI Occasional Paper 47. Part 4: Public Housing by D. J. Smith and G. Chambers.

ROBILLIARD, St. J. A., 1984. *Religion and the Law: Religious liberty in Modern English Law*, Manchester, Manchester University Press.

SACHR (Standing Advisory Commission on Human Rights), 1987. *Religious and Political Discrimination and Equality of Opportunity in Northern Ireland: Report on Fair Employment*, London, HMSO.

SACHR, 1990. *Religious and Political Discrimination and Equality of Opportunity in Northern Ireland, Second Report*, London, HMSO.

SMYTH, M., 1990. *Race, Sectarianism and Social Work Training in Northern Ireland, a discussion document*, Derry, Working Group on the Teaching of Inequality.

SOLOMOS, J., 1988. *Black Youth, Racism and the State*, Cambridge, Cambridge University Press.

SUTTON, M., 1994. *Bear in mind these dead: an Index of Deaths from the Conflict in Ireland 1969-1993*, Belfast, Beyond the Pale.

WALLIS, R. (ed.), 1975. *Sectarianism, analyses of religious and non-religious sects*, London, Owen.

WALLER, P. J., 1981. *Democracy and Sectarianism; a political and social history of Liverpool 1868-1939*, Liverpool University Press.

WHITE, J., 1975. *The Protestant Community in the Irish Republic*, Dublin, Gill and Macmillan.

WHYTE, J., 1980. *Church and State in Modern Ireland*, Dublin, Gill and Macmillan.

WILSON, R. M., 1989. *Ripley Bogle*, Belfast, Blackstaff.

WORKING PARTY ON SECTARIANISM, 1993. *Sectarianism: A Discussion Document*, Belfast, Inter-Church Centre.

21
The Social Shaping of the Environmental Movement in Ireland*

STEVEN YEARLEY

Introduction: the greening of social science in Ireland

Until recently, sociologists in Ireland and Britain had shown little interest in ecological problems. However, two main factors have helped to alter this state of affairs in the last few years. Firstly, in the late 1980s, there was a large and rapid rise in popular and political concern about widespread, sometimes global, ecological threats – threats such as the likelihood of global warming, the Europe-wide effects of acid rain and the increasing depletion of the world's protective ozone layer. Internationally, the membership of campaigning organisations such as Greenpeace, Friends of the Earth and the World Wide Fund for Nature soared (McCormick, 1991, p. 152) and political parties hurried to incorporate some green thinking into their party programmes. As commentators and journalists, teachers, advertisers and the marketing personnel of large corporations caught on to these issues and

---

* The research on which this chapter is based was supported by a research grant from the Science Policy Support Group/Economic and Social Research Council (UK) and by a McCrea Research Award from the University of Ulster.

began to examine their social impact, social scientists too became interested (for an overview see Yearley, 1992a). Although growth in commercial and popular interest in the environment has since been checked by the economic reverses widespread in Europe and North America, these countries' governments have generally accepted that environmental policy is an enduring responsibility. In a similar vein, social scientists have taken the view that environmental considerations must play a part in any comprehensive approach to society, its problems and needs.

The second stimulus developed over a longer time span. Social scientists noticed that, throughout Ireland, groups – usually locally based and relatively small – were organising to protest about environmental damage or hazards in specific localities. Whether it was proposed lignite mining in County Tyrone, uranium extraction in Donegal or an asbestos factory and associated disposal site in County Cork, groups of local residents were forming to combat the perceived threat to their environment (Baker, 1990; Tovey, 1992). On many occasions groups such as these were led to oppose what appeared to be economic development for their regions. Their protest was at odds with the state's intentions and brought them into conflict with state agencies (such as the Industrial Development Authority) and powerful industrial interests. The groups drew on a variety of supporters, from newly arrived rural dwellers to long-established families, from politically experienced campaigners to those with no history of protest. Sociologists and political scientists were interested in the nature of these groups and in the factors which influenced the growth and success of their campaigns.

There is a third factor which has also played a part in prompting the interest of social scientists although this factor exhibits less 'human interest' than the previous two and its influence comes from outside Ireland: it is the growing role of the European Union in affecting member states' environmental policies. Increasingly the EU is acting as a broker for cross-national agreements as well as issuing guidelines and directives which substantially determine large aspects of member states' environmental legislation and policy. In part this expansion in the EU's role has been justified by the impact of environmental issues on trade. If the Irish Republic had looser environmental controls than, say, Germany this would mean that Irish manufacturers would be able to produce goods more cheaply which, in turn, would put German industry at a comparative disadvantage – something the EU is bent on eliminating. But the EU has also acted on environmental issues as a way of advancing its political and social mission. EU institutions are generally keen to see their power and influence increased and this is one area where they can be seen to act in the common good. Students of political and social change could not help but notice the impact of the EU when it led to innovations, both in the Irish Republic and in the UK, governing such areas as planning, agriculture, the emission of acidic gases and waste management.

New social movements and the re-shaping of politics in the industrialised world

In attempting to account for the growth of environmental awareness in Ireland, the obvious first place to turn is towards sociological studies of the 'new social movements' (NSMs). In the last quarter century such movements, including the feminist, peace and environmental movements, have developed throughout the industrialised capitalist world. The generally accepted interpretation of the growth of these movements points to the social basis for their support. In the second half of this century there has been a marked change in the overall class structure of the western world. The traditional industrial working classes have shrunk from over half the workforce to something around a third. For example, in a major British survey conducted in 1984, the working class was reckoned at just over 35 per cent (Marshall *et al*, 1988, p. 22). At the same time, there has been a corresponding growth in the middle classes to about 50 per cent (1988, p. 22; see also Abercrombie and Urry, 1983). Accordingly the social basis of support for the 'old' social movements (the labour movement and various traditional trade union organisations), based on the interests of labour, has declined dramatically. By contrast, new social movement issues have exerted their strongest appeal on the middle classes, particularly those sections described by Berger as the 'knowledge class'.

Berger has argued that this knowledge class is a new phenomenon, a 'new middle class ... of people whose occupations deal with the production and distribution of symbolic knowledge' (1987, p. 66). Most of these people have occupations which have only recently come into being. They can be defined as the intellectuals and service workers whose knowledge is not generally directed towards material production. They work in education, counselling, communications and – as he archly puts it – in the 'bureaucratic agencies planning for the putative non-material needs of the society (from racial amity to geriatric recreation)' (1987, p. 67). These people tend to argue for the value of such 'non-material' values as education, personal development and self realisation. The crucial issue is that this knowledge class tends, in Berger's view, to be antagonistic to the core values of free-market capitalism, a fact which he attributes chiefly to two factors. Firstly, this class has an interest in having 'privilege based on educational credentials' rather than on naked wealth. Secondly, this class has an interest in expanding the role of the welfare state in which its members find work.

> [T]he knowledge class has an interest in the distributive machinery of government, as against the production system, and this naturally pushes it to the left in the context of western politics (1987, p. 69).

Accordingly, in Berger's view, this section of the middle classes tends to align itself with social democratic or labour-type parties.

While this class offers a new source of support for such parties, the situation the parties face is still difficult. There remains a tension between pursuing the interests of the parties' (dwindling) traditional members (creating jobs, retaining industry and so on) and pursuing the more 'progressive' interests of the knowledge class. The two may come into direct conflict over, for example, dirty but job-creating industries or over the arms industry, where shipyards or tank factories employ thousands of working class people but few members of the knowledge class. Such tensions have had various political consequences but among them has been the fact that members of the knowledge class have not been completely assimilated into these leftist parties. Instead they have often pursued their values and political objectives through social movements and pressure groups and through non-traditional parties such as the Greens.

However, this analysis of the social background to the emergence of sustained environmental awareness needs two final amendments (Yearley, 1992b, pp. 132-5). The first supplementary consideration is that, as Berger points out, the knowledge class is huge – far larger than the membership of NSMs. Even a generous definition of 'supporters' of the movement in the UK put peak numbers considerably below 10 per cent of the available population (McCormick, 1991, p. 152). Thus while this class makes up much of the social basis for the green movement, membership of the class is not by itself sufficient to specify that people will support particular NSMs. Other people with an identical class profile to that of keen environmentalists may support different movements or causes, promoting – for instance – community arts or alternative therapies.

Secondly, by no means all supporters of environmentalism derive from this class. According to data from the most recent British Social Attitudes Survey, while the majority of members of ecological organisations are drawn from middle-class occupations, 7 per cent of members are from the unskilled manual class, with similar percentages in the other manual-class groupings. Or, to take an example from the other end of the social spectrum, it is worth noting that the executive director of Greenpeace UK is a (Labour) peer, Lord Melchett (McCormick, 1991, p. 77). Equally, the World Wide Fund for Nature (WWF), founded in the 1960s, was largely established by business leaders. The British 'royals' have had a long and close association with environmental bodies, the Duke of Edinburgh with WWF and the Prince of Wales with the Royal Society for Nature Conservation (RSNC) (Pye-Smith and Rose, 1984, pp. 187-9).

Since membership of the knowledge class does not narrowly determine participation in particular NSMs, other factors must be involved too and prominent amongst these is the active 'marketing' role undertaken by environmental voluntary agencies such as Friends of the Earth and the Royal Society for the Protection of Birds. These are the organisations (known in the literature as 'social movement organisations' or SMOs) which take the lead in 'selling' the environmental message to its target audience. Their respective successes in attracting media attention, in devising popular campaigns, in fundraising and in recruitment inevitably influence the size and shape of the movement. Any analysis of the development of environmental awareness in particular countries must take account of the role played by these entrepreneurial movement organisations and of the SMOs' interaction with government, the media, and other national and international agencies.

This leaves one final factor to be taken into account, the state of the environment itself. In a country with no ecological problems green campaigners would probably have a steeply uphill struggle. But it would be wrong to suppose that environmental awareness stems in any automatic way from ecological despoliation. There are several reasons for this.

Firstly, some forms of pollution are not easily visible. Global warming may be a colossal ecological threat but climate changes are likely to be so slow that it is not readily detectable except by using extremely elaborate scientific tests. Thus, whether or not people worry about this problem is very unlikely to be determined by their personal experience of the build-up of carbon dioxide. Secondly, some people or countries may be so eager for economic development that they are willing to tolerate pollution. What is unacceptable in one place may well be given a cautious welcome elsewhere. The key role of *social* variables is also demonstrated by the fact that many physical problems arising from industrial pollution are likely to be the same in very many countries, even though public responses are strikingly different. For example, the risks from nuclear power installations are presumably similar in France, Germany, Sweden, Britain and the USA, yet the degree of public opposition has varied very widely. The same argument holds true for related installations such as waste incinerators and even for hazardous agrochemicals. In these cases we can be pretty confident that disparities between people's responses are attributable to social and political variations much more than to physical differences in the nature of the threat. This is, of course, not to deny that ecological problems lead people to worry about the environment. Air quality problems in Dublin, for example, did finally give rise to popular support for policy changes. My point, however, is that the degree of active public concern about the environment is not determined in any straightforward way by the extent of physical ecological problems.

In short, a growing knowledge class and a dwindling working class have brought about a demographic transformation of the political left in the advanced, industrial nations. The knowledge class tends to supply a disproportionate support for NSMs including the environmental movement. Traditional left-wing parties cannot fully transform themselves to accommodate these new interests since they still depend on the working class vote. Supporters of NSMs are therefore attracted to movement organisations and 'alternative' Green parties. The fate of environmental politics in any particular country also depends on the performance of its SMOs and, to a vital but limited degree, on the nature and severity of that country's ecological problems.

The shaping of the environmental movement in the Irish Republic

The development of the environmental movement in Ireland, in both the Republic and in Northern Ireland, can be understood in terms of the three factors outlined so far: the changing social and economic structure, the role of SMOs and the agencies with which they interact, and the ecological base itself. In part the Irish case can be understood in terms of its conformity with the claims outlined above but of equal importance are the ways in which it is exceptional. This is true both north and south of the border although the exceptional features differ. I will deal first with the Irish Republic.

As Baker (1990, p. 47) notes, although Ireland shares:

> . . . many of the features common to west European democracies, the pattern of [its] environmental destruction suggests that it has more in common with third world countries than with its more developed European neighbours.

In other words, the way in which the Irish Republic has sought to pursue rapid industrialisation since the 1950s, primarily by encouraging investment by overseas companies (typically from the USA), has led to distinctive environmental threats. Most notoriously, although far from typically, this is because some foreign companies have seen Ireland as a country in which they can locate processes which have been rendered uneconomical or even been outlawed by changing environmental regulations in their home countries (Leonard, 1988, pp. 122-32). The Irish Republic has had more lax environmental controls and has been so keen to attract investment that operations effectively exiled from the USA have turned up there; the asbestos industry is a case in point (Baker, 1987). Of course, given the less strict regulatory environment, once foreign firms arrived in Ireland – even if they had not come there to pollute – they found that they could cut costs by not adhering to the pollution-control and health and safety standards to which they would have had to subscribe in the USA. In a related way, there was a concern that economic development agencies were so keen to encourage investment that in any tight calculation it would be economic advancement and not the environment which was given the benefit of the doubt.

Less sinisterly, foreign firms excited environmental protest because they were often the first big factories to come to development areas. Any pollution they caused was thus likely to be on a scale unprecedented in that locality. The fact that green-field sites were a common choice for incoming companies increased the likelihood that such factories and their attendant hazards were a new phenomenon for local residents. Several factors contributed to the popularity of green-field locations, including official support for bringing employment to depressed rural areas, the comparative cheapness and convenience of the land, and the advantages for the firm arising from a relatively dependent local workforce. Rural locations also brought industry into close proximity with farm production, still a major source of employment and of exports. In time (Yearley, 1994, p. 165), local objectors and environmental campaigners were to argue that threats to agriculture from pollution (especially from chemical and pharmaceutical plants) outweighed the economic rationale for bringing industry in at all.

Since these issues had a potentially deep effect on local communities, much of the initial environmental protest in the Irish Republic had three noteworthy features. It was directed at industrial pollution or associated mining and dumping; it was targeted to a large degree at foreign firms; and it involved local, usually community-based organisations. On this last point, it is worth emphasising Tovey's obser-vation, that the values espoused in many successful antipollution protests were those of family and community, not those of the international conservation movement (1999, p. 285). This profile of environmental protest differs from that typical in, say, Britain or Germany in all three respects. In the latter cases, environmental activism quickly became associated with professionalised campaign organisations. Equally, protest tended to focus on a wider range of environmental features rather than on factory pollution. Correspondingly, organised opposition targeted the state (over rural planning, nuclear power, nature conservation, pollution from power stations and so on) at least as much as private industry; where it did focus on industry, its targets tended to be domestic companies at least as much as foreign firms. Loosely expressed, the concern was over what 'we' or 'our government' was doing to 'ourselves' rather than – in the Irish case – what 'others' were doing to 'us'.

It is peculiarities such as these which lead Baker to associate Ireland's environmental situation and its environmental protest groups with corresponding phenomena in the third world. The similarity is also brought out by the 'anti-imperialist' vocabulary often deployed during environmental protest in the 1980s and subsequently (see for example Allen and Jones, 1990, pp. 174 and 160-61). Indeed, as Baker points out (1990, pp. 67-8), this general orientation influenced responses to foreign capital even before environmental concerns came to be highlighted. Early anxieties about mining at the beginning of the 1970s were directed at the loss of Ireland's resources to overseas capitalists rather than at the ecological consequences of mining (see also Curtin and Shields, 1988). The difference between the Irish situation and that in, say, Germany or France was further accentuated because the main stimulus to domestic environmental agitation, the anti-nuclear campaign, was resolved in the Irish Republic by 1980 (Baker, 1988). After that date there were no serious political backers for a nuclear industry, quite unlike the French or even the British position where there was an established nuclear industry and plans for nuclear expansion.

662   Irish Society: Sociological Perspectives

Thus, the distinctiveness of environmental protest in Ireland is clearly associated with the nature of the ecological threats, with the characteristics of the agencies responsible for them and, lying behind these two factors, with the pattern of industrialisation. But this distinctiveness is reinforced by a second consideration – the nature of the class composition of Irish society.

The account already given of sociologists' explanation for the rise of new social movements applies most readily to advanced western nations. Less economically developed countries have not experienced the dwindling of the working class (in extreme cases they may not have yet had its growth) or the rise of a substantial knowledge class. They are not characterised by an influential and wealthy class with distinctive values associated with the 'non-material' values of education and personal development mentioned earlier – the class which forms the natural audience for the environmental message.

Of course, the Irish Republic has many members of the knowledge class. Indeed the middle classes in general have grown extraordinarily rapidly in the last two decades from a shade over 23 per cent of the workforce in 1961 to nearly 39 per cent in 1985 (Breen *et al*, 1990, p. 57).[1] As these authors comment:

> The changes in the class composition of the Irish workforce emerged from industrial development that was more rapid, occurred later, and was more state-inspired than in most western societies. So intense were the changes that it is easy to overlook their incompleteness (1990, p. 59).

The societal make-up of the Irish Republic, in terms of the relative sizes of the social classes, in relation to the persistence of a large agricultural sector and in terms of the geographical spread of the members of its social classes is still different from that typical of western industrial societies. Judging by the pattern of support for NSMs elsewhere in the west, one would expect support for the environmental message to smaller in Ireland.

One indirect test of this notion can be carried out by looking at the comparative sizes of environmental SMOs in Britain and the Irish Republic. A number of such organisations can be approximately paired: Greenpeace Ireland/UK; Earthwatch and Friends of the Earth; the Irish Wildlife Federation and the Royal Society for Nature Conservation; the Irish Wildbird Conservancy and the Royal Society for the Protection of Birds. None of these pairings contains exact partners but they are close, and in each case the early-1990s membership of the Irish organisation per head of population was significantly smaller than the British SMO by at least a factor of four and sometimes much more. Thus, Greenpeace Ireland had around 5,000 members, its UK equivalent grouping some 350,000.[2] Of course, some of this difference may be attributable to the publicity and entrepreneurial skills of an SMO's staff. A large size may itself be a benefit – in terms of publicity and so on – which is self-reinforcing. But the consistent imbalance between the two countries' SMOs suggests that there are general factors accounting for the difference as well as ones specific to the organisations. Different 'audience' sizes is a likely and suitable, though not proven, explanation.

None the less, professional campaign organisations have grown in size and influence in the Irish Republic. But as they have grown, their relationships with local community-based groups have not always developed smoothly, in part for the reasons highlighted by Tovey (1992). These larger groups' professionalism and relative wealth can earn them some resentment as well as what local campaigners may see as an undue share of media attention. They also tend to have longer-term objectives than community organisations which are opposing a particular factory or incinerator. Thus Allen, a journalist whose accounts tend to champion the cause of local campaigners, notes that:

... the immediate aims of the communities are often

incompatible with the global aims of [Greenpeace]. [A local campaign leader] made the point, following a meeting addressed by a Greenpeace speaker, that the community wanted to know how to deal with the problem of the incinerator up the road, not hear about clean technology which might solve the problem in years to come (1992, p. 221).

In any country there are likely to be conflicts between local campaigners with urgent, immediate objectives and campaign bodies which are seeking to elaborate long-term policy alternatives. In Britain the centralised nature of political decision making and the growth of environmental pressure groups has tipped the balance conspicuously in favour of the larger campaigning bodies. The more local, clientelistic politics of the Republic together with the nature of environmental problems leaves the balance much more even.

There is one remaining significant form of ecological organisation which needs to be included in this review, Comhaontas Glas or the Green Party. Formed in 1981 as the Ecology Party, Comhaontas Glas expanded during the 1980s in the form of an alliance of reform-minded greens and more radical ecologists. But, following internal disputes over direction, the alliance dissolved and Comhaontas Glas became a parliamentary Green Party, its resolve and increasing professionalism yielding one member of parliament (TD) in the 1989 elections (Baker, 1990, p. 73). This performance was repeated in the 1992 poll. Such electoral success was largely made possible by the system of proportional representation used. Both successful candidates stood in Dublin. Although a comparatively minor success, the election of the party's first TD in 1989 was of great symbolic importance for the party (and contrasts strongly with the situation in Britain where the Greens are handicapped by the electoral system). It gave Comhaontas Glas a taste of success and encouraged growth of the party in the early 1990s to a size roughly comparable to Earthwatch and Greenpeace, a far happier state than that of the UK Greens.

Consideration of parliamentary activity leads us on to the final issue in relation to the Irish Republic. As Breen *et al* stated in the passage cited above, the Irish state has been very influential in shaping Ireland's development. And in the last three decades the primary role of the state and of its associated agencies (the IDA and EOLAS, now re-organised into Forfás, Forbairt and IDA Ireland, and the training agencies) has been to encourage job creation and economic expansion (Breen *et al*, 1990, p. 48). Given that the nature of the stimulus to much environmental protest has been industrial or mining development, this has often cast the state more or less directly as the villain's sidekick in environmental struggles.

This issue came to a head very publicly over a large-scale fire at Hickson Pharmachem in Ringaskiddy, just outside Cork, in August 1993. Overseas chemical companies around Cork had been involved in repeated environmental controversies in the preceding two decades (Peace, 1993). What made this case stand out was that the supposedly-independent Environmental Protection Agency had been set up only the previous month. Its first major public act was thus to investigate the fire (Peace, 1994).[3] According to Peace's analysis, there were two main kinds of difficulty with the EPA's response. First, there were a set of problems around the notion of the agency's 'independence'. These arose, among other things, from the fact that the EPA board members were selected by the minister, and because of the reliance of the EPA on external expertise. More direct concerns over political independence were also stimulated because the junior Minister for Environmental Protection arranged that the EPA should not hold a public inquiry on the fire, but only an in-house investigation. Second, the EPA's response was confined to a study of issues amenable to 'hard' scientific investigation. But since many of the possible adverse consequences of the fire were of a long-term nature and would be likely to come about through subtle effects which are hard to measure, the tone of the EPA's report was seen by some local residents as bland and unjustifiably reassuring. The absence of hard proof of damage was apparently being offered as a reason to believe that there was no danger. This could be seen as dubious reassurance.

In all, successive governments' partiality towards economic development and the preference shown towards industrial interests by some state agencies was commonly presented as evidence that the state could not be entrusted with the care of the environment. It appeared now that even the EPA's independence from 'development' interests was suspect.

Official agencies have also attracted criticism for their role in planning and heritage protection and there have also been scandals associated with planning permission and property development. For this reason, environmentalists have been inclined to look to European legislation as an environmentally 'progressive' force since it has tended to demand higher standards of, for example, environmental impact assessment or water quality than have domestic laws (Coyle, 1994). Certainly, there are pressures from the EU encouraging tighter environmental regulation on the European periphery, not least because uniform standards favour free trade. However, examples already given remind us of the limits of 'progress' flowing from Europe. For one thing, the creation of the EPA was itself stimulated by European requirements. Its origins in the EU do not, however, guarantee its practical independence. Secondly, the EU is committed to socio-economic development in its periphery, and some of the largest recent planning controversies (for example over interpretative centres in the Burren) have concerned developments which are backed by EU funds.

The shaping of environmentalism in Northern Ireland

If the development of environmentalism in the Irish Republic can be said to have been shaped by the country's exceptional characteristics, we would expect this to be even more markedly the case for Northern Ireland. Its claims to exceptional status are very strong indeed (Yearley and Milton, 1990; Yearley, 1995).

In the first place, nearly a quarter of a century of political unrest has had an impact on people's political and social objectives. The Northern Irish have been understandably preoccupied with the 'troubles' and much of the campaigning energy which elsewhere might have gone into new social-movement-type concerns has been diverted by the unrest. The sectarian divide has also largely monopolised politics, dividing parties chiefly on confessional lines and has prevented the emergence of class politics. Any political realignment around 'movement' issues or even in favour of the Northern Ireland Green Party must be extremely unlikely. Worse still from the environmentalists' point of view, none of the leading parties has much of a political interest in advancing green reforms – greening just won't add significantly to their votes. Only the smaller parties, such as the Alliance Party and the Workers' Party, have made much of an effort to publicise their environmental credentials.

But the exceptions extend far beyond the nature of political parties. Business decline, due to ageing industries but hastened by the troubles, has produced an economic situation which not even an extremely anti-interventionist Conservative administration could tolerate. Through the civil service, particularly the Department of Economic Development, but also through state-backed agencies (such as the Industrial Development Board), the government has played a far greater role in economic initiatives in Northern Ireland than almost anywhere else in the UK. The authorities' other priority has been security, important both for the government's political agenda and for encouraging investment.

On the face of it, this commitment by the state to bring in investment might appear similar to objectives in the Republic and one might expect that it would have led to similar

environmental problems and, therefore, protests. This however has not happened. In part this is due to the, understandable, difficulties which the IDB has experienced in
bringing in large-scale foreign investors. A recent IDB listing
cites twenty-six US companies and seven other 'overseas' (i.e.
non-European) investors. None of these firms is involved in
the chemicals or pharmaceutical businesses which have given
rise to the bulk of the protest in the Republic. Indeed, many
of them are in conspicuously traditional sectors such as
tobacco, clothing and light engineering and components
manufacture.[4] By and large, community protest has not been
stirred up in the same way. Furthermore, the leading
experience in Northern Ireland has been one of de-industrialisation. There are few areas awaiting industrial investment which could plausibly present themselves as 'unspoilt'
environments, in the way open to some communities in the
Republic.

There have been some protests over mining and mineral
prospecting. For example, Baker (1989) discusses the community response to the possibility that lignite could be mined
on the western shores of Lough Neagh. The fact that the
threatened area had a largely Roman Catholic population
lent an added intensity to locals' distrust of government and
of official agencies and complicated the residents' relation to
their local (Unionist) MP (1989, p. 66). Sectarian issues
aside, the pattern of protest was very similar to anti-mining
agitation in the Republic. A second significant case was the
proposal by Du Pont (a US multinational) to install a waste
incinerator at its Derry site. The incinerator would have
burned the company's own waste together with hazardous
waste brought in from elsewhere in Ireland, including the
Republic (for a breathless account see Allen, 1992, pp. 3-37).

Successive proposals to site an incinerator in the Republic
of Ireland have been thwarted by local opposition supported
by local TDs and, usually, councils. The frequency of closely
fought general elections has also helped to prevent this kind
of development since, as soon as an election is called,

controversial plans tend to get dropped for fear of losing votes. An incinerator in the North would have suited the Republic's politicians almost more than its industrialists. But Derry's politicians came very close to unity in opposing these plans (the unionists not wanting the Republic's toxins and nationalists joining the general opposition to incineration in Ireland). Community opposition was strong too, reinforced by campaigning expertise offered by experienced community campaigners from the Republic and by Greenpeace Ireland. In early 1992 the proposals were dropped, although it is unclear whether this was because of the strength of local opposition or because of lack of subsidies for the capital cost of the plant. Thus, where circumstances were close to those prevalent in the Republic, environmental protest took much the same form. Typically, however, the circumstances were not similar.

A further significant issue is that, just as in the Republic prior to the EPA, while – on the one hand – the state is active in trying to encourage economic development, at the same time another branch of the civil service is in charge of environmental protection. The government is both poacher and game-keeper. Probably only the lack of opportunities for industrial development has prevented this conflict of interest from being much publicised by protesters.

However, the dual roles of the government have come in for criticism from a different quarter. Just as in Britain, but unlike in the Irish Republic, until recently the dominant environmental SMOs in Northern Ireland have been groups concerned with nature conservation. In particular the Royal Society for the Protection of Birds, the Ulster Wildlife Trust and the National Trust had quite large memberships and healthy incomes. In England an independent body has for many years stood outside the civil service to monitor wildlife conservation. But this arrangement does not hold in Northern Ireland, where one part of the Department of the Environment (DoE) is supposed to undertake this role. However, civil service rules prevent this pro-wildlife element in the

DoE speaking out in public against the Department's actions (over planning, for example) even when these are injurious to the environment (Yearley and Milton, 1990, p. 196). This limitation, along with other setbacks to the cause of wildlife in Northern Ireland, has led the conservation SMOs to be rather more militant and campaigning than would otherwise probably have been the case. At the same time these groups, but particularly the Ulster Wildlife Trust (UWT), were able to take advantage of reasonably generous funding from the government through job creation and employment training schemes. Such groups had the opportunity to gain a higher profile and comparatively greater income than the corresponding groups in Britain. Thus, in the late 1980s and early 1990s the UWT had around fifty employees while neither Friends of the Earth nor Greenpeace had any in Northern Ireland. The UWT was able to build on this favourable position to move into areas which might have been thought to be the natural prerogative of other SMOs, starting an aluminium can recycling scheme and beginning to do environmental consultancy work (Yearley, 1988).

As in the Republic, general levels of participation in environmental organisations remain lower than in Britain, probably for the same reasons of lower income levels and proportionately fewer members of the knowledge class than the European average. But the distribution of membership between these organisations is rather skewed away from Friends of the Earth and Greenpeace towards the more traditional groups. In early 1992 Friends of the Earth established a Belfast office managed and financed through its London headquarters; World Wide Fund for Nature have had a staff member in Northern Ireland for just over a year longer. It remains to be seen whether a full-time presence in Northern Ireland for such groups will lead to a replication of the British profile of environmental SMOs. There is also a Green Party operating in Northern Ireland but it has been largely occupied with working out its policies on the future of Northern Ireland since, on public platforms, its representatives were constantly asked whether it was a unionist or a republican green party.

Finally, the dominance of the state in the Northern Ireland economy is bound to continue unless there are unprecedented political changes. But the state shows little sign of moving away from the poacher-and-gamekeeper model. Although a House of Commons Environment Committee report recommended that Northern Ireland should have an independent Environmental Protection Agency, this was straight-away rejected by the government (DoE NI, 1991). As with the Republic, campaigners are increasingly inclined to look to Europe for the kind of legislative lead they cannot secure domestically.

Concluding remarks

In this chapter we have seen how the development of environmental protest and ecological politics in the Irish Republic and Northern Ireland both deviate from the pattern typical of other advanced western nations. But we have also seen how a focus on certain peculiar characteristics of these two regions – their class structures, their leaders' industrialisation policies and the action of their environmental SMOs and Green parties – allows us to make sense of these deviations. The political and socio-economic conditions in both parts of Ireland shape the environmental challenges they face and the nature of the responses which have been forthcoming. These two cases are thus a test and a vindication of the sociology of new social movements and of SMOs. However, this is not to imply that sociological understanding of Irish environmental sensibilities is now complete; far from it. As this chapter indicates, there is still much to be done on – among other topics – the social and gender structure of support for environmental organisations, on the role of the media in stimulating and shaping the public perception of environmental issues, and on cultural values, religious organisations and environmental concerns (on this last topic see Eipper, 1986 and Tovey, 1992). This chapter is offered as an incitement to further study.

Notes

1. Although derived in a slightly different way, these figures are generally comparable with those given for Britain earlier on; I should like to thank Richard Breen for his assistance in making these comparisons. My thanks go also to the editors and to an anonymous reviewer for very instructive comments on the text.
2. Exact figures for size are very hard to come by partly because memberships fluctuate and because groups are keen to give the impression that they have large memberships. The figures are, though, accurate enough to make the limited point about the relative imbalance in size.
3. I would like to thank Patrick O'Mahony, Ger Mullally, Elaine McCarthy and Tracey Skillington at the Centre for European Social Research at University College Cork for their advice on this aspect of the account. Their current work examines sustainability policies in the Irish Republic.
4. Listing of 'Overseas Investment' supplied by the IDB, Belfast in 1991.

References

ABERCROMBIE, NICHOLAS and JOHN URRY, 1983. *Capital, Labour and the Middle Classes*, London, Allen and Unwin.

ALLEN, ROBERT, 1992. *Waste Not, Want Not*, London, Earthscan.

ALLEN, ROBERT and TARA JONES, 1990. *Guests of the Nation: People of Ireland versus the Multi-nationals*, London, Earthscan.

BAKER, SUSAN, 1987. 'Dependent Industrialisation and Political Protest: Raybestos Manhattan in Ireland', *Government and Opposition*, Vol. 22, No. 3, pp. 352-358.

BAKER, SUSAN, 1988. 'The nuclear power issue in Ireland: the role of the Irish anti-nuclear movement', *Irish Political Studies*, Vol. 3, pp. 3-17.

BAKER, SUSAN, 1989. 'Community Survival and Lignite Mining in Ireland',

The Ecologist, Vol. 19, No. 2, pp. 63-67.

BAKER, SUSAN, 1990. 'The Evolution of the Irish Ecology Movement', in Wolfgang Rüdig (ed.), *Green Politics One 1990*, Edinburgh, Edinburgh University Press, pp. 47-81.

BERGER, PETER L., 1987. *The Capitalist Revolution*, Aldershot, Wildwood House.

BREEN, RICHARD *et al*, 1990. *Understanding Contemporary Ireland*, London, Macmillan.

COYLE, CARMEL, 1994, 'Administrative capacity and the implementation of EU environmental policy in Ireland', in Susan Baker *et al* (eds.), *Protecting the Periphery: Environmental Policy at the European Periphery*, London, Frank Cass.

CURTIN, CHRIS and DAN SHIELDS, 1988. 'The legal process and the control of mining development in the west of Ireland', in Mike Tomlinson *et al* (eds.), *Whose Law and Order? Aspects of Crime and Social Control in Irish Society*, Belfast, Sociological Association of Ireland, pp. 109-28.

DoE NI, 1991. *The Government's Response to the First Report from the House of Commons Select Committee on the Environment*, Cmnd 1484, London, HMSO.

EIPPER, CHRIS, 1986. *The Ruling Trinity – A Community Study of Church, State and Business in Ireland*, Aldershot, Gower.

LEONARD, H. JEFFREY, 1988. *Pollution and the Struggle for the World Product*, Cambridge, CUP.

McCORMICK, JOHN, 1991. *British Politics and the Environment*, London, Earthscan.

MARSHALL, GORDON *et al*, 1988. *Social Class in Modern Britain*, London, Unwin Hyman.

PEACE, ADRIAN, 1993. 'Environmental protest, bureaucratic closure: the politics of discourse in rural Ireland', in Kay Milton (ed.), *Environmentalism: the View from Anthropology*, London, Routledge, pp. 189-204.

PEACE, ADRIAN, 1994. 'Chemicals, conflicts and the Irish Environmental Protection Agency', *CEA News* (Cork Environmental Alliance), No. 9, Spring, pp. 17-22.

PYE-SMITH, CHARLIE and CHRIS ROSE, 1984. *Crisis and Conservation*, Harmondsworth, Penguin.

TOVEY, HILARY, 1992. 'Environmentalism in Ireland: modernisation and identity', in Patrick Clancy *et al* (eds.), *Ireland and Poland, Comparative Perspectives*, Dublin, University College Dublin, pp. 275-87.

YEARLEY, STEVEN, 1988. 'The Greening of Ulster', *Fortnight*, No. 267, pp. 14-15.

YEARLEY, STEVEN, 1992a. *The Green Case*, London, Routledge.

674   Irish Society: Sociological Perspectives

YEARLEY, STEVEN, 1992b.
'Environmental challenges',
in Stuart Hall *et al* (eds.),
Modernity and its Futures,
Cambridge, Polity, pp. 117-67.

YEARLEY, STEVEN, 1994.
'Social movements and
environmental change', in
Michael Redclift and Ted
Benton (eds.), *Sociology and
Global Environmental Change*,
London, Routledge, pp. 150-
168.

YEARLEY, STEVEN, 1995. 'UK
environmental policy and the
politics of the environment in
Northern Ireland', in Tim
Gray (ed.), *UK Environmental
Policy in the 1990s*,
Basingstoke, Macmillan,
forthcoming.

YEARLEY, STEVEN and
KAY MILTON, 1990.
'Environmentalism and Direct
Rule', *Built Environment*,
Vol. 19, No. 3, pp. 192-202.

22
From Democracy to Femocracy: the Women's Movement in the Republic of Ireland

EVELYN MAHON

Introduction

Until recently Ireland was regarded as a predominantly patriarchal society. It had earned this reputation because of its traditional stance on reproductive rights and the low participation of women in the labour force (Pyle, 1990). Hegemonic Catholicism, a poor demand for labour and a state employment policy which discriminated against women in employment prolonged this private patriarchal phase (Mahon, 1994). However, the seventies in Ireland saw the development of the second wave of the women's movement and Ireland's accession to the European Community. The latter required the introduction of equal pay and equal treatment legislation. However, reproductive rights, one of the main issues of the European women's movement, had a complicated and protracted campaign in Ireland. In this article the Irish women's movement from the seventies to the nineties will be examined with some comparative references to women's movements elsewhere.

The women's movement

The women's movement is the best example of a post-World War II social movement which brought about a transformation of social and political life. A social movement is a 'conscious, collective activity to promote social change, representing a protest against the established norms and values' (Dahlerup, 1986, p. 2). One of the necessary conditions for a social movement is structural strain, where people observe social inequalities and explain them in terms of social structural conditions. This explanation grows and emerges as a definition (Smelser, 1963, p. 47). J. Freeman's analysis of the women's movement in the US explains the structural strain which gave rise to feminism there, by invoking Gurr's (1970) concept of relative deprivation. A sense of deprivation is only likely to occur when people are exposed to the possibility of a better way of life. It also explains why the leaders of the women's movement were more likely to be middle class.

The post-war entry of women into the US labour market, and in particular the demand for well-educated low paid clerical and service workers, drew married women into the labour force. The birth rate had declined, especially for second and third children, and fewer women married. There was a considerable increase in the proportion of women being awarded degrees. By 1968 the participation of women aged over sixteen in the labour force had increased to 42 per cent, partly accounted for by the fact that 37 per cent of married women were working (Freeman, 1975, pp. 29-30). In turn, the daughters of these working mothers had aspirations to work, and generally received a college education. This led to a competitive labour market for women in which many could not obtain the kinds of jobs that lived up to their expectations. So women were working, and educated, but in comparison with their husbands they were underpaid, or unable to obtain the jobs they wanted. The result was structural strain and active support among women for a women's movement which would improve their position in society. Structurally then, a high female participation rate in the labour force, especially of married women, can be deemed a pre-condition of women's liberation since it generates feelings of relative deprivation. According to Freeman its other essential elements are:

- a pre-existing network which is cooptable to the ideas of the new movement,
- a series of crises and
- subsequent organisation.

The second wave of the women's movement, an international phenomenon, began in the late sixties and early seventies, almost simultaneously in the US and in Northern Europe. It was facilitated in the US by The President's Commission on the Status of Women in 1961, and in Ireland by a Commission on the Status of Women in 1969. The latter generated a number of politicians and bureaucrats with an interest and concern in women's inequalities.

While not all those in the women's movement necessarily describe themselves as feminist, feminist scholarship provided the ideas and concepts on which the movement was based. Feminism has been characterised as an ideology, and as a doctrine (Dahlerup, 1986, p. 6). Dahlerup used an inclusive definition of feminism which included all ideologies, activities and policies whose goal it is to remove discrimination against women and to break down the male domination of society. Feminist scholarship introduced new concepts, a new form of knowledge, which brought about an entirely new way of examining society. Initially the task was to make women's lives visible, examining their unequal position in society. The exclusion of married women from the workplace, discrimination in pay and promotion, a lack of reproductive rights, the low participation of women in political life, were on the academic and political agendas. Women used the concept of patriarchy to explain their own unequal status in society. Their response was feminism which provided the intellectual basis of the women's movement.

One of the major feminist works of this second wave was Simone de Beauvoir's *Le Deuxieme Sexe* (translated in 1952 as *The Second Sex*), published in France in 1949. This work explicitly differentiated between the concepts of sex (nature) and gender (nurture): 'One is not born, but becomes, a woman. No biological, psychological or economic fate determines the figure that the human female presents in society; it is civilisation as a whole that produces this creative intermediate between male and eunuch, which is described as feminine' (de Beauvoir, 1952, p. 249). The book was translated into many languages, and sold millions of copies world-wide. It greatly influenced young women of the time who later became well-known feminists (Forster and Sutton, 1989). A second major work was Betty Friedan's *The Feminine Mystique*, published in the US in 1974. This work captured effectively the lack of self-identity and the isolation of white suburban middle-class American women. Other important works were Germaine Greer's *The Female Eunuch* (1970), Kate Millett's *Sexual Politics* (1970), and Juliet Mitchell's *Woman's Estate* (1971). The feminism of these works meant that society was examined in terms of patriarchy, i.e. in terms of society being dominated and controlled by male leaders and male values.

The demands of the women's movement varied internationally according to the particular branches of feminism which dominated the movement (Kaplan, 1992). Liberal feminism, or 'equal rights feminism', demands that women participate equally with men in the public world. 'Public' here means paid work, politics and involvement at the decision-making level of business and industry. Radical feminism demands that the traditional male value system be overthrown and replaced by the female values of care and empowerment. It argues that central to patriarchy is the control over women's sexuality and reproductive organs; it demands freedom of sexual orientation and full reproductive rights including the right to abortion. Socialist feminism shares many of the concerns of radical feminism, but has developed from a Marxist perspective, incorporating a class dimension to feminist theory. It incorporates domestic (or 'private') work into the Marxist labour theory of value, and demands the public socialisation of childcare and domestic services (Tong, 1989; Jaggar, 1983).

The women's movement in the US was initially dominated by 'equal rights feminism', which placed particular emphasis on the admission of women to all levels of education, to the professions and to politics. It aligned itself with the civil rights movement, which had campaigned for equal rights for people of different racial origins and had legally secured that in the Equal Rights Amendment Act of 1972. Abortion was permitted in limited circumstances since 1967 in the US and a Supreme Court ruling in 1973 limited the legal control a state could have in restricting abortions and effectively gave a right to choose to the mother (see Bishop, 1989). While the emphasis and success of the movement varied from country to country the following were the major issues addressed: equal pay and equal treatment in employment; family planning services including availability of contraceptives (in Catholic countries); the right to abortion on demand; the recognition of rape (including rape within marriage) as a crime; protection of women against domestic violence and sexual harassment; and the provision of child-care and equal treatment for women under social welfare legislation (Kaplan, 1992; Lovenduski and Randall, 1993; Dahlerup, 1986).

The women's movement in Ireland

In Ireland we can identify two active peaks in the women's movement. The first occurred in the early seventies and focused on equal rights for women at work and for the legalisation of contraception. The second occurred in the early nineties, and in Ireland especially addressed abortion. To put the movement in a social context we must first describe the socio-economic position of women in Ireland in the early seventies.

Ireland was a late industrialising economy. It failed to surmount many of the obstacles to late industrialisation and consequently failed to generate an extensive industrial labour force (O'Malley, 1989). Thus for women there were few opportunities for industrial work. The fertility rate also remained very high until the late eighties, so there was never a critical labour shortage that might have drawn women into the labour force. When Ireland embarked on an export-oriented industrial development phase in the sixties, the state gave preferential treatment to male-dominated employment, at the ratio of 75:25 (Pyle, 1990; Mahon, 1994). There was also a ban on married women working in the civil service, the trade unions, and the banks; this lasted until 1973, when EC accession obliged the state to remove it. Subsequent state taxation policy however exerted a negative impact on married women's participation in the labour force (Callan and Farrell, 1991; Mahon, 1992).

Ireland was a deeply religious country. The emergent nationalist state in the thirties needed the legitimating support of the Catholic Church. Catholic social teaching was incorporated into the constitution, which contained a prohibition on divorce and an acknowledgement of the special position of women in the home. Later legislation (Censorship of Publications Act 1929) forbade the dissemination of information on family planning and censored the content of films and literature. Since the Catholic Church had control of Irish education, people continued to be educated into Catholic values. The Criminal Law (Amendment) Act of 1935 prohibited the sale and importation of contraceptives.

It has been argued that there was an excessive emphasis placed on matters of sexual morality in Catholic education (Lee, 1989). This could be explained by the post-famine restructuring of Irish society, in which high fertility rates within families were balanced by high levels of celibacy. The latter was ideologically supported by an intense religious value being placed upon virginity, chastity and religious vocations (Inglis, 1987). A European values study conducted in 1981 showed that the Irish differed from other Europeans on issues relating to life and death. Strong disapproval was expressed of abortion and adultery, moderate disapproval of euthanasia, prostitution and homosexuality, and mild

disapproval of divorce. As regards gender differences, housewives emerged as more conservative than men, although
housewives working part-time proved to be the most radical
of all. All women expressed strong disapproval of abortion
with a slight variation between full-time and part-time
housewives (Fogarty *et al*, 1984). Religious practices and
beliefs, while declining among younger cohorts, were still
high in the eighties (Chubb, 1992).

The first meeting of the founders of the women's movement took place in 1970, shortly after the First Commission
on the Status of Women was initiated. A 'Late, Late Show' TV
show on the topic, followed by a meeting in the Mansion
House which attracted 1,500 women, launched the women's
movement. The leaders of the movement were journalists
and writers, and they were able to generate extensive media
coverage of their protests which included a picket on the Dáil
(where they chanted 'we shall not conceive'), a picket on the
Eurovision song contest where they protested about the payment of children's allowances to fathers, and the infamous
condom purchasing train excursion to Belfast. Ardent
demonstrations on highly controversial issues and in
particular the opposition to the Forcible Entry Bill proved
too radical for many women (Levine, 1982; Mahon, 1987).

One of the leaders, Nuala Fennell, charged that anyone
who was not anti-American, anti-clerical, anti-government,
anti-Irish Countrywomen's Association, anti-police and anti-
men, had no place in the Irish women's movement. In her
view, it was necessary to create a group like the American
group NOW, interested in bringing about legal reforms and
concessions for women (Mahon, 1987). It is not surprising
that the women's movement in Ireland did not concentrate
on the issue of abortion, as their European sisters did
(Lovenduski and Outshoorn, 1986). Their initial demands,
published in the 1971 manifesto *Chains or Change?* were as
follows: equal pay; equality before the law; equal education;
contraception; justice for deserted wives, unmarried mothers
and widows; and one house, one family. The last might be

described as a socialist demand. It proved subsequently to be divisive. The demand for contraception was to be the most controversial issue of all.

A subsequent split ended the original broad women's movement. Two groups emerged in the early seventies: Fennell's liberal reformists, and a more socialist group which later diversified into pressure groups like Irish Women United, Contraception Action Campaign (CAP) and Women's Right to Choose Group (WRCG).

Fennell set up the Action, Information and Motivation (AIM) organisation, whose main purpose was to seek legal reforms for women. The Dublin AIM group founded the Irish Women's Aid Committee, which in 1974 established the first hostel for 'battered' wives in Ireland. Additional hostels were opened by AIM groups throughout the country. Members of these groups advised women on their legal rights and helped seek barring orders or find temporary refuge accommodation from violent husbands. Their task was assisted by the Free Legal Aid Committee (FLAC), much of whose work was concerned with family law.

The liberal reformist approach produced positive legal changes. The Juries Act (1976) made women eligible for jury service. The Family Home Protection Act (1976) ensured that a home could not be sold by one spouse without the consent of the other. The Family Law (Maintenance of Spouses and Children) Act (1976) legally obliged the spouse to support partner and children. The Family Law (Protection of Spouses and Children) Act (1981) permitted the legal barring of a violent spouse from the family home. These laws were all designed to protect wives who had been deserted or who were the victims of violence. In 1986, the Domicile and Recognition of Foreign Divorces Act was passed. A married woman no longer had to take the domicile of her husband. These laws were achieved in a gradual reformist way and were successful in granting individual rights to married women. Women legally were no longer their husbands' chattels.

Irish Women United (IWU) was established in 1975 by

some of the founding members of the women's movement, along with a number of socialist groups. It was led by Anne Speed, a trade union activist. Their charter repeated the first six demands of the founders' group, but added demands for women's centres and freedom of sexual orientation. They invaded the male-only bathing place, the Forty Foot in Sandycove and daubed their insignia on the courts of the all-male Fitzwilliam Lawn Tennis Club. They occupied the offices of the Federated Union of Employers in protest against the delay in implementing equal pay. By 1977-78 however, the IWU was fragmented. In addition to conflicts between radical, lesbian and socialist members, they were divided by the national question, i.e. what attitude Irish feminists should adopt towards nationalism (Randall, 1986). They eventually gravitated towards single-issue groups or woman-oriented services such as the Rape Crisis Centres. When IWU petered out in 1977 it was 'the last radical feminist group to attempt a national profile' (Fennell and Arnold, 1987). From then on, instead of a unified broadly-based women's movement, women formed a number of special-interest or campaign groups.

Legislative and labour force changes

The comparative social and economic position of Irish women must be emphasised at this point. In 1971 Ireland had a female labour force participation rate of 28 per cent, as compared with (in 1970): 43 per cent in Canada; 48 per cent in France; 48 per cent in West Germany; 59 per cent in Sweden; 50 per cent in UK; and 49 per cent in US (Bakker, 1988, p. 19). Until the Civil Service (Employment of Married Woman) Act 1973, there was a ban on the recruitment or employment of married women in the civil service, local authorities and health boards. Contraception was illegal so Irish fertility rates were also appreciably higher (Clancy, 1992). From the sixties onwards, Ireland witnessed great social development in employment and economic growth, but patriarchal state policy restricted opportunities for women (Pyle, 1990; Mahon, 1994).

However, from the seventies onwards, progressive employment legislation was introduced. Ireland's accession to the EEC in 1973 was a modernising influence as membership demanded compliance with EEC social directives. In addition to the removal of the marriage bar, the Anti-Discrimination (Pay) Act (1974) established women's right to equal pay which was made legally binding from February 1976. The Employment Equality Act (1977) was introduced to eliminate discrimination in employment or promotion on grounds of sex or marital status and gave a legal basis to the establishment of the Employment Equality Agency. These legal changes facilitated a gradual increase in married women's participation in the labour market (Table I).

From the seventies onwards several statutory and voluntary organisations committed to improving the position of women in Irish society were founded. In 1972-73, CHERISH and ADAPT were established to advance the rights of lone parents and their children. The Council for the Status of Women, a statutory co-ordinating body for women's organisations, was founded in 1973. In 1977 the first Rape Crisis Centre was opened in Dublin. In the early eighties the Joint Oireachtas Committee on Women's Rights was established and in 1984,

Table 1: **Women in the labour force, 1971-1991**

	1971	1981	1987	1989	1991
Women as % of total labour force	25.7	29.1	30.9	30.7	32.1
Married women as % of female labour	13.6	30.2	39.6	41.5	44.4
Women as % of employed labour force	26.3	29.4	32.4	32.3	35.5
Women as % of unemployed	18.2	25.2	23.8	22.2	25.0

Source: NESC 1991, p. 32 and Labour Force Survey 1991

a programme for action to remove sexism in education was published by the government. These all helped to generate a more progressive role for women in Irish society.

In parallel with these developments there was a campaign to establish women's rights to information on family planning and to legalise contraception. This was a very controversial issue. When it was accomplished, a conservative movement emerged demanding that the constitution be amended to introduce a ban on abortion. The demand was met, making abortion information and referral services illegal. This was followed by a liberal attempt to remove the constitutional prohibition on divorce, an attempt which was unsuccessful. Finally, in the nineties there was a campaign to legalise abortion information and referral and to introduce abortion in very limited circumstances. The following is a brief account of these contentious campaigns for contraception, divorce and abortion.

The campaign for contraception

The Criminal Law (Amendment Act) of 1935 prohibited the sale, advertising, or importation of contraceptives. In 1969, however, the Fertility Guidance Clinic, supported by the International Planned Parenthood Association, opened in Dublin. Because of a loop-hole in the law, the clinic could dispense contraceptives freely, while at the same time requesting 'donations' from its clients. Though at first such clinics existed only in Dublin, eventually they were established in large regional towns. The contraceptive pill was also prescribed by more liberal doctors, as a cycle regulator for health reasons. A Supreme Court case in 1973, McGee *vs* Attorney-General, declared that the right to marital privacy included the right to import contraceptives for personal use. Section 17 of the 1935 Act was therefore ruled to be unconstitutional. The Labour Party and the Contraception Action Campaign (CAP), set up by Ann Speed and other members of the IWU, called for new legislation. In

1979 the Health (Family Planning) Act came into force. Contraceptives could be supplied on prescription to married couples, but were only allowed for medical reasons, or for *bona fide* family planning purposes. Doctors and nurses, if they were conscientious objectors, could opt out of the scheme.

CAP were unhappy with the Act because they considered it to be too restrictive. The view was expressed that it was absurd to require prescriptions for condoms. At this stage family planning centres were operating in five cities outside of Dublin, selling condoms without prescription, and providing a mail order service. They were legally ignored until 1985, when the Fine Gael-Labour government amended the legislation to permit the sale of condoms. In 1992, in response to the AIDS crisis, legislation was extended to permit supermarkets to sell condoms. Few have done so but a number of clubs and public houses have installed condom vending machines.

The Catholic Church remains opposed to the use of contraceptives. Despite Catholic Church teaching, the extent of the use of contraceptives in Ireland among married couples is similar to that which prevails in other European countries (Clancy and Nic Ghiolla Phádraig, 1991). This is reflected in the marked decline in fertility rates, particularly since 1986 (Table 2). The first part of this decline can be explained by a decline in large families. There were fewer high order births after 1960. They fell from just under a half to just over a quarter by late seventies and by the late eighties fourth and higher order births had fallen further to little more than a fifth of the total (Coleman, 1992, p. 67). Completed family size has fallen, there is a delay in childbearing and the mean age of marriage has increased by a year since 1980. These two latter factors will in the short term reduce the birth rate. However, the 1990 European values study indicates that the ideal family size in Ireland is four or more, as compared to the general European two or less (Whelan and Fahey, 1994, p. 61). We will have to await

Table 2: **Age specific marital fertility rate 1961, 1981, 1986, 1988 and annual percentage change 1961-81, 1981-86 and 1986-88**

Age group	1961	1981	1986	1988	1961-81	1981-86	1986-88
					*Annual percentage change**		
15-19	600.6	549.5	537.7	491.8	–0.4	–0.4	–4.3
20-24	478.0	365.5	302.1	263.7	–1.6	–1.5	–6.4
25-29	372.3	262.5	235.2	210.2	–1.5	–2.1	–5.3
30-34	298.6	188.2	170.2	148.4	–1.8	–1.9	–6.4
35-39	202.4	105.7	84.6	71.6	–2.4	–4.0	–7.7
40-44	71.1	30.7	24.6	19.7	–3.0	–4.0	–10.0
45-49	5.8	2.9	1.9	1.3	–2.5	–6.9	–8.0
15-49	195.4	154.1	124.2	104.4	–1.1	–3.9	–8.0

*gross percentage change over the period divided by number of years.

Source: P. Clancy, 'Continuity and Change in Irish Demographic Patterns' in *Ireland and Poland*; Ed. P. Clancy, M. Kelly, J. Wiatr and R. Zoltaniecki, p. 167.

later cohort analysis to assess whether we are seeing reduced fertility or delayed childbearing. Meanwhile delayed fertility enables women to remain active for longer in the labour market.

The campaign for a constitutional prohibition of abortion

Abortion is illegal in Ireland, under the 1861 Offences against the Person Act. However, for years Irish women have gone to England to procure abortions (Jackson, 1986). Because Irish women who needed abortions could go to England, Ireland did not have a 'backstreet abortion' problem which might have exerted pressure for legislative change. In 1980 the Woman's Right to Choose Group (WRCG) was formed, demanding the right to abortion in the context of fertility control in general. WRCG set up the Irish Pregnancy Counselling Centre in 1980; this included an abortion referral service, the legality of which was unclear. WRCG held their first public meeting in March 1981 (Beale, 1986).

This meeting was also attended by women from the Society for the Protection of the Unborn Child (SPUC), which had been formed in June of the previous year. It attracted conservative Catholics who felt threatened by liberal interpretations of the constitution and the introduction of EC equality legislation. SPUC sought to prevent any further escalation of liberalism, particularly with respect to abortion. They decided to campaign for a constitutional amendment that would prevent the legalisation of abortion in Ireland, since a constitutional amendment could not be overruled by the European Court of Justice.

The campaign spanned more than two years, from April 1981 to September 1983. SPUC exhibited human embryos in schools, and waged philosophical battles in the media over when human life began. It formed the Pro-Life Amendment Campaign (PLAC), which insisted that the constitution should guarantee the absolute right to life of the embryo from the moment of conception. The two major political parties, Fianna Fáil, which was in government, and Fine Gael, supported the proposed amendment. Labour was generally non-committal, although some of its members declared their opposition. SPUC organised meetings all over the country, gave anti-abortion talks in schools, and was supported by the Catholic Church, along with some Catholic doctors and gynaecologists.

The Pro-Life Amendment Campaign (PLAC) initiative put its opponents on the defensive. Differences over strategy led to a split into two groups. The Woman's Right to Choose Campaign (WRCC) advocated working with the general public. The Woman's Right to Choose Group (WRCG), however, advocated working with academics, professors and media people. It formed an anti-amendment group which opposed the amendment on the broad liberal grounds that: it would do nothing to solve the problem of unwanted pregnancies; it would allow of no exceptions; it was sectarian; it would prevent possible legislation on abortion; and it was a waste of public funds.

This approach was successful. Groups of doctors and lawyers supported the anti-amendment campaign and argued against their pro-life colleagues. In response, the government proposed a compromise wording. However, the original, more restrictive wording of the amendment to the Constitution was eventually put forward. It read as follows:

> The State acknowledges the right to life of the unborn, and with due regard for the equal right to life of the mother, guarantees in its laws to respect and as far as it is practicable by its laws to defend and vindicate that right.

The amendment was put to the people in a referendum in 1983. The amendment was carried by 66 per cent ('yes votes') to 33 per cent ('no votes'). There was a low turnout at just under 50 per cent. The 'No' vote was highest in Dublin and large towns, and lowest in the west.

Abortion information and referral services

Encouraged by their success in the referendum SPUC proceeded to legally challenge abortion referral and information services, arguing that such services were unconstitutional under Article 40.3.3. In SPUC & Attorney General *vs.* Open Line Counselling and Well Woman Centre, Justice Hamilton ruled in the High Court that these services were unlawful. His judgment was upheld by the Supreme Court. The Open Line Counselling had to be closed and the Well Woman Centre had to suspend its pregnancy counselling services.

In 1988, SPUC successfully gained a Supreme Court injunction to prevent UCD students from publishing abortion information in student handbooks. In 1989 a similar injunction was granted by the Supreme Court against Trinity College students. In a High Court case which proceeded it

Justice Carroll had referred the matter to the European Court of Justice. The latter in June 1991 upheld the ban on abortion information. At the beginning of the nineties all information on abortion, even in magazines and books, was illegal. Some women's health books were removed from public libraries and English magazines had to produce censored Irish editions.

The Open Door Counselling lodged an appeal to the European Court of Human Rights in Strasbourg, arguing that the ban on information on abortion available abroad contravened Article 10 of the Convention which provides a right to freedom of information. This appeal was eventually successful but its verdict was superseded by the unexpected aftermath of the 1992 'X' abortion case to which I will return later.

The campaign for divorce

Article 41.3.2 of the constitution prohibits divorce. While many members of the women's movement were in favour of divorce, it was not until 1986 that any attempts were made to end this prohibition. Initially, opinion polls showed a majority (60 per cent) in favour of removing the prohibition. Divorce, it was argued, was a civil right. The Divorce Action Group (DAG) was small and lacked funding. Strongest in Dublin, it included women involved in AIM, professional people, and separated and deserted wives. It was led by Jean Tansey, a feminist and member of the Labour Party.

The campaign against changing the constitutional prohibition on divorce was spearheaded by Family Solidarity. They drew some of its members from the previously successful PLAC group, and benefited from that group's organisational and media skills. William Binchy, Family Solidarity's legal spokesperson, argued cogently against the legalisation of divorce. Extensive literature opposing divorce was delivered to every home. Sermons exhorted the laity to oppose its introduction. Liberal priests who spoke out in support of divorce legislation were silenced by the Catholic Church hierarchy. Among the political parties, only the Labour Party declared itself in favour of divorce. Fianna Fáil and Fine Gael allowed its members to vote and canvass as they wished.

The proposed legislation for divorce drawn up by the Fine Gael-Labour government was comparatively liberal: in effect, a no-fault divorce after five years of marital breakdown. But the government had failed to work out many of the legal and economic aspects of the proposed legislation. In the week before the referendum, last minute revisions were still being made about pension rights, benefits and inheritance. The anti-divorce campaign continued to frighten people, claiming that men would flee their wives, that farms would be divided in divorce settlements, that women and children would be abandoned, and that large demands would be made on the already strained social welfare system. The amendment was defeated by 63 per cent to 36 per cent (the turnout was 63 per cent) in 1986. Only in four Dublin constituencies and in Dún Laoghaire was there a majority vote in favour of divorce (Department of Environment 1992, p. 26).

There were four principal reasons for the defeat of the divorce amendment: the central role of the family in the lives of Irish Catholic women; the exploitation of dependency or the real fear of poverty; the character of the proposed divorce legislation; the lack of any theoretical feminist direction on the issue.

The defence of the family

The voting results in the referenda on divorce and abortion were virtually the same. There is no absolute evidence that the same people voted in the same way, but it is likely that there was a considerable overlap. American research on opposition to abortion is important here. Luker argues that women's hostility to abortion and support for traditional relationships are rooted in deep anxieties about male abandonment (Luker, 1984). She links this world-view with their traditional roles in society (most are housewives, have low family incomes, married at an early age, work in traditional female jobs). For them, she suggests, the abortion argument concerns the place and meaning of motherhood. Similarly, Petchesky has argued that in a situation of economic stress and social change, for those women who make up the pro-life movement, the 'loss of a protective conjugal family structure and motherhood as the core of women's fulfilment is a menacing spectre' (Petchesky, 1984). Ehrenreich claims that in the economic stresses of the seventies in the US, women were divided into two groups: those who went out to fight for some measure of economic security, and those who stayed at home to hold on to what they had (Ehrenreich, 1981).

These arguments could equally apply to the Irish referenda. Women were for instance more supportive than men of a 'yes' vote in the closing stages of the 1983 campaign on the 'pro-life' amendment, with 75 per cent stating an intention to vote in favour as against 62 per cent of men (Girvin, 1986, p. 79). Polls taken during the divorce debate also revealed a gender gap in voting intentions towards the end of the campaign, with women adopting a more conservative position (Galligan, 1992).

Structural factors, as already outlined, restricted women's participation in the labour force in Ireland. The majority of women – over 50 per cent – were engaged full-time in home duties. They had large families. The low participation rate of married women in the labour force was accompanied by attitudinal differences. A study in 1978 revealed that 75 per cent of non-employed mothers agreed that being a wife and mother were the most fulfilling roles any mother could want (Fine Davis, 1983). Sixty per cent felt it was bad for young children if their mothers went out to work, even if they were well taken care of by an adult. In 1978, 70 per cent of the total sample agreed that if there was high unemployment, married women should be discouraged from working – and this view was still held by 60 per cent of non-employed mothers and 30 per cent of employed mothers in 1981. This suggests that women in particular voted to protect the family and their position within it. They were frightened by warnings that the mere existence of divorce legislation would increase the number of divorces.

During the campaign, the poverty of families headed by single women in the US was used as an example of what might befall women if divorce was introduced. The government had not anticipated this exploitation of women's economic dependency and had failed to work out in advance any detailed proposals on financial matters. It wrongly assumed that the latter could be left until after the referendum had cleared the way for legislation. The absence of a Matrimonial Properties Act and the feared economic consequences of a patriarchal property law, meant that opponents of divorce were able to play upon women's fears of these very consequences. The liberal character of the proposed legislation only served to heighten these fears, providing as it did for no-fault divorce after five years of marital breakdown. No doubt this formulation was influenced by amendments to divorce legislation in other countries – particularly the idea of non-adversarial courts for the benefits of children. In practice it meant that the Anti-Divorce Campaign was able to spread fears of widespread easy divorce, 'divorce through boredom'. They would have found it more difficult to oppose a more restrictive divorce legislation for which there appeared to be greater support. For instance the value study mentioned earlier showed that divorce was considered justifiable by over 50 per cent of respondents if there was family violence or unfaithfulness. In addition, at that time, 1978, legal separations were not available so people were not acquainted with post-divorce outcomes. The result was a fear of divorce or at least some ambiguity about its introduction.

The arguments of economic dependency, which resonated among middle-class women, might also have accounted for the ambivalence towards divorce of female journalists. Noticeably absent too, was any worked-out feminist stance in favour of divorce. There was no attempt to develop a pro-divorce policy document that would ensure the financial protection of dependent wives, so there was no basis on which to build up support among women for the legislation. The result was that women, in Ehrenreich's terminology, voted to hold on to what they had.

Educational developments in the eighties

While divorce and abortion dominated the media in the eighties there were progressive changes in the education and employment of women. The first report of the First Joint Oireachtas Committee on Women's Rights stressed equity in education. A study on Schooling and Sex Roles (Hannan *et al*, 1983), generated much discussion and was followed by a Gender Equity in Education programme in the Department of Education. In 1990/91 a 'Girls into Technology' project was initiated, in addition to an action project on the Integration of Equal Opportunities in the Curriculum of Teacher Education (TENET). At second level, gender differences in both provision and uptake of mathematics and science have been considerably reduced over time (Drudy and Lynch, 1993, Chap. 8). Entrance to third level became increasingly competitive especially in the traditionally high status professions such as medicine and law. While women constituted only 27 per cent of full-time higher education students in 1955, by 1990/91, they accounted for 47 per cent. In 1991/92 girls comprised 53 per cent of first time entrants to third level university courses (Department of Education, 1993, Table 5.1). A parity now exists in areas once male dominated: medicine, law, science and commerce/business studies. It seems that the demands of achievement and class reproduction are prevailing over those of gender repro-duction as the achievement principle dominates entry.

There are still some differences, notably in engineering which remains a male enclave, with only 10 per cent of engineering graduates in 1989 being women (HEA, 1990,

p. 44). In regional colleges, 60 per cent of students attending science and business studies courses are female but they comprise only 6 per cent of electrical and electronic and 3 per cent of mechanical engineering students.

Of special interest are gender differences in the hidden curricula in Ireland, which deviated from research findings in other countries. Lynch (1989) found that the ethos in girls' schools was slightly more achievement-oriented than in boys' schools. Girls' schools differed also in the greater emphasis they placed on moral/religious development and the personal development of their students. In boys' schools there was a strong emphasis on sport, defined in terms of physical strength, team spirit and the will to succeed. Lynch argued that these qualities are very conducive to the pursuit of instrumental success in the labour market (Lynch, 1989). But girls' schools present girls with 'two contradictory role models: on the one hand they were educated to compete and succeed in the formal educational system with a view to gaining labour market advantages that go with it; on the other hand they were socialised to be guardians of the moral order, to be unselfish, non-assertive and appreciative of the cultural rather than purely material products of the age' (Lynch, 1989, p. 27; see also Morgan and Lynch in this volume). To an extent a girl's education reflects the changing environment and the expectation that middle-class girls will be oriented to the labour market. There are class differences and reports which show that girls who leave school without any qualifications were poorly catered for in the training sector and were likely to be absorbed into 'home duties' (Hannan and Shorthall, 1991). As gender differences begin to decline, class differences between women increase.

Increased labour force participation of women in the eighties

Since the seventies women's labour force participation in Ireland steadily increased as the female services sector grew extensively (Callander, 1990). Between 1975 and 1991 the number of economically active women increased by 36 per cent. The labour force participation of married women increased from 15 per cent to 24 per cent. Among younger cohorts the changes were more dramatic: from 16 per cent to 37 per cent among women aged 25-44 and from 25 per cent to 46 per cent among women aged 20-24. The mean age at marriage increased and marital fertility declined.

Also since the seventies, women's studies courses emerged in all universities. Community women's groups mushroomed in both rural and urban areas. While women were still engaged predominantly in home duties, many were also active in voluntary organisations such as the Rape Crisis Centres, Irish Countrywomen's Association, Zonta, Professional Women's Networks. Such groups created an awareness of women's needs and raised consciousness of their inequalities. The statutory body, The Council for the Status of Women, which is a federation of all such voluntary groups, became a more active lobby group on behalf of women. The civil service initiated an equal opportunities policy in 1986 (Mahon, 1991). These changes are comparable to those which occurred in the US in the late sixties and support the pre-conditions for social change.

Changing values

A European values study conducted in 1990 measured attitudes towards the traditional sex role of women (the researchers – all male – did not investigate attitudes to the traditional sex roles of men). Three attitudinal dimensions were identified: career cost (translated to mean impact of working mother on her children!); pro-homemaker (house-wife role) and anti-employment. On the first item Irish people held similar attitudes scores to the average European figures, being even less likely to think that a pre-school child suffers if his/her mother works. As regards homemaker, the Irish were more likely to claim that being a housewife was just as fulfilling as working for pay, and accordingly more likely to disagree that a job was the best way for a woman to be independent. However, if somewhat inconsistent with the endorsement of the housewife role, the Irish were more likely to agree that husband and wife should contribute to family income. The authors argue that the Irish scores do not differ appreciably from the European. For this author, it would seem the Irish view housewife *versus* working-mother as a matter of choice or opportunity and retain a respect for the housewife role. Younger cohorts are less traditional in their views on the housewife as are the more educated. All men, even younger men, are more traditional and are more likely to see negative effects on children if mothers work outside the home (Whelan and Fahey, 1994, p. 53). This shows an emergent cleavage between young men and women, women wishing to adopt new roles but men with negative attitudes towards same. Women in employment held less traditional attitudes than full-time homemakers on all items.

The feminisation of politics

By 1990 therefore more women, especially married women, were in the labour force and attitudes towards women were more progressive. However, there was as yet little public evidence of all this, until the extraordinary and historic election of Mary Robinson as the first woman President of Ireland in November 1990 (O'Sullivan, 1991; Mahon, 1991).

The election of Ireland's seventh President

In the presidential election of 1990, Ireland defied all its stereotypes. Mary Robinson was the nominee of the Labour Party. Brian Lenihan was the candidate for the incumbent Fianna Fáil/Progressive Democrat coalition, while Austin Curry was the Fine Gael candidate. Mary Robinson conceived of the role as that of a 'president with a purpose' (Finlay, 1991). From being an almost complete outsider at the beginning of the campaign, she was eventually elected. While the Fianna Fáil candidate was beset by campaign problems related to his credibility, Mary Robinson's central strength was her own standing as a leading lawyer who had previously supported and won cases on women's rights. Feminists recognised her as a feminist but she won the respect of others who might have been slightly scared of feminism. Her reconstruction of 'women's interests' (in electoral broadcasts) as issues which should concern all, revealed her ability to extend her concerns in a way with which all, male and female, young and old could empathise. Her victory was overwhelming, signalling a dramatic change for women in Ireland. For that reason 1990 proved to be a turning point for Irish politics.

The abortion crisis

In 1992, a crisis known as the 'X' case put abortion once more on the political agenda. A fourteen-year-old school girl revealed to her parents that she had been repeatedly molested by a friend of the family, culminating in rape in December 1991. She was pregnant as a result of that rape. Her parents went to the police to report the rape and to make arrangements to procure foetal evidence in advance of an abortion in England, that could be used in court against the man to support her case. The Gardaí sought legal advice which reported that such evidence was inadmissible in an Irish court. In addition the attorney general issued a temporary injunction restraining her from leaving the country, so preventing her obtaining an abortion as she and her parents had intended. At that stage the girl and her parents had already gone to England but they returned in compliance with the injunction. The latter was upheld by Justice Costello in the High Court, who restrained the girl from leaving the jurisdiction of the court for nine months and from procuring an abortion within or without the jurisdiction.

There was an immediate public outcry against her internment. Meetings and protests, culminating in a massive demonstration, indicated the extent of public support for the young girl. In addition questions were raised about the 4,000 women who went annually to England for abortions and whether this internment would be followed by pregnancy testing for all women leaving the country.

The family appealed their case to the Supreme Court, arguing that the girl had suicidal tendencies as a result of the pregnancy and that her life was therefore at risk. The Supreme Court decided by a majority of four to one that 'if it is established as a matter of probability that there is a real risk to the health of the mother which can only be avoided by the termination of her pregnancy, then such termination is permissible, having regard to the true interpretation of Article 40.3.3'. Surgical intervention was permissible under the constitution where there was a threat to the mother's life: abortion was not unconstitutional in certain limited circumstances. According to the Supreme Court the government would have to introduce appropriate legislation on the issue.

While this was seen as a progressive judgment by many, the court in its judgment said that the right to travel did not take precedence and only pregnant women whose lives were endangered could legally travel to secure an abortion. This was a new restriction.

Referendum on Maastricht Treaty of Accession

Coinciding with this case was a public discussion on the forthcoming Maastricht Treaty of Accession . The 'X' case exposed the fact that a protocol guaranteeing the constitutional protection of the unborn had been introduced into the Maastricht Treaty in December 1991. This protocol had been inserted quite surreptitiously under pressure from right-wing groups and without any public discussion. The implications of the protocol for Irish women were threefold: they could not seek to assert a Community right to travel to another member state for an abortion; they could not receive abortion information; and the law on abortion in Ireland, up to then unaffected by Community law, would remain unchanged (Reid, 1992). Its aim was to protect the Irish constitutional position on abortion from any European liberalising influences.

However, following the Supreme Court judgment in the 'X' case, the implications of this protocol had to be reinterpreted. It would now protect the pro-abortion ruling of the Supreme Court while also prohibiting travel and quite possibly information. The liberal community were on the one hand pleased about the abortion or 'substantive' issue but concerned about the restrictions placed on the right to travel and information. Those opposed to abortion under any circumstances were shocked at the legal endorsement of abortion even in limited circumstances.

At European Community level, the government tried to renegotiate the protocol but this was rejected. The best that could be achieved was an insertion of a Solemn Declaration which permitted travel to procure and information on services legally available in the other member states. It included an agreement that if a future amendment of Article 40.3.30 was voted on in Ireland, the protocol could be amended. This was designed to please both sides, women who did not want to vote away their rights under EC legislation and the anti-abortion group who hoped to have a new referendum that would revert matters to the way they were understood to be, prior to the Supreme Court decision. The government wanted, at all costs, to ratify the Maastrict Treaty in June 1992. At that stage, the Danes had voted against ratification so it was portrayed as if the future of the European Union depended on Ireland endorsing the Maastrict Treaty. Ireland was also to receive six billion pounds in Structural Funds subsequent to the ratification of the Treaty.

Council for the Status of Women

A most interesting development was the role played by the Council for the Status of Women, under the leadership of Frances Fitzgerald, in the campaign leading up to the Maastricht Treaty. The council at no stage endorsed abortion but cogently argued that women should be able to make up their own minds on the matter. Furthermore, the council and its affiliated groups had a long and consistent history in supporting women and mothers. It raised questions about the motives of certain pressure groups who presumed to tell Irish women about their responsibilities as mothers. The council both identified and generated 'a middle ground' on the issue. Prior to the Maastrict referendum, they held that they could not recommend that women support the referendum unless women could be formally included in decisions relating to EC expenditure. They also wanted a referendum that would give women a right to travel and to information on abortion. Meantime anti-abortion groups wanted a referendum on 'the substantive issue', abortion.

The government pledged that it would have three related referenda in the Autumn of 1992 on the right to travel, the right to information and the substantive issue of abortion *per se.* With this guarantee the council encouraged women to vote in favour of Maastricht. The Society for the Protection of the Unborn Child (SPUC) called for a 'no' vote. The electorate (almost 70 per cent) voted in favour of the Maastricht Treaty. But the abortion issue was still on the agenda. The three referenda were planned for November 1992. They were preceded by vigorous arguments from both sides, all producing articulate spokespersons with far more women active on both sides than in the past. The debate was more controlled. The pro-choice Women's Coalition group effectively held a middle ground. A 'Late, Late Show' TV debate on abortion at the end of the campaign revealed that the anti-abortion group were split, some urging a 'yes' vote in favour of abortion in very restricted circumstances. Others disagreed and urged that only a 'no' vote was a consistently anti-abortion one. Unexpected political upheavals meant that the three referenda were held on the same day as the 1992 general election. The wording of the Twelfth Amendment was as follows:

It will be unlawful to terminate the life of an unborn unless such termination is necessary to save the life, as distinct from the health, of the mother where there is an illness or disorder of the mother giving rise to a real and substantial risk to her life, not being a risk of self-destruction.

This was rejected by the electorate. The rejection implied that the people did not want the Supreme Court's decision – which included abortion if there was a threat of suicide – changed. Irish women were procuring the constitutional preconditions of legal rights to abortion in restricted circumstances.

The Thirteenth Amendment proposed an amendment to Article 40 by the addition of the following:

This subsection shall not limit freedom to travel between the State and another state.

The Fourteenth Amendment to Article 40 was:

This subsection shall not limit freedom to obtain or make available, in the State, subject to such conditions as may be laid down by law, information relating to services lawfully available in another state.

Both of these amendments were approved by the people and were signed by the President in December 1992 and promulgated as law. Women had a constitutional right to travel (to procure an abortion) and to information on abortion.

The referendum result on the substantive issue (Twelfth) is not surprising in the light of the European values study carried out in 1990 which revealed that 65 per cent of the total sample and 80 per cent of woman under thirty-five approved of abortion when the mother's health was at risk from pregnancy (Whelan and Fahey, 1994, p. 72). This coupled with the plight of the 'X' case – a very young woman often referred to as a child – made abortion a personalised issue rather than an abstract moral one. But the Irish support for abortion is a restrictive one; only 8 per cent approved of it on the grounds of the mother being unmarried or because a married couple did not want any more children (Fahey and Whelan, 1992, p. 237).

At the time of writing no legislation on abortion information or referral has been introduced but a Bill regulating the availability of abortion information has been passed in March 1995. The provision of non-directive information is no longer illegal according to the Minister for Justice (*The Connaught Tribune* 29-5-94). The Pro-Life Campaign argues that the provision of addresses and details of abortion clinics amounts to abortion referral (*The Irish Times* 13-5-1994). At least 4,000 women go to England for abortions annually. While the referenda showed that people did not want the Supreme Court verdict overturned, legislation on abortion *per se*, given prevalent attitudes, will be controversial.

Local and general elections

The number of women elected in local elections in 1991 rose to 11 per cent (Gardiner, 1992). The general election results also signalled change. It returned the highest ever number of Labour deputies to the Dáil and the highest number of women, twenty or 12 per cent. The latter was further confirmation of a new era for Irish women. The Labour Force survey for 1991 revealed the highest ever participation rate of women in the labour force and for the first time less than 50 per cent of women were described as 'engaged in home duties'.

The report of the Second Commission on the Status of Women, under Justice Mella Carroll as chairperson, was published in early 1993. It made extensive recommendations, endorsing a more individualistic future for Irish women, with an emphasis on employment and the provision of child care and increased rights and benefits for women in the home. There is increasing support for women's rights helped by the formation of an *ad hoc* 'Group 84' of women TDs. As many women topped the poll in the last general election, this has now led to greater nominations of, and encouragement of, female candidates.

Conclusion

Irish women's liberation was comparatively delayed. EC membership had a very definite modernising influence principally on women in the workplace. Ironically resistance to the EC's modernising influences generated conflict on the issues of divorce and abortion, with traditional outcomes in the eighties.

In the nineties, Irish society has become more complex. The 1992 Fianna Fáil/Labour coalition espoused a more liberal agenda. A female Minister for Justice legalised homosexuality and introduced additional measures to help wives who are victims of violence. A divorce referendum is planned and some restricted abortion legislation will sooner or more likely, later, be introduced. The slow, gradual but very significant changes made in areas such as education under female ministers, the activities of women active in community groups, in adult education and in voluntary organisations have created a supportive infrastructure or 'submerged networks' (Melucci, 1988, p. 248). They have generated an informed woman-centred constituency. This is now being recognised as a politically powerful grouping among the electorate with an increased number of female candidates in the 1994 European elections and increased references to women's rights in the literature of male candidates. Women have become empowered in the public domain. Given such empowerment, Irish women will make considerable gains in the future.

References

BAKKER, I., 1988, 'Women's employment in Comparative Perspective' in J. Jenson, E. Hagen and C. Reddy (eds.), *Feminization of the Labour Force*, Cambridge, Polity Press, pp. 17-44.

BEAUVOIR, S. de. *The Second Sex*, 1953 translation, London, Jonathan Cape.

BEALE, J., 1986. *Women in Ireland, Voices of Change*, Dublin/London, Macmillan.

BISHOP, N, 1989. 'Abortion:

The Controversial Choice',
in J. Freeman (ed.), Women:
a Feminist Perspective,
California, Mayfield
Publishers, pp. 45-56.

CALLAN, T. and B. FARRELL,
1991. *Women's Participation in
the Irish Labour Market,* Dublin,
National Economic and Social
Council.

CALLENDER, R., 1990.
'Women and Work: the
appearance and Reality of
Change', *Labour Market Review*
1, June, pp. 17-36.

CHUBB, B., 1992. *Government
and Politics of Ireland,* Essex,
Longman.

CLANCY, P., 1988. *Who goes to
College,* Dublin, Higher
Education Authority.

CLANCY, P., 1992.
'Continuity and Change in
Irish Demographic Patterns',
in P. Clancy, M. Kelly,
J. Wiatr and R. Zoltaniecki
(eds.), *Ireland and Poland,*
Dublin, Dept. of Sociology,
University College, Dublin.

CLANCY, P. and Nic GHIOLLA
PHÁDRAIG, M., 1991.
'Marital Fertility and Family
Planning', paper presented at
the Sociological Association of
Ireland Conference,
Termonfeckin.

COLEMAN, D.A., 1992. 'The
Demographic Transition in
Ireland in International
Context', in J. Goldthorpe
and C. Whelan, *The
Development of Industrial
Society in Ireland,* Oxford,

Oxford University Press,
pp. 53-77.

DAHLERUP, D., 1986. *The New
Women's Movement: Feminism
and Political Power in Europe
and the USA,* London, Sage.

DEPT OF ENVIRONMENT,
1992. Referenda in Ireland
1937-87 and addendum,
Dublin, Stationery Office.

DRUDY, S. and K. LYNCH,
1993. *Schools and Society in
Ireland,* Dublin, Gill and
Macmillan.

EHRENREICH, B. 1981. 'The
Women's Movement, Feminist
and Antifeminist', *Radical
America,* Spring 1981.

FENNELL, N. and
M. ARNOLD, 1987.
Irishwomen in Focus, Dublin,
Office of the Minister of State
for Women's Affairs.

FINE DAVIS, M., 1983. *Women
and work in Ireland,* Dublin,
Council for the Status of
Women.

FINLAY, F., 1990. *Mary Robinson
– A President with a Purpose,*
Dublin, O'Brien Press.

FORSTER, P. and I. SUTTON,
1989. *Daughters of de Beauvoir,*
London, Women's Press.

FOGARTY, M., L. RYAN and
J. LEE, 1984. *Irish Values and
Attitudes: The Report of the
European Value Systems Study,*
Dublin, Dominican
Publications.

FREEMAN, J., 1975. *The Politics
of Women's Liberation,* New
York, Longman.

FREIDAN, B., 1981. *The*

Feminine Mystique, New York, Dell.

GALLIGAN, Y., 1992. 'Women in Irish Politics', in J. Coakley and M. Gallagher (eds.), *Politics in the Republic of Ireland*, Galway, PSAI Press.

GARDINER, F., 1992. 'Political Interest and Participation of Irish Women 1922-1992: The Unfinished Revolution', *The Canadian Journal of Irish Studies*, Vol. 18, No. 1, pp. 15-39.

GARDINER, F., 1993. 'Women in the Election' in M. Gallagher and M. Laver (eds.), *How Ireland Voted*, Dublin, Folens and PSAI Press, pp. 79-92.

GIRVIN, B., 1986. 'Social Change and Moral Politics: The Irish Constitutional Referendum 1983', *Political Studies* 34, 1, pp. 61-81.

GREER, G., 1970. *The Female Eunuch*, London, MacGibbon and Kee.

GURR, T., 1970. *Why Men Rebel*, Princeton, N.J., Princeton University Press.

HANNAN, D., R. BREEN, B. MURRAY, D. WATSON, N. HARDIMAN and K. O'HIGGINS, 1983. *Schooling and Sex Roles: Sex Differences in subject provision and subject choice in Irish post-primary schools*, Dublin, Economic and Social Research Institute, Paper No. 113.

HANNAN, D. and S. SHORTALL, 1991. *The Quality of their Education*, Dublin, Economic and Social Research Institute, Paper No. 153.

HIGHER EDUCATION AUTHORITY, 1990. First Destinations of Award Recipients in Higher Education (1989), Dublin, Government Publications Office.

INGLIS, T., 1987. *Moral Monopoly: The Catholic Church in Modern Irish Society*, Dublin, Gill and Macmillan.

JACKSON, P., 1986. 'Outside the Jurisdiction – Irish Women Seeking Abortion', in C. Curtin, P. Jackson and B. O'Connor (eds.), *Gender in Irish Society*, Galway, Galway University Press.

JAGGAR, A., 1988. *Feminist Politics and Human Nature*, Totowa, New Jersey, Rowmand and Allenheld.

KAPLAN, G., 1992. *Contemporary Western European Feminism*, London, UCL Press and Allen and Unwin.

LABOUR FORCE SURVEY 1991. Dublin, Stationery Office.

LEE, J., 1989. *Ireland 1912-1985: Politics and Society*, Dublin, Gill and Macmillan.

LEVINE, J., 1982. *Sisters. The Personal Story of an Irish Feminist*, Dublin, Ward River Press.

LOVENDUSKI, J. and J. OUTSHOORN (eds.), 1986. *The New Politics of Abortion*, London, Sage.

LOVENDUSKI J. and
V. RANDALL, 1993.
Contemporary Feminist Politics,
Oxford, Oxford University
Press.

LUKER, K., 1984. *Abortion and
the Politics of Motherhood*,
Berkeley and Los Angeles,
University of California Press.

LYNCH, K., 1989. 'The Female
Ethos of Girls' Schools: an
Analysis of Differences
between Male and Female
Schools', *Social Studies*, Vol. 10,
Nos. 1-2, pp. 11-31.

MAHON, E., 1987. 'Women's
Rights and Catholicism in
Ireland', *New Left Review*,
No. 166, pp. 53-78.

MAHON, E., 1991. *Motherhood,
Work and Equal opportunity:
A Case Study of Irish Civil
Servants*, Dublin, Stationery
Office

MAHON, E., 1991. 'The
Election of Ireland's Seventh
President: Mary Robinson',
paper presented to the
European Consortium for
Political Research Joint
Sessions, Essex.

MAHON, E., 1992. 'Women still
being kept out of the
Workforce', *The Irish Times*,
9 September.

MAHON, E., 1994. 'Ireland: A
Private Patriarchy?', in The
Diverse Worlds of European
Patriarchy, Special edition of
Environment and Planning,
Vol. 26, July, pp. 1277-1296.

MELUCCI, A., 1988. 'Social
Movements and the
Democratisation of Everyday
Life' in J. Keane (ed.), *Civil
Society and the State*, London
and New York, Verso, pp. 245-
260.

MITCHELL, J., 1971. *Woman's
Estate*, Harmondsworth,
Penguin.

MILLETT, K., 1978. *Sexual
Politics*, London, Virago,

O'MALLEY, E., 1989. *Industry
and Economic Development:The
Challenge for the Latecomer*,
Dublin, Gill and Macmillan.

O'SULLIVAN, E., 1991. 'The
1990 Presidential Election
in the Republic of Ireland',
Irish Political Studies, No. 6,
pp. 85-98.

PETCHESKY, R., 1984. *Abortion
and Woman's Choice*, London,
Verso.

PYLE, J., 1990. *The State and
Women in the Irish Economy*,
Albany, State University of
New York Press.

RANDALL, V., 1986. 'The
Politics of Abortion in
Ireland', in J. Lovenduski and
J. Outshoorn (eds.), *The New
Politics of Abortion*, London,
Sage.

REID, M., 1992. 'Abortion Law
in Ireland after the Maastricht
Referendum', in A. Smyth
(ed.), *The Abortion Papers*,
Dublin, Attic Press, pp. 25-39.

SMELSER, N., 1963. *Theory of
Collective Behaviour*, New York,
Free Press.

TONG, R., 1989. *Feminist
Thought*, London, Unwin
Hyman.

WHELAN, C. and T. FAHEY, 1994. 'Marriage and the Family' in C. Whelan (ed.), *Values and Social Change in Ireland*, Dublin, Economic and Social Research Institute, pp. 3.1-3.45.

WHELAN, C. and T. FAHEY, 1994. 'Marriage and the Family' in C. Whelan, *Values and Social Change in Ireland*, Dublin, Gill and Macmillan.

Index

Authors' names are given in the index when there is a discussion of their work. The bibliography at the end of each chapter lists all the works relevant to each chapter. RI: Republic of Ireland. NI: Northern Ireland.

Investment in Education 468,
479-85 *passim*
Irish Journal of Sociology 18
Irish Republican Army (IRA) 29,
435, 441-51 *passim*, 457; 574-86
passim
Irish Women's Aid Committee 682
Irish Women United (IWU) 682,
683, 685
Laissez faire: in education 497, 498

Kelly, Mary 31
Kimball, Solon T. 23, 208, 212, 223,
229

Labour *see* work
Law: and court decision making
423-4; and the legal system 412-5;
selective enforcement of 415-23;
see also crime
Law enforcement *see* law
LEADER programme 196-7, 434;
see also European Union
Legal system *see* law
Leisure: and work 255-7
Lemass, Seán 91, 92, 110, 370
Leonard, Madeleine 23, 24
Le Play 23, 206-7, 224
Love Labour: nature of 256-65;
see also women, work
Lynch, Kathleen 24, 31

McCullagh, Ciaran 28, 29
McDyer, Fr James 395-6, 403
McLaughlin, Eithne 24
McVeigh, Robbie 33
Mahon, Evelyn 35
Malthus' theory of population 40,
41, 42
Mansholt, Sicco (Mansholt Plan),
184, 186, 201
Marriage mobility *see* social mobility
Marital breakdown 23, 225-6
Marx, Karl 4-9, 14, 15, 207, 236,

263, 299-305 *passim*, 308, 317, 318
Marxism 325 678; and education
469-72; *see also* structuralism
Mead, G.H. 6, 11
Media *see* broadcasting
Middleclass *see* class
MI5 436, 441-5, 457, 458; *see also*
Northern Ireland
MI6 441, 442; *see also* Northern
Ireland
Migration 20, 65-73
Mjoset, Lars 114-118
Modernisation: process of 20, 90,
91, 101, 108, 109, 111, 116, 205,
212, 365, 594, 599
Modernisation theory, 40, 41
Morgan, Valerie 31
Mortality, 62-5
Muintir na Tíre: and community
action 27, 379, 383, 384-6, 399
Multinationals *see* transnational
corporations

National Council for the Elderly
282
National Identity: and broadcasting
563-76, 590
New coverage *see* broadcasting
Nic Giolla Phadraig, Máire 32
Non-marital parenthood 225-6
Northern Ireland: armed forces in
437-40; demographic structure
and change in 37-87 *passim*;
education in 495- 528;
environmentalism in 666-71;
equality issues in 146- 60, 495-524
passim, 529-62 *passim*; and
European social control strategies
435, 456-60; fortifying the border
448-52; informal economic
activity in Belfast 235-249;
intelligence operations in 436,
440-8; monitoring state power in
452-6; negative economic effects

of conflict 133, 135, 144, 145;
sectarianism in 620-51; state,
economy and society in 132-172
Nuptiality 51-61

Occupation: and class 297-306
passim, 312, 314, 317; and
education 482, 483; and social
mobility 326, 332, 343, 345
Odds ratio *see* social mobility
O'Dowd, Liam 20, 21
O'Hearn, Denis, 20, 21, 119-20
O'Malley, Eoin 113-14
Osborne, Robert 30

Parsons, Talcott 23, 209, 469-70
Peillon, Michel 26, 27
People action against
unemployment project (PAUL)
see community action
Pluralism: and the state 364-75
passim, 402
Population 19, 20; composition of
74-7; by denomination 79-82;
dependency levels in 78-9;
statistics 44-5, 49, 55, 58, 63, 71,
76-7; structure and change in 39-
89 *passim; see also* demography
Poulantzas, N. 301-4, 318
Poverty: and community action 380-
90 *passim,* 402
Pro-Life Amendment Campaign
(PLAC) 688, 703
Protestants: and education 499-524,
530, 533; and the media 564-72
passim, and sectarianism 620-51
passim
Pressure groups *see* interest groups

Racism 622, 623, 627, 639-42, 643,
644
Radio Éireann 564-71; *see also*
broadcasting
Radio Telefís Éireann (RTÉ) 574-80

passim, 589; and self censorship
581-84, 586, 587; *see also*
broadcasting
Rape 225, 227
Religion: and education 474-9
passim, 495-524 *passim,* 530-3; in
RI 593-619 *passim;* and inequality
in NI 153-58
Republic of Ireland: broadcasting in
563-592; community action in
379-409; class transformation and
social mobility in 324-57;
demographic structure and
change in 39-85; education in
467-94; environmental movement
in 659-71; family and household
in 205-34; power of Catholic
Church in 593-619; sectarianism
in 631-6; women's movement in
675-708
Robinson, Mary 35, 697-698
Rolston, Bill 31
Roscommon Hospital Campaign
see community action
Royal Ulster Constabulary (RUC)
437-54; *see also* Northern Ireland
Rural economy: and Europe
(EEC/EC/EU) 178-204 *passim*

Save the West movement *see*
community action
Schools: ethos of 549-52; funding of
511-514; levels of attainment in
505-8; management of 552-6;
types of 532-4; *see also* education
Sectarianism 620-51: and class 634,
639, 642, 643; and the colonial
process 33, 624-9; definition of
644-5; and gender 625, 639, 642-
3; and racism 622, 623, 627, 639-
42, 643, 644; and religion 637-9;
sociology of 622-5; and the state
634-6; as a structure 632-634
Sexual abuse 225